# RESEARCH HANDBOOK ON THE ECONOMICS OF CORPORATE LAW

T0305212

RESEARCH HANDBOOKS IN LAW AND ECONOMICS

**Series Editors:** Richard A. Posner, *Judge, United States Court of Appeals for the Seventh Circuit and Senior Lecturer, University of Chicago Law School, USA* and Francesco Parisi, *Oppenheimer Wolff and Donnelly Professor of Law, University of Minnesota, USA and Professor of Economics, University of Bologna, Italy*

Edited by highly distinguished scholars, the landmark reference works in this series offer advanced treatments of specific topics that reflect the state-of-the-art of research in law and economics, while also expanding the law and economics debate. Each volume's accessible yet sophisticated contributions from top international researchers make it an indispensable resource for students and scholars alike.

Titles in this series include:

Research Handbook on Public Choice and Public Law
*Edited by Daniel A. Farber and Anne Joseph O'Connell*

Research Handbook on the Economics of Property Law
*Edited by Kenneth Ayotte and Henry E. Smith*

Research Handbook on the Economics of Family Law
*Edited by Lloyd R. Cohen and Joshua D. Wright*

Research Handbook on the Economics of Antitrust Law
*Edited by Einer R. Elhauge*

Research Handbook on the Economics of Corporate Law
*Edited by Claire A. Hill and Brett H. McDonnell*

Research Handbook on the Economics of European Union Law
*Edited by Hans-Bernd Schäfer and Thomas Eger*

# Research Handbook on the Economics of Corporate Law

*Edited by*

Claire A. Hill

*Professor and James L. Krusemark Chair in Law, University of Minnesota Law School, USA*

Brett H. McDonnell

*Professor of Law and Solly Robbins Distinguished Research Fellow, University of Minnesota Law School, USA*

RESEARCH HANDBOOKS IN LAW AND ECONOMICS

**Edward Elgar**
Cheltenham, UK • Northampton, MA, USA

Published by
Edward Elgar Publishing Limited
The Lypiatts
15 Lansdown Road
Cheltenham
Glos GL50 2JA
UK

Edward Elgar Publishing, Inc.
William Pratt House
9 Dewey Court
Northampton
Massachusetts 01060
USA

A catalogue record for this book
is available from the British Library

Library of Congress Control Number: 2011942540

ISBN 978 1 84844 958 9 (cased)
ISBN 978 1 78100 547 7 (paperback)

Printed and bound by CPI Group (UK) Ltd, Croydon, CR0 4YY

# Contents

# Contributors

**Robert B. Ahdieh**
Vice Dean, Professor of Law and Director, Center on Federalism and Intersystemic Governance, Emory University School of Law.

**Vladimir Atanasov**
Associate Professor of Business and Richard C. Kraemer Term Chair at the Mason School of Business, College of William and Mary.

**Stephen M. Bainbridge**
William D. Warren Distinguished Professor of Law, UCLA School of Law.

**Bernard Black**
Nicholas D. Chabraja Professor, Northwestern University School of Law and Professor of Finance, Kellogg School of Management.

**Margaret M. Blair**
Milton R. Underwood Chair in Free Enterprise, Vanderbilt University Law School.

**Matthew T. Bodie**
Associate Dean for Research and Faculty Development, Professor of Law, Saint Louis University School of Law.

**Conrad S. Ciccotello**
Associate Professor, Robinson College of Business, Georgia State University and Director, Personal Financial Planning Program.

**Donald C. Clarke**
David Weaver Research Professor of Law, George Washington University Law School.

**Lawrence A. Cunningham**
Henry St. George Tucker III Research Professor of Law, George Washington University Law School.

**Aline Darbellay**
Research Fellow, University of Zurich Faculty of Law and Research Associate, University of San Diego School of Law.

**Steven M. Davidoff**
Associate Professor, Michael E. Moritz School of Law, University of Ohio.

**Lisa M. Fairfax**
Leroy Sorenson Merrifield Research Professor of Law, George Washington University Law School and Director of Conference Programs, C-LEAF.

**Fabrizio Ferri**
Assistant Professor, Columbia Business School.

**Jill E. Fisch**
Perry Golkin Professor of Law and Co-Director, Institute for Law and Economics, University of Pennsylvania Law School.

**Tamar Frankel**
Michaels Faculty Research Scholar and Professor of Law, Boston University School of Law.

**Ronald J. Gilson**
Charles J. Meyers Professor of Law and Business, Stanford University Law School and Marc and Eva Stern Professor of Law and Business, Columbia Law School.

**Sean J. Griffith**
T.J. Maloney Professor in Business Law and Director, Fordham Corporate Law Center, Fordham University School of Law.

**Claire A. Hill**
Professor and James L. Krusemark Chair in Law, University of Minnesota Law School.

**Reinier Kraakman**
Ezra Ripley Thayer Professor of Law, Harvard Law School.

**Donald C. Langevoort**
Thomas Aquinas Reynolds Professor of Law, Georgetown University Law Center and Co-Director, Joint Degree in Law and Business Administration.

**Ian B. Lee**
Associate Professor of Law, University of Toronto Faculty of Law.

**Brett H. McDonnell**
Professor of Law and Solly Robins Distinguished Research Fellow, University of Minnesota Law School.

**Richard W. Painter**
S. Walter Richey Professor of Corporate Law, University of Minnesota Law School.

**Frank Partnoy**
George E. Barrett Professor of Law and Finance and Co-Director, Center for Corporate and Securities Law, University of San Diego School of Law.

**D. Gordon Smith**
Associate Dean and Glen L. Farr Professor of Law, Brigham Young University Law School.

**Randall S. Thomas**
John S. Beasley II Professor of Law and Business and Director, Law and Business Program, Director, LL.M. Program and Professor of Management, Vanderbilt University.

**Robert B. Thompson**
Peter P. Weidenbruch Jr. Professor of Business Law, Georgetown University Law Center.

**David I. Walker**
Maurice Poch Faculty Research Scholar and Professor of Law, Boston University School of Law.

**Charles K. Whitehead**
Professor of Law, Cornell Law School.

# 1. Introduction: The evolution of the economic analysis of corporate law

*Claire A. Hill and Brett H. McDonnell*

## 1. INTRODUCTION

Economic analysis plays a crucial role in contemporary scholarly writing on corporate law. Indeed, although doctrinal analysis remains important and other interdisciplinary perspectives can occasionally be seen, economic analysis dominates most current corporate law scholarship. Sometimes the economics involves formal mathematical modeling; increasingly frequently, it involves econometric data analysis, while even more frequently it takes a softer, more informal form. Still, whatever the form, there is usually some reliance on ideas drawn from economics.

Thus, a research handbook on the economics of corporate law is hard to distinguish from a research handbook on corporate law, period. And indeed, in this volume we have felt little need to try to make that distinction. The collected contributions give an overview of some of the leading lines of research that scholars today are pursuing in trying to understand and critique legal developments in corporate law.

This volume is part of a new series of *Research Handbooks in Law and Economics*, directed by Francesco Parisi and Judge Richard Posner. As the editors of an earlier volume said, '[e]ach volume in the series aims to serve as a reference, providing helpful introductions to important topics, and as a provocateur, suggesting weaknesses and important areas for further exploration.' (Farber & O'Connell 2010, 1)

We hope that several different audiences will find this volume useful. Scholars in the field can look to it for a useful gathering of leading research, and also for suggestions as to possible directions for further research. Students and scholars just starting on the path of research into corporate law can look to it for an introductory overview. Practitioners in the field may be curious what scholars are saying, and can find that brought together in a quick reference guide. Policymakers may find leads on ideas for reforms.

In this Introduction we give a quick historical overview of the economic analysis of corporate law as well a description of the book that follows. Part II sketches the origins of the economic analysis of corporate law. Part III sketches how that analysis has developed over the last two decades. Part IV gives an overview of this volume.

A caution: many persons have contributed to a vast scholarly body of work on corporate law. Even this not-thin volume cannot hope to be anything close to comprehensive. There are important areas of law and research that we do not address at all, and within the areas that are addressed, the chapters can only sample some of the leading contributions. Large amounts of extremely good work must go unmentioned.

## 2.   ORIGINS OF THE ECONOMIC ANALYSIS OF CORPORATE LAW

We can look for the origins of the economic analysis of corporate law within both economics and legal scholarship. Much of our current understanding of the core problems of the field go back to an early collaboration between a law professor and an economist: Berle and Means (1932). They identified the separation of ownership and control, with public corporations owned by a dispersed group of shareholders, none of whom owned enough shares to have the incentive to rigorously monitor managerial behavior. A problem thus arose as to what, if anything, keeps managers from exploiting corporate resources for their own ends – what economists call an agency problem. The key question for scholars has been how corporate law does and should regulate this agency problem.

For a long time, academic economists largely treated firms as a black box, not saying much about the incentive issues within firms. But gradually they developed a theory of the firm. Ronald Coase (1937) began by asking what explains the boundaries between transactions that occur within firms and transactions between firms. He pointed to different transaction costs of the two types of transactions, arguing that boundaries would adjust to minimize transaction costs.

Coase left the concept of transaction costs rather vague. A subsequent school of transaction cost economics began to fill in the gaps. Oliver Williamson (1975, 1985), the leader of this school, focused on asset specificity. Where investments in assets are much more valuable within specific relationships, firms are more likely to form. A related property rights approach formalized similar ideas, with a focus on who has the right to decide how particular assets are used (Grossman & Hart 1986; Hart & Moore 1990; Hart 1995).

A somewhat different line of research used agency theory and corporate finance to shape the theory of the firm. Alchian and Demsetz (1972) is a key early work in this line, but the most influential contribution is Jensen and Meckling (1976). Jensen and Meckling coined the idea of the firm as a nexus of contracts, which became extremely important to the application of economic ideas within the legal academy.

The modern application of economic thinking within corporate law scholarship started in the 1960s with several papers by Henry Manne (1965, 1967). Others began to contribute in the 1970s and 1980s, and the volume of papers accelerated. By the beginning of the 1990s, corporate law and economics had reached its mature initial form, with important books by Frank Easterbrook and Daniel Fischel (1991) and Roberta Romano (1993) summarizing the approach. Several features stand out in what one can call the Chicago School approach. It applied relatively basic microeconomic theory to an understanding of corporations and corporate law. Most of the work was theory, often informal (non-mathematical) theory, with relatively little empirical research (Romano was an important exception). The theory generally assumed strong individual rationality and well-functioning markets. It analyzed many ways in which markets effectively constrained managerial self-dealing. As a result, its normative tilt usually viewed strong regulations with skepticism. The approach painted most state corporate law as creating enabling default rules rather than mandatory regulations, and it approved. By the 1990s, this sort of economic theorizing dominated corporate law scholarship.

## 3.   DEVELOPMENTS IN LAW AND IN ECONOMICS

That scholarship has evolved significantly over the last two decades. Some of that evolution reflects responses to changes in the law and in corporate governance practices. Other parts of that evolution reflect changes within economic scholarship. We discuss each source of change in turn.

There have been many major developments in corporate law and corporate governance. One area that had already begun to evolve significantly in the 1980s as the first wave of economic analysis hit was the market for corporate control (Davidoff Ch. 12). Public corporations faced a wave of hostile takeover bids. Target management and their lawyers developed a variety of innovative defenses, and the courts needed to address legal changes to those defenses. Although Delaware courts attempted to craft a balanced approach, by the end of the 1980s they had left enough latitude for effective defenses that a well-advised board could generally ward off any direct hostile assault. But hostile overtures continue, and courts have continued over the last few decades to refine the legal standards developed in the 1980s.

The main way in which contemporary state corporate law attempts to police managerial misbehavior is via shareholder suits claiming breaches of fiduciary duty (Hill & McDonnell Ch. 8; Thomas & Thompson Ch. 9). Fiduciary duty law has evolved significantly in recent decades. Once there were just two main standards of judicial review: the duty of loyalty and the duty of care. But a variety of intermediate standards have arisen, many but not all in the change of control context. A particularly notable development has been the development of the law of good faith. Scholars have analyzed and debated this and other developments in fiduciary law.

A leading change has been the growth of institutional investors and shareholder activism (Smith Ch. 4; Ferri Ch. 11). Over half of the shares of American public corporations are now owned by institutions such as mutual funds, pension funds, and hedge funds. Some of these institutions have better incentives to become involved in corporate governance than the isolated small shareholders described in the Berle & Means picture of the corporation. Simultaneously, the decline in the market for corporate control and the dim prospects for most fiduciary duty suits have, together, reduced the effectiveness of other forms of control. As a result, some institutional investors have sought to become actively involved in corporate governance matters, and to change the law to make it easier to do so. Some corporate scholars have applauded this development and called for legal change to encourage it (Bebchuk 2005), while others are skeptical of activist investors and want to limit their ability to intervene (Bainbridge 2006).

Another key development has been the growing emphasis on the role of outside, independent directors (Fairfax Ch. 10). In the paradigmatic managerialist company of the post-war decades, most directors were inside managers or otherwise tied to the company (e.g., as company counsel or investment bankers). The board was nominally the source of legal authority in the corporations, but in fact it was not very important. Both best practice and the law have over the last few decades led to our current situation, where most public corporation directors are now outsiders with no significant ties to the company beyond their position on the board. Multiple studies consider what effect, if any, this has had on corporate actions.

While the above developments have been mostly of interest to those who specialize in corporate law and governance, the explosion in executive compensation is a trend that has received much public attention. Economists and legal scholars have explored this trend thoroughly

(Walker Ch. 13). Some see this trend as reflecting optimal contracting, with new forms of compensation contracts giving executives better incentives to look after shareholder interests (Core et al. 2003). Others see the trend as reflecting managerial power, with the result that it often leads to worse, not better, incentives (Bebchuk & Fried 2004).

Another trend in both corporate governance and law has been a growing focus on the role of a variety of gatekeepers. These are professionals who act as informational and reputational intermediaries. They gather information about companies, and help to warrant to outsiders the validity of information made public. Gatekeepers who are doing their jobs properly can thus help prevent managerial misbehavior. The legal responses to the two great financial crises of the past decade heavily implicate gatekeepers: much of the Sarbanes-Oxley Act focuses on a variety of gatekeepers, and the corporate governance elements of the Dodd-Frank Act also cover several types of gatekeepers. Important gatekeepers include corporate lawyers (Painter Ch. 14), rating agencies (Darbellay & Partnoy Ch. 15), auditors and accountants (Cunningham Ch. 16), securities analysts (Fisch Ch. 17), D & O insurers (Griffith Ch. 18), and investment banks (Frankel Ch. 19).

Mention of Sarbanes-Oxley and Dodd-Frank points to another key legal development: the federalization of important parts of corporate law. American corporate law scholars have traditionally focused on state law. A much discussed question has long been whether competition between states for corporate charters leads to a race to the bottom (Cary 1974) or to the top (Romano 1993). But now, important scholarship suggests that Delaware's main competition is not other states but rather the federal government (Roe 2003, 2005). Much debate swirls over both the nature of the federal–state interaction and whether or not it tends to lead to better or worse law (Ahdieh Ch. 20).

A final notable development in practice is globalization. American business and law firms are increasingly global in nature, and hence must care about the rules of other countries. The corporate laws of the leading industrial countries (Europe, Japan) are of most importance, but with the growth of emerging markets other countries are becoming important too, with China as the most obvious example. Corporate law scholarship has not ignored this development, and there has been much writing on comparative corporate governance (Clarke Ch. 21).

The above refers to notable developments in the law and the practice of corporate governance, which have been reflected in legal scholarship that analyzes their significance. That is, the scholarship of law and economics has changed as the law has changed. It has also changed as economics has changed. The remaining most notable developments in corporate legal scholarship reflect developments within economics scholarship.

One area where there has been less significant development over the last two decades within economics than one might expect is the theory of the firm. A significant exception is the work of Rajan and Zingales (1998) on the allocation of power within firms. Within legal scholarship there has been some significant evolution as two new broad theoretical approaches appeared, drawing upon both older and newer theories of the firm. The director primacy theory of Stephen Bainbridge (Ch. 2) draws upon the work of Kenneth Arrow (1974). It stresses the central role of the board of directors, and while Bainbridge describes a tradeoff between authority and accountability, he generally comes down on the side of board authority. The team production theory of Margaret Blair and Lynn Stout (Blair Ch. 3) moves the focus away from agency theory and instead draws more upon team production economic models, including both older (Alchian & Demsetz 1972) and newer (Rajan & Zingales 1998) models.

A pronounced trend within economics over the last few decades has been a greater emphasis on empirical work. Legal scholars have followed that trend, with a lag. Much of the most visible and influential corporate law scholarship today involves econometric examination of data bases. This is true for many topics, but areas of particular concentration include studies of shareholder lawsuits (Thomas & Thompson Ch. 9), the effect of outside directors (Fairfax Ch. 10), shareholder activism (Ferri Ch. 11), executive compensation (Walker Ch. 13), the effect of various gatekeepers (Fisch Ch. 17; Griffith Ch. 18), and the law and finance literature within studies of comparative corporate governance (Clarke Ch. 21).

Economic theory in recent decades has made important moves away from the old Chicago School story of well-functioning markets. Those moves came in two main steps. First, scholars such as Joseph Stiglitz (2002) developed the theory of asymmetric information. If market participants lack complete information about the relevant good or service, and if persons on one side of a transaction have more information than the other, then traditional conclusions as to the efficiency of markets become suspect and complicated. Asymmetric information certainly characterizes the relationship between corporate insiders and shareholders of public corporations, and so this theory has had an important effect on corporate law scholarship. Scholars like Lucian Bebchuk (2005) have used this theory to develop reasons why shareholders may need more regulatory protection than most participants in the first wave of corporate law and economics advocated.

The second step away from the Chicago School came with the development of behavioral economics. Behavioral economics, starting with the important experiments and insights of Tversky and Kahneman (1974), called into question the assumption of rational behavior that underlies neoclassical economics. As applied within the theory of finance, this movement has focused on various theoretical and empirical challenges to the efficient capital market hypothesis (Shleifer 2000). Applied within corporate law scholarship, behavioral finance has provided more arguments to question the efficiency of unregulated markets (Langevoort Ch. 23), although behavioralist arguments further complicate matters by providing new insights into ways that government may fail as well.

We mention one other influential development in economics which has affected recent corporate law scholarship, although of course there are many more that we lack space to consider here. Economists have begun to focus more on comparison of economic institutions across countries. A particularly influential strand has been the law and finance literature (La Porta et al. 1997), although there have been other strands as well within a broad development of comparative institutional analysis (Aoki 2001). This literature has informed the large growth within law schools of writing on comparative corporate governance (Clarke Ch. 21).

Where will the economic analysis of corporate law go from here? Who are we to say? If we were good at anticipating that sort of thing, our lives would probably look different. The dominant development as we write is an ongoing reaction to the recent financial crisis. To a large extent the main legal developments have (appropriately) been in the different albeit related field of banking law and financial regulation. However, securities and corporate law have not been unaffected. The Dodd-Frank Act has many provisions affecting these fields, including the regulation of derivatives, hedge funds, credit rating agencies, executive compensation, and proxy access.

These regulations, and the crisis itself, have brought a new concern to the fore: systemic risk. Some financial markets are subject to bouts of excessive optimism followed by panics which can have severe consequences for the economy as a whole, especially where excessive leverage becomes widespread. Decisions by individual companies and investors may ignore the impact they have on these waves of optimism and panic: systemic risk is thus a type of externality. Corporate and securities law scholars in the past have paid little attention to this issue, but that has begun to change in the wake of the crisis (Schwarcz 2008). This will require drawing upon scholarship on the theory of networks (Cohen & Havlin 2010) and complex evolving systems (Arthur et al. 1997).

We also suspect we may see more scholarship in an area that crosses two of the trends from economics discussed above. We have already seen a large growth in empirical scholarship, and also much research in both behavioral economics and behavioral finance. Some ideas from behavioralism can be explored well using regressions, the traditional empirical tool of economics. However, other ideas may be better explored using a range of other empirical tools, such as experiments, surveys, interviews, case studies, and participant-observer studies. In this exploration, the large existing literature on organizational behavior (Greenberg & Baron 2007) is a resource that has probably been under-used by corporate law scholars.

## 4.   OVERVIEW OF THIS BOOK

We have divided this book into five parts. Part I lays out the core constituency groups who are involved in a corporation and hence are most centrally affected by corporate law. Parts II and III explore the main governance rules and accountability mechanisms which are at the heart of corporate law. Part II considers mechanisms which give power to inside constituents, mainly directors, shareholders, and officers. Part III considers a variety of other corporate gatekeepers. Part IV looks at corporate law in different jurisdictions, including American states, the federal government, and different national governments. Part V looks at a few new theoretical developments.

### Part I: Corporate Constituencies

Part I considers the core constituencies at the heart of the corporation, including directors, officers, shareholders, creditors, and employees, as well as the role (or lack thereof) of the interests of the public at large. It starts with Stephen Bainbridge's (Ch. 2) elaboration of his influential theory of director primacy. This theory attempts to both explain and defend the broad grant of authority to boards of directors that is at the heart of American corporate law. Drawing heavily on Arrow (1974), it argues that this grant of authority is essential to ameliorating the informational demands a large corporation faces. The grant of authority, however, creates the potential for abuse of that authority, creating a need for accountability mechanisms to limit such abuses. The tradeoff between authority and accountability is at the heart of corporate law. Bainbridge argues, though, that a presumption should generally favor authority, and he opposes most proposals to increase shareholder power. In his chapter Bainbridge lays out the basic logic of his position, and also responds to some criticisms of that position.

A leading competitor to director primacy is the team production theory of Margaret Blair and Lynn Stout (1999). Blair (Ch. 3) explicates this theory in her contribution to this volume. Like director primacy, team production theory defends the broad grant of authority to boards. However, it draws upon a different theoretical framework in doing so. The team production problem arises when multiple parties must contribute to the production process. One very useful solution to this problem involves a mediating hierarch with ultimate authority to direct production decisions and to mediate the conflicting preferences of the different parties. Although Blair and Stout agree with Bainbridge on the desirability of granting significant authority to boards, they disagree on the proper ultimate aims of the board in exercising that authority. Bainbridge believes boards should focus on maximizing the value of the corporation for shareholders. Blair and Stout believe boards should focus on maximizing the net value created for all corporate constituencies collectively.

The leading broad opposition to these approaches which defend broad board authority comes from proponents of shareholder primacy, with Lucian Bebchuk (2005) as the most prominent example. In his chapter Gordon Smith (Ch. 4) examines the role of shareholders in the modern American public corporation. He starts with the Berle and Means (1932) problem of the separation of ownership and control, but notes that the rise of institutional investors has changed the situation. Shareholders have three main sets of rights through which they can protect themselves: the right to vote, to sell, and to sue. Each of these rights has evolved significantly in recent years. Smith describes some of the changes and debates, and also briefly addresses the question of the proper beneficiaries of corporate decisions.

In his chapter, Charles Whitehead (Ch. 5) examines a corporate constituency that has received less, but increasing, attention: creditors. Not only do creditors provide an important source of financing, but they also play a significant role in corporate governance. Particularly important are covenants within debt agreements. Whitehead traces how corporate debt markets have become increasingly liquid, with the growth of syndication, securitization, and derivatives. This increased liquidity creates challenges for traditional means of monitoring and governance. Traditionally, banks with long-term relationships with creditor corporations were able to use private information to monitor and affect behavior. More liquid markets have weakened those ties, but created new potential governance mechanisms through the use of public signals such as the price of debt on the secondary market or credit ratings.

Another major corporate constituency that usually receives little attention in American law and scholarship is employees. Matthew Bodie (Ch. 6) analyzes their role within corporations. He notes that although employees have almost no formal role within American corporate law, they are a quite significant part of the subject matter of the economic theory of the firm. He analyzes how other areas of the law help shape the relationship between employees and the corporations for which they work, including agency law, intellectual property law, tax law, and employment law. He suggests that corporate law might provide a larger role for employees, but notes that as the traditional large corporation/long-term employee relationship rapidly evolves, laws and scholarly understandings will need to adapt in response.

Part I concludes with Ian Lee's (Ch. 7) examination of the role of the public interest in corporate law. This reviews the ongoing debate between shareholder primacy versus stakeholder conceptions of the corporation and the progressive critique of traditional law and economic theories which put shareholder interests first. The conventional view defends shareholder primacy by arguing that shareholders are the residual claimants of a corporation, and hence in need of special protection. Lee considers what he calls 'public facility' and 'powerful institution' critiques of this position. He then considers various proposals for expanding the role of the public interest in corporate law. These include modifying the board's mandate, non-shareholder board representation, using corporate law to control externalities, and encouraging socially responsible shareholder engagement.

## Part II: Insider Governance

Part II examines various mechanisms by which some of the insider constituencies discussed in Part I help to monitor and deter misbehavior by corporate officers and directors. Perhaps the leading such mechanism within state corporate law is the existence of fiduciary duties enforceable by shareholder suits. Claire Hill and Brett McDonnell (Ch. 8) discuss the evolution in recent decades of the law of fiduciary duty. Traditionally, fiduciary duties came in two varieties, the duty of loyalty, which applied to conflicts of interests, and the duty of care, which very rarely led to liability given the protection of the business judgment rule. A variety of intermediate standards of review and doctrines have arisen in Delaware law, which the cognoscenti will recognize in the shorthand of case names such as *Unocal, Revlon, Zapata, Blasius, Caremark*, and *Disney*. We argue that these represent an attempt by the courts to address concerns about structural bias in a variety of contexts where we expect directors to not be fully motivated to pursue the best interests of shareholders, while still granting boards the wide discretion that is a core element of American corporate law.

Randall Thomas and Robert Thompson (Ch. 9) provide an overview of the growing empirical literature on shareholder litigation under both federal securities law and state corporate law. Such suits are an important part of the enforcement scheme of both securities and corporate law, but there has been much concern about plaintiff lawyer abuse in shareholder litigation. For Delaware state law suits, class actions in the context of an acquisition have become the dominant form of litigation – a type of situation in which judicial oversight has been seen as critically needed. Studies suggest that litigated deals have higher premia, although it is not clear whether the reason is the litigation or the independent committees of directors typically formed in such transactions. In studies of federal cases, much attention has focused on the effects of the Private Securities Litigation Reform Act of 1995, with scholars reaching varied conclusions. Some studies suggest that some provisions of this Act have improved results for plaintiffs, while others find little effect.

One striking change in recent decades has been a strong emphasis on using outside, independent directors as monitors of corporate actions. Much scholarship has focused on whether outside directors are in fact able to act independently and improve corporate performance. Lisa Fairfax (Ch. 10) reviews the evidence in her chapter. She finds that the empirical evidence is mixed and, on the whole, does not show that boards with more outside directors are more effective at monitoring. Many factors limit the effectiveness of outside directors as monitors, including structural bias, selection bias, informational asymmetries, and a lack of legal liability as a spur. She argues for a larger role for both inside directors and external oversight.

Another striking change has been the growth of institutional investors and a related move towards increasing shareholder activism. There has been much debate over the effectiveness of that activism and whether or not it should be encouraged. In his chapter, Fabrizio Ferri (Ch. 11) reviews the empirical evidence on the effects of some kinds of shareholder activism. He focuses on what he calls 'low-cost' activism, as contrasted with 'activism via large ownership' in which a shareholder gains a large equity stake. Ferri looks particularly at two activism tools: director elections and shareholder proposals under Rule 14a-8. There is some evidence that vote withholding campaigns in board elections have reduced agency costs. A future development of potential significance is new rules on proxy access; event studies on the effect of the adoption of proxy access on share prices have been mixed. Early evidence on shareholder proposals suggested they were a weak governance mechanism. More recently they have become a more powerful tool, with their effect depending upon the degree of voting support they receive.

A governance mechanism that received much attention in early corporate law and economics scholarship was the market for corporate control (Manne 1965). The threat and reality of hostile takeovers was supposed to act as a significant deterrent to managerial misbehavior. However, the legal and institutional landscape for takeovers has changed greatly in recent decades, and scholarship has had to react to those changes. Steven Davidoff's chapter (Ch. 12) surveys that reaction. The main thrust of early scholarship was that takeovers and the threat thereof enhanced shareholder value, and hence the law should discourage takeover defenses. For the most part, courts and legislators have not followed that advice. Scholars have had to react to that fact. Reaction has been mixed. Some argue that takeovers remain viable, albeit in changed forms. Others argue that the law has gone too far in allowing defenses and should be reformed. Yet others argue that other accountability mechanisms have taken the place of the market for corporate control. Davidoff argues that takeover theory should become more nuanced, recognizing the greater complexity of modern capital markets and corporate governance practices.

One of the most publicly debated developments in corporate governance has been the explosion of executive compensation, due mainly to the growth in use of options and other forms of equity-based compensation. David Walker (Ch. 13) surveys the scholarly debate. There are two basic positions. One holds that equity compensation represents an efficient approach to align the incentives of corporate officers with the interests of shareholders. The other holds that increased compensation is a sign that officers have captured boards. Walker surveys studies of the amount of compensation, its design, and the impact of tax and accounting rules. He examines various reform attempts and proposals, including changes in board structure, disclosure, compensation consultants, and shareholder say on pay. Walker finds that executive pay is complex, and that each of the opposing theoretical approaches sheds significant light on elements of that pay.

## Part III: Gatekeepers

A major development within corporate practice has been the increased prominence of a variety of corporate gatekeepers. The two main federal legislative developments of the past decade, Sarbanes-Oxley and the corporate governance elements of Dodd-Frank, have focused heavily on these gatekeepers. Part III contains chapters analyzing the role of six different sets of gatekeepers. The first of these is Richard Painter's (Ch. 14) chapter on business lawyers. Painter considers three different accounts of business lawyers within legal scholarship. Some describe lawyers as 'transaction cost engineers' who help increase the net value of transactions by allocating risk to those best able to evaluate and bear it. Others describe them as 'loophole engineers' who help clients get around the law. Yet others describe them as 'gatekeepers' who help certify their clients as suitable for interaction; Sarbanes-Oxley section 307 focused on this gatekeeping role. Each role helps explain aspects of what business lawyers do. Painter observes that as we learn more about the role lawyers played in the financial crisis, the next question will be whether they should have a legal or moral responsibility to behave differently.

Credit rating agencies played a central role in the growth of securitization, and their poor performance during the financial crisis made them a major target for criticism and for legal reform in the Dodd-Frank Act. Aline Darbellay and Frank Partnoy (Ch. 15) analyze their role and that reform. Traditionally, theorists understood credit rating agencies as informational intermediaries, but Darbellay and Partnoy argue that they are now better understood as providing 'regulatory license' due to the key role that ratings have played in many financial regulations. They review research on the potential for changes in regulatory oversight, increasing accountability through liability, and reduced regulatory reliance on ratings. They argue that Dodd-Frank contains some potentially beneficial reforms, but much will depend upon how the Act is implemented and more remains to be done.

Lawrence Cunningham (Ch. 16) reviews developments in the scholarship of law and accounting. Modern finance theory has greatly affected the understanding of accounting. Finance theory helped encourage the adoption of forward-looking disclosure in federal securities regulation. Cunningham argues that on balance this has helped reduce agency costs. Finance theory has also helped re-shape accounting standards, including those applicable to cash flow statements and fair value measures. Within state corporate law, finance theory has helped shape how and when court-ordered appraisals will be done. Finance and agency theory pointed to a role for outside auditors in helping monitor corporations, a role which became the focus for many reforms in the Sarbanes-Oxley Act of 2002.

Jill Fisch (Ch. 17) examines the role and regulation of another gatekeeper, the research analyst. Sarbanes-Oxley, along with the global research settlement between ten investment banks, the SEC, the New York Attorney General, and several others, instituted reforms which attempt to keep research analysts independent from the investment bankers who often work at the same firm. Research suggests that these reforms have led to reduced analyst coverage. Analyst recommendations have become less optimistic, with fewer buy recommendations, but they have also become less informative. The push for independence has put serious pressure on the business model for the research analyst industry.

Sean Griffith (Ch. 18) examines the role of providers of directors and officers (D & O) insurance. This insurance may decrease the deterrence effect of insurance litigation, insofar as it prevents individuals from being personally liable. On the other hand, D & O insurers may themselves play a role in monitoring corporate governance, since premia should depend upon how vulnerable a company is to suits. Griffith reviews empirical evidence on D & O insurance, and suggests that the pricing of governance risk in insurance policies does not make up for the decrease in deterrence effect of such insurance. The evidence also suggests that selective payment of claims also does little to re-create a deterrence effect. Griffith suggests some policy reforms that could help strengthen deterrence, including disclosure of D & O policy details or of settlement details.

Tamar Frankel (Ch. 19) considers the influence of investment banks on corporate governance. Corporate finance has become an increasingly large and influential industry, and this has affected corporate governance. Investment banks have played an important role in the rise of finance. They provide an array of services, including underwriting, securities trading, advising on mergers and acquisitions, and asset management. In providing these services, they have played a major role in advising and influencing corporate management.

**Part IV: Jurisdiction**

Competition between states for charters has long been a major topic within corporate law scholarship. Robert Ahdieh (Ch. 20) surveys recent developments in the scholarship of corporate law federalism. The traditional literature focused on the relationship between states, and asked whether the ability to choose one's state of incorporation tends to lead to a race to the bottom or to the top. Ahdieh argues that to a large extent this debate recapitulates an underlying debate concerning more basic assumptions about how well capital markets constrain managers. He suggests that state competition, however, can plausibly be seen as a check on regulatory abuse. The most dramatic element in recent scholarship is an emphasis on the vertical element of federalism, with the federal government a leading player. Here too, much of the debate as to the value of the federal role turns on differences as to whether mandatory rules are needed, or whether choice among rules is better. Scholarship now must focus on the relationship between actors at different levels of the federal scheme and on achieving an optimal balance between state and federal roles.

Donald Clarke (Ch. 21) surveys comparative corporate governance (CCG) scholarship. CCG scholarship has used a variety of methodologies, but Clarke characterizes, and to some extent criticizes, functionalism as the prevailing methodology. An important more recent methodological trend, seen particularly in the law and finance literature (La Porta et al. 1997), has been quantitative empirical studies using standardized measures of corporate governance. Clarke describes some important lessons learned from CCG, including the extent to which economics, law, history, politics, culture, and property rights matter in shaping corporate governance. Clarke concludes by describing major challenges facing CCG scholarship. The vast literature on whether or not national systems are converging to the same model of corporate governance may have reached its useful limits. In contrast, CCG scholars could usefully pay more attention to topics such as non-corporate forms and law and practice in emerging countries like China and India. CCG scholars should also take into account that countries differ in their view of what corporate governance is trying to accomplish – they should be less quick to assume that all laws should be judged by how well they handle the type of agency problems on which American scholars focus.

**Part V: New Theory**

Recent economic theory has given a twist on the concept of agency costs with the idea of tunneling, namely that managers and controlling shareholders can extract (tunnel) wealth from firms using a variety of methods. Vladimir Atanasov, Bernard Black, and Conrad Ciccotello (Ch. 22) analyze how effectively US rules limit tunneling in public corporations. They categorize tunneling into three types. In cash flow tunneling, insiders extract current cash flow. In asset tunneling, insiders buy corporate assets at below-market prices, or sell assets to the corporation at above-market prices. In equity tunneling, insiders acquire equity at below-market prices. They examine how many kinds of rules, including corporate, securities, accounting, tax, and creditor protection, affect each of these kinds of tunneling. Such a broad perspective is necessary, because to the extent that these rules collectively constrain some forms of tunneling well but not others, insiders will tend to gravitate to less-constrained forms.

Donald Langevoort (Ch. 23) explores how ideas from behavioral economics and finance have affected corporate law scholarship. Behavioral economics uses ideas from psychology to modify standard economic assumptions about the rationality of individual behavior. A crucial question for applying such ideas within corporate law is why persons behaving closer to the standard assumptions of rationality are not able to drive others out of the market, given the large amounts of money at stake and the competitiveness of financial markets. Langevoort suggests that in some cases, some sorts of heuristics have adaptive value. He surveys how scholars have applied the psychological literature to study board behavior and to question the efficient markets hypothesis.

Ronald Gilson and Reinier Kraakman (Ch. 24) examine what remains of the efficient market hypothesis in the wake of the financial crisis. While many have proclaimed that the crisis has discredited the hypothesis, Gilson and Kraakman argue that properly conceived the hypothesis remains viable. They distinguish informational and fundamental efficiency, acknowledging that the distinction is hard to put into practice. Efficiency should be conceived as a relative concept, with markets more or less efficient depending upon the costs to market participants of obtaining and effectively using information. The financial crisis revealed that those costs were quite high in some important markets. The efficient market hypothesis can help guide policy by pointing to measures that may help reduce those informational costs, thereby improving market efficiency.

## ACKNOWLEDGMENTS

Many people have helped make this project possible. We would like to thank some of them here. First of course is each of the contributors. We also thank Francesco Parisi and Judge Richard Posner, the editors of the overall *Research Handbooks in Law and Economics* series, for asking us to compile this volume.

The good people at Edward Elgar have also been indispensable. Tara Gorvine has been our main contact, and she has provided assistance and advice repeatedly at each stage of the project. Rebecca Wise did great work in copyediting the volume.

At the University of Minnesota, Julie Hunt, Bria Goldman and Alia El Bakri provided exceptional administrative assistance. Suzanne Thorpe and other staff at the Law Library provided wonderful help on several chapters. Jamie Kastler provided excellent research assistance on our own chapter. Our dean, David Wippman, provided summer research funding which helped us work on the volume.

Last on the page but first in our hearts, we thank our partners, Eric Hillemann (Hill) and Paul Rubin (McDonnell), for all the emotional and household support that gave us the time and energy to get this done.

## REFERENCES

Alchian, Armen A. & Harold Demsetz (1972), 'Production, Information Costs, and Economic Organization', *American Economics Review*, 62, 777–795.
Aoki, Masahiko (2001), *Towards a Comparative Institutional Analysis*, Boston: MIT Press.
Arrow, Kenneth J. (1974), *The Limits of Organization*, New York: W.W. Norton & Co.
Arthur, W. Brian, Steven N. Durlauf & David A. Lane (1997), *The Economy as a Complex Evolving System II*, Reading, Mass.: Addison-Wesley.
Bainbridge, Stephen M. (2006), 'The Case for Limited Shareholder Voting Rights', *UCLA Law Review*, 53, 601–36.
Bebchuk, Lucian A. (2005), 'The Case for Increasing Shareholder Power', *Harvard Law Review*, 118, 833–914.
Bechuk, Lucian A. & Jesse Fried (2004), *Pay Without Performance: The Unfulfilled Promise of Executive Compensation*, Boston: Harvard University Press.
Berle, Adolf A. & Gardiner C. Means (1932), *The Modern Corporation and Private Property*, New York: Commerce Clearing House, Inc.

Blair, Margaret M. & Lynn A. Stout (1999), 'A Team Production Theory of Corporate Law', *Virginia Law Review*, 85, 247–328.

Cary, William L. (1974), 'Federalism and Corporate Law: Reflections Upon Delaware', *Yale Law Journal*, 83, 663–705.

Coase, Ronald H. (1937), 'The Nature of the Firm', *Economica*, 4, 386–405.

Cohen, Reuven & Shlomo Havlin (2010), *Complex Networks: Structure, Robustness, and Function*, Cambridge: Cambridge University Press.

Core, John E., Wayne R. Guay & David F. Larcker (2003), 'Executive Equity Compensation and Incentives: A Survey', *FRBNY Economic Policy Review*, 9, 27–50.

Easterbrook, Frank & Daniel Fischel (1991), *The Economic Structure of Corporate Law*, Boston: Harvard University Press.

Farber, Daniel A. & Anne Joseph O'Connell (2010), 'Introduction: A Brief Trajectory of Public Choice and Public Law', in Daniel A. Farber & Anne Joseph O'Connell, *Research Handbook on Public Choice and Public Law*, Northampton, Mass.: Edward Elgar.

Greenberg, Jerald & Robert A. Baron (2007), *Behavior in Organizations*, 9th ed., New York: Prentice Hall.

Grossman, Sanford J. & Oliver D. Hart (1986), 'The Costs and Benefits of Ownership: A Theory of Vertical and Lateral Integration', *Journal of Political Economy*, 94, 691–719.

Hart, Oliver (1995), *Firms, Contracts, and Financial Structure*, Oxford: Oxford University Press.

Hart, Oliver D. & John Moore (1990), 'Property Rights and the Nature of the Firm', *Journal of Political Economy*, 98, 1119–58.

Jensen, Michael C. & William H. Meckling (1976), 'Theory of the Firm: Managerial Behavior, Agency Costs, and Ownership Structure', *Journal of Financial Economics*, 3, 305–60.

La Porta, Rafael, Florencio Lopez-de-Silanes, Andrei Shleifer & Robert Vishny (1997), 'Legal Determinants of External Finance', *Journal of Finance*, 52, 1131–1150.

Manne, Henry G. (1965), 'Mergers and the Market for Corporate Control', *Journal of Political Economy*, 73, 110–20.

Manne, Henry G. (1967), 'Our Two Corporation Systems: Law and Economics', *Virginia Law Review*, 53, 259–284.

Rajan, Raghuram G. & Luigi Zingales (1998), 'Power in the Theory of the Firm', *Quarterly Journal of Economics*, 113, 387–432.

Roe, Mark J. (2003), 'Delaware's Competition', *Harvard Law Review*, 117, 588–646.

Roe, Mark J. (2005), 'Delaware's Politics', *Harvard Law Review*, 118, 2491–2543.

Romano, Roberta (1993), *The Genius of American Corporate Law*, New York: AEI Press.

Schwarcz, Steven L. (2008), 'Systemic Risk', *Georgetown Law Journal*, 97, 193–249.

Shleifer, Andrei (2000), *Inefficient Markets: An Introduction to Behavioral Finance*, Oxford: Oxford University Press.

Stiglitz, Joseph E. (2002), 'Information and the Change in the Paradigm in Economics', *American Economic Review*, 460–501.

Tversky, Amos & Daniel Kahneman (1974), 'Judgment Under Uncertainty: Heuristics and Biases', *Science*, 185, 1124–31.

Williamson, Oliver E. (1975), *Markets and Hierarchies: Analysis and Antitrust Implications*, New York: The Free Press.

Williamson, Oliver (1985), *The Economic Institutions of Capitalism*, New York: The Free Press.

# PART I

# CORPORATE CONSTITUENCIES

# 2.  Director primacy
## Stephen M. Bainbridge[*]

## 1.  INTRODUCTION

Ownership and control rights typically go hand in hand. A homeowner may eject trespassers, for example, even using force in appropriate cases.[1] A principal is entitled to control his agent.[2] Each partner is entitled to equal rights in the management of the partnership business.[3]

In the corporation, however, ownership and control are decisively separated. Control is vested by statute in the board of directors. The Delaware General Corporation Law, for example, provides that the corporation's 'business and affairs ... shall be managed by or under the direction of the board of directors'.[4] In contrast, the firm's nominal owners – the shareholders – exercise virtually no control over either day-to-day operations or long-term policy. Shareholder voting rights are limited to the election of directors and a few relatively rare matters such as approval of charter or bylaw amendments, mergers, sales of substantially all of the corporation's assets, and voluntary dissolution. As a formal matter, moreover, only the election of directors and amending the bylaws do not require board approval before shareholder action is possible (Dooley 1995). In practice, of course, even the election of directors (absent a proxy contest) is predetermined by virtue of the existing board's power to nominate the next year's board (Manning 1958). The shareholders' limited control rights thus are almost entirely reactive rather than proactive.

These direct restrictions on shareholder power are supplemented by a host of other rules that indirectly prevent shareholders from exercising significant influence over corporate decision making. Three sets of statutes are especially noteworthy: (1) disclosure requirements pertaining to large holders;[5] (2) shareholder voting and communication rules;[6] and (3) insider

---

[*]   Portions of this chapter are adapted with permission from my book Stephen M. Bainbridge (2008) *The New Corporate Governance in Theory and Practice*, Oxford: Oxford University Press.
[1]   *See, e.g., State v. Zajac*, 767 N.W.2d 825 (N.D. 2009).
[2]   *See, e.g.,* Official Committee of Unsecured Creditors of Allegheny Health, 989 A.2d 313 (Pa. 2010).
[3]   Unif. Partnership Act § 401(f) (1997) [hereinafter cited as UPA (1997)].
[4]   Del. Code Ann., tit. 8, § 141(a).
[5]   Securities Exchange Act § 13(d) and the SEC rules thereunder require extensive disclosures from any person or group acting together which acquires beneficial ownership of more than 5 percent of the outstanding shares of any class of equity stock in a given issuer. 15 U.S.C. § 78m. The disclosures required by § 13(d) impinge substantially on investor privacy and thus may discourage some investors from holding blocks greater than 4.9% of a company's stock. US institutional investors frequently cite Section 13(d)'s application to groups and the consequent risk of liability for failing to provide adequate disclosures as an explanation for the general lack of shareholder activism on their part (Black 1998).
[6]   *See* 17 C.F.R. § 240.14a-1-14b-2 (proxy rules). To the extent shareholders exercise any control over the corporation, they do so only through control of the board of directors. As such, it is the share-

trading and short swing profits rules (Bainbridge 1995). These laws affect shareholders in two respects. First, they discourage the formation of large stock blocks.[7] Second, they discourage communication and coordination among shareholders (Bainbridge 1995).

Contrary to what some commentators have argued,[8] shareholders not only lack significant managerial rights, they also lack most of the other categories of rights associated with control. Shareholders have no right to use or possess corporate property, for example. As one court explained, 'even a sole shareholder has no independent right which is violated by trespass upon or conversion of the corporation's property'.[9] Indeed, to the extent that possessory and control rights are the indicia of a property right, the board of directors is a better candidate for identification as the corporation's owner than are the shareholders. As an early New York opinion put it, 'the directors in the performance of their duty possess [the corporation's property], and act in every way as if they owned it'.[10]

## 2.   DIRECTOR PRIMACY: BOARD-CENTRIC GOVERNANCE

Taken together, the rules empowering directors and disempowering shareholders create a board-centric form of corporate governance that I named 'director primacy' (Bainbridge 2008). In this model, the board of directors is not a mere agent of the shareholders, but rather is a *sui generis* body whose powers are 'original and undelegated'.[11] To be sure, the directors are obliged to use their powers towards the end of shareholder wealth maximization,[12] but the decisions as to how that end shall be achieved are vested in the board not the shareholders.[13]

Separation of ownership and control and director primacy have been key characteristics of corporate governance in the United States since early in the nineteenth century (Werner 1981).[14] They have served the US economy well (Bainbridge 2008, 152–53).

---

holders' ability to affect the election of directors that determines the degree of influence they will hold over the corporation. The proxy regulatory regime discourages large shareholders from seeking to replace incumbent directors with their own nominees (Bainbridge 1992).

   [7]    *See* 15 U.S.C. § 78j, 78p; 17 C.F.R. §§ 240.10b-5, 16b-1-16b-8 (insider trading and short swing profit rules). Large block formation may also be discouraged by state corporate law rules governing minority shareholder protections. Under Delaware law, a controlling shareholder has fiduciary obligations to the minority. *See, e.g., Zahn v. Transamerica Corp.*, 162 F.2d 36 (3d Cir. 1947). A controlling shareholder who uses its power to force the corporation to enter into contracts with the shareholder or its affiliates on unfair terms can be held liable for the resulting injury to the minority. *See, e.g., Sinclair Oil Corp. v. Levien*, 280 A.2d 717 (Del. 1971). A controlling shareholder who uses its influence to effect a freeze-out merger in which the minority shareholders are bought out at an unfairly low price likewise faces liability. *See, e.g., Weinberger v. UOP, Inc.*, 457 A.2d 701 (Del. 1983).

   [8]    Eisenberg (1999, 825), for example, claims that shareholders possess most of the incidents of ownership, including 'the rights to possess, use, and manage, and the rights to income and capital'.

   [9]    *W. Clay Jackson Enterprises, Inc. v. Greyhound Leasing and Financial Corp.*, 463 F. Supp. 666, 670 (D. P.R. 1979).

   [10]    *Manson v. Curtis*, 119 N.E. 559, 562 (N.Y. 1918).

   [11]    *Ibid.*

   [12]    Admittedly, the text's claim with respect to the ends of corporate governance is contested on both descriptive and normative grounds by many of those who favor corporate social responsibility. For a defense of the text's claims, which space does not permit here, *see* Bainbridge (2008, 57–72).

   [13]    My work in this area was prompted by and has been much influenced by Dooley (1992), which in turn built on Arrow (1974).

   [14]    As Jennifer Hill observes, 'there are a number of important differences in the balance of power

The American Bar Association's Committee on Corporate Laws, which has drafting responsibility for the widely adopted Model Business Corporation Act, recently affirmed that 'the deployment of diverse investors' capital by centralized management maximizes corporate America's ability to contribute to long-term wealth creation' (ABA 2010, 4). As the Committee explains, the 'board centric' model gives shareholders 'the regular opportunity to elect the members of the board, but during the directors' terms, the board has the power, informed by each director's decisions in the exercise of his or her fiduciary duties, to direct and oversee the pursuit of the board's vision of what is best for the corporation' (ABA 2010, 4) Accordingly, although the drafters acknowledged the need to offer some concessions to shareholder activism, they also reaffirmed the Act's basic commitment to vesting 'the power to direct and oversee the management of the corporation in the board of directors, rather than in the shareholders' (ABA 2010, 5).

The Committee justified its board-centric approach by explaining that:

> If corporations were directly managed by shareholders, and the actions of management were the subject of frequent shareholder review and decision-making, the ability to rely on management teams would be diluted and the time and attention of managers could, in many cases, be diverted from activities designed to pursue sustainable economic benefit for the corporation. For example, valuable board time might have to be diverted to address referenda items propounded by particular shareholders who may have interests that diverge from those of other shareholders or interests other than sustainable economic benefit. In addition, since shareholders generally do not owe fiduciary duties to each other or the corporation, such power would not be accompanied by corresponding accountability. (ABA 2010, 5)

All of which is consistent with the claims of the director primacy model advanced herein.

## 3.    CHALLENGES

Despite director primacy's distinguished pedigree, the board-centric model is under attack from many directions. Influential academics like Lucian Bebchuk advocate 'readjusting the balance of power between shareholders and the board of directors in some key areas of US corporate law, including the corporate election process … and amendment of the' corporation's organic documents (Hill 2010, 10). Powerful institutional investors have pressed a similar agenda, advocating a number of forms of shareholder empowerment (Hill 2010).

The activists have had some considerable successes to date. 'As a response to a "growing push from institutional investors and other shareholder activist groups for a majority vote standard for the election of directors", the Delaware legislature amended' key sections of the General Corporation Law to facilitate the use of majority voting in the election of directors (Razzouk 2008, 404), as have the drafters of the Model Business Corporation Act. In an advisory opinion requested by the Securities and Exchange Commission (SEC), arising out of a shareholder proposal put forward by an activist union pension fund, the Delaware Supreme

---

between shareholders and directors in the US and UK, which have arguably produced different levels of shareholder activism in these countries'. She further explains that 'US corporate law is strikingly different to that in other common law jurisdictions, such as the UK and Australia, in terms of the ability of shareholders to alter the constitution'. (Hill 2010) The claimed domain for director primacy is limited to publicly held US corporations without a controlling shareholder.

Court expansively authorized shareholder-sponsored bylaws relating to the director election process.[15]

The Dodd-Frank Wall Street Reform and Consumer Protection Act[16] effects even more sweeping changes in corporate governance, all of which will empower shareholders vis-à-vis boards of directors. Among other things, the Act:

- mandates a 'say on pay' advisory shareholder vote on executive compensation;[17]
- authorizes the SEC to adopt rules granting shareholders access to the company's proxy statement to nominate directors;[18] and
- requires new disclosures relating to such issues as executive compensation and the structure of the board of directors.[19]

In light of these on-going challenges to director primacy, it is worth exploring some foundational questions, such as: do the constraints on shareholder control provided by corporate and securities law have an efficiency justification? Why are corporate decisions made through the exercise of authority rather than by consensus? What is the appropriate balance between authority and accountability?[20]

## 4.   AUTHORITY OR CONSENSUS?

Any organization needs a governance system that facilitates efficient decision-making. Although firms can choose amongst a wide array of options, most decision-making structures fall into one of two categories: 'consensus' and 'authority' (Arrow 1974, 68–70). Consensus is utilized where each member of the organization has comparable information and interests. Under such conditions, assuming no serious collective action problems, decision-maker preferences can be aggregated at low cost. In contrast, authority-based decision-making structures arise where team members have different interests and amounts or types of information. Such structures are characterized by the existence of a central agency to which all relevant information is transmitted and which is empowered to make decisions binding on the whole.

### On the Necessity of Authority

To be sure, Armen Alchian and Harold Demsetz (1972, 777) famously claimed that the firm 'has no power of fiat, no authority, no disciplinary action any different in the slightest degree from ordinary market contracting between any two people'. Hence, they argued, an

---

[15]   *CA, Inc. v. AFSCME Employees Pension Plan*, 953 A.2d 227, 237 (Del. 2008) ('The context of the Bylaw at issue here is the process for electing directors – a subject in which shareholders of Delaware corporations have a legitimate and protected interest.').

[16]   Pub. L. 111–203 (2010).

[17]   § 951.

[18]   § 971.

[19]   § 952–56, 972.

[20]   I have elsewhere addressed a closely related pair of questions, which space does not permit me to revisit herein; namely, why is corporate authority exercised hierarchically? Why is the firm's ultimate decision maker a collective rather than an individual? *See generally* Bainbridge (2008, Ch. 2).

employer's control over its employees differs not at all from the power of a consumer over the grocer with whom the consumer does business.

If fiat were not an essential attribute of 'firm-ishness', however, the firm would be just a legal fiction describing the space within which the set of contracts are worked out. Self-evidently, this is not the case insofar as public corporations are concerned. The public corporation has a central decision-maker – the board of directors – that wields powers of coordination within the firm quite different from those of a consumer vis-à-vis a grocer. Indeed, economic activity shifts from being conducted across markets to within firms precisely because it is sometimes more efficient to substitute entrepreneurial coordination for the price mechanisms of the market (Coase 1937).[21]

Coordination need not imply authority, of course. To the contrary, American business law allows one to choose between off-the-rack governance systems ranging from an almost purely consensus-based model to an almost purely authority-based model.[22] At one extreme, the decision-making structure provided by partnership law is largely a consensus model. Partners have equal rights to participate in management of the firm on a one-vote per partner basis. This outcome is predictable because all partners are also entitled to share equally in profits and losses,[23] giving them essentially identical interests (namely higher profits), and are entitled to equal access to information,[24] giving them essentially identical levels of information. In addition, the small size characteristic of most partnerships means that collective action problems generally are not serious in this setting.

At the other extreme, a publicly held corporation's decision-making structure is principally an authority-based one. As we have seen, the statutory separation of ownership and control means that shareholders have essentially no power to initiate corporate action and,

---

[21]   There are several ways in which organizing economic activity via fiat can reduce transaction costs vis-à-vis markets. Where production requires some form of team effort, for example, bringing economic activity within the boundaries of firm can reduce search and related bargaining costs (Coase 1937, 392). Bringing together employees, creditors, equity investors, and other necessary factors of production requires on-going interactions too complex to be handled through a price mechanism. The firm solves that problem by creating a centralized contracting party – some team member is charged with seeking out the necessary inputs and bringing them together for productive labor.

Fiat can also lower costs associated with uncertainty, opportunism, and complexity. Given the limits on cognitive competence implied by bounded rationality, incomplete contracts are the inevitable result of the uncertainty and complexity inherent in on-going business relationships. In turn, incomplete contracts leave greater room for opportunistic behavior. *See* Williamson (1975, 23), who argues that, under conditions of uncertainty and complexity, it becomes 'very costly, perhaps impossible, to describe the complete decision tree'. According to the Coasean theory of the firm, firms arise when it is possible to lower these costs by delegating to a team member the power to direct how the various inputs will be utilized by the firm. In other words, one team member is empowered to unilaterally rewrite terms of the contract between the firm and its various constituents.

The necessity for a centralized decision maker capable of making adaptive changes by fiat thus emerges as the defining characteristic of the Coasean firm. Obviously, fiat within firms has limits. Some choices are barred by contract, such as negative pledge covenants in bond indentures. Other choices may be barred by regulation or statute. Still other choices may be unattractive for business reasons, such as those with potentially adverse reputational consequences. Within such bounds, however, adaptation effected through fiat is the distinguishing characteristic of the firm.

[22]   See Dooley (1992, 466–68), which compares partnership and corporate law.

[23]   UPA (1997) § 401(b).

[24]   UPA (1997) § 403.

moreover, are entitled to approve or disapprove only a very few board actions. The statutory decision-making model thus is one in which the board acts and shareholders, at most, react.

Authority – a center of power capable of exercising fiat – within the corporation follows as a matter of course from the asymmetries of information and interests among the corporation's various constituencies. Shareholders care about the value of the residual claim on the corporation. Customers care about the quality and quantity of the goods produced by the corporation. Workers care about salary and conditions of employment. And so on. Under such conditions, efficient decision-making demands an authority-based governance structure.

Consider the problems faced by shareholders, who are conventionally assumed to be the corporate constituency with the best claim on control of the decision-making apparatus. At the most basic level, the sheer mechanical difficulties of achieving consensus amongst thousands of decision-makers impede shareholders from taking an active role. Just as cities get too big to be run by New England-style town meetings, so do corporations.

In large corporations, authority-based decision-making structures are also desirable because of the potential for division and specialization of labor (Clark 1986). Bounded rationality and complexity, as well as the practical costs of losing time when one changes jobs, make it efficient for corporate constituents to specialize. Directors and managers, for example, specialize in the efficient coordination of other specialists. In order to reap the benefits of specialization, all other corporate constituents should prefer to specialize in functions unrelated to decision-making, such as risk bearing (shareholders) or labor (employees), delegating decision-making to the board and senior management.[25] This natural division of labor, however, requires that the chosen directors and officers be vested with discretion to make binding decisions. Thus separating ownership and control by vesting decision-making authority in a centralized body distinct from the shareholders and all other constituents is what makes the large public corporation feasible.

Even if one could overcome the seemingly intractable collective action problems plaguing shareholder decision-making, the shareholders' widely divergent interests and distinctly different levels of information would still preclude active shareholder participation in corporate decision-making. Although neoclassical economics assumes that shareholders come to the corporation with wealth maximization as their goal, and most presumably do, once uncertainty is introduced it would be surprising if shareholder opinions did not differ on which course will maximize share value.[26] More prosaically, shareholder investment time horizons are likely to vary from short-term speculation to long-term buy-and-hold strategies, which in turn is likely to result in disagreements about corporate strategy. Even more prosaically, shareholders in different tax brackets are likely to disagree about such matters as dividend policy, as are shareholders who disagree about the merits of allowing management to invest the firm's free cash flow in new projects (Klein 1982).

---

[25]   *See* Arrow (1991), who argues that economies of scale in the information transmission process can be achieved only by elite control of organizations.

[26]   As my colleague Iman Anabtawi (2006) observes: 'On close analysis, shareholder interests look highly fragmented.' She documents divergences among investors along multiple fault lines: short-term versus long-term, diversified versus undiversified, inside versus outside, social versus economic, and hedged versus unhedged. My colleague Lynn Stout (1995, 616) similarly argues that 'in a world of costly and imperfect information, rational investors are likely to form heterogeneous expectations – that is, to make different forecasts of stocks' likely future performance'.

As to Arrow's information condition, shareholders lack incentives to gather the information necessary to actively participate in decision-making (Clark 1986). A rational shareholder will expend the effort necessary to make informed decisions only if the expected benefits of doing so outweigh its costs. Given the length and complexity of corporate disclosure documents, the opportunity cost entailed in making informed decisions is both high and apparent. In contrast, the expected benefits of becoming informed are quite low, as most shareholders' holdings are too small to have significant effect on the vote's outcome. Corporate shareholders thus are rationally apathetic. Instead of exercising their voting rights, disgruntled shareholders typically adopt the so-called Wall Street Rule – it's easier to switch than fight – and sell out.

The efficient capital markets hypothesis provides yet another reason 'for shareholders to eschew active participation in the governance process' (Dooley 1995, 483). If market prices are a valid indicator of performance, as the efficient capital markets hypothesis claims, 'investors can easily check the performance of companies in which they hold shares and compare their current holdings with alternative investment positions' (Dooley 1995, 483). An occasional glance at the stock market listings in the newspaper is all that is required. Because it is so much easier to switch to a new investment than to fight incumbent managers, a rational shareholder will not even care why a firm's performance is faltering. With the expenditure of much less energy than is needed to read corporate disclosure statements, he will simply sell his holdings in the struggling firm and move on to other investments.

Consequently, it is hardly surprising that the modern public corporation's decision-making structure precisely fits Arrow's model of an authority-based decision-making system. Overcoming the collective action problems that prevent meaningful shareholder involvement would be difficult and costly. Even if one could do so, moreover, shareholders lack both the information and the incentives necessary to make sound decisions on either operational or policy questions. Under these conditions, it is 'cheaper and more efficient to transmit all the pieces of information to a central place' and to have the central office 'make the collective choice and transmit it rather than retransmit all the information on which the decision is based' (Arrow 1974, 68–69).

Put another way, the public corporation succeeded as a business organization form because it provides a hierarchical decision-making structure well suited to the problem of operating a large business enterprise with numerous employees, managers, shareholders, creditors, and other inputs. In such a firm, someone must be in charge: 'Under conditions of widely dispersed information and the need for speed in decisions, authoritative control at the tactical level is essential for success' (Arrow 1974, 69). In other words, someone must possess the right to make decisions by fiat that are binding on the whole.

## 5.   AUTHORITY VERSUS ACCOUNTABILITY

A model of corporate governance premised on the value of authority necessarily raises the question of who will monitor the monitors. In any team organization, one must have some ultimate monitor who has sufficient incentives to ensure firm productivity without having to be monitored himself. Otherwise, one ends up with a never ending series of monitors monitoring lower-level monitors. Alchian and Demsetz (1972) solved this dilemma by consolidating the roles of ultimate monitor and residual claimant: if the constituent entitled to the firm's residual income is given final monitoring authority, he is encouraged to detect and punish shirking by the firm's other inputs because his reward will vary exactly with his success as a monitor.

Unfortunately, this elegant theory breaks down precisely where it would be most useful. Because of the separation of ownership and control, it simply does not describe the modern publicly held corporation. Because shareholders are the corporation's residual claimants, the Alchian and Demsetz theory predicts that shareholders should act as the firm's ultimate monitors. As we have seen, however, shareholder control rights are minimal. While the law provides shareholders with some enforcement and electoral rights, these are reserved for fairly extraordinary situations (Dooley 1992).

Berle and Means (1932, 6) thus famously claimed that 'the separation of ownership from control produces a condition where the interests of owner and of ultimate manager may, and often do, diverge and where many of the checks which formerly operated to limit the use of power disappear'. Jensen & Meckling (1976) formalized this concern by developing the concept of agency costs. In their wake, several generations of scholars have come to 'believe that the fundamental concern of corporate law is "agency costs"' (Greenfield 1998, 295).

In doing so, however, these scholars allow the tail to wag the dog. To be sure, deterrence and punishment of misconduct by the board and senior management is a necessary function of corporate governance. Accountability standing alone, however, is an inadequate normative account of corporate law. As explained above, a fully specified account of corporate law must incorporate the value of authority, i.e., the need to develop a set of rules and procedures that provides the most efficient decision-making system (Dooley 1992). At the core of the director primacy model therefore lies the normative claim that the virtues of authority, in terms of corporate decision-making efficiency, can be ensured only by respecting the board's decision-making.

The problem is that achieving an appropriate mix between authority and accountability is a daunting task. Ultimately, authority and accountability cannot be reconciled. At some point, greater accountability necessarily makes the decision-making process less efficient, while highly efficient decision-making structures necessarily entail non-reviewable discretion.

This is so because the power to review is the power to decide. As Arrow (1974, 78) observed: 'If every decision of A is to be reviewed by B, then all we have really is a shift in the locus of authority from A to B and hence no solution to the original problem.' Shareholder oversight of board decisions – whether through the vote or in courts – would effect just such a shift. It contemplates outside review of management decisions, with shareholders or judges stepping in to make corrections and changes when management performance falters. If it were easy for shareholders to obtain such reviews, directors might be more accountable, but the board's power of fiat would become merely advisory, rather than authoritative. The efficient separation of ownership and control that makes the modern corporation possible thus is inconsistent with routine shareholder review of board decisions.

The predictive power of director primacy is demonstrated in the host of legal doctrines and governance structures that resolve the tension between authority and accountability in favor of the former. Because only shareholders are entitled to elect directors, for example, boards of public corporations are insulated from pressure by non-shareholder corporate constituencies, such as employees or creditors. At the same time, the diffuse nature of US stock ownership and regulatory impediments to investor activism insulate directors from shareholder pressure. As such, the board has virtually unconstrained freedom to exercise business judgment.

Corporate law's respect for the board's authority is especially evident in its central doctrine; namely, the business judgment rule (Bainbridge 2008, 106–29):

> To encourage freedom of action on the part of directors, or to put it another way, to discourage inter-
> ference with the exercise of their free and independent judgment, there has grown up what is known
> as the 'business judgment rule.' Questions of policy of management, expediency of contracts or
> action, adequacy of consideration, lawful appropriation of corporate funds to advance corporate
> interests, are left solely to their honest and unselfish decision, for their powers therein are without
> limitation and free from restraint, and the exercise of them for the common and general interests of
> the corporation may not be questioned, although the results show that what they did was unwise or
> inexpedient.[27]

In a passage from its leading *Van Gorkom* decision that has received less attention than it deserves, the Delaware Supreme Court explained that:

> Under Delaware law, the business judgment rule is the offspring of the fundamental principle, codi-
> fied in [DGCL] § 141(a), that the business and affairs of a Delaware corporation are managed by or
> under its board of directors … The business judgment rule exists to protect and promote the full and
> free exercise of the managerial power granted to Delaware directors.[28]

In other words, the business judgment rule exists to protect director primacy. It permits authority to trump accountability absent bad faith or self-dealing.

## 6. THE DIRECTOR PRIMACY APPROACH TO SHAREHOLDER ACTIVISM

As we have seen, the board-centric model of corporate governance is currently under attack. The financial crisis of 2008 and the ascendancy of the Democratic Party in Washington have created an environment in which proponents of expanded shareholder corporate governance rights are making considerable progress. Even before the crisis hit, of course, there had been a number of efforts to extend the shareholder franchise, principally so as to empower institutional investors. The crisis, however, has given them new momentum (Bainbridge 2009).

The logic behind the shareholder empowerment project is that institutional investors will behave quite differently from dispersed individual investors. Because they own large blocks, and have an incentive to develop specialized expertise in making and monitoring investments, institutional investors could play a far more active role in corporate gover-nance than dispersed individual investors traditionally have done. Institutional investors holding large blocks thus have more power to hold management accountable for actions that do not promote shareholder welfare. Their greater access to firm information, coupled with their concentrated voting power, might enable them to more actively monitor the firm's performance and to make changes in the board's composition when performance lags (Roe 1994).

---

[27]   *Bayer v. Beran*, 49 N.Y.S.2d 2 (1944) (citations omitted).
[28]   *Smith v. Van Gorkom*, 488 A.2d 858 (Del. 1985).

In fact, however, institutional investor activism is rare and limited primarily to union and state or local public employee pension funds (Black 1998). As a result, institutional investor activism has not – and cannot – prove a panacea for the pathologies of corporate governance.

First, activist investors pursue agendas not shared by and often in conflict with those of passive investors. With respect to union and public pension fund sponsorship of shareholder proposals under existing law, for example, Roberta Romano observes that:

> It is quite probable that private benefits accrue to some investors from sponsoring at least some shareholder proposals. The disparity in identity of sponsors – the predominance of public and union funds, which, in contrast to private sector funds, are not in competition for investor dollars – is strongly suggestive of their presence. Examples of potential benefits which would be disproportionately of interest to proposal sponsors are progress on labor rights desired by union fund managers and enhanced political reputations for public pension fund managers, as well as advancements in personal employment … Because such career concerns – enhancement of political reputations or subsequent employment opportunities – do not provide a commensurate benefit to private fund managers, we do not find them engaging in investor activism. (Romano 2001, 231–32)

Second, activism by investors undermines the role of the board of directors as a central decision-making body, thereby making corporate governance less effective. While some argue that shareholder activism 'differs, at least in form, from completely shifting authority from managers to' investors (Roe 1994, 184), it is in fact a difference in form only. Shareholder activism necessarily contemplates that institutions will review management decisions, step in when management performance falters, and exercise voting control to effect a change in policy or personnel. For the reasons identified above, giving investors this power of review differs little from giving them the power to make management decisions in the first place. Even though investors probably would not micromanage portfolio corporations, vesting them with the power to review board decisions inevitably shifts some portion of the board's authority to them. This remains true even if only major decisions of A are reviewed by B.

Finally, relying on activist institutional investors will not solve the principal-agent problem inherent in corporate governance but rather will merely shift the locus of that problem. The vast majority of large institutional investors manage the pooled savings of small individual investors. From a governance perspective, there is little to distinguish such institutions from corporations. The holders of investment company shares, for example, have no more control over the election of company trustees than they do over the election of corporate directors. Nor do the holders of such shares have any greater access to information about their holdings, or ability to monitor those who manage their holdings, than do corporate shareholders. Worse yet, although an individual investor can always abide by the Wall Street Rule with respect to corporate stock, he cannot do so with respect to such investments as an involuntary, contributory pension plan (Bainbridge 2009).

## 7.   CRITICISMS

### Director Primacy Lacks Predictive Power

A theory is properly judged by its predictive power with respect to the phenomena it purports to explain, not by whether it is a valid description of an objective reality (Friedman 1953). With respect to legal theories, the key question thus is whether it facilitates accurate predictions about the content of the law. In particular, the predictive power of any model of the corporation must be measured by the model's ability to predict the separation of ownership and control, the formal institutional governance structures following from their separation, and the legal rules responsive to their separation.

This mode of analysis suggests a rather different approach to corporate law scholarship than is typical in the literature. Like most legal scholarship, corporate law scholarship tends to be critical of the status quo. Few self-respecting legal academics will end an article or book without some sort of reform proposal. This is perfectly understandable, of course. Academic rewards skew towards the new and novel. A rather different concern, however, motivated my work on director primacy; namely, to understand the existing statutory framework of corporate governance in US law.

I set out not to reform the statutory allocation of power, but simply to understand it. My premise is that corporate law tends towards efficiency. A state generates revenue from franchise and other taxes imposed on firms that incorporate in the state. The more firms that choose to incorporate in a given state, the more revenue the state generates. Delaware, the runaway winner in this competition, generates so much revenue from incorporations that its resident taxpayers reportedly save thousands of dollars a year.

In order to attract capital, managers must offer investors attractive terms. Among those terms are the corporate governance rules imposed on investors by the law of the state of incorporation. Accordingly, managers have an incentive to incorporate in states offering terms preferred by investors. In turn, states have an incentive to attract incorporations by offering such terms. State competition for charters therefore results in a race to the top, driving corporate law towards efficient outcomes.[29] Accordingly, the task was to develop a model that explains and predicts the structure of corporate law as it exists today.

Apropos of which, Christopher Bruner (2008) argues that director primacy fails to account for certain key aspects of corporate law. If true, this would be a significant criticism.

First, Bruner asserts that director primacy has 'a difficult time accounting for the law of corporate takeovers, and the absence of any clear mandate to maximize the wealth of shareholders under any but the most limited circumstances' (Bruner 2008, 1398). In fact, however, I addressed those issues in detail in an article entitled *Unocal at 20: Director Primacy in Corporate Takeovers*, which acknowledged that Delaware's takeover jurisprudence is almost universally condemned in the academic corporate law literature. Building on my director primacy model, however, I offered a defense of that jurisprudence. Specifically, I argued that Delaware courts struck an appropriate balance between two competing but equally legitimate goals of corporate law: on the one hand, because the power to review differs only in degree and not in kind from the power to decide, the discretionary authority of the board of directors must be insulated from shareholder and judicial oversight in order to promote efficient corporate decision-making. On the other hand, because directors are obligated to maximize shareholder wealth, there must be mechanisms to ensure director accountability. The framework developed by the Delaware courts provides them with a mechanism for filtering out those cases in which directors have abused their authority from those in which directors have not (Bainbridge 2006b).

---

[29]   These are, of course, highly contested claims. I defend them in detail in Bainbridge (2002, 14–16).

Second, Bruner argues that:

> The very existence of any shareholder voting power inevitably proves problematic for those who identify the board as the very essence of the corporate enterprise itself. Bainbridge, for example, who depicts the board as a 'sui generis body' and 'a sort of Platonic guardian,' justifies giving voting power to shareholders by reference to the disciplinary effects of the market for corporate control (made possible by the transferability of their interests), but then proves amenable to 'sharply constrain[ing]' the market for control through takeover defenses in favor of the efficiency of board governance – an account that undercuts its own explanation for the existence of even minimal shareholder voting rights. (Bruner 2008, 1399)

In a world of pure director primacy, in which directors could be counted on to be faithful to the shareholder wealth maximization norm, shareholder voting rights likely would not exist. Hence, in *The Case for Limited Shareholder Voting Rights*, I argued that shareholder voting is properly understood not as an integral aspect of the corporate decision-making structure, but rather as an accountability device of last resort to be used sparingly, at best. Why sparingly? As we have just seen, corporate governance is made at the margins of an unending competition between two competing values; namely, authority and accountability. Both are essential to effective corporate governance, but they are ultimately irreconcilable. Efforts to hold someone to account inevitably limit their discretion. The inconsistency Bruner claims to see in my work arises inherently out of this tension between authority and accountability. Shareholder voting is an accountability mechanism, exercised mainly through the takeover market, but preservation of the board's authority requires that both the franchise and the market for corporate control have limits (Bainbridge 2006a).

Even if Bruner is correct that director primacy fails to explain all aspects of the current corporate legal regime, I've believed for a long time that there is no unified field theory that explains all of corporate governance. In *Executive Compensation: Who Decides?*, for example, I wrote that:

> Physicists have long sought a unified field theory, which would provide a single set of simple laws that explain the four interactions or forces that affect matter – i.e., the strong, electromagnetic, weak, and gravitational forces. To date, they have failed, which provides a strong cautionary tale for anyone seeking a unified field theory of social interactions among fallible humans, whose behavior is far harder to predict than is that of, say, an electron. (Bainbridge 2005, 1628)

But so what? Elegant and parsimonious models are more important for economists than for lawyers. Instead, situation-specific mini-theories often are more useful for making legal decisions than a single unified theory. I thus do not claim that director primacy explains everything about corporate governance. My claim is only that director primacy does a better job explaining the separation of ownership and control, the formal institutional governance structures following from their separation, and the legal rules responsive to their separation than any other theory on the market. It thus satisfies Friedman's test for the utility of a model.

**The Persistence of Imperial CEOs**

George Dent (2008) argues that managerialism remains the reality of modern corporate governance. Imperial CEOs remain the dominant force rather than boards of directors. One answer to this argument is that I set out not to explain the real world dynamics of the

CEO–board relationship, but rather to provide an explanation of why corporate statutes contemplate director primacy. From this perspective, the Imperial CEO phenomenon is a perversion of the statutory ideal to be criticized as such.

In addition, the real world dynamics of the board–CEO relationship seem to be shifting in the former's favor. As I argued in Bainbridge (2002, 206):

> During the 1980s and '90s, several trends coalesced to encourage more active and effective board oversight. Much director compensation is now paid in stock, for example, which helps align director and shareholder interests. Courts have made clear that effective board processes and oversight are essential if board decisions are to receive the deference traditionally accorded them under the business judgment rule, especially insofar as structural decisions are concerned (such as those relating to corporate acquisitions). Third, director conduct is constrained by an active market for corporate control, ever-rising rates of shareholder litigation, and, some say, activist shareholders. In sum, modern boards of directors are smaller than their antecedents, meet more often, are more independent from management, own more stock, and have better access to information ...
>
> In any event, the institutional structure created by corporate law allows but does not contemplate one-man rule. If it comes to overt conflict between board and top management, the former's authority prevails as a matter of law, if not always in practice.

## The Arrowian Moment

Critics of the director primacy model sometimes suggest that it overstates the importance of authority. Brett McDonnell (2009, 143), for example, argues that 'Bainbridge moves very, very quickly from recognizing the tension between authority and accountability to arguing that we should presume a legal structure that favors authority over accountability, unless there are strong arguments against that presumption'. Apropos the discussion in the preceding section, however, I contend that the utility of director primacy is confirmed by its ability to explain one of the truly striking things about US corporation law; namely, the extent to which the balance between authority and accountability in fact leans towards the former. As we've seen, for example, a host of rules serve to limit the power of shareholders vis-à-vis directors. As we've also just seen, the business judgment rule is designed precisely 'to protect and promote the full and free exercise of the managerial power granted to Delaware directors'.[30]

In the closely related context of the procedural rules governing shareholder derivative litigation, the New York Court of Appeals stated in *Marx v. Akers* that 'By their very nature, shareholder derivative actions infringe upon the managerial discretion of corporate boards ... Consequently, we have historically been reluctant to permit shareholder derivative suits, noting that the power of courts to direct the management of a corporation's affairs should be "exercised with restraint".'[31] The *Marx* court further noted the need to strike 'a balance between preserving the discretion of directors to manage a corporation without undue interference, through the demand requirement, and permitting shareholders to bring claims on behalf of the corporation when it is evident that directors will wrongfully refuse to bring such claims', which is precisely the balance between authority and accountability the director primacy model predicts.

---

[30] *Smith v. Van Gorkom*, 488 A.2d 858, 872 (Del. 1985).
[31] *Mark v. Akers*, 666 N.E.2d 1034, 1037 (N.Y. 1996) (quoting *Gordon v. Elliman*, 119 N.E.2d 331, 335 (N.Y. 1954)); see also *Pogostin v. Rice*, 480 A.2d 619, 624 (Del. 1984) ('[T]he derivative action impinges on the managerial freedom of directors ...').

We observe similar rules seemingly designed to protect the board's authority in statutory provisions, such as those governing transactions in which the directors are personally interested, including management buyouts, which involve a significant conflict of interest and therefore tend to get close judicial scrutiny, but which receive judicial deference in appropriate cases (Bainbridge 1993, 1074–81). The same is true for the similar problem of target board of director resistance to unsolicited takeover bids (Bainbridge 2006b).

On the other hand, I have never claimed that the board should have unfettered authority. In some cases, accountability concerns become so pronounced as to trump the general need for deference to the board's authority. Once again, I turn to Arrow (1974, 78):

> To maintain the value of authority, it would appear that [accountability] must be intermittent. This could be periodic; it could take the form of 'management by exception,' in which authority and its decisions are reviewed only when performance is sufficiently degraded from expectations …

Given the significant virtues of discretion, however, I continue to believe that one must not lightly interfere with the board's decision-making authority in the name of accountability.

McDonnell (2009, 143) contends that this argument proves too much when applied to real-world problems, however:

> The argument that Bainbridge borrows from Arrow only tells us that there is a trade-off between authority and accountability, and that both have real value. It also tells us that it will generally be unwise to choose a structure that eliminates authority completely in favor of accountability, or vice versa. None of the major pro-accountability reform proposals currently in play, however, comes even close to eliminating board authority. In the world in which we live today, Arrow's argument is not able to tell us whether reform in favor of somewhat more accountability at the expense of some, but far from a total, loss in authority is a good idea or not.

It's certainly the case that to say a particular proposed reform would shift authority from directors to shareholders is more of a description than an argument. Even so, however, I find McDonnell's critique ultimately unpersuasive.

I have never denied that the argument McDonnell (2009, 143) calls my 'Arrowian moment' does much more than establish a general presumption in favor of respecting director authority.[32] Each doctrinal problem must be carefully analyzed to determine where to strike the balance between authority and accountability. The necessary analysis typically requires one to go beyond the 'Arrowian moment' to consider other policies. Hence, for example, my analysis of the business judgment rule acknowledged that:

> Critics of the [Arrowian moment] likely would concede that judicial review shifts some power to decide to judges, but contend that that observation is normatively insufficient. To be sure, they might posit, centralized decision making is an essential feature of the corporation. Judicial review could serve as a redundant control on board decision making, however, without displacing the board as the primary decision maker. (Bainbridge 2008, 114)

---

[32]   As we have just seen, however, such a presumption has considerable explanatory value when one reviews the many corporate law doctrines that enshrine deference to boards. If one grants my starting hypothesis that corporate law tends towards efficient solutions, those doctrines are persuasive evidence for director primacy.

To explain why the presumption in favor of authority prevails in this context, accordingly, I moved on to consider other policies, such as encouraging risk taking, preventing hindsight bias, and so on.

Similarly, I acknowledge that it's not enough to point out that proposals to change the shareholder voting process would shift the balance towards accountability. One must go on to ask why such a shift is undesirable (or, preferably, to defend the presumption against such a shift). Hence, in Bainbridge (2008, Ch. 5), for example, I went on to consider such questions as whether the shareholders would use the powers activists propose to give them, whether certain shareholders are more likely to do so than others, and whether those shareholders are likely to use their new powers to pursue private gains at the expense of other shareholders.

In sum, director primacy sets the stage. It defines the parameters within which the debate over particular issues takes place. It enables one to make broad predictions about the law and foundational critiques of legal rules that depart from those predictions. The fact that specific problems sometimes require additional fine tuning is hardly proof that the basic model is flawed.

Having made that concession, however, I must immediately, by way of analogy, recall Benjamin Cardozo's famous dictum that the legal duties of a fiduciary should not be undermined by 'the "disintegrating erosion" of particular exceptions'.[33] Just so, if one believes that authority has survival value, one should protect the board of directors' decision-making authority from the 'disintegrating erosion' of reform.

This does not mean that one should always reject reforms that shift the balance towards accountability. It does, however, suggest one must pay attention to the cumulative impact of repeated reform proposals, lest one subject the board's authority to the legal equivalent of death by a thousand cuts. It also suggests that there ought to be at least a presumption in favor of authority. In light of the huge advantages authority offers the corporate form, the burden of rebutting that presumption should be on those who wish to constrain the board's authority.

## 8.   CONCLUSION

In sum, there are significant economic advantages to vesting ultimate decision-making authority in a small group rather than either a single executive or a dispersed body of shareholders. For much of the last century, persistent market failures allowed for managerial domination. In recent years, however, pressures for greater accountability have enabled the economic advantages of board-centered governance to overcome those market failures. The problem now is to solidify those gains and to continue empowering the board of directors.

## REFERENCES

Alchian, Armen A. & Harold Demsetz (1972), 'Production, Information Costs, and Economic Organization', *American Economics Review*, 62, 777–795.
Anabtawi, Iman (2006), 'Some Skepticism About Increasing Shareholder Power', *UCLA Law Review*, 53, 561–99.

---

[33]   *Meinhard v. Salmon*, 249 N.Y. 458, (N.Y. 1928).

Arrow, Kenneth J. (1974), *The Limits of Organization*, New York: W. W. Norton & Co.

Arrow, Kenneth J. (1991), 'Scale Returns in Communication and Elite Control of Organizations', *Journal of Law, Economics, and Organization*, 7, 1–6.

Bainbridge, Stephen M. (1992), 'Redirecting State Takeover Laws at Proxy Contests', *Wisconsin Law Review*, 1992, 1071–1145.

Bainbridge, Stephen M. (1993), 'Independent Directors and the ALI Corporate Governance Project', *George Washington Law Review*, 61, 1034–83.

Bainbridge, Stephen M. (1995), 'The Politics of Corporate Governance', *Harvard Journal of Law and Public Policy*, 18, 671–734.

Bainbridge, Stephen M. (2002), *Corporation Law and Economics*, New York: Foundation Press.

Bainbridge, Stephen M. (2005), 'Executive Compensation: Who Decides?', *Texas Law Review*, 83, 1615–1662.

Bainbridge, Stephen M. (2006a), 'The Case for Limited Shareholder Voting Rights', *UCLA Law Review*, 53, 601–636.

Bainbridge, Stephen M. (2006b), 'Unocal at 20: Director Primacy in Corporate Takeovers', *Delaware Journal of Corporate Law*, 31, 769–863.

Bainbridge, Stephen M. (2008), *The New Corporate Governance in Theory and Practice*, Oxford: Oxford University Press.

Bainbridge, Stephen M. (2009), 'Shareholder Activism in the Obama Era', available at SSRN: http://ssrn.com/abstract=1437791 (last accessed October 2011).

Berle, Adolf A. & Gardiner C. Means (1932), *The Modern Corporation and Private Property*, New York: Commerce Clearing House, Inc.

Black, Bernard S. (1998), 'Shareholder Activism and Corporate Governance in the United States', in *The New Palgrave Dictionary of Economics and the Law*, London: Palgrave Macmillan.

Bruner, Christopher M. (2008), 'The Enduring Ambivalence of Corporate Law', *Alabama Law Review*, 59, 1385–1449.

Clark, Robert C. (1986), *Corporate Law*, Boston: Little, Brown & Co.

Coase, Ronald (1937), 'The Nature of the Firm', *Economica*, 4(16), 386–405.

Committee on Corporate Laws of the American Bar Association Section of Business Law (2010) 'Report on the Roles of Boards of Directors and Shareholders of Publicly Owned Corporations', available at: http://www.abanet.org/media/nosearch/task_force_report.pdf (last accessed October 2011).

Dent, George W. (2008), 'Academics in Wonderland: The Team Production and Director Primacy Models of Corporate Governance', *Houston Law Review*, 44, 1213–1274.

Dooley, Michael P. (1992), 'Two Models of Corporate Governance', *Business Lawyer*, 47, 461–528.

Dooley, Michael P. (1995), *Fundamentals of Corporation Law*, Westbury, NY: Foundation Press.

Eisenberg, Melvin A. (1999), 'The Conception that the Corporation is a Nexus of Contracts, and the Dual Nature of the Firm', *Journal of Corporation Law*, 24, 819–836.

Friedman, Milton (1953), 'The Methodology of Positive Economics', in *Essays in Positive Economics*, Chicago: University of Chicago Press.

Greenfield, Kent (1998), 'The Place of Workers in Corporate Law', *Boston College Law Review*, 39, 283–328.

Hill, Jennifer G. (2010), 'The Rising Tension between Shareholder and Director Power in the Common Law World,' available at SSRN: http://ssrn.com/abstract=1582258 (last accessed October 2011).

Jensen, Michael C. & William H. Meckling (1976), 'Theory of the Firm: Managerial Behavior, Agency Costs, and Ownership Structure', *Journal of Financial Economics*, 3, 305–60.

Klein, William A. (1982), 'The Modern Business Organization: Bargaining Under Constraints', *Yale Law Journal*, 91, 1521–64.

Manning, Bayless (1958), 'Book Review', *Yale Law Journal*, 67, 1477–1496.

McDonnell, Brett H. (2009), 'Professor Bainbridge and the Arrowian Moment: A Review of "The New Corporate Governance in Theory and Practice"', *Delaware Journal of Corporate Law*, 34, 139–190.

Razzouk, Jay (2008), 'The Momentum, Motive, and Mouse-Kapades of the Majority Vote Movement', *Journal of Business, Entrepreneurship and the Law*, 1, 391–420.

Roe, Mark J. (1994), *Strong Managers, Weak Owners: The Political Roots of American Corporate Finance*, Princeton, N.J.: Princeton University Press.

Romano, Roberta (2001), 'Less Is More: Making Shareholder Activism a Valued Mechanism of Corporate Governance', *Yale Journal on Regulation*, 18, 174–251.

Stout, Lynn A. (1995), 'Are Stock Markets Costly Casinos? Disagreement, Market Failure, and Securities Regulation', *Virginia Law Review*, 81, 611–712.

Werner, Walter (1981), 'Corporation Law in Search of its Future', *Columbia Law Review*, 81, 1611–1666.

Williamson, Oliver E. (1975), *Markets and Hierarchies: Analysis and Antitrust Implications*, New York, N.Y.: The Free Press.

# 3. Corporate law and the team production problem
*Margaret M. Blair*[1]

## 1. INTRODUCTION

Should corporations be managed for the sole purpose of maximizing share value for corporate shareholders? While for much of the last three decades the dominant perspective in corporate law scholarship and policy debates about corporate governance has adopted this view, the corporate scandals of 2001 and 2002, followed by the disastrous performance of financial markets 2007–2009, has left many observers uneasy about this prescription. A number of strong shareholder value advocates have shifted their recommendations. Michael Jensen (2001), one of the leading advocates of share value maximization in the 1980s and 1990s, has recognized that shareholder value can be increased without adding to social wealth by extracting value from other corporate participants, such as creditors. He now argues that corporate managers should maximize 'not just the value of the equity but also ... the market values of all other financial claims including debt, preferred stock, and warrants' (Jensen 2001). Likewise, former GE CEO Jack Welch, considered by some to be the 'father of the "shareholder value" movement' among corporate boards and managers now says that 'shareholder value is a result, not a strategy ... your main constituencies are your employees, your customers, and your products' (Guerrera 2009). Among academics, Lucian Bebchuk, one of the most outspoken and prolific advocates of enhanced shareholder rights now concedes that 'the common shareholders in financial firms do not have an incentive to take into account the losses that risks can impose on preferred shareholders, bondholders, depositors, taxpayers underwriting governmental guarantees of deposits, and the economy' (Bebchuk & Spamann 2010, 2–3).

As advocates back away from a commitment to shareholder value maximization as the exclusive goal of corporate governance, some scholars and practitioners have considered the 'team production' framework for understanding the social and economic role of corporations and corporate law (Blair & Stout 1999) as a leading candidate for a viable alternative (Hansmann & Kraakman 2000–2001; Hamilton & Macey 2009; Frey & Osterloh 2005; Gelter 2009; Daily et al. 2003; Boatright 2009; Sharfman & Toll 2009; Bainbridge 2008).[2] The team production problem in economics refers to the problem of organizing productive activity that involves complex inputs from a number of different people (Alchian & Demsetz 1972) – a problem that pervades nearly all business enterprises. The problem is how to get

[1]    Professor Blair would like to thank the Alfred P. Sloan Foundation and the Vanderbilt University Law School Law & Business program for financial support. She would also like to thank Tim Mitchell and Lin Hou for helpful research assistance. All errors are those of the author.
    [2]    Not all of these scholars whole-heartedly support adopting the team production framework, but they acknowledge that it is a leading contender. *See also Citizens United v. Federal Election Commission*, 558 U.S. (2010), dissent, at note 72.

the contributors of all the different inputs to fully cooperate with each other in situations that don't lend themselves to drafting and enforcing complete, detailed contracts – precisely the situations most likely to lead to production being governed within a firm rather than by contract (Williamson 2002).

The team production framework challenges the 'principal-agent' framework, which dominated corporate law and economics scholarship in the 1980s and 1990s, and continues to be influential today (Jensen & Meckling 1976; Easterbrook & Fischel 1991; Shleifer & Vishny 1997). The principal-agent framework provided a strong justification for the focus on share value. This framework is premised on the idea that the central problem to be solved in the governance of corporations is getting the managers and directors of the corporation to be faithful 'agents' of shareholders. Shareholders are understood to be the 'owners' or 'principals' of the business enterprise undertaken by the corporation. The principal-agent framework has been used by many scholars to model the problem first identified by Adolf Berle and Gardiner Means (1932) as the 'separation of ownership from control'. Scholars who have tried to explain or analyze corporate law using the principal-agent approach, therefore, have generally assumed that the social goal of corporations is to generate profits for shareholders, an assumption which has been called 'shareholder primacy'. Using the principal-agent framework, scholars have analyzed a number of features of corporate law, from shareholder voting rights, to executive compensation arrangements, to takeover rules, in terms of whether they serve to maximize the value of equity shares, or provide incentives to corporate directors and managers to do this.[3]

The team production framework, by contrast, does not incorporate an a priori assumption about who, among parties to a common enterprise, should be regarded as the 'principal' and who should be regarded as the 'agent'. For this reason, it can be seen as a generalization of the principal-agent problem that is symmetric: all of the participants in a common enterprise have reason to want all of the other participants to cooperate fully. A team production analysis thus starts with a broader assumption that all of the participants hope to benefit from their involvement in the corporate enterprise, and that all have an interest in finding a governance arrangement that is effective at eliciting support and cooperation from all of the other participants whose contributions are important to the success of the joint enterprise.

Insights from a team production analysis provide a rationale for a number of features of corporate law that are problematic under a principal-agent framework. As such, it does a somewhat better job of explaining how many aspects of corporate law actually work, as well as provides a better normative framework for understanding what corporate directors are supposed to do. Below, I explain the economic theory of teams, and review various institutional arrangements that, in theory at least, can help solve the contracting problems that arise in team production. Next, I review six features of the corporate form that distinguish corporations from other organizational forms. While a principal-agent analysis of these features suggests that most of them would tend to exacerbate agency costs rather than reduce them, I argue that these features of modern corporations may provide remedies to the mutual co-operation problems that arise in team production. In the following section, I discuss several recent developments in corporate law that have tilted in the direction of shareholder primacy,

---

³   For further discussions in this volume, *see* Smith (voting rights), Ferri (same), Walker (executive compensation), and Davidoff (takeover rules).

even as corporate law scholarship has increasingly recognized that maximizing value for shareholders of corporations does not always lead to the optimal social outcome. I then address some of the criticisms that have been aimed at the team production framework and argue that those problems are no more troubling than the problems that plague shareholder primacy.

## 2.  THE ECONOMIC THEORY OF TEAMS AND TEAM PRODUCTION

The team production problem arises when a productive activity involves multiple parties, each contributing complex inputs that are difficult to contract over. Alchian and Demsetz (1972) defined team production as 'production in which 1) several types of resources are used … 2) the product is not a sum of separable outputs of each cooperating resource … [and] 3) not all resources used in team production belong to one person' (Alchian & Demsetz 1972, 779).

When these conditions hold, as is often the case in business ventures, it may not be possible to organize this kind of production by contracting over the inputs, because it may not be possible to clearly specify and measure the inputs ex ante. Likewise, equal-sharing or fixed-sharing contracts would also be problematic because they would give each participant an incentive to shirk, or to free ride on other participants. This is because, under an ex ante rule, each participant will get the same share of output whether she fully contributes or not. On the other hand, if the participants try to write open-ended contracts in which the output shares will be determined ex post, all will have incentives to expend resources in 'rent-seeking' – haggling and competing for a larger share of the pie once the size of the pie has been determined (Blair & Stout 1999).

In their initial analysis of the team production problem, Alchian and Demsetz argued that a solution is to establish a hierarchy, in which one member of the team specializes in monitoring all of the other members to make sure that all are contributing adequately (Alchian & Demsetz 1972). To be sure that the monitor has appropriate incentives to do this well, Alchian and Demsetz proposed that the monitor should have hiring and firing authority, that the other team members should be employees of the monitor who are paid according to their opportunity costs, and that the monitor should receive all the economic surplus or profits created by the enterprise.

Alchian and Demsetz argued that this solution to the team production problem provides a 'theory of the firm', and that it helps explain why people organize productive activity in 'firms'. Their proposed solution, however, resembles an individual proprietorship, where the same party has both 'ownership' and 'control' over the business. It does not resemble a corporation in which the parties who have hiring and firing authority (as well as other decision-making authority) are not the same as the parties who capture the profits from the enterprise. Thus this initial attempt to analyze the team production problem does not shed light on what distinguishes corporate law from law governing other business forms.

Subsequent analyses of the team production problem have generally focused on production that requires each team member to contribute some specialized skills, or make specialized ('firm-specific') investments in the joint enterprise. When all team members have team-specific investments at risk, the contracting problem is especially hard to solve, and participants generally cannot write complete contracts to cover all of the possible scenarios that the business will face over its life. Nonetheless, by bringing some real world complexity to the economic models, the 'solutions' that economic theorists produce begin to look more like real world firms. Economist Oliver Hart and various co-authors (Grossman & Hart 1986; Hart & Moore 1990; Hart 1988, 1989) have proposed, for example, that the contracting problem can be solved by assigning property rights over assets used in production to one of the participants. This gives the 'owner' the right to make decisions that have not previously been specified by contract. But which of the participants should be the 'owner'? Hart and his co-authors concede that there is no first-best solution to this problem if multiple parties must make specific investments. The best solution that can be achieved, they claim, is to assign property rights over the enterprise to the party whose specialized investments are most critical to the success of the enterprise (Grossman & Hart 1986; Blair & Stout 1999).

This solution, however, may not be adequate if the contributions of more than one person are critical to the success of the enterprise. Moreover, the proposed solution again looks more like an individual proprietorship than a publicly-traded corporation in which control rights and rights to receive the residual benefits have been split up, with the former going to managers and the latter going, at least in part, to shareholders.

In considering a similar problem, economists Raghuram Rajan and Luigi Zingales (1998) note that assigning property rights over the firm's assets to one member of the team might not solve the problem if those rights also give the 'owner' the right to sell the assets. This is because an 'owner' who can sell the assets might be able to capture more of the team surplus by arranging to sell the assets than by making the critical specialized investments that she needs to make in order for the team to be as productive as possible. Thus, if one member of the team is given ownership rights (as Hart and co-authors propose), the other members may be reluctant to make specific investments in the enterprise.

Rajan and Zingales (1998) suggest that instead of giving control rights to one team member, all of the team members might be better off if they agree to give up certain critical decision rights to an outsider, someone who is not a member of the team and has no other stake in the enterprise.[4] The decision-rights that the outsider should get include the right to

---

    [4]    The role of outsider in Rajan and Zingales's model is similar, but not identical, to the role of the 'budget breaker' in an early effort by Bengt Holmstrom (1982) to model a solution to the team production problem. Holmstrom studied the problem that arises if the members of the team bring specialized skills, or must make specialized ('firm-specific') investments. Holmstrom asked whether it would be possible to write a contract as a function of the output of the enterprise (rather than trying to contract over inputs, which would be hard to monitor) that provides incentives that will discourage all team members from shirking. His conclusion, sometimes known as 'Holmstrom's impossibility theorem' (see http://en.wikipedia.org/wiki/Holmstr%C3%B6m's_theorem (last accessed November 2011)) was that to provide correct incentives for team members, each team member must bear the full cost of his own shirking. But he showed that it is mathematically impossible to create a contract that allocates the full cost of each team member's shirking to that team member, unless all team members are punished for the shirking if any one team member shirks. The math is complicated, but the intuition is simple. If there are, say, n team members, and each team member is to receive 1/n of the total output, then all team members would have an incentive to shirk, because each would bear only 1/n of the cost of shirking. The solution is to set a target output level, a level that can only be reached if no one shirks, then agree that each team member will receive 1/n of the output only if the output reaches the target level. If output fails to reach the target level, this would be taken as evidence that at least one team member shirked, say by withholding some fraction, $\alpha$, of the expected contribution. Since a monitor will not be able to discern which team member shirked, all team members would have their compensation

choose the members of the team (hiring and firing rights), and the right to allocate economic surpluses created by the team. But this outsider would not be an 'owner' since it is important that she may not lay claim personally to the assets of the enterprise, nor be able to sell those assets. According to Rajan and Zingales (1998), the outsider in such an arrangement should be compensated with a small fraction of the total surplus created by the enterprise, to give her an incentive to choose the team that can generate the largest surplus.

Rajan and Zingales (1998) interpret their decision-maker model as offering an explanation for the role of outside shareholders in publicly-traded corporations. But the role played by their decision-maker does not resemble the role of outside shareholders in actual corporations. Outside shareholders are highly unlikely to be involved in most decisions. Blair and Stout (1999), instead, propose that the role of outside decision-maker identified by Rajan and Zingales (1998) looks more like the role played by a board of directors in a publicly-traded corporation. Directors do not own the assets of a corporation, and they may not sell those assets and pocket the proceeds. They could, acting as a body, direct the managers to sell the assets, but the proceeds of such a sale would go to the corporation, not to the directors. Directors (except for so-called 'inside directors' who are members of the management team) are usually generalists who do not make substantial specialized investments in the firm. But corporate law provides that they are the ultimate decision-makers for the corporation. Thus by starting with a symmetric team production problem, with its agnostic perspective about whose interests should be served by a corporation, rather than with an asymmetric principal-agent problem in which shareholders are assumed to be the principals, Blair and Stout argue that a role for an independent board of directors in a corporation, with substantial decision-making authority, emerges endogenously.[5] The separation of control rights and decision rights from the ownership of assets is, therefore, not an infirmity of the corporate form that

---

cut by $\alpha$. This would effectively punish the shirker (so the shirker would not have an incentive to shirk), but it would also mean that $n*\alpha$ of the output would not be distributed. What should happen to this left-over output? Holmstrom's solution requires that some outsider be solicited who would serve as what he called a 'budget breaker' (Holmstrom 1982, 325). That person's only role would be to take the excess output when some team member shirks. Holmstrom argued that his model explained why it might be beneficial to separate ownership from control in capitalist business enterprises, but his solution does not look quite like any institutional arrangements that we see in practice. In fact, if the budget breaker is assumed to be a person, this solution would have the perverse effect of creating a situation in which it would be in the interest of the budget breaker to conspire with one of the team members to shirk a bit, to ensure that the team does not meet its target level of output. The Holmstrom solution, hence, has not often been discussed as part of the economics of corporate law, although Blair and Stout (1999) suggested that the corporation itself – a legal person that cannot conspire on its own behalf – could serve as the budget breaker by retaining output – failing to pay dividends or give raises, for example – when output is low.

    5    Oliver Williamson (1985, 306) has also argued that the institution of the board of directors 'arises endogenously, as a means by which to safeguard the investments of [shareholders] who face a diffuse but significant risk of expropriation.' Steven Bainbridge has made a similar point, though for different reasons. 'Separating ownership and control by vesting decision-making authority in a central-ized nexus distinct from the shareholders and all other constituents is what makes the large corporation feasible' (Bainbridge 2002, 202). It should not be surprising that some of the same institutional arrange-ments might arise under team production analysis as well as under principal-agent analysis because, as noted earlier, team production analysis is a generalization of principal-agent analysis (or, alternatively, principal-agent analysis is a special case of team production analysis). But in both Williamson's and Bainbridge's analysis, the board of directors would be answerable to shareholders, whereas corporate law in the US typically makes boards quite autonomous.

needs to be corrected or offset by other institutional arrangements. Rather, it is, under a team production analysis, an essential aspect of the corporate form that makes it attractive for organizing certain kinds of productive enterprises.

## 3.    THE CORPORATE FORM AS A SOLUTION TO THE TEAM PRODUCTION PROBLEM

Corporate law scholars have identified a number of features that distinguish corporations from other business organizations. In recent years, business entity law has evolved to permit business people to form a growing variety of hybrid organizational forms that combine features from partnerships with features more typical of corporations. But to understand why business organizers might want to choose a corporate characteristic rather than a partnership characteristic, it is useful to consider the function of each feature. This part reconsiders several widely recognized features of classical business corporations. When these features are assessed within a principal-agent framework, they are often seen as problematic in that they appear to lead to increased agency costs (even though they may help solve other problems). But considering them within a team production framework sheds light on how they may help to reduce transactions costs associated with team production.

John Armour, Henry Hansmann and Reinier Kraakman (2009) identify five legal features that are characteristic of business corporations across most national jurisdictions: 'legal personality, limited liability, transferable shares, delegated management under a board structure, and investor ownership' (Armour et al. 2009, 1).[6] In addition to these five, this chapter will also consider a sixth feature, 'indefinite existence'.

### Legal Personality, or Separate Existence, or Separate Entity Status for the Corporation

Corporations (unlike individual proprietorships or common law partnerships), are legal entities, separate under the law from their managers, shareholders, creditors, employees, and even from individual board members. As such, they can purchase, own, and sell property, enter into contracts, and sue and be sued in the name of the corporation rather than in the name of any of its participants.[7] Separate entity status is the most important of the characteristics of corporations, because most of the other distinguishing attributes are a consequence of the fact that the corporation has a separate existence (Blair forthcoming).

---

6    In fact, Armour et al. (2009, 2) assert that 'a principal function of corporate law is to provide business enterprises with a legal form that possesses these five core attributes'. The last of these attributes, 'investor ownership' does not seem well-defined in the context of corporations, so this problem will be considered below.

7    Armour et al. (2009, 9) define 'legal personality' as organizational forms that share the attributes of being 'capable of entering into contracts and owning its own property; capable of delegating authority to agents; and capable of suing and being sued in its own name'. Yet it seems odd and imprecise to say that corporations 'delegate authority to agents'. Instead, the law, in creating the entities, delegates all authority to act and decide for corporations to their boards of directors. Directors, then, acting as a board, may delegate authority to managers.

Separate existence of the corporation serves a number of important functions, from facilitating contracting among the participants in the corporation, to keeping corporate assets separate from the personal assets of the participants,[8] to permitting the business and assets of the corporation to continue, even as various participants come and go. Separate legal existence, however, is hard to explain under the standard agency theory account of corporate law, in which shareholders are viewed as principals in a complex set of interlocking contracts in which other key participants – especially directors, managers, and employees – are supposed to be pursuing the best interest of the shareholders. In fact, the earliest literature on the principal-agent theory of the firm (Jensen & Meckling 1976) assumed away separate legal existence by postulating that a firm (and a corporation in particular) is no more than a legal fiction that serves as a nexus of contracts. Subsequent corporate law scholarship adopting a principal-agent analysis has frequently denied that separate entity status is important.

Yet separate legal existence (entity status) precedes, and is even more fundamental to the nature of the corporation than shareholders. A corporation must come into existence as a separate entity before it can issue and sell stock to shareholders. Moreover, corporations can exist without shareholders. The earliest corporations were eleemosynary institutions (such as churches, hospitals, and universities), or civil institutions (such as townships and municipalities) that did not have shareholders. Modern non-profit corporations (which own a sizeable share of total wealth in the US) also have no shareholders. While for-profit corporations have shareholders, those shareholders do not legally own the assets of the corporation, and they cannot compel a corporation to distribute its assets to shareholders. The exception is in corporations that have only a single shareholder, and even in this case, there are legal limits on how much of the assets the shareholder may take out.[9]

While separate entity status fits uncomfortably with shareholder-centric principal-agent theories of the firm, it serves a critical function in team production theories. The team production theory of corporate law emphasizes that all of the participants in a corporation are mutually interested in fostering the cooperation of, and protecting themselves from any dishonest tendencies of all of the other participants (Blair & Stout 1999). In this context, separate entity status serves a number of valuable purposes. It provides a mechanism by which the team assets used in production can all be owned by the same entity; it commits the assets to use by the team for team purposes because those assets are not owned directly by any of the team members; and it ensures that no team members have the right to take the assets out of the corporation or expropriate them for personal use. This makes it easier for all of the participants to credibly commit to working toward a common goal (Blair 2003a). It may also be easier to elicit mutual cooperation by all of the participants if that goal is understood to be maximizing the total value generated by the enterprise, rather than the total value captured by one group of participants.

---

8    Hansmann and Kraakman (2000) have called this function 'asset partitioning', which is a combination of limited liability and what I have elsewhere called 'capital lock-in' (Blair 2003a).

9    See e.g., MBCA §6.40 (Imposing constraints on distributions to shareholders). In corporations with a single shareholder, the primary purpose of corporate form is to enable the single investor/entrepreneur to separate out assets that are available to pay the personal creditors of the entrepreneur from those that are available to pay the creditors of the business. This situation could alternately be characterized as a solution to a specific type of 'team production problem' between the entrepreneur and her business creditors, in which the commitment of assets by the entrepreneur to the separate legal entity which is carrying out the business helps to reassure business creditors that the entrepreneur will use business assets to repay the creditor before she takes out assets for herself.

## Limited Liability

The idea that shareholders do not have personal liability for debts of the corporation is hard to square with an assertion that shareholders are the 'owners' of corporations. Ownership of property in every other context implies not only that the owner can possess the property, use it for his own purposes, or dispose of it, but also that the owner can be held liable for misuse of property that harms others (Restatement (Second) of Torts §281 (1977)). But limited liability for shareholders makes perfect sense if we understand the corporation as a separate legal entity that supports team production. If the entity is separate, then it follows more or less naturally that, while all of the participants can lose what they contributed to the entity (the creditors their loaned funds, the managers and employees their time and human capital, the suppliers their as yet unpaid-for supplies, the shareholders their initial capital investment), none can be held personally responsible for compensating any of the other participants, or third parties such as tort claimants, for losses that the corporation cannot pay. Limited liability for shareholders makes their contribution to the joint enterprise quite similar to the contribution of creditors, except in the order of priority in which they are paid in any final disposition or settlement.[10]

## Transferable Shares

Because a corporation is a separate legal entity, shareholders have limited liability, and the contribution of shareholders qua shareholders is simply money, the identity of the shareholders may be a matter of complete indifference to the enterprise and to the other participants. The contribution (and associated claims) of shareholders can thus be divided up into completely fungible units, which can be parsed, or held in portfolios, or traded among various investors without having any direct impact on the enterprise or its other participants. This is one of the truly brilliant innovations of the corporate form of organizing businesses. Having fungible shares separates the task of contributing capital from any other contribution that a specific investor might make, and ensures that capital can be committed to the enterprise without requiring a commitment by any particular capital provider to continue to participate. The ability to 'lock-in' the capital without locking in the capital provider makes it vastly easier for entrepreneurs to raise committed capital (Blair 2003a).

The ready transferability of shares is quite problematic, however, for a principal-agent theory of the corporation in which shareholders are supposed to be the 'principals'. Shareholders are not all alike in terms of their goals for their investments, or their values or views about what the goals should be for the corporations in which they invest (Rose 2010). Moreover, as shareholdings turn over in any given corporation, the goals of shareholders will

---

[10]    In bankruptcy settlements, however, it is commonly the case that shareholders recover some positive amount even if creditors have not recovered every dime of value that they are owed (Longhofer & Carlstrom 1995). The frequency of this outcome is evidence that shareholders are not the only 'residual claimants' in a corporation, and that other participants in the corporation are not fully protected by contract with the corporation. In many other contexts, too, events and actions that benefit shareholders may have a negative effect on other corporate participants. Klein and Zur (2011), for example, show that when a hedge fund activist takes an equity stake in a corporation, the share price of the target company goes up, but the firm's bondholders lose almost as much value as the shareholders gained.

likely be in continuous flux. Numerous observers have commented that the share turnover rate of corporations listed on the major stock exchanges in the US is very high (Strine 2010). Thus, any mandate or expectation that the corporation should be run solely in the interest of shareholders would be impossible to satisfy.

Multiple goals and frequent turnover among shareholders is less problematic under team production analysis, however. This approach starts from the premise that various team members will have multiple, sometimes competing goals that must be negotiated and balanced as team members work through what they are doing, how they will do it, and how any value created is going to be divided.[11] The most important constraint on how the proceeds of the enterprise are divided up is that each participant or team member must capture sufficient value to cause him to stay on the team and continue to contribute (Blair & Stout 1999). This means that the team must try to ensure that shareholders receive a satisfactory return on investment including adequate compensation for risk. But it notably does not mean that boards of directors or managers must try to 'maximize share value', as is often asserted by advocates of shareholder primacy. Consistent with team production analysis, but contrary to principal-agent analysis and shareholder primacy, corporate law does not require that directors or managers must maximize share value.[12]

**Delegated Management Under a Board Structure**

The role of the board of directors in corporations has been the subject of much debate (Blair & Stout 2001). Under a shareholder-centric principal-agent analysis, it has been argued that control rights in corporations have been delegated to boards to take advantage of the benefits of specialization, with some corporate participants providing risk capital, while others provide management expertise (Jensen & Meckling 1976; Easterbrook & Fischel 1991; Meese 2002). The same theorists who extol the benefits of specialization also argue that the

---

[11]   This same analysis would thus apply even if the only team members being considered were various shareholders (Bratton & Wachter 2009–2010).

[12]   A narrow exception applies in what has been called the 'Revlon' context, *Revlon, Inc.* v. *MacAndrews & Forbes Holdings, Inc.* Del. S.C. 506 A.2d 173 (1986). When, in the midst of a negotiation regarding the acquisition of a corporation by another corporation, it becomes inevitable that the target corporation will be acquired, at that point, the board of directors of the target firm must try to get the highest price they can get for the target company shares. But even in the opinion in *Revlon*, the court was clear that this is an exception, and that the duty 'changes' once the Revlon conditions apply. In most other contexts, courts have repeatedly affirmed that directors may balance the interests of shareholders against the interests of other corporate participants. E.g., *Unocal Corp.* v. *Mesa Petroleum Co.* Del. S.C. 493 A.2d 946 (1986) (providing that directors may consider the 'impact on "constituencies" other than shareholders' in deciding how to respond to an unsolicited tender offer). The Delaware Chancery Court, in a recent case involving eBay and Craigslist (*eBay Domestic Holdings, Inc.* v. *Craig Newmark*, A.2d, 2010 WL 3516473 (Del.Ch.), at 21) found that a poison pill adopted by Craigslist was not valid because the interest it was intended to protect – Craigslist's 'values, culture and business model, including [Craigslist's] public-service mission', was not a 'proper corporate purpose' because the Craigslist executives and controlling shareholders who implemented the pill failed to show 'that there was a sufficient connection between the Craigslist "culture" (however amorphous and intangible it might be) and the promotion of stockholder value'. *Ibid.*, at 22. This finding raises questions I will address later in this chapter, but even here, the court did not clearly say that controlling shareholders have a duty to 'maximize' share value, only that 'the corporate form … is not an appropriate vehicle for purely philanthropic ends'. *Ibid.*, at 23.

role of directors is to serve as faithful agents of shareholders in directing the firm in such a way as to maximize share value.

This latter assertion, however, is at odds with the legal description and duties of directors. Under corporate law, directors are not agents of any particular group of participants in the corporation (Clark 1985).[13] If directors were indeed legal agents of shareholders, then ownership would not be separated from control, because shareholders could dictate to their agents what they are supposed to do. Corporate law makes it clear, however, that directors are neither agents of shareholders nor of any other corporate participants. Directors acting as a body (and not individually) are authorized by the law to exercise 'all corporate powers' and to manage or direct 'the business and affairs of the corporation'.[14] The board of directors is thus the human decision-maker and nerve center of the corporation. Corporate officers and managers are agents of the corporation (not of the shareholders) and are subject to the oversight of directors. But the board itself is empowered to act for the corporation without being subject to the oversight or direction of any of the other participants in the corporation. Moreover, corporate law holds that directors and officers have fiduciary duties to the corporation itself and sometimes to the corporation and the shareholders,[15] but it does not specify how the interests of the corporation are to be determined.[16] Enriques et al. argue that such duties are 'most naturally understood as a command to maximize the net aggregate returns (pecuniary and non-pecuniary) of *all* corporate constituencies ...' (Enriques et al. 2009, 103).[17]

This legal description of board governance is completely consistent with the team production theory of corporate law. Under team production theory the participants in a corporate enterprise agree to yield ultimate decision-making authority to the board so that they can more easily overcome mutual shirking and rent-seeking problems. The internal hierarchy of the corporation, according to Blair and Stout (1999), must coordinate the activities of the team members, allocate the resulting production, and mediate disputes among team members over that allocation. 'At the peak of this hierarchy sits a board of directors whose authority over the use of corporate assets is virtually absolute and whose independence from individual team members is protected by law' (Blair & Stout 1999, 753).

---

[13]    In *New York Dock Co.* v. *McCollum*, 16 N.Y.S. 2d 844, 847 (N.Y. Sup. 1939) the court found that 'a director of a corporation is not an agent either of the corporation or of its stockholders ... [Rather] his office is a creature of the law'.

[14]    MBCA Sec. 8.01(b).

[15]    In older cases, courts often found that directors' fiduciary duties ran to 'the corporation' (e.g., *Sterling* v. *Mayflower Hotel Corp.*, 93 A.2d 107, 109 (Del. 1952)). But more recently, courts have found that the duties run to 'the corporation and its shareholders' (e.g., *North American Catholic Educational Programming Foundation, Inc.* v. *Gheewalla*, 930 A.2d 92, 99 (Del. 2007)). Occasionally courts have said that the duties run only 'to shareholders', but this formulation is applied primarily when the concern of the courts is protection of minority shareholders in a closely held corporation (e.g. *eBay Domestic Holdings, Inc.* v. *Newmark*).

[16]    Enriques et al. (2009) observe that 'the corporate law of many jurisdictions provides that directors owe their duty of loyalty to the company rather than to any of its constituencies, including its shareholders.' (Enriques et al. 2009, 103).

[17]    Enriques et al. (2009) fret, however, that because courts cannot enforce a duty to maximize aggregate private welfare, 'the injunction to boards to pursue their corporations' interests is less a species of equal sharing than, at best, a vague counsel of virtue, and, at worst, a smokescreen for board discretion'.

**Investor Ownership**

The idea that shareholders are the 'owners' of corporations at first seems more consistent with a principal-agent interpretation of corporate law than it is with a team production interpretation. But Armour et al. (2009), who identify 'investor ownership' as a distinguishing characteristic of the corporate form, have adopted a very narrow and specialized notion of 'ownership'. As they use the term, the statement that investors are the 'owners' of corporations is intended to capture two ideas, that parties who contribute capital to the firm in the form of equity shares have the right to 'control the firm' and that they also have the right to 'receive the firm's net earnings'.

These authors equate 'controlling the firm', however, with the right to vote in elections for directors, and to vote on certain other corporate transactions. While shareholders typically do get these rights, these rights hardly constitute 'control', given that normally only the board of directors nominates individuals for election to the board,[18] and only the board of directors may plan and propose corporate transactions (such as a mergers) that require shareholder approval. In fact, one of the great puzzles of corporate law, if one starts from a principal-agent perspective, is why shareholders have the right to vote on so few things (Blair 2003b; Bebchuk 2007).

Likewise shareholders get pro-rata shares of any distributions that the board of directors decides to pay out to shareholders, but this is hardly the same thing as having the right to a firm's net earnings. Corporate law makes it clear that shareholders only get what is paid out to them, and that the decision about when and what to pay out resides solely with directors. As long as the net earnings are retained in the firm, they do not belong to the shareholders. And, while it would be true in theory that shareholders would get the 'residual value' that is left after payment to all other corporate participants in a complete liquidation of the firm, it is notable that the 'residual value' claim applies in practice only at the time when the corporation is being wound up and its existence coming to an end (and is often violated even then, with shareholders often receiving some value for their shares even when creditors have not all been paid, dollar for dollar, all that was owed to them) (Longhofer & Carlstrom 1995). For example, Mark Roe and David Skeel (2010) describe how this happened recently in the restructuring of Chrysler in bankruptcy.

Armour et al. note that the default rule for business corporations is that both voting rights and the rights to receive dividends are allocated in proportion to capital contributions by shareholders, taking this as evidence that 'the law of business corporations is principally

---

[18]   Shareholders have the right to nominate persons to serve as directors, but in publicly-traded corporations, it is very costly to for shareholders to do so unless they have access to the proxies that will be mailed to all shareholders. Pursuant to the Dodd-Frank Wall Street Reform and Consumer Protection Act of 2010, the SEC in August of 2010 amended federal proxy rules to make it easier for shareholders who meet certain conditions to have their nominees for board elections placed on the company's proxy. The new rule was immediately challenged by the US Chamber of Commerce and the Business Roundtable, and in the summer of 2011, the US Court of Appeals for the District of Columbia struck down the new rule on the grounds that the SEC had not adequately considered the rule's effects on companies. In September of 2011, the SEC announced that it would not appeal this decision (Statement by SEC Chairman Mary L. Schapiro on Proxy Access Litigation, available at http://www.sec.gov/newws/press/2011/2011-179.htm (last accessed November 2011). The decision left in place amendments to Rule 14a-8 which allow shareholders to propose proxy access bylaw amendments.

designed to facilitate the organization of investor-owned firms' (Armour et al. 2009, 14–16). But proportional allocation of voting rights and distributions may simply be a product of the fact that the shares are designed to be fungible and transferable.[19] If shares have any voting rights or claims to distributions, those rights and claims must be allocated proportionately in order for the shares to be fungible.

If one starts with a team production framework, however, there is no particular need to identify one or another group of participants as 'owners'. Instead, all participants are seen to bring different contributions and any or all may have some specific contractual rights. But the allocation of any surplus value is left to the board of directors, and the board itself retains all unallocated control rights. When the corporation is doing well, most of the firm's participants will also do well, and when times are not so good, many of the firm's participants will experience losses.

**Indefinite Existence**

In addition to the five distinguishing characteristics of business corporations identified by Armour et al. (2009), another important feature is that corporations can continue to exist long after the initial organizers, directors, and investors are gone and have been replaced by others. This feature has been called 'indefinite existence' or 'indefinite duration' (Klein et al. 2010, 109). It facilitates the accumulation of assets in a firm that are dedicated to the team enterprise, and is closely associated with a feature of corporate law that I have elsewhere called 'capital lock-in' (Blair 2003a; Bank 2006). Once shareholders have paid capital into a corporation to purchase shares, shareholders cannot compel the firm to buy back the shares or even to pay dividends, and neither can any of the creditors or heirs of the shareholders. The assets stay 'locked in' the corporation until the board of directors decides to distribute them. While these legal rules are problematic from the perspective of a principal-agent model, they are easy to explain under a team production model of the firm because they protect all of the parties who make specific investments in the firm, making it possible for the corporation to commit both capital and the earnings from capital over time to the enterprise that the firm is undertaking, while encouraging similar commitments on the part of providers of human capital.

## 4.   CRACKS IN THE DOMINANCE OF SHAREHOLDER PRIMACY

Recent scholarship on corporate governance increasingly acknowledges problems with viewing corporate governance issues solely through the shareholder-centric principal-agent model (Frey & Osterloh 2005; Daily et al. 2003; Boatright 2009; Sharfman & Toll 2009). After early excitement about findings by Gompers et al. (2003) and Bebchuk (2005) that suggested that superior stock market performance could be predicted in corporations by indices of the strength of shareholder rights in a firm (constructed by counting up the presence or absence of certain governance provisions), more recent work suggests that this relationship has not

---

[19]    Only shares of the same class are expected to be fungible. Thus different classes of shares may get different voting rights that are not necessarily proportional to capital contribution.

held up over time (Core et al. 2006; Bhagat & Bolton 2008). While Gompers et al. (2003) found that corporations with weak shareholder rights had relatively poor stock price performance, and firms with strong shareholder rights had strong stock price performance, they found no evidence of correlation between weak shareholder rights and weak operating performance. By contrast, Core et al. (2006) and Bhagat & Bolton (2008) find the opposite, that firms with weak shareholder rights tend to have poor operating performance, but not poor stock price performance. Core et al. (2006) argue that their findings are consistent with the relationship between shareholder rights and stock price performance in the 1990s not being a causal relationship – with poor shareholder rights leading to poor performance – but resulting instead from some kind of anomaly of the 1990s. An important mechanism by which weak shareholder rights are thought to lead to weak corporate performance is that firms with weak shareholder rights are harder for outsiders to take over, and thus are less likely to be disciplined by the market for corporate control (Core et al. 2006). But Core et al. (2006) find that 'weak governance firms are taken over at about the same rate as strong governance firms' (2006, 657) (these studies define 'weak governance firms' as those with weak shareholder rights and strong protections for existing management).

In addition to studies by finance scholars that cast doubt on the hypothesized causal relationship between weak (strong) shareholder rights and weak (strong) stock price performance, management and finance scholars have expressed concern that the empirical facts of how corporations are organized and governed do not fit the principal-agent model (Garvey & Swan 1994; Daily et al. 2003), and note that most empirical studies based on principal-agent models have had little or no ability to predict financial performance or other measures of performance consistently (Daily et al. 2003; Bhagat & Bolton 2008).[20] Evidence is at best mixed on whether reforms based on enhancing shareholder power, or making boards of directors more independent, succeed in enhancing non-financial corporate performance (Bhagat & Bolton 2008; Core et al. 2006; Bhagat & Black 2002; Daily et al. 2003; Kaufman & Englander 2005; Stout 2007; Arlen & Talley 2003–2004). Meanwhile, scholars have found no systematic evidence of a significant negative effect on the performance of share prices in firms where employees have explicit influence on the boards of directors, through co-determination (Aguilera & Jackson 2010).

While it is not clear that shareholder primacy reforms enhance corporate performance, an exclusive focus on share value may actually harm corporate performance. Legal scholars have noted lately that shareholders do not all have the same interests, and that this raises challenges for simple principal-agent models of corporate governance (Rose 2010). And finance and legal scholars have begun examining the implications of the fact that shareholders who hedge away their financial interest in a corporation can have interests that are diametrically opposed to all of the other participants in the corporation, including the other shareholders (Partnoy 2000; Hu & Black 2006, 2007). Financial derivatives now make it possible for all of the claims and rights associated with share ownership to be broken apart

---

[20]    Although Bhagat & Bolton (2008), like Core et al. (2006) do find a positive correlation between measures of strong shareholder rights and operating performance, they find no relationship between the same measures of shareholder rights and stock market performance. This is the reverse of what Gompers et al. (2003) and Bebchuk et al. (2005) found. Notably, none of these studies include data on the performance of firms in the years leading up to and including the financial market crisis of 2008–2009.

and traded separately (Partnoy 2000), which raises numerous questions about what is in the interest of any given shareholder, let alone shareholders as a group.

Moreover, individuals and financial firms that hold or acquire significant holdings in a corporation may encourage the firm to engage in a variety of speculative activities that are not aligned with society's best interests, as became painfully apparent during the widespread series of financial crises that began in 2007. Klein and Zur (2011), for example, find that when hedge funds acquire a significant stake in a target corporation, the stock price of the target firm's shares increases, but the firm's bonds lose almost as much value as the shareholders gain. In fact, Bratton & Wachter (2010) argue that an analysis of the tendency of shareholders to encourage managers to take excessive risks (thereby imposing costs on other corporate stakeholders as well as the society at large) would likely show that the financial firms that were most responsive to pressures from the market for increases in share prices were the firms that took on excessive leverage and consequently fell the furthest during the crisis. Countrywide Financial Corp., they note 'was [a] clear market favorite [among banks] at least until mid-2007' but quickly turned into 'one of the clear villains in the story' (Bratton & Wachter 2010, 718). Similarly, the *New York Times* has documented that while Washington Mutual Inc. ('WaMu') internally tracked and documented the extraordinary amount of risk it was undertaking as it continued to purchase mortgages that had little or no documentation behind them well into 2008, it did not abjure this business because to do so 'would have devastated profits' in the short run (Norris 2011). WaMu was another poster child of the failures in the financial markets. Both Countrywide and WaMu collapsed in 2008 and had to be taken over by other banks, at considerable cost to taxpayers.

In the wake of the corporate scandals of the early 2000s, and at an accelerating pace in the last few years, prominent shareholder rights advocates have conceded that it may not always be in society's best interests for corporations to be run solely to maximize share value. Michael Jensen, for example, now argues that corporate managers should try to maximize 'the market values of all other financial claims including debt, preferred stock, and warrants' (Jensen 2001). Similarly, Lucian Bebchuk and Holger Spamann (2010) now admit that maximizing value for shareholders can impose costs on other participants in the firms and on society generally. In particular, they now propose that bankers should be compensated in ways that encourage them to take into account risks on 'preferred shareholders, bondholders, depositors, and taxpayers' as well as on shareholders, by, for example, tying compensation not just to the performance of common shares, but to a 'broader basket of securities' (Bebchuk & Spamann 2010, 6). Although Bebchuk and Spamann (2010) apply their reasoning solely to banks, the same logic applies to all corporate enterprises.[21] More generally, some scholars have proposed alternative models for understanding corporate governance in which boards and managers are said to be agents for multiple principals (Rose 2010, 1375–7), while others have begun to consider the agency costs associated with shareholder empowerment (Bratton & Wachter 2010).

---

[21]   Some might object that this argument only applies to banks because a bank's downside risk is borne in part by the government, but Bebchuk and Spamann (2010) specifically say that they believe their argument would hold even without deposit insurance. 'Even if they [depositors] were not protected by insurance, the vast majority of small depositors would have neither the incentives nor the resources to monitor the bank's behavior' they observe (Bebchuk & Spamann 2010, 11).

None of these problems, or their proposed solutions, is surprising under a team production analysis. Team production theory would predict that corporate governance reforms designed to tie the incentives of boards and managers to those of shareholders, or to give shareholders more access to or influence over directors or managers, will not necessarily improve the overall performance of the firms. Team production theory accommodates the fact that shareholders are not monolithic, and that the task of managing and governing a corporation requires a balancing of interests, rather than a commitment to benefit one set of interests, even at the expense of the others.

Only a few leading law and economics scholars have explicitly adopted the team production framework to address the problems with shareholder primacy. But, once it is conceded that it may not be in society's interests for corporate managers and directors to focus exclusively on 'maximizing share value', or, indeed, that a mandate to maximize share value even has the same meaning for all shareholders, theories about the role of corporate directors in the face of competing interests among shareholders and other stakeholders take on most of the important features of the team production model as laid out by Blair & Stout (1999).

These cracks in the intellectual dominance of the shareholder-centric principal-agent approach to analyzing corporate law and corporate governance come even as corporate governance law and policy itself moves in various ways toward increasing shareholder power in corporations. In the early 1990s, the SEC relaxed rules that restricted institutional shareholders from exchanging information with each other about corporate governance matters in portfolio companies. This made it easier for institutional shareholders to freely communicate with each other and with other shareholders without triggering filing requirements with the SEC (Blair 1995; Monks & Minow 1995). Similarly, the emergence of proxy advisory services has offered a market solution to the collective action problem that inhibited shareholder action in the past (US GAO 2007). Rose has developed evidence that institutional shareholders now have some significant influence on corporate policies (Rose 2010). In particular, institutional investors have become increasingly active in pressuring portfolio companies to eliminate poison pills and staggered boards, to disclose executive compensation arrangements and to give shareholders a chance to approve or disapprove of them, and to change voting rules so that directors can only be elected by the affirmative vote of a majority of outstanding shares. In the wake of the corporate scandals of 2001–2002, Congress passed the Sarbanes-Oxley Act[22] that imposed new requirements for director independence at publicly-traded corporations.

The US Congress was apparently also persuaded that shareholders should be given even more clout in corporate governance arrangements, rather than less, and enshrined in the Dodd-Frank Wall Street Reform and Consumer Protection Act[23] that the SEC should rewrite its rules to ensure that corporations must give shareholders the right to approve compensation packages for executives, and to give shareholders easier access to proxies for nominating directors. The SEC acted on this during the summer of 2010, but two prominent business groups immediately challenged the new rules. In the summer of 2011 the US Court of Appeals for the District of Columbia struck down the proxy access rule that the SEC had put in place, and in September 2011 the SEC announced that it would not appeal this decision.[24]

---

[22]   Pub. L.107–204, 116 Stat.745.
[23]   Pub. L. 111–203.
[24]   Statement by SEC Chairman Mary L. Schapiro on Proxy Access Litigation available at http://www.sec.gov/news/press/2011/2011-179.htm (last accessed November 2011).

Finally, there may even be a shift under way in the approach of the Delaware Courts, which have long given deference to the 'business judgment' of directors and officers of corporations when they make decisions that benefit other corporate stakeholders, even at some short-term cost to shareholders, as long as there is some reason (however weak) to believe that shareholders will benefit in the long run (Blair & Stout 1999). In a decision reached in September, 2010 (*eBay Domestic Holdings, Inc.* v. *Craig Newmark*, A.2d., 2010 WL 3516473), the Chancery Court announced that 'a corporate policy that specifically, clearly, and admittedly seeks not to maximize the economic value of a for-profit Delaware corporation for the benefit of its stockholders' cannot be a valid corporate purpose'.[25] This finding has not yet been confirmed by the Delaware Supreme Court, and there are reasons to believe that its application may be limited to a close corporation context in which majority shareholders are harming the interest of a minority shareholder by consciously refusing to pursue profit opportunities. Nonetheless, it represents the most explicit adoption of share value maximization language by Delaware courts to date.

If a widespread corporate commitment to maximizing share value, despite the risks and costs imposed on others, was one of the factors that contributed to the financial bubble and subsequent collapse, these legal and regulatory changes are going in the wrong direction (Blair 2011; Bratton & Wachter 2010).

## 5.  CONCLUSION

More than a decade ago, Professors Margaret Blair and Lynn Stout developed an alternative framework for understanding corporate law that was well grounded in economic theory, but that did not reify 'share value' as the most important goal of corporations. Their framework recognized and accommodated interests of other corporate participants as well as shareholders. Although the team production framework has been criticized (from both the Right and the Left) on the grounds that it does not provide clear directions for boards of directors (Meese 2002; Millon 2000), there is growing reason to believe that leaving the direction of corporations to the business judgment of directors (while bidding them to be responsible corporate citizens and to pay attention to the larger social costs and benefits of corporate action) may not be worse, and may be better in many instances, than instructing them and incentivizing them to do whatever it takes to make share prices higher. As the weaknesses in the shareholder primacy view of corporate governance have become increasingly apparent, this alternative, the 'team production theory', may be seen as increasingly relevant.

---

[25]    Under the facts of this case, which Chancellor Chandler repeatedly noted were 'unique', the controlling shareholders in Craigslist, Inc., Craig Newmark and James Buckmaster, adopted a 'poison pill' that harmed the interest of minority shareholder eBay by making it nearly impossible for eBay to sell or transfer its holdings in Craigslist to some other party. Newmark and Buckmaster defended their adoption of the pill on the grounds that it protected Craigslist 'culture' using an argument that Delaware Courts had accepted in *Time* v. *Paramount*, 571 A.2d 1140 (Del. 1989). Part of that 'culture' was the idea that Craigslist should be operated as a public service, rather than to make a profit, and Newmark and Buckmaster claimed that they wanted to make sure that this commitment to public service continued even after they died, even if their heirs were to sell out to eBay or another party. The case is, thus, a classic case of shareholder 'oppression' in a closely-held corporation.

# REFERENCES

Aguilera, Ruth V. & Gregory Jackson (2010), 'Comparative and International Corporate Governance', *Academy of Management Annals*, 4, 485–556.

Alchian, Armen A. and Harold L. Demsetz (1972), 'Production, Information Costs, and Economic Organization', *American Economic Review*, 62, 777–795.

Arlen, Jennifer and Eric Talley (2003–2004), 'Unregulable Defenses and the Perils of Shareholder Choice', *University of Pennsylvania Law Review*, 152, 577–666.

Armour, John, Henry Hansmann and Reinier Kraakman (2009), 'What is Corporate Law?', in Reinier Kraakman, John Armour, Paul Davies, Luca Enriques, Henry Hansmann, Gerard Hertig, Klaus Hopt, Hideki Kanda, & Edward Rock (2009), *The Anatomy of Corporate Law: A Comparative and Functional Approach*, New York: Oxford University Press, 1–34.

Bainbridge, Steven M. (2002), 'The Board of Directors as a Nexus of Contracts', *Iowa Law Review*, 88, 1–33.

Bainbridge, Steven M. (2008), *The New Corporate Governance in Theory and Practice*, Oxford: Oxford University Press.

Bank, Steven A. (2006), 'A Capital Lock-In Theory of the Corporate Income Tax', *Georgetown Law Journal*, 94, 889–947.

Bebchuk, Lucian A. (2005), 'The Case for Increasing Shareholder Power', *Harvard Law Review*, 118, 835–914.

Bebchuk, Lucian A. (2007), 'The Myth of the Shareholder Franchise', *Virginia Law Review*, 93, 675–732.

Bebchuk, Lucian A. & Holger Spamann (2010), 'Regulating Bankers' Pay', *Georgetown Law Journal*, 98, 247–87.

Berle, Jr., Adolf A. & Gardiner C. Means (1932), *The Modern Corporation and Private Property*, Piscataway, N.J.: Transaction Publisher.

Bhagat, Sanjai & Bernard S. Black (2002), 'The Non-Correlation Between Board Independence and Long Term Firm Performance', *Journal of Corporation Law*, 27, 231–73.

Bhagat, Sanjai and Brian J. Bolton (2008), 'Corporate Governance and Firm Performance', *Journal of Corporate Finance*, 14, 257–273.

Blair, Margaret M. (1995), *Ownership and Control: Rethinking Corporate Governance for the Twenty-first Century*, Washington D.C.: Brookings.

Blair, Margaret M. (2003a), 'Locking in Capital: What Corporate Law Achieved for Business Organizers in the Nineteenth Century', *UCLA Law Review*, 51, 387–455.

Blair, Margaret M. (2003b), 'Shareholder Value, Corporate Governance, and Corporate Performance: A Post-Enron Reassessment of the Conventional Wisdom', in Peter K. Cornelius and Bruce Kogut (eds) *Corporate Governance and Capital Flows in a Global Economy*, Oxford: Oxford University Press.

Blair, Margaret M. (2011), 'Financial Innovation, Leverage, Bubbles, and the Distribution of Income', *Journal of Banking and Financial Law*, 30, 225–311.

Blair, Margaret M. (forthcoming), 'The Four Functions of Corporate Personality', in Anna Grandori (ed) (forthcoming) *Handbook of Economic Organization*, Northampton, Mass.: Edward Elgar Publishing Inc.

Blair, Margaret M. & Lynn A. Stout (1999), 'A Team Production Theory of Corporate Law', *Virginia Law Review*, 85, 247–328.

Blair, Margaret M. & Lynn A. Stout (2001), 'Director Accountability and the Mediating Role of the Corporate Board', *Washington University Law Quarterly*, 79, 403–47.

Boatright, John R. (2009), 'From Hired Hands to Co-Owners: Compensation, Team Production, and the Role of the CEO', *Business Ethics Quarterly*, 19, 471–96.

Bratton, William W. & Michael L. Wachter (2010), 'The Case Against Shareholder Empowerment', *University of Pennsylvania Law Review*, 158, 653–728.

Clark, Robert C. (1985), 'Agency Costs versus Fiduciary Duties', in John W. Pratt & Richard J. Zeckhauser (eds) (1985) *Principals and Agents: The Structure of Business*, Boston: Harvard Business School Publishing.

Core, John E., Wayne R. Guay & Tjomme O. Rusticus (2006), 'Does Weak Governance Cause Weak Stock Returns? An Examination of Firm Operating Performance', *Journal of Finance*, 61(2), 655–687.

Daily, C.M., D.R. Dalton & A.A. Cannella (2003), 'Introduction to special topic forum corporate governance: Decades of dialogue and data', *Academy of Management Review* 28, 371–382.

Easterbrook, Frank H. & Daniel R. Fischel (1991), *The Economic Structure of Corporate Law*, Boston: Harvard University Press.

Enriques, Luca, Henry Hansmann & Reinier Kraakman (2009), 'The Basic Governance Structure: Minority Shareholders and Non-Shareholder Constituencies', in Reinier Kraakman, John Armour, Paul Davies, Luca Enriques, Henry Hansmann, Gerard Hertig, Klaus Hopt, Hideki Kanda & Edward Rock (eds) (2009), *The Anatomy of Corporate Law: A Comparative and Functional Approach*, New York: Oxford University Press, 89–113.

Frey, Bruno S. & Margit Osterloh (2005), 'Yes, Managers Should Be Paid Like Bureaucrats', *Journal of Management Inquiry*, 14, 96–111.

Garvey, Gerald T. & Peter L. Swan (1994), 'The Economics of Corporate Governance: Beyond the Marshallian Firm', *Journal of Corporate Finance*, 1, 139–74.

Gelter, Martin (2009), 'Dark Side of Shareholder Influence: Managerial Autonomy and Stakeholder Orientation in Comparative Corporate Governance', *Harvard International Law Journal*, 50, 129–194.

Gompers, Paul, Joy Ishii & Andrew Metrick (2003), 'Corporate Governance and Equity Prices', *Quarterly Journal of Economics*, 118, 107–155.

Grossman, Sanford J. & Oliver D. Hart (1986), 'The Costs and Benefits of Ownership: A Theory of Vertical and Lateral Integration', *Journal of Political Economy*, 94(4), 691–719.

Guerrera, Francesco (2009), 'Welch Rues Short-Term Profit "Obsession"', *Financial Times*, March 12, 2009.

Hamilton, Robert W. & Jonathan R. Macey (2009), *Cases and Material on Corporations*, (10th ed.), New York: Thomson West.

Hansmann, Henry & Reinier Kraakman (2000), 'The Essential Role of Organizational Law', *Yale Law Journal*, 110, 387–440.

Hansmann, Henry & Reinier Kraakman (2000–2001), 'The End of History for Corporate Law', *Georgetown University Law Review*, 89, 439–468.

Hart, Oliver D. (1988), 'Incomplete Contracts and the Theory of the Firm', *Journal of Law, Economics, and Organization*, 4, 119–40.

Hart, Oliver D. (1989), 'An Economist's Perspective on the Theory of the Firm', *Columbia Law Review*, 89, 1757–1774.

Hart, Oliver D. & John Moore (1990), 'Property Rights and the Nature of the Firm', *Journal of Political Economy*, 98, 1119–58.

Holmstrom, Bengt (1982), 'Moral Hazard in Teams', *Bell Journal of Economics*, 13, 324 –340.

Hu, Henry T.C. & Bernard S. Black (2006), 'The New Vote Buying: Empty Voting and Hidden (Morphable) Ownership', *Southern California Law Review*, 79, 811–908.

Hu, Henry T.C. & Bernard S. Black (2007), 'Hedge Funds, Insiders, and the Decoupling of Economic and Voting Ownership: Empty Voting and Hidden (Morphable) Ownership', *Journal of Corporate Finance*, 13, 343–67.

Jensen, Michael C. (2001), 'Value Maximization, Stakeholder Theory, and the Corporate Objective Function', *European Financial Management Review*, 14(3), 297–317.

Jensen, M.C., & W.H. Meckling (1976), 'Theory of the Firm: Managerial Behavior, Agency Costs and Ownership Structure', *Journal of Financial Economics*, 3, 305–60.

Kaufman, Allen & Ernie Englander (2005), 'A Team Production Model of Corporate Governance', *Academy of Management Executive*, 319, 9–22.

Klein, April & Emanuel Zur (2011), 'The Impact of Hedge Fund Activism on the Target Firm's Existing Bondholders', *Review of Economic Studies*, 4, 1735–1771.

Klein, William A., John C. Coffee, Jr. & Frank Partnoy (2010), *Business Organization and Finance: Legal and Economic Principles*, New York: Foundation Press.

Kraakman, Reinier, John Armour, Paul Davies, Luca Enriques, Henry Hansmann, Gerard Hertig, Klaus Hopt, Hideki Kanda & Edward Rock (2009), *The Anatomy of Corporate Law: A Comparative and Functional Approach*, New York: Oxford University Press.

Longhofer, Stanley D. & Charles T. Carlstrom (1995), 'Absolute Priority Rule Violations in Bankruptcy', *Economic Review*, 31, 21–33.

Meese, Alan J. (2002), 'The Team Production Theory of Corporate Law: A Critical Assessment', *William and Mary Law Review*, 43, 1629–1702.

Millon, David (2000), 'New Game Plan or Business as Usual? A Critique of the Team Production Model of Corporate Law', *Virginia Law Review*, 86, 1001–1004.

Monks, Robert A.G. & Nell Minow (1995), *Corporate Governance*, Hoboken, N.J.: Wiley-Blackwell.

Norris, Floyd (2011), 'Eyes Open, WaMu Still Failed', *New York Times*, March 24, 2011, available at http://www.nytimes.com/2011/03/25/business/25norris.html?page (last accessed November 2011).

Partnoy, Frank (2000), 'Adding Derivatives to the Corporate Law Mix', *Georgia Law Review*, 34, 599–629.

Rajan, Raghuram G. & Luigi Zingales (1998), 'Power in the Theory of the Firm', *Quarterly Journal of Economics*, 113, 387–432.

Roe, Mark J. and David Skeel (2010), 'Assessing the Chrysler Bankruptcy', *Michigan Law Review*, 108, 721–772.

Rose, Paul (2010), 'Common Agency and the Public Corporation', *Vanderbilt Law Review*, 63, 1355–1417.

Sharfman, Bernard S. & Steven J. Toll (2009), 'A Team Production Approach to Corporate Law and Board Composition', *Northwestern University Law Review Colloquy*, 103, 380–92.

Shleifer, Andrei & Robert W. Vishny (1997), 'A Survey of Corporate Governance', *Journal of Finance*, 52, 737–83.

Stout, Lynn A. (2007), 'The Mythical Benefits of Shareholder Control', *Virginia Law Review*, 93, 789–810.

Strine, Jr., Leo E. (2010), 'One Fundamental Corporate Governance Question We Can Face: Can Corporations Be Managed for the Long Term Unless Their Powerful Electorates Also Act and Think Long Term?', *Business Lawyer*, 66, 1–26.

US GAO (US Government Accountability Office) (2007), 'Corporate Shareholder Meetings: Issues Relating to Firms that Advise Institutional Investors on Proxy Voting', Report to Congressional Requesters, GAO-07-765, June.

Williamson, Oliver (1985), *The Economic Institutions of Capitalism*, New York: The Free Press.

Williamson, Oliver (2002), 'Theory of the Firm as a Governance Structure: From Choice to Contract', *Journal of Economic Perspectives*, 16, 171–95.

# 4. The role of shareholders in the modern American corporation

*D. Gordon Smith*[*]

## 1. INTRODUCTION

Shareholders participate in the governance of the modern American corporation in three principal ways: they vote, they sell, and they sue (Thompson 2000). Large shareholders also exert informal influence in public corporations (Smith 1996). In closely held corporations, shareholders often exercise control through contracts (Easterbrook & Fischel 1986).[1] This chapter describes the evolving governance role of shareholders in the modern American corporation, focusing on public corporations.

The ability of shareholders to participate in corporate governance depends partly on the legal rules defining shareholder rights and partly on the transaction costs of collective action. For most of the past century, corporate law and corporate scholarship in the United States were based on a stylized view of the corporation in which shareholders were widely dispersed (Berle & Means 1932). Under this traditional conception of corporations, shareholders were passive investors who relied on directors and officers to manage the corporation's assets and on various market forces to provide the directors and officers with incentives for good behavior (Bebchuk 2007). The 'Wall Street Rule' dictated that dissatisfied shareholders 'vote with their feet' by selling their shares, rather than attempting to participate in governance of the corporation.

State corporate laws and federal securities laws impose obligations on directors and officers to be honest, diligent, and loyal in discharging their responsibilities. When they stray, shareholders may pursue a remedy through litigation, either in the form of a 'derivative action', in which shareholders sue managers on behalf of the corporation, seeking compensation for harm to the corporation, or a 'direct action', in which shareholders sue managers on their own behalf. Typically, the direct actions of numerous shareholders are aggregated into a class action. In recent decades, the derivative action has declined in importance, displaced by federal securities class actions and acquisition-oriented class actions (Thompson & Thomas 2004a). Institutional investors – including public pension funds, labor unions, and hedge funds – play a pivotal role in shareholder litigation, often monitoring that litigation for other shareholders.

While selling and suing remain important to the corporate governance system, shareholders in the modern American corporation have come to rely more on voting. The central focus

---

[*] Marcus Hintze and Matt Hall provided excellent assistance.

[1] 'Public corporations' have shares owned by a large number of investors, and those shares are traded in the public securities markets. 'Closely held corporations' have shares owned by a small number of shareholders without access to the public securities markets.

of law reform efforts in this area has been on the right of shareholders to elect directors, though many shareholders also manifest a desire to participate in policy decisions through referenda on particular business issues or the adoption of bylaws (Bebchuk 2005; Smith et al. 2011).

This chapter proceeds with a description of three categories of theoretical frameworks that dominate the analysis of corporate governance in a world with dispersed shareholders: political theories, theories of the firm, and legal origins theory. The next section describes the rise of institutional investors in the United States and shows how the increased concentration of shareholdings has led to changes in the right to vote, the right to sell, and the right to sue. This chapter concludes with a brief discussion of shareholder primacy.

## 2.   A WORLD WITH DISPERSED SHAREHOLDERS (THEORETICAL FRAMEWORKS)

In *The Modern Corporation and Private Property*, Adolf Berle and Gardiner Means famously described 'the separation of ownership and control' (Berle & Means 1932). Although dispersed shareholders have the right to vote their shares, corporation statutes allocate to boards of directors the power of initiation for most corporate actions, consigning shareholders to a ratifying role (Fama & Jensen 1983, 303–4). Even when shareholders are permitted to initiate, the costs inherent in collective action make the exercise of control through voting impractical in many circumstances (Olson 1971). As a result, when shareholders are widely dispersed, they are often content to influence corporate affairs through their right to sell, including in a hostile takeover, and, less frequently, through their right to sue the managers of a corporation for a breach of fiduciary duty. These observations about dispersed shareholders have motivated the theoretical frameworks used to analyze corporate law in the United States.

### Political Theories

While the separation of ownership and control has served as the consummate description of the modern American corporation, the causal forces behind the creation of strong capital markets that make the separation possible are much debated. Berle and Means viewed the separation of ownership and control as a solution to the problem of illiquidity: 'The owner of a non-liquid property is, in a sense, married to it' (Berle & Means 1932, 284). The solution to this problem was to divide property into ownership 'participations' while leaving the management and the 'integral quality' of the property undisturbed. Under this system, 'management is more or less permanent, directing the physical property which remains intact while the participation privileges of ownership are split into innumerable parts – "shares of stock" – which glide from hand to hand, irresponsible and impersonal' (Berle & Means 1932, 250). Thus, the shareholder 'has exchanged control for liquidity' (Berle & Means 1932, 251).

What makes liquidity possible is a vibrant capital market, but for Berle and Means, the big story was the concentration of power in the hands of corporate managers, and this was at root a political story. Berle and Means viewed the concentration of power as a dangerous development facilitated by nineteenth-century legal reforms, and Berle and Means viewed their primary task as explaining these developments. The 'checks which formerly operated to limit the use of power' (Berle & Means 1932, 6), they argued, were systematically dismantled 'to facilitate the appearance and success of the large, mass-producing, management-controlled corporation' (Bratton & Wachter 2008, 119).

Mark Roe has advanced an updated political theory of the separation of ownership and control that, instead of focusing on the concentration of power, focuses on the creation of strong capital markets (Roe 2000, 2006). Roe argues that strong capital markets are essential to ensuring that managers remain loyal to shareholders, and this loyalty is said to be an essential prerequisite to the dispersed ownership that enables the separation of ownership and control. In Roe's words, '[i]f shareholders strongly fear managers' disloyalty or incompetence, they invest warily; if sufficiently fearful, they do not invest at all, and other ownership structures will prevail' (Roe 2000, 541). Thus, capital markets are strong when they provide incentives for managers to favor shareholders over other constituencies, most importantly, the corporation's employees.

The crux of Roe's political account is that some countries are better able to encourage shareholder primacy than other countries. In the United States, for example, the corporate governance system employs myriad tools to ensure managerial loyalty, including 'the independent and active board, incentive compensation, hostile takeovers and proxy contests, securities markets signaling from securities analysts, competitive capital and product markets, and socialization in business schools and at work to a shareholder-wealth maximization norm' (Roe 2000, 546). By contrast, social democracies in continental Europe systematically favor employees over shareholders, thus constraining the development of capital markets because employees are risk averse 'as their human capital is tied up in the firm and they are not fully diversified' (Roe 2000, 551).

Roe's work is part of an extensive literature on the political economy of finance (Haber & Perotti 2008). The basic thrust of this literature is that the laws regulating corporate governance in continental Europe are the result of democratic processes in which labor gained social security and worker protection, while economically powerful families succeeded in limiting legal protections for outside (minority) shareholders to ensure the entrenchment of the families (La Porta et al. 2008). In the United States and England, by contrast, the laws regulating corporate governance offered robust protections for minority shareholders. Of course, minority shareholders would rely on these robust protections only if the government could credibly commit to retaining the rules (North & Weingast 1989).

For present purposes, the important lesson of the political theories of corporate finance is that legal rules in the United States are designed to facilitate the formation of public capital markets. Strong capital markets are associated with dispersed shareholders.

## Theories of the Firm[2]

Modern theories of the firm developed in reaction to the impoverished concept of the firm in neoclassical economics. Prior to the publication of Ronald Coase's *The Theory of the Firm* in 1937, economists did not suspect that the theory of the firm was impoverished. Oliver Williamson described the neoclassical firm as a production function, a 'technology to which a profit maximization purpose was ascribed' (Williamson 1999, 365). With profit maximiza-

---

[2]   This section relies heavily on Thompson & Smith (2001).

tion as the goal, firms would be forced to pursue strategies dictated by markets or perish. Under this view, price theory was the only requirement for a theory of the firm.

Against this intellectual backdrop, Coase asked a question that continues to intrigue economists today: 'Why is there any organization?' (Coase 1937, 35–6). In answering that question, Coase reasoned that firms exist to economize on transaction costs, and he hypothesized that firms would integrate to the extent required to take advantage of savings in transaction costs.

Armen Alchian and Harold Demsetz strove to 'move the theory forward' by describing more specifically when the costs of managing resources were likely to be high relative to the costs of market transactions (Alchian & Demsetz 1972). They argued that firms were most useful in solving the 'team-production' problem, which occurs when two or more people work jointly, and their respective inputs are 'unobservable'. The key feature of team production is the inability of an outsider to reward team members based on their inputs because direct observation of those inputs is impossible or prohibitively costly or because the inputs of one team member are indistinguishable from the inputs of other team members. In this circumstance, team members have an incentive to shirk. Alchian and Demsetz argued that the costs associated with shirking could be mitigated by monitoring. Such monitoring would be performed by a principal, who specialized in monitoring, and the monitor's incentives would derive from the fact that he was entitled to the residual earnings of the team.

Many scholars have relied on this description of the residual claimant as a powerful explanation for shareholders in the modern corporation, but the description has one rather obvious flaw: if the inputs of team members are unobservable, an outside monitor will be ineffective (Aoki 1994). Despite this shortcoming, a modified version of team production theory (which drops the assumption of unobservable inputs) has enjoyed some popularity in corporate law discourse through the work of Margaret Blair and Lynn Stout (Blair & Stout 1999), who view shareholders, employees, creditors, and other corporate constituencies as team members. Under this view, boards of directors serve as 'mediating hierarchs' whose task is to 'coordinate the activities of the team members, allocate the resulting production, and mediate disputes among team members over that allocation' (Blair & Stout 1999, 251).

The emphasis on monitoring in team production theory is shared by agency theory. In the seminal work on the agency theory of the firm, Michael Jensen and William Meckling described the firm as a 'legal fiction which serves as a nexus for contracting relationships and which is also characterized by the existence of divisible residual claims on the assets and cash flows of the organization which can generally be sold without permission of the other contracting individuals' (Jensen & Meckling 1976, 310). This view of the firm has dominated corporate law scholarship, teaching, and policy making for more than three decades.

The central focus of agency theory is the conflict created when one person acts on behalf of another. In the context of corporate law, the directors are viewed as 'agents' of the shareholders, who are the 'principals'. The probability that self-interested agents will deviate from the best interests of their principals will prompt parties in an agency relationship to provide incentives for loyalty. Principals may monitor agents, or agents may bond their own performance. In either event, the parties will not be able to align the agent's performance perfectly with the principal's preferences, and any divergences are referred to as residual loss. Taken together the monitoring costs, bonding costs, and residual losses are the total agency costs of the relationship. For many, the function of corporate law is to minimize the total agency costs inherent in the relationship between directors and shareholders.

Incomplete contract theory presents 'both a substantive and methodological break' from agency theory (Bolton & Dewatripont 2005, 489). Beginning from the proposition that all contracts are incomplete (i.e., contracts do not specify the obligations of the contracting parties for all potential outcomes), this theory shifts the focus from monitoring and bonding to decision-making procedures and institutional design. Incomplete contract theory takes two forms: transaction cost economics, associated with the work of Oliver Williamson (Williamson 1985, 1999), and property rights theory, associated with the work of Sanford Grossman, Oliver Hart, and John Moore (Grossman & Hart 1986; Hart & Moore 1988, 1990).

Transaction cost economics views the firm as a governance structure that minimizes transaction costs. Transaction cost analysis is founded on two behavioral assumptions, 'bounded rationality' and 'opportunism'. Bounded rationality is the notion that actors strive to act rationally, but are simply incapable of fulfilling the requirements of strict rationality because of limited information and limited ability to process information. Opportunism is familiar from agency theory, but Williamson offers the most commonly quoted definition: 'self-interest seeking with guile' (Williamson 1985, 47). He elaborates that this 'includes but is scarcely limited to more blatant forms, such as lying, stealing, and cheating. Opportunism more often involves subtle forms of deceit'. Transactions are examined along three dimensions: asset specificity,[3] frequency, and uncertainty. Where transaction costs are high, the relationships are brought inside the firm subject to its hierarchy and internal governance. Within the corporation, the board of directors is viewed as a governance instrument of shareholders, an instrument 'whose principal purpose is to safeguard those who face a diffuse but significant risk of expropriation because the assets in question are numerous and ill-defined, and cannot be protected in a well-focused, transaction-specific way' (Williamson 1984, 1210).

Property-rights theorists argue that the key to understanding the nature of firms is to focus on assets. Given the inevitability of incomplete contracts, ownership – defined as the residual right to control assets – will determine the decisions made in situations that are outside of any existing contracts. When ownership relates to specialized assets, it leads to control over human capital. Under this view, decision-making within the firm is determined by ownership because owners have power. Firms are created when the exercise of such power produces efficiencies. Stated differently, firms solve the problems posed by incomplete contracts, but not by reducing transaction costs. Rather, firms solve those problems by encouraging the appropriate level of relationship-specific investment by removing the opportunity for expropriation of assets after formation of the relationship, thus improving the incentive to invest in the relationship in the first place.

For all of the attention that they receive, shareholders are still slighted in the theory of the firm. Whether because of 'rational apathy' (Easterbrook & Fischel 1991, 197; Jensen & Meckling 1976, 337–38; Olson 1971, 55–6) or lack of business expertise (Shleifer & Vishny 1997, 741), shareholders are inevitably cast as passive constituents of the firm. While they nominally possess residual control rights of the firm, actual control is said to reside in the managers.

Agency theorists leave surprisingly little to the shareholders. 'Surprising' because agency theory is erected on the notion that a principal (the shareholders) monitors an agent (the

---

[3]   Williamson has helpfully defined 'asset specificity' to mean '[a] specialized investment that cannot be redeployed to alternative uses or by alternative users except at a loss of productive value' (Williamson 1999, 377).

managers). Nevertheless, agency theory routinely invokes the power of product markets, capital markets, employment markets, and takeover markets to 'monitor' managers, thus supplanting the shareholders. When these market mechanisms fail, shareholders may sue. Voting is viewed as important, but not terribly effective in most contexts; therefore, the domain of shareholder self-help under this view is limited.

Property-rights theory provides less guidance than agency theory on the role of shareholders in corporate governance. Hart and Moore assert that shareholders have the *residual right to control* assets, which they define as 'the right to decide how these assets are to be used except to the extent that particular usages have been specified in an initial contract' (Hart & Moore 1990, 1120). Within this definition lie the seeds of confusion for those attempting to delineate the respective roles of shareholders and directors. While it is widely accepted that shareholders have the residual right of control over a corporation, it is equally well established that shareholders 'delegate' some of those control rights to the board of directors. Incorporation subjects the assets of the firm to the default rules of the incorporation statute, which empowers the board of directors with management authority over the firm. In many of the most difficult problems in corporate law (including the allocation of control rights when facing a hostile takeover bid), the issue is whether directors or shareholders should have decision-making power. Suggesting that shareholders have decision-making power 'except to the extent that particular usages have been specified in an initial contract' (Hart & Moore 1990, 1120) merely leads to the next question: what usages have been specified in the initial contract (that is, the statutory default rules)? On this issue, property rights theorists provide no explicit guidance.

Transaction-cost economics appears more helpful in defining the shareholder role because of its emphasis on *ex post* governance of the firm. Under this view, the statutory default rules are not complete contingent contracts, but governance mechanisms. Even as governance mechanisms, however, the statutory default rules are incomplete because they do not precisely specify the decision-making roles of directors, shareholders, and courts.

## Legal Origins Theory

Legal Origins Theory has developed over the past 15 years from the path-breaking work on comparative corporate governance of Rafael La Porta, Florencio Lopez-de-Silanes, Andrei Shleifer, and Robert W. Vishny ('LLSV') (La Porta et al. 1997, 1998, 2008). The initial motivation for the work was the rather mundane observation that some countries have larger capital markets than other countries. LLSV attempted to explain the differences by reference to legal origins, that is, whether the legal system of the country was based in the common law or the civil law. According to LLSV, this distinction mattered because common law countries provide greater legal protections to external investors than civil law countries.

Perhaps the most innovative aspect of Legal Origins Theory is LLSV's effort to measure and quantify legal rules. Like the other theoretical frameworks described above, Legal Origins Theory assumes that the role of law in economic development is to protect dispersed shareholders, and LLSV have attempted to quantify this protection. In the early papers, LLSV developed a new measure of shareholder protection, which they called the Antidirector Rights Index. This early attempt to codify corporate law was criticized for being too simplistic (Coffee 2001), and LLSV subsequently developed two new quantitative measures of shareholder protection, a measure of shareholder protection through securities laws in the offerings of new issues (La Porta et al. 2006) and a measure of shareholder protection from self-dealing by corporate insiders through corporate law (Djankov et al. 2008). While these subsequent efforts have also been criticized (Armour et al. 2009), 'leximetrics' has reinvigorated the study of comparative corporate law.

In the process of refining their measures of shareholder protection, LLSV have revised their claim about the importance of legal origins. What started as a focused examination of connections between law and finance has evolved into a broad-based endorsement of private ordering. In a recent survey article, three members of the original LLSV describe their thesis as follows: 'common law stands for the strategy of social control that seeks to support private market outcomes, whereas civil law seeks to replace such outcomes with state-desired allocations' (La Porta et al. 2008, 286).

## 3.  THE RISE OF INSTITUTIONAL INVESTORS

The theoretical frameworks described above all assume an environment with dispersed shareholders, but in the last half century, that environment in the United States has changed dramatically. Over the past few decades, the emergence of institutional investors has shifted public policy debates regarding the role of shareholders. Rather than relying primarily on the shareholders' right to sell their shares, large institutional investors have evinced a desire to participate directly in corporate decision-making. As a result, public policy debates have shifted from a focus on capital and takeover markets to a focus on voting and private ordering.

In the 1980s, institutional investors often participated in corporate governance only informally, backed by the threat of a hostile takeover. As late as the early 1990s, two prominent commentators identified only three ways in which institutional investors had become active in corporate governance: (1) by protecting 'the market for corporate control by seeking to block or dismantle takeover defenses erected by portfolio companies without shareholder approval'; (2) by urging 'the creation of shareholder advisory committees'; and (3) by seeking 'direct input into the selection of outside directors' (Gilson & Kraakman 1991, 868). Despite increased interest in shareholder activism among scholars in the early 1990s, even proponents of institutional investor activism were conceding in the mid-1990s that the hopes for shareholder governance were 'largely aspirational' (Bratton & McCahery 1995, 1871). By the late 1990s, however, the landscape was changing dramatically, and activist institutions were gaining more traction in corporate governance. This section describes recent developments relating to the rights of large institutional shareholders to vote, sell, and sue.

### The Right to Vote

While shareholders have sought more active participation in the affairs of the corporation, the avenues for initiating action granted by state corporation laws are limited. Under most state codes, shareholders vote on the election and removal of directors and on certain fundamental transactions, including amending the corporation's charter, amending the corporation's bylaws, approving a merger or consolidation, approving the sale of assets not in the ordinary course of business (i.e., selling all or most of the assets of the company), and approving the dissolution of the company. Shareholders also may vote to ratify conflict-of-interest transactions. Most of these votes must be initiated by the board of directors. Indeed, of the shareholder actions listed in most state corporation laws, only the election and removal of directors and the amendment of bylaws are initiated by shareholders.[4]

Even when shareholders have the right to initiate action, placing items before the other shareholders for a vote can be challenging. In closely held corporations, most shareholder votes are conducted in person, but in corporations with a large number of shareholders, most votes are cast by proxy. A 'proxy' is the authorization given by a shareholder to another person to vote the shareholder's shares. If most shareholders voted by proxy, then shareholders who wished to initiate corporate action would need to place their proposal on the corporation's proxy ballot to have any realistic chance of success. Of course, an initiating shareholder could simply pay the costs of soliciting votes directly from other shareholders, but this expensive process is generally reserved for hostile takeovers, where the stakes are high enough to justify the large expenditures.

Generally, the board of directors controls access to a corporation's proxy ballot. For most shareholders, therefore, the only practical means of placing a proposal on the ballot is Rule 14a-8, promulgated under the Securities Exchange Act of 1934, which entitles shareholders to have their proposals included on a proxy ballot, unless those proposals are properly excluded by the company.[5] Rule 14a-8 was adopted in 1942, and over the past decade, it has become the most important battleground in the shareholder empowerment debate.

Shareholder empowerment has been at the center of corporate governance debates since the early 1990s, corresponding with the increased prominence of institutional investors. Much of the early work in this area compared corporate governance systems having dispersed shareholders – the United States and England – with corporate governance systems having concentrated or 'block' shareholders – Germany and Japan (Baums 1992; Black & Coffee 1994; Buxbaum 1991; Gilson & Roe 1993). As institutional investors in the United States became more active, demanding and receiving more power vis-à-vis managers, commentators have been keen to explore the limits of shareholder power.

On one side of this debate stand those who would insulate the board of directors from shareholder influence. As noted above, Margaret Blair and Lynn Stout describe boards of directors as 'mediating hierarchs' whose task is to represent the interests of all members of the corporate 'team', not just the shareholders (Blair & Stout 1999). The implication of this view is that shareholder power should be limited. Stephen Bainbridge also views the board of directors as the proper decision-maker in a corporation, but argues that directors should serve the interests of the shareholders (Bainbridge 2008). Shareholders should be content with this centralization of power, Bainbridge contends, because most shareholders are rationally apathetic about corporate decisions, and those who are not apathetic are likely to misuse any powers allocated to them (Bainbridge 2006). Iman Anabtawi makes a similar point, arguing that 'shareholders will use any incremental power conferred upon them to pursue those interests to the detriment of shareholders as a class' (Anabtawi 2005), and a substantial literature examining such claims has developed with specific regard to hedge funds (Kahan & Rock 2007, 2010; Anabtawi & Stout 2008; Bratton 2007). With increasingly sophisticated shareholders, the potential for opportunism may be greater than ever. Henry Hu and Bernie Black

---

[4]    For further discussion in this volume of studies on shareholder votes in director elections, see Ferri (Ch. 11).

[5]    For a discussion of studies on shareholder activism under Rule 14a-8, see Ferri (Ch. 11).

have explained how 'empty voting' and 'hidden ownership' – both forms of 'decoupling of shareholder voting rights from shareholder economic interests' – would threaten the integrity of shareholder voting (Hu & Black 2006, 2008). William Bratton and Michael Wachter claim that the case against shareholder empowerment is particularly convincing in the wake of the recent financial crisis, which demonstrated the need for managers to focus on risk management, not maximization of stock prices in the near term (Bratton & Wachter 2010).

On the other side of the debate stand those who would expand shareholder power. In early contributions to the literature on institutional investor activism, Bernie Black described the case for increased shareholder monitoring through the right to vote (Black 1990), and Jayne Barnard considered the case for shareholder access to the proxy (Barnard 1990). The debate over proxy access took on new urgency during the 2000s as the SEC thrice proposed new proxy access rules to facilitate shareholder nominations of director candidates. In 2010 the SEC adopted new Rule 14a-11 that required companies to include shareholder-nominated directors in their proxy materials, subject to certain requirements. The regulation also amended Rule 14a-8, requiring companies to include in their proxy materials proposals from qualifying shareholders for new procedures in the companies' governing documents that would include shareholder director nominees in the company's proxy statements. Shortly after the SEC adopted the rules, the US Chamber of Commerce and the Business Roundtable sued the SEC to invalidate 14a-11. The plaintiffs argued, among other things, that the SEC adopted the rules through a 'fundamentally flawed' process, particularly that it did not adequately consider the costs of the rules. On July 22, 2011, a unanimous panel of the DC Circuit agreed with the Business Roundtable, holding that the SEC was 'arbitrary and capricious in promulgating Rule 14a-11'.[6] The Court vacated the new rule (but not the amendments to Rule 14a-8 allowing shareholder proxy access proposals), but the debate over proxy access promises to remain active (Smith et al. 2011; Kahan & Rock 2010; McDonnell 2011; Grundfest 2010; Bebchuk & Hirst 2010).

Beyond the election of directors, shareholders may also be interested in participating in various policy decisions. Gordon Smith has argued that the right to vote on policy matters should generally be constrained (Smith 1996), though Robert Thompson and Gordon Smith suggested an expansion of shareholder power in the context of takeovers (Thompson & Smith 2001). Robert Thompson and Paul Edelman developed an argument that shareholder voting is best employed to correct errors committed by the board of directors (Thompson & Edelman 2009). The implication of this theory is that shareholders should be allowed to replace directors in a contested election and approve mergers, but Thompson and Edelman are not enamored with shareholder nominations of directors or precatory votes. Lucian Bebchuk has offered a more ambitious proposal for shareholder empowerment, under which shareholders could initiate two categories of decisions beyond the election and removal of directors: 'rules-of-the-game' decisions to amend the corporate charter or to change the company's state of incorporation and specific business decisions of substantial importance (Bebchuk 2005). Gordon Smith, Matthew Wright, and Marcus Hintze take shareholder empowerment one step further, proposing 'to empower shareholders in public corporations by facilitating their ability to contract' through the adoption of shareholder bylaws (Smith et al. 2011, 127).

As shareholdings have become more concentrated in institutional investors, voting has

---

6   *Business Roundtable v. SEC*, 647 F.3d 1144 (D.C. Cir. 2011).

become the control mechanism of choice. As noted above, however, under state corporation statutes, shareholders have only limited options to initiate change through voting, including shareholder-adopted bylaws. For many years, the most important unanswered question about Delaware corporate law was: what is the scope of shareholder power to adopt, alter, or repeal the bylaws of a Delaware corporation? Commentators offered numerous possible answers (McDonnell 2005; Coates & Farris 2001; Hamermesh 1998; Gordon 1997), and in *CA v. AFSCME*,[7] the Delaware Supreme Court finally took a turn, holding that shareholders can adopt 'procedural' bylaws as long as they do not 'commit the board of directors to a course of action that would preclude them from fully discharging their fiduciary duties to the corporation and its shareholders'. In the wake of *CA v. AFSCME*, the Delaware legislature adopted two new sections of the Delaware General Corporation Law allowing shareholders to adopt bylaws granting stockholders greater access to the corporate ballot for director elections, but the law relating to shareholder-adopted bylaws remains in its infancy.[8]

Congress has also taken to encouraging shareholder activism. The Dodd-Frank Wall Street Reform and Consumer Protection Act, passed in 2010, contains a number of corporate governance provisions to this end. For example, companies must allow shareholders to have a non-binding vote on executive compensation at least once every three years ('say-on-pay').[9] The Act also requires companies to have different individuals serving as the Chief Executive Officer and the Chairman of the Board of Directors or, failing to adopt this separation, to explain the reasons for a unified executive in the annual proxy statement.[10]

### The Right to Sell

Generally, shares of stock in a corporation are freely transferable. Despite this default rule, shares in closely held corporations often are subject to contractual transfer restrictions. Even if contractual constraints are absent, shares in closely held corporations may not have a ready market (Hetherington & Dooley 1977). Shares in public corporations, by contrast, typically may be sold into a public capital market and, with some important exceptions (e.g., restricted stock used as executive compensation and lock-up agreements with existing shareholders entered into before an initial public offering) usually are not subject to any contractual or regulatory transfer restrictions.

For most shareholders, the right to sell shares into the public market makes the right to vote shares relatively unimportant. As noted by Robert Thompson and Paul Edelman, 'Shareholders seldom seem to care much about the vote even when they have it, usually preferring the "Wall Street rule" (i.e., sell) when they disagree with a decision made by the corporation's managers' (Thompson & Edelman 2009, 130). Many institutional investors view selling as a form of shareholder activism that they call 'voting with their feet' (McCahery et al. 2010; Admati & Pfleiderer 2009), and there is both theoretical and empirical support for the notion that institutional sales affect firm governance (Edmans 2009; Gopalan 2008).

Despite the free transferability of shares in public corporations, some large shareholders

---

7   953 A.2d 227 (Del. Supr. 2008).
8   DEL. CODE ANN. tit. 8, §§ 112 and 113.
9   Dodd-Frank Wall Street Reform and Consumer Protection Act, H.R. 4173, 111th Cong., § 951 (2010).
10   *Ibid.* at § 972.

find that their stakes are so large that transferability is limited as a practical matter. As noted by Alfred Conard, 'Selling out is a good alternative only for the holder of a small block of shares who gets the news before it is public or before others have time to act on it. The holding of a large fund or a large family of funds may be too large to liquidate without pushing down the price' (Conard 1988, 145). Even in this circumstance, some institutional investors engage in 'share dumping' (Parrino et al. 2003). Share dumping results in lower share prices, which serve as a 'signal to the relationship investor that management is weak and thus activism may be profitable' (Attari et al. 2006, 183).

One circumstance in which all shareholders might sell their shares, whether voluntarily or by coercion, is a hostile takeover. One legal issue that has bedeviled courts and legal scholars in this area is whether the board of directors can deprive shareholders of the right to sell their shares to a hostile acquirer. The mechanism by which the board of directors typically stands in the way of a hostile bid is the so-called 'poison pill'. The Delaware courts often are asked to review actions by a target board of directors that takes defensive action in the face of a hostile bid. While a review of this complex area of law is beyond the scope of this chapter,[11] it is worth noting that Chancellor Chandler of the Delaware Court of Chancery recently ruled that the board of directors of Airgas, Inc. was justified in resisting a hostile bid by Air Products and Chemicals Inc. According to the Chancellor:

> a board of directors found to be acting in good faith, after reasonable investigation and reliance on the advice of outside advisors, which articulates and convinces the Court that a hostile tender offer poses a legitimate threat to the corporate enterprise, may address that perceived threat by blocking the tender offer and forcing the bidder to elect a board majority that supports its bid.[12]

The implication of this decision is that the shareholders of a Delaware corporation may not be able to sell their shares in a hostile takeover, even if the shareholders believe that the hostile bid is generous.

**The Right to Sue**

In addition to voting and selling, shareholders have attempted to exert influence on corporate affairs through litigation.[13] Shareholder suits have the potential to increase the value of a corporation in two ways: (1) providing compensation to shareholders (in the case of direct actions) or the corporation (in the case of derivative actions) for wrongs committed by corporate officers and directors; and (2) deterring corporate officers and directors from wrongdoing (Kraakman et al. 1994, 1736). Despite these potential benefits, shareholder litigation has been viewed with skepticism by courts and commentators in the United States because it depends on an 'entrepreneurial' model that encourages unmeritorious litigation, otherwise known as 'strike suits' (Coffee 2010). Shareholders engage in three major forms of litigation

---

[11]    For further discussion in this volume, see Davidoff (Ch. 12).

[12]    *Air Products and Chemicals, Inc. v. Airgas, Inc.*, CIV.A. Nos. 5249-CC, 5256-CC, 2011 WL 806411 at *1 (Del. Ch. February 15, 2011).

[13]    For further discussion in this volume of shareholder litigation, see Thomas & Thompson (Ch. 9).

with corporate governance implications: federal securities class actions, state court acquisition-oriented class actions, and derivative suits (Thomas 2008). This section briefly reviews all three forms with special attention to the role of institutional investors.

The purpose of federal securities class actions is to deter fraud by corporate managers. Concerns over the potential for strike suits in this context caused Congress in the Private Securities Litigation Reform Act of 1995 to adopt various procedural reforms, including the implementation of 'lead plaintiff provisions' proposed by Elliott Weiss and John Beckerman (Weiss & Beckerman 1995). As a technical matter, the lead plaintiff is simply the class member whose lawyer is designated lead counsel for the class. As a practical matter, however, the lead plaintiff is expected to serve as the litigation monitor, ensuring that the litigation is conducted for the benefit of the class members and not only for the benefit of the attorneys. Congress adopted the lead plaintiff provisions with an eye toward encouraging institutional investors to take a larger role in securities class actions.

Initially, institutional investors were reluctant to serve as lead plaintiffs (Choi et al. 2005), but participation rates have grown significantly over time (Choi & Thompson 2006). Reflecting on developments over the first decade or so of the PLSRA, Elliott Weiss wrote, 'Over the years, though, institutional investors in steadily increasing numbers have become more comfortable with the idea of serving as lead plaintiff, and have sought and received appointment to that position' (Weiss 2008, 551).

State court acquisition-oriented class actions are now 'the dominant form of corporate litigation and outnumber derivative suits by a wide margin' (Thompson & Thomas 2004a, 135). Claims in these lawsuits typically arise under fiduciary law.[14] While these lawsuits share attributes of the other forms of aggregate litigation – multiple lawsuits filed quickly by a well-known group of plaintiffs' lawyers 'in the name of a professional cadre of plaintiff shareholders' (Thompson & Thomas 2004a, 138) – the settlements tend to be for larger amounts than in other aggregate litigation. It also appears that the cases are most successful in contexts when self-dealing would be expected to be greatest. Also, '[i]nstitutional investors have almost no monitoring role in this litigation' (Thompson & Thomas 2004a: 138).

Derivative suits have traditionally played a central role in the corporate governance system, serving as 'the primary mechanism for enforcing the fiduciary duties of corporate managers' (Kraakman et al. 1994, 1733). While derivative litigation is present in closely held corporations, most shareholder suits in that context pursue other remedies or theories of liability (Davis 2008). Even in public corporations, however, the number of derivative suits is small. Robert Thompson and Randall Thomas hypothesize that derivative litigation has been 'strangled by procedural hurdles, such as the demand requirement and other constraints that make ultimate recovery unlikely, including special litigation committees and Delaware's statutory limitation on monetary recovery for duty of care claims' (Thompson & Thomas 2004b, 1792). Nevertheless, 'the associated litigation agency costs are low in comparison to other forms of representative litigation and ... there are significant benefits' (Thompson & Thomas 2004b, 1792).

---

[14]   *See, e.g., Revlon, Inc. v. MacAndrews & Forbes Holdings, Inc.*, 506 A.2d 173 (Del. 1986); *Weinberger v. UOP, Inc.*, 457 A.2d 701 (Del. 1983).

## 4.   SHAREHOLDER PRIMACY

The discussion about the three traditional roles of shareholders in corporate governance made an implicit assumption that shareholders are the primary beneficiaries of corporate action. The debate over whether corporate directors should act for the sole purpose of maximizing shareholder profit (shareholder primacy) or whether their managerial powers should be employed by and used to benefit a larger group of stakeholders (stakeholder governance) has been ongoing for many decades.[15] The shareholder primacy model is based principally on the notion of private property – the shareholders, as the owners of the corporation, are entitled to direct the corporation's activities toward profit-maximizing activities. The stakeholder governance perspective views corporations as social entities with a public purpose, existing by the grace of government to promote social welfare. Stakeholder governance advocates argue that shareholders are not the only 'investors' in the corporation, and that because employees, creditors, communities, and other constituencies all provide some level of investment, corporate law should be structured to encourage directors to take into account their goals as well as shareholder goals.

'Corporations are collective enterprises, drawing on investments from various stakeholders who contribute to the firm's success' (Greenfield 2008, 1043). Stakeholders include employees, local communities, and shareholders, all of whom invest resources because they believe that the collective action benefits provided by the corporate structure will allow them to make more money than they could apart. Corporate law can support, enhance, and encourage this collective action by removing barriers to investment by the various stakeholders and by allocating the corporation's financial surplus. Stakeholder governance advocates believe that by reforming corporate law such that corporate directors take into account *all* stakeholder interests, rather than just those of shareholders, more collective action will result and society will be better off. They further believe that internal mechanisms for protecting the interests of stakeholders are more efficient than the current external regulatory scheme. Finally, they believe that when management considers the interests of all investors, corporations will be better managed.

## REFERENCES

Admati, Anat Ruth & Paul Pfleiderer (2009), 'The Wall Street Walk and Shareholder Activism: Exit as a Form of Voice', *Review of Financial Studies*, 22, 2245–85.
Alchian, Armen A. & Harold Demsetz (1972), 'Production, Information Costs, and Economic Organization', *American Economic Review*, 62, 777–95.
Aoki, Masahiko (1994), 'The Contingent Governance of Teams: Analysis of Institutional Complementarity', *International Economic Review*, 35, 657–76.
Armour, John, Simon Deakin, Viviana Mollica & Mathias Siems (2009), 'Law and Financial Development: What We Are Learning from Time-Series Evidence', *BYU Law Review*, 2009, 1435–1500.
Anabtawi, Iman (2005), 'Some Skepticism About Increasing Shareholder Power', *UCLA Law Review*, 53, 561–99.
Anabtawi, Iman & Lynn Stout (2008), 'Fiduciary Duties for Activist Shareholders', *Stanford Law Review*, 60, 1255–1308.
Attari, Mukkaram, Suman Banerjee & Thomas Noe (2006), 'Crushed by rational stampede: Strategic share dumping and shareholder insurrections', *Journal of Financial Economics*, 79, 181–222.

---

[15]   For further discussion in this volume, see Lee (Ch. 7).

Bainbridge, Stephen M. (2003), 'Director Primacy: The Means and Ends of Corporate Governance', *Northwestern University Law Review*, 97, 547–606.
Bainbridge, Stephen M. (2006), 'Director Primacy and Shareholder Disempowerment', *Harvard Law Review*, 119, 1735–58.
Bainbridge, Stephen M. (2008), *The New Corporate Governance in Theory and Practice*, New York: Oxford University Press.
Barnard, Jayne W. (1990), 'Shareholder Access to the Proxy Revisited', *Catholic University Law Review*, 40, 37–103.
Baums, Theodor (1992), 'Corporate Governance in Germany: The Role of the Banks', *American Journal of Comparative Law*, 40, 503–26.
Bebchuk, Lucian A. (2005), 'The Case for Increasing Shareholder Power', *Harvard Law Review*, 118, 833–914.
Bebchuk, Lucian A. (2007), 'The Myth of the Shareholder Franchise', *Virginia Law Review*, 93, 675–732.
Bebchuk, Lucian A. & Scott Hirst (2010), 'Private Ordering and the Proxy Access Debate', *Business Lawyer*, 65, 329–59.
Berle Jr., Adolf A. & Gardiner Means (1932), *The Modern Corporation and Private Property*, New York: Macmillan.
Black, Bernard S. (1990), 'Shareholder Passivity Reexamined', *Michigan Law Review*, 89, 520–608.
Black, Bernard S. & John C. Coffee, Jr. (1994), 'Hail Britannia?: Institutional Investor Behavior Under Limited Regulation', *Michigan Law Review*, 92, 1997–2087.
Blair, Margaret M. & Lynn A. Stout (1999), 'A Team Production Theory of Corporate Law', *Virginia Law Review*, 85, 247–328.
Bolton, Patrick & Mathias Dewatripont (2005), *Contract Theory*, Cambridge, Mass.: MIT Press.
Bratton, William W. (2007), 'Hedge Funds and Governance Targets', *Georgetown Law Journal*, 95, 1375–433.
Bratton, William W. & Joseph A. McCahery (1995), 'Regulatory Competition, Regulatory Capture, and Corporate Self-Regulation', *North Carolina Law Review*, 73, 1861–1948.
Bratton, William W. & Michael Wachter (2008), 'Shareholder Primacy's Corporatist Origins: Adolf Berle and the Modern Corporation', *Journal of Corporation Law*, 34, 99–152.
Bratton, William W. & Michael L. Wachter (2010), 'The Case Against Shareholder Empowerment', *University of Pennsylvania Law Review*, 158, 653–728.
Buxbaum, Richard M. (1991), 'Institutional Owners and Corporate Managers: A Comparative Perspective', *Brooklyn Law Review*, 57, 1–53.
Choi, Stephen J., Jill E. Fisch & A.C. Pritchard (2005), 'Do Institutions Matter? The Impact of the Lead Plaintiff Provision of the Private Securities Litigation Reform Act', *Washington University Law Quarterly*, 83, 869–904.
Choi, Stephen J. & Robert B. Thompson (2006), 'Securities Litigation and Its Lawyers: Changes During the First Decade After the PSLRA', *Columbia Law Review*, 106, 1489–533.
Coase, Ronald H. (1937), 'The Nature of the Firm', *Economica*, 4, 386–405.
Coates, John C. & Bradley C. Farris (2001), 'Second-Generation Shareholder Bylaws: Post-Quickturn Alternatives', *Business Lawyer*, 56, 1323–79.
Coffee, Jr., John C. (1997), 'The Bylaw Battlefield: Can Institutions Change the Outcome of Corporate Control Contests', *University of Miami Law Review*, 51, 605–21.
Coffee, Jr., John C. (2001), 'The Rise of Dispersed Ownership: The Role of Law in the Separation of Ownership and Control', *Yale Law Journal*, 111, 1–82.
Coffee, Jr., John C. (2010), 'Litigation Governance: Taking Accountability Seriously', *Columbia Law Review*, 110, 288–351.
Conard, Alfred (1988), 'Beyond Managerialism: Investor Capitalism?', *University of Michigan Journal of Law Reform*, 22, 117–78.
Davis, Jr., Kenneth B. (2008), 'The Forgotten Derivative Suit', *Vanderbilt Law Review*, 61, 387–451.
Djankov, Simeon, Rafael LaPorta, Florencio Lopez-de-Silanes & Andrei Shleifer (2008), 'The Law and Economics of Self-Dealing', *Journal of Financial Economics*, 88, 430–65.
Easterbrook, Frank H. and Daniel R. Fischel (1986), 'Close Corporations and Agency Costs', *Stanford Law Review*, 38, 271–301.
Easterbrook, Frank H. & Daniel R. Fischel (1991), *The Economic Structure of Corporate Law*, Cambridge, Mass.: Harvard University Press.
Edmans, Alex, (2009), 'Blockholder trading, market efficiency, and managerial myopia', *Journal of Finance*, 64, 4881–917.
Edmans, Alex & Gustavo Manso (2010), 'Governance through trading and intervention: A theory of multiple block-holders', *Review of Financial Studies*, 24.
Fama, Eugene F. & Michael C. Jensen (1983), 'Separation of Ownership and Control', *Journal of Law and Economics*, 26, 301–25.
Gilson, Ronald J. & Reinier Kraakman (1991), 'Reinventing the Outside Director: An Agenda for Institutional Investors', *Stanford Law Review*, 43, 863–905.

Gilson, Ronald J. & Mark J. Roe (1993), 'Understanding the Japanese Keiretsu: Overlaps Between Corporate Governance and Industrial Organization', *Yale Law Journal*, 102, 871–906.

Gopalan, Radhakrishnan (2008), 'Institutional stock sales and takeovers: the disciplinary role of voting with your feet', available at http://papers.ssrn.com/sol3/papers.cfm?abstract_id=891515 (last accessed November 2011).

Gordon, Jeffrey N. (1997), '"Just Say Never?" Poison Pills, Deadhand Pills, and Shareholder-Adopted Bylaws: An Essay for Warren Buffett', *Cardozo Law Review*, 19, 511–52.

Greenfield, Kent (2008), 'Defending Stakeholder Governance', *Case Western Reserve Law Review*, 58, 1043–65.

Grossman, Sanford J. & Oliver D. Hart (1986), 'The Costs and Benefits of Ownership: A Theory of Vertical and Lateral Integration', *Journal of Political Economy*, 94, 691–719.

Grundfest, Joseph A. (2010), 'The SEC's Proposed Proxy Access Rules: Politics, Economics, and the Law', *Business Lawyer*, 65, 361–94.

Haber, Stephen & Enrico C. Perotti (2008), 'The Political Economy of Finance', available at http://fic.wharton.upenn.edu/fic/sicily/19%20haberperotti.pdf (last accessed November 2011).

Hamermesh, Lawrence A. (1998), 'Corporate Democracy and Stockholder Adopted By-Laws', *Tulane Law Review*, 73, 409–93.

Hart, Oliver & John Moore (1988), 'Incomplete Contracts and Renegotiation', *Econometrica*, 56, 755–85.

Hart, Oliver & John Moore (1990), 'Property Rights and the Nature of the Firm', *Journal of Political Economy*, 98, 1119–58.

Hetherington, J.A.C. & Michael P. Dooley (1977), 'Illiquidity and Exploitation: A Proposed Statutory Solution to the Remaining Close Corporation Problem', *Virginia Law Review*, 63, 1–75.

Hu, Henry T.C. & Bernard Black (2006), 'The New Vote Buying: Empty Voting and Hidden (Morphable) Ownership', *Southern California Law Review*, 79, 811–908.

Hu, Henry T.C. & Bernard Black (2008), 'Equity and Debt Decoupling and Empty Voting II: Importance and Extensions', *University of Pennsylvania Law Review*, 156, 625–739.

Jensen, Michael & William Meckling (1976), 'Theory of the Firm: Managerial Behavior, Agency Costs and Capital Structure', *Journal of Financial Economics*, 3, 305–60.

Kahan, Marcel & Edward B. Rock (2007), 'Hedge Funds in Corporate Governance and Control', *University of Pennsylvania Law Review*, 155, 1021–93.

Kahan, Marcel & Edward B. Rock (2010), 'Embattled CEOs', *Texas Law Review*, 88, 987–1051.

Kraakman, Reinier, Hyun Park & Steven Shavell (1994), 'When Are Shareholder Suits in Shareholder Interests?', *Georgetown Law Journal*, 82, 1733–75.

La Porta, Rafael, Florencio Lopez-de-Silanes, Andrei Shleifer & Robert W. Vishny (1997), 'Legal Determinants of External Finance', *Journal of Finance*, 52, 1131–50.

La Porta, Rafael, Florencio Lopez-de-Silanes, Andrei Shleifer & Robert W. Vishny (1998), 'Law and Finance', *Journal of Political Economy*, 106, 1113–55.

La Porta, Rafael, Florencio Lopez-de-Silanes & Andrei Shleifer (2006), 'What Works in Securities Laws?', *Journal of Finance*, 61, 1–32.

La Porta, Rafael, Florencio Lopez-de-Silanes & Andrei Shleifer (2008), 'The Economic Consequences of Legal Origins', *Journal of Economic Literature*, 46, 285–332.

McCahery, Joseph, Zacharias Sautner & Laura T. Starks (2010), 'Behind the Scenes: The Corporate Governance Preferences of Institutional Investors', available at http://papers.ssrn.com/sol3/papers.cfm?abstract_id=1571046 (last accessed November 2011).

McDonnell, Brett H. (2005), 'Shareholder Bylaws, Shareholder Nominations, and Poison Pills', *Berkeley Business Law Journal*, 3, 205–64.

McDonnell, Brett H. (2011), 'Setting Optimal Rules for Shareholder Proxy Access', *Arizona State Law Journal*, 43, 67–123.

North, Douglass C. & Barry R. Weingast (1989), 'Constitutions and Commitment: The Evolution of Institutions Governing Public Choice in Seventeenth-Century England', *The Journal of Economic History*, 44, 803–32.

Olson, Jr., Mancur (1971), *The Logic of Collective Action: Public Goods and the Theory of Groups* (revised edition), Cambridge, Mass.: Harvard University Press.

Parrino, Robert, Richard W. Sias & Laura T. Starks (2003), 'Voting With Their Feet: Institutional Ownership Changes Forced CEO Turnover', *Journal of Financial Economics*, 68, 3–46.

Rock, Edward B. & Michael L. Wachter (2001), 'Islands of Conscious Power: Law, Norms, and the Self-Governing Corporation', *University of Pennsylvania Law Review*, 149, 1619–1700.

Roe, Mark J. (2000), 'Political Preconditions to Separating Ownership from Control', *Stanford Law Review*, 53, 539–606.

Roe, Mark, J. (2006), 'Legal Origins, Politics, and Modern Stock Markets', *Harvard Law Review*, 120, 460–527.

Rogers, Brishen (2008), 'The Complexities of Shareholder Primacy: A Response to Sanford Jacoby', *Comparative Labor Law and Policy Journal*, 30, 95–109.

Shleifer, Andrei & Robert W. Vishny (1997), 'A Survey of Corporate Governance', *Journal of Finance*, 52, 737–83.

Siems, Mathias & Simon Deakin (2010), 'Comparative Law and Finance: Past, Present and Future Research', *Journal of Institutional and Theoretical Economics*, 166, 120–40.

Smith, D. Gordon (1996), 'Corporate Governance and Managerial Incompetence: Lessons From Kmart', *North Carolina Law Review*, 74, 1037–1139.

Smith, D. Gordon, Matthew Wright & Marcus Kai Hintze (2011), 'Private Ordering with Shareholder Bylaws', *Fordham Law Review*, 80, 126–88.

Thomas, Randall S. (2008), 'The Evolving Role of Institutional Investors in Corporate Governance and Corporate Litigation', *Vanderbilt Law Review*, 61, 299–313.

Thompson, Robert B. (2000), 'Preemption and Federalism in Corporate Governance: Protecting Shareholder Rights to Vote, Sell, and Sue', *Law and Contemporary Problems*, 62, 215–42.

Thompson, Robert B. & D. Gordon Smith (2001), 'Toward a New Theory of the Shareholder Role: "Sacred Space" in Corporate Takeovers', *Texas Law Review*, 80, 261–326.

Thompson, Robert B. & Randall S. Thomas (2004a), 'The New Look of Shareholder Litigation: Acquisition-Oriented Class Actions', *Vanderbilt Law Review*, 57, 133–209.

Thompson, Robert B. & Randall S. Thomas (2004b), 'The Public and Private Faces of Derivative Lawsuits', *Vanderbilt Law Review*, 57, 1747–93.

Thompson, Robert B. & Paul H. Edelman (2009), 'Shareholder Voting', *Vanderbilt Law Review*, 62, 129–74.

Weiss, Elliott J. (2008), 'The Lead Plaintiff Provisions of the PSLRA After a Decade, Or "Look What's Happened To My Baby"', *Vanderbilt Law Review*, 61, 543–77.

Weiss, Elliott J. & John S. Beckerman (1995), 'Let the Money Do the Monitoring: How Institutional Investors Can Reduce Agency Costs in Securities Class Actions', *Yale Law Journal*, 104, 2053–127.

Williamson, Oliver E. (1984), 'Corporate Governance', *Yale Law Journal*, 93, 1197–1230.

Williamson, Oliver E. (1985), *The Economic Institutions of Capitalism*, New York: The Free Press.

Williamson, Oliver E. (1999), *The Mechanisms of Governance*, New York: Oxford University Press.

# 5.  Creditors and debt governance
## *Charles K. Whitehead*

## 1.  INTRODUCTION[1]

Most corporate debt is private, and most private lenders are banks (although increasingly they include non-bank lenders) (Kahan & Tuckman 1993; Amihud et al. 1999; Wilmarth 2002).[2] Even among public firms, which typically have access to larger pools of capital, roughly 80% maintain private credit agreements (Nini et al. 2009). Consequently, debt's role in corporate governance (sometimes referred to as 'debt governance') has mirrored changes in the private credit market.[3]

Within the traditional framing, bank lenders tend to rely on covenants and monitoring as the most cost-effective means to minimize agency costs and manage a borrower's credit risk.[4] Loans were historically illiquid, and so lenders had a direct and long-term say in how a firm was managed. As liquidity increased, banks began to manage credit risk through purchases and sales of loans and other credit exposure, lowering capital costs, but potentially weakening their incentives and ability to monitor and enforce covenant protections. The 2007–2008 financial crisis – and recognition that shareholder oversight, without the offsetting discipline provided by creditors, could cause financial firms to incur socially suboptimal levels of risk[5] – re-focused attention on the importance of debt governance.[6]

---

[1]  Portions of this chapter are derived from Whitehead (2009).

[2]  Many firms use both public and private sources of debt capital, including bank debt, program debt (such as commercial paper), and public bonds. Investment-grade firms often rely on senior unsecured debt and equity, while lower-credit firms are more likely to rely on a combination of secured bank debt, senior unsecured debt, subordinated bonds, convertible securities, and equity (Rauh & Sufi 2010).

[3]  'Corporate governance,' in this chapter, is defined as a mechanism to reduce or deter agency costs arising from management incentives or actions that impede the maximization of firm value.

[4]  'Credit risk' is defined as the possibility that a borrower will fail to perform its obligations under a loan or other credit instrument, mainly the payment of principal and interest.

[5]  Some portion of that risk may be managed directly through financial regulation (Whitehead 2010). New proposals also focus on the balancing effect of debt holders. Creditors tend to be more conservative risk-takers than shareholders, and to the extent debt (by its terms) converts into equity upon a financial firm's credit downgrade, those debt holders would have an incentive to oversee how the firm is managed and minimize risk-taking (Coffee 2010).

[6]  New credit instruments have been blamed for the 2007–2008 financial crisis, calling into question the viability of a corporate governance mechanism that relies, in part, on an increasingly liquid credit market. There are, however, important differences between those instruments – primarily tied to subprime mortgages – and unsecured corporate debt. By their nature, subprime mortgage instruments relied principally on collateral to manage credit risk. Unsecured loans, however, are much more dependent on covenants and monitoring without any offsetting protection. As described later in this chapter, changes in the credit market may result in the introduction of alternative means for lenders to help oversee borrowers (Whitehead 2009).

There is relatively little 'law' in the law and economics of debt governance beyond the legal infrastructure necessary to implement debt's oversight function (including contract law, enforcement of contract rights, and bankruptcy law) and a greater reliance on debt (with shorter maturities) in countries with higher levels of corruption (La Porta et al. 1998; Fan et al. 2010). Governance, in most corporation codes, is typically relegated to a firm's shareholders. No state, for example, affirmatively grants debt holders the right to vote, although a few state codes – such as, for example, California Corporation Code § 204(a)(7) and Delaware General Corporation Law § 221 – expressly make it optional. Creditors, nevertheless, can significantly influence how a firm is governed – through contractual protections and self-interested actions that protect their investment, as well as the disciplining effect that debt can have on a firm's budget and use of free cash flow.

The traditional construct distinguishes between public and private debt, although how each is structured turns on many issues (described below) that are common to both. As noted earlier, bank lenders traditionally have relied on covenants and monitoring in the private credit market. Borrowers in the public market are often larger, more profitable, and have higher credit ratings than private firms, and so benefit less from bank monitoring (Diamond 1991; Bolton & Freixas 2000). Rather, public bonds are widely held and easily transferable, increasing agency costs – due to the collective action problem of dispersed ownership – but permitting holders to inexpensively diversify, manage, and transfer credit risk. Balanced against greater liquidity, public debt typically has less restrictive covenants in light of the public availability of information, the higher cost to directly monitor and enforce compliance, and a decline in the ability (or, for higher-quality borrowers, the need) to mitigate credit risk through contract (Smith & Warner 1979; James 1987; Carey et al. 1993; Triantis & Daniels 1995; Amihud et al. 1999; Rauh & Sufi 2010). Consequently, a firm that initially issues public debt may see a decline in its share price – reflecting a drop in debt governance, which can be even more pronounced if, at the same time, the borrower reduces bank monitoring (perhaps by paying down its bank debt) (Denis & Mihov 2003).

This chapter traces changes in the private credit market. It begins with a look at the traditional role of debt, focusing on the impact of debt on corporate governance and, in particular, the effect of an illiquid credit market on creditors' reliance on covenants and monitoring – a reliance that has continued even as the credit market has evolved. It then turns to changes in the private credit market and their effect on lending structure. Greater liquidity raises its own set of agency costs. In response, loans and lending relationships have adjusted to mitigate those costs, providing new means by which debt can influence corporate governance.[7]

Going forward, a firm's decision to borrow must increasingly take account of the costs and benefits of a liquid credit market. How firms are governed is closely related to how they raise capital (Williamson 1988). Thus, actions that affect a firm's credit quality are likely to be reflected in changes in the secondary price at which its loans and other credit instruments trade. Those changes, in turn, may affect a borrower's cost of capital, providing managers with a real incentive to minimize risky behavior. The intuition, which I describe at the end of

---

[7]    There is a substantial literature on why firms choose to fund with varying amounts of debt, beginning with the Miller-Modigliani claim that, absent frictions, capital structure is irrelevant to firm value. Scholarship regarding tax and other real world frictions demonstrate that firm value may be enhanced through a capital structure that includes both debt and equity. I do not address that scholarship in this chapter, except to the extent it relates to our principal focus on debt governance.

this chapter, is that a liquid private credit market may begin to provide a discipline that complements the traditional protections of contract. Changes in the cost of private credit may provide a governance function similar to that provided by changes in the price of public equity.

## 2.   DEBT'S ROLE IN CORPORATE GOVERNANCE

In a perfect world, investors would be as familiar as managers with projects that require new financing. Investors often have less information, however, permitting managers to invest in less profitable projects that benefit them personally or that favor one class of investors over another, without investors being aware of the project's value or the managers' actions (Jensen & Meckling 1976; Smith & Warner 1979; Arrow 1981). Thus, in order to attract new capital at low cost, managers must credibly commit to behave in a manner consistent with investor interests.

Debt can help curb management excess, in large part through its reliance on contractual provisions, like loan covenants, that require the debtor to make specified payments (principal and interest), meet minimum financial criteria, report periodically, and operate within bounds specified by creditors (Williamson 1988).[8] In addition, debt financing increases the risk of bankruptcy because payouts are compulsory. For example, although the board can choose to suspend dividend payments, suspending interest payments is typically a breach of the firm's debt obligations and may trigger a bankruptcy filing. Consequently, greater leverage increases a firm's risk of incurring the real costs of financial distress – the actual costs of bankruptcy, as well as a rise in risk premiums demanded by customers, suppliers, and employees. The likelihood that a borrower will fail to repay or otherwise meet its debt obligations can, in turn, lower a firm's stock price and increase the risk of takeover.[9] In order to reduce those risks, managers are motivated to maximize profitability, including by reducing business expenses, working harder, and investing more carefully (Grossman & Hart 1982; Jensen 1989; Harris & Raviv 1990; Zwiebel 1996). Managers also have a direct interest in avoiding bankruptcy, since directors and officers of bankrupt firms tend to do poorly in the labor market (Gilson 1989, 1990).

Debt also affects a borrower's investment policies. Start-up firms with high growth opportunities, for example, are likely to benefit if management's hands remain untied, permitting them to allocate capital to the most profitable projects. Such firms often have fewer tangible assets, with lenders relying on more costly loan restrictions or shorter maturities to manage risk (Billett et al. 2007). Slower-growing firms, by contrast, face a greater possibility of managers making unprofitable investments, perhaps in areas outside their expertise, driven by an interest in building empires for personal benefit. In those cases, covenants that restrict overinvestment or a borrower's ability to incur more debt may benefit both creditors and shareholders. Thus, explicitly limiting a firm's capital expenditures, particularly after its

---

8    A description of standard loan covenants appears in Tung (2009).

9    Greater leverage can also be used to deter a hostile takeover, perhaps incurred to finance a defensive self-tender offer that increases management's percentage of voting control, with entrenched managers weighing the benefits of continued control against the potential cost and disciplining effect of greater indebtedness (Harris & Raviv 1988; Stulz 1988; Zwiebel 1996).

credit quality has declined, is likely to result in an increase in operating performance and a rise in stock price (Nini et al. 2009). At the very least, new capital investments that extend beyond existing limits – either investment or leverage limits, or both – will need to be reviewed and agreed by a firm's creditors before they can go forward. In addition, by contractually committing to make future payments, increased debt reduces the agency costs of free cash flow, making less cash available to be spent at management discretion (Jensen 1986; Stulz 1990). Here, again, a significant change in a borrower's cash flow – perhaps prompted by a change in its business operations – may require its creditors' consent, providing them with the ability to oversee and influence certain fundamental business decisions.[10]

Debt maturity can also affect corporate governance. For example, a firm that is focused on maximizing shareholder value may underinvest in new projects whose benefits accrue only to the firm's creditors.[11] If funding is short-term, however, the projects' success is likely to be reflected in a lower cost of refinancing, resulting in a decline in the firm's overall cost of capital that benefits shareholders (Myers 1977; Barclay & Smith 1995). Short-term debt also motivates managers to invest in profitable projects or risk the loss of future, near-term financing. Before 'rolling over' existing loans, or financing new ones, lenders must be convinced of management's capability and may increase the cost of financing (including adding more restrictive terms) to reflect any rise in credit risk (Rajan & Winton 1995; Stulz 2002; Nini et al. 2009). Long-term debt, by contrast, postpones a borrower's need for refinancing, potentially reflecting concerns over the borrower's future credit quality (Flannery 1986). Its repayment, however, is dependent on future earnings and, therefore, longer maturities may also help to motivate managers to pursue value-additive projects (Hart & Moore 1995).

By incurring more debt, managers can commit to making profitable investments and operating improvements, also signaling their willingness to pay out cash flows or be monitored by lenders, or both (Leland & Pyle 1977; Diamond 1991). The result can be a boost in the borrower's stock price, enhancing management's job security (Zwiebel 1996; Berger et al. 1997). Higher leverage also gives superior managers the ability to signal their quality, separating them from managers who suffer a greater risk of bankruptcy (Grossman & Hart 1982). Conversely, entrenched managers may prefer less leverage than is optimal in order to reduce the firm's risk of financial distress (and, in turn, the risk of losing private benefits). They may also limit their reliance on debt financing or choose only longer-term debt in order to minimize the limitations imposed by creditors and reduce external monitoring (Garvey & Hanka 1999; Datta et al. 2005; Lundstrum 2009).

Notwithstanding the incentive to understate leverage, recent research suggests that under some circumstances entrenched managers – those whose interests may be less aligned with shareholders – may actually incur greater debt than less-entrenched managers. Managers whose interests are aligned with shareholders (for example, whose compensation may be tied to stock price) may make riskier policy choices whose returns are more likely to benefit shareholders at the expense of creditors, particularly as the firm nears insolvency (Coles et al.

---

10    Note that lenders have an incentive to over-regulate a firm's risk-taking in an effort to protect their own investments, potentially causing managers to forego value-enhancing projects that would otherwise benefit shareholders (John et al. 2008).

11    This might occur if the project's payouts are positive – resulting in an overall increase in firm value – but only sufficient to make payments of interest and other amounts owed to the firm's creditors (who are paid first before the shareholders receive anything) (Myers 1977).

2006).[12] Lenders, therefore, may consider entrenched managers to be less risky – for example, by adopting more conservative investment policies (John et al. 2008) – and so be willing to provide them with better financing terms, resulting in an overall increase in leverage (John & Litov 2010). From that perspective, a greater reliance on debt may reflect weaker governance rather than a mechanism to improve management performance (Denis & Mihov 2003).

Debt can contractually limit managerial discretion through restrictive covenants, with lenders monitoring compliance in order to minimize exposure to the borrower's credit risk. With the protection of limited liability, shareholders of a leveraged firm have incentives to increase the firm's risk-taking once debt is in place. Lenders, therefore, also rely on covenants to mitigate conflicts with managers who may favor the interests of equity over debt (Smith & Warner 1979; Sufi 2007).[13] To that end, covenants act as early warning 'trip wires' (Triantis & Daniels 1995) that enable lenders to reassess a borrower's credit risk under weakened financial conditions and mitigate loss by renegotiating loans (and reducing leverage) following a breach (Fischel 1989; Hart & Moore 1998; Dichev & Skinner 2002). Covenant violations can be costly, typically resulting in tighter restrictions, lower caps on capital expenditures, and an increase in real costs. For those reasons, managers have a strong incentive to ensure the firm complies with their terms (Smith & Warner 1979; Roberts & Sufi 2009a; Nini et al. 2009). Tighter covenants, in turn, can result in a decline in real borrowing costs. A firm can also improve its borrowing capacity and increase its share price through the debt capital available to fund new projects and the positive signal provided by new lending (Fama 1985; Myers 1989).

Covenants, however, are imperfect predictors of management behavior, reflecting the difficulty of assessing a borrower's future actions and performance (Triantis & Daniels 1995). Covenant violations are not uncommon, but typically do not result in lenders accelerating repayment of the loan or taking control of the borrower. Instead, those violations are often waived, but prompt closer scrutiny of credit quality and tighter restrictions on the borrower in both renegotiated and future loans (Tung 2009). Through covenants, creditors can also limit expenditures that might otherwise be available to repay a loan in order to ensure a fair return on their investment (Chava & Roberts 2008). Although there is a risk that some covenants will limit profitable activity, that cost is offset by the ability, among a small group of lenders, to inexpensively renegotiate covenants that have become too restrictive, as well as to exercise control rights (Myers 1977; Smith & Warner 1979; Bolton & Scharfstein 1996).

A loan agreement may include pre-agreed contingencies that trigger modification of a term (or terms) of the loan.[14] A pricing grid provides one example. Under normal circumstances, a decline in cash flow may cause the borrower, in light of its riskier position, to be better off under the loan's original terms than if it entered into a new loan, creating a strong incentive

---

[12]   A well-known example is found in footnote 55 of the Delaware Chancery Court's decision in *Credit Lyonnais Bank Nederland, N.V. v. Pathe Communications Corp.*, 1991 WL 277613 (1991). There, Chancellor Allen posed a hypothetical where a corporation's sole asset was a judgment ($51 million) against a solvent debtor. The case was on appeal, with the corporation receiving offers to settle for an amount that would satisfy both shareholders and debt holders. Diversified shareholders, nevertheless, would be likely to reject the offers, since the additional upside if the corporation won would be theirs, whereas the downside of losing would be borne by both shareholders and debt holders.

[13]   Examples of the tension between debt and equity, and potential risk-shifting by managers, are set out in Amihud et al. (1999).

[14]   Examples of loan agreement contingencies appear in Roberts & Sufi (2009b) and Tung (2009).

for it to avoid renegotiation. A pricing grid can adjust the amount of interest payable by the borrower based on changes in its financial ratios or credit rating. Thus, by increasing interest payments, a pricing grid shifts relative bargaining power to the lender, which can then restructure the loan to reflect the borrower's changed circumstances. Conversely, improved performance can cause a drop in interest payments, reflecting the borrower's better credit quality (Roberts & Sufi 2009b). Loan covenants are typically tied to the same measures used in setting the pricing grid. Together, they establish minimum performance standards for the borrower, but also reward actions that improve its credit quality (Tung 2009).

In order to minimize agency costs, private debt relies on long-term relationships between lenders and borrowers – very often tied to the traditional relationship between banks and customers (Diamond 1984; Baird & Rasmussen 2006). Banks often take deposits from, and give financial advice to, their borrowers, which provide them with ready access to quasi-public information (Black 1975; Fama 1985). As a result, banks can assess credit quality and monitor compliance with covenants at a lower cost than others, particularly with small- and medium-sized firms. They are also better able to detect and deter managerial slack at an early stage, providing shareholders and other investors with a credible signal of the firm's performance (Smith & Warner 1979; Triantis & Daniels 1995).[15] The resulting benefits can be tangible – a decline in the overall cost of capital as other investors, including shareholders, free-ride on the enhanced oversight provided by self-interested bank monitors. Reflecting a bank's superior knowledge, the renewal of an existing loan facility can result in an increase in the borrower's stock price. Less-informed creditors, by contrast, are more likely to seek stricter covenants than banks in order to more closely control a borrower's future actions in light of the higher cost of monitoring (Rajan & Winton 1995; Denis & Mihov 2003; Shepherd et al. 2008).

Note that a bank's superior information can give it greater bargaining power over the borrower than a more arm's-length lender – a potential hold-up problem if the bank demands surplus from successful projects as a condition to continued lending. Borrowers, as a result, may choose to diversify sources of capital in order to reduce the bank's ability to appropriate rents (Rajan 1992). Likewise, having made a loan, a bank may be compelled to extend further credit to a shaky borrower, or otherwise forestall a default, rather than risk losing the value of its original investment. Granting the bank a preference over the borrower's assets may address part of the problem, but the bank may still be reluctant to call a default if it results in a drop in the value of its original loan (Boot 2000).

Reputation can also affect covenant levels.[16] A firm that repeatedly accesses the credit market has an economic interest in developing a reputation as a 'good' borrower. If it can benefit (for example, through fewer covenants), then it has an incentive – even if not contractually obligated to do so – to act in a manner consistent with the lender's interests. Lenders may, in turn, begin to relax their reliance on covenants and monitoring in loans to borrowers with established reputations (Diamond 1991; Boot et al. 1993; Sufi 2007).[17]

---

[15]   Recent research suggests that banks may also facilitate acquisitions through the information they receive as lenders and transmit to potential acquirers, possibly in order to reduce their default risk by seeking to transfer debt from weak to strong borrowers (Ivashina et al. 2009).

[16]   Credit ratings historically have provided an important assessment of market reputation, even though recent findings regarding conflicts of interest, inadequate staffing, and a failure to follow their own guidelines have drawn the credibility of rating agencies into question (Partnoy 1999; Hill 2004).

[17]   As Jensen & Meckling (1976) famously noted, although reputation can reduce agency costs,

A bank's informational advantage makes it less costly for it to extend loans than a more arm's-length creditor. Yet, it also makes it more difficult to resell loans to less knowledgeable purchasers, a classic 'lemons problem' that originally impeded the creation of a liquid credit market. The inability to transfer loans, in turn, reinforced the value to lenders of covenants and monitoring (Diamond 1984). To be sure, the traditional agency cost model considered diversification as one means to manage risk. Portfolio theory suggested there should be a less costly means for banks to manage credit risk than covenants and monitoring.[18] Doing so effectively, however, required a liquid market for the purchase and sale of credit, which did not exist at the time the agency cost analysis of corporations was first introduced.[19] Thus, the benefits of diversification were understood to be principally tied to public equity, with banks instead relying on contractual protections to manage credit exposure.

## 3.   PRIVATE CREDIT LIQUIDITY

The business of banking began to transform in the 1970s and 1980s, driven by increasing competition, innovation in the marketplace, and changes in financial regulation. In particular, new regulatory requirements encouraged banks to change their business models, making it more expensive to continue as they had before.[20] Banks began to reassess lending, with many adopting strategies to minimize their overall credit cost (Berger et al. 1995; Allen & Gale 1997; Allen & Santomero 2001).

Debt's role in corporate governance has remained largely unchanged even as the credit market has evolved. The traditional tools that have helped minimize agency costs and curb management excess remain applicable. Differences in lending structure, however, have prompted changes in how creditors oversee borrowers. They have also raised their own set of agency costs, which market participants have needed to address.

Banks began to diversify their credit risk, requiring a new approach to risk management, as well as a liquid market to buy and sell loans and other credit instruments. New technologies were developed to measure risk and diversification across loan portfolios – enabling banks to decide which assets to buy and sell, and at what price, in order to optimize a portfolio's return-to-risk relationship (Whitehead 2009). The costs traditionally associated with the resale of loans were offset by the real benefits of managing credit risk. Banks that participated in the loan market were required to raise less capital against riskier loans and more profitable loan portfolios (Berger & Udell 1993; Simons 1993; Cebenoyan & Strahan 2004). A portion of the gains could be passed on to borrowers, for example, through increased lending

---

even 'sainthood' will not drive those costs to zero. Moreover, lenders and borrowers have short memories, and so the incentives that make reputation valuable can shift with changes in the marketplace (Bratton 1989).

[18]   Markowitz first demonstrated the benefits of portfolio diversification in the early 1950s, for which he won the Nobel Prize in Economics in 1990 (Markowitz 1952).

[19]   I mark the introduction of the agency cost framework as the publication of Jensen & Meckling (1976).

[20]   For example, the greater regulatory capital requirements imposed on banks prompted an increase in loan securitizations and syndications, as banks moved assets from their balance sheets in order to reduce their effective capital requirements (Basel Committee on Banking Supervision 1999; Whitehead 2006; Wilmarth 2002).

or lower interest rates, potentially resulting in an overall decline in a borrower's real cost of capital (Hughes & Mester 1998; Güner 2006; Duffie 2008). The lending business evolved as banks originated loans for sale to others and bought and sold credit risk in order to better manage their overall exposures (Llewellyn 1996; Caouette et al. 1998; Bolton & Freixas 2000; Calomiris 2000).

Today's private credit market is increasingly liquid. Banks have an incentive to minimize the agency costs of lending to private borrowers for whom there is limited public information. Spanning that gap – by designing resale arrangements that help address the problems of limited information – can reduce the lemons problem, increasing a bank's ability to transfer loans at lower cost, as well as enhancing profitability (Pennacchi 1988). Thus, beyond the traditional bank-borrower relationship, a firm's decision to borrow must increasingly take account of the costs and benefits of a liquid credit market, with the resulting changes likewise shaping the role that debt plays in corporate governance (Whitehead 2009).

Bank lenders can arrange for others to participate in a loan at origination, as well as sell all or part of a loan at a later date. In loan syndications, one or more 'lead banks' (or 'arrangers') negotiates the terms of the loan and invites other creditors to participate at origination. Interests in a loan, whether or not syndicated, can also be sold in the secondary market, which riskier borrowers and non-bank investors tend to dominate.[21] Through collateralized loan obligations (CLOs), a portfolio of loans can be sold to a special purpose vehicle that, in turn, issues multiple tranches of CLO securities to diversified investors in order to fund the purchase. Converting loan assets to securities, and then transferring an undivided interest through the capital market, enhances their liquidity (Frankel 1999).

In addition, credit derivatives enable lenders to transfer credit risk to other investors, permitting the separation of a loan's working capital from its risk capital. Using a credit default swap (CDS),[22] for example, a lender can buy or sell all or a portion of a borrower's credit risk without transferring the loan itself, enabling the lender to more efficiently manage and diversify its credit exposure. In effect, a CDS permits the lender to outsource credit risk to a new group of CDS investors, who can assume (and manage) the borrower's credit risk without funding the working capital component of the loan (Whitehead 2010).[23] The benefits to a creditor of greater liquidity could not be replicated at low cost by a creditor's or borrower's shareholders, providing value-maximizing managers with an incentive to continue to support and grow the private credit market (Merton 1992; Merton & Bodie 2005; Gilson & Whitehead 2008).

The new credit market has been concentrated among large banks (Wilmarth 2002; Minton et al. 2009). Part of the reason may be the informational asymmetry that historically has given

---

[21]    A description of the syndicated loan market, and how it differs from secondary trading, can be found in Sufi (2007).

[22]    A CDS permits a counterparty to a swap contract to buy or sell all or a portion of the credit risk tied to a loan or bond. The CDS customer pays the 'writer' of the swap a periodic fee in exchange for a contingent payment in the event of a credit default. If a credit event occurs, typically involving default by the borrower, the CDS writer must pay the counterparty an amount sufficient to make it whole or purchase the referenced loan or bond at par. Although there are important differences, a CDS is economically similar to a term insurance policy written against the credit downgrade of the referenced borrower (Masters & Bryson 1999; Glantz 2003; Sjostrom 2009).

[23]    A description of different credit derivatives appears in Masters & Bryson (1999) and Glantz (2003).

banks a competitive edge over non-bank lenders (Acharya & Johnson 2007). Trading among a small group of informed investors, however, can still result in the public release of a substantial amount of private information through competitive pricing. Others can rely on that information to make their own investment decisions, resulting in an overall increase in market size (Holden & Subrahmanyam 1992). Greater and more diverse information may also be reflected in price as more participants enter the market.

Balanced against liquidity's benefits is the risk that the 'decoupling' of economic and control rights – for example, through securitization and credit derivatives – may result in less effective governance. Having transferred the credit risk of a loan to someone else, a lender – who, nevertheless, retains full contractual rights – may have less incentive to monitor the borrower or act in the interest of those who own interests in the loan. Accordingly, while purchasers of credit risk may be better able to manage it through diversification, they may be less able to oversee borrowers as effectively, resulting in an increase in agency costs and decline in corporate governance (Partnoy & Skeel 2007). Transferring credit risk, however, may also enable a creditor to more effectively enforce its covenant protections. The decline in risk exposure raises the lender's relative bargaining power, enabling it to more easily refuse to renegotiate a loan unless the terms are attractive. In the extreme, a creditor who transferred its economic risk may have less incentive to renegotiate or restructure a loan altogether, potentially reducing the value of the borrower's outstanding debt or even pushing the borrower into bankruptcy (Hu & Black 2008; Bolton & Oehmke 2010).

Likewise, covenant levels may drop if creditors are unable at low cost to monitor a borrower's compliance with its loan obligations or renegotiate a loan following its breach. As noted earlier, public bonds typically contain less restrictive covenants than loans, in part due to the higher cost of monitoring. Banks, in turn, have an incentive to transfer lower quality assets to third parties – with the result that covenants and oversight may decline for those borrowers most in need of closer monitoring. The outcome reflects a trade-off, with the lower cost of managing credit risk being offset by greater agency costs.[24]

Those costs are similar to costs that arise in the public market, but with a critical difference: Unlike firms that typically issue public bonds, information regarding private borrowers is often less well known. Some portion of the cost is offset by the creditors' ability to manage credit risk more efficiently. Yet, as covenants and monitoring decline, investors are likely to demand higher returns to compensate for the greater risk – a result that is consistent with the drop in governance, but unlikely to be sustained if there are less costly means to miti-

---

[24]   That description is consistent with the decline in commercial loan covenants that began in 1995. For over a decade, federal bank regulators cautioned banks against weakening covenants in syndicated loans to risky borrowers (Wilmarth 2002). Covenants tightened as the US markets entered a recessionary period in 2001–2002, but by 2006, lending standards had eased considerably to the earlier, lower levels. In particular, before the beginning of the financial crisis in 2007, private equity sponsors saw a substantial rise in 'covenant-lite' (or 'cov-lite') loans – which, as the name suggests, had substantially fewer covenants than most commercial loans – jumping from four loans in 2005 to over 100 in 2007. Competition among bankers for new business and among investors for new loan assets is likely to have contributed. Reputation may have also played a role. The private equity market is comprised of a limited group of participants that interact frequently, suggesting that a reputation as a 'good' borrower can have substantial and positive economic consequences. Market participants also attributed a portion of the decline in covenant levels to the increased ability to hedge risk in the credit market and the weakening incentives of banks to screen and monitor borrowers (Whitehead 2009).

gate the increase in agency costs (Black 1975; Ashcraft & Santos 2007). Market participants, therefore, have looked to change how loans are structured and, by extension, have shaped new forms of corporate governance (Pennacchi 1988). A key to that change has been the response of the private credit market to shifts in the source of capital, as providers have moved from bank lenders within the traditional framing to bank and non-bank investors in an increasingly liquid credit market.

## Syndication

A loan is more likely to be syndicated as information about the borrower becomes more transparent (for example, through a credit rating or listing on a stock exchange) (Dennis & Mullineaux 2000). For less well-known borrowers, the number of lenders may be capped and resales restricted in order to encourage direct monitoring and renegotiation if a covenant is breached (Demsetz 1999; Lee & Mullineaux 2004). Participants in the original syndicate are more likely than later purchasers to have long-term relationships with the borrower and syndicate manager, enabling them to monitor the borrower at lower cost and facilitating coordination (Haubrich 1989; Sufi 2007). Thus, a lead bank's traditional governance role may be replaced by the collective oversight of a syndicate's members.

In addition, as a condition of sale, a purchaser may require the lead bank to continue to hold a portion of the loan until it matures.[25] By retaining economic risk, the bank can credibly commit to continued monitoring and, as necessary, enforcing a loan's covenants (Diamond 1984; Pennacchi 1988; Gorton & Pennacchi 1990). A lender can also commit to monitoring if, as is often the case, other relationships with the borrower continue to motivate oversight. Those relationships, however, may be of questionable value to the extent they potentially result in conflict between the economic interests of the loan purchasers and the originating lender (Hu & Black 2008).

## Covenant Levels

Greater liquidity (as in the public debt market) is typically accompanied by a decline in covenants and monitoring. Information about private borrowers, however, tends to be less available than for public issuers, reinforcing the need to rely on covenants. Covenants levels, therefore, may also increase in order to offset the greater monitoring costs tied to more opaque firms. Non-syndicated loans structured for resale (typically leveraged, risky loans to non-bank, institutional investors) may contain higher covenant levels tied to observable public information. By tightening covenants, lenders can more quickly discover changes – including relatively discrete changes – in a borrower's financial position. In addition, by tying covenants to observable data, purchasers can mitigate the increased cost of direct monitoring.

---

[25]   That condition is now mandatory for most securitizations, even though not a legal requirement for loan syndications. Section 941 of the Dodd–Frank Wall Street Reform and Consumer Protection Act, Pub. L. No. 111-203, 124 Stat. 1376 (2010) (Dodd-Frank Act) added new Section 15G of the Securities Exchange Act of 1934, which generally requires securitizers to retain a portion of the credit risk of assets included in a securitization. Securitizers are prohibited from directly or indirectly hedging or transferring the credit risk they are required to retain, unless permitted by regulation.

Investors, as a result, may be better able to manage credit risk and provide greater levels of funding (Drucker & Puri 2009).

Growing liquidity has also prompted the rise of specialist investors (sometimes referred to as 'vultures') that look to influence a firm's management through its debt covenants. Loans purchased by those investors are often distressed, with the discount in purchase price (and potential for substantial return) offsetting the greater cost of monitoring (Hotchkiss & Mooradian 1997). Investors use the borrower's breach of its covenants to force change in its policies or a change in control – providing another pair of eyes over distressed borrowers, where the potential for management opportunism can be the greatest (Harner 2008).

**Reputation**

Reputation can also help mitigate agency costs. A reputable borrower is more likely to be able to obtain loans with fewer restrictions than a borrower with a less well-known credit history. Consequently, like in the traditional model, a borrower may be more inclined to act in a manner consistent with its lenders' interests to the extent it benefits from an improved reputation.

Bank reputation can also be important (Dennis & Mullineaux 2000; Drucker & Puri 2009). For investors, how a bank structures a loan or monitors a borrower may not be apparent at the time the loan is sold. The purchaser, instead, must rely on the lender's reputation based on prior sales. Structuring a bad loan, or failing to monitor a borrower, can hurt that reputation – and so, as long as loan sales are a significant part of its business, concerns over reputation may induce an originating bank to continue to monitor a borrower, even after its credit risk has been transferred (Preece & Mullineaux 1996; Rajan 1998; Lee & Mullineaux 2004). Transferring credit risk secretly, while possible, exposes the bank to a potential loss of reputation and a costly decline in its ability to sell loans in the future (Duffie 2008).

## 4.   DEBT'S EVOLUTION

So far, we have considered how loan structure has changed in response to greater liquidity in the private credit market. Syndicate structure, covenant levels, and reputation are all means to reduce the resulting agency costs and balance the potential decline in debt governance.

A further possibility is prompted by increasing liquidity in the credit market itself. For public debt, secondary trading prices inform the issuer's managers of how the market assesses the borrower's credit quality (Amihud et al. 1999). Likewise, in a more complete market, actions that affect a firm's credit risk will increasingly be reflected in changes in the price at which a firm's loans and other private credit instruments trade. Those changes may affect a borrower's cost of capital – including a change in the price and non-price terms on which the loans are made – providing a discipline through the feedback furnished by market participants that complements the traditional protections provided by contract (Whitehead 2009).

In a frictionless world, a firm's equity and debt prices should move in tandem when new information is discovered. A loan, in that world, is economically equivalent to the lender owning a riskless claim on the borrower and also issuing a put option on the borrower to the borrower's shareholders. If the value of the borrower's assets falls below the face value of the loan, then the borrower defaults – with the shareholders, in effect, exercising their right to 'put' the firm to the lender in satisfaction of its claims. The implication is that there is a corre-lation between the value of a firm's debt (including credit derivatives tied to that debt) and equity, so that market prices should adjust at the same time and to the same information (Merton 1974).

In practice, however, credit derivatives often react first to new credit information – with their prices moving ahead of changes in both equity and debt (Chan-Lau & Kim 2004; Norden & Weber 2004; Blanco et al. 2005), as well as in advance of the public announce-ment of a negative change in a firm's credit rating (Hull et al. 2004). Thus, for a public firm, a change in derivatives pricing may mirror an increase or decrease in its credit quality *before* a change in its debt or equity pricing – providing more accurate feedback on the perceived riskiness of the firm's policies and projects (Glantz 2003). No doubt, part of the difference in response reflects the special access of market participants, like banks, to private information about borrowers (Acharya & Johnson 2007). Part of it also reflects the close relationship between the value of a credit derivative and changes in a firm's default risk (Andritzky & Singh 2006).

The growth in private credit may, in turn, affect the terms on which subsequent loans are made (Norden & Wagner 2008). Loan agreements already include features, like pricing grids (described earlier), that can adjust the real cost of capital based upon pre-agreed changes in a borrower's financial condition or credit rating. Going forward, lenders can rely on the pri-cing of credit instruments to assess a firm's credit quality and, if necessary, determine the cost of hedging their credit exposure. A borrower's actions that change the price at which its exist-ing loans or other credit instruments trade can alter the terms of a loan or influence the price and non-price terms on which lenders make subsequent loans. Since most loan pricing over the riskless rate is tied to default risk, actions that increase credit risk will result in a corres-ponding increase in a borrower's cost of capital (Longstaff et al. 2005).

One outcome is that secondary trading in private credit may begin to overtake covenants and monitoring as an efficient form of governance. Covenants may be over- or under-inclu-sive, reflecting the difficulty of anticipating future events and drafting covenants that prop-erly reflect them. By contrast, since firms access the credit market on a regular basis (Triantis & Daniels 1995), changes in credit pricing that directly affect a firm's cost of capital may provide a more efficient alternative.[26] The impact of more costly debt can be reflected shortly after a change in the firm's credit risk, either through a higher interest rate on an existing loan or the increased cost of a new loan. That cost, in turn, may lower the firm's share price and, like public equity, discipline managers by affecting compensation, retention decisions based on share price performance, and the likelihood of a hostile takeover. To be clear, covenants will continue to play an important role in corporate governance, but some portion of the tradi-tional reliance may be offset by the feedback provided by an increasingly liquid credit market. The trick, as the markets become more complete, will be to balance that new disci-pline against the traditional role played by covenants and monitoring.

---

[26]   As Judge Easterbrook has noted, 'Additional ways to price or trade financial instruments ought to strengthen the capital market as a disciplinary force. What makes the capital market more efficient not only makes governance less important – in what field does it retain a comparative advantage? – but also makes governance better' (Easterbrook 2002)

## 5.  CONCLUSION

Debt governance is an important piece of the corporate governance puzzle. Understanding its effects is a principal challenge for the theory of the firm. Some have been concerned, in the wake of the 2007–2008 financial crisis, that leverage – and, in particular, new credit instruments – can weaken the general economy. No doubt, excessive leverage can be problematic. Debt, however, can also assist productivity through its ability to control agency costs and discipline sub-optimal managers. Properly managed, it can result in the effective use of available capital, enhancing profitability and raising stock prices.

Debt governance may be particularly important for traditional financial intermediaries, like banks, that rely on debt (including deposits) for capital. Unlike traditional lenders, consumer creditors – such as depositors – are unable to effectively monitor a financial intermediary's credit quality. They tend to have limited information (and, with government-sponsored insurance, less incentive) to assess whether a firm is investing their capital profitably. To date, an important function of financial regulation has been to bridge that gap (Whitehead 2010). Financial firms may also benefit through mechanisms that increase the role of debt governance. A greater focus on creditor interests may help balance some of the apparent weaknesses resulting from the particular focus on equity governance leading up to the financial crisis (Coffee 2010).

The traditional view of debt governance has been premised on debt's relative illiquidity. Banks with access to private information were able to extend loans at lower cost than other lenders, but looked to covenants and monitoring as a principal means to manage credit risk. The last three decades have witnessed a transformation in the traditional bank–borrower relationship, resulting in growth in the private credit market. Over time, with greater liquidity, changes in a firm's credit quality may increasingly be reflected in the pricing of its credit instruments, creating a more efficient 'real time' alternative that supplements a lender's traditional reliance on covenants and monitoring. In short, changes in the capital market have affected capital structure and corporate governance, and will likely continue to do so.

It may be useful, therefore, to consider the extent to which financial regulation – beyond its traditional focus on market integrity, customer protection, and systemic risk – may affect how firms are governed. Consider, for example, the increased regulation of the credit rating agencies.[27] A principal focus has been on the role of the agencies in informing prospective investors of the quality of the securities they purchase. Yet, just as important is the role they play in corporate governance. Changes in a firm's credit rating affect its real cost of capital, as well as the relative mix of debt funding it relies on, providing managers with an incentive to minimize risky activities (Rauh & Sufi 2010). To what extent should the impact on corporate governance be reflected in the new regulation? Consider also a bank's regulatory capital requirements. Changes in minimum capital levels may help minimize systemic risk, but they

---

[27]   Subtitle C of Title IX of the Dodd-Frank Act institutes reforms in the regulation, oversight and accountability of nationally recognized statistical rating organizations. It reflects concerns over conflicts of interest faced by credit rating agencies and that 'inaccurate' ratings played a role in the mismanagement of risk by large financial institutions and investors leading up to the financial crisis. Its purpose is to identify and eliminate conflicts of interest and restore confidence in the ratings process. Accordingly, Subtitle C substantially expands credit rating agency accountability and the scope of Securities and Exchange Commission regulation and oversight.

will also affect how private credit instruments are structured and traded (Nicolò & Pelizzon 2008). Should the effect of those instruments on debt governance also inform policymakers' deliberations over new regulation? Those questions mirror the evolving nature of debt and debt governance. They suggest, as well, that debt governance must become an increasingly important consideration in regulating the private credit market.

# REFERENCES

Acharya, Viral V. & Timothy C. Johnson (2007), 'Insider Trading in Credit Derivatives', *Journal of Financial Economics*, 84, 110–41.

Allen, Franklin & Douglas Gale (1997), 'Financial Markets, Intermediaries, and Intertemporal Smoothing', *Journal of Political Economy*, 105, 523–46.

Allen, Franklin & Anthony M. Santomero (2001), 'What do Financial Intermediaries do?', *Journal of Banking & Finance*, 25, 271–94.

Amihud, Yakov, Kenneth Garbade & Marcel Kahan (1999), 'A New Governance Structure for Corporate Bonds', *Stanford Law Review*, 51, 447–92.

Andritzky, Jochen & Manmohan Singh (2006), 'The Pricing of Credit Default Swaps During Distress', International Monetary Fund Working Paper WP/06/254.

Arrow, Kenneth (1981), 'Pareto Efficiency with Costly Transfers', in N. Assorodobraj-Kula, C. Bobrowski, H. Hagemejer, W. Kula & J. Los (eds) *Studies in Economic Theory and Practice: Essays in Honor of Edward Lipinski*, Amsterdam: North Holland Publishing Company.

Ashcraft, Adam B. & João A.C. Santos (2007), 'Has the Credit Default Swap Market Lowered the Cost of Corporate Debt?', Federal Reserve Bank of New York Staff Report No. 290.

Baird, Douglas G. & Robert K. Rasmussen (2006),'Private Debt and the Missing Lever of Corporate Governance', *University of Pennsylvania Law Review*, 154, 1209–51.

Barclay, Michael J. & Clifford W. Smith, Jr. (1995), 'The Maturity Structure of Corporate Debt', *Journal of Finance*, 50, 609–31.

Basel Committee on Banking Supervision (1999), 'Capital Requirements and Bank Behaviour: The Impact of the Basel Accord', Working Paper No. 1.

Berger, Allen N. & Gregory F. Udell (1993), 'Securitization, Risk, and the Liquidity Problem', in Michael Klausner & Lawrence J. White (eds) *Structural Change in Banking*, Homewood, IL: Irwin Publishing.

Berger, Allen N., Anil K. Kashyap & Joseph M. Scalise (1995), 'The Transformation of the U.S. Banking Industry: What a Long, Strange Trip It's Been', *Brookings Papers on Economic Activity*, 55–218.

Berger, Phillip G., Eli Ofek & David L. Yermack (1997), 'Managerial Entrenchment and Capital Structure Decisions', *Journal of Finance*, 52, 1411–38.

Billett, Matthew T., Tao-Hsien Dolly King & David C. Mauer (2007), 'Growth Opportunities and the Choice of Leverage, Debt Maturity, and Covenants', *Journal of Finance*, 62, 697–730.

Black, Fischer (1975), 'Bank Funds Management in an Efficient Market', *Journal of Financial Economics*, 2, 323–39.

Blanco, Roberto, Simon Brennan & Ian W. March (2005), 'An Empirical Analysis of the Dynamic Relationship between Investment-Grade Bonds and Credit Default Swaps', *Journal of Finance*, 60, 2255–81.

Bolton, Patrick & David S. Scharfstein (1996), 'Optimal Debt Structure and the Number of Creditors', *Journal of Political Economy*, 104, 1–25.

Bolton, Patrick & Xavier Freixas (2000), 'Equity, Bonds, and Bank Debt: Capital Structure and Financial Market Equilibrium Under Asymmetric Information', *Journal of Political Economy*, 108, 324–51.

Bolton, Patrick & Martin Oehmke (2010), 'Credit Default Swaps and the Empty Creditor Problem', National Bureau of Economic Research Working Paper 15999.

Boot, Arnoud (2000), 'Relationship Banking: What Do We Know?', *Journal of Financial Intermediation*, 9, 7–25.

Boot, Arnoud W.A., Stuart I. Greenbaum & Anjan V. Thakor (1993), 'Reputation and Discretion in Financial Contracting', *American Economic Review*, 83, 1165–83.

Bratton, Jr., William W. (1989), 'Corporate Debt Relationships: Legal Theory in a Time of Restructuring', *Duke Law Journal*, 1989, 92–172.

Calomiris, Charles W. (2000), *U.S. Bank Deregulation in Historical Perspective*, New York, NY: Cambridge University Press.

Caouette, John B., Edward I. Altman & Paul Narayanan (1998), *Managing Credit Risk: The Next Great Financial Challenge*, New York, NY: John Wiley & Sons.

Carey, Mark, Stephen Prowse, John Rea & Gregory Udell (1993), 'The Economics of the Private Placement Market', Board of Governors of the Federal Reserve System, Staff Study No. 166.

Cebenoyan, A. Sinan & Philip E. Strahan (2004), 'Risk Management, Capital Structure and Lending at Banks', *Journal of Banking & Finance*, 28, 19–43.

Chan-Lau, Jorge A. & Yoon Sook Kim (2004), 'Equity Prices, Credit Default Swaps, and Bond Spreads in Emerging Markets', International Monetary Fund Working Paper WP/04/27.

Chava, Sudheer & Michael R. Roberts (2008), 'How Does Financing Impact Investment? The Role of Debt Covenants', *Journal of Finance*, 63, 2085–2121.

Coffee, Jr., John C. (2010), 'Bail-ins Versus Bail-outs: Using Contingent Capital to Mitigate Systemic Risk', Columbia Law and Economics Working Paper No. 380.

Coles, Jeffrey L., Naveen D. Daniel & Lalitha Naveen (2006), 'Managerial Incentives and Risk-Taking', *Journal of Financial Economics*, 79, 431–68.

Datta, Sudip, Mai Iskander-Datta & Kartik Raman (2005), 'Managerial Stock Ownership and the Maturity Structure of Corporate Debt', *Journal of Finance*, 60, 2333–50.

Demsetz, Rebecca S. (1999), 'Bank Loan Sales: A New Look at the Motivations for Secondary Market Activity', Federal Reserve Bank of New York Staff Report No. 69.

Denis, David J. & Vassil T. Mihov (2003), 'The Choice Among Bank Debt, Non-bank Private Debt, and Public Debt: Evidence from New Corporate Borrowings', *Journal of Financial Economics*, 70, 3–28.

Dennis, Steven A. & Donald J. Mullineaux (2000), 'Syndicated Loans', *Journal of Financial Intermediation*, 9, 404–26.

Diamond, Douglas W. (1984), 'Financial Intermediation and Delegated Monitoring', *Review of Economic Studies*, 51, 393–414.

Diamond, Douglas W. (1991), 'Monitoring and Reputation: The Choice Between Bank Loans and Directly Placed Debt', *Journal of Political Economy*, 99, 689–721.

Dichev, Ilia D. & Douglas J. Skinner (2002), 'Large-Sample Evidence on the Debt Covenant Hypothesis', *Journal of Accounting Research*, 40, 1091–1123.

Drucker, Steven & Manju Puri (2009), 'On Loan Sales, Loan Contracting, and Lending Relationships', *Review of Financial Studies*, 22, 2835–72.

Duffie, Darrell (2008), 'Innovations in Credit Risk Transfer: Implications for Financial Stability', Bank for International Settlements Working Paper No. 255.

Easterbrook, Frank H. (2002), 'Derivative Securities and Corporate Governance', *University of Chicago Law Review*, 69, 733–47.

Fama, Eugene F. (1985), 'What's Different About Banks?', *Journal of Monetary Economics*, 15, 29–39.

Fan, Joseph P.H., Sheridan Titman & Garry Twite (2010), 'An International Comparison of Capital Structure and Debt Maturity Choices', *Journal of Financial and Quantitative Analysis*, forthcoming.

Fischel, Daniel R. (1989), 'The Economics of Lender Liability', *Yale Law Journal*, 99, 131–54.

Flannery, Mark J. (1986), 'Asymmetric Information and Risk Debt Maturity Choice', *Journal of Finance*, 41, 19–37.

Frankel, Tamar (1999), 'Securitization: The Conflict Between Personal and Property Law (Contract and Property)', *Annual Review of Banking Law*, 18, 197–219.

Garvey, Gerald T. & Gordon Hanka (1999), 'Capital Structure and Corporate Control: The Effect of Antitakeover Statutes on Firm Leverage', *Journal of Finance*, 54, 519–46.

Gilson, Ronald J. & Charles K. Whitehead (2008), 'Deconstructing Equity: Public Ownership, Agency Costs, and Complete Capital Markets', *Columbia Law Review*, 108, 231–64.

Gilson, Stuart (1989), 'Management Turnover and Financial Distress', *Journal of Financial Economics*, 25, 241–62.

Gilson, Stuart (1990), 'Bankruptcy, Boards, Banks, and Blockholders', *Journal of Financial Economics*, 27, 355–87.

Glantz, Mortan (2003), *Managing Bank Risk: An Introduction to Broad-Base Credit Engineering*, San Diego, CA, and London, England: Academic Press.

Gorton, Gary & George Pennacchi (1990), 'Banks and Loan Sales: Marketing Non-marketable Assets', National Bureau of Economic Research Working Paper No. 3551.

Grossman, Sanford J. & Oliver D. Hart (1982), 'Corporate Financial Structure and Managerial Incentives', in John J. McCall (ed.) *The Economics of Information and Uncertainty*, Chicago, IL: University of Chicago Press.

Güner, A. Burak (2006), 'Loan Sales and the Cost of Corporate Borrowing', *Review of Financial Studies*, 19, 687–716.

Harner, Michelle M. (2008), 'Trends in Distressed Debt Investing: An Empirical Study of Investors' Objectives', *American Bankruptcy Institute Law Review*, 16, 69–110.

Harris, Milton & Artur Raviv (1988), 'Corporate Control Contests and Capital Structure', *Journal of Financial Economics*, 20, 55–86.

Harris, Milton & Artur Raviv (1990), 'Capital Structure and the Informational Role of Debt', *Journal of Finance*, 45, 321–49.

Hart, Oliver & John Moore (1995), 'Debt and Seniority: An Analysis of the Role of Hard Claims in Constraining Management', *American Economic Review*, 85, 567–85.

Hart, Oliver & John Moore (1998), 'Default and Renegotiation: A Dynamic Model of Debt', *Quarterly Journal of Economics*, 113, 1–41.

Haubrich, Joseph G. (1989), 'Financial Intermedation – Delegated Monitoring and Long Term Relationships', *Journal of Banking & Finance*, 13, 9–20.

Hill, Claire A. (2004), 'Regulating the Rating Agencies', *Washington University Law Quarterly*, 82, 43–94.

Holden, Craig W. & Avanidhar Subrahmanyam (1992), 'Long-Lived Private Information and Imperfect Competition', *Journal of Finance*, 47, 247–70.

Hotchkiss, Edith S. & Robert M. Mooradian (1997), 'Vulture Investors and the Market for Control of Distressed Firms', *Journal of Financial Economics*, 43, 401–32.

Hu, Henry T.C. & Bernard Black (2008), 'Debt, Equity, and Hybrid Decoupling: Governance and Systemic Risk Implications', *European Financial Management*, 14, 663–709.

Hughes, Joseph P. & Loretta J. Mester (1998), 'Bank Capitalization and Cost: Evidence of Scale Economies in Risk Management and Signaling', *Review of Economics and Statistics*, 80, 314–25.

Hull, John, Mirela Predescu & Alan White (2004), 'The Relationship between Credit Default Swap Spreads, Bond Yields, and Credit Rating Announcements', *Journal of Banking & Finance*, 28, 2789–2811.

Ivashina, Victoria, Vinay B. Nair, Anthony Saunders, Nadia Massoud & Roger Stover (2009), 'Bank Debt and Corporate Governance', *Review of Financial Studies*, 22, 41–77.

James, Christopher (1987), 'Some Evidence on the Uniqueness of Bank Loans', *Journal of Financial Economics*, 19, 217–35.

Jensen, Michael C. (1986), 'Agency Costs of Free Cash Flow, Corporate Finance, and Takeovers', *American Economic Review*, 76, 323–9.

Jensen, Michael C. (1989), 'Active Investors, LBOs, and the Privatization of Bankruptcy', Statement Before the US House Ways and Means Committee, reprinted in *Journal of Applied Corporate Finance*, 22, 77–85.

Jensen, Michael C. & William H. Meckling (1976), 'Theory of the Firm: Managerial Behavior, Agency Costs and Ownership Structure', *Journal of Financial Economics*, 3, 305–60.

John, Kose, Lubomir Litov & Bernard Yeung (2008), 'Corporate Governance and Risk-Taking', *Journal of Finance*, 63, 1679–1728.

John, Kose & Lubomir Litov (2010), 'Managerial Entrenchment and Capital Structure: New Evidence', *Journal of Empirical Legal Studies*, 7, 693–742.

Kahan, Marcel & Bruce Tuckman (1993), 'Private vs. Public Lending: Evidence from Covenants', UCLA, Anderson Graduate School of Management, Working Paper.

La Porta, Florencio Lopez-de-Silanes, Andrei Shleifer & Robert W. Vishny (1998), 'Law and Finance', *Journal of Political Economy*, 106, 1113–55.

Lee, Sang Whi & Donald J. Mullineaux (2004), 'Monitoring, Financial Distress, and the Structure of Commercial Lending Syndicates', *Financial Management*, 33, 107–30.

Leland, Hayne E. & David H. Pyle (1977), 'Informational Asymmetries, Financial Structure, and Financial Intermediation', *Journal of Finance*, 32, 371–87.

Llewellyn, David T. (1996), 'Banking in the 21st Century: The Transformation of an Industry', in Malcom Edey (ed.) *The Future of the Financial System*, Reserve Bank of Australia.

Longstaff, Francis A., Sanjay Mithal & Eric Neis (2005), 'Corporate Yield Spreads: Default Risk or Liquidity? New Evidence from the Credit-Default Swap Market', *Journal of Finance*, 60, 2213–53.

Lundstrum, Leonard L. (2009), 'Entrenched Management, Capital Structure Changes and Firm Value', *Journal of Economics and Finance*, 33, 161–75.

Markowitz, Harry (1952), 'Portfolio Selection', *Journal of Finance*, 7, 77–91.

Masters, Blythe & Kelly Bryson (1999), 'Credit Derivatives and Loan Portfolio Management', in Jack Clark Francis, Joyce A. Frost & J. Gregg Whittaker (eds) *Handbook of Credit Derivatives*, New York, NY: McGraw-Hill.

Merton, Robert C. (1974), 'On the Pricing of Corporate Debt: The Risk Structure of Interest Rates', *Journal of Finance*, 29, 449–70.

Merton, Robert C. (1992), 'Financial Innovation and Economic Performance', *Journal of Applied Corporate Finance*, 4, 12–22.

Merton, Robert C. & Zvi Bodie (2005), 'The Design of Financial Systems: Towards a Synthesis of Function and Structure', *Journal of Investment Management*, 3, 1–23.

Minton, Bernadette, René M. Stulz & Rohan Williamson (2009), 'How Much Do Banks Use Credit Derivatives to Hedge Loans?', *Journal of Financial Services Research*, 35, 1–31.

Myers, Stewart C. (1977), 'Determinants of Corporate Borrowing', *Journal of Financial Economics*, 5, 147–75.

Myers, Stewart C. (1989), 'Still Searching for Optimal Capital Structure', in Richard W. Kopcke & Eric S. Rosengren (eds) *Are the Distinctions between Debt and Equity Disappearing?*, Federal Reserve Bank of Boston.

Nicolò, Antonio & Loriana Pelizzon (2008), 'Credit Derivatives, Capital Requirements and Opaque OTC Markets', *Journal of Financial Intermediation*, 17, 444–63.

Nini, Greg, David C. Smith & Amir Sufi (2009), 'Creditor Control Rights and Firm Investment Policy', *Journal of Financial Economics*, 92, 400–20.

Norden, Lars & Martin Weber (2004), 'Informational Efficiency of Credit Default Swap and Stock Markets: The Impact of Credit Rating Announcements', *Journal of Banking & Finance*, 28, 2813–43.
Norden, Lars & Wolf Wagner (2008), 'Credit Derivatives and Loan Pricing', *Journal of Banking & Finance*, 32, 2560–9.
Partnoy, Frank (1999), 'The Siskel and Ebert of Financial Markets?: Two Thumbs Down for the Credit Rating Agencies', *Washington University Law Quarterly*, 77, 619–712.
Partnoy, Frank & David A. Skeel, Jr. (2007), 'The Promise and Perils of Credit Derivatives', *University of Cincinnati Law Review*, 75, 1019–52.
Pennacchi, George G. (1988), 'Loan Sales and the Cost of Bank Capital', *Journal of Finance*, 43, 375–96.
Preece, Dianna & Donald J. Mullineaux (1996), 'Monitoring, Loan Renegotiability, and Firm Value: The Role of Lending Syndicates', *Journal of Banking & Finance*, 20, 577–93.
Rajan, Raghuram (1992), 'Insiders and Outsiders: The Choice between Informed and Arm's-Length Debt', *Journal of Finance*, 47, 1367–1400.
Rajan, Raghuram (1998), 'The Past and Future of Commercial Banking Viewed through an Incomplete Contract Lens', *Journal of Money, Credit and Banking*, 30, 524–50.
Rajan, Raghuram & Andrew Winton (1995), 'Covenants and Collateral as Incentives to Monitor', *Journal of Finance*, 50, 1113–46.
Rauh, Joshua D. & Amir Sufi (2010), 'Capital Structure and Debt Structure', *Review of Financial Studies*, 23, 4242–80.
Roberts, Michael R. & Amir Sufi (2009a), 'Control Rights and Capital Structure: An Empirical Investigation', *Journal of Finance*, 64, 1657–95.
Roberts, Michael R. & Amir Sufi (2009b), 'Renegotiation of Financial Contracts: Evidence from Private Credit Agreements', *Journal of Financial Economics*, 93, 159–84.
Shepherd, Joanna M., Frederick Tung & Albert H. Yoon (2008), 'What Else Matters for Corporate Governance: The Case of Bank Monitoring', *Boston University Law Review*, 88, 991–1041.
Simons, Katerina (1993), 'Why Do Banks Syndicate Loans?', *New England Economic Review*, Jan–Feb 1993, 45–52.
Sjostrom, Jr., William K. (2009), 'The AIG Bailout', *Washington and Lee Law Review*, 66, 943–94.
Smith, Jr., Clifford W. & Jerold B. Warner (1979), 'On Financial Contracting: An Analysis of Bond Covenants', *Journal of Financial Economics*, 7, 117–61.
Stulz, René (1988), 'Managerial Control of Voting Rights: Financing Policies and the Market for Corporate Control', *Journal of Financial Economics*, 20, 25–54.
Stulz, René (1990), 'Managerial Discretion and Optimal Financing Policies', *Journal of Financial Economics*, 26, 3–27.
Stulz, René (2002), 'Does Financial Structure Matter for Economic Growth? A Corporate Finance Perspective', in Asli Demirgüç-Kunt & Ross Levine (eds) *Financial Structure and Economic Growth: A Cross-Country Comparison of Banks, Markets, and Development*, Cambridge, MA, and London, England: MIT Press.
Sufi, Amir (2007), 'Information Asymmetry and Financing Arrangements: Evidence from Syndicated Loans', *Journal of Finance*, 62, 629–68.
Triantis, George G. & Ronald J. Daniels (1995), 'The Role of Debt in Interactive Corporate Governance', *California Law Review*, 83, 1073–113.
Tung, Frederick (2009), 'Leverage in the Board Room: The Unsung Influence of Private Lenders in Corporate Governance', *UCLA Law Review*, 57, 115–81.
Whitehead, Charles K. (2006), 'What's Your Sign? – International Norms, Signals, and Compliance', *Michigan Journal of International Law*, 27, 695–741.
Whitehead, Charles K. (2009), 'The Evolution of Debt: Covenants, the Credit Market, and Corporate Governance', *Journal of Corporation Law*, 34, 641–77.
Whitehead, Charles K. (2010), 'Reframing Financial Regulation', *Boston University Law Review*, 90, 1–50.
Williamson, Oliver E. (1988), 'Corporate Finance and Corporate Governance', *Journal of Finance*, 43, 567–91.
Wilmarth, Jr., Arthur E. (2002), 'The Transformation of the U.S. Financial Services Industry, 1975–2000: Competition, Consolidation, and Increased Risks', *University of Illinois Law Review*, 2002, 215–476.
Zwiebel, Jeffrey (1996), 'Dynamic Capital Structure under Managerial Entrenchment', *American Economic Review*, 86, 1197–1215.

# 6. Employees and the boundaries of the corporation

*Matthew T. Bodie*

## 1. INTRODUCTION

United States corporate law has little to say about employees.[1] Employees are simply one category of the many parties who form contracts with the corporation. Although individual states have their own separate sets of corporate law, states uniformly delineate the roles of directors, officers, and shareholders in governing the entity. The relationships between these three groups constitute the purpose and function of corporate law (Clark 1986; Smith & Williams 2008). The 'employee' category is not a meaningful one when it comes to creating, sustaining, or dissolving the corporation (Greenfield 1998).

When it comes to the firm, however, as opposed to the corporation, employees take on a much more central role. In *The Nature of the Firm*, Ronald Coase singled out the relationship between the firm and its employees as the firm's defining feature (Coase 1937). This relationship has continued to be a focal point in the development of the theory of the firm – particularly in differentiating between firms and market transactions (Greenfield 1998). In subject areas such as tort law, intellectual property law, and tax law, the employer–employee relationship provides the necessary contours in separating the firm from the market. And when it comes to other business organizations, especially partnerships, the providers of labor can have a critical role in the ownership and governance of the firm.[2] Corporate law stands out in its exclusion of employees in defining and establishing the legal shape of the firm.[3]

This result is somewhat ironic, since corporate law is the area of law most influenced by the theories of the firm. Since the 1970s, scholars have focused on the interrelationship between the theory of the firm and the construction of corporate law. The 'nexus of contract' theory of the corporation comes from Jensen & Meckling's work on the firm (1976), and it remains foundational in the field (Easterbrook & Fischel 1991; Bainbridge 2002). This theory, in brief, seeks to disaggregate our notion of the corporation as an entity and break it down into its component parts. These parts are the contractual relationships between the various sets of people involved with the firm: executives, directors, shareholders, creditors,

---

[1]   This chapter concerns corporate law and scholarship in the United States. Other countries have had a greater role for employees in governance, with Germany's system of codetermination the most prominent example (Hansmann 1996; Pistor 1999; Roe 1999).

[2]   For example, a partnership can be formed, and a partner can join a partnership, solely through labor contributions. Moreover, a partnership may be formed without an explicit agreement or even contrary to specific agreement, based on joint labor between two parties looking to share the fruits of their labor. *Holmes v. Lerner*, 74 Cal. App. 4th 442 (1999); *Fenwick v. Unemployment Compensation Commission*, 44 A.2d 172 (N.J. Err. & App. 1945).

[3]   Other forms of business organizations, especially workers' cooperatives, allow for significant employee participation in governance (Hansmann 1996; Gulati et al. 2002). This chapter, however, discusses the role of employees in corporations and corporate law.

suppliers, customers, and employees. The 'corporation' itself doesn't really exist; it is merely the 'nexus' (or connection) amongst these various corresponding relationships (Easterbrook & Fischel 1989). Thus, the further irony: research into the theory of the firm has been used to establish that the corporation really is not a firm at all, but rather a series of contracts.

There is, however, a countervailing view. This chapter seeks to recenter the notion of the corporation around the theory of the firm as a separate institution from the market. It will first provide a brief summary of the conventional view of the corporation and the role of employees within the corporation. It will then look to developments in the theory of the firm (both old and new) that provide for a more meaningful role for employees in defining the corporation. The chapter then looks to other areas of law – tort law, intellectual property law, and tax law – for examples of how the employee-centered theory of the firm has already played a role in shaping the law. The chapter concludes with a review of recent works that point to radically different possibilities for the future of firms and the employees within them.

## 2.   THE ROLE OF EMPLOYEES IN STATE AND FEDERAL CORPORATE LAW

Corporations are fictional persons that are created through state corporate law. In order to form a corporation, individuals must follow the procedures established by the individual states. These procedures generally require the incorporating individuals to file a corporate charter, also known as the articles or certificate of incorporation.[4] This charter provides the firm's basic structure: the corporation's name, information regarding the incorporators, the total number of shares the corporation may issue, and the nature of the business to be conducted.[5] Other provisions regarding the governance structure are permitted but are not necessary.[6] Once the corporation is up and running, control transitions from the incorporators to the board of directors. The board manages the firm and may bind the corporation through contracts and transfers of property.[7] Shareholders select the directors at the annual shareholders' meeting.[8] Directors are bound to act in the interests of the firm through common law fiduciary duties of care, good faith, and loyalty. This structure – shareholders select the directors, who in turn run the corporation – represents the crux of corporate law.

Corporate law does sketch out rights and responsibilities for officers, who are employees of the firm. Delaware law, for example, appears to require the corporation to choose officers, including one (generally the secretary) to record the proceedings of shareholders' and directors' meetings.[9] However, the corporation has the power to determine the exact number and nature of the officer positions. Officers owe fiduciary duties to the corporation, and they may be indemnified under corporate law for their acts in the corporation's service.[10] They are

---

[4]   Del. Code tit. 8, § 101(a).
[5]   *Ibid.* § 102.
[6]   Such structures may include a limitation on the liability of directors for breaches of the duty of care (*ibid.* § 102(b)(7)) or the provision for a staggered board of directors (Klausner 2006).
[7]   *Ibid.* § 141.
[8]   *Ibid.* § 211.
[9]   *Ibid.* § 142.
[10]   *Ibid.* § 145.

selected by the board and generally serve at the pleasure of the board, but they have no formal decision-making roles in annual meetings, board decisions, mergers and acquisitions, or dissolution.

Employees are generally hired by the officers and other employees on behalf of the corporation; their role within the corporate structure is purely contractual. The permeability of these categories means that employees can also play a role as shareholders, as directors, or both. These roles are often intermixed in closely-held corporations,[11] but it is also common for the chief executive officer of a public corporation to hold a position on the board as well as a large number of shares.[12] Employees can hold stock directly through a 401(k) plan, or indirectly through a money market account or even an employee stock ownership plan (ESOP).[13] These overlapping roles do create a ripple in the securities laws, as, for example, employees may be offered the corporation's securities without the need for certain registration requirements.[14] For the most part, however, employees are treated as regular investors.[15]

Of course, corporations can be structured in myriad ways. They can provide for employee board representatives by structuring classes of stock to provide for such representation. In perhaps the most famous example of employee board representation, the board for United Airlines had three employee representatives (out of twelve directors) when it underwent its 1994 restructuring (Blair 2001; Gordon 1999; Hansmann 2006). Given that employees owned 55% of the company through an ESOP, three directors gave employees less than their proportional allocation. However, the structure was still controversial. The ESOP and concomitant board structure was eventually unwound when the company entered bankruptcy. United is the exception that proves the rule. Nothing requires an ESOP plan to put employee representatives on the board, and it is in fact a fairly unusual structure to find.[16]

Why do employees have no role in corporate law? The simple – and perhaps tautological – answer is that corporate law does not concern employees. Corporate law focuses on the structure of firm governance, which involves shareholders, directors, and officers. Employees can take on the roles of shareholders and directors, but the employment relationship is contractual and outside the scope of corporate law. Of course, this begs the follow-up question: how can the corporation be constructed without reference to employees? As explained in the following sections, employees are crucial to our understanding of the firm not only in the academic literatures, but in many other areas of the law.

---

[11]   In fact, the doctrine of 'minority oppression' in closely-held corporations often concerns the ability of the majority to deprive the minority of some of its rightful stake in the corporation, particularly employment (Moll 1999).

[12]   Some statutory schemes may exclude management or supervisors from the definition of employee. For example, the National Labor Relations Act excludes supervisors and managers: 29 U.S.C. § 152(11). However, the more common meaning covers anyone who works for the 'employer' (i.e., the corporation).

[13]   Gordon (1997) discusses the dynamics of employee equity ownership through pension funds. For further discussion of employee ownership interests, particularly stock options, see Bodie (2003).

[14]   17 C.F.R. § 230.701.

[15]   See *SEC v. Ralston Purina Co.*, 346 U.S. 119 (1953) (refusing to exempt offerings to employees from securities registration requirements).

[16]   As one example, during its existence as an ESOP-owned company, Avis did not have any employee representatives on its board (Hirsch 1995).

## 3.    EMPLOYEES AND THE THEORY OF THE FIRM

Employees have been central to our conception of the firm from the start. The neoclassical theory of the firm is renowned for its emptiness; neoclassical economics simply saw the firm as a black box which took in inputs and produced outputs. However, this theory did differentiate between what was inside the firm and what was outside: employees and capital assets were inside, while customers and suppliers were outside (Rock & Wachter 2001, 1631; Milgrom & Roberts 1992). Although this conception of the firm was useful in early economic modeling and retains that purpose even today, it was ripe for a reinvestigation that endeavored to give it substance.

Coase offered a new theory in *The Nature of the Firm* (1937). In a passage that has been oft-quoted, Coase framed the issue in this manner:

> Outside the firm, price movements direct production, which is coordinated through a series of exchange transactions on the market. Within a firm these market transactions are eliminated, and in place of the complicated market structure with exchange transactions is substituted the entrepreneur-coordinator, who directs production. It is clear that these are alternative methods of coordinating production. Yet, having regard to the fact that, if production is regulated by price movements, production could be carried on without any organization at all, well we might ask, why is there any organization? (Coase 1937, 388)

Coase's answer is that the price mechanism can be costly. For certain transactions, it is cheaper to simply direct the production to occur rather than contracting separately for it. In order to avoid the transaction costs of contracting, such transactions will occur within a firm rather than on an open market (Coase 1937, 390–92).

The firm-based transactions described by Coase involve the purchase of labor for a particular endeavor. In explaining these transactions, Coase states: 'If a workman moves from department Y to department X, he does not go because of a change in relative prices, but because he was ordered to do so' (Coase 1937, 387). The relationship between the entrepreneur-coordinator and the employee is the primary distinction between the firm and the market. It is the reason for the firm's existence. Coase seems to be arguing that firms would be unnecessary, but for the need to remove the employment relationship from the vagaries of market transactions.

This conclusion is cemented when Coase considers 'whether the concept of a firm which has been developed fits in with that existing in the real world' (Coase 1937, 403). His answer? 'We can best approach the question of what constitutes a firm in practice by considering the legal relationship normally called that of "master and servant" or "employer and employee"' (Coase 1937, 403). He then quotes at length from a treatise concerning the common law 'control' test, which provides that '[t]he master must have the right to control the servant's work, either personally or by another servant or agent' (Coase 1937, 404). He concludes: 'We thus see that it is the fact of direction which is the essence of the legal concept of "employer and employee", just as it was in the economic concept which was developed above' (Coase 1937, 404).

For Coase, the firm is defined by the employer–employee relationship (Orts 1998a). For Alchian & Demsetz (1972), Coase's focus on control and authority is misleading. As they argue: 'To speak of managing, directing, or assigning workers to various tasks is a deceptive way of noting that the employer continually is involved in renegotiation of contracts on terms that must be acceptable to both parties' (Alchian & Demsetz 1972, 777). They frame their argument in these terms:

> Telling an employee to type this letter rather than to file that document is like my telling a grocer to sell me this brand of tuna rather than that brand of bread. I have no contract to continue to purchase from the grocer and neither the employer nor the employee is bound by any contractual obligations to continue the relationship. Long-term contracts between employer and employee are not the essence of the organization we call a firm. (Alchian & Demsetz 1972, 777)

However, Alchian and Demsetz's critique of Coase's theory does not mean that employees are no longer central to the idea of the firm. They argue that the importance of the firm (as separate from the market) stems from the need to coordinate production in the midst of a variety of inputs. The need for a system of team production is what differentiates firms from markets. Alchian and Demsetz define team production as 'production in which 1) several types of resources are used and 2) the product is not a sum of separable outputs of each cooperating resource' (Alchian & Demsetz 1972, 779). As a result, team production is used when the team method increases productivity, after factoring out the costs associated with monitoring and disciplining the team.

Alchian and Demsetz's model seems even more amenable to employee involvement in the firm than Coase's model. The primary concern of team production is to make sure that the team members do not shirk their responsibilities to the team. The inability to measure individual contributions to productivity is what makes the firm possible, but it is also the firm's central governance problem. Alchian and Demsetz argue that a specialized, independent monitor may be the best way of insuring that the team members all contribute appropriately and are rewarded appropriately. That central monitor – the recipient of the residual profits – is the firm. Although both Coase and Alchian and Demsetz personify this monitor in the role of an entrepreneur-coordinator, such a collapse of powers into one human being is only possible in the smallest of firms. In order to meet the criteria set down by the model,[17] the central component of team production is the firm itself: a 'person' who contracts for all other team inputs.

It could be argued that Alchian and Demsetz conceived of a firm detached from employees, since the Alchian-Demsetz monitor must be outside the production process while being able to negotiate with all team members for their input and compensation. However, unless the 'firm' is a sole proprietor, that monitor is merely a mechanism for providing coordination of inputs. And employees are the primary source of the inputs. It is true that Alchian and Demsetz seem to believe that the firm will be represented by a central figure who has claim to the entire residual, and thus an interest in coordinating the firm most efficiently. But they say nothing about who can appoint such a central figure. And in a lengthy discussion in footnote 14, they express skepticism about the ability of shareholders to perform the monitoring function. Rather than characterize shareholders as owners, they argue that shareholders should be viewed merely as investors, like bondholders, albeit 'more optimistic' ones. They ask:

---

[17]   Alchian and Demsetz (1972) set forth the following characteristics of the firm: (a) joint input production, (b) several input owners, (c) one party is common to all the contracts of the joint inputs, (d) who has the rights to renegotiate any input's contract independently of contracts with the other input owners, (e) who holds the residual claim, and (f) who has the right to sell his central contractual residual status.

In sum, is it the case that the stockholder-investor relationship is one emanating from the *division* of *ownership* among several people, or is it that the collection of investment funds from people of various anticipations is the underlying factor? If the latter, why should any of them be thought of as the owners in whom voting rights, whatever they may signify or however exercisable, should reside in order to enhance efficiency? Why voting rights in any of the outside, participating investors? (Alchian & Demsetz 1972, 789 n.14)

Thus, the Alchian-Demsetz team production model does not exclude employees from the definition of the firm. Although their model, with its focus on 'inputs', broadens the scope of the firm to include investors as well as employees, the purpose of the Alchian-Demsetz firm remains the management of employees through the coordination of team production.

As theorists moved beyond these foundational works and into empirical research, the identification of transaction costs, monitoring costs, and team production have remained central concepts. The two primary theories of the firm in play today are the 'transaction-costs' model and the 'property rights' model. Using the transaction-costs model, Williamson and others have identified the types of contractual difficulties which are likely to lead to firm governance, rather than market solutions (Williamson 1985; Macher & Richman 2008). In situations where contributions and compensation can be harder to define, the parties will be left with incomplete contracts that require a governance structure to prevent opportunism. This opportunism will be particularly problematic where one or both of the parties must invest significant resources in assets specific to the particular firm, project, or transaction. This asset specificity makes the parties susceptible to hold-ups from their contractual partners in the absence of a system of governance. Firms can be useful in providing the structures that deter opportunism (Williamson 1985, 1996).

The focus on assets has carried over into the 'property rights' theory of the firm. This theory, developed in a series of articles by Grossman, Hart, and Moore, argues that firms are necessary as a repository of property rights for assets used in joint production (Hart 1995; Grossman & Hart 1986; Hart & Moore 1988, 1990). By owning the property outright, the firm prevents the problem of the commons (in which no one holds property rights over valuable assets) as well as the problem of the anticommons (in which property rights are divvied up amongst too many disparate actors). The Grossman-Hart-Moore model dictates that the firm should be owned by those who contribute the most valuable and most asset-specific property to the joint enterprise. They are not only most necessary to the firm's success, they are also the most vulnerable to hold-up problems as the joint enterprise moves forward in time.

These theories have not enumerated the role of the employee in the firm, instead focusing on contracts and property rights. But the role of the employee in these models still remains critical. In the transaction costs model, employees' contributions must be recognized as assets of both the firm and the employee – often described as 'human capital'. Some types of human capital are transferable, such as education or general skills, but other types are specific to the firm and generally worthless outside it. To the extent an employee has invested in firm-specific skills, she is subject to opportunistic behavior, since she has little leverage to get the full value of those skills. In the transaction-cost model, employees may be precisely the vulnerable yet valuable contributors to the joint enterprise who have the most to fear from opportunistic behavior.[18]

---

[18]    Indeed, Blair offers the following critique: 'The tendency of the transactions costs literature

The property-rights model is also concerned with the relationship of employees to the firm. Although the property rights discussed in the model are generally nonhuman assets, the assets are 'the glue that keeps the firm together' (Hart 1995, 57) and thus keep employees within the firm. Hart poses the following hypothetical: if firm 1 acquires firm 2, what is to stop workers at former firm 2 from quitting and forming a new entity?

> For firm 1's acquisition of firm 2 to make any economic sense, there must be some source of firm 2 value over and above the workers' human capital, i.e. some 'glue' holding firm 2's workers in place. The source of value may consist of as little as a place to meet; the firm's name, reputation, or distribution network; the firm's files, containing important information about its operations or its customers; or a contract that prohibits firm 2's workers from working for competitors or from taking existing clients with them when they quit ... [W]ithout something holding the firm together, the firm is just a phantom. (Hart 1995, 57)

Thus, the property-rights theory of the firm is designed in part to explain why the firm's employees remain with the firm.[19]

Recent scholarship has taken the role of human capital even further. The broad macroeconomic shift within the United States from manufacturing to service and creative industries has led one group of scholars to develop a knowledge-based theory of the firm (Gorga & Halberstam 2007). According to the knowledge-based theory, '[t]he way the firm develops the knowledge it will use in its production process and the extent that the firm can bind this knowledge to its structure will influence its organizational structure' (Gorga & Halberstam 2007, 1140). Rather than emphasize the ownership of physical assets, which can be fungible and non-specific, the knowledge-based theory focuses on the need to produce, distribute, and ultimately retain valuable knowledge-based assets within the firm. The primary generators of this knowledge are employees. Similarly, another approach known as the capability-based theory of the firm focuses on firm-specific knowledge and learning that can be translated into joint production (McInerney 2004). This theory also emphasizes the role of employees as holders of the firm's capabilities.

Perhaps the model based on human capital that has been most well received is Rajan and Zingales' 'access' model of power within the firm (1998).[20] The model defines a firm 'both in terms of unique assets (which may be physical or human) and in terms of the people who have access to these assets' (Rajan and Zingales 1998, 390). Access to the unique assets is what defines the power of the individuals within and without the firm. Rajan and Zingales define access as 'the ability to use, or work with, a critical resource' (Rajan and Zingales 1998, 388). Examples of critical resources include machines, ideas, and people. As Rajan and Zingales make clear, '[t]he agent who is given privileged access to the resource gets no new residual rights of control. All she gets is the opportunity to specialize her human capital to the resource and make herself valuable' (Rajan and Zingales 1998, 388). Combined with her right to leave the firm, access gives the employee the ability to 'create a critical resource that she

---

has been to recognize that firm-specific human capital raises similar questions, but then to sidestep the implications of these questions for corporate governance' (Blair 1999, 66).

19    But see Rajan & Zingales (1998, 388), 'The property rights view does not consider employees part of the firm because, given that employees cannot be owned, there is no sense in which they are any different from agents who contract with the firm at arm's length'.

20    Blair (1999) refers to this as the 'nexus of specific assets' model, based on an earlier version of the paper (p. 82 & n. 50).

controls: her specialized human capital'. Control over this critical resource is a source of power. Rajan and Zingales argue that '[s]ince the amount of surplus that she gets from this power is often more contingent on her making the right specific investment than the surplus that comes from ownership, access can be a better mechanism to provide incentives than ownership' (Rajan and Zingales 1998, 388). Given the importance of access, the role of the firm is to allocate access efficiently amongst the firm's agents. Again, employees play the most critical role.

Tellingly, perhaps, the theory of the firm which has had the most purchase on corporate law cares least about the role of employees within the firm. The 'nexus of contracts' theory, originated by Jensen and Meckling (1976), argues that the firm is merely a central hub for a series of contractual relationships. Jensen and Meckling emphasize that the firm is a 'legal fiction'; it is *'not an individual'* and has no real independent existence. The 'nexus of contracts' theory has been extremely influential in shaping corporate law theory in the past three decades (Easterbrook & Fischel 1991; Ulen 1993; Bainbridge 2002). It has driven corporate law theorists to emphasize the non-mandatory nature of corporate law, both as a descriptive and a normative manner, and it has counseled against changes to the status quo based on the contractual nature (and arguable Pareto optimality) of that status quo (Ulen 1993).

Although Jensen and Meckling's model focuses on agency costs, it largely ignores employees as a whole. The agents in question are the upper-level managers who are tasked to do the bidding of principals. Their theory defines agency costs as the costs associated with monitoring by the principal, bonding expenditures by the agent, and the residual loss (Jensen & Meckling 1976). The monitoring they describe does look a lot like the 'control' that Coase focused on as the key element in defining the firm.[21] However, Jensen and Meckling turn their attention to the relationship between shareholders (principals) and management (agents), rather than the relationship of employees to the firm. Their model seeks to describe the financial structure of the firm in conjunction with the management structure of corporate governance.

The nexus of contract theory is thus not really a theory of the firm at all, but rather a theory of agency costs within a certain type of firm (Hart 1989; Rock & Wachter 2001, 1624). As McInerney has pointed out, 'Scholars working in this paradigm do not offer theories of the firm so much as theories of who controls the firm' (2004, 137–8). Jensen and Meckling might argue that they make no bones otherwise, and that their project was primarily an analysis of the positive aspect of agency costs theory in the corporate setting. But if we use the theory of the firm to determine the reasons why we have firms at all, the assumption of an investor-controlled firm defeats the purpose of the exercise. Thus, the nexus of contracts paradigm isolates corporate law, as it 'leaves corporate law focused entirely on financial transactions that are cut off from the primary strategic operating transactions of the corporation' (Rock & Wachter 2001, 1629).

Economic theories of the firm have generally considered the employer–employee relationship to be critical, if not central, to the definition and purpose of the firm. This relationship is also critical to the definition of the firm in areas of the law beyond corporate law. The following section explores some of these areas.

---

[21]    And indeed, Jensen and Meckling observe in a footnote: 'As it is used in this paper the term monitoring includes more than just measuring or observing the behavior of the agent. It includes efforts on the part of the principal to "control" the behavior of the agent through budget restrictions, compensation policies, operating rules etc' (1976, 308).

## 4.   THE IMPORTANCE OF EMPLOYEES TO THE FIRM IN OTHER AREAS OF THE LAW

Although this chapter is a contribution to a volume on corporate law, I ask the reader's indulgence as we take a brief exploration into the role of the firm in other areas of the law. The purpose of this diversion is to show that unlike corporate law, other areas of the law regard the firm–employee relationship as central in defining the boundaries of the firm.

### Agency Law and *Respondeat Superior*

As discussed above, the law of master–servant was for Coase the defining legal element of the firm. Since servants/employees were under the 'control' of the master/employer, they followed the theory's predictions about what transactions would be within the firm (employment) and what transactions would be outside the firm (all others). This aspect of agency law has remained remarkably durable. The common law test for the employment relationship remains the control test.[22]

The control test states that when determining whether a person hired for labor is an employee, the primary factor is the hiring party's 'right to control the manner and means by which the product is accomplished'.[23] However, other factors are also taken into account, including 'the skill required; the source of the instrumentalities and tools; the location of the work; the duration of the relationship between the parties; whether the hiring party has the right to assign additional projects to the hired party; [and] the extent of the hired party's discretion over when and how long to work'.[24] These factors also relate to the degree of independence of the worker from the firm.

Employees are also agents of the employer, and they fit within the general agency relationship (Restatement Third of Agency 2006, § 1.01). An agent can operate on behalf of the principal and can bind the principal by his or her actions (§ 2.01). An agent can act for the principal even when authority has not been expressly granted, as long as a third party reasonably believes the agent has the authority (§ 2.03). Agency relationships can operate outside of the firm, and thus seem to contradict the notion that control is central in differentiating the firm from the market.

However, the distinction between employees and mere agents remains critical for the doctrine of *respondeat superior*. Under that doctrine, employers are liable for the torts committed by their employees within the scope of employment (Restatement Third of

---

22   *Clackamas Gastroenterology Assocs. v. Wells*, 538 U.S. 440 (2003); *Nationwide Mutual Insurance Co. v. Darden*, 503 U.S. 318 (1992). The Restatement Third of Employment Law has modified this by describing employees as those who work in the interests of the employer when 'the employer's relationship with the individual effectively prevents the individual from rendering the services as part of an independent business' (Restatement Third of Employment Law (2009), § 1.01(1)). Those who work outside of the relationship are distinguished because they exercise 'entrepreneurial control over the manner and means by which the services are performed' (§ 1.01(2)).

23   *Darden*, 503 U.S. at 323.

24   *Ibid.* The court also includes 'the method of payment; the hired party's role in hiring and paying assistants; whether the work is part of the regular business of the hiring party; whether the hiring party is in business; the provision of employee benefits; and the tax treatment of the hired party' ibid. 323–4.

Agency § 2.04). This doctrine does not extend to principals' liability for the actions of agents. The reason is that the principal does not have the level of control over an agent that the employer has over its employees. As the Restatement describes: 'Agents who are retained as the need arises and who are not otherwise employees of their principal normally operate their own business enterprises and are not, except in limited respects, integrated into the principal's enterprise so that a task may be completed or a specified objective accomplished. Therefore, respondeat superior does not apply' (§ 2.04 cmt. b).

When it comes to tort, in a very real sense employees mark the outer boundaries of the firm. The firm is responsible for the actions of its employees but not for the acts of its mere agents. A corporation is not liable for the torts of its creditors, its customers, or its share-holders – only its employees. Interestingly, the doctrine of *respondeat superior* has generally been justified on risk-allocative or retributivist theories (Keeton et al. 1984, § 69). The employer may be seen as the best party to absorb the risk, either to deter the employee from harmful activity or to bear the costs of the injuries caused by the tort (Posner 2007; Baty 1916). The doctrine has apparently never been justified based on a theory of the firm. However, under a theory of the firm that seeks to explain joint production, the employee's effort on the part of the employer makes the conduct in question fall under the umbrella of the firm. The firm's scope is defined by its employees.

## Intellectual Property Law

The relationship between employees and intellectual property is a fairly complex one. The term 'intellectual property' refers to a wide range of information to which specific legal rights have attached. In some cases, intellectual property is generated by a single individual: an author writing alone in her home, or an inventor toiling away in the garage. However, in many cases, intellectual property is generated by specific individuals who are working within the context of a larger firm. How the rights to that 'property' are divvied up has significant legal and economic ramifications, particularly for firms and individual employees (Stone 2004).

The role of the employee within intellectual property law is perhaps most evident in the work-for-hire doctrine. Under this statutory default rule, the employer is considered the author of any copyrighted work created by employees.[25] The common law control test is used to determine whether the work was made by an employee or an independent contractor, and like *respondeat superior*, work-for-hire applies only to work produced within the scope of employment.[26] Thus, for purposes of copyright, the employee once again marks the boundaries of the firm; works made by employees within the scope of their employment are considered property of the firm, while works made by independent contractors are not (by default). The default rule for patent law is that the employee who invents the patent is the author, not the employer.[27] However, the employer is free to contract with employees explicitly for the

---

[25]   17 U.S.C. § 201(b) ('In the case of a work made for hire, the employer or other person for whom the work was prepared is considered the author for purposes of this title, and, unless the parties have expressly agreed otherwise in a written instrument signed by them, owns all of the rights comprised in the copyright.')

[26]   *Community for Creative Non-Violence v. Reid*, 490 U.S. 730 (1989).

[27]   The patent must be registered by the individual inventor. See 35 U.S.C. § 111, 115 (discussing oath taken as part of patent process that the registrant is the 'original and first inventor').

rights to all inventions created within the scope of employment. Even without an explicit contract, courts have found something akin to a work for hire doctrine when an employee is hired to work on a specific invention or problem (Fisk 2009). In addition, under the shop-right doctrine, employers enjoy a non-exclusive right to use the patent without having to compensate the employee. A shop right arises when the employee has created the invention on the job using the employer's materials (Fisk 2009). Once again, the firm provides the context: if the employee creates the invention at work while using the employer's tools, the employer has a right to use that invention without cost.

Recent scholarship has made significant forays in using the theory of the firm to explain intellectual property law (Bar-Gill & Parchomovsky 2009; Burk 2004; Burk & McDonnell, 2007a, 2007b, 2009; Heald 2005; Merges 1999; Miller 2007). These theories use both the transaction-costs model and the property-rights model in demonstrating the connections between intellectual property, employees, and the firm. Using the transaction-costs model, Merges (1999) points to the concern about opportunism and holdups to explain why employers generally hold intellectual property rights over employee inventions. Heald (2005) focuses on transaction costs in explaining the patent system. Comparing a system of registered patents to a system based solely on trade secret protection, Heald argues that patent law makes it easier to buy and sell the information at issue. The patent buyer need not enter into a costly array of contractual protections in order to keep others (especially the sellers) from using the information.[28] He also argues that patent facilitates the creation of technical information and the use of that information in team production. Patents enable the critical information to be used within the team without fear that one of the team members will defect. The alternative would again be costly contracts with all employees in the team. Without the need to monitor these contracts, the firm can facilitate team production more efficiently.[29]

The property-rights theory of the firm explicitly alludes to the importance of intellectual property. In describing the theory, Hart uses forms of intellectual property as examples of the 'glue' that binds employees to the firm (Hart 1995). The protections for this type of property are designed to manage the interactions between firms as well as amongst the firm and its employees. For Burk & McDonnell (2007a), intellectual property rights are a way to balance property interests between firms as well as within firms. Employees have an interest in exploiting information they have created on the job, both within the firm and outside the firm when on the job market. Patent, copyright, and trade secrets each balance the firm's needs and the individual employee's needs in separating employee information 'assets' from firm assets. Burk and McDonnell point out that this division mirrors that of agency law and the corporate opportunity doctrine, in that the critical factors are whether the information/opportunity arose in the context of employment with the use of firm resources. Moreover, they point out that the weakest form of intellectual property protection – trade secrets protection – applies to the type of information most likely to overlap with an employee's own information capital (Burk & McDonnell 2007a, 609). This balancing of rights within firms and between firms leads to their 'Goldilocks' hypothesis: the level of legal protection of intellectual property rights that minimizes transaction costs will be somewhere between a system that provides

---

[28]   Such contractual efforts would likely encounter difficulties, for example, if one of the seller's former employees sought to use the information.
[29]   Heald (2005) also notes that some companies use patent applications, which must be filed by individuals, as a way of monitoring employee performance.

strong rights to firms and a system of weak rights for firms.[30] And that balance includes the treatment of employee covenants not to compete, since their impact intersects with intellectual property, particularly trade secrets (Burk & McDonnell 2007a; Bar-Gill & Parchomovsky 2009).

Trademark presents a special connection between the firm, its employees, and intellectual property. Trademark protection is what enables a group of people to join together and be recognized as a common enterprise without fearing that their reputation will be poached by outsiders. Burk and McDonnell (2009) point out that just as patent, copyright, and trade secret protections concern the allocation of information rights between employee and firm, trademark concerns the allocation of good will and reputational rights between employee and firm. Trademarks enable firms to transfer reputational assets over to the firm, and thus deprive individual employees of their ability to hold up the firm over their own reputational assets (Burk & McDonnell 2009, 376–9). As in their discussion of informational property rights, Burk and McDonnell advocate for an intermediate approach, as depriving employees of any reputation rights would lead them to under-invest in reputation. They also discuss the critical role of trademark to franchise agreements. Allowing franchise entities to use the national firm's trademark permits a bifurcation between elements common to all users of the trademark (advertising, brand reputation) and elements handled individually by franchisees (hiring being the most prominent). Thus, franchising is an effort to restructure employment: it enables separate entities to break off into individual firms while maintaining the ability to share reputational assets with a national group. Franchisees need not be employees of the national firm in order to use the trademark.

In sum, these efforts to discuss intellectual property in terms of the theory of the firm demonstrate the importance of the firm to intellectual property law. And again, the boundaries of the 'firm' are shaped by the relationship between the firm and its employees.

## Tax Law

Tax law has a well-known role in shaping choice of business organization, as certain organizational types such as partnerships and Limited Liability Companies (LLCs) enjoy 'pass through' taxation while most corporations are taxed as separate entities. Indeed, it was the changes in entity taxation that opened up the LLC revolution in the late 1980s and early 1990s (Ribstein 2010). However, when it comes to taxing based on the theory of a firm, the relationship between firm and employee also has an important role to play. Firms are expected to differentiate between employees and independent contractors over a host of provisions, including whether taxes need to be withheld,[31] whether the firm must pay a share of Social Security and Medicare (FICA) and unemployment (FUTA) taxes for the worker,[32] and whether the workers count as employees for benefit plan purposes.[33]

---

[30]    Burk and McDonnell (2007a) argue that the level for interfirm transactions is calculated independently from the level for intrafirm transactions, although these levels could overlap or even be identical once calculated. Moreover, they indicate that employees are critical not only to intrafirm analysis, but also to interfirm analysis.

[31]    26 U.S.C. § 3402.

[32]    26 U.S.C. § 3101 et seq. (FICA); 26 U.S.C. § 3301 et seq. (FUTA).

[33]    26 U.S.C. § 410.

The IRS defines employees based on the common law control test.[34] The consequences of a misclassification can be extremely costly, as the business is then subject to the mandatory back-tax formula.[35] In fact, Congress was moved to create a 'safe harbor' for employers when it came to the employee-independent contractor distinction.[36] The upshot of these requirements is to give the firm tax responsibilities for its employees, while giving independent contractors tax responsibilities for themselves. We thus see the differentiation between employee and independent contractor determining society's expectations about the firm's role in the worker's financial life. The firm is expected to manage and even pay some taxes for its employees, while it must leave independent contractors to their own devices. This responsibility accords with the broader picture of the myriad employment protections afforded under federal and state law only to employees. These employment-related protections – and the motivations behind them – are discussed more below in the final section.

## 5.   RECONSIDERING THE ROLE OF EMPLOYEES IN THE FIRM AND CORPORATE LAW

### The Firm and Employment Law

Employment law also does work in binding the employee to the firm. As Coase (1937) recognized in his seminal article, the common law control test for employees is the foundation for the firm. The control test defines an employee based on control and loyalty, and provides the legal apparatus for that structure (Masten 1991). All employees owe duties to the firm, including the duty of obedience, the duty of loyalty, and the duty to disclose relevant information to the employer. Masten likely overstates the importance of these doctrines to average employees, as they are unlikely to be enforced in that context. However, the duty of loyalty, when considered in context with covenants not to compete and trade secret protections, does bind the employee to the firm in meaningful ways. To the extent that the firm is meant to bind employees to a common enterprise, the common law duties required of employees reinforce this 'glue' (Hart 1995).

The employment relationship is also defined by the 'at-will' doctrine, which sets out the presumption that employees can be fired for any reason unless specified otherwise. This doctrine may seem unremarkable in this form, as it only creates a default rule, and the default is the general contractual default as well (Masten 1991). However, the at-will presumption is more than just a default rule; it is a presumption so strong that it sometimes can overrun contracting efforts that would normally be upheld.[37] Other jurisdictions have looser forms of

---

[34]   Treas. Regs. § 31.3121(d)-1(c) (finding an employment relationship 'when the person for whom services are performed has the right to control and direct the individual who performs the services, not only as to the result to be accomplished by the work but also as to the details and means by which that result is accomplished').

[35]   26 U.S.C. § 3509.

[36]   Revenue Act of 1978, § 530.

[37]   For example, in New York oral evidence is not sufficient to overcome the presumption; the employment term must be established through specific written terms and there must be reliance on those terms. See *Wanamaker v. Columbian Rope Co.*, 907 F.Supp. 522, 539 (N.D.N.Y. 1995).

the presumption, and in some situations implicit terms or good faith protections will come to the aid of the employee. However, the presumption itself is a form of insulation to allow for greater managerial freedom. Rock and Wachter (2001) have argued that the at-will doctrine, like the business judgment rule in corporate law, is designed to create space for the operation of non-legally enforceable rules and standards essential to firm governance. Regardless of those norms – which are arguably weakening – the at-will rule allows the legal space for the firm to easily separate itself from employees.

Employment law protections are perhaps then an attempt to provide certain benefits to employees based on their status within the firm. Employees do not control whether they can take time off for sickness or care of a newborn; employees cannot control whether they are subject to discrimination in promotions or whether they are paid overtime. We expect that those operating outside of a firm, however, do not have their time or activities controlled in such a manner that these remedies are necessary. The common law control test is used within many employment statutory schemes to differentiate between those who are entitled to the statute's protections and those who are not.[38] Only employees can sue under Title VII for discrimination based on race, sex, or religion,[39] or under the Age Discrimination in Employment Act for age discrimination,[40] or under Title I of the Americans with Disabilities Act for discrimination based on disability.[41] Only employees have their investment and retirement expectations protected under ERISA.[42] Only employees have contractual minimums for wages and overtime.[43] Only employees are allowed to take time off from their contractual responsibilities to care for a newborn, tend to sick relatives, or recuperate from an illness.[44]

In considering why employees are protected by these statutory schemes, one might be tempted to say, 'Well, of course these laws protect only employees; they're employment laws.' But that overlooks an interesting question: why do we distinguish employees from other contractual partners when it comes to these laws? The answer is primarily that employees – because of the employer's control over their labor – lack the market and legal power to

---

[38]    The Supreme Court assumes that Congress meant to use the common law test if the statute provides an unhelpful and/or tautological definition of employee. See *Nationwide Mutual Insurance v. Darden*, 503 U.S. 318, 322–4 (1992). An example of such a statutory definition is 'The term "employee" means an individual employed by an employer' Title VII.

[39]    42 U.S.C. § 2000e(f). In contrast, contractual exchanges are protected much more generally under 42 U.S.C. § 1981(a) ('All persons within the jurisdiction of the United States shall have the same right in every State and Territory to make and enforce contracts').

[40]    29 U.S.C. § 630(f).

[41]    42 U.S.C. § 12111(4).

[42]    29 U.S.C. § 1002(6); *Darden*, 503 U.S. at 328.

[43]    Fair Labor Standards Act (FLSA), 29 U.S.C. § 203(g). The FLSA defines employ as 'to suffer or permit to work'. Courts have interpreted this definition more expansively under the 'economic realities' test. *Sec'y of Labor v. Lauritzen*, 835 F.2d 1529, 1535 (7th Cir. 1989). However, the economic realities test largely overlaps with the control test; in fact, 'control' is the first factor in the economic realities test. *Ibid.*1535–6.

[44]    The Family and Medical Leave Act uses the FLSA's definition of employee, which as noted above, is broader than the control test. The Department of Labor's regulations concerning the FMLA state: 'In general an employee, as distinguished from an independent contractor who is engaged in a business of his/her own, is one who "follows the usual path of an employee" and is dependent on the business which he/she serves' 29 C.F.R § 825.105.

meet their needs contractually. This disempowerment has been particularly acute in the corporation. Corporate law has definitively separated employees from the governance of the firm. As such, the corporation can control the fruits of individual employees' labor without interference from the laborers themselves. In order to balance out the employment relationship, the power that the firm has taken unto itself to better coordinate joint production must be mitigated through specific substantive protections that apply only to employees.[45]

## The Separation of Employees from the Corporation

Firms need not have the effect of disempowering those who work for them or within them. The purpose of the firm is to overcome the effects of market-induced transaction costs and to facilitate team production around a core of common property. These purposes, in and of themselves, do not dictate that employees will be 'servants' of the firm. In fact, the firm could be used as a device of employee empowerment. It allows a group of participants – workers and investors – to cumulate their resources under a common banner. Rather than competing against each other in a market or seeing their joint efforts held up by the opportunism of one person, employees could work together under a firm's collectivizing umbrella to produce as a team.

Intellectual property law provides a nice example of the employee-affirming possibilities of the firm. As described by Burk and McDonnell (2007a, 2009), intellectual property protections for information and reputation are designed (at least in part) to avoid holdups by individual employees. Patent, copyright, and trade secret law divvy up control and ownership of information assets between the firm and individual employees, and trademark divvies up reputational rights. Strong firm intellectual property protections are anti-employee only if the firm is separate from employees. If the firm represents the employees collectively, then assigning rights to the firm makes the employees as a whole better off. If all employees had individual rights, one employee looking to act opportunistically could hurt the other employees who have been following the rules and working cooperatively. Assigning ownership to individual employees would produce an anticommons that fostered holdups and a breakdown of coordinated production (Merges 1999). Team production needs a place to assign ownership outside the individual participants, and the firm serves that function.

Why then do so many scholars (Fisk 2009; Noble 1977) lament the transfer of intellectual property rights from employee to firm? The issue, I would argue, has less to do with the ideal intellectual property system, and more to do with the governance of firms. If employees participated more robustly in firm ownership and governance, firms would act as a repository of employee collective rights. Instead, firms – constructed primarily as corporations – act as a tool for prying assets away from employees and into the hands of managers and investors. The construction of the firm as a business organization, which has been managed largely through corporate law, has been entirely different than the construction of the firm when it comes to agency law, property law, intellectual property law, and tax. So if we look at the

---

[45]    Greenfield makes this point, by noting that when employees are subject to employer opportunism, '[t]hey may demand a higher wage; they may demand more explicit job security protections; they may moderate their effort; they may solicit their legislators to protect them in other ways' (2008, 1064). Of course, whether each of these statutes properly recalibrates the balance is subject to debate. I merely cite to their intent to address the balance.

firm not as a legal tool to facilitate team production, or not as an abstract placeholder for collective rights, but rather as a corporation, we see that the law has been taking rights away from employees and giving them to the corporation. The corporation, in turn, is governed by directors who are elected entirely by shareholders and who are charged with governing in the shareholders' interests.

Burk and McDonnell explicitly recognize this tradeoff when it comes to property rights in information:

> In transactions that involve inchoate firm-specific assets embodied in employees' human capital, both firms and employees face a hold-up problem. We have seen why the law might best assign rights to firms in such circumstances. However, this leaves employees open to exploitation, so that the opposite assignment might be better. Even if assigning rights to the firm is best, it is possible that protection of employees then requires assigning more power to employees within firms than we observe. (Burk & McDonnell 2007a, 634–45)

This concern applies in other areas as well. In trademark, employees assign over their individual reputation rights to the collectivizing brand. Property law and corporate law assign any collective property to the corporation. Employees enjoy no property rights in what they produce or in their positions within the firm. And yet employees owe duties to the firm of obedience and loyalty, and their mobility may be constrained by covenants not to compete and trade secret law.

It is true that some employee-oriented doctrines favor society over the firm. The doctrine of *respondeat superior*, for example, makes the firm liable for the actions of all of its employees when they act within the scope of employment. However, when the firm becomes instantiated as the corporation, there is an answer: limited liability. Although investors may lose all that they invested, they are liable for no more. Limited liability is the one doctrine that had differentiated the corporation from other business forms for many years, and it is a direct response to one of the legal weaknesses of the firm. Tax law is the one area where corporations have been treated more harshly than other business organizations. Perhaps that taxation – so beneficial from a revenue perspective – is what drove legislators to give corporations such advantages in other realms of the law (Ribstein 2010).[46]

Under our current system, employees hand over assets to the firm, but then the firm – established as a corporation – directs those assets to the shareholders. This dynamic provides the answer to those who insist that progressives should leave corporate law alone and instead focus on changes in labor and employment law (Smith 2008). A properly constructed corporation might not need layers of employment protections. A corporation can be described as 'an association of stockholders formed for their private gain' (Dodd 1932, 1146–7) only because the law established the corporation in that manner. The thesis of this chapter is that the firm is naturally made up of employees, and it is corporate law that has divorced the employees from the firm.

---

[46]   This is a blunter version of a more complicated public choice argument that both corporate managers and Congress made peace over double taxation as it gave corporations an incentive to retain their earnings within the firm (Arlen & Weiss 1995; Bank 2006).

## Moving from Firms to Markets?

For those interested in reinvigorating an employee-centric view of the corporation, there is a further complication: both the corporation and the employment relationship seem to be declining in importance. The corporation is under siege by a plethora of new organizational structures, most notably the LLC. When the Treasury moved to 'check-the-box' taxation for these new entities, they became viable alternatives to the corporation in a variety of different fields (Ribstein 2010). The flexibility of the LLC form is in contrast to many of the requirements, state and federal, placed upon the corporation.[47] It seems, perhaps, as if Jensen & Meckling's 'nexus of contracts' model is coming to life in the LLC, and the corporation's failure to live up to the model is bringing it down.

The employment relation is moving from firm to market as well. In the mid-twentieth century, labor economists identified internal labor markets as a deviation from neoclassical labor market theory (Stone 2004). These economists found that employees largely stayed within one firm for their lifetime of employment, and that firms generally used internal promotion to fill vacancies. These findings established an empirical basis for Coase's notion of the importance of the employment relation to the firm. Moreover, internal labor markets are an instantiation of the separateness of the firm from the market; they demonstrate that the firm is truly a different set of relationships.

However, economists are finding that the importance of internal labor markets has been dwindling. Beginning in the 1970s, firms began to hire more temporary and contingent workers (Stone 2004). This trend accelerated through the 1990s, and continues apace. Recent reports indicate that the 2008 recession has turned many employees into 'permanent' temporary workers, with as much as 26% of the workforce now having 'nonstandard' jobs (Coy et al. 2010). And the effects go beyond low-skill and low-wage employment; executive officers, lawyers, and scientists are all among the temporarily employed (Coy et al. 2010; Greenhouse 2008). Moreover, 'outsourcing' – a word of relatively recent vintage – continues to break down relationships that were traditionally within the firm (Geis 2009, 2010; Blair & O'Hara 2009). What Alan Hyde said in 1998 continues to be true today: 'Increasingly, labor is hired through short-term, market-mediated arrangements that may not be "employment" relations in any legal or technical sense of that word' (Hyde 1998, 99).

If the corporation is giving way to a more contractually-oriented form of business enterprise, and the employment relationship is dissolving back into the market, then perhaps corporations (or their successor organizational forms) will exist only to structure financial relationships and confer limited liability. There is reason to believe, however, that the firm and the corporation will remain relevant to our economic system. As even Ribstein (2010) acknowledges, the role of the 'uncorporation' remains limited under current law. It seems likely that not only will the public corporation survive, but it will be made even less contractual after the passage of finance reform legislation.[48] And in the employment context, the

---

[47]  Moreover, when it comes to the public corporation, commentators have suggested that more firms are going private because of the regulatory requirements layered upon the public corporation (Carney 2006). Bartlett (2009) argues, however, that Sarbanes-Oxley is not to blame for the high-profile 'going private' transactions of the last decade.

[48]  The legislation paves the way for new regulations on compensation committees, say-on-pay proposals, and proxy access for director nominations, Dodd-Frank Act, Pub. L. 111-203, §§ 951–2, 971.

flight from employment seems driven by an effort to avoid employment-related regulations and restrictions, rather than the disappearance of the firm itself. In fact, many employers are looking to tie their employees even more closely to the firm and its image. The importance of 'brand' for businesses means that employees are critical to reifying and promoting the brand, especially in service industries. Firms have used branding to draw out psychological commitments from employees that are not reciprocal on the part of the employer. Scholars have criticized this branding as too invasive, as it dictates what employees wear, what they say, and what they do when not on the job (Avery & Crain 2007; Crain 2010). Control over employees in these industries is becoming more important to the role of the firm, not less.

In fact, it may be that the tide is turning back to a more employee-oriented workplace. Popular management literature emphasizes the importance of the employee (Bodie 2007). Companies like Costco and Patagonia are winning praise and success with an employee-focused orientation (Greenhouse 2008). Small startups, particularly in the tech industry, are once again blurring the line between entrepreneur and employee (Shafrir 2010). Academia is evolving, as well. As discussed earlier, recent research into the theory of the firm has focused on the importance of knowledge-based assets and the distribution of access top those assets within the firm (Rajan & Zingales 1998; Gorga & Halberstam 2007). In the corporate law literature, scholars such a Margaret Blair, Lynn Stout, Kent Greenfield, and Brett McDonnell are theoretizing a team-production and employee-centric approach to the corporation (Blair & Stout 1999; Blair 1999; Greenfield 2007; McDonnell 2008). As we learn more about the importance of trust, norms, and procedural justice within the corporation, employees will grow even more in importance (Blair & Stout 2001; Tyler & Blader 2000).

It is possible to envision a radically individualized future, in which each worker is a 'corporation' unto herself and firms are merely temporary agglomerations within the global market. It is also possible to envision a future in which employees participate at the highest levels of governance, and corporations are tools of team production rather than investor enrichment. Perhaps both of these futures are in store, to varying degrees within different industries. Further exploration into the role of the firm will make our choices in these regards more informed and thus more likely to be efficient.

## 6.   CONCLUSION

Inquiries into the relationship between employer and employee are what drive the theory of the firm. Yet corporate law and corporate law theory spend little attention on this relationship. This chapter is not meant as an argument for employee ownership, or even to advocate for specific forms of employee empowerment.[49] Rather, it is to remind theoreticians of the importance of employees to the firm, and to re-center our studies of the firm around this relationship. Corporate law is where this neglect has been felt most keenly. Like the curious incident of the dog that didn't bark (McDonnell 2000), the puzzle of employees – silent within corporate law – has resisted a solution. Here's to hoping that bark is heard soon.

---

[49]   For a fuller treatment of the pros and cons of employee ownership, see Hansmann (1996). His concern about worker heterogeneity, however, overstated the dire consequences of employee governance (Hayden & Bodie 2009).

# REFERENCES

Alchian, Armen A. & Harold Demsetz (1972), 'Production, Information Costs, and Economic Organization', *American Economic Review*, 62, 777–95.

Arlen, Jennifer & Deborah M. Weiss (1995), 'A Political Theory of Corporate Taxation', *Yale Law Journal*, 105, 325–90.

Asher, Cheryl C., James M. Mahoney & Joseph T. Mahoney (2005), 'Towards a Property Rights Foundation for a Stakeholder Theory of the Firm', *Journal of Management and Governance*, 9, 5–32.

Avery, Dianne & Marion Crain (2007), 'Branded: Corporate Image, Sexual Stereotyping, and the New Face of Capitalism', *Duke Journal of Gender Law & Policy*, 14, 13–123.

Bainbridge, Stephen (2002), 'The Board of Directors as Nexus of Contracts', *Iowa Law Review*, 88, 1–34.

Bainbridge, Stephen (2003), 'Director Primacy: The Means and Ends of Corporate Governance', *Northwestern University Law Review*, 97, 547–606.

Baldwin, Carliss (2007), 'Where Do Transactions Come From? Modularity, Transactions, and the Boundaries of Firms', *Industrial and Corporate Change*, 1–41.

Bank, Steven A. (2006), 'A Capital Lock-In Theory of the Corporate Income Tax', *Georgetown Law Journal*, 94, 889–947.

Bar-Gill, Oren & Gideon Parchomovsky (2009), 'Law and the Boundaries of Technology-Intensive Firms', *University of Pennsylvania Law Review*, 157, 1649–89.

Bartlett III, Robert P. (2009), 'Going Private But Staying Public: Reexamining the Effect of Sarbanes-Oxley on Firms' Going-Private Decisions', *University of Chicago Law Review*, 76, 7–44.

Baty, Thomas (1916), *Vicarious Liability*, Oxford: Oxford University Press.

Blair, Margaret M. (1995), *Ownership and Control: Rethinking Corporate Governance for the Twenty-First Century*, Washington, D.C.: The Brookings Institution.

Blair, Margaret M. (1999), 'Firm-Specific Human Capital and Theories of the Firm', in Margaret M. Blair & Mark J. Roe (eds), *Employees and Corporate Governance*, Washington, D.C.: The Brookings Institution, 58–90.

Blair, Margaret M. (2001), 'Director Accountability and the Mediating Role of the Corporate Board', *Washington University Law Quarterly*, 79, 403–47.

Blair, Margaret M. (2005), 'Closing the Theory Gap: How the Economic Theory of Property Rights Can Help Bring "Stakeholders" Back Into Theories of the Firm', *Journal of Management and Governance*, 9, 33–39.

Blair, Margaret M. & Lynn A. Stout (1999), 'A Team Production Theory of Corporate Law', *Virginia Law Review*, 85, 247–328.

Blair, Margaret M. & Lynn A. Stout (2001), 'Trust, Trustworthiness, and the Behavioral Foundations of Corporate Law', *University of Pennsylvania Law Review*, 149:6, 1735–1810.

Blair, Margaret M. & Erin O'Hara (2009), 'Outsourcing, Modularity and the Theory of the Firm,' Working Paper No. 09-19, Vanderbilt University Law School, Law & Economics Series, available at: http://ssrn.com/abstract=1318263, 1–41.

Bodie, Matthew T. (2003), 'Aligning Incentives with Equity: Employee Stock Options and Rule 10b-5', *Iowa Law Review*, 88:3, 539–600.

Bodie, Matthew T. (2007), 'Workers, Information, and Corporate Combinations: The Case for Nonbinding Employee Referenda in Transformative Transactions', *Washington University Law Review*, 85(4), 871–929.

Burk, Dan L. (2004), 'Intellectual Property and the Firm', *University of Chicago Law Review*, 71, 3–20.

Burk, Dan L. & Brett H. McDonnell (2007a), 'The Goldilocks Hypothesis: Balancing Intellectual Property Rights at the Boundary of the Firm', *University of Illinois Law Review*, 2007, 575–636.

Burk, Dan L. & Brett H. McDonnell (2007b), 'Patent, Tax Shelters, and the Firm', *Virginia Tax Review*, 26, 981–1004.

Burk, Dan L. & Brett H. McDonnell (2009), 'Trademarks and the Boundaries of the Firm', *William & Mary Law Review*, 51, 345–94.

Carney, William J. (2006), 'The Costs of Being Public after Sarbanes-Oxley: The Irony of "Going Private"', *Emory Law Journal*, 55, 141–60.

Clark, Robert Charles (1986), *Corporate Law*, Boston: Little, Brown and Co.

Coase, Ronald (1937), 'The Nature of the Firm', *Economica*, 4(4), 386–405.

Coy, Peter, Michelle Conlin & Moira Herbst (2010), 'The Disposable Worker', *Bloomberg BusinessWeek*, Jan. 28, 2010, 33–39.

Crain, Marion (2010), 'Managing Identity: Buying Into the Brand at Work', *Iowa Law Review*, 95, 1179–1258.

Demsetz, Harold (2002), 'Toward a Theory of Property Rights II: The Competition Between Private and Collective Ownership', *Journal of Legal Studies*, 31(S)2, S653–72.

Dibadj, Reza (2005), 'Reconceiving the Firm', *Cardozo Law Review*, 26(4), 1459–1534.

Dodd, E. Merrick, Jr. (1932), 'For Whom Are the Corporate Managers Trustees?', *Harvard Law Review*, 45, 1145–63.

Easterbrook, Frank & Daniel Fischel (1989), 'The Corporate Contract', *Columbia Law Review*, 89, 1416–48.
Easterbrook, Frank & Daniel Fischel (1991), *The Economic Structure of Corporate Law*, Cambridge, Mass.: Harvard University Press.
Fisk, Catherine L. (2009), *Working Knowledge: Employee Innovation and the Rise of Corporate Intellectual Property, 1800–1930*, Chapel Hill, North Carolina: The University of North Carolina Press.
Foss, Nicolai & Peter Klein (2006), 'The Emergence of the Modern Theory of the Firm', SMG Working Paper No. 1/2006, 1-57, available at: http://papers.ssrn.com/sol3/papers.cfm?abstract_id=982094 (last accessed November 2011).
Geis, George S. (2009), 'The Space Between Markets and Hierarchies', *Virginia Law Review*, 95, 99–153.
Geis, George S. (2010), 'An Empirical Examination of Business Outsourcing Transactions', *Virginia Law Review*, 96:2, 241–300.
Gordon, Jeffrey N. (1997), 'Employees, Pensions, and the New Economic Order', *Columbia Law Review*, 97, 1519–66.
Gordon, Jeffrey N. (1999), 'Employee Stock Ownership in Economic Transitions: The Case of United and the Airline Industry', in Margaret M. Blair & Mark J. Roe (eds) *Employees and Corporate Governance*, Washington, D.C.: The Brookings Institution, 317–54.
Gorga, Érica & Michael Halberstam (2007), 'Knowledge Inputs, Legal Institutions and Firm Structure: Towards a Knowledge-Based Theory of the Firm', *Northwestern University Law Review*, 101(3), 1123–1206.
Grandori, Anna (2005), 'Neither Stakeholder Nor Shareholder "Theories": How Property Right and Contract Theory Can Help in Getting Out of the Dilemma', *Journal of Management and Governance*, 9, 41–46.
Greenfield, Kent (1998), 'The Place of Workers in Corporate Law', *Boston College Law Review*, 39, 283–327.
Greenfield, Kent (2007), *The Failure of Corporate Law: Fundamental Flaws and Progressive Possibilities*, Chicago, IL: University of Chicago Press.
Greenfield, Kent (2008), 'Defending Stakeholder Governance', *Case Western Reserve Law Review*, 58, 1043–65.
Greenhouse, Steven (2008), *The Big Squeeze: Tough Times for the American Worker*, New York, NY: Alfred A. Knopf.
Grossman, Sanford & Oliver Hart (1986), 'The Costs and Benefits of Ownership: A Theory of Vertical and Lateral Integration', *Journal of Political Economy*, 94, 691–719.
Gulati, G. Mitu, William Klein & Eric Zolt (2000), 'Connected Contracts', *UCLA Law Review*, 47, 887–948.
Gulati, G. Mitu, T.M. Thomas Isaac & William A. Klein (2002), 'When a Worker's Cooperative Works: The Case of Kerala Dinesh Beedi', *UCLA Law Review*, 49, 1417, 1453.
Hansmann, Henry (1996), *The Ownership of Enterprise*, Cambridge, Mass.: Belknap Press.
Hansmann, Henry (2006), 'Corporation and Contract', *American Law & Economics Review*, 8, 1–19.
Hart, Oliver (1989), 'An Economist's Perspective on the Theory of the Firm', *Columbia Law Review*, 89, 1757–74.
Hart, Oliver (1995), *Firms, Contracts, and Financial Structure*, Oxford: Clarendon Press.
Hart, Oliver & John Moore (1988), 'Incomplete Contracts and Renegotiation', *Econometrica*, 56, 755–85.
Hart, Oliver & John Moore (1990), 'Property Rights and the Nature of the Firm', *Journal of Political Economy*, 98, 1119–58.
Hayden, Grant & Matthew Bodie (2009), 'Arrow's Theorem and the Exclusive Shareholder Franchise', *Vanderbilt Law Review*, 62(4), 1217–43.
Heald, Paul J. (2005), 'A Transaction Cost Theory of Patent Law', *Ohio State Law Journal*, 66(3), 473–509.
Hirsch, James S. (1995), 'Avis Employees Find Stock Ownership is a Mixed Blessing', *Wall Street Journal*, May 2, 1995, B1.
Hyde, Alan (1998), 'Employment Law After the Death of Employment', *University of Pennsylvania Journal of Labor & Employment Law*, 1(1), 99–115.
Jensen, Michael C. and William Meckling (1976), 'Theory of the Firm: Managerial Behavior, Agency Costs and Capital Structure', *Journal of Financial Economics*, 3, 305–80.
Keeton, W. Page (general editor), Dan B. Dobbs, Robert E. Keeton & David G. Owen (1984), *Prosser & Keeton on Torts*, 5th ed., St. Paul, Minn.: West Group.
Klausner, Michael (2006), 'The Contractarian Theory of Corporate Law: A Generation Later', *Journal of Corporate Law*, 31, 779–97.
McDonnell, Brett H. (2000), 'The Curious Incident of the Workers in the Boardroom', *Hofstra Law Review*, 29, 503–28.
McDonnell, Brett H. (2008), 'Employee Primacy, or Economics Meets Civic Republicanism at Work', *Stanford Journal of Law, Business & Finance*, 13(2), 334–83.
McInerney, Thomas (2004), 'Theory of the Firm and Corporate Governance', *Columbia Business Law Review*, 135–96.
Macher, Jeffrey T. and Barak D. Richman (2008), 'Transaction Cost Economics: An Assessment of Empirical Research in the Social Sciences,' *Business and Politics*, 10(1), 1–63.
Masten, Scott E. (1991), 'A Legal Basis for the Firm', *Journal of Law, Economics, and Organization*, 4, Spring

1988, pp. 181–98, reprinted in Oliver E. Williamson and Sidney G. Winter (eds), *The Nature of the Firm: Origins, Evolution, and Development*, New York: Oxford University Press.

Means, Benjamin (2010), 'A Contractual Approach to Shareholder Oppression Law,' *Fordham Law Review*, 79:3, 1161–1210.

Merges, Robert P. (1999), 'The Law & Economics of Employee Inventions', *Harvard Journal of Law & Technology*, 13, 1–54.

Meurer, Michael (2004), 'Law, Economics, and the Theory of the Firm', *Buffalo Law Review*, 52, 727–55.

Milgrom, Paul and John Roberts (1992), *Economics, Organization and Management*, Englewood Cliffs, NJ: Prentice Hall.

Miller, Joseph S. (2007), 'Standard Setting, Patents, and Access Lock-In: RAND Licensing and the Theory of the Firm', *Indiana Law Review*, 40, 351–95.

Moll, Douglas K. (1999), 'Shareholder Oppression v. Employment at Will in the Close Corporation: The Investment Model Solution', *University of Illinois Law Review*, 1999, 517–81.

Noble, David F. (1977), *America by Design: Science, Technology, and the Rise of Corporate Capitalism*, New York: Alfred A. Knopf.

Orts, Eric W. (1998a), 'Shirking and Sharking: A Legal Theory of the Firm', *Yale Law & Policy Review*, 16, 265–329.

Orts, Eric W. (1998b), 'The Future of Enterprise Organization', *Michigan Law Review*, 96, 1947–74.

Osterloh, Margit & Bruno S. Frey (2006), 'Shareholders Should Welcome Knowledge Workers as Directors', *Journal of Management and Governance*, 10, 325–45.

Pistor, Katharina (1999), 'Codetermination: A Sociopolitical Model with Governance Externalities', in Margaret M. Blair & Mark J. Roe (eds) *Employees and Corporate Governance*, Washington, D.C.: The Brookings Institution, 163–93.

Posner, Richard A. (2007), *Economic Analysis of Law*, 7th ed., New York, N.Y.: Aspen Publishers.

Rajan, Raghuram G. & Luigi Zingales (1998), 'Power in a Theory of the Firm', *The Quarterly Journal of Economics*, 113, 387.

Rajan, Raghuram G. & Luigi Zingales (2001), 'The Firm as a Dedicated Hierarchy: A Theory of the Origins and Growth of Firms', *The Quarterly Journal of Economics*, 116(3), 805–51.

Ribstein, Larry E. (2010), *The Rise of the Uncorporation*, New York: Oxford University Press.

Rock, Edward B. & Michael L. Wachter (2001), 'Islands of Conscious Power: Law, Norms, and the Self-Governing Corporation', *University of Pennsylvania Law Review*, 149, 1619–1700.

Roe, Mark J. (1999), 'Codetermination and the German Securities Markets', in Margaret M. Blair & Mark J. Roe (eds) *Employees and Corporate Governance*, Washington, D.C.: The Brookings Institution, 194–205.

Shafrir, Doree (2010), 'Tweet Tweet Boom Boom', *New York Magazine*, April 26, 2010, 34–41, 91–2.

Smith, D. Gordon (2008), 'Response: The Dystopian Potential of Corporate Law', *Emory Law Journal*, 57, 985–1010.

Smith, D. Gordon & Cynthia A. Williams (2008), *Business Organizations: Cases, Problems, and Case Studies*, Austin: WoltersKluwer Law & Business.

Stone, Katherine V.W. (2004), *From Widgets to Digits: Employment Regulation for the Changing Workplace*, Cambridge, UK: Cambridge University Press.

Tyler, Tom R. & Steven L. Blader (2000), *Cooperation in Groups: Procedural Justice, Social Identity, and Behavioral Engagement*, Philadelphia, PA: Psychology Press.

Ulen, Thomas (1993), 'The Coasean Firm in Law and Economics', *Journal of Corporate Law*, 18, 301–31.

Williamson, Oliver E. (1985), *The Economic Institutions of Capitalism: Firms, Markets, Relational Contracting*, New York: The Free Press.

Williamson, Oliver E. (1996), *The Mechanisms of Governance*, New York: Oxford University Press.

# 7.   The role of the public interest in corporate law
## *Ian B. Lee*

The concept of the 'public interest' has little, if any, direct doctrinal presence in corporate law and, for the majority of corporate law scholars, this is as it should be. In addition, the concept of the public interest does not play a prominent role in most normative corporate law scholarship. Although few scholars would deny that corporate law should ultimately serve the public interest (that it should maximize social welfare, in one manner of expressing this idea), it is largely taken for granted that the way in which corporate law advances the public interest is by facilitating transactions in which individuals pursue their private interest. As a result, when evaluating actual or proposed corporate law provisions, analysts do not typically return to the basic question whether the provision is in the public interest; rather, the question asked is whether the provision serves the interests of the participants in corporations, especially shareholders, in particular by minimizing their costs of transacting with one another.

A challenge to the dominant view comes from a 'progressive' school of thought (Mitchell 1995) according to which the public interest should play a greater role within corporate law doctrine and corporate law should constrain, in the name of the public interest, the pursuit by corporate actors of their private interest. Progressive policy prescriptions include, depending on the author, reforms to the mandate and manner of selection of the board of directors and the facilitation of socially-motivated shareholder engagement.

In this chapter, I shall describe the limited role of the concept of the 'public interest' in corporate law doctrine;[1] review the standard account of the manner in which corporate law serves the public interest, and its implications for policy; describe two different progressive understandings of the relationship between the public interest and corporate law; and comment on the degree to which these alternative understandings are capable of generating persuasive arguments for corporate law reform.

## 1.   THE 'PUBLIC INTEREST' IN CORPORATE LAW DOCTRINE

Although it might be thought that the 'public interest' is too vague to serve as a legal standard, the term is no more shapeless than other frequently employed legal standards, such as 'fair' and 'reasonable'. The phrase 'public interest' in fact appears 1,739 times in the United States Code and 180 times in the Delaware Code. However, the concept does not appear in the Delaware General Corporation Law and it plays virtually no role in corporate law doctrine.

---

[1]    Except where the laws of non-US jurisdictions are used for illustrative purposes, the jurisdictional scope of the discussion in this chapter will be limited to the United States, especially Delaware.

There are a number of ways in which the public interest could, but, for the main part, does not, figure in corporate law doctrine: it could be a standard for the exercise of corporate powers by the board of directors or by the shareholders; and it could serve as a standard for the exercise of power in relation to corporations by public officials.

## The Directors' Duty of Loyalty

Corporate law vests the power to manage or supervise the management of the corporation in its board of directors. The directors owe duties of care and loyalty; the latter is an obligation to pursue the 'best interests of the corporation'.[2] It is endlessly debated whether the directors' duty of loyalty to the corporation amounts to a duty to maximize profits for the shareholders, or whether it is instead a duty to advance some broader conception of the corporate interest. A further question is whether this duty, however defined, is subject to any independent duty or discretion to consider the public interest.

### The 'best interests of the corporation'
The classic statement of the position that the shareholders' interests come first remains that in *Dodge v. Ford*, in which the Michigan Supreme Court wrote:

> A business corporation is organized and carried on primarily for the profit of the stockholders. The powers of the directors are to be employed for that end. The discretion of directors is to be exercised in the choice of means to attain that end, and does not extend to a change in the end itself.[3]

Many scholars read *Dodge* as articulating, in uncompromising terms, a directorial duty to maximize profits. However, subsequent case law has been more nuanced and even ambiguous. For instance, in explaining why reasonable corporate charitable contributions are permissible, the Delaware courts have hedged: the leading judicial decision on this point provides support both for the position that the law recognizes the intrinsic appropriateness of corporate support for public causes,[4] and for the seemingly contrary position that corporate donations are legitimate only because they are ultimately beneficial to the shareholders.[5] As a practical matter, courts rarely interfere with corporate philanthropy or social responsibility because there is almost always a plausible argument that actions considerate of a corporation's employees, customers, or creditors, or the environment, are in the long-term interests of the corporation's stockholders. Also, board decisions, in the absence of self-dealing, receive deference under the business judgment rule.[6]

---

[2]    *Guth v. Loft*, 5 A.2d 503, 510 (Del. 1939) (articulating a duty of 'undivided and unselfish loyalty to the corporation').

[3]    *Dodge v. Ford Motor Co.*, 170 N.W. 668, 684 (Mich. 1919).

[4]    *Theodora Holding Corp. v. Henderson*, 257 A.2d 398, 404 (Del. Ch. 1969) ('The recognized obligation of corporations towards philanthropic, educational and artistic causes is reflected in the statutory law of all of the states, other than the states of Arizona and Idaho.')

[5]    *Ibid.* 405 ('[T]he relatively small loss of immediate income otherwise payable to ... [the shareholders because of the donation] is far out-weighed by the overall benefits flowing from ... [the donation, which in providing] justification for large private holdings, thereby ... [benefits the shareholders] in the long run.')

[6]    *Aronson v. Lewis*, 473 A.2d 805 (1984).

When the future of the corporation as a going concern is in doubt, it may be difficult to rationalize an act undertaken for the benefit of a non-shareholder constituency as being also, ultimately, in the interests of the shareholders. For instance, when a corporation is in financial distress, the stockholders' interests might well be served by the taking of severe risks that, if they pay off, will produce profits for the corporation and its shareholders but, if they turn out badly, will leave creditors unpaid. Delaware law does not require corporate management to prefer the stockholders' interests in such circumstances. On the contrary, 'at least in the vicinity of insolvency, the board is not merely the agent of the residue [*sic*] risk bearers, but owes its duty to the corporate enterprise'.[7]

A similar conflict can arise in connection with a hostile takeover, because the economic interest of the shareholders lies in having access to an above-market bid for their shares even if the takeover is expected to be detrimental to employees or another non-shareholder constituency. Here, too, the Delaware Supreme Court has expressed a nuanced position. On the one hand, management may take into account the impact of the takeover on its non-shareholder constituencies, provided that there are 'rationally related benefits accruing to the stockholders'.[8] On the other hand, if the directors decide to sell the business or otherwise abandon their long-term strategy, a focus on obtaining the best price for the stockholders must prevail over other considerations.[9]

It is a matter of dispute how to interpret these authorities and characterize their net legal effect. Does the fact that the interests of the shareholders are seemingly paramount in the takeover context shed light on the ambiguous dicta on corporate philanthropy and permit us, ultimately, to conclude that the duty to pursue the 'best interests of the corporation' amounts to a duty to maximize the shareholders' wealth? Or, can the hostile takeover context be viewed as special on the ground that it involves an offer by a third party to the stockholders to purchase the latter's interest? The fact that managerial interference in dealings between the shareholders and a third party concerning the shareholders' sovereign right to sell their shares must be governed by the shareholders' interests does not imply that the same is true where there is no risk of the managers' treading on the shareholders' exit rights (Lee 2006b).

Similarly, is insolvency special, on the theory that residual risk in an insolvent enterprise is also borne by non-shareholders (Macey & Miller 1993); or does the Court's use of the hedging phrase, 'at least', not leave the door open to a whole-enterprise understanding of the best interests of the corporation, even when the corporation is not in financial distress?

For present purposes, it is not necessary to choose between these interpretations.[10] It

---

[7]   *Credit Lyonnais Bank Nederland N.V. v. Pathé Communications Corp.*, No. 12150, 1991 Del. Ch. LEXIS 215, 108 (Dec. 30, 1991). The directors' fiduciary duties in the vicinity of insolvency are owed to the 'corporate enterprise' and not directly to the creditors. See *North American Catholic Educational Programming Foundation v. Gheewalla*, 930 A.2d 92 (Del. 2007) (rejecting direct claim by creditors for breach of fiduciary duties against directors of corporation in the vicinity of insolvency).

[8]   *Revlon v. MacAndrews*, 506 A.2d 173 at 176 (Del. 1986); *Unocal v. Mesa Petroleum* 493 A.2d 946 (Del. 1985).

[9]   *Revlon*, above; *Paramount Communications, Inc. v. Time, Inc.*, 571 A.2d 1140 (Del. 1989); *Paramount Communications, Inc. v. QVC Network Inc.*, 637 A.2d 34 (Del. 1994).

[10]   The debate has been resolved by statute in 30 states (although not Delaware), in favour of the broader interpretation, through the enactment of other-constituency statutes. These statutes authorize (and in one case require) directors and officers to take into account the interests of non-shareholder constituencies under certain circumstances, such as in the context of a hostile takeover. It is noteworthy

suffices to observe that, even if one is drawn to a position towards the broader end of the spectrum of reasonable interpretations, there is little support for the view that the 'best interests of the corporation' is synonymous with the 'public interest'.[11] Instead, at its broadest, the 'best interests of the corporation' appears to refer to the community of interest of the members of the corporate enterprise, a group which is smaller than the public. For example, under Margaret Blair and Lynn Stout's (1999; 2001) influential 'team production theory', the group would consist of parties having made voluntary, irrevocable investments in firm-specific assets.[12]

### An independent discretion to consider the public interest?

Einer Elhauge (2005) has argued that directors possess 'discretion to sacrifice profits in the public interest'. There is some truth in the statement, but its implicit reformulation of the duty to pursue the 'best interests of the corporation' in terms of a primary duty to maximize profits and a secondary discretion to advance the public interest is potentially misleading.

It is, I have said, controversial whether the 'best interests of the corporation' concept is synonymous with the maximization of the shareholders' wealth. Let us first suppose that it is. In that case, what is meant by 'discretion' to sacrifice profits in the public interest is the practical freedom enjoyed by the board as a consequence of the ease with which generosity can be rationalized in the terms of the shareholders' long-term interests, and the reluctance of courts to second-guess the directors' business judgment. It is important not to confuse this practical freedom with legal discretion. The legal position of the board may be contrasted with that of non-controlling shareholders, who are legally entitled to prefer their own partial interests to the common interests of the shareholders when exercising their powers under corporate law (e.g., casting a vote).[13]

In fact, this practical freedom extends to unprofitable behavior of all kinds, and not only to that which is directed toward the public interest. For instance, executive perks, such as first class air travel and corporate retreats at luxury resorts, subtract from the bottom line but can also be rationalized in terms of the shareholders' interests, and courts are highly unlikely to question them. The result is that executives enjoy a similar practical freedom to consume excessive perquisites, but it would be a mischaracterization of their legal powers and responsibilities to

---

that these statutes were almost always enacted as a result of lobbying by corporate directors and officers. This fact has given rise to the view, informed by public choice theory, that the intended and actual beneficiaries of the constituency statutes are not the employee and other constituencies named in the statutes, but rather incumbent management teams, whose discretion to resist a hostile takeover the statutes expand.

[11]    Even if one reads the philanthropy cases as recognizing the intrinsic appropriateness of corporate support for public causes, it does not follow that the support of such causes is the very end to which the directors' powers are to be employed.

[12]    Constituency statutes typically include 'communities' in the list of constituencies whose interests may be taken into account. Although some might view the interest of the community as a synonym for the public interest, the term could also be interpreted, in light of the other enumerated constituencies (workers, suppliers, customers), as referring to the community's interest in a fair return on any firm-specific investments (e.g., roads, tax holidays). The latter remains a narrower interest than the 'public interest'. In Canada, the Supreme Court has been less ambiguous in narrowing the gap between the best interests of the corporation and the public interest, indicating in a recent ruling that the interests of 'inter alia ... governments and the environment' may also be considered by a board of directors in seeking to advance the 'best interests of the corporation'. *Peoples Department Stores v. Wise*, [2004] 3 S.C.R. 461.

[13]    See below.

say that they possess a legal discretion to favor their own comfort and pleasure over the share-holders' interests.

The situation does not change if we make the contrary assumption that the expression 'best interests of the corporation' refers to a community of interest that extends beyond the share-holders to embrace other participants. The directors continue to enjoy a practical freedom to advance the public interest (or, indeed, their own personal interests) at the corporation's expense, because of imperfections in legal accountability mechanisms. It nevertheless remains misleading to suggest that they have a legal discretion to prefer the public interest over the best interests of the corporation.

## The Shareholders' Powers

The shareholders' bundle of rights under corporate law includes a right to participate in and vote at shareholders' meetings, either in person or by proxy (Thompson & Edelman 2009). While the management of the corporation's business is vested in the board, and not in the shareholders, the latter are entitled to elect and remove directors, and to approve amendments to the corporate charter or by-laws, mergers, and other specified fundamental changes.

As a general matter,[14] non-controlling shareholders[15] are legally entitled to exercise their voting rights as they see fit. They are under no legal obligation to be guided by the common interest of the shareholders, but may act upon their self-interest or even upon 'whims and caprice'.[16] *A fortiori*, there is no requirement for shareholders to have regard to the public interest when casting a vote; but neither is there any legal impediment to being motivated in casting one's vote by the public interest rather than by self-interest or the collective interest of the shareholders.

It is, presumably, the hope that at least some shareholders will be guided by the public inter-est that underpins the use of the shareholder proposals in corporate social responsibility campaigns.[17] Although some have suggested that a public-interest motivation should disqualify

---

[14]   One limit to this general freedom is the rule, found in the statutory or common law of many jurisdictions, that prohibits vote selling. In *Schreiber v. Carney*, 447 A. 2d 17, the Delaware Court of Chancery held that vote-selling agreements are not *per se* invalid, but are voidable subject to ratifica-tion by the disinterested stockholders. See also *Crown EMAK Partners, LLC v. Kurz*, 992 A.2d 377 (Del 2010) (suggesting that restrictions on vote selling are based on the premise that shareholder voting should 'reflect rational, economic self-interest arguably common to all shareholders' – that is, the share-holders' common economic interest).

[15]   Controlling shareholders are subject to a fiduciary duty owed to the corporation, the applica-tion of which is nebulous in practice but in relation to which the underlying principle is that a control-ling shareholder may not use its control to transfer wealth from the corporation to itself. See, e.g., *Abraham v. Emerson Radio Corp.* 901 A.2d 751, 759 (Del. Ch. 2006) ('the premise for contending that the controlling stockholder owes fiduciary duties in its capacity as a stockholder is that the controller exerts its will over the enterprise in the manner of the board itself').

[16]   *Ringling Bros.-Barnum & Bailey Com. Shows v. Ringling*, 53 A.2d 441, 447 (Del. 1947).

[17]   Pursuant to Rule 14a-8 under the Exchange Act of 1934, 17 C.F.R. § 240.14a-8, an eligible shareholder is entitled to require that management include in the annual proxy circular, sent to share-holders at the corporation's expense, a 'proposal' submitted by the shareholder together with a brief supporting statement. Proposals on social responsibility matters often argue both that a particular change in the corporation's conduct is socially or morally called for (an appeal to the public interest) and that it will have beneficial reputational or other monetizable consequences for the corporation, at

a proposal (Manne 1972; Fischel 1982),[18] this is not the current position. Rather, provided that a proposal is significantly related to the corporation's business[19] and concerns significant policy issues rather than 'ordinary business',[20] the fact that the public interest, rather than the shareholders' economic interests, motivates the proposal is not a ground of exclusion.[21]

Although the 'ordinary business' exclusion is a serious hurdle for proposals on social responsibility matters,[22] it appears to be more easily crossed when the social proposal in question relates to employment policies. In explaining its more welcoming attitude towards employment-related proposals, the SEC cites the emergence of 'certain social issues relating to employment matters … as a consistent topic of widespread public debate' and the interest of shareholders generally in 'having an opportunity to express their views to company management' on such matters.[23] In other words, the public significance of the issue, especially as perceived by shareholders, contributes to bringing employment discrimination outside the scope of the 'ordinary business' exclusion.

## The Revocation of Corporate Charters

In addition to allocating powers among various corporate institutions, especially the board of directors and the shareholders, corporate law also confers powers and responsibilities upon public officials and judges, such as the Court of Chancery. Here again, the role played by the concept of the public interest is very limited.

One place where the concept appears is in connection with a provision, sometimes mentioned hopefully by proponents of greater corporate social accountability,[24] authorizing the Court of Chancery to revoke the corporate charter for 'abuse, misuse or nonuse of its corporate powers' in a proceeding brought by the state Attorney General.[25] What is an 'abuse … of corporate powers'? Some early cases have referred to acts that 'threaten or harm the public welfare'.[26]

However, the leading Delaware case notes that courts are 'reluctant to take a subjective position on what ultra vires activities injure the general welfare or contravene public policy,

---

least in the long term, that outweigh any short-term sacrifice of profits (an appeal to the collective economic interests of the shareholders).

[18] A Canadian court upheld the exclusion of a shareholder proposal on this basis in *Varity Corporation v. Jesuit Fathers of Upper Canada*, (1987) 59 OR (2d) 459. The decision has effectively been reversed by amendments to the Canada Business Corporations Act, R.S.C. 1985, C-44, s. 137(5).

[19] Rule 14a-8(i)(5). This is arguably the successor to the historical requirement that proposals relate to something the corporation is actually doing (or should be doing) rather than simply calling for social or legal reform. In *Lovenheim v. Iroquois Brands*, 618 F.Supp. 554 (D.C. Dist. 1985), a federal district court ruled against the excludability of a shareholder proposal seeking the discontinuance of the sale of *pate de foie gras*, on the basis of concerns about animal cruelty. The proposal was held to be significantly related to the corporation's business even though the economic stakes for the corporation were negligible.

[20] Rule 14a-8(i)(7).

[21] *Medical Committee for Human Rights v. Securities and Exchange Commission*, 432 F.2d 659 (C.A.D.C. 1970).

[22] See *Apache Corp. v. NYCERS*, 621 F.Supp.2d 444 (S.D.Tex., 2008).

[23] Amendments to Rules on Shareholder Proposals, 63 Fed. Reg. 29106, 29108 (May 28, 1998).

[24] See, e.g., Greenfield (2007, 97–8).

[25] 8 Del. Code Sec. 284.

[26] *People v. North River Sugar Refining Co.*, 24 N.E. 834 (N.Y. 1890).

[and instead] look for and find a sustained course of fraud, immorality or violations of statutory law before deciding that there has been an abuse of charter privileges'.[27] Moreover, although the legal possibility of charter revocation is clear, its practical significance as a feature of contemporary corporate law is diminished by the overwhelming reluctance of state Attorneys General to make use of it.[28]

## 2.   HOW CORPORATE LAW SERVES THE PUBLIC INTEREST: THE STANDARD VIEW

### The Purpose of Corporate Law

The immediate purpose of corporate law is to provide a mechanism for the formation of corporations. Why is it in the public interest to provide such a mechanism?

The standard answer begins with the insight that firms – of which corporations are one type – are an alternative to market transactions (Coase 1937). When some activity requires the inputs of several people, there are, in principle, two ways of proceeding: the owners of the inputs can trade them with one another, or they can agree to work under the direction of a coordinator. The coordinator's instructions are a substitute for the chain of contracts that would otherwise be required: production becomes centralized within a firm.

Obviously, most real-world productive efforts rely in part on each method. Much production takes place within firms, but virtually every firm purchases some of its inputs from outsiders. This reality reflects the fact that there is a trade-off between the costs of organizing activity within firms (for instance, agency costs) and the costs of transacting. Coase hypothesized that wealth-seeking actors (entrepreneurs and suppliers of factors of production) are guided by their self-interest to provide for the coordination of a given activity within a firm if, and only if, the costs of doing so are less than the costs of leaving coordination to markets.

One thing that corporate law provides is a template for the organization of firms: a significant proportion of most corporations' statutes consists of provisions concerning the respective roles of the board of directors and the shareholders, for instance. According to the standard view, these provisions anticipate the arrangements that parties seeking to associate within a firm would arrive at in any event (Easterbrook & Fischel 1991). It is not difficult to believe that the public interest is served by facilitating productive arrangements (a social good) that economize on transaction costs (a deadweight loss).

---

[27]   *Young v. National Ass'n for Advancement of White People*, 109 A.2d 29 (Del. Ch. 1954); see also *Craven v. Fifth Ward Republican Club, Inc.*, 146 A.2d 400, 402 (Del. Ch. 1958).

[28]   Virtually all Attorney-General proceedings for dissolution for abuse of corporate powers date from the first half of the twentieth century. Exceptions include *Surrogate Parenting Associates, Inc. v. Com. ex rel. Armstrong*, 704 S.W.2d 209, 54 USLW 2435, Ky., February 06, 1986 (NO. 85-SC-421-DG) (dissolution refused); and *State v. Cortelle Corp.*, 38 N.Y.2d 83, 341 N.E.2d 223, 378 N.Y.S.2d 654 (1975). More recently, New York brought abuse-of-powers proceedings in 1998 seeking the dissolution of two corporations, the Council for Tobacco Research and the Tobacco Institute. The subject corporations were ultimately dissolved by consent pursuant to the *Attorneys General Master Settlement Agreement*, subsection III(o), available at http://www.naag.org/backpages/naag/tobacco/msa/msa-pdf/ (last accessed November 2011).

And what of the 'bundle of privileges' that distinguish corporations from other firms, especially legal personality and limited liability? At first, economics-influenced scholars dismissed legal personality as a mere notational convenience.[29] More recently, theorists have pointed to a more substantial advantage: legal personality shelters the assets contributed to a venture from unilateral withdrawal by the shareholders (and from claims by the shareholders' creditors) (Hansmann & Kraakman 2000; Blair 2003). This feature, which distinguishes corporations from unincorporated firms such as partnerships and proprietorships, makes the venture less vulnerable to changes in the identity and personal circumstances of the shareholders. This in turn enables the suppliers of other inputs to participate with greater confidence in the firm, for example, in the case of employees, by investing in the acquisition of specialized skills.

As for limited liability, it is important to remember that, with respect to any creditors whose relationship with the corporation is contractual, limited liability is only a default rule. If a given creditor attaches more value to the possibility of recourse to the shareholders' wealth than the latter attach to the reduction of their exposure, the former may demand and the latter may consent to a personal guarantee. Shareholder guarantees are not uncommon in the small business context. They are, however, unheard-of in corporations with many shareholders. Economic theorists of the corporation suppose that this is because unlimited liability would be dysfunctional where there are many shareholders. The value of a share, taking into account liability risk, would depend in part on the wealth of the other shareholders. The need to ascertain the wealth of the members of a changing group adds to the cost of investing in, and holding, shares. 'In the extreme, securities markets will not exist' (Halpern et al. 1980, 136).

In summary, the conventional view supposes that people are motivated to engage in productive activity with one another, and that such activity is desirable in principle. They face inherent obstacles in doing so – this is what transaction costs are – and the law can mitigate these costs or aggravate them. It is in the public interest for the law to mitigate them.

## The Position of the Shareholders

To many critics, it seems that mainstream corporate law discourse is obsessed with the shareholders (Greenfield 2007). Major fault lines within contemporary US corporate law scholarship, for example in debates about executive compensation and directorial nominations, do not concern whether the shareholders' interests should be at the centre of the policymaker's concerns, but whether a given policy reform would increase or decrease shareholder value. The focus on shareholders might seem especially anomalous when it is considered that, according to the conventional economic understanding of the corporation, the shareholders are merely the suppliers of a factor of production. They are just one of a number of groups whose contributions are coordinated within the firm.

The explanation for the focus on the shareholders is that corporate law constructs shareholders as the residual claimants within the corporation. They are entitled to whatever corporate assets are left once the 'fixed claims' – contractual obligations to creditors, employees,

---

[29]   See, e.g., Easterbrook & Fischel (1991): 'It would be silly to attach a list of every one of Exxon's investors to an order for office furniture just to ensure that all investors share their percentage of the cost'.

customers, and other participants in the corporation – have been met.[30] This structure is, according to the conventional account, in the interests of all participants in the corporation. A venture is worth more in the aggregate if there is a single group of residual claimants because of lower agency costs compared to a venture in which there are multiple residual claimants (Macey & Miller 1993). It follows that if all of the participants are acting rationally and with a view to their respective interests, they will agree that (1) one of the groups (let us call them shareholders) will enjoy the status of sole residual claimant; (2) management's powers should be exercised towards the end of maximizing the value of the shareholders' investment; and (3) the other participants will receive fixed terms that compensate them prospectively for agreeing to (1) and (2).

When matters are viewed in this way, the central policy problem in corporate law becomes whether, and to what extent, intervention by the state is necessary to ensure that those who control the corporation (the board and executive management) act consistently with the maximization of shareholder value.[31] Corporate law focuses on this problem, not because the shareholders are more 'deserving' than any other group, but because their status as residual claimants is the basis on which reasonable people who commit resources to the corporation have parted with their money.

## Other Purposes

As for other ingredients of the public interest – say, the economic or dignitary interests of workers or consumers – the conventional corporate law narrative does not deny that they may be important. However, it argues that they are not what corporate law is about.

One strategy for responding to the concern about non-shareholder interests is to point to the possibility of contractual protections. For instance, the firm's workforce is in a voluntary relationship with the other participants in the venture, and it can be presumed that the negotiated terms of that relationship represent the most advantageous bargain possible for the workers that is consistent with the requirement of the other parties to consent to it. By contrast, the shareholders' position as the residual claimant, and the design of corporate governance so as to promote the maximization of the value of this claim, *are* the substance of the shareholders' contract with the other parties.

There may be a role for state intervention in light of, for example, market failures in the labor market or the market for consumer products, or collective action problems in relation to environmental harm. In the standard narrative, those interventions are called labor law, consumer protection law, and environmental law, respectively (Hansmann & Kraakman 2001).

The last point reflects the notion that, while all public power should ultimately be directed at the advancement of the public interest, governmental action in different spheres of policy may be directed at different aspects of the public interest. The prevailing view among corporate law scholars and policymakers is that the manner in which the law of corporations

---

[30]    In corporate law, this idea is captured in the rules governing the distribution to shareholders of net liquidation proceeds and prohibiting the payment of dividends by an insolvent corporation.

[31]    In countries where publicly-traded corporations tend to have a controlling shareholder, the central problem is how to deal with the conflict between controlling shareholders' interests and the value of the minority shares. *See, e.g.,* Enriques and Volpin (2007).

advances the public interest is by facilitating a particular form of coordination among private participants who are pursuing their own ends in connection with a business venture.

## 3.   SHOULD THE PUBLIC INTEREST PLAY A GREATER ROLE IN CORPORATE LAW?

### Alternative Paradigms: Corporate Law as Public Law

We have seen that the public interest plays a limited role (at best) in corporate law doctrine. Moreover, according to the conventional understanding, corporate law advances the public interest in a very specific respect: it facilitates a form of cooperation among private parties that reduces their costs of engaging in productive activity together. Most corporate law scholars believe that other desirable policy goals should be pursued under other regulatory heads, such as environmental law, labour law, and consumer protection law, rather than by diverting corporate law from its mission.

There are two basic alternatives to this understanding of the relationship between the corporate law and the public interest. I shall refer to them as the 'public facility' and the 'powerful institution' paradigms, respectively.

### The 'public facility' paradigm

The first alternative acknowledges that the corporation may be a vehicle for the pursuit of private ends, but analogizes the state's role in providing this vehicle to the provision of other public facilities, such as parks and highways. The state contemplates, to be sure, that citizens will use these facilities for their own purposes. Nevertheless, both legal and informal norms reflect society's expectation that users show consideration for the interests of other users as well as non-users who may be affected by the activity; no one thinks it unusual if the use of a public facility is made subject to rules designed to promote or protect these interests. Just as a municipal park bylaw may include rules to protect non-users living in the vicinity from excessive noise, so too might corporate law impose requirements for reasons beyond the convenience of the parties to the 'corporate contract'.

A variation on this perspective characterizes the corporate form as a 'concession' or privilege, the conferral of which entails 'reciprocal … public responsibilities'.[32] This is a more extreme characterization, in that it implies that the use of the corporate form entails heightened social obligations. By contrast, the public facility characterization does not invite us to see consideration for the public interest as a quid pro quo, a sort of 'fee' levied on the users of the corporate form. Its underlying principle is simply that whatever consideration society is entitled to expect citizens to show for the public interest, even as they pursue their own ends, can also be reflected in rules governing the use of public facilities such as the corporate form.

To be sure, the fact that the public interest 'can' be pursued through the imposition of internal limits on the private use of public facilities does not mean that such limits are preferable as compared with external regulation. The public facility perspective merely calls into

---

[32]   Hutchinson (2005, 9).

question the peremptory dismissal of such limits as a diversion of corporate law from its mission. It recommends instead that we consider, in relation to any given public goal and the instruments available for achieving it, whether the goal would be achieved more completely, or at lower social cost, through internal or external regulation.

### The 'powerful institution' paradigm

As for the second alternative paradigm, at its core is the principle that power should be the trigger for the passage of a relationship from the private sphere to the public sphere. The principle implies that what is significant about corporations is not that their existence is enabled by the state, but that they consist of relationships in which some participants exercise power over other participants and, in some cases, over non-participants (Fraser 1998; Hutchinson 2005).

The notion that corporate relationships involve the exercise of power finds support in Coase's theory of the firm as a small planned economy: they are, he wrote, 'islands of conscious power' (Coase 1937).[33] However, it runs against an influential current of scholarly opinion that downplays 'fiat' and instead emphasizes the importance of market forces in determining the behaviour of corporations and corporate officials (Alchian & Demsetz 1972). A different objection to the power paradigm is that the relationships that make up the corporation are consensual (hence, the use of the contractual metaphor), such that the legitimacy issues that arise in connection with the state's exercise of power are avoided.[34] Actual consent obviates the quest for hypothetical consent. Critics respond to this objection by casting doubt on the quality of the consent, or by insisting that the exercise of power can be fair or unfair even if it was acquired consensually.

In addition to the power they wield over the corporation's voluntary participants, such as its employees and shareholders, the people who command the resources pooled within the corporation wield power in relation to the outside world. For instance, with control over greater economic resources comes a greater ability to influence political outcomes, for example through lobbying, campaign donations or political advertising.

The control over aggregated resources may also confer a degree of market power, the power to set the terms of access to those resources (Avi-Yonah 2004). Milton Friedman (1972) himself recognized that 'the monopolist ... has power. It is easy to argue that he should discharge his power not solely to further his own interests but to further socially desirable ends'.[35] The link between market power and the corporate form is open to question: unincorporated firms can be monopolists, and many corporations operate in competitive markets. Nonetheless, the fact that the corporate form facilitates the aggregation of resources, and that the latter is one source of market power, may cast doubt on the proposition that the

---

[33]   See also Dodd (1932, 1157) ('Modern large-scale industry has given to the managers of our principal corporations' enormous power over the welfare of wage earners and consumers, particularly the former.')

[34]   See Rodrigues (2006, 1398) (contrasting the voluntary nature of investment with involuntary nature of political citizenship).

[35]   Friedman (1972, 120). After stating the proposition, of course, Friedman denounced it as 'destr[uctive of] a free society' (*ibid.*). He warned that once it is conceded that pricing decisions are 'public ... as the doctrine of social responsibility declares', then it will not be long before the authority to make such decisions is transferred to the state and we find ourselves living under a 'centrally controlled system' (134–5).

only public interest consideration relevant to corporate law is the reduction of the transaction costs associated with team production.

How 'public' is corporate law? From the conventional neoclassical perspective, the answer is: hardly at all. Corporate law is a vehicle for the pursuit of private ends. In fact, it is best described as a subset of contract law (Easterbrook & Fischel 1991). The answer is different, however, if corporate law is analogized to a public facility. The fact that the state makes corporate law available to citizens for them to use more or less as they wish does not rule out the imposition of conditions for the use of the corporate form, for the protection of the public interest. The line between corporate law and public law becomes further blurred if one attaches significance to the effect of the corporate contract – the formation of 'islands of conscious power' – and not only to the origin of the power in the voluntary adhesion of the participants in the venture.

**What's in a paradigm?**

It can be tempting to suppose that one of these ways of looking at corporate law is correct and that the others are mistaken. If this assumption were correct, then it would seem to follow that choosing the correct paradigm is a step towards arriving at the correct answer to some related policy question, and that choosing an incorrect paradigm is a recipe for policy error. Much might appear to ride, therefore, on whether corporate law *really is* just private law.[36]

However, a more nuanced approach to corporate law paradigms has much to recommend it. Each of the models just described – the contractual paradigm, the public facility paradigm and the powerful institution paradigm – singles out for emphasis certain aspects of the corporate form. There is no ground on which one may state categorically that one of these aspects is the 'most important' and that the corresponding paradigm is therefore the most correct.

It is worth recalling that the contractual paradigm originates in the economic literature as a framework for the generation of testable predictive hypotheses about how the characteristics of organizations differ depending on the characteristics of their members or the nature of the organization's activities (Coase 1937; Jensen & Meckling 1976; for discussion see Lee 2008). For that type of inquiry, it was useful to make simplifying assumptions that have the effect of emphasizing some considerations and obscuring others – such as the role of the state in providing the corporate form, and considerations of fairness in relationships characterized by power. However, the utility of making simplifying assumptions in connection with the generation of predictive hypotheses does not imply the irrelevance for policy, let alone the non-existence, of the obscured considerations.

In the next section, we shall encounter and evaluate a series of proposals for the enhancement of the role of the public interest. These proposals will not be considered to be disqualified at the outset by the fact that they draw upon alternatives to the conventional contractual paradigm.

---

[36]   See, e.g., Butler (1989, 99–100) ('economists have come to view the firm as a "nexus of contracts" ... [Where this view prevails,] the role of the state is limited to enforcing contracts ... [and] freedom of contract requires that parties to the "nexus of contracts" must be allowed to structure their relations as they desire.'); Ribstein (1992, 109) ('if, as many scholars now believe, a corporation is a nexus of contracts [rather than an artificial person],' then certain policy consequences follow.). For a progressive example, see Mitchell (1993), esp. 875–6 (criticizing the ALI Principles of Corporate Governance for evading the fundamental choice between the public and private conceptions of the corporation).

## Proposals for the Expansion of the Role of the Public Interest in CorporateLaw

The critical literature contains countless proposals for reforming corporate law and governance so as to enhance its 'public' character. For example, a reader of this literature is likely to encounter proposals:

- For modifying the mandate of the board of directors, for example by relaxing the shareholder wealth maximization norm (Greenfield 2007; Hutchinson 2005; O'Connor 1991);
- For worker or public interest representation on the board of directors (Greenfield 2007; McDonnell 2008; Hutchinson 2005; Nader et al. 1976; Schwartz 1971);
- For the use of corporate law to control externalities, such as environmental harms (Sneirson 2009), human rights abuses (Bilchitz 2009), or the economy-wide risks said to be associated with certain forms of executive compensation (Bratton & Wachter 2010; Mitchell 2009); and
- For the facilitation of socially-motivated shareholder engagement, for instance through mandatory social disclosure (Hess 1999; Dhir 2009).

### Modification of the board's mandate

Critics of the status quo commonly emphasize that corporations are institutions with a social function. However, such critics virtually never propose specifically to redefine the mandate of the board of directors to advance the 'best interests of the corporation' so that it amounts simply to a mandate to pursue the 'public interest'. In other words, few recommend assigning to the board the task of maximizing aggregate social welfare. What is more usually advocated is a definition of the 'best interests of the corporation' that embraces an enlarged subset of the general public. The subset is sometimes described in terms of the corporation's 'stakeholders' (Green 1993) or the members of a 'team' (Blair & Stout 1999). We may also describe this group as consisting of the various parties to the 'corporate nexus of contracts'. Typically, employees, creditors, suppliers, and customers are included alongside shareholders.[37] The broader public interest appears, if at all, as a secondary element, in the form of a permissive discretion on the part of the board to consider the impact of its decisions on society.

Consider, for instance, Merrick Dodd's (1932) famous argument that the corporation was coming to be seen 'as an economic institution which has a social service as well as a profit-making function'. Dodd's prescription was only for 'some degree of legal freedom' on the part of managers to act upon 'a sense of social responsibility toward ... the general public' in the same manner as the owners of an unincorporated business.[38] Dodd did not suggest, in other words, that managers' primary duty would be to advance the public interest. Rather, in the pursuit of the corporation's business, Dodd urged that managers have legal discretion to show whatever consideration a normal businessperson would have for the public interest.

So let us consider two distinct normative propositions: first, that the 'best interests of the corporation' should be understood to refer to a community of interests that stretches beyond

---

[37]   Sometimes 'local communities' are also included. Regarding the distinction between 'local communities' and the general public interest, see note 12 above.

[38]   Dodd (1932, 1160–61).

the shareholders to encompass all of the parties to the corporate nexus of contracts; and, second, that boards of directors should have legal discretion to give independent consideration to the impact of their decisions on the general public interest.

*Best interests of the corporation*   As noted in the descriptive part of this chapter, the law in Delaware is ambiguous as to whether the board must pursue the shareholders' interests exclusively, or whether the 'best interests of the corporation' instead refers to the corporate enterprise as a whole. In assuming the former, some critics, such as Bakan (2004), are prematurely conceding defeat on the legal question.

At present, our focus is on the normative question. There are at least two ways of approaching the question: as a question of efficiency, and as a question of contractual interpretation.

1   *Efficiency:* From the standpoint of efficiency, the basic social trade-off concerns, on the one hand, the costs imposed upon non-shareholders by corporations' pursuit of shareholder wealth, and, on the other hand, the agency costs (borne in the first instance by shareholders) resulting from the increased managerial discretion that a broader mandate would entail.

It is an unresolved question as to which of these two types of cost is greater, but it may be observed that both are smaller than is often assumed. On the one hand, the proponents of shareholder wealth maximization argue strenuously that market forces in any event provide incentives for managers to pay heed to the interests of non-shareholders: doing so may be a cost-effective way of purchasing customers' patronage, employees' loyalty, and so on (Meese 2002).

On the other hand, the agency costs entailed by pluralistic legal duties may also be less than is sometimes understood. In particular, one may question the importance of managers' duties under corporate law in controlling agency costs, given the ease with which consideration for and even generosity to non-shareholder members of the team can be rationalized in terms of the shareholders' long-term interests. In controlling agency costs, it is the market for corporate control, rather than directors' duties, that does the heavy lifting (Manne 1965).[39]

2   *Contract:* As explained earlier, many proponents of a narrow, shareholder-focused definition of the 'best interests of the corporation' place a contractual gloss on the argument. Non-shareholders, they argue, have agreed to assume the risk of harm to their interests that comes from the corporation's pursuit of the shareholders' advantage. They do so because the enterprise is worth more as a whole if a single constituency with homogeneous interests is designated to be the exclusive beneficiary of the managers' allegiance, than if the managers' allegiance is dispersed among numerous constituencies. The other constituencies receive 'fixed' terms adequate to compensate them for their participation in the enterprise. Indeed, because the value of the enterprise is greater, non-shareholder constituencies may receive richer (albeit fixed) terms for their participation in an enterprise in which the shareholders' interests come first than they would in a less focused enterprise.

---

[39]   Managers are also constrained by other markets, such as product and labor markets.

In disputing this argument, one strategy for the critics is to question the magnitude of the agency costs problem.[40] In addition, experimental evidence suggests that many people underestimate the probability that negative outcomes will happen to them (Jolls et al. 1998); and this may provide reasons not to accept, uncritically, the assumption that non-shareholders have consented to bear them (Lee 2005a).

Margaret Blair and Lynn Stout (1999, 2001) offer a rival to the conventional interpretation of the corporate contract. They argue that, if directors' duties were articulated solely in terms of the shareholders' interests, it would be more difficult to attract firm-specific investments from employees, suppliers, and other non-shareholder parties. It is helpful, for instance, if workers put in more than the minimum amount of effort that prevents their dismissal, but they will be reluctant to do so if they are not certain that these investments, once made, will be rewarded. Extra effort is often better generated through implicit understandings than through explicit contracting (Shleifer & Summers 1988; Chapman 1993). The guardian of these implicit understandings is a board of directors, which is responsible for coordinating the team's activities and dividing up the fruits of its labour among the members of the team. A shareholder-focused duty of loyalty would be inconsistent with the board's necessary role, and we should therefore not read such a duty into the corporate contract.

*Discretion to consider the public interest*   Should there be a legal discretion on the part of corporate boards to give independent consideration to the effect of their decisions on the public interest? This question presents a trade-off similar to that which arises in the context of the choice between broader and narrower formulations of the 'best interests of the corporation'. On the one hand, permitting directors to consider the public interest may reduce social externalities. On the other hand, with discretion come reduced accountability and increased agency costs.

As in the debate about the definition of the 'best interests of the corporation', there may be somewhat less to this trade-off than meets the eye. As the opponents of a discretion to consider the public interest point out, the additional social costs entailed by its absence are mitigated by market forces and external regulation. However, on the other side of the ledger, the incremental agency cost advantage of non-discretion may be modest, in light of the business judgment rule and the market for corporate control.

Einer Elhauge (2005) has argued for managerial discretion to 'sacrifice profits in the public interest', on the basis that it is a necessary condition for the availability of 'moral and social sanctions' as a means of regulating corporate behavior. The argument is that social reprobation, feelings of guilt, and internalized 'private values' can sometimes be more effective or less costly than legal sanctions as modalities of social control. However, within public corporations, the shareholders are insulated from such impulses because of their anonymity and lack of information. It follows that, if social and moral sanctions are to have any impact in regulating public corporations, it must be through their effect on managers. A 'discretion to sacrifice profits in the public interest' provides the necessary space within which managers can act upon their moral and social impulses.

---

[40]   Greenfield (2007, 138) (describing the agency costs argument as the 'Emperor's New Clothes of corporate law scholarship').

Elhauge's conclusion is framed as a categorical recommendation that the law provide for managerial discretion to advance the public interest. In reality, his contribution is more fairly viewed as providing a theoretical explanation of the manner in which the benefits of discretion are realized, namely through the operation of moral and social norms. These benefits remain to be weighed against the costs of discretion: reduced managerial accountability.[41]

### Non-shareholder board representation

Should corporate law mandate the representation of workers and the public interest on boards of directors? The assumption underlying proposals for the representation of non-shareholder interests on the board of directors is that, as currently constituted, boards represent the shareholder interest. It is a reasonable enough assumption, as the directors are elected by the shareholders.

Yet, there is a near-consensus, among critics and proponents of the conventional view alike, that the shareholders' voting rights are 'so weak that they scarcely qualify as part of corporate governance' (Bainbridge 2008, 53).[42] The shareholder franchise is derided as a 'myth' (Bebchuk 2007). According to this consensus, the significance of shareholder voting resides almost exclusively in the role it plays in enabling the market for corporate control. It is not the right of the dispersed shareholders in a public corporation to vote per se, but rather their combined right to sell a majority of the voting rights to a hostile bidder, which motivates the board of directors to attend to the shareholders' interests.[43]

It would appear, therefore, that in proposals for representation for non-shareholder interests and a corresponding diminution of the voting power of the shareholders, there could be two distinct, though related objectives. The first could be to disrupt the operation of the market for corporate control. The second is to exploit the gaps left by that market.

*Non-shareholder board representation and the market for corporate control*   Let us first consider the disruption of the market for corporate control. Proponents of non-shareholder representation rarely discuss the effect of their proposals on the market for corporate control. However, we may presume that the determining factor is whether directors chosen by the shareholders continue to have majority voting power on the board; if they do, then the market for corporate control continues to function. Thus, for instance, McDonnell's (2007, 380) recommendation for 'minority employee representation' would leave the market for corporate control unaffected. By contrast, Hutchinson's (2005) proposal to reduce the shareholders to one-third of the seats on the board, and to fill the remaining seats with representatives of labour and the public interest, would make hostile takeovers impossible.

A compelling objection to eliminating the market for corporate control is that it would remove the main source of assurance for the shareholders in widely-held corporations that their interests will be attended to. Unlike other stakeholders, the shareholders receive no

---

[41]   Elhauge appears to claim that the benefits of discretion can be obtained at no incremental cost to the shareholders (2005, 806–807). This claim is unpersuasive (for discussion, see Lee 2006b).

[42]   See also Macey (2008, 201) (endorsing Bainbridge's view); Mitchell (2001, 125) ('stockholder voting is not very effective'); Blair and Stout (1999, 310) ('shareholders' voting rights ... are so weak as to be virtually meaningless').

[43]   See Coates (1999, 851); Bainbridge (2003, 568–9).

legally binding promise of cash flow – no promise of wages, interest or return of principal.[44] When, in addition to the absence of any legal claim on the corporation's cash flow, and the absence of any binding promise to maximize profits, one deprives the shareholders of the power to replace the managers if profits and cash flows are unsatisfactory, it becomes unclear what shareholders are receiving in exchange for their contributions. This is not a point about fairness, but about whether equity survives as a distinct mode of financing. For if both majority voting control and a promise to maximize profits are off the table, it becomes unclear what commitment a firm can make that is capable of attracting capital, other than the promise of a fixed return akin to that made to creditors (Lee 2005b).

*Worker representation*    Let us now assume instead that the proposal is for worker or public interest representation that leaves intact the market for corporate control. The proposal might achieve the latter by ensuring that the shareholder representatives are in the majority, or by having the worker and/or public interest representatives chosen by the shareholders (e.g., Nader et al. 1976). The assumption underlying such reforms would be that the existing constraints imposed by market forces leave space for board deliberation to affect outcomes.[45] It may be that, currently, deliberations are structured around a norm of shareholder wealth maximization that the presence of non-shareholder representatives on the board could help to counteract.[46]

In the case of worker representation, would such a broadening be desirable? From a democratic perspective, the reflexive answer might be in the affirmative, for 'more participation is better than less participation' (Hutchinson 2005, 282–3). A more considered response might depend on additional information. Do employees want seats on the board? Do they want them as much as they want other things, such as subsidized day care or more money? What trade-off among these wants is reflected in the corporate 'bargain,' that is, in the provisions of corporate law to which all have adhered, as modified by the terms of any issued securities, and the employees' job contracts?

After all, worker representation can be achieved contractually. For instance, management can undertake to nominate a worker representative as part of its slate, confident that the shareholders will rubber-stamp the nomination at the annual meeting (Fraser 1982). Within a more formal constitutional framework, worker representation could be achieved by providing for the issuance to employees of a class of preferred shares conferring the right to vote for a certain number of directors.[47] Given that worker representation is contractually available, but rarely observed in practice, the neoclassical reflex is to suspect that the status quo better suits the needs of the parties to the corporate contract, workers included.[48]

---

[44]    The so-called right to receive dividends is only a right to receive such dividends as have been declared by the board in its discretion, and the right to receive the net proceeds of liquidation arises only upon the dissolution of the corporation, which is to say, in most cases, never.

[45]    This is the space which Coaseans (1937) believe is occupied by 'fiat.' (For discussion of the relationship between fiat and deliberation, see Lee 2009.)

[46]    See, e.g., Fraser (1982, 956–7) (anecdote illustrating impact of constituency director on other board members' thinking about plant closing and on subsequent outcome). See also Hunter (1998, 571); Greenfield (2007, 149).

[47]    The shares could be subject to redemption upon the termination of the worker's employment, and (for greater conformity with democratic principles) could provide for per-capita voting.

[48]    For the sake of simplicity, I am ignoring the principal-agent problem as between workers and

Some might think the neoclassical analysis insufficiently respectful of a democratic entitlement. After all, 'citizens are entitled to basic economic protections by virtue of their membership in society, and not only through their efforts at contractual negotiations' (Hutchinson 2005, 151). However, from the standpoint of autonomy we might question whether a policymaker would be doing any favors to the employees by making representation on the board a mandatory term of the employment relationship. The overall balance of advantage in the transaction between the employees and employer is determined by conditions of supply and demand in the labor market; thus, a regulatory adjustment to one term will prompt a compensating adjustment in some other term, such as wages. The balance of advantage in the relationship will not change, but both parties will wind up with a package different from the one they would have chosen in the absence of the policymaker's well-intentioned interference.[49]

*Public interest representation*   The question whether there should be representative directors for the public interest raises different issues. On the one hand, the neoclassical response – if it were optimal, the parties would choose it voluntarily – has no application. Unlike the workforce, the general public is not a party to the corporate contract. Instead, on its behalf, the state dictates the terms on which private parties may cooperate using the corporate form. The question here under consideration is whether one of these terms should be board representation for the public interest.

On the other hand, the case for public interest representation faces an objection that the case for worker representation does not: worker representation is compatible with the preservation of the corporation and the public as distinct communities of interest, while public interest representation sits uneasily with that distinction. Because employees are members of the corporate enterprise, an employee director arguably speaks to the 'best interests of the corporation' as an insider. Her constituents' interests are a component of the best interests of the corporation, according to a defensible, if disputed, interpretation of the latter concept. By contrast, a representative of the public interest on the board of directors will, by definition, be speaking to the 'best interests of the corporation' as an outsider, unless one is willing to collapse the conceptual distinction between the corporation's interests and those of society.[50]

## Use of corporate law to control externalities

In the debate between defenders and critics of the conventional understanding of the relationship between corporate law and the public interest, an important theme concerns the distinction between external and internal approaches to the regulation of corporate behaviour. The conventional understanding does not deny that the pursuit by individuals of their private interest, including through their participation in incorporated businesses, may cause social

---

their collective bargaining agents. See Conard (1977, 958) (discussing lack of enthusiasm on the part of US union leaders for codetermination, and mentioning the conflict of interest between those leaders and the membership).

[49]   For discussion, see Lee (2006a). McDonnell's (2008) recommendation that the state encourage employee representation through subsidies, rather than mandating it, avoids this criticism.

[50]   Even if one proceeds on the basis that corporate law is a public facility or that corporations are loci of power within society, one need not abandon the idea that the corporation is a vehicle for private initiative and that there is therefore a distinction between the corporation's interests and those of society as a whole.

harms. It does not deny that state intervention may sometimes be preferable to reliance upon market forces in avoiding those harms. It only holds that such intervention should be external to corporate law.

Modifying the mandate or composition of the board of directors is an internal strategy for the corporate behaviour modification. Internal strategies need not be so intrusive, however. In general, internal regulation includes any mandatory provision of corporate law the purpose of which is to limit the parties' contractual freedom because of its impact on non-parties. For instance, in the wake of the financial crisis of 2008, some are suggesting that limits be placed on executive compensation – not for the protection of the shareholders, but because of the economy-wide risks believed to be caused by compensation arrangements that were congenial to the interests of both the managers and shareholders of individual firms (Bratton & Wachter 2010). The enactment of such limits within corporate law would be an internal strategy for regulating corporate activity.

It might seem that the dichotomy between internal and external strategies is a distinction without a difference. If everyone agrees that, in some cases, corporate behaviour requires regulation, what difference does it make whether the label attached to such regulation is 'corporate law' or (for example) 'environmental law'?[51]

The principal drawback of an internal strategy, according to the conventional view, is that it weakens the wealth-producing capacities of the firm. By contrast, when external regulation is used, these capacities can be 'conscript[ed]' in the service of the public good:

> Given wealth as a maximand, society may change corporate conduct by imposing monetary penalties. These reduce the venturers' wealth, so managers will attempt to avoid them. So, for example, a pollution tax would induce the firm to emit less. It would behave as if it had the interests of others at heart. Society thus takes advantage of the wealth-maximizing incentives built into the firm in order to alter its behavior at least cost. (Easterbrook & Fischel 1991, 37–8)

However, matters are not so cut and dried; in fact, there a trade-off involved. The downside of external regulation is that managers may view the restrictions as constraints to be worked around (Conard 1977). By contrast, provisions embedded within corporate law might influence the managers' conception of their role, with the result that the norms underlying such provisions are capable of guiding managers even within the gaps left by legal enforcement mechanisms.[52]

Another difference between internal and external strategies concerns jurisdiction. Corporate law is the law of the place of incorporation, not the place or places where the

---

[51]   Greenfield argues for internal regulation on the basis that 'it is often cheaper to avoid a problem than to rectify it later, and it is often better to give the responsibility to avoid a problem to the person who knows most about it and can avoid it at the least expense' (2007, 141). These arguments appear to miss their mark. As to the first point, external regulation often seeks to prevent (e.g., through deterrence) rather than simply to 'rectify'. As for the second point, if the suggestion is that certain individuals within the corporation (such as its directors) are in the best position to avoid the social harm, it is not uncommon for environmental laws to be drafted in such a way as to ascribe personal liability upon individuals, including those acting in corporate roles, for their personal failures.

[52]   This is, of course, one way of thinking about shareholder primacy. The norm of shareholder wealth maximization guides managers' exercise of discretion within the substantial gaps left by their fiduciary duties and the market for corporate control (Bainbridge 1993).

corporation carries on business.[53] By contrast, 'external regulation' is typically imposed by the jurisdiction where the activities take place. For instance, the applicable labour rules are those of the places where the workers perform their duties; the applicable consumer protection laws are those of the places where the transactions with consumers occur.

In principle, the choice of whether or how to regulate a harm-causing activity should be made by the governmental authorities with jurisdiction over the place where the harm occurs or, alternatively, the place where the activity occurs. In contrast, governmental authorities in the jurisdiction of incorporation may not be well situated to make the cost-benefit calculations involved in evaluating the necessity of regulation: they are responsible to electorates that neither incur the harm nor obtain the benefit of the regulated activity. Moreover, regulation by the jurisdiction of incorporation may be ineffective at limiting the incidence of the conduct. Simply by choosing to incorporate elsewhere, the restrictions can be avoided.[54] Sometimes, the proponents of internal regulation simultaneously urge that corporate law be nationalized (Nader et al. 1976), which – for domestic harms, at least – solves both problems, although at the cost of depriving shareholders of the benefits of jurisdictional competition.

### Facilitation of shareholder engagement

Many critics of the status quo in corporate law think that shareholders are part of the problem (e.g., Dodd 1932; Bratton & Wachter 2010; Mitchell 2001; Fraser 1998). For these commentators, it is because of the managers' single-minded focus on the shareholders' interests and, in particular, on the maximization of their wealth, that corporations sometimes act detrimentally to the interests of society at large. This view of the nature of the problem generates recommendations to reduce the shareholders' rights, for example by limiting the shareholder franchise (Mitchell 2001). The problem with these proposals is that if you disenfranchise the shareholders, you cut the managers loose – the proposals require a heroic belief in the wisdom and incorruptibility of managers.

A less drastic strategy is to try to improve the shareholders' performance as responsible actors. In this connection, some commentators propose the enactment of rules requiring 'social disclosure' by public corporations, such as disclosure of the corporation's pattern of compliance with domestic and foreign law and of information concerning employment practices and the earning of income from 'controversial products' (Williams 1999; Dhir 2009). A policy of making the shareholder proposal mechanism available for socially motivated proposals is also consistent with the encouragement of shareholder responsibility (Lee 2005a).

A standard response to the suggestion of policies to facilitate shareholder engagement is that shareholder passivity is not a weakness of the corporate structure, but one of its strengths

---

[53]    Some countries have sought to challenge this principle. For instance, German law deprived foreign corporations of legal capacity if their 'place of administration' was in Germany. The so-called 'real seat doctrine' ensured, for instance, that labor's participatory rights under German corporate law could not be easily evaded by incorporation outside Germany. However, the real seat doctrine is now inoperative in Germany, following a ruling by the European Court of Justice that it contravenes EU law: Case C-208/00, *Überseering BV v Nordic Construction Co Baumanagement GmbH* [2002] E.C.R. I-9919.

[54]    It is arguable that one state – Delaware – possesses monopoly power in the market for incorporations such that it has some margin for imposing conduct requirements without becoming subject to a corporate exodus. Regarding Delaware as monopolist, see Bebchuk and Hamdani (2002).

(Bainbridge 2008). The *raison d'être* for firms is to substitute authority for costly transactions; corporate law rightly vests this authority in the board of directors, not the shareholders, for several reasons. One is that separating the role of exercising authority from that of providing equity financing enables people who have capital, but no managerial inclination or expertise, to be shareholders. Another is that it facilitates the use of legally unenforceable understandings ('implicit contracts') as a way of incentivizing irrevocable investments of effort and other resources by non-shareholder participants in the venture (Blair & Stout 1999, 2001). Finally, the costs of collective decision-making increase with the size of the deliberating body. One might expect these costs to be so great, if the decision-making body consists of the shareholders in a public company, as to rival or exceed the transaction costs that authority is supposed to avoid. It follows that the last thing that most economic analysts of corporate law want to encourage is shareholder social activism, which they characterize as the exploitation of the many (indifferent shareholders) by the few (activists) (Manne 1972).

*Shareholder social proposals*   In reality, the shareholder proposal mechanism is not much of a threat to the authority of the board. Proposals are framed as recommendations only, and the only direct claim such proposals make on the corporate treasury is the cost of including a few hundred words in management's proxy circular.[55]

Moreover, a shareholder is not without reasons to feel that she has an ethical stake in the conduct of the corporation's business, as she occupies voluntarily the position of ultimate beneficiary of that conduct (Brandeis 1965 [1934]). If it is permissible for management to be guided by ethical considerations,[56] in the discharge of its duty of loyalty to a community of interests including the shareholders, it is not unreasonable for shareholders to wish to provide input on the question of what should be done in their name (Lee 2005a).

*Mandatory social disclosure*   A somewhat different analysis is called for in the case of mandatory social disclosure. On the one hand, relative to the proposal mechanism, mandatory disclosure causes less offense to orthodox sensibilities because it is not necessarily a vehicle for shareholder activism: a shareholder may simply use the information in deciding whether to continue in or exit from her role as shareholder. On the other hand, a mandatory social disclosure regime is likely to be much more expensive to administer and comply with than Rule 14a-8. As a result, one cannot simply treat as immaterial the costs the regime would impose upon the indifferent majority, as it seems defensible to do in relation to Rule 14a-8.

The debate about mandatory social disclosure is a variant of the more general debate about mandatory disclosure by capital-raising corporations (about which, see Easterbrook & Fischel 1991). In this debate, an important argument against mandatory disclosure is that the operation of the capital market in any event ensures that corporations disclose information valued by investors. Moreover, some information that is not forthcoming directly from issuers but that is valued by investors is likely to be provided to willing purchasers by analysts and other private actors.

---

[55]   The SEC has estimated its own costs of complying with Rule 14a-8 (not limited to social proposals) at one staff-year. See Proposed Amendments to Rule 14a-8, Exchange Act Release No. 34-19135, 47 Fed. Reg. 47420, at 47423 n.15 (Oct. 26, 1982).

[56]   Even Milton Friedman (1970) conceded that managers should conform to 'the basic rules of the society, both those embodied in law and those embodied in ethical custom'.

There is, however, a possible argument in favor of mandatory social disclosure beyond those that may be offered in support of mandatory disclosure generally: namely, that investors *ought to* want social information more than they do. To put the point less paternalistically, to the extent that the acquisition of social information by investors contributes positively to the corporate responsibility, it produces external benefits for society. Assuming that we can quantify these benefits, they must be weighed against the costs of mandatory social disclosure, including the costs for the state of determining what disclosure to require,[57] the costs of complying with the disclosure regime, and the possibility that shareholders and managers acting upon the disclosed information might be mistaken in their judgment as to where the social interest really lies (Lee 2005a).

## 4. CONCLUSION

For a century or more, American law has oscillated between private and public conceptions of the corporation (Allen 1992). For the past two decades, it would appear that the private, contractual paradigm has been in the ascendancy. At present, the concept of the public interest plays a very limited role in corporate law doctrine, and most corporate law scholarship is supportive of its marginalization. With the spotlight cast by the financial crisis of 2008 upon the social impact of private arrangements, conditions are perhaps ripe for a resurgence of alternative paradigms more supportive of a role for the public interest in corporate law.[58]

## REFERENCES

Alchian, Armen A. & Harold Demsetz (1972), 'Production, Information Costs, and Economic Organization', *American Economic Review*, 62, 777–95.
Allen, William T. (1992), 'Our Schizophrenic Conception of the Business Corporation', *Cardozo Law Review*, 14, 261–81.
Avi-Yonah, Reuven S. (2004), 'Corporations, Society, and the State: A Defense of the Corporate Tax', *Virginia Law Review*, 90, 1193–1255.
Bainbridge, Stephen M. (1993), 'In Defense of the Shareholder Wealth-Maximization Norm', *Washington & Lee Law Review*, 50, 1423–47.
Bainbridge, Stephen M. (2003), 'Director Primacy: the Means and Ends of Corporate Governance', *Northwestern University Law Review*, 97, 547–606.
Bainbridge, Stephen M. (2008), *The New Corporate Governance in Theory and Practice*, New York: Oxford University Press.
Bakan, Joel (2004), *The Corporation: The Pathological Pursuit Of Profit And Power*, New York: Simon & Schuster.
Bebchuk, Lucian (2007), 'The Myth of the Shareholder Franchise', *Virginia Law Review*, 93, 675–732.
Bebchuk, Lucian & Assaf Hamdani (2002), 'Vigorous Race or Leisurely Walk: Reconsidering the Debate on State Competition over Corporate Charters', *Yale Law Journal*, 112, 553–615.
Bilchitz, David (2009), 'Corporate law and the Constitution: towards binding human rights responsibilities for corporations', *South African Law Journal*, 125, 754–89.
Blair, Margaret M. (2003), 'Locking in Capital: What Corporate Law Achieved for Business Organizers in the Nineteenth Century', *UCLA Law Review*, 51, 387–455.
Blair, Margaret M. & Lynn A. Stout (1999), 'A Team Production Theory of Corporate Law', *Virginia Law Review*, 85, 247–328.

---

[57]  Donald Langevoort (1998, 98), warns of 'intensely political and ideological' balancing exercises within the SEC if its mandate were expanded to include consideration of non-investor interests.
[58]  Not everyone welcomes this prospect: see, e.g., Manne (2008), predicting dark days ahead.

Blair, Margaret M. & Lynn A. Stout (2001), 'Director Accountability and the Mediating Role of the Corporate Board', *Washington University Law Quarterly*, 79, 403–47.

Brandeis, Louis D. (1965 [1934]), 'On Industrial Relations', in Osmond K. Frankel (ed.) (1965) *The Curse Of Bigness: Miscellaneous Papers Of Louis D. Brandeis*, Port Washington, N.Y.: Kennikat Press.

Bratton, William M. & Michael L. Wachter (2010), 'The Case against Shareholder Empowerment', *University of Pennsylvania Law Review*, 158, 653–728.

Butler, Henry N. (1989), 'The Contractual Theory of the Corporation', *George Mason University Law Review*, 11(4), 99–123.

Calabresi, Guido (1991), 'The Pointlessness of Pareto: Carrying Coase Further', *Yale Law Journal*, 100, 1211–37.

Chapman, Bruce (1993), 'Trust, Economic Rationality and the Corporate Fiduciary Obligation', *University of Toronto Law Journal*, 43, 547–88.

Coase, Ronald H. (1937), 'The Nature of the Firm', *Economica*, 4, 386–405.

Coates, John C., IV (1999), 'Measuring the Domain of Mediating Hierarchy: How Contestable are U.S. Public Corporations?', *Journal of Corporation Law*, 24, 837–67.

Conard, Alfred F. (1977), 'Reflections on Public Interest Directors', *Michigan Law Review*, 75, 941–61.

Dhir, Aaron A. (2009), 'The Politics of Knowledge Dissemination: Corporate Reporting, Shareholder Voice, and Human Rights', *Osgoode Hall Law Journal*, 2009, 47–82.

Dodd, E. Merrick (1932), 'For Whom are Corporate Managers Trustees?', *Harvard Law Review*, 45(7), 1145–63.

Easterbrook, Frank H. & Daniel R. Fischel (1991), *The Economic Structure of Corporate Law*, Cambridge: Harvard University Press.

Elhauge, Einer (2005), 'Sacrificing Corporate Profits in the Public Interest', *N.Y.U. Law Review*, 80, 733–869.

Enriques, Luca & Paolo Volpin (2007), 'Corporate Governance Reforms in Continental Europe', *Journal of Economic Perspectives*, 21(1), 117–40.

Fischel, Daniel R (1982), 'The Corporate Governance Movement', *Vanderbilt Law Review*, 35, 1259–92.

Fraser, Douglas A. (1982), 'Worker Participation in Corporate Government: The U.A.W. Chrysler Experience', *Chicago-Kent Law Review*, 58, 949–80.

Fraser, Andrew (1998), *Reinventing Aristocracy: The Constitutional Reformation of Corporate Governance*, Aldershot: Ashgate Dartmouth Publishing.

Friedman, Milton (1970), 'The Social Responsibility of Business is to Increase its Profits,' *New York Times Magazine*, Sept. 13, p. 6.

Friedman, Milton (1972), *Capitalism and Freedom*, Chicago: University of Chicago Press.

Green, Ronald M. (1993), 'Shareholders as Stakeholders: Changing Metaphors of Corporate Governance', *Washington & Lee Law Review*, 50, 1409–22.

Greenfield, Kent (2007), *The Failure of Corporate Law: Fundamental Flaws and Progressive Possibilities*, Chicago: University of Chicago Press.

Halpern, Paul, Michael Trebilcock & Stuart Turnbull (1980), 'An Economic Analysis of Limited Liability in Corporation Law', *University of Toronto Law Journal*, 30, 117–50.

Hansmann, Henry & Reinier Kraakman (2000), 'The Essential Role of Organizational Law', *Yale Law Journal*, 110, 387–440.

Hansmann, Henry & Reinier Kraakman (2001), 'The End of History for Corporate Law', *Georgetown Law Journal*, 89, 439–68.

Hess, David W. (1999), 'Social Reporting: A Reflexive Law Approach to Corporate Social Responsiveness', *Journal of Corporation Law*, 25, 41–84.

Hunter, Larry W. (1998), 'Can Strategic Participation be Institutionalized? Union Representation on American Corporate Boards', *Industrial & Labor Relations Review*, 51 557–78.

Hutchinson, Allan C. (2005), *The Companies We Keep: Corporate Governance for a Democratic Society*, Toronto: Irwin Law.

Jensen, Michael C. & W.H. Meckling (1976), 'Theory of the Firm: Managerial Behavior, Agency Costs and Ownership Structure', *Journal of Financial Economics*, 3, 305–60.

Jolls, Christine, Cass Sunstein & Richard Thaler (1998), 'A Behavioural Approach to Law and Economics', *Stanford Law Review*, 50, 1471–1550.

Langevoort, Donald C. (1998), 'Commentary: Stakeholder Values, Disclosure and Materiality', *Catholic University Law Review*, 48, 93–100.

Lee, Ian B. (2005a), 'Corporate Law, Profit Maximization and the "Responsible" Shareholder', *Stanford Journal of Law, Business & Finance*, 10, 31–72.

Lee, Ian B. (2005b), 'Is There a Cure for Corporate "Psychopathy"?', *American Business Law Journal*, 42, 65–90.

Lee, Ian B. (2006a), 'Democracy Versus Economics in Corporate Governance', *Canadian Business Law Journal*, 44, 130–146.

Lee, Ian B. (2006b), 'Efficiency and Ethics in the Debate about Shareholder Primacy', *Delaware Journal of Corporate Law*, 31, 533–87.

Lee, Ian B. (2008), 'Implications of Sen's Concept of Commitment for the Economic Understanding of the Corporation', *Canadian Journal of Law & Jurisprudence*, 21, 97–127.

Lee, Ian B. (2009), 'Citizenship and the Corporation', *Law & Social Inquiry*, 34, 129–68.

Macey, Jonathan R. (2008), *Corporate Governance: Promises Kept, Promises Broken*: Princeton: Princeton University Press.

Macey, Jonathan R. & Geoffrey P. Miller (1993), 'Corporate Stakeholders: A Contractual Perspective', *University of Toronto Law Journal*, 43, 401–24.

Manne, Henry G. (1965), 'Mergers and the Market for Corporate Control', *Journal of Political Economy*, 73, 110–20.

Manne, Henry G. (1972), 'Shareholder Social Proposals Viewed by an Opponent', *Stanford Law Review*, 24, 481–506.

Manne, Henry G. (2008), 'A Voice From The Friedmanite Wilderness', *Forbes*, October 13, available at http://www.forbes.com/2008/10/13/crisis-economy-friedman-oped-cx_hm_1014manne_print.html (last accessed Novmeber 2011).

McDonnell, Brett (2008), 'Employee Primacy, or Economics Meets Civic Republicanism at Work', *Stanford Journal of Law, Business & Finance*, 13, 334–83.

Meese, Alan J (2002), 'The Team Production Theory of Corporate Law: A Critical Assessment', *William & Mary Law Review*, 43 1629–1702.

Mitchell, Lawrence E. (1993), 'Private Law, Public Interest: The ALI Principles of Corporate Governance', *George Washington Law Review*, 61, 871–97.

Mitchell, Lawrence E. (1995), *Progressive Corporate Law*, Boulder, Col.: Westview Press.

Mitchell, Lawrence E. (2001), *Corporate Irresponsibility: America's Latest Export*, New Haven: Yale University Press.

Mitchell, Lawrence E. (2009), 'The Legitimate Rights of Public Shareholders, George Washington University Legal Studies Research Paper No. 461, available at http://papers.ssrn.com/sol3/papers.cfm ?abstractid=1352025 (last accessed Novmeber 2011).

Nader, Ralph, Mark J. Green & Joel Seligman (1976), *Taming the Giant Corporation*, Norton, New York.

O'Connor, Marleen A. (1991), 'Restructuring the Corporation's Nexus of Contracts: Recognizing a Fiduciary Duty to Protect Displaced Workers', *North Carolina Law Review*, 69, 1189–1260.

Ribstein, Larry E. (1992), 'Corporate Political Speech', *Washington & Lee Law Review*, 49, 109–59.

Rodrigues, Usha (2006), 'The Seductive Comparison of Shareholder and Civic Democracy', *Washington and Lee Law Review*, 63, 1389–1406.

Schwartz, Donald E. (1971), 'The Public-Interest Proxy Contest: Reflections on Campaign GM', *Michigan Law Review*, 69, 419–538.

Shleifer, Andrei & Lawrence Summers (1988), 'Breach of Trust in Hostile Takeovers', in Alan Auerbach (ed.) *Corporate Takeovers: Causes and Consequences*, Chicago: University of Chicago Press.

Sneirson, Judd F. (2009), 'Race to the Left: A Legislator's Guide to Greening a Corporate Code', *Oregon Law Review*, 88, 491–514.

Thompson, Robert B. & Paul H. Edelman (2009), 'Corporate Voting', *Vanderbilt Law Review*, 62, 129–75.

Williams, Cynthia A. (1999), 'The Securities and Exchange Commission and Corporate Social Transparency', *Harvard Law Review*, 112, 1197–1311.

# PART II

# INSIDER GOVERNANCE

# 8. Fiduciary duties: The emerging jurisprudence
## *Claire A. Hill and Brett H. McDonnell*

## 1. INTRODUCTION

Fiduciary duties are at the heart of corporate law. Directors manage corporations, and officers do the day-to-day work; both are directed and constrained by the fiduciary duties they owe to their corporations and to shareholders (and perhaps other constituencies as well). In this chapter, we provide a brief overview of where fiduciary duty law has been, where it is now, and where we believe it is and should be going.

A stylized version of fiduciary duty history carves the world into two types of duties: the duty of care and the duty of loyalty. The duty of care covers attentiveness; the duty of loyalty covers self-dealing. The former is a duty with few teeth, given that certificates of incorporation typically contain provisions relieving directors of liability for what would otherwise be breaches of the duty. Moreover, where decisions (or omissions) are at issue that might implicate the duty of care, courts are extremely deferential, in most cases declining to second-guess what directors and officers did. That being said, the duty of care remains enormously influential as a guide to and constraint on director and officer conduct. The duty of loyalty covers matters that appropriately invite significant scrutiny by courts – and carry a real risk of liability (Hill & McDonnell 2007a).

But these two duties as classically articulated leave open a wide middle ground, where neither inattentiveness nor self-dealing is implicated, but director and officer conduct is not properly serving the interests it should be serving. The courts[1] have crafted doctrines for recurring fact patterns, often those involving possible takeovers, but have not articulated precisely where these fit in the classically articulated fiduciary duties. They have, however, recently and energetically begun to develop the doctrine of good faith, characterizing it as part of the duty of loyalty.

In this chapter we discuss the trajectory of fiduciary duty law over time, starting with the classical articulation, continuing with the development of intermediate standards between care and loyalty, and continuing further with the development of good faith jurisprudence. In the recent renaissance of good faith jurisprudence, the doctrine seemed at first poised to deal with the elephant in the room of corporate law, structural bias – conduct that is not lacking in attentiveness, and that does not involve self-dealing as classically conceived, but seems to reflect directors viewing the world through management-friendly eyes or self-interest in pleasing management. But the more recent jurisprudence has been narrowing the scope of the doctrine; what remains overall is the toothless care, the stricter oversight of true self-dealing, and a hodge-podge in between.

---

[1]   We mainly consider Delaware courts. Delaware is the leading state of incorporation for public corporations; Delaware courts' decisions are important not only for their direct effect but also for their influence on decisions in other states.

In the next section of this chapter we discuss the classical articulation of fiduciary duties. In the succeeding section we discuss the more recent trajectory. The following section discusses the present state of affairs and finally, we discuss where we think law is going, and where we think it should go.

## 2.   CLASSICAL FIDUCIARY DUTIES

Once upon a time, many substantive provisions in corporate law operated to restrict the ability of directors or officers to take actions that might harm shareholders or others. Over time, as corporate law has become more and more enabling, these rules have disappeared completely, narrowed considerably, or become easy to evade. The main mechanism by which state corporate law today attempts to patrol the behavior of those running the corporation is the law of fiduciary duty. This law is enforced by shareholder actions, derivative or direct, against those alleged to have violated a duty to the corporation. The law of fiduciary duty has evolved primarily through a common law process, especially in Delaware, although in many states the basic principles have also been codified.[2]

Traditionally, fiduciary duties came in two main forms: the duty of loyalty and the duty of care (Allen et al. 2001). The duty of loyalty traditionally applies where a director, officer, or controlling shareholder has a material financial stake in a transaction at odds with the interest of the corporation.[3] A paradigmatic case is the corporation providing a loan to a director. The history generally recounted is that at early common law, such conflicted transactions were simply void or voidable (Marsh 1966); some scholars, though, disagree with that characterization (Beveridge 1992). Over time, the law has evolved to allow corporations to undertake such transactions under certain circumstances.

By a combination of statute and common law, all states now allow corporations to engage in conflicted transactions in three kinds of circumstances: where there has been approval by disinterested and independent directors, where there has been approval by disinterested shareholders, and where the transaction can be proved to be fair to the corporation.[4] Board or shareholder approval must comply with a variety of procedural requirements, most importantly that all material facts concerning the transaction and conflict have been disclosed to the directors or shareholders. Assuming approval in compliance with the required procedure, courts will still review the transaction, but more leniently than had there been no approval. In Delaware, the state with the most developed case law, a transaction that has received appropriate board or shareholder approval will be reviewed under lenient standards such as business judgment or waste, unless the transaction involves the interest of a controlling shareholder. In the case of a controlling shareholder, after board or shareholder ratification the transaction still receives fairness review, but ratification shifts the burden to the plaintiff to prove unfairness.[5] The fairness standard involves testing the transaction for both procedural and substantive fairness.[6]

---

[2]   E.g. Mod. Bus. Corp. Act §§ 8.30, 8.31, 8.60–63.
[3]   *Rales v. Blasband*, 634 A.2d 927 (Del. 1993); Mod. Bus. Corp. Act § 8.60(1)).
[4]   Del. Gen. Corp. L. 144; Mod. Bus. Corp. Act §§ 8.60–63.
[5]   *Kahn v. Lynch Commc'n Sys., Inc.*, 669 A.2d 79 (Del. 1995); *In re Wheelabrator Techs. Inc. S'holders Litig.*, 663 A.2d 1194 (Del. Ch. 1995).
[6]   *Weinberger v. UOP, Inc.*, 457 A.2d 701 (Del. 1983).

Under the traditional approach, where there was no material conflict of interest, a corporate decision would be reviewed under the duty of care. The duty of care requires directors and officers to adequately inform themselves before making a decision. Decisions subject to the duty of care are protected by the business judgment rule. Under the standard formulation in Delaware, this rule is 'a presumption that in making a business decision the directors of a corporation acted on an informed basis, in good faith, and in the honest belief that the action taken was in the best interests of the company'.[7] The chances of plaintiffs succeeding in attacking a decision protected by the business judgment rule are exceedingly slim (Black et al. 2006). The most notorious instance in which plaintiffs succeeded in obtaining a judgment in a care case was *Smith v. Van Gorkom*.[8] Van Gorkom quickly elicited a legislative response: corporations were to be allowed to include in their charters a provision limiting or eliminating director liability for a violation of the duty of care.[9] These provisions do not allow limits on liability for violations of the duty of loyalty, and they typically also do not allow limits on liability for behavior that is not in good faith – a limit which we shall see has become important.

Scholars have applied economic concepts to analyze fiduciary duty in corporate law (Easterbrook & Fischel 1991; Smith 2002). They have asked why fiduciary duty limits on board and officer behavior exist at all, and also why the legal limits are not stricter than described above. This analysis has occurred primarily through the lens of principal-agent theory (Frankel 2007; Easterbrook & Fischel 1993; Cooter & Freedman 1991; Jensen & Meckling 1976; Berle & Means 1932). The concept of a principal-agent relationship in economics is somewhat more expansive than the legal definition. For an economist, an agency relationship exists where one person acts on behalf of another (Ross 1973). That is an element of the legal definition, but the legal definition also requires that the agent act subject to the control of the principal, and that both principal and agent assent to the relationship (Restatement Third of Agency § 1.01). Under the economics definition directors are agents of shareholders, while under the legal definition they are not because shareholders lack the requisite control. The economics of agency focuses on the incentive for advantage-taking by the agent created by asymmetric information (Milgrom & Roberts 1992).

Under an economic approach, fiduciary duty law is seen as one mechanism among many for reducing the transaction costs created by that asymmetric information and the resulting advantage-taking, or threat thereof. The threat of being sued for violation of one's fiduciary duty helps deter agents from taking advantage of their principals. The possible ways in which an agent may take advantage of a principal are nearly infinite, and it is not remotely possible to fully anticipate in advance and contract for all possible circumstances. The law of fiduciary duty sets forth a broad standard limiting agents' behavior, and then allows courts to interpret that standard in particular circumstances (Easterbrook & Fischel 1991).

The foregoing sets forth a widely-accepted reason for why fiduciary duties exist, but does not explain why the duties are so limited. The business judgment rule makes liability for violating the duty of care extremely unlikely – why? Many explanations have been offered. One explanation is that other mechanisms may sufficiently motivate the desired conduct: there may be little need for the additional deterrence offered by the existence of fiduciary duty

---

[7]   *Aronson v. Lewis*, 473 A.2d 805 (Del. 1984).
[8]   488 A.2d 858 (Del. 1985).
[9]   Del. Gen. Corp. L. §102(b)(7); Mod. Bus. Corp. Act §2.02(b)(4).

suits. Compensation contracts may provide strong incentives to pursue the interests of the corporation. There is a large economics literature on optimal compensation contracts, and much work has been done applying that literature to compensation within corporations (Murphy 2002), although some believe that executive compensation contracts have themselves been hijacked by corporate officers to enrich themselves at the expense of shareholders (Bebchuk & Fried 2004).[10]

Another mechanism which may constrain directors from being bad agents for their principals is the threat of a hostile takeover. A poorly-run corporation will see its stock price fall, making it vulnerable to a possible takeover (Manne 1965). However, boards have found effective ways to block hostile takeovers, greatly reducing this threat. Responding to such antitakeover defenses has itself become a major topic of fiduciary duty law, discussed in the next section and elsewhere in this volume (Davidoff Ch. 12). Product market competition and the threat of bankruptcy also limit executive incompetence (Hart 1983; Nickell 1996). Shareholder voting for directors also helps focus directors on the interests of shareholders, although in US public corporations, boards themselves have traditionally dominated the director nomination process – a situation about which there is now considerable debate.[11] Norms of good behavior may also help guide executive behavior (Eisenberg 1993; Rock 1997; Rock & Wachter 2001; Hill & McDonnell 2009; Gold 2009).

That costly shareholder lawsuits may be brought to enforce fiduciary duties also helps explain judicially-imposed limits on those duties. Plaintiffs' lawyers may bring such suits even when they have little merit, as a way of extorting payments from boards that wish to avoid the hassles, expenses, and bad press that arise out of such suits (Swanson 1993). That substantial liability may arise simply because a decision turns out badly may make boards and officers unduly risk averse even if the chance of liability is small. This is especially true for public corporations, since in such corporations, directors and officers capture only a relatively small fraction of the gains from decisions that turn out well (Bainbridge 2002). Hindsight bias on the part of courts and juries may also increase the risk of liability where decisions turn out badly even though ex ante those decisions are justified, so that doctrines limiting liability may help counter-balance such a tendency (Arkes & Schipani 1994).

Courts and legislatures have tried to reduce the costs of abusive suits by weeding them out of the judicial system at an early stage. In Delaware, the shareholder demand requirement does this.[12] Since making demand will very likely lead to demand being rejected and a court upholding that rejection,[13] plaintiffs will claim that demand is excused. To do so, however, in their complaints they need to present particularized facts which suggest either that a majority of the board is interested or lacking in independence or else that the board does not deserve the protection of the business judgment rule.[14] If they cannot produce particularized facts at the beginning of the case, the case is dismissed.

An important recent explanation of the business judgment rule arises from the director primacy theory of Stephen Bainbridge (Bainbridge 2003, 2004). Bainbridge argues that boards in public corporations provide a way to centralize authoritative decision-making and

---

[10]   Executive compensation is explored further in this volume in Walker (Ch. 13).
[11]   In this volume, *see* Ferri (Ch. 11) and Smith (Ch. 4).
[12]   This requirement only applies for cases characterized as derivative actions.
[13]   *Levine v. Smith*, 591 A.2d 194 (Del. 1991).
[14]   *Aronson v. Lewis*, 473 A.2d 805 (Del. 1984).

thereby reduce transaction costs. If courts have the power to review too many board decisions, however, the locus of authority is transferred away from the board. The business judgment rule thus operates as an abstention doctrine by which courts refuse themselves the power to review unconflicted board decisions, and thus leave authority with the board.[15]

Why, then, are boards and officers not protected by the business judgment rule in cases involving a conflict of interest? The standard answer is that in such cases, those with the conflict have a strong incentive to make a decision that is not in the best interests of the corporation. The sorts of incentive mechanisms described above may often not be strong enough to induce appropriate behavior in the face of serious temptation. Moreover, there are often good unconflicted alternatives to conflict transactions. Rules which impose barriers to conflict transactions thus address situations where the threat of misbehavior is particularly high and where the costs associated with judicial intervention are often relatively low.

But the barrier the law imposes is not insurmountable. The law has moved from the old common law practice of voiding conflicted transactions altogether. As described above, board or shareholder approval of a conflicted transaction or court approval of the transaction as fair will allow a corporation to carry out the transaction without giving rise to a cause of action. Is this approach appropriate, given the justification we have just seen for greater scrutiny of such transactions? The argument in favor is that at least some conflicted transactions may be quite good for the corporation, and there may not be good unconflicted alternatives available. Clearly directors and officers must receive compensation, which creates inevitable conflicts. Manager or controlling shareholder buyouts of a corporation may often put control in the hands of those best able to make decisions, and give them a greater stake in the consequences of their decisions. And so on – a complete ban on conflicted transactions would ban many worthwhile dealings.

The question then becomes: who should be able to approve conflict transactions, and how much scrutiny should courts give to the process? Many different answers to those questions exist both in the law and in scholarship. In Delaware, where the transaction does not involve a controlling shareholder, if adequate disclosure is made, the courts are relatively deferential to decisions made by the disinterested directors to approve a transaction (Brown 2006–2007). This involves a judgment that directors are generally to be trusted in making decisions that affect the interests of fellow directors or top officers. The ALI suggests a somewhat closer review in such circumstances, requiring that the transaction be one that the directors could reasonably believe to be fair to the corporation.[16] This suggests a judgment that directors may not be able to be objective regarding the interests of their fellow directors. The Delaware courts trust board approval less in cases where the interests of a controlling shareholder are at stake.[17] The judgment is that directors will find it hard to be objective about the interests of a shareholder who has the power to install and remove members of the board. If disinterested shareholders give their approval, courts will review the transaction under either the business judgment standard or, if the transaction is with a controlling shareholder, under the fairness standard but with a burden shift (Brown 2003).

Some scholars think that courts should be more skeptical of board decisions approving conflicted transactions because of concerns about objectivity in such cases (Hill &

---

[15]   For more on board primacy in this volume, *see* Bainbridge (Ch. 2).
[16]   American Law Institute (1994) § 5.02(a)(2)(B).
[17]   *Kahn v. Lynch Communication Systems, Inc.*, 638 A.2d 1110 (Del. 1994).

McDonnell 2012). Some argue that the fairness standard as applied is too weak (Mitchell 1993). Others argue that moving to business judgment review after disinterested director approval (Brown 2006–2007; Eisenberg 1988; Brudney 1982) or shareholder approval (Brown 2003) is inappropriate. Others defend the prevailing practice (Bainbridge 2002; Dooley 1992; Hansen et al. 1990). The debates are closely related to concerns about structural bias that we discuss in the remaining sections of this chapter.

## 3.  THE PROLIFERATION OF STANDARDS OF REVIEW

A contemporary analysis of fiduciary duty standards, particularly in Delaware, is considerably more complicated than that laid out in the previous section. Over the last few decades, a variety of standards of review beyond those used for the duty of care and the classical duty of loyalty have proliferated. The Delaware courts have developed these standards in situations not covered by the classical duty of loyalty in which distrusting board decision-making nevertheless seems appropriate. But in these situations, courts are not well positioned to make independent judgments about what is best for the corporation. This creates a dilemma for the courts. The new standards thus attempt to balance judicial scrutiny and restraint in ways appropriate to particular types of circumstances (Velasco 2004, 2009; Hill & McDonnell 2007a, 2007b). This section analyzes the standards created starting in the 1980s; the next section examines how those standards have developed in the last half-decade or so.

### Changes of Control

Several important lines of cases emerged in Delaware in the 1980s in response to the wave of hostile and friendly takeovers. The *Unocal* standard applies where a corporation adopts measures intended to defend against the threat of a hostile takeover.[18] It involves a two-step analysis. In the first step, the court asks if the measure was adopted in response to a legitimate threat to corporate policy and effectiveness. If so, the court then asks if the response is reasonable in relation to the threat posed. This two-step analysis was deliberately crafted to occupy a middle ground between lenient business judgment review and the stricter scrutiny of the duty of loyalty. In responding to hostile takeovers, the threat that the directors and officers are acting to entrench themselves is ever-present. Officers' positions, salaries, and perks are at risk, as are their earnings as directors. Outside directors also have some stake in keeping their positions, albeit a smaller one than officers do. Moreover, they may identify too closely with the interests of officers. Still, there may be good business reasons for adopting anti-takeover measures. Whether or not a takeover should be discouraged involves a complex business calculation that courts are not well-placed to carry out. The intermediate standard of review in *Unocal* was intended to give boards some breathing room to make those judgments, while still providing closer judicial scrutiny than under the business judgment rule because of the danger of the entrenchment motivation (Balotti et al. 2005). No consensus exists as to whether the appropriate balance has been achieved (Gordon 1997; Loewenstein 2001; Bainbridge 2006; Gilson 2001; Gilson & Kraakman 1989).

---

[18]   *Unocal Corp. v. Mesa Petroleum Co.*, 493 A.2d 946 (Del. 1985).

Another standard of review developed in Delaware at approximately the same time applies where the board puts a corporation up for sale or the corporation's break-up is inevitable. Here the *Revlon* standard applies,[19] and judicial review is more searching than under *Unocal*. The board must show that it has taken steps to assure that shareholders are receiving the best price available in selling the corporation. The concern in these situations is that corporations under pressure from a number of potential suitors will choose one which offers the best deal for its officers and directors rather than for its shareholders. Moreover, sales of corporate control are crucial events in the life of a corporation which may drastically change the nature of the shareholders' investment.

The general understanding is that as applied, the *Unocal* standard has little bite, and rarely constrains boards from adopting antitakeover mechanisms (Balotti et al. 2005). The *Revlon* standard has more constraining power when applied, although the courts have interpreted the circumstances that trigger *Revlon* relatively narrowly,[20] and have interpreted what Revlon requires quite narrowly as well.[21] There is debate as to the effects of giving boards much discretion in change of control transactions, and whether the courts should review such transactions more strictly or leniently than they currently do (Bainbridge 2006; Bebchuk 2002; Thompson & Smith 2001). Corporate changes of control are discussed in more detail in this volume in Davidoff (Ch. 12).

Freezeouts by controlling shareholders have received stricter judicial scrutiny than takeovers by other acquirers. The potential for abuse is obvious when a controlling shareholder can force the minority to surrender their shares at whatever price the controller chooses. Delaware courts have applied the traditional duty of loyalty/entire fairness standard to such transactions, although procedurally adequate approval by independent directors or a majority of the minority shareholders could shift the burden of proof.[22] More recently, controlling shareholders have attempted to avoid this scrutiny by using tender offers to reach a 90% ownership threshold, and then consummating a short-form merger to freeze out the remaining shareholders. Initial cases suggested this procedure would not be subject to fairness review,[23] although we shall see in the next section that this law has evolved. Some scholars have questioned whether this procedure has been made too easy (Stevelman 2007; Gilson & Gordon 2005), and early evidence suggested that it led to lower shareholder premia (Subramanian 2005).

**The Shareholder Franchise**

The *Blasius* standard of review, developed in Delaware in the 1980s, is also typically related to battles over corporate control.[24] This standard applies where the court determines that a board's action is intended to impede the shareholder franchise. If so, the action violates the board's fiduciary duty unless the board can show a compelling justification for what it did.

---

[19]    *Revlon, Inc. v. MacAndrews & Forbes Holdings, Inc.*, 506 A.2d 173 (Del. 1986).
[20]    *Paramount Communications, Inc. v. Time, Inc.*, 571 A.2d 1140 (Del. 1989).
[21]    *Lyondell Chemical Co. v. Ryan*, 970 A.2d 235 (Del. 2009), *see infra* text at n. 43.
[22]    *Weinberger v. UOP, Inc.*, 457 A.2d 701 (Del. 1983).
[23]    *In re Siliconix Shareholders' Litig.*, 2001 WL 716787 (Del. Ch. 2001); *Glassman v. Unocal Exploration Corp.*, 777 A.2d 242 (Del. 2001).
[24]    *Blasius Industries, Inc. v. Atlas Corp.*, 564 A.2d 651 (1988).

Attempts to impede the shareholder franchise became important in hostile takeover battles during the 1980s – as boards adopted effective takeover defenses, bidders moved to using proxy contests to try to remove incumbent directors, and those incumbents in turn sought ways to stop or delay the efforts to oust them (Klein 1991; Warren & Abrams 1992). Courts are, and arguably should be, more willing to scrutinize board action that limits shareholder collective action than board action involving ordinary operating decisions (Stone 2006). Several scholars have suggested that courts do and should exercise heavier scrutiny where boards limit shareholder power to vote or sell their shares (Paredes 2003; Thompson & Smith 2004).

**Special Litigation Committees**

Another stringent standard of review also emerged in the 1980s in a different kind of circumstance where skepticism of board decisions seems justified: recommendations from special litigation committees (SLCs). Boards use SLCs to try to wrest control of shareholder derivative litigation, especially in cases where the demand requirement has been excused or is likely to be excused, i.e., there is some substantive evidence that the board is compromised. Boards appoint new directors uninvolved in the underlying case to an SLC, which reviews the claims and makes a recommendation as to whether or not the case should continue. Generally the SLC recommends dismissing the case. The question then arises: how should a court should treat that recommendation?

In some states, the courts give business judgment deference to SLC recommendations so long as the SLC members have disinterested independence.[25] However, in Delaware SLC recommendations get less deference. Under the *Zapata* standard, the SLC must first prove that its members were disinterested and independent and that they reasonably informed themselves before recommending dismissal.[26] This step resembles business judgment review, but the burden is on the SLC to show an informed and independent judgment, rather than upon the plaintiff to show that the judgment was uninformed or showed a lack of independence. Even if the SLC satisfies this burden, the court may (and generally will) move to a second step, in which the board exercises its own independent judgment to determine whether the case should be dismissed.

The Delaware courts adopted the *Zapata* standard out of a concern over structural bias (Davis 2005). Even though the members of the SLC do not have a personal stake in the litigation, they decide whether or not a case should continue against fellow board members, and those defendant board members are often the persons who appointed the SLC members to the board. There are very good reasons to doubt the SLC members are likely to exercise independent judgment under these circumstances. Moreover, the business value in allowing boards to stop cases in which there is enough evidence to excuse demand is dubious if one believes that shareholder derivative suits are at least sometimes valuable for shareholders, giving less reason to defer to director judgment in these cases.[27]

---

[25]   *Auerbach v. Bennett*, 47 N.Y.2d 619, 393 N.E.2d 994 (1979).

[26]   *Zapata Corp. v. Maldonado*, 430 A.2d 779 (Del. 1981).

[27]   For an empirical study of SLCs, *see* Myers (2009). Myers finds that cases involving SLCs are resolved faster than other cases, usually ending in settlements, and suggests they may be seen as a form of alternative dispute resolution.

## Disclosure

Another fiduciary duty, somewhat murkily related to other duties, has emerged over the last several decades: a duty to disclose material facts to shareholders under certain circumstances (Hamermesh 1996). Where shareholders approve transactions in which a director or controlling shareholder has conflicting interests, this duty requires disclosure of all material facts in order for shareholder approval to have a cleansing effect. The duty is weaker where directors are not interested (Hamermesh 1996). This duty to disclose overlaps substantially with federal securities law requirements, and Robert Thompson has argued that it provides a way for Delaware to assert authority in an area mostly claimed by the federal government, while linking disclosure to substantive shareholder protection in a way only Delaware can under existing law (Thompson 2009).

## Good Faith

A more recent and important development in fiduciary duty law is elaboration of the requirement of good faith. Over the last two decades, shareholder plaintiffs in Delaware have increasingly come to argue that the defendants' behavior was not in good faith. Several features of fiduciary duty law have encouraged them to do so. If a plaintiff can succeed in demonstrating that a particular action was in bad faith, that action is no longer protected by the business judgment rule (see above formulation of the rule in *Aronson*). Even more important, action in bad faith is not exculpable under Section 102(b)(7) of Delaware corporate law.

As plaintiffs started to plead bad faith more frequently, Delaware courts have gradually been forced to delineate what sorts of actions qualify. The leading statement to date comes from the *Disney* case.[28] *Disney* dealt with the hiring and firing of Michael Ovitz, who received over $130 million in severance after a year in which he did a very bad job, which is quite a winning payday even by the standards of contemporary American corporate officers. The plaintiffs argued that the actions of the board in approving his contract were so far from appropriate best practices that they were in bad faith. The Chancery Court allowed the case to go to trial on this theory, but ultimately found the behavior was not in bad faith.

In the process, the Chancery Court stated what is now the leading standard in Delaware for when action is in bad faith, saying that a 'failure to act in good faith may be shown … where the fiduciary intentionally fails to act in the face of a known duty to act, demonstrating a conscious disregard for his duties'.[29] The Supreme Court affirmed this as an appropriate standard.

Another important context where good faith has been applied is in board monitoring of behavior by lower-level corporate employees. In the well-known *Caremark* case,[30] the Chancery Court held that even in the absence of red flags, the board has a duty to put in place some sort of system for monitoring whether employees are complying with relevant laws. However, the Court gave great latitude to boards to determine what such a system should look

---

[28]   The three leading opinions in the case are *In re Walt Disney Co. Derivative Litig.*, 825 A.2d 275 (Del. Ch. 2003); *In re Walt Disney Co. Derivative Litig.*, 907 A.2d 693 (Del. Ch. 2005); and *In re Walt Disney Co. Derivative Litig.*, 906 A.2d 27 (Del. 2006).

[29]   *Disney* 906 A.2d at 67.

[30]   *In re Caremark Int'l Inc. Derivative Litig.*, 698 A.2d 959 (Del. Ch. 1996).

like: 'only a sustained or systematic failure of the board to exercise oversight – such as an utter failure to attempt to assure a reasonable information and reporting system exists – will establish the lack of good faith that is a necessary condition to liability'.[31] Thus, as long as a board has any sort of legal compliance monitoring system in place at all, it is extremely unlikely to be held liable for how it designs or implements that system.

The Delaware Supreme Court affirmed that *Caremark* is good law in *Stone v. Ritter*.[32] More controversially, it placed the obligation to act in good faith as an element of the duty of loyalty, thereby upsetting the flow charts in many a corporations class.

Scholars in recent years have spent considerable effort analyzing Delaware's emerging good faith jurisprudence.[33] Hillary Sale argues that the concept of good faith should be developed along lines similar to the scienter requirement in federal securities law; she argues as well that good faith doctrine can provide a way to prod directors to more actively monitor corporate behavior (Sale 2004). Sean Griffith analyzes good faith as a rhetorical device that allows Delaware courts to alternate between greater and lesser scrutiny of boards in response to pressures from competing states and the federal government (Griffith 2005). Christopher Bruner argues that the law of good faith, and Delaware fiduciary duty law generally, have evolved in a convoluted way reflecting a tension between, on the one hand, the need to reduce agency costs and police board misbehavior and on the other, the need for boards to attract strong director candidates and to limit risk aversion (Bruner 2006).

In our writing on good faith, we have suggested that the courts may be using the concept to police various forms of structural bias (Hill & McDonnell 2007a, 2007b). We characterize a range of circumstances where self-interest may be more attenuated than in traditional loyalty cases, or where directors may defer to officers because that's how they would like to be treated in their own companies – what we call a 'pernicious golden rule'. Executive compensation, at issue in *Disney*, is a leading example of an important recurring kind of circumstance in which structural bias may be present. Changes of corporate control are another crucial example. Understood broadly, structural bias can arise for a wide range of corporate decisions. We will see, though, that Delaware courts seem to have backed off from aggressively using good faith to police structural bias (or much of anything else).

Indeed, the range is too wide for courts to provide searching scrutiny in all cases where structural bias is traditionally present – doing so would involve courts much more deeply in corporate decision-making than they are at present, contrary to all the strong policy arguments underlying the business judgment rule. And yet there are good reasons to be concerned about the objectivity of board decision-making in situations involving structural bias. The various intermediate standards of review discussed in this section are attempts by the Delaware courts to calibrate judicial scrutiny for different sorts of situations involving structural bias. Where the potential for bias is high and the benefits of allowing unfettered board discretion are relatively low, courts set a stricter standard of review (e.g. *Zapata*). Where the potential for bias is low and the benefits of allowing unfettered board discretion are high, courts set a weaker standard of review (e.g. *Caremark*). We array the leading Delaware cases and standards of review along a continuum from traditional care cases to traditional loyalty

---

[31]   *Ibid*, 971.
[32]   *Stone v. Ritter*, 911 A.2d 363 (Del. 2006), *see infra* 56.
[33]   Others beyond those discussed here include Bishop (2006), Duggin & Goldman (2006), Eisenberg (2006), Hintmann (2005), Nowicki (2007), and Rosenberg (2004).

cases, with the cases discussed in this section aligned in between (Hill & McDonnell 2007b). Velasco also views fiduciary duties at various levels of abstraction, but argues that arranging standards along a continuum is misleading, and that good faith is not intermediate between care and traditional loyalty (Velasco 2009).

## 4. WHERE ARE WE NOW?

There have been significant developments in the bodies of case law and standards of review discussed above over the last several years, and scholarship has begun to respond.

In the takeover context of the *Unocal* and *Revlon* standards, several cases have modified how courts creatively fashion equitable remedies, while others have added further nuance to the vexed question of poison pills. The *Blasius* standard, governing action that threatens the shareholder franchise, has been softened somewhat. There have been interesting analyses of director independence in the context of special litigation committees, where the *Zapata* standard applies. Finally, the doctrine surrounding good faith has continued to evolve significantly. One other notable recent development is increasing focus on the fiduciary duties of officers, as opposed to directors.

### Changes of Control

Applying the *Revlon* standard, several recent cases in the takeover context demonstrate how courts can find director behavior to be defective, but ultimately provide ways for the directors to cure the defect.[34] In all these cases, the court required corrective disclosures before shareholder votes could be held. A source of concern has been how companies structure provisions requiring or limiting shopping for other potential buyers. Some evidence suggests that properly-structured 'go-shop' provisions can increase shareholder premia (Subramanian 2008).

Several other cases involve takeover defenses, in particular the poison pill, and hence involve the ongoing development of the *Unocal* standard. In *Yucaipa American Alliance Fund II L.P. v. Riggio et al.,*[35] the court allowed a poison pill whose trigger was 20% ownership, but which grandfathered the 30% holdings of the controlling shareholder, Riggio. It noted that the pill was adopted to prevent a creeping acquisition of shares that did not yield a control premium, a valid purpose, and that Yucaipa in any event had a good enough chance of winning control by mounting a proxy fight. In *Selectica, Inc. v. Versata, Inc.*, C.A. No. 4241-VCN (Del. Ch. 2010), the court validated a poison pill intended to help a company preserve its net operating losses using the Unocal standard. The pill was not preclusive notwithstanding that its trigger was acquisition of 4.99% of the company's shares. The standard for preclusiveness is deliberately high: 'Such a high standard operates to exclude only the most egregious defensive responses' (see http://courts.delaware.gov/opinions/list.aspx?ag=court+of+chancery (60)). The directors' action need not be perfect – it need only be

---

34    *See In Re the Topps Company Shareholder Litigation*, C.A. No. 2786-VCS (Del. Ch. 2007); *In Re Lear Corporation Shareholder Litigation*, CA No. 2728-VCS, (Del. Ch. 2007); and *In Re Netsmart Technologies Inc. Shareholder Litigation*, C.A. No. 2563-VCS, (Del. Ch. 2007).
35    C.A. No. 5465-VCS, Del. Ch. 2010.

reasonable, where the standard of reasonableness is construed broadly. Requiring such a high standard for preclusiveness, and allowing a poison pill with a 5% trigger, has been criticized as favoring financial acquirers over strategic acquirers, and increasing the power of proxy voting advisors (Edelman & Thompson 2010).

While courts have generally allowed poison pills, there are times when poison pills have been deemed to violate fiduciary duties. In *eBay Domestic Holdings v. Newmark*,[36] the Delaware Chancery Court rescinded a poison pill enacted by Craigslist majority shareholders to prevent Craigslist minority shareholder eBay from acquiring more shares. Ebay had established a rival online classified ad site, as it was expressly allowed to do under a shareholders' agreement; the pill limited eBay's ability to acquire more shares or sell their shares to third parties. The court concluded that the pill did not pass muster under *Unocal*. The purpose the shareholders claimed to be threatened, one that maintains a culture eschewing shareholder wealth-maximization, was not cognizable under Delaware law and even if it was cognizable, the pill was not reasonable in relation to the threat posed.[37]

As noted above, several cases at the turn of the century suggested that companies could avoid fairness review in freezeouts if they used a tender offer to increase their ownership to 90% and then used a short-form merger. More recent Chancery Court cases have applied a different framework to such transactions, however. Vice-Chancellor Strine in 2005 held that fairness review would apply unless the transaction received both independent director approval and approval by the disinterested shareholders.[38] Vice-Chancellor Laster approved this standard in 2010, and noted that the Delaware Supreme Court was needed to resolve the law in this area.[39] Cain and Davidoff (2011) find evidence that the sort of procedural safeguards encouraged by this case law provide added value for shareholders.

### Shareholder Franchise

One recent case pushes management deference, in a context where courts historically had been less deferential. The court established a new and more deferential standard towards management in the context of the shareholder franchise. In previous jurisprudence (the *Blasius* standard discussed above) on the 'shareholder franchise,' where the franchise was threatened boards bore a significant burden of showing a 'compelling justification' for doing so. It was generally considered that this standard would be nearly impossible, if not impossible, to meet. But a recent decision, *Mercier v. Inter-tel*,[40] indicated that a compelling justification might be easier to find than previously thought; it also indicated that where what was at issue was not a director election that was purportedly being interfered with, a compelling justification might not be needed. Rather, it might be sufficient to demonstrate a legitimate and reasonable corporate objective, so long as the 'interference' (typically taking the form of a postponement of a shareholder vote) wasn't preclusive or coercive – meeting the Unocal test will apparently suffice. One commentator has argued that *Blasius* should remain the default rule, subject to shareholder ability to opt out ex ante, in cases where the board seeks

---

36   CA No. 3705-CC (Del. Ch., 2010).
37   The court also rescinded a right of first offer, but left intact a staggered board.
38   *In re Cox Communications, Inc. Shareholders' Litig.*, 879 A.2d 604 (Del. Ch. 2005).
39   *In re CNX Gas Corp. Shareholders' Litig.*, 4 A.3d 397 (Del. Ch. 2010).
40   929 A.2d 786 (Del. Ch. 2007).

to postpone a shareholder vote required under state law for a transaction. The potential for managerial misconduct is high enough in such circumstances to warrant the extra costs imposed (Kling 2010).

## Special Litigation Committees

In *London v. Tyrrell*[41] the Court applied the *Zapata* standard of review, for special litigation committee recommendations, in an interesting way. This case involved a special litigation committee formed to respond to a shareholder's attempt to bring a derivative lawsuit. Under *Zapata*, the committee has the burden of showing its independence and the reasonableness of its investigation; to appraise reasonableness, the court uses its 'independent business judgment'. While neither member of the SLC had a personal stake in the transactions at issue in the case, one was the husband of the defendant's cousin (as to which the court noted: 'appointing an interested director's family member to an SLC will always position a corporation on the low ground' (see http://courts.delaware.gov/opinions/list.aspx?ag=court+of+chancery (35)) and the other was the defendant's former employer, who had 'a great respect' for the defendant. The defendant was, the SLC member said, 'very helpful in helping me get a good price for my company' (see http://courts.delaware.gov/opinions/list.aspx?ag=court+of+chancery (37)). The court found that the SLC had not met its burden of showing its independence. In an older case, *Oracle*,[42] the court also denied the SLC's motion to terminate derivative litigation on grounds that the SLC had not met its burden of showing independence. The SLC members were Stanford professors, Grundfest and Garcia-Molina. One director who was a defendant in the derivative litigation was a Stanford professor as well, and had long-standing professional ties with Grundfest. Another director, Lucas, was a Stanford alumnus who had given significant amounts to Stanford, some of which had funded Grundfest's research. Yet another director, Ellison, one of the richest men in America and a prominent figure in Silicon Valley, where Stanford is located, had given large amounts to Stanford and was publicly considering giving more to Stanford in the future.

## Good Faith

Good faith jurisprudence has evolved considerably in recent years (Strine et al. 2010). After some language that suggested good faith might have real force in addressing structural bias, the more recent cases have stressed a very limited conception of intentional violations and derelictions of duty, a standard that will be very hard to meet in most cases. Consider in this regard *Lyondell Chem. Co. v. Ryan*,[43] a case involving an acquisition proposal accepted by the Board. The Court of Chancery was poised to find directors in violation of their Revlon duties, pointing to the following facts: the acquired company knew it was 'in play' given that a 13D filing had been made, and didn't do much in response; the Board's meetings considering the acquisition proposal lasted no more than seven hours; the transaction was negotiated and finalized in less than a week; the company did not shop itself or otherwise conduct a market check, and the deal given to the acquirer gave the acquirer considerable deal

---

41  C. A. No. 3321-CC (Del. Ch. March 11, 2010).
42  *In Re Oracle Corp. Derivative Litig.*, 824 A. 2d 917 (2003).
43  970 A.2d 235 (Del. 2009).

protections.[44] The Supreme Court found for the directors, noting that notwithstanding that they had not done a market check, they generally knew about market value of the company and the industry; they had tried to negotiate a higher price (albeit not 'seriously' pressing the bidder); Deutsche Bank, the company's investment banker, said the price was fair and that no other bidder was likely to offer more; and finally, on many metrics, the price was quite high (characterized in the opinion as a 'blowout price'). The court further noted that 99% of share-holders voted in favor of the transaction. The court held that '[o]nly if [the directors] *knowingly and completely failed to undertake their responsibilities* would they breach their duty of loyalty.' '[T]he inquiry should have been whether those [disinterested] directors *utterly failed* to attempt to obtain the best sale price.'[45]

With such language, it's hard to imagine a case in which directors would be found liable for breaching their duty of good faith. Indeed, despite some ambiguity in the language of the earlier good faith cases, especially *Disney*, the duty of good faith is clearly being interpreted as a duty not to act in bad faith rather than an affirmative duty to act in good faith. See also *Wayne County Employees' Ret. Sys.* v. *Corti*[46] in which the court applied *Lyondell v. Ryan.* Again it held that the applicable standard was that the directors must have 'utterly failed' to attempt to obtain the best sale price (see http://courts.delaware.gov/opinions/list.aspx?ag= court+of+chancery (38)). *Wayne County* also reiterated the holding in *Lyondell* and other cases that there was 'no single blueprint' boards must follow to fulfill their Revlon duties (see http://courts.delaware.gov/opinions/list.aspx?ag=court+of+chancery (25)). Plaintiffs in Wayne County argued that the failure to get a control premium violated the board's Revlon duties; the court held to the contrary:

> Thus, plaintiff's allegation that the board failed to obtain a 'control premium' for Activision share-holders is, at most, a thinly veiled attack on the adequacy of the price the board obtained in the sale of control. If the directors fulfilled their fiduciary duties in the sale of control, however, the Court will not second guess the business decision of the board ... . This process-based approach to evaluating director action in a sale of control is consistent with the business judgment rule and the foundational principle of Delaware corporate law that the directors, and not the court, properly manage the corporation. (See http://courts.delaware.gov/opinions/list.aspx?ag=court+of+chancery (40))

Some commentators have argued vigorously that the duty of good faith should be interpreted narrowly. One commentator has argued that courts lack the institutional competence to aggressively oversee good faith and furthermore, that 'best practices' are being followed in today's boardrooms without the specter of liability (Bratton 2010). Another commentator has argued that the duty should be interpreted more broadly, but that companies should be allowed to opt out of that standard (Lund 2010).

The constricted duty of good faith leads to continuing deference to boards where there is no taint of self-interest. This is true not only for director decisions, but also for failures to monitor. In *In Re Citigroup Inc. Shareholder Derivative Litigation*,[47] plaintiffs were suing the Citigroup directors for not having monitored Citigroup's risk-taking behavior. The firm lost billions, and was bailed out by the US Government. The court held that:

---

[44]  *Lyondell Chem. Co. v. Ryan*, 317-VCN (Del. Ch. 2008).
[45]  970 A. 2d. 235, 243-4.
[46]  C.A. No. 3534-CC (Del. Ch. July 24, 2009).
[47]  964 A. 2d. 106 (Del. Ch. 2009).

[t]o establish oversight liability a plaintiff must show that directors *knew* they were not discharging their fiduciary obligations or that the directors demonstrated a *conscious* disregard for their responsibilities such as by failing to act in the fact of a known duty to act. The test is rooted in concepts of bad faith; indeed, a showing of bad faith is a *necessary condition* to director oversight liability.[48]

It noted that 'Citigroup was in the business of taking on and managing investment and other business risks … Oversight duties under Delaware law are not designed to subject directors, even expert directors, to *personal liability* for failure to predict the future and to properly evaluate business risk.'[49] Another case, *In Re Dow Chemical Company Derivative Litigation*,[50] involving a company (Dow) failing to complete a merger with another company, Rohm & Haas, stressed that the standards described in Citigroup were not higher when the transaction at issue effectively 'bet the company' (see http://courts.delaware.gov/opinions/list.aspx?ag=court+of+chancery (25)). The court noted that 'A business decision made by a majority of disinterested, independent board members is entitled to the deferential business judgment rule regardless of whether it is an isolated transaction or part of a larger transformative strategy.' (See http://courts.delaware.gov/opinions/list.aspx?ag=court+of+chancery (26)). Some scholars have defended this unwillingness to extend liability for business oversight (Bainbridge 2009; Miller 2010), while others have suggested courts should be less deferential (Neres 2010).

*Stone v. Ritter* and *Disney* might have heralded a new age in which director behavior was looked at more carefully, not just for obvious types of conflicted behavior, but for behavior that furthered directors' own interests more expansively construed. Expanding the scope of the 'duty of loyalty' could have brought to bear the rhetoric of loyalty, in its more expansive constructions, on the way in which directors comported themselves: consider in this regard the memorable phrase from the famous *Meinhard v. Salmon* case about the duty of loyalty requiring 'the punctilio of an honor the most sensitive'. The concept of good faith could have been developed to mean something closer to affirmative good faith. But this did not happen. Indeed, quite the opposite did: courts have used the expansive rhetoric of loyalty to create a high bar for liability, requiring utter failure to act in the face of a known duty to act, intentional violations and so on. In *Lyondell v Ryan*, the Court quoted approvingly from *Lear*: 'In the transactional context, *[an] extreme set of facts* [is] required to sustain a disloyalty claim premised on the notion that disinterested directors were intentionally disregarding their duties'.[51] The duty of good faith has become a duty not to act in bad faith; where self-interest in any traditional sense is not at issue, directors enjoy considerable deference. But courts have sometimes articulated at considerable length in dicta guidance as to how directors ought to behave; as we have argued in our other work, especially given the role of corporate lawyers in ensuring roles for themselves in advising clients on the intricacies of the courts' pronouncements, we expect this guidance to have an effect well beyond what might be expected if the dicta only had the force of a prediction of future outcomes in litigation.

---

48   *In Re Citigroup Inc. Shareholder Derivative Litigation*, 123.
49   *Ibid*, 131.
50   No. 4349-CC (Jan. 11, 2010).
51   *Lyondell v. Ryan*, 243 (emphasis added), *see supra* text at n. 21.

**Officers**

Most case law and scholarship on corporate fiduciary duty has focused on the duties of directors or controlling shareholders. Recently there has been somewhat increased focus on the duties of corporate officers. At least two factors explain this new attention. First, the Delaware long-arm jurisdiction statute was amended to grant jurisdiction over all officers of Delaware corporations after January 1, 2004.[52] Second, the Delaware exculpation clause applies only to directors, not officers.[53] Thus, attacking the behavior of a defendant as an officer rather than a director now provides an alternative, and in some ways easier, way to hold her personally liable. This raises the question of what standards of liability should apply to officers, and in particular whether or not the business judgment rule should protect officers in the same way that it protects directors.

Some argue that officers should be held to a stricter standard of care, and that the business judgment rule should not apply, or at least should apply more weakly. The business judgment rule is justified in part as a way to encourage directors to serve and take risks, and to protect the authority of the board, but these rationales are weaker for officers (Johnson 2005; Johnson & Millon 2005). Others argue that those policy justifications for the business judgment rule apply just as well to officers (Hamermesh & Gilchrist 2005). Some argue for an intermediate position, e.g., that the business judgment rule should not be available to officers for cases favored by the board, but not in cases in which the board objects to the litigation (Crespi 2006). In a recent case, the Delaware Supreme Court held that officers have the same fiduciary duty as directors,[54] but case law as yet gives little guidance as to how to apply that duty to the behavior of officers. One area where suits against officers could have particular traction is where the worst that can be alleged against directors is a failure to monitor. *Caremark*,[55] *Stone v. Ritter*[56] and *Citigroup*[57] come immediately to mind. Vice-Chancellor Strine has called these cases among the hardest for plaintiffs to win.[58] Showing that someone who did not act should have acted in a particular way is difficult. But *someone* acted, causing the bad result that motivates a shareholder suit – the government fines in *Caremark* and *Stone v. Ritter*, and the massive losses in *Citigroup*. The action may not constitute a breach of the duty of loyalty, but it is more likely to do so than inaction in most cases.

## 5.    WHERE IS FIDUCIARY DUTY LAW GOING? WHERE SHOULD IT BE GOING?

We can expect a steady accretion of precedents on good faith. These precedents are not apt to expand what good faith requires – indeed, quite the contrary, given the language in cases such as *Lyondell*. More generally, we can expect that absent showings of self-interest, courts

---

52    10 Del. Code § 3114(b).
53    8 Del. Code § 102(b)(7).
54    *Gantler v. Stephens*, 965 A.2d 695 (Del. 2009).
55    *See supra* text at n. 30.
56    *Stone v. Ritter*, 911 A.2d 362, 370 (Del. 2006).
57    *See supra* text at n. 48.
58    *See supra* text at n. 30, 967.

will continue to be deferential to management, as they historically have been. We also expect that judges will continue to make what is effectively law via expansive dicta and pronouncements in articles and speeches; the 'law' thereby made will have a penumbra that extends further than the law on the books.

But the law's penumbra may not be broad enough. We think law should do a better job of coming to terms with the pervasiveness of structural bias. We mean here structural bias broadly construed – not just identifiable relationships such as family or direct money ties, but the more ephemeral ties of a shared community and a shared mindset. Corporations and their shareholders deserve boards that are truly critically minded, conducting themselves without strongly biased prior beliefs favoring management deference. Law has made some inroads towards encouraging, if not requiring, directors to be more critically-minded monitors, but not enough. One area we think is particularly worthy of attention is executive compensation and in particular, the sensitivity of pay to performance. The various initiatives in the area of executive compensation, together with the stunningly bad results many firms have had in the crisis period, have had some effect; there are some indications that compensation levels may have slowed their increase, if not actually decreased, at some firms (Lublin 2010). We will soon see how short investor and policymaker memories are.

# REFERENCES

Allen, William T., Jack B. Jacobs & Leo E. Strine, Jr. (2001), 'Function Over Form: A Reassessment of Standards of Review in Delaware Corporation Law', *Business Lawyer*, 56, 1287–1321.

American Law Institute (1994), *Principles of Corporate Governance: Analysis and Recommendations*, St. Paul, Minn.: American Law Institute Publishers.

Arkes, Hal R. & Cindy A. Schipani (1994), 'Medical Malpractice v. the Business Judgment Rule: Differences in Hindsight Bias', *Oregon Law Review*, 73, 587–638.

Bainbridge, Stephen M. (2002), *Corporation Law and Economics*, New York, N.Y.: Foundation Press.

Bainbridge, Stephen M. (2003), 'Director Primacy: The Means and Ends of Corporate Governance', *Northwestern Law Review*, 97, 547–606.

Bainbridge, Stephen M. (2004), 'The Business Judgment Rule as Abstention Doctrine', *Vanderbilt Law Review*, 57, 83–130.

Bainbridge, Stephen M. (2006), '*Unocal* at 20: Director Primacy in Corporate Takeovers', *Delaware Journal of Corporate Law*, 31, 769–863.

Bainbridge, Stephen M. (2009), '*Caremark* and Enterprise Risk Management', *Journal of Corporation Law*, 34, 967–90.

Balotti, R. Franklin, Gregory V. Varallo & Brock E. Czeschin (2005), 'Unocal Revisited: Lipton's Influence on Bedrock Takeover Jurisprudence', *The Business Lawyer*, 60, 1399–1417.

Bebchuk, Lucian Arye (2002), 'The Case against Board Veto in Corporate Takeovers', *University of Chicago Law Review*, 69, 973–1035.

Bebchuk, Lucian & Jesse Fried (2004), *Pay Without Performance: The Unfulfilled Promise of Executive Compensation*, Cambridge, Mass.: Harvard University Press.

Berle, Adolf A. & Gardiner C. Means (1932), *The Modern Corporation and Private Property*, New York, N.Y.: Harcourt, Brace, and World.

Beveridge, Norwood P. (1992), 'The Corporate Director's Fiduciary Duty of Loyalty: Understanding the Self Interested Director Transaction', *DePaul Law Review*, 41, 655–688.

Bishop, Carter G. (2006), 'A Good Faith Revival of Duty of Care Liability in Business Organization Law', *Tulsa Law Review*, 41, 479–511.

Black, Bernard, Brian Cheffins & Michael Klausner (2006), 'Outside Director Liability', *Stanford Law Review*, 58, 1055–1158.

Bratton, William W. (2010), 'Lyondell: A Note of Approbation', *New York Law Review*, forthcoming.

Brown, Jr., J. Robert (2003), 'Speaking With Complete Candor: Shareholder Ratification and the Elimination of the Duty of Loyalty', *Hastings Law Journal*, 54, 641–94.

Brown, Jr., J. Robert (2006–2007), 'Disloyalty without Limits: "Independent" Directors and the Elimination of the Duty of Loyalty', *Kentucky Law Journal*, 95, 53–105.

Brudney, Victor (1982), 'The Independent Director – Heavenly City or Potemkin Village?', *Harvard Law Review*, 95, 597–659.

Bruner, Christopher M. (2006), 'Good Faith, State of Mind, and the Outer Boundaries of Director Liability in Corporate Law', *Wake Forest Law Review*, 141, 1131–1887.

Cain, Matthew & Steven M. Davidoff (2010), 'Form Over Substance? The Value of Corporate Process and Management Buy-outs', *Delaware Journal of Corporate Law*, forthcoming.

Cooter, Robert & Bradley J. Freedman (1991), 'The Fiduciary Relationship: Its Economic Character and Legal Consequences', *New York University Law Review*, 66, 1045–75.

Crespi, Gregory Scott (2006), 'Should the Business Judgment Rule Apply to Corporate Officers, and Does It Matter?', *Oklahoma City University Law Review*, 31, 237–55.

Davis Jr., Kenneth B. (2005), 'Structural Bias, Special Litigation Committees, and the Vagaries of Director Independence', *Iowa Law Review*, 90, 1305–60.

Dooley, Michael P. (1992), 'Two Models of Corporate Governance', *The Business Lawyer*, 47, 461–527.

Duggin, Sarah Helene & Stephen M. Goldman (2006), 'Restoring Trust in Corporate Directors: The Disney Standard and the "New" Good Faith', *American University Law Review*, 56, 211–74.

Easterbrook, Frank H. & Daniel Fischel (1991), *The Economic Structure of Corporate Law*, Cambridge M.A.: Harvard University Press.

Easterbrook, Frank H. & Daniel R. Fischel (1993), 'Contract and Fiduciary Duty' *Journal of Law and Economics*, 36, 425–446.

Edelman, Paul H. & Randall S. Thomas (2010), 'Resetting the Trigger on the Poison Pill: Where Should the Delaware Courts Go Next?', *Indiana Law Journal*, forthcoming.

Eisenberg, Melvin Aron (1988), 'Self-Interested Transactions in Corporate Law', *Journal of Corporation Law*, 13, 997–1009.

Eisenberg, Melvin Aron (1993), 'The Divergence of Standards of Conduct and Standards of Review in Corporate Law', *Fordham Law Review*, 62, 437–68.

Eisenberg, Melvin A. (2006), 'The Duty of Good Faith in Corporate Law', *Delaware Journal of Corporate Law*, 31, 1–75.

Frankel, Tamar (2007), *Fiduciary Law*, New York: Oxford University Press.

Gilson, Ronald (2001), '*Unocal* Fifteen Years Later', *Delaware Journal of Corporate Law*, 26, 491–514.

Gilson, Ronald & Reinier Kraakman (1989), 'Delaware's Intermediate Standard', *The Business Lawyer*, 44, 247–274.

Gilson, Ronald & Jeffrey Gordon (2005), 'Controlling Controlling Shareholders', *University of Pennsylvania Law Review*, 152, 785–843.

Gold, Andrew S. (2009), 'The New Concept of Loyalty in Corporate Law', *U.C. Davis Law Review*, 43, 457–528.

Gordon, Jeffrey N. (1997), '"Just Say Never?" Poison Pills, Deadhand Pills, and Shareholder-Adopted Bylaws: An Essay for Warren Buffett', *Cardozo Law Review*, 19, 511–52.

Griffith, Sean J. (2005), 'Good Faith Business Judgment: A Theory of Rhetoric in Corporate Law Jurisprudence', *Duke Law Journal*, 55, 1–73.

Hamermesh, Lawrence A. (1996), 'Calling off the Lynch Mob: The Corporate Director's Fiduciary Disclosure Duty', *Vanderbilt Law Review*, 49, 1087–1178.

Hamermesh, Lawrence A. & A. Gilchrist Sparks III (2005), 'Corporate Officers and the Business Judgment Rule: A Reply to Professor Johnson', *The Business Lawyer*, 60, 865–76.

Hansen, Charles, John F. Johnston & Frederick H. Alexander (1990), 'The Role of Disinterested Directors in "Conflict" Transactions: The ALI Corporate Governance Project and Existing Law', *The Business Lawyer*, 45, 2083–2103.

Hart, Oliver D. (1983), 'The Market Mechanism as an Incentive Scheme', *Bell Journal of Economics*, 14, 366–382.

Hill, Claire A. & Brett H. McDonnell (2007a), 'Disney, Good Faith & Structural Bias', *Journal of Corporation Law*, 32, 833–64.

Hill, Claire A. & Brett H. McDonnell (2007b), '*Stone v. Ritter* and the Expanding Duty of Loyalty', *Fordham Law Review*, 76, 1769–96.

Hill, Claire & Brett McDonnell (2009), 'Executive Compensation and the Optimal Penumbra of Delaware Corporation Law', *Virginia Law and Business Review*, 4, 333–72.

Hill, Claire A. & Brett H. McDonnell (2012), 'Sanitizing Interested Transactions', *Delaware Journal of Corporate Law*, forthcoming.

Hintmann, C.G. (2005), 'You Gotta Have Faith: Good Faith in the Context of Directorial Fiduciary Duties and the Future Impact on Corporate Culture', *Saint Louis University Law Journal*, 49, 571–604.

Jensen, Michael & William Meckling (1976), 'Theory of the Firm: Managerial Behavior, Agency Costs, and Ownership Structure', *Journal of Financial Economics*, 3, 305–60.

Johnson, Lyman P.Q. (2005), 'Corporate Officers and the Business Judgment Rule', *The Business Lawyer*, 60, 439–69.

Johnson, Lyman P.Q. & David Millon, (2005), 'Recalling Why Corporate Officers Are Fiduciaries', *William and Mary Law Review*, 46, 1597–1653.

Klein, Robert J. (1991), 'The Case of Heightened Scrutiny in Defense of the Shareholders' Franchise Right', *Stanford Law Journal*, 44, 129–77.

Kling, Jacob A. (2010), 'Disenfranching Shareholders: The Future of Blasius After Mercier v. Inter-Tel', *Yale Law Journal*, 119, 2040–94.

Loewenstein, Mark J. (2001), 'Unocal Revisited: No Tiger in the Tank', *Journal of Corporation Law*, 27, 1–28.

Lublin, Joann S. (2010), 'CEOs see pay fall again', *Wall Street Journal*, March 29, 2010.

Lund, Andrew C.W. (2010), 'Opting Out of Good Faith', *Florida State University Law Review*, 393–449.

Manne, Henry G. (1965), 'Mergers and the Market for Corporate Control', *Journal of Political Economy*, 73, 110–20.

Marsh Jr., Harold, (1966), 'Are Directors Trustees? Conflict of Interest and Corporate Morality', *Business Lawyer*, 22, 35–76.

Milgrom, Paul & John Roberts (1992), *Economics, Organization, and Management*, Englewood Cliff, N.J.: Prentice Hall.

Miller, Robert T. (2010), 'Oversight Liability for Risk-Management Failures at Financial Firms', *Southern California Law Review*, 84, 47–123.

Mitchell, Lawrence E. (1993), 'Fairness and Trust in Corporate Law', *Duke Law Journal*, 43, 425–91.

Murphy, Kevin J. (2002), 'Explaining Executive Compensation: Managerial Power Versus the Perceived Cost of Stock Options', *University of Chicago Law Review*, 69, 847–69.

Myers, Minor (2009), 'The Decisions of the Corporate Special Litigation Committees: An Empirical Investigation', *Indiana Law Journal*, 84, 1309–36.

Neres, Ann Tucker (2010), 'Who's the Boss? Unmasking Oversight Liability within the Corporate Power Puzzle', *Delaware Journal of Corporate Law*, 35, 199–258.

Nickell, Stephen J. (1996), 'Competition and Corporate Performance', *Journal of Political Economy*, 104, 724–46.

Nowicki, Elizabeth A. (2007), 'A Director's Good Faith', *Buffalo Law Review*, 55, 457–535.

Paredes, Troy A. (2003), 'The Firm and the Nature of Control: Toward a Theory of Takeover Law', *Journal of Corporation Law*, 29, 103–78.

Rock, Edward B. (1997), 'Saints and Sinners: How Does Delaware Corporate Law Work?', *UCLA Law Review*, 44, 1009–1107.

Rock, Edward B. & Michael L. Wachter (2001), 'Islands of Conscious Power: Law, Norms, and the Self-Governing Corporation', *University of Pennsylvania Law Review*, 1619–1700.

Rosenberg, David (2004), 'Making Sense of Good Faith in Delaware Corporate Fiduciary Law: A Contractarian Approach', *Delaware Journal of Corporate Law*, 29, 491–516.

Ross, Stephen A. (1973), 'The Economic Theory of Agency: The Principal's Problem', *American Economic Review*, 63, 134–9.

Sale, Hillary A. (2004), 'Delaware's Good Faith', *Cornell Law Review*, 89, 456–95.

Smith, D. Gordon (2002), 'The Critical Resource Theory of Fiduciary Duty', *Vanderbilt Law Review*, 55, 1399–1497.

Stevelman, Faith Kahn (2007), 'Going Private', *The Business Lawyer*, 62, 775–912.

Stone, Ethan G. (2006), 'Business Strategists and Election Commissioners: How the Meaning of Loyalty Varies with the Board's Distinct Fiduciary Roles', *The Business Lawyer*, 31, 893–947.

Strine, Jr., Leo E., Lawrence A. Hamermesh, R. Franklin Balotti & Jeffrey M. Gorris (2010), 'Loyalty's Core Demand: The Defining Role of Good Faith in Corporation Law', *Georgetown Law Journal*, 98, 629–96.

Subramanian, Guhan (2005), 'Fixing Freezeouts', *Yale Law Journal*, 115, 2–70.

Subramanian, Guhan (2008), 'Go-Shop Provisions in Private Equity Deals: Evidence and Implications', *The Business Lawyer*, 63, 729–60.

Swanson, Carol B. (1993), 'Juggling Shareholder Rights and Strike Suits in Derivative Litigation: The ALI Drops the Ball', *Minnesota Law Review*, 77, 1339–92.

Thompson, Robert B. (2009), 'Delaware's Disclosure: Moving the Line of Federal-State Corporate Regulation', *University of Illinois Law Review*, 2009, 167–90.

Thompson, Robert B. & D. Gordon Smith (2001), 'Toward a New Theory of the Shareholder Role: "Sacred Space" in Corporate Takeovers', *Texas Law Review*, 80, 261–326.

Velasco, Julian (2004), 'Structural Bias and the Need for Substantive Review', *Washington University Law Quarterly*, 82, 821–917.

Velasco, Julian (2009), 'How Many Fiduciary Duties Are There in Corporate Law?', *Southern California Law Review*, 83, 1231–1318.

Warren, Irwin H. & Kevin G. Abrams (1992), 'Evolving Standards of Judicial Review of Procedural Defenses in Proxy Contests', *The Business Lawyer*, 47, 647–70.

# 9. Empirical studies of representative litigation[1]
## Randall S. Thomas and Robert B. Thompson

## 1. INTRODUCTION

Shareholder litigation has long played a prominent role in corporate governance as a check on possible management misconduct. As compared to other possible constraints – markets, private ordering via monitors and incentives, norms, and government regulation, to name a few – shareholder litigation has been used more in the United States than elsewhere. In an economy of public companies with large numbers of shareholders and few large block holders, there have been recurring concerns about the incentives of those who bring such litigation (and their lawyers) and the outcomes that result. From the Wood report in the 1940s to the Private Securities Litigation Reform Act of 1995, legislatures and courts have responded to these concerns with new regulation of such litigation. As empirical work has grown over the last several decades to assume a core position in the study of corporate law, representative shareholder litigation has been a frequent topic. This chapter seeks to explain what empirical studies have told us about representative litigation and how such studies have shaped our understanding of corporate law.

## 2. OVERVIEW

### Litigation Embedded Within a Nexus of Managerial Constraints

American corporate governance is a combination of state and federal law in a mix that has changed over time (usually in the direction of a greater role for federal law). Understanding the role of litigation in corporate law therefore requires coverage of two sets of laws and the integration of the two as they affect corporations. We begin with state law and follow up with the federal discussion, seeking to emphasize the common threads that appear in both.

### State law
State law is the usual legal source for the creation of corporations, in defining their key members, and for providing the core governance structure. The small mid-Atlantic state of Delaware has maintained a dominant position in the market for incorporations of public companies over the last century (Bebchuk & Cohen 2003). Under the prevailing state law model (in Delaware and elsewhere), virtually all corporate power is placed in the hands of the directors or under their direction. For most of the twentieth century, a regular concern of academics was that managers have effective control of their corporations, triggering a variety

---

[1]    Portions of this chapter draw significantly from Cox and Thomas (2009a).

of suggested responses to protect shareholders and other constituencies (Berle & Means 1932). This power given by law to directors (and through them to managers) is itself subject to limits from corporate law and elsewhere. An array of market constraints – for example, the product market, the capital market, the market for employees, and the market for corporate control – limits the exercise of broad director and managerial power (Easterbrook & Fischel 1982). Government regulation in turn constrains a variety of corporate activities and quasi-government regulation, such as stock exchange listing standards, further impacts managers. Markets, the government, or the directors themselves, insert a variety of gatekeepers – e.g. auditors, analysts, lawyers, investment bankers, credit rating agencies – who in turn provide monitoring of director and managerial behavior.[2]

Shareholder litigation is one of the few structural limits on managerial power provided within corporate law itself. While Delaware corporation law explicitly puts control of the entity under the directors, it recognizes three limited but important roles for shareholders (Thompson 1999). First, they can sell their shares. As the market for corporate control has grown in the last three decades, the impact of this power has increased substantially. Second, they can vote. With the recent upswing in the influence of institutional investors (often interacting with the market for corporate control), the exercise of the shareholder franchise looks more powerful than a decade or two ago. Third, they can sue. Delaware's common law imposes fiduciary duties on managers and directors as a significant judicial check on their behavior. Such litigation, while decided by the Delaware judiciary, is brought by a shareholder against publicly held corporations, either as a derivative suit (in the name of and on behalf of the corporation with any recovery going to the corporate treasury) or as a direct suit, normally a class action. Both kinds of litigation are representative litigation as discussed here in that there is a plaintiff acting as a representative of the entire group in seeking relief.

**Federal law**
The principal federal source for litigation relating to corporations is the proscription against manipulative or deceptive acts in Section 10(b) of the Securities Exchange Act of 1934 and Rule 10b-5 promulgated by the Securities and Exchange Commission (SEC) pursuant to that section.[3] The prohibition of fraud in connection with the purchase or sale of a security covers deception practiced on a counterparty in a securities transaction. Federal law impacts corporate governance by creating liability for misstatements made to the market by managers or others who are not necessarily trading in the firm's shares. In such a setting, the class of investors who bought or sold after the misstatement was made but before its correction ensued can sue the company, its officers and its directors. In a world in which the 'turnover' rate of public company stocks has increased dramatically over a generation or two ago, a misstatement or omission made by a company about its products, financial position or other material matters, that goes uncorrected for many months, can generate a class of allegedly deceived investors that makes up a large percentage of the company's shareholders, creating enormous potential damages. In such a setting, the line between improper disclosure and improper corporate governance activities of managers fades substantially.

---

2   *See* Part III of this volume.
3   The Securities Exchange Act of 1934 §10(b) codified in 15 U.S.C. §78j and Rule 10b-5 published at 17 C.F.R. §240.10b-5.

A significant difference between the state and federal realms as to representative litigation is that the federal space overlaps with a substantial public enforcement presence that is not normally replicated at the state level. The SEC regularly brings civil proceedings for violations of the securities laws, and the Department of Justice backs up that civil action with criminal proceedings in particular circumstances. The United States spends more on public enforcement than any other country in the world in absolute dollar terms and remains near the top for expenditures adjusted by the size of stock markets in the country (Jackson & Roe 2009). The traditional justification for private securities fraud causes of action as a necessary supplement to limited Commission resources has survived even as public resources have increased. Studies suggest that SEC and private litigation diverge as to the companies that are the targets of each type of proceeding (Cox & Thomas 2003).[4]

## Specific Issues of Representative Litigation in a Corporate Law Context

When litigation is brought in a corporate context on behalf of a large group, either a derivative action on behalf of the entity, or a class action on behalf of a large portion of shareholders or former shareholders of the entity, there are specific issues beyond those that arise in litigation generally. We focus here on two: the litigation agency costs that arise in such a setting in terms of the dominating interest of the lawyers and plaintiffs who bring the suit as opposed to the larger group of shareholders; and the possible circularity of any recovery in a corporate setting when any payment comes out of the corporate treasury.

### Litigation agency costs

In the typical American corporation with numerous, dispersed shareholders, the average size of individual shareholdings is small enough that any potential recovery is so low as to be easily surpassed by the costs of bringing the lawsuit, thereby providing only minimal incentive for a shareholder to pursue litigation either for an individual return or on behalf of a group. In American representative litigation, attorneys have filled this gap where claims that are individually small, but collectively significant, are joined; in this context, attorneys often advance the expenses of the litigation and take their fee as a portion of recovery when the suit is resolved. Indeed, because the class counsel customarily invests substantial out-of-pocket costs to prosecute the suit, and incurs even more substantial opportunity costs by devoting time to the suit rather than to other matters, it has often been the attorney, and not the class representative, that has the largest economic interest in the suit and who we would therefore expect to be the key decision-maker in litigation. While the possibility of significant fees for attorneys provides them incentives to ferret out fraud, punish wrongdoers, and compensate the injured, representative litigation introduces factors that can put daylight between the interests of lawyers and investors.

---

[4]   In that study of public and private enforcement actions between 1990 and 2001, there was an overlap between public and private plaintiffs in 15% of cases; in part the small overlap reflects that only about half of the SEC prosecutions could have given rise to a private action given broader SEC jurisdiction, but there remain substantial differences among the potential overlap group. This study found the SEC more likely to target smaller firms and those in financial distress. *See also*, Cox and Thomas (2005a) for an updated and expanded version of the earlier paper using data from 1990 to 2003.

For example, attorneys can manage the risk of a lack of success in a particular action by maintaining a portfolio of suits, so the attorney may be more willing than shareholders to initiate suits, including those that have low chances of recovery. At the same time, the class counsel may advocate an early, and low, settlement, not viewing the marginal benefits of pursuing a larger settlement as worth expending the additional time and costs necessary to obtain the uncertain benefits of pushing the case further. Similarly, the assured payment from an existing insurance policy, or even the corporation's treasury, may be much more promising to the contingent fee counsel than continuing the case against the defendant firm's officers, the likely alleged perpetrators of any fraud. From this perspective, if suits were being driven too much by lawyer interests, representative litigation could result in the attorney initiating suits with little merit, settling strong suits for too little, and structuring the settlement so that the costs are not borne by the actual wrongdoers.

Courts and commentators have recognized these distinct agency costs that can arise in representative litigation. The Wood study in New York in the 1940s focused particularly on derivative suits and led to new legislation as to those suits, for example, requiring a bond to be posted before a derivative suit could be brought (Thompson & Thomas 2004a). Empirical studies in the late twentieth century broadened the empirical examination to include federal and state law (Jones 1980; Romano 1991). One conclusion was that these suits resulted in a relatively small percentage recovery for plaintiffs, but larger recoveries for the lawyers (Romano 1991). Commentators worried about troubling signs of representative suits being driven by lawyer interest: suits were filed quickly, often in the first day or days after an event that could trigger liability, and multiple suits were filed based on the same facts. Both trends suggest lawyers seeking to file in ways that would maximize their role in the litigation. A recurring group of law firms produced a large number of these filings, and there was evidence of repeat involvement by the plaintiffs themselves who often had very little economic interest in the company targeted. More recent scholarship has confirmed these claims empirically (Thompson & Thomas 2004a).

In recent years, federal securities fraud has become the focus for the policy debate over representative litigation and the source for multiple empirical studies. In 1995, on the heels of Republicans gaining majorities in both the House of Representatives and the Senate on a platform that included new limits on securities class actions, Congress, over a presidential veto, passed the Private Securities Litigation Reform Act of 1995 (PSLRA).[5] A lead plaintiff provision was added that sought to avoid the race to the courthouse by providing a presumption that the representative of the class would not necessarily be the first to file, but rather the plaintiff(s) with the largest economic interest. Other provisions were inserted to check perceived frivolous claims by plaintiff's lawyers and plaintiffs. Heightened pleadings standards were added both as to allegations of scienter and misstatements. In addition, discovery was barred until the defendant had the opportunity to have a motion to dismiss heard before a judge. A loss causation requirement was made explicit by the statute and a limit on damages was specified. A safe harbor was added largely blocking liability based on forward-looking statements made by the company and its officers.

---

[5]    Pub. L. No. 104-67, 109 Stat. 737 (codified, as amended, in scattered sections of 15 and 18 U.S.C.).

## Circularity

Securities fraud class actions pose a possible circularity problem. To the extent that recoveries are paid by the corporation (on whose behalf officers are said to have made misleading statements), money is moving from one investor pocket to another, after subtraction of a substantial transaction cost in terms of fees paid to the attorneys. Such recovery largely from the corporate treasury reduces the asset base of the current group of shareholders with payment going to investors who were shareholders at the (somewhat earlier) time of the misrepresentation or omission.

Even if there has been a substantial turnover of the shareholders of the corporation so that the exact shareholders at the two times are different, the wide footprint of most institutional investors in today's market and the fact that some of these investors diversify their holdings means that securities fraud litigation has been claimed by some to be moving money from one pocket of institutional investors to another pocket of institutional investors, albeit after the sum has been depleted by a substantial portion having been paid to attorneys.

Derivative suits could be less susceptible to this claim in that these claims have been traditionally brought against individual directors and officers for breach of their fiduciary duties leading to settlements in which these parties sometimes paid money into the corporate treasury. But to the extent that indemnification and insurance cover these claims, these costs too come indirectly (via higher insurance premiums) out of the corporate treasury, raising again the problem of circularity at least indirectly. With insurance, however, undiversified investors, such as employees with significant dollar amounts in shareholdings, are benefiting from the small contributions paid by all investors.

A similar argument can be made about all forms of intra-firm litigation where the firm's shares are held by diversified investors. As in the context of securities class actions, the circularity argument would be that money resulting from settlements merely flows out of one pocket of the institutional holders and into the other pocket of that same institution; the lawyers prosecuting and defending the suits impose non-trivial transaction costs that ultimately reduce the wealth of the institutional holders.

The policy result that would flow from such an argument would be to limit representative suits, or all litigation among corporations with diversified shareholders.[6] A similar conclusion follows from Easterbrook and Fischel's argument suggesting there is no harm to the investor from the underlying conduct that gave rise to the litigation. They argue that management misbehavior that affects any specific firm should not necessarily cause a loss to investors if all investors held diversified portfolios because the randomness of firm-specific gains or losses would inevitably sum to zero (Easterbrook & Fischel 1982).

These arguments blend into a larger debate of whether securities law should be designed to provide compensation to the investors harmed by the fraud or to deter those performing the alleged fraudulent act. On the deterrence side of the argument, Nobel laureate Gary Becker has shown that the frequency of anti-social behaviour is a function, in part, of the probability of conviction per offense and the punishment per offense (Becker 1968). Under this view, the sanctions incurred by fraudsters impart a message to those who might consider following the fraudster's crooked path and should discourage others, depending on the actual experience

---

[6]   An alternative policy result would be to limit or disallow indemnification. See the SEC's views on indemnification in an IPO setting in Item 512 of Regulation S-K, 17 CFR §229.512(h).

with sanctions, from deceiving investors. Thus, the frequency and magnitude of sanctions are important in the deterrence of deceptive financial behaviour. At the same time, we should be concerned that sanctions are consistently applied and proportional to the harm caused by the violation; otherwise enforcement may take on a random, overly harsh, appearance and thereby erode deterrence and lead to wasteful precautionary action.

## 3. EMPIRICAL WORK ON REPRESENTATIVE LAW SUITS

### State Law

A study of all corporate law filings in Delaware (the state where the large majority of American public corporations are incorporated) over a two-year period showed that 85% of corporate suits versus public companies alleging claims of breach of fiduciary duty were class actions arising in the context of an acquisition (Thompson & Thomas 2004a). Such class action acquisition litigation exceeded derivative suits, the traditional state law form of representative litigation, by a factor of 8 to 1. Only a few of the fiduciary duty claims were brought by parties to the acquisition. There were also corporate suits which were not fiduciary duty suits, for example, actions for inspection of records or those seeking fair value in a statutory appraisal.

For the class action suits, there is some evidence of litigation agency costs. Almost 70% of the suits were filed on the same day as the announcement of the deal or within the next three days. Multiple suits were often filed in the same transaction with the average being about three cases and many deals generated suits in the double digits. There were repeat plaintiffs in some of the suits and 16 law firms filed three-fourths of the class action cases. These factors together suggest that the law firm is the most interested party and that the lawyers are jockeying for position to be the lead counsel or to gain a controlling position in the litigation that might be consistent with the traditional story told about litigation agency costs.

However, the actual results of the litigation run counter to the litigation agency cost story. While all sorts of acquisitions trigger the filing of suits, the set of suits in which cash recovery occurs (as opposed to non-cash relief or dismissal without any affirmative relief) is tilted toward mergers initiated by a controlling shareholder to cash out the minority at a price chosen by the controlling shareholder, or a management buyout in which the officers' interest as purchasers prevents the selling shareholders from having the disinterested advice of the agents best positioned to act on their behalf. Of 31 suits producing affirmative dollar relief, 25 (80%) were either control shareholder acquisitions, or MBOs, even though these two categories made up only half of the cases actually filed. That suggests that state class action litigation is doing its most work in settings where fiduciary duty has traditionally been seen as most useful – where the fiduciaries are conflicted and entering into transactions with the corporation. When focusing on the subset of control share transactions, the lawsuits in that subset that produce a cash settlement started out with a lower premium over market price in the offer made to shareholders, but ended up producing a larger premium over market price. Taken as a whole, these results suggest there is a greater chance of litigation in conflict of interest deals and that it concerns facts that would raise conflict of interest issues to judges.

The litigation cases which produced the affirmative results just discussed usually had another characteristic that may well have contributed to a financial recovery. Under a

Delaware practice encouraged by *Weinberger v. UOP, Inc.*,[7] such conflicted transactions are usually negotiated by an independent litigation committee sometimes known as a special litigation committee. Thus, the management will be simultaneously negotiating with both the special litigation committee and the lawyers for the class. One Delaware case suggests the first set of negotiations is the most intense and that the second often adds little, or even no, value.[8] An empirical study (Weiss & White 2004) examines the same process and concludes this litigation is not adding value. Yet, even if negotiations with the class lawyers are less intense, it may still be that the presence of the litigation is enough of a monitor to drive the settlement price up in those cases. The higher premium in cases with a monetary settlement would be consistent with either hypothesis.

A study of all takeover litigation in 1999 and 2000 (90% of which occurred in state courts) showed that 12% of all deals attracted litigation. Moreover, the deals with litigation have a lower completion rate as compared to deals without litigation, although those that are completed yield higher premiums. The authors find that the additional premium more than offsets the reduction in completion rate, suggesting that deal litigation creates overall higher returns for shareholders (Krishnan et al. 2011). Data from subsequent periods shows a greater percentage of deals attracting litigation and more of the suits being filed outside of Delaware, suggesting evolving law firm strategies in M&A litigation (Armour et al. 2011).

**Federal Law**

The period since the passage of the PSLRA in 1995 has produced the largest number of empirical studies of representative litigation. PSLRA has had a clear impact on shareholder litigation after 1995: the number of cases filed has gone down, although perhaps not as much as some might have expected (Cornerstone 2009);[9] the percentage of cases dismissed has gone up (Buckberg et. al 2005; Miller 2006);[10] and the characteristics of the cases brought seem to have changed somewhat with, for example, fewer against hardware/software firms and fewer involving auditor liability (Johnson et al. 2006). There are some examples of the changes having a positive effect in reducing litigation agency costs, as with the lead plaintiff provision discussed below, and some where the statutory changes have not had much effect. The impact on the companies themselves is disputed with different papers reaching opposite results about whether the passage of the PSLRA resulted in an increase in stock value at the time of the adoption of the Act. There is also evidence concerning the effect on targeted companies' value when fraud cases are brought and a suggestion of false negatives – cases no longer brought that could be viewed as meritorious. The interaction of these private class suits with the SEC and gatekeepers continues to evolve. We summarize much of this work below.

---

[7]   457 A.2d 701 (Del. 1983).
[8]   *In re Cox Communications, Inc. Shareholders Litigation*, 879 A.2d 604 (Del. 2008).
[9]   This study reports that for 1996–2007, the number of securities fraud class action suits averaged 192 (with a range from 111 to 242) about the same as the number of suits in one study of the pre-1995 period. See Perino (2003). There have been several spurts of litigation including backdating that may skew the numbers. Without such one-time claims, the average number of cases post-1995 drops to 110 per year (Cox & Thomas 2009a).
[10]   Buckberg reports a pre-1995 dismissal rate in securities class actions of about 20%; Miller reports a dismissal rate in the 1998–2003 period of about 40%.

**Did the 1995 statute change anything? Greater participation of institutional investors as lead plaintiffs**

The PSLRA creates a rebuttable presumption that the shareholder with the largest financial interest in the firm should be named the lead plaintiff in a federal securities class action law suit. Congress intended this provision to harness the power of institutional investors, especially public pension funds, to act as monitors of plaintiffs' attorneys in these cases (Cox & Thomas 2009a). After a slow start, institutional investors began appearing more frequently as lead plaintiffs so that by 2007 institutional investors appeared in roughly 60% of all securities class action settlements (Simmons & Ryan 2008). Cox, Thomas & Bai (2008) establish that institutional investors are appearing in a larger number of securities class actions over time, and that public pension funds and labor union funds are the most commonly observed participants.

Several studies have consistently found a strong correlation between the appearance of a public pension fund as a lead plaintiff and higher settlements. The earliest academic work, Choi, Fisch and Pritchard's (2005) study using 122 post-PSLRA settlements 1996–2000, found that the presence of a public pension fund acting as a lead plaintiff is correlated with higher settlements for investors. The absence of control variables for the presence of an accounting restatement, or for an SEC investigation, led the authors to conclude they could not reject the possibility that institutional investors 'cherry pick' the highest-valued cases in which to appear. More recent papers control for these variables, yet still find strong linkages between the presence of public pension fund lead plaintiffs and higher settlement values, pointing in favor of finding a causal linkage. Perino (2006a), the most thorough academic study done to date, uses a sample of 501 post-PSLRA cases 1995–2004 to study the relationship between public pension fund participation as lead plaintiffs and settlement size. Controlling for accounting restatements and SEC investigations, as well as numerous other potential influences on settlement size, he concludes that 'there is at least some reason to believe that self-selection [i.e. cherry picking] is not a significant problem here' (Perino 2006a, 23).

Cox & Thomas (2006), examining the 1995–2002 time period for a sample of 260 post-PSLRA settlements, controlled for a variety of other factors, including the presence of an SEC investigation; they find a positive and significant relationship between institutional lead plaintiffs and higher settlements. Cox, Thomas and Bai (2008) examined 627 post-PSLRA settlements for the 1996–2004 time period and found public pension fund lead plaintiffs are associated with the largest positive impact on settlement size; labor union funds showed a similar relationship, albeit the magnitude of their impact is smaller than that of public pension funds.

Institutional investor plaintiffs appear to be using the same law firms that brought cases before 1995 (Choi & Thompson 2006). Yet, the interaction may have changed. Perino (2006a) suggests some monitoring by these lead plaintiffs of attorney conduct. He finds that cases with public pension fund lead plaintiffs show a greater number of docket entries and a higher ratio of settlement value to docket entries. In a related paper, Perino (2006b) evaluates the effect of competition and the participation of experienced repeat players as lead plaintiffs on the level of attorneys' fees in securities class actions. He finds 'a significant negative correlation between public pension fund participation as lead plaintiffs and the size of fee requests and fee awards' (Perino 2006b). He further uncovers negative correlations between fee levels and experienced courts, as well as the correlation of fees to repeat players in securities litigation. These results are consistent with the claim that there is stronger plaintiffs' side litigation agency cost monitoring by institutional lead plaintiffs and experienced judges.

Empirical studies show the conduct of institutional investors has also changed in another way. Cox & Thomas (2002) and Cox & Thomas (2005b) examined samples of securities class action settlements to assess whether institutional shareholders were filing claims with the settlement administrators to collect their portion of the settlement proceeds. They found 28–33% of institutional investors filed such claims. Perhaps due to the publicity surrounding these studies, or learning from them, a later survey of self-selected respondents, itself a limiting constraint, found public pension funds to be filing all of their claims in securities fraud class actions (Choi & Fisch 2008).

In sum, these papers show that the lead plaintiff provision has had many of its intended effects. Institutional lead plaintiffs are appearing in large numbers, raising settlement values and decreasing attorneys' fees. In essence, institutional lead plaintiffs are proving to be socially useful monitors of securities class action prosecutions. This supports a belief that the PSLRA has been successful in this regard.

In contrast, other portions of the 1995 Act aimed at adding new monitors of attorney conduct in class actions do not appear to have had a noticeable effect. In the PSLRA, Congress sought to ratchet up judicial supervision of lawyers by mandating in every securities class action judicial review of possible attorney and client misconduct, including greater sanctions (Choi & Thompson 2006). In the hundreds of securities class actions studied, there were only 22 reported opinions discussing sanctions in the first decade of the PSLRA and only four instances of sanctions being imposed, or one case every two and a half years.

### Heightened pleading standards and bar on discovery

In 1995 Congress also chose to influence representative litigation by making changes in what must be shown for a class to recover. These included new requirements for pleading scienter, a bar on discovery until after a judge's opportunity to rule on a motion to dismiss, and greater specificity as to the causation and damages elements necessary to prove a Rule 10b-5 action.

*Scienter and how scienter must be pleaded*   The scienter element has received the most empirical attention. The 1995 legislation did not specify the mental state required for a Rule 10b-5 violation, leaving in place the ambiguity of a two decades-old Supreme Court decision that said the federal action required a mental state greater than negligence, but not further defining whether that might be some form of recklessness, knowledge or specific intent.[11] The PSLRA did say that whatever the particular mental state required, facts must be pled with particularity giving rise to a strong inference that the defendant acted with the requisite state of mind. The various circuit courts of appeals thereafter set out different phrasings of the substantive standard and sought to define what constitutes a strong inference. The only subsequent Supreme Court action was the *Tellabs* case, where it interpreted the 'strong inference' to mean cogent and at least as compelling as any opposing inference.[12]

---

[11]   *Ernst & Ernst v. Hochfelder*, 425 U.S. 185 (1976).
[12]   *Tellabs, Inc. v. Makor Issues and Rights, Ltd.*, 551 U.S. 308 (2007).

The Ninth Circuit, which contains Silicon Valley and many of the high technology firms, adopted a very stringent pleading standard for alleging fraud, in *In Re Silicon Graphics Inc. Securities Litigation*.[13] An event study by Johnson, Nelson and Pritchard (2000) investigated the effect of the announcement of this decision upon the stock prices of 277 high technology companies both in the Ninth Circuit and elsewhere. They found a statistically significant positive stock price reaction for the sample firms, with a greater increase for the firms located in the Ninth Circuit. They explain the observed difference in returns as supporting their hypothesis that the higher pleading standard increased shareholder wealth by decreasing the likelihood of these firms being sued successfully.

Pritchard and Sale (2005) studied the effect of different circuit courts' interpretation of the PSLRA's requirements on the outcome of motions to dismiss. Using cases decided by the Second and Ninth Circuit, they find that the more stringent *Silicon Graphics* fraud pleading standard in the Ninth Circuit correlated with a higher dismissal rate for securities fraud class actions. They also uncover several significant differences in how the two circuits react to allegations of accounting principle violations, claims of false forward looking statements, and allegations of violations of the 1933 Securities Act.

*Greater protection for forward looking statements; less exposure for technology firms & auditors*   Before the PSLRA, there was a good deal of litigation focused on allegedly false forward looking statements regarding the firm's, or its products', likely performance. Technology firms residing in Silicon Valley were frequent targets. One central provision of the PSLRA was a safe harbor provision for companies making such forward looking statements.

Johnson, Nelson and Pritchard (2006), using a data base comprised exclusively of suits filed during 1991–2000 against computer hardware and software firms, find a decided shift away from such litigation following the enactment of the PSLRA. Post-PSLRA, they show that securities class actions increasingly target accounting fraud (rising from 31% of the cases in the pre-PSLRA era to 61% in the post-PSLRA era), while relatively few post-PSLRA suits focus on forward looking statements. They attribute the latter result to the safe harbor Congress provided for forward looking statements.

The same authors find that firms that announce an accounting restatement are more likely to be sued as are firms whose insiders engage in abnormal stock sales (Johnson et al. 2006). Each of these considerations may well reflect the impact of the heightened pleading requirement which demands objective evidence to be set forth with particularity in the complaint supporting allegations of fraudulent reporting. Courts responding to this approach have, among other things, embraced evidence of the managers' possible motive for false reporting which is strongly supported by allegations they traded on inside information. Similarly, an accounting restatement, which by itself creates no inference of fraud, does strengthen the inference that can be drawn from other factors set forth in the complaint. Interestingly, accounting restatements are not associated with settlement outcomes in the pre-PSLRA era but are for the post-PSLRA era.

---

[13]   *In re Silicon Graphics Inc. Securities Litigation*, 183 F.3d 970 (9th Cir.1999). A recent Ninth Circuit decision suggests *Tellabs* might require a relaxation of the strict pleading standard in *Silicon Graphics*. See *South Ferry LP #2 v. Killinger*, 542 F.3d 776 (9th Cir.2008).

The extra legal protection for the disclosure of forward looking information provided by the PSLRA's safe harbor provisions could provide an incentive for companies to increase the amount of this type of information that they provide to the public. Johnson, Kasznik and Nelson (2001), using a sample of high technology and pharmaceutical firms' disclosures 1994–1996, determine that, controlling for other factors that may affect the disclosure decision, there were significant increases in both the frequency of firms issuing forecasts and the mean number of forecasts issued in the first year after the passage of the PSLRA. These authors also find no evidence of any decrease in the quality of the forecasts issued by firms, determining that these forecasts did not appear to be either more optimistic or noisier. In contrast, Brown, Hillegeist and Lo (2005) find that increased litigation risk for a company is associated with forecasts being released earlier and being more precise. They also find that higher litigation risk is 'associated with a higher proportion of news being released when firms have bad news'.

*The possibility of a false negative: Are meritorious suits being shut out by the new rules?* Even if the PSLRA has successfully reduced the number of unmeritorious suits, there is also the possibility that at the same time it has blocked what may be meritorious suits that lack the necessary outward indicia of fraud to satisfy these more difficult filing hurdles. Choi (2007), using a data set containing all IPOs of US corporations 1990–1999, finds that pre-PSLRA non-nuisance suits without 'hard evidence' of fraud, such as an SEC investigation, or an accounting restatement, would be less likely to be filed in the post-PSLRA period and have a greater likelihood of being dismissed. Choi concludes that, while the PSLRA made it harder to bring frivolous actions, it also made it harder to bring meritorious ones. Choi, Nelson and Pritchard (2009) make a number of complementary findings, including that the PSLRA had the effect of discouraging suits that would have produced positive, non-nuisance settlements in the pre-PSLRA time period.

**The larger question: Did the PSLRA produce value for investors?**

*Stock market event studies at the time of passage*   Several papers have looked at the stock market's reaction to the passage of the PSLRA. Johnson, Kasznik and Nelson (2000) examined 489 high technology firms to observe how their stock prices reacted to the passage of the PSLRA. They found that on average the value of these firms increased with the enactment of the statute, with a more significant increase in firms that faced higher expected likelihoods of being sued.

Other broader studies have reached conflicting results. Two studies drawn from four high litigation industries – electronics, computers, retailing and pharmaceuticals/biotechnology – find contrasting results in terms of shareholder return. Spiess and Tkac (1997) find similar results to those just discussed in terms of increase in prices. In contrast, Ali and Kallapur (2001) find that investors in these industries reacted negatively to the passage of the statute. Ali and Kallapur (2001) point out numerous confounding events that render ambiguous the interpretation of the stock price changes relied upon by the two earlier studies just discussed. Instead, they conduct additional analyses of several other legislative events, calculating the cumulative abnormal returns to investors over the legislative period and an additional analysis of other events affecting investors' ability to sue for fraud. They conclude that shareholders lost wealth because of the passage of the PSLRA. These conflicting results make it difficult to conclude whether the enactment of the PSLRA was perceived by the market as a value increasing or decreasing event (Cox & Thomas 2009a).

*Returns associated with litigation; factors affecting litigation returns*   A pre-PSLRA study, itself widely cited during the Congressional debate of that legislation, suggested that settlements in securities fraud cases (more particularly a small sample of initial public offerings (IPOs)) were not based on the strength of the plaintiff's case, but settled for a similar percentage (about 25%) (Alexander 1991). Empirical studies since drawn from broader and more diverse samples have identified factors related to the merits of securities fraud cases that are correlated with higher settlement values.

Cox and Thomas (2006) find that settlement size is highly and positively correlated with the presence of an SEC enforcement action, the length of the class period, the size of the defendant corporation, the presence of an institutional lead plaintiff and the amount of the estimated losses for the class. Perino (2006b) reports similar results, finding that the presence of a public pension fund, longer class periods, greater total assets of the defendant firm, SEC enforcement actions, accounting restatements, the presence of an underwriter defendant and estimated damages are all positively and significantly related to settlement size, while bankruptcy filing by the defendant firm is negatively and significantly related to settlement size. Simmons and Ryan (2008), from the defense side consulting firm Cornerstone Research, also report that a large number of variables are correlated with settlement size, including the defendant firm's total assets, restatements, the presence of an SEC enforcement action, accountant or underwriter defendants, public pension fund lead plaintiff, and estimated losses of the shareholder class. All of these studies are consistent with the view that the merits of the plaintiff's case impact the overall settlement size.

Empirical work on the correlation of good corporate governance to shareholder return remains subject to debate. There have been empirical studies linking weaker corporate governance to greater likelihood of being sued and also improvements in governance that follow such suits. Firms that commit fraud generally have poor corporate governance structures relative to other firms in terms of fewer outside board members, a lower number of audit committee meetings, more frequently join the positions of CEO and Chair of the Board, and are less likely to use Big Four accounting firms (Farber 2005). Bohn and Choi (1996) provide similar findings that firms with weak corporate governance structures are more likely to face such a suit than a set of matched firms.[14] A similar substantive result follows from the inverse relationship: firms with stronger corporate governance practices make better disclosures, and this leads to a reduced risk of being sued in a securities fraud class action (Mohan 2007).

Strahan (1998), who also finds that firms with greater ex ante levels of corporate governance problems are more likely to be sued in securities fraud class actions, shows that class actions can lead to corporate governance improvements with the likelihood of CEO turnover increasing by almost 14% when an above average quality securities fraud class action is filed, controlling for other factors. Marciukaityte et al. (2006) conclude that firms improve their internal monitoring systems after experiencing corporate fraud (e.g. raise the number of independent directors on their boards and oversight committees) and that these changes help to

---

[14]   Their data shows that the sued firms had fewer outside directors on their boards and that these firms' directors held relatively fewer directorships at other firms than the matched sample firms (Bohn & Choi (1996, 962).

mend the harm caused by the fraud and restore the firm's reputation, although operating performance and stock price performance did not improve compared to a matched sample of firms that were not accused of fraud.[15]

Executive compensation, one of the most highly visible and debated corporate governance topics, has also been the subject of possible connections to securities fraud class actions with several studies finding correlations between high levels of executive compensation, financial fraud and the likelihood of a company being targeted by a securities fraud class action. For example, Mohan (2004) finds that companies that have high levels of total managerial compensation and option grants compared to a set of other industry and size matched firms are more likely to be sued in a securities fraud class action. She also finds that the presence of a large institutional block holder reduces this litigation risk. Peng and Roell's study reaches a slightly different, although similar conclusion: 'the option component in executive compensation is positively and significantly associated with the incidence of class action lawsuits' holding constant a wide range of firm characteristics (Peng & Roell 2008, 142). Another study ties the likelihood of fraud to another compensation characteristic – unrestricted stock (Johnson et al. 2009). Controlling for firm corporate governance structures, firm characteristics and CEO specific variables, they find that 'the likelihood of fraud is positively related to incentives from unrestricted stock, and is unrelated to incentives from vested options, unvested options and restricted stock'.

The incentives from compensation are sometimes linked to upward earnings manipulation and other conduct (Johnson et al. 2009). Data from Talley and Johnsen (2004) develop more specific connections; their analysis shows that a one percent increase in the quantity of a manager's incentives predicts a 0.3% increase in the likelihood of her firm being targeted with a securities law suit and increases the expected settlement costs by $3.4 million.

In summary, these studies are consistent with the view that where compensation packages create strong incentives to manipulate accounting earnings, or stock price, stock prices are more likely to be manipulated by false reporting, and this leads to an increased likelihood of shareholder litigation (Cox & Thomas 2009a). More positively, the studies report that good corporate governance structures, such as institutional blockholders, or better designed compensation systems, may reduce or even eliminate the risk of fraud, and therefore of litigation, and that securities fraud class actions may serve as ex post substitutes for these systems.

**Circularity**

One study of the circularity thesis concludes that before considering recoveries through litigation, large institutions generally break even from their investments in common stocks impacted by fraud allegations (Thakor et al. 2005). With litigation included, the study finds such institutions are *overcompensated* as a result of the litigation.[16] Another study, using

---

[15]    This study of corporate fraud was not specifically focused on securities fraud class actions, which are the topic of this chapter.

[16]    While these findings are quite intriguing, their generality is impossible to verify given the authors' unwillingness to disclose even the names of the companies in their sample. It also bears mentioning the funding source for this study is an organization that has publicly spearheaded a campaign to eliminate the private enforcement of the federal securities laws.

In addition, there are non-diversified institutional holders, such as a hedge fund whose holdings are concentrated in a few companies, for which this finding would not hold.

observational data and simulated trading data, finds not only that undiversified individual investors are likely to suffer net losses from securities fraud, but also that large numbers of diversified institutional investors may also be harmed (Davis 2009).

Even if there were overcompensation, the learning on deterrence would suggest that in a world where a substantial number of frauds go unpunished, then overcompensation of investors in cases that do lead to a recovery will help to bolster compensation more in the direction of optimal deterrence (Becker 1968). This broader literature encourages an examination of the effect of litigation on the behavior of the firm, gatekeepers and deterring individuals. Karpoff et al. (2008a) find that while the litigation sanctions are far from trivial, averaging $23.5 million, the reputational sanction suffered by the offending entity for committing fraud is huge, with the decline in the present value of future cash flow being in excess of 7.5 times the litigation sanction. The authors' calculation is that for every dollar that the fraudulent representation inflates its market value upon disclosure of the violation it loses a dollar plus an additional $3.08 and the loss is larger than this if the firm survives (about 88% of this amount is reputational cost with the balance being legal defense costs). In a related paper, the same investigators follow the impact of the identified action on individuals; they report that nearly 94% of the individuals identified as being responsible for the false statements lose their jobs by the end of the enforcement proceedings and a majority of these are fired by their firms (Karpoff et al. 2008b). Culpable managers are more likely to lose their jobs when their misconduct is accompanied by insider trading, the firm is young or financially troubled, their conduct was harmful to the company, and when the firm has an independent board. These findings suggest that markets do play an important role in punishing fraud, and that shareholder litigation serves a secondary function is this regard, although it does add meaningful additional monetary sanctions and may serve to stimulate the firm to discipline the wrongdoers harshly (Cox & Thomas 2009a).

**State Law in Federal Court**

There is a third set of representative litigation cases beyond the securities fraud class actions and the class actions or derivative suits in state courts. These are derivative suits brought in federal court, which have received less attention than the federal and state representative claims discussed earlier, but which share some of the same issues as the other types of representative litigation. Derivative suits, generally, are suits brought by an individual shareholder on behalf of the corporation, seeking a recovery for the corporation from defendants said to have breached their fiduciary duties to the firm. The source of the duty is usually state law, but the suit arises in federal court because of diversity of citizenship. Plaintiffs in these cases prefer to be in federal court than Delaware or whichever state is the place of incorporation of the firm.

Erickson's study of derivative suits filed in federal courts in a 12-month period spanning 2005–2006 suggests that derivative suits are frequently filed in federal court (Erickson 2010). She found 141 suits against 126 public companies over a one-year period in federal courts across the country. A study a few years earlier of derivative suits filed in Delaware found about 50 suits against less than 30 public companies per year (Thompson & Thomas 2004a).[17] The federal derivative count includes a substantial number (40) that arose from the

---

[17]    There has not been a study of derivative suits in state courts outside of Delaware other than in

backdating of options scandal that was concentrated in the time period during which the study was conducted.

These representative suits brought as federal derivative claims reflect some of the same indicia that have given rise to litigation agency costs in other contexts. There are repeat law firms, with a strong overlap with firms that bring other representative litigation.

The results achieved in these cases are bifurcated. Overall, about 30% of the public company suits settled, but less than 10% of public company cases resulted in a settlement that included some monetary relief paid to the company (Erickson 2010). Almost all of these payments occurred in the cases related to option backdating. For federal derivative suits that did not involve option backdating, there was a 'meaningful financial benefit' in only two of 101 remaining suits (Erickson 2010). There were an additional 35 settlements in total providing some corporate governance changes. This type of benefit is more difficult to evaluate, but seems sufficient to provide courts with a basis for an award of attorneys' fees and is not generally available in class action suits. Finally, the non-backdating cases frequently appear to be companion suits to federal securities fraud class actions, raising the question of whether the federal derivative suits may be a way for plaintiffs' attorneys to get a seat at a negotiating table dominated by the federal securities class action suits.

## 4.   CONCLUSIONS

There is a wealth of empirical studies on federal class actions in the US, and an increasing number of papers that examine state law representative litigation and federal derivative cases. The studies tell us that legislation such as the PSLRA has reshaped who brings suits and the kinds of claims that are brought. In state litigation, debate continues about litigation agency costs and how litigation interacts with other managerial constraints such as special litigation committees. As with much empirical work, gaps remain in the data that would fill out our understanding such as in the interaction of representative litigation in different courts, the role that legal rules have in influencing the plaintiffs' selection of forum and type of suit filed on any given fact pattern, the size of defense side attorneys' fees and potential agency cost issues related to them, and the long-term consequences for targeted firms of representative litigation.[18] These and other issues provide future scholars with important areas for future research.

## REFERENCES

Alexander, Janet Cooper (1991), 'Do The Merits Matter? A Study of Settlements in Securities Class Actions', *Stanford Law Review*, 43, 497–598.
Ali, Ashiq & Sanjay Kallapur (2001), 'Securities Price Consequences of the Private Securities Litigation Reform Act of 1995 and Related Events', *The Accounting Review*, 76(3), 431–60.

---

the acquisition context, which makes up a very small portion of derivative litigation (Krishnan et al. 2010), but the pattern of acquisition litigation in Delaware and the other states (where the rate of derivative suits in the other states is about 80% of the Delaware number) suggests that the federal forum for derivative suits is the most significant numerically.

[18]    Bai, Cox and Thomas (2010) provides some insight into the effect of securities fraud class action settlements on targeted firms.

Armour, John, Bernard S. Black and Brian R. Cheffins (2011), 'Delaware's Balancing Act', available at http://papers.ssrn.com/sol3/papers.cfm?abstract_id=1677400 (last accessed December 2011).

Bai, Lynn, James D. Cox & Randall Thomas (2010), 'Lying and Getting Caught: An Empirical Study of the Effect of Securities Class Action Settlements on Targeted Firms', *University of Pennsylvania Law Review*, 158, 1877–1914.

Bebchuk, Lucian A. & Alma Cohen (2003), 'Firms' Decisions Where to Incorporate', *Journal of Law and Economics*, 46, 383–425.

Beck, James D. & Sanjai Bhagat (1997), 'Shareholder Litigation: Share Price Movements, News Releases and Settlement Amounts', *Managerial and Decision Economics*, 18, 563–86.

Becker, Gary (1968), 'Crime and Punishment: An Economic Approach', *Journal of Political Economy*, 76, 169–217.

Berle Jr., Adolf A. & Gardiner Means (1932), *The Modern Corporation and Private Property*, New York: Macmillan.

Bhagat, Sanjai & James Beck (1996), 'Share Price Drops and Shareholder Litigation', available at http://papers.ssrn.com/sol3/papers.cfm?abstract_id=956499 (last accessed October 2011).

Bohn, James and Stephen Choi (1996), 'Fraud in the New Issues Market: Empirical Evidence on Securities Class Actions', *University of Pennsylvania Law Review*, 144, 903–82.

Brown, Stephen, Stephen A. Hillegeist & Kin Lo (2005), 'Management Forecasts and Litigation Risk', available at http://papers.ssrn.com/sol3/papers.cfm?abstract_id=709161 (last accessed October 2011).

Buckberg, Elaine, Todd Foster & Ronald I. Miller (2005), 'Recent Trends in Shareholder Class Action Litigation: Are WorldCom and Enron the New Standard?', NERA Economic Consulting.

Cao, Zhiyan & Ganapathi Narayanamoorthy (2011), 'Accounting and Litigation Risk: Evidence from Directors' and Officers' Insurance Pricing', available at http://papers.ssrn.com/sol3/papers.cfm?abstract_id=853024 (last accessed October 2011).

Choi, Stephen J. (2004), 'The Evidence on Securities Class Actions', *Vanderbilt Law Review*, 57, 1465–1526.

Choi, Stephen J., Jill E. Fisch & Adam C. Pritchard (2005), 'Do Institutions Matter? The Impact of the Lead Plaintiff Provision of the Private Securities Litigation Reform Act', *Washington University Law Quarterly*, 83, 869–906.

Choi, Stephen J. & Robert B. Thompson (2006), 'Securities Litigation and Its Lawyers: Changes During the First Decade after the PSLRA', *Columbia Law Review*, 106, 1489–1533.

Choi, Stephen J. (2007), 'Do The Merits Matter *Less* After the Private Securities Litigation Reform Act?', *Journal of Law, Economics, and Organization*, 23, 598–626.

Choi, Stephen J. & Jill E. Fisch (2008), 'On Beyond CalPERS: Survey Evidence on the Developing Role of Public Pension Funds in Corporate Governance', *Vanderbilt Law Review*, 61, 315–54.

Choi, Stephen J., Karen K. Nelson & A.C. Pritchard (2009), 'The Screening Effect of the Private Securities Litigation Reform Act', *Journal of Empirical Legal Studies*, 6, 35–68.

Coffee, Jr., John C. (1986), 'Understanding the Plaintiffs' Attorney: The Implications of Economic Theory for Private Enforcement Through Class and Derivative Actions', *Columbia Law Review*, 86, 669–727.

Cornerstone Research (2009), 'Securities Class Action Filings – 2008: A Year in Review'.

Cox, James D. & Randall S. Thomas (2002), 'Leaving Money on the Table; Do Institutional Investors Fail to File Claims in Securities Class Actions', *Washington University Law Quarterly*, 80, 855–82.

Cox, James D. & Randall S. Thomas (2003), 'SEC Enforcement Heuristics: An Empirical Inquiry', *Duke Law Journal*, 53, 737–80.

Cox, James D. & Randall S. Thomas (2005a), 'Public and Private Enforcement of the Securities Laws: Have Things Changed Since Enron?', *Notre Dame Law Review*, 80, 893–908.

Cox, James D. & Randall S. Thomas (2005b), 'Letting Billions Slip Through Your Fingers: Empirical Evidence and Legal Implications of the Failure of Financial Institutions to Participate in Securities Class Action Settlements', *Stanford Law Review*, 58, 411–54.

Cox, James D. & Randall S. Thomas (2006), 'Does the Plaintiff Matter? An Empirical Analysis of Lead Plaintiffs in Securities Class Actions', *Columbia Law Review*, 106, 1587–1640.

Cox, James D., Randall S. Thomas & Lynn Bai (2008), 'There Are Plaintiffs and … There Are Plaintiffs: An Empirical Analysis of Securities Class Action Settlements', *Vanderbilt Law Review*, 61, 355–86.

Cox, James D. & Randall S. Thomas (2009a), 'Mapping the American Shareholder Litigation Experience: A Survey of Empirical Studies of the Enforcement of the U.S. Securities Law', *European Company and Financial Law Review*, 6, 164–203.

Cox, James D., Randall S. Thomas & Lynn Bai (2009b), 'Do Differences in Pleading Standards Cause Forum Shopping in Securities Class Actions?: Doctrinal and Empirical Analyses', *Wisconsin Law Review*, 2009, 421–54.

Davis, Alicia J. (2009), 'Are Investors' Gains and Losses from Securities Fraud Equal Over Time?', available at http://papers.ssrn.com/sol3/papers.cfm?abstract_id=1121198 (last accessed October 2011).

Easterbrook, Frank & Daniel J. Fischel (1982), 'Corporate Control Transactions', *Yale Law Journal*, 91, 698–738.

Erickson, Jessica (2010), 'Corporate Governance in the Courtroom: An Empirical Analysis', *William and Mary Law Review*, 51, 1749–1832.

Farber, David B. (2005), 'Restoring Trust After Fraud: Does Corporate Governance Matter?', *The Accounting Review*, 80, 539–61.

Green, D.L. (1999), 'Litigation Risk for Auditors and Society', *Critical Perspectives on Accounting*, 10, 339–53.

Jackson, Howell E. & Mark J. Roe (2009), 'Public and Private Enforcement of Securities Laws: Resource-Based Evidence', *Journal of Financial Economics*, 91, 207–38.

Johnson, Marilyn F., Ron Kasznik & Karen K. Nelson (2000), 'Shareholder Wealth Effects of the Private Securities Litigation Reform Act of 1995', *Review of Accounting Studies*, 5, 217–33.

Johnson, Marilyn F., Karen K. Nelson & A.C. Pritchard (2000), 'In re Silicon Graphics Inc.: Shareholder Wealth Effects Resulting from the Interpretation of the Private Securities Litigation Reform Act', *Southern California Law Review*, 73, 773–810.

Johnson, Marilyn F., Ron Kasznik & Karen K. Nelson (2001), 'The Impact of Securities Litigation Reform on the Disclosure of Forward Looking Information by High Technology Firms', *Journal of Accounting Research*, 39, 297–327.

Johnson, Marilyn F., Karen K. Nelson & A.C. Pritchard (2006), 'Do the Merits Matter More? The Impact of the Private Securities Litigation Reform Act', *Journal of Law, Economics, and Organization*, 23, 627–52.

Johnson, Shane A., Harley E. Ryan, Jr., & Yisong S. Tian (2009), 'Managerial Incentives and Corporate Fraud: The Sources of Incentives Matter', *Review of Finance*, 13, 115–45.

Jones, Thomas M. (1980), 'An Empirical Examination of the Resolution of Shareholder Derivative and Class Action Lawsuits', *Boston University Law Review*, 60, 542–74.

Karpoff, Jonathan M. & John R. Lott, Jr. (1993), 'The Reputational Penalty Firms Bear from Committing Criminal Fraud', *Journal of Law and Economics*, 36, 757–802.

Karpoff, Jonathan M., D. Scott Lee & Gerald S. Martin (2007), 'The Legal Penalties for Financial Misrepresentation', available at http://papers.ssrn.com/sol3/papers.cfm?abstract_id=933333 (last accessed October 2011).

Karpoff, Jonathan M., D. Scott Lee & Gerald S. Martin (2008a), 'The Cost to Firms of Cooking the Books', *Journal of Financial and Quantitative Analysis*, 43, 581–611.

Karpoff, Jonathan M., D. Scott Lee & Gerald S. Martin (2008b), 'The Consequences to Managers for Financial Misrepresentation', *Journal of Financial Economics*, 88, 193–215.

Krishnan, C.N.V., Ronald W. Masulis, Randall S. Thomas & Robert B. Thompson (2011) 'Litigation in Mergers and Acquisitions', available at http://papers.ssrn.com/sol3/papers.cfm?abstract_id=1722227 (last accessed October 2011).

Marciukaityte, Dalia, Samuel H. Szewczyk, Hatice Uzun & Raj Varma (2006), 'Governance and Performance Changes after Accusations of Corporate Fraud', *Financial Analysts Journal*, 62, 32–41.

Miller, Ronald I., (2006), 'Recent Trends in Shareholder Class Action Litigation: Beyond the Mega-Settlements, Is Stabilization Ahead?', NERA Economic Consulting.

Mohan, Saumya (2004), 'Corporate Governance Monitoring and Litigation as Substitutes to Solve Agency Problems', available at http://ssrn.com/abstract=606625 (last accessed October 2011).

Mohan, Saumya (2007), 'Disclosure Quality and Its Effect on Litigation Risk', available at http://papers.ssrn.com/sol3/papers.cfm?abstract_id=956499 (last accessed October 2011).

Palmrose, Zoe-Vonna & Susan Scholz (2000), 'Restated Financial Statements and Auditor Litigation', available at http://papers.ssrn.com/sol3/papers.cfm?abstract_id=248455 (last accessed October 2011).

Peng, Lin & Ailsa Roell (2008), 'Executive Pay and Shareholder Litigation', *Review of Finance*, 12, 141–84.

Perino, Michael A. (2003), 'Did the Private Securities Litigation Reform Act Work?', *University of Illinois Law Review*, 2003, 913–78.

Perino, Michael A. (2006a), 'Institutional Activism Through Litigation: An Empirical Analysis of Public Pension Fund Participation in Securities Class Actions', *St. John's Legal Studies*, Research Paper No. 06-055, available at http://papers.ssrn.com/sol3/papers.cfm?abstract_id=938722 (last accessed October 2011).

Perino, Michael A. (2006b), 'Markets and Monitors: The Impact of Competition and Experience on Attorneys' Fees in Securities Class Actions', *St. John's Legal Studies*, Research Paper No. 06-0034, available at http://papers.ssrn.com/sol3/papers.cfm?abstract_id=870577 (last accessed October 2011).

Pritchard, Adam C. & Hillary A. Sale (2005), 'What Counts As Fraud? An Empirical Study of Motions to Dismiss Under the Private Securities Litigation Reform Act, *Journal of Empirical Legal Studies*, 2, 125–49.

Romano, Roberta (1991), 'The Shareholder Suit: Litigation Without Foundation?', *Journal of Law, Economics and Organization*, 7, 55–87.

Simmons, Laura E. & Ellen M. Ryan (2008), 'Securities Class Action Settlements: 2007 Review and Analysis', Cornerstone Research, 10.

Spiess, D. Katherine & Paula A. Tkac (1997), 'The Private Securities Litigation Reform Act of 1995: The Stock Market Casts its Vote', *Managerial and Decision Economics*, 18, 545–61.

Strahan, Philip E. (1998), 'Securities Class Actions, Corporate Governance and Managerial Agency Problems', available at http://papers.ssrn.com/sol3/papers.cfm?abstract_id=104356 (last accessed October 2011).

Talley, Eric L. (2006), 'Cataclysmic Liability Risk Among Big Four Auditors', *Columbia Law Review*, 106, 1641–97.

Talley, Eric L. & Gudrun Johnsen (2004), 'Corporate Governance, Executive Compensation and Securities Litigation', USC L. Sch., Olin Research Paper No. 04–7, available at http://papers.ssrn.com/sol3/papers.cfm?abstract_id=536963 (last accessed October 2011).

Thakor, Anjan V., Jeffrey S. Nielsen & David A. Gulley (2005), 'The Economic Reality of Securities Class Action Litigation', Navigant Consulting, prepared for US Chamber of Commerce Institute for Legal Reform, October 26, 2005.

Thompson, Robert B. (1999), 'Preemption and Federalism in Corporate Governance: Protecting Shareholder Rights to Vote, Sell and Sue', *Law and Contemporary Problems*, 62, 215–42.

Thompson, Robert B. & Randall S. Thomas (2004a), 'The New Look of Shareholder Litigation: Acquisition-Oriented Class Actions', *Vanderbilt Law Review*, 57, 133–210.

Thompson, Robert B. & Randall S. Thomas (2004b), 'The Public and Private Faces of Derivative Lawsuits', *Vanderbilt Law Review*, 57, 1745–93.

Weiss, Elliott J. & Lawrence J. White (2004), 'File Early, then Free Ride: How Delaware Law (Mis)Shapes Shareholder Class Actions', *Vanderbilt Law Review*, 57, 1797–1882.

# 10. The elusive quest for director independence[1]
## Lisa M. Fairfax

## 1. INTRODUCTION

The inside director – a director currently employed with the corporation on whose board she serves – is a dying breed. Although the inside director once dominated corporate boards, today the inside director has been painted as biased, untrustworthy, and generally antithetical to the best interests of shareholders and the corporation. As a result, inside directors have been banished altogether from many board committees and reduced to holding a minimal number of seats on the board as a whole (Bhagat & Black 1999, 2002; Chandler 1999; Millstein 1993).

This virtual elimination of inside directors' role on corporate boards is inextricably linked to the overwhelming consensus that boards should be dominated by 'independent' directors. Such consensus stems from a belief that independent directors are better equipped to monitor the corporation, detect fraud, and protect shareholders' interests. However, the evidence accumulated from our increased experience with independent directors calls into question such a belief. Surveying that evidence, this chapter argues that the independent director's value has been vastly overstated, while the inside director has been under-appreciated and under-examined. This has important implications for corporate governance and our system of external regulation.

The second part of this chapter reveals the manner in which the corporate landscape has shifted to exclude inside directors from the board, and the rationale for that shift. The following sections pinpoint the limits of independent directors' ability to be truly independent and to effectively perform their monitoring role, while highlighting the difficulties associated with overcoming those limitations. The penultimate section examines the empirical evidence on independent directors' impact. Finally, the last section makes the affirmative case for the inside director while considering the principal drawbacks associated with reliance on such directors.

## 2. THE VIRTUAL DISAPPEARANCE OF THE INSIDE DIRECTOR

Despite its prominence in corporate and securities law, the term 'independent director' has no uniform definition; instead judges and legislators define the term differently. Moreover, the term is used differently in various contexts (Clarke 2007; Brudney 1982; Rodrigues 2008).

At the federal level, SOX and various federal listing standards define an independent director by reference to a bright-line test that excludes inside directors. For example, under

---

[1]  Reprinted with edits from Fairfax (2010).

New York Stock Exchange (NYSE) and NASDAQ Stock Market (NASDAQ) rules, no direc-tor can qualify as independent if she has a material relationship with the company.[2] The first such disqualifying material relationship is serving as an employee of the company.[3] Similarly, SOX automatically excludes from the definition of 'independent' any director who receives direct compensation from the company on whose board she sits.[4] These standards distinguish an 'inside director' from an 'outside director' who does not have an employment position with the company, and make being an outside director a prerequisite for being considered independent.

In contrast to this bright-line test for independence at the federal level, Delaware courts define 'independence' contextually. As an initial matter, Delaware courts distinguish between a 'disinterested director' and an 'independent director'. A disinterested director is a director who will not benefit financially from a transaction unless shareholders more generally enjoy the benefit.[5] Hence, disinterest is narrower than independence. However, a director's disin-terest is a necessary, but not sufficient, condition for independence. Thus, in addition to demonstrating that a director is disinterested, proving independence requires showing that a director has no ties to a particular interested individual and is not otherwise controlled by that individual in a manner that compromises her ability to make objective decisions with respect to the individual.[6] Delaware's situational approach to independence means that a director's independence cannot be determined *ex ante*; instead a director's independence can be deter-mined only after examining the specific transaction at issue and the directors or officers impacted by the transaction (Veasey 2001; Rodrigues 2008). Nevertheless, both Delaware and federal rules define independence to exclude inside directors.

Historically, inside directors played a dominant role on corporate boards, holding most of the seats (Bhagat & Black 1999). While their numbers gradually declined, inside directors still held some 50% of board seats in the 1950s. Moreover, as recently as 1989, it was rare for a board to have fewer than three inside directors (Gordon 2007).

In recent years, insiders' early dominance has diminished completely. By the 1990s, inde-pendent directors began holding an increasingly larger portion of corporate board seats. The most recent Korn/Ferry study on corporate boards found that, on average, 80% of directors are independent. This figure has remained unchanged for at least a decade (Korn/Ferry Inst. 2004, 2008).

This change has been accelerated by federal legislation. SOX essentially requires that a board have an audit committee comprised entirely of independent directors. SOX also requires each national securities exchange and national securities association to adopt rules compatible with SOX.[7] Pursuant to this requirement, listing agencies such as the NYSE and NASDAQ not only adopted rules requiring each member of the audit committee to be independent, but also mandated that each member of the nominating and compensation committee be independent.

---

2   *See Listed Company Manual* § 303A.08, NYSE (last approved by the SEC in July 2009), http://www.nyse.com/lcm/lcm_section.html; NASDAQ, Marketplace Rules, at Rule 4200(a)(15) (2004), available at www.nasdaq.com/about/MarketplaceRules.pdf (last accessed October 2011).
3   *See Listed Company Manual, supra* note 2, § 303A.02(b)(i); NASDAQ, *supra* note 2, at Rule 4200(a)(15).
4   *See* 15 U.S.C. § 78-1(m)(3)(B) (2006).
5   *See Aronson v. Lewis*, 473 A.2d 805, 812 (Del. 1984).
6   *See Cede & Co. v. Technicolor, Inc.*, 634 A.2d 345, 362 (Del. 1993).
7   *See* Sarbanes-Oxley Act of 2002 § 301, 15 U.S.C. § 78j-1(m) (2006).

Finally, the NYSE and NASDAQ require their listed companies to have a majority of independent directors on their boards.[8] Federal rules passed in the wake of the recent financial meltdown also incorporate director-independence provisions. Thus, the Dodd-Frank Act requires compensation committee members to be independent.[9] Federal rules already required that the compensation committees of companies receiving funding pursuant to the Troubled Asset Relief Program (TARP) be comprised of independent directors.[10] By mandating the presence of independent directors, these rules hastened the shift away from inside directors.

This shift is prompted by the belief that independent directors are better monitors than inside directors and hence respond to the corporate agency problem. In the corporation, shareholders (or those perceived to 'own' the corporation) are distinct from directors and officers (or those charged with managing the corporation). The separation of ownership and control in the corporation means that while corporate officers have tremendous discretion to make decisions, there exist few mechanisms to hold them accountable for those decisions and ensure that they use their discretion in a manner that benefits the corporation and its shareholders. Importantly, there is nothing to prevent corporate officers from self-dealing – that is, engaging in transactions that benefit themselves at the expense of the corporation. Therefore, corporate law's perpetual challenge has been to develop mechanisms that can reduce agency costs (Berle & Means 1932; Bratton 2001; Jensen & Meckling 1976).

The principal corporate governance response to the agency problem has been the independent director. The independent director's primary function is to monitor the corporation and its officers with an eye towards ensuring that managers do not abuse their authority by engaging in self-dealing or fraud, or otherwise shirking their responsibilities (Cox 2003; Mitchell 2005a). Independent directors' monitoring role encompasses several functions. Such directors guard against self-dealing by closely examining conflict-of-interest transactions to ensure that they benefit the corporation (Cox 2003). Independent directors also are supposed to detect and prevent fraud because their active oversight decreases managers' ability to engage in wrongdoing. In addition, such directors should prevent managerial shirking and thus enhance corporate performance because they can proactively examine corporate affairs, not only to ensure that managers are productive, but also to ensure that managers make the most efficient and effective decisions.

Importantly, it is believed that in order to perform this monitoring function effectively, directors must be independent from management and the corporation. Their independence ensures that directors do not feel beholden to managers and hence can monitor them without unwarranted influences. In other words, a director's independence means that she can be trusted to critically examine decisions made by officers, as opposed to simply rubber-stamping those decisions.

Monitoring by independent directors has served as an alternative to external regulation. Courts and regulators historically have embraced the view that they are not in the best position to judge the conduct of corporate officers and directors for at least two reasons. The first is that they are not businesspeople and hence are ill-equipped to judge business decisions.

---

[8]   *See Listed Company Manual*, § 303A; NASDAQ, Rules 4200, 4350.

[9]   *See* Dodd-Frank Wall Street Reform and Consumer Protection Act, Pub. L. No. 111-203, § 952, 124 Stat. 1376, 1900 (2010) (codified at 15 U.S.C. 78j-3).

[10]   *See* TARP Standards for Compensation and Corporate Governance, 31 C.F.R. pt. 30 (2009).

Indeed, given the inherent risk associated with business decisions, judges' *ex post* analysis of those decisions may discourage directors from engaging in appropriate, though risky, behavior (Cunningham 2007; Velasco 2004). Moreover, courts should prefer the decisions of directors because such directors (and not judges) were elected by shareholders to govern (Velasco 2004). The second reason courts and regulators have been reluctant to intervene in business decisions is that they cannot be proactive in monitoring corporate decisions – at best they serve as an *ex post* check on board behavior (Borowski 1984). This reluctance is exemplified by the standard pursuant to which courts review most corporate conduct. This standard, known as the 'business judgment rule', presumes that directors' decisions are made in the best interests of the corporation and requires shareholders to overcome a tremendous hurdle in order to hold directors liable for such decisions (Allen et al. 2001; Johnson 2000).

Importantly, however, courts and regulators recognize that the deference afforded corporate decisions is only appropriate if they can be assured that those decisions will be made free from inappropriate influences. This recognition means that deference is afforded mainly to independent directors. Courts and legislatures defer to decisions made by independent directors not just with respect to ordinary transactions, but also with respect to transactions that pose particular risks of managerial abuse (Mitchell 2005b; Bainbridge 1993). Conflict-of-interest transactions receive heightened review under the 'entire fairness' test, but if the transaction is approved by independent directors, courts reinstate review under the business judgment rules. Courts similarly defer to independent directors in the context of shareholder derivative actions.

## 3. THE INTRACTABILITY OF COMPROMISING TIES

Conventional wisdom suggests that in order for directors to be effective monitors, they must be free from all compromising ties to the corporation. In fact, prior scandals have revealed that even directors deemed independent under an *ex ante* standard because they lacked employment relationships with a corporation nevertheless received advisory or similar fees from the corporation, or otherwise had significant relationships with the corporation or its board that jeopardized their ability to be impartial (Breeden 2003). As a result, reform efforts have focused on eliminating those relationships and thereby strengthening the definition of 'director independence'. Notwithstanding those efforts, the current conception of director independence continues to fall short of capturing all of the ties that compromise a director's ability to be objective. This section indicates that this failure may be impossible to rectify in a manner that enhances directors' ability to be truly impartial.

**Social Ties**

All of the recent reforms define 'independence' with reference to the financial ties between a director and the corporation. Thus, SOX excludes from the definition of 'independent director' anyone who receives compensation from the corporation. Along these same lines, the NYSE and NASDAQ's definition of independence essentially filters out compromising financial relationships between the corporation and the director. New financial reforms also focus on financial ties, determining independence by reference to the source of a person's compensation. Then too, while Delaware's independence definition appears to capture more than just financial relationships, Delaware courts historically have defined independence in a manner that fails to give significant weight to anything but financial ties.

By contrast, the current definition of director independence does not in any meaningful manner encompass social or professional ties between directors and the corporation. Outside of familial ties, federal rules do not consider social or professional connections in the independence inquiry. Similarly, Delaware courts essentially have dismissed allegations of social ties from the independence analysis. To be sure, on the heels of the 2002 corporate-governance scandals, it appeared that Delaware courts would allow social ties to play a significant role in the independence inquiry (Fairfax 2005). Thus, two lower Delaware court cases affirmatively recognized the impact that social and professional ties could play in a director's ability to be independent.[11] In so doing, Delaware courts acknowledged that such recognition represented a departure from earlier cases that failed to consider the compromising nature of social relationships. However, recent decisions from the Delaware Supreme Court make clear that evidence regarding social, professional, or business relationships would normally be insufficient to discredit a director's independence, essentially minimizing the role such relationships play in the independence inquiry.[12]

Of course, some discount the impact of social ties on a director's objectivity, and hence independence. Accordingly, judges and corporate-governance experts alike have insisted that it would be a mistake to presume that directors would subordinate their professional reputation and business judgment in order to favor the interests of friends or business associates. Instead, we should presume that other considerations, particularly professional reputation, will eclipse any potential for bias stemming from social ties (Veasey 1997).

This presumption, however, seems dubious for at least three reasons. First, it is not clear that directors' business and professional reputations suffer as a result of 'favoring' the social relationships they have with managers and board members. Indeed, anecdotal and empirical evidence indicates that directors may not experience significant harm when they make decisions based on such social relationships. At least some studies reveal that directors continue to hold board seats and be accepted within the business community even after evidence that they may have acquiesced in large frauds (Agrawal et al. 1999; Helland 2006; Fich & Shivdasani 2007).

Second, favoring these social relationships might enhance a director's reputation in business circles. Indeed, not only does being a board member often depend upon one's social and professional connections, but remaining on the board also depends upon ensuring that those connections are not damaged. Thus, directors have strong incentives to behave in ways that ensure their continued presence on the board, and such behavior often includes compliance with norms against questioning managerial policies (Borowski 1984).

Third, social science research and other prevailing evidence regarding board conduct indicate that social ties can have a profound impact on a person's ability to behave objectively. Anecdotal evidence from corporate scandals reflects the compromising nature of social ties. For example, congressional investigations regarding Enron and WorldCom found that directors had extensive social and professional ties with corporate officers and their fellow direc-

---

[11]    *See Beam ex rel. Martha Stewart Living Omnimedia, Inc. v. Stewart*, 833 A.2d 961, 979–82 (Del. Ch. 2003); *In re Oracle Corp. Derivative Litig.*, 824 A.2d 917, 938–39 (Del. Ch. 2003).

[12]    *See Beam ex rel. Martha Stewart Living Omnimedia, Inc. v. Stewart*, 845 A.2d 1040, 1051–52 (Del. 2004).

tors that compromised their ability to be impartial and undermined their ability to provide an adequate check on directors' and officers' conduct (Breeden 2003). Then too, even some Delaware judges have recognized the fallacy in assuming that corporate directors' independence would not be jeopardized as a result of social connections they have with other directors or officers.[13] In their view, such an assumption ignores the social nature of humans.

That nature has been documented by social science literature, revealing that groups with strong social or personal ties experience difficulties impartially assessing one another's behavior (Brudney 1982; O'Connor 2003). Instead, people with strong social ties seek to avoid conflict out of concern that such conflict would undermine their friendship and 'social capital' – the network of relationships they have with fellow board members (Jehn & Shah 1997; Nahapiet & Ghoshal 1998; Nelson 1989). Applying this literature to corporate boards, corporate-governance experts have found that when board members have strong social or professional relationships, those relationships reduce their capacity to critically scrutinize one another's conduct (O'Connor 2003). This finding confirms that social ties likely impact the ability of board members to impartially assess each other's actions. Other research supports the notion that business relationships undermine true independence, increasing directors' and officers' ability to engage in corporate fraud (Uzun et al. 2004). In this regard, the failure to consider these relationships impedes directors' ability to be truly independent.

This is true even if such ties may have some advantages. For example, social psychologists who study board behavior have argued that social ties may be beneficial in the boardroom because such ties increase trust and openness among board members, thereby promoting honest feedback (Westphal & Zajac 1997). Other corporate-governance scholars concur that people in close social relationships may have more candid dialogue because they feel free to criticize one another's actions (Olson & Adams 2004). A strong social relationship between directors and the CEO may be especially important because without such a relationship, directors may feel reluctant to critique such a powerful officer. Then too, CEOs may be more likely to seek out advice from people with whom they are close and share strong social bonds. In this regard, social relationships among board members promote better communication in the boardroom. Moreover, studies reveal that the collegiality among board members with strong social ties enhances their productivity (Langevoort 2001). Therefore, there may be benefits to social ties in the boardroom, though some question their strength (Velasco 2004).

These benefits do not negate the drawbacks of such ties. In fact, even those who tout the benefits of social ties acknowledge that they come at the expense of the drawbacks discussed above, some of which can be significant (Olson & Adams 2004). Courts' and regulators' failure to acknowledge those drawbacks means that the compromising nature of those ties is not appropriately examined, let alone appropriately balanced against any potential benefits. Hence, that failure impedes the extent to which any director truly can be regarded as independent.

### Structural Bias

Even if courts gave due consideration to social ties, the current understanding of director independence fails to consider appropriately the ramifications of structural bias. 'Structural

---

[13]   *See In re Oracle Corp. Derivative Litig.*, 824 A.2d 917, 938 (Del. Ch. 2003).

bias' refers to the bias resulting from board members' interactions with one another after join-ing the board. This bias stems from the natural collegiality that emerges as a result of working together in a group, as well as the empathy resulting from being a part of the group (Velasco 2004). As one court noted, when directors are forced to pass judgement upon the behavior of their fellow directors, they cannot help but to approach the inquiry from a 'there but for the grace of God go I' mentality, ensuring that their decisions will not be free from bias.[14]

Federal rules fail to acknowledge this structural bias at all. By comparison, Delaware has recognized the effects of structural bias in the context of shareholder derivative suits. In *Zapata*, the court acknowledged the negative impact of structural bias by reserving the ability to reject an independent committee's dismissal decisions. That reservation recognizes that independent directors may find it difficult to be impartial when faced with the decision whether to allow their fellow directors or officers to be sued. However, before shareholders can receive the benefit of a Delaware court's substantive analysis of their suit, they must establish demand futility under *Aronson*. Because proving demand futility is difficult, most shareholder-plaintiffs do not get the benefit of a *Zapata* review. Even when shareholders do get *Zapata* review, courts overwhelm-ingly defer to the committees' decisions. This diminishes the importance of courts' considera-tion of structural bias in the independence inquiry (Velasco 2004).

Psychological research confirms the prevalence of structural bias and suggests that such bias is extremely relevant to the question of director independence (Velasco 2004). Thus, Professors Cox and Munsinger (1985) studied the impact of structural bias on board behav-ior in the context of shareholder derivative actions. They concluded that structural bias can have 'subtle, but powerful' effects on decision-making within a boardroom, prompting direc-tors to insulate their colleagues from legal sanctions. Professor O'Connor similarly concluded that the psychological research with respect to structural bias is particularly relevant in the context of boards, highlighting the degree to which such bias undermines directors' ability to be critical of their fellow directors (O'Connor 2003).

The existence and impact of structural bias makes it normatively difficult to have truly independent directors. To be sure, such bias can be minimized. For example, reducing direc-tors' length of service may reduce the effects of structural bias by minimizing the strong social affinity that hinders impartiality (Bhagat & Black 1999). Furthermore, increasing board diversity – the number of women and people of color on the board – could reduce the impact of structural bias because such bias is understood to flourish in homogeneous and highly cohesive groups (O'Connor 2003). As a descriptive matter however, the failure of courts and regulators to meaningfully acknowledge the relevance of structural bias makes it difficult to implement mechanisms that could minimize such bias. More importantly, research suggests that even if such bias can be minimized, it cannot be eradicated. As a result, such bias makes it 'virtually impossible for directors to be unconflicted in all meaningful respects' (Velasco 2004, 870).

**Director Compensation**

While courts and commentators at least acknowledge the potentially compromising nature of social ties and structural bias, they generally do not acknowledge the problematic ties that

---

[14]   *See Zapata Corp. v. Maldonado*, 430 A.2d 779, 787 (Del. 1981).

may stem from directors' cash compensation. It should come as no surprise that directors are compensated for their board service. In 2009, the average compensation of directors at S&P 500 companies was more than $200,000, with cash compensation reaching an average of about $75,000 (Stuart 2009). This compensation gets ignored when considering a director's independence. Hence, although federal rules provide that a director's receipt of fees from the corporation on whose board she serves prevents her from being viewed as independent, these rules exclude board compensation. Delaware courts similarly do not take board compensation into account when examining a director's independence.

This failure to account for director compensation runs counter to the clear consensus regarding the bias-producing nature of financial ties. In the independence inquiry, receipt of financial fees from the corporation is the quintessential disqualifying tie. Indeed, while courts and regulators differ on their definition of independence, they are uniform in their view that receipt of financial fees automatically disqualifies someone from being deemed independent. All compensation (other than directors' fees) disqualifies a director from being considered independent under SOX. The listing agencies only exclude directors if they receive direct compensation, other than directors' fees, in excess of a certain threshold. Under NASDAQ, for example, direct compensation in excess of $60,000 disqualifies a director from being viewed as independent, while the NYSE threshold is $120,000.[15] Based on these rules, if directors' board fees were not excluded, the current amount of such fees would exclude the average director from being considered independent under both SOX and NASDAQ. On the one hand, these rules reveal that we view the potential for bias from financial fees as so strong that receipt of such fees merits categorically disqualifying people from being deemed independent. On the other hand, the rules' exclusion regarding director fees suggests that merely characterizing such fees as director compensation eradicates any potential for bias. Such a suggestion seems problematic at best.

To be sure, one can offer several reasons why director compensation is excluded from the independence inquiry. First, director compensation is often characterized as nominal, and hence it may not warrant serious concern. Concededly, director compensation is nowhere near the levels of executive compensation. However, the fact that the average directorial compensation package exceeds the thresholds for independence under federal rules suggests that such compensation should not be considered nominal. Second, directors generally have other sources of compensation, thereby reducing any concern that board compensation may jeopardize directors' impartiality. Of course, consultants and advisors likely have additional sources of income but nevertheless are excluded from the definition of independence if they receive funds from the corporation on whose board they sit. This fact undercuts the theory that an outside director's alternative source of income minimizes the compromising nature of director compensation.

To be sure, the most pragmatic rationale behind the failure to consider board fees in the independence inquiry is that such consideration would result in no one being viewed as independent. Hence, such compensation cannot be used to measure a director's independence. In light of the compromising nature of financial ties, however, the fact that we cannot consider those ties underscores the inherent limitations in the quest for true director independence.

---

[15]   *See* NASDAQ, *supra* note 2, at 4200(a)(15). The NYSE disqualifies directors only if they receive direct compensation in excess of $120,000. *See Listed Company Manual, supra* note 2, § 303A.02.

**Climate Changes**

When viewed in context of the current demands on independent directors, the prospects for meaningfully minimizing any of the aforementioned ties seem bleak. Such ties, particularly those resulting from structural bias and director fees, are an inevitable feature of board service. Moreover, as we increase our reliance on independent directors, such ties deepen. Thus, as directors have greater responsibility, they inevitably spend more time together. Hence, the current climate likely increases the strength of directors' social ties while enhancing the potential for structural bias. Then too, independent directors are being paid more. This is because it is difficult to increase directors' responsibilities without a corresponding increase in compensation (Korn/Ferry Inst. 2008). Indeed, because many directors are paid on a per-meeting basis, their compensation increases with the frequency of their meetings. Therefore, like social ties and structural bias, these financial ties not only appear to be an inevitable feature of board service, but also are likely to increase as we continue to rely on independent directors. Hence, as we increase our dependence on independent directors, we reduce our ability to minimize these compromising ties, thereby reducing the extent to which independent directors can be characterized as truly independent.

## 4.   SELECTION BIAS

The current director-selection process in public corporations also undermines a director's ability to be truly independent and perform her monitoring roles with sufficient rigor. In public corporations, most shareholders vote by proxy, which means that they vote without being physically present at the annual meeting. To obtain shareholders' proxies, the corporation must send them a proxy statement.[16] Currently, only the names of candidates supported by incumbent managers and directors appear on a corporation's proxy statement; corporations can and do exclude the names of candidates supported by shareholders.[17] This exclusion means that although shareholders can nominate their own candidates, the only way that those candidates can be voted upon is if shareholders distribute their own proxy statement. The expenses associated with such a distribution can be prohibitive, making it extremely difficult for most shareholders to nominate and elect candidates of their choice (Bebchuk 2005; Eisenberg 1970). The inability of shareholders to nominate their candidates on the corporation's proxy statement means that the vast majority of directors are chosen by incumbent officers and directors and run unopposed (Bebchuk 2005).

This process undermines director independence and the corresponding monitoring function. Shareholders' ability to vote directors out of office or refuse to elect them into office should prompt directors to pay heed to their monitoring responsibilities. Moreover, shareholders' power to replace directors should encourage them to make decisions beneficial to shareholders (Bebchuk 2005). However, the director-selection process means that such power does not exist in any meaningful respect. Instead, directors may feel beholden to their fellow

---

[16]    *See* Exchange Act Rule 14a-3, 17 C.F.R. § 240.14a-3(a)(8) (2010). The proxy statement also contains information about the candidates to be voted on.

[17]    *See* Exchange Act Rule 14a-8, 17 C.F.R. § 240.14a-8(i)(8) (2010) (providing exclusions for shareholder proposals related to election of directors).

directors because those directors nominate them and therefore control their ability to remain on the board (Bebchuk 2005; Blair & Stout 1999; Cosenza 2007; Eisenberg 1970). In fact, studies reveal that CEOs often dominate the director nomination process, causing directors to feel beholden to CEOs (Bebchuk 2005; Borowski 1984; Cosenza 2007). Thus, the director selection process does little to incentivize effective monitoring and instead increases the potential for managerial and CEO capture (Bebchuk 2005; Borowski 1984). Then too, this process enhances the structural bias within the boardroom because it increases the extent to which directors view their fate as linked with their fellow officers and directors. Therefore, the director-selection process impedes the ability of directors to be truly independent (Brudney 1982; Cosenza 2007).

Recognizing the potential for managerial and CEO capture inherent in the director-selection process, reforms have not only required boards to create nominating committees, but also have required that those committees be comprised of independent directors (Gordon 2007). A nominating committee is charged with locating and nominating qualified directorial candidates. Separate nominating committees are designed to ensure that directors locate qualified candidates without unwarranted influence from management in general and the CEO in particular. The belief was that eliminating managers and CEOs from the selection process would ensure the independence of directors, realigning directors' interests with shareholders and enhancing the efficacy of their monitoring (Borowski 1984).

Unfortunately, this solution may not alleviate the capture problem. First, notwithstanding the creation of independent nominating committees, evidence reveals that CEOs continue to influence the director-nomination process through informal consultations and recommendations of directorial candidates (Uzun et al. 2004). Boards continue to appoint people with social and professional connections to the CEO and other managers. Second, even if nominating committees alleviate the concerns associated with managerial and CEO capture, they fail to ensure that directors are free from bias with respect to other directors. Thus, evidence reveals that directors have substantial social and professional ties with their fellow directors. In fact, even when boards rely on search firms, they gravitate towards candidates with whom they have some shared history or relationships (Uzun et al. 2004). At best, therefore, we may have exchanged managerial capture for board capture.

Some corporate scholars contend that the solution to selection bias is to increase shareholders' role in the nomination process by allowing them access to the corporation's proxy statement (Bebchuk 2005; Cosenza 2007). Such access ensures that shareholder-supported candidates have an opportunity to be included on the corporate proxy statement, increasing the chances that directors' interest will be aligned with that of the shareholders. Because it creates the potential that shareholders can replace directors, proxy access also incentivizes all directors to pay heed to shareholder interests, thereby invigorating directors' monitoring role.

In August 2010, the SEC passed a proxy-access rule for the first time in its history.[18] The rule included both a provision requiring all public corporations to provide proxy access to its shareholders under certain circumstances and a provision allowing shareholders to adopt proxy access bylaws. However, the SEC halted implementation of the rule in the face of legal challenges to its legitimacy. Pursuant to such challenges, the DC Circuit overturned the

---

[18]   *See, e.g.*, Facilitating Shareholder Director Nominations, Exchange Act Release Nos. 33-9136, 34-62764 (Aug. 25, 2010), available at http://www.sec.gov/rules/final/2010/33-9136.pdf (last accessed October 2011).

portion of the rule mandating proxy access. The decision does not impact the validity of that portion of the SEC's proxy access rule allowing for the adoption of proxy access bylaws. Nevertheless, it remains unclear what form, if any, proxy access will take.

Additionally, recently, shareholders have been more active and have waged more proxy contests (Institutional Shareholder Services 2006). But often such contests only seek to replace a percentage of the board, typically less than a majority (SharkRepellent 2008). Moreover, many proxy contests result in negotiated settlement agreements, pursuant to which the board is expanded to accommodate one or two shareholder-supported candidates. This suggests that proxy access is not likely to reverse the status quo, pursuant to which board-rooms are largely populated with directors selected by management as opposed to sharehold-ers. As a result, proxy access may not decrease the number of people on the board that may be impacted by selection bias, except indirectly. Then too, evidence suggests that once share-holder-supported candidates secure election to the board, they tend to adapt to board culture rather than becoming forceful advocates for shareholders (SharkRepellent 2008). In other words, the nature of their selection does not negate the bias that occurs as a result of being a board member (Borowski 1984). Given the literature related to structural bias, this result should not be surprising. Consequently, while increased access to the proxy may result in increased director independence at the margins, it does not significantly reduce the bias of board members, and thus may not significantly enhance directors' monitoring abilities.

## 5.   INFORMATIONAL ASYMMETRIES

Informational asymmetries inherent in the role of independent directors further limit such directors' ability to be effective monitors. In order for a director to be effective, she needs accurate information (Eisenberg 1975; Bainbridge 1993). As one scholar acknowledges, 'Uninformed independence has limited value ...' (Gordon 2007, 1541). However, the fact that independent directors are outsiders, and hence not engaged in the daily affairs of the corporation, means that they are dependent on the insiders they must monitor to supply them with the information necessary to discharge their responsibilities (Cox 2003). To the extent we are concerned that insiders may inappropriately filter or otherwise manipulate the infor-mation, independent directors may not alleviate this concern. This is because such directors' outsider status makes it difficult for them to verify the accuracy of the information, and thus difficult to be effective monitors.

The primary corporate governance response to the informational asymmetry problem has been reliance on 'gatekeepers' such as advisors, attorneys, and accountants (Cox 2003; Cunningham 2007). These gatekeepers should reduce the problems associated with informa-tional asymmetries by providing independent directors with an alternate and impartial source of information, thereby ensuring that they are not wholly dependent on insiders. Moreover, these gatekeepers are supposed to verify the integrity of the information provided by company insiders.

However, reliance on gatekeepers does not necessarily reduce the problem of informa-tional asymmetries, nor does it adequately enhance the efficiency of corporate monitoring. First, even gatekeepers depend upon insiders for their supply of information (Eisenberg 1975). Thus, gatekeepers' presence does not negate the insider's ability to dominate, and therefore potentially manipulate, the flow of information. Second, gatekeepers may be unreliable because they are subject to their own conflicts of interest that could lead them to manipulate data or otherwise rubber-stamp decisions made by managers (Cunningham 2004). The unreliability of gatekeepers reflects one of the principal insights of the corporate governance scandals of 2002 (Cunningham 2004; Coffee 2004; Gordon 2007). Those scandals also indicated that when gatekeepers fail in their responsibility, independent directors are unable to take up the slack, not only because such directors cannot monitor gatekeepers to ensure their impartiality, but also because such directors cannot ensure the integrity and clarity of financial reporting without the assistance of gatekeepers (Gordon 2007; Wilmarth 2007). Third, evidence suggests that these gatekeepers are also impacted by structural bias and therefore find it difficult to be truly objective. Indeed, such gatekeepers come to view themselves as a part of the managerial team, reducing their ability to criticize that team (Baysinger & Butler 1985; Elson & Gyves 2003). Hence, reliance on gatekeepers does not overcome directors' informational disadvantage.

Another solution to the informational asymmetries problem focuses on public disclosure of corporate information. Indeed, over the last fifty years, the SEC has sought to require better and more accurate disclosure from public companies (Gordon 2007). Such disclosure is aimed at ensuring that directors are not wholly dependent on insiders, but instead can rely on the accuracy and integrity of corporate information. To the extent the disclosure regime imparts accurate information, that regime ensures that independent directors will not be at an informational disadvantage. According to Professor Gordon, the disclosure regime ensures that the stock market is well informed, increasing the informativeness of stock price. As a result, Professor Gordon argues that the disclosure regime ameliorates independent directors' information deficit, therefore enhancing such directors' ability to perform their oversight functions (Gordon 2007).

However, this argument appears flawed for a variety of reasons. First, many scholars maintain that stock price is not accurate. Instead, the price incorporates noise. Consequently, many have asserted that stock price fails to reflect fundamental value (Black 1986; Gerding 2006; Langevoort 1992; Stout 1995). The existence of noise undermines the informativeness of stock price and undermines the reliability of the information such price imparts to independent directors. Second, the focus on short-term stock price encourages independent directors to acquiesce in management's price-manipulation practices for at least two reasons. The first is because independent directors come to view stock price as a measure of success and thus have incentives to ensure that the measure remains high. The second is that the increase in stock-based compensation for directors increases directors' bias in favor of practices that augment, if not manipulate, stock price. Evidence reveals that independent directors not only were complicit in stock-based fraud such as option backdating, but also that they benefited from them through the receipt of opportunistically timed stock-option grants (Bebchuk et al. 2007; Gordon 2007). In this regard, the focus on stock price may undermine independent directors' objectivity, while the potential for fraud undermines the integrity of information reflected by the stock price.

Third, even if stock price conveys accurate information, it is not narrowly tailored enough to assist independent directors in making or monitoring strategic decisions (Abramowicz & Henderson 2007). Finally, the notion that the disclosure regime overcomes the independent directors' informational disadvantages is somewhat circular. In order for the disclosure regime to overcome independent directors' informational disadvantage, the regime must convey accurate information. However, the conveyance of accurate information depends upon the independent directors' ability to verify the accuracy and integrity of such information. In other words, independent directors can only verify the accuracy of the information by reliance on the disclosure regime, which in turn relies upon the directors for its efficiency. The circularity of this problem illuminates the flaws in the presumption that the disclosure regime overcomes the informational-asymmetries problem (Abramowicz & Henderson 2007).

As this discussion reveals, informational asymmetries may significantly curtail independent directors' effectiveness as monitors. Because the solutions aimed to overcome this problem are flawed at best, independent directors' monitoring abilities may also be flawed at best.

## 6.   THE KNOWLEDGE DEFICIT

The fact that the current conception of an independent director fails to consider the necessary expertise of a director further undermines the directors' ability to be effective. Except in the audit committee, no reform focuses on the affirmative skills or knowledge directors need in order to properly perform their responsibilities. Thus, studies reveal that while many directors have knowledge about general business matters, few have knowledge regarding the particular industry on whose board they sit, and even fewer have knowledge about the specific company on whose board they sit (Bancroft 2006).

This knowledge deficit is troubling. Recently, scholars have argued that corporate governance literature has largely ignored the knowledge resources necessary to enhance corporate governance. Such scholars maintain that a monitoring system that relies on people without sufficient knowledge is not only inefficient, but potentially damaging (Gorga & Halberstam 2007). In other words, even if directors received accurate and adequate information, they may lack the ability to understand that information, and thus they may also lack the ability to detect deficiencies with respect to that information (Olson & Adams 2004). Corporate governance scandals tend to confirm that many directors lack the knowledge and expertise to sufficiently appreciate the complexities associated with their business, and that such lack of knowledge impedes the effectiveness of their oversight (Forelle & Bandler 2006). The knowledge deficit also increases the likelihood that independent directors will acquiesce in managerial decisions because their lack of knowledge will prompt inappropriate deference.

To be sure, some corporations have sought to overcome the knowledge deficit by focusing on director expertise during recruitment. However, this focus is difficult in light of the requirements for director independence. Those requirements not only limit the overall pool of qualified directors, but also limit the pool of candidates with needed industry expertise, since such candidates are most likely to be insiders.

## 7.   INDEPENDENT DIRECTOR LIABILITY, OR LACK THEREOF

This section contends that the reluctance to impose liability on independent directors also may reduce their effectiveness. The law imposes responsibilities on independent directors but essentially fails to impose any legal sanctions on such directors for their failure to adhere to those responsibilities. In an effort to ensure adherence to their various monitoring duties, the law imposes various fiduciary duties on directors. At the state level, those duties encompass the duty of care, which demands that directors make decisions in the best interest of the corporation, and the duty of loyalty, which regulates director conduct when there is some conflict of interest. Delaware recently made clear that the duty of loyalty includes the duty of oversight, encompassing the obligation to effectively monitor the actions of officers and directors.[19] The federal securities laws also impose obligations on independent directors, holding them responsible for accurate and reliable disclosures (Sale 2006). All of these duties are aimed at ensuring that independent directors carry out their jobs in a diligent fashion and do not place their interests ahead of corporate interests. However, independent directors rarely face liability, either civil or criminal, for breaching their duties.

This rarity significantly reduces the extent to which independent directors are deterred from shirking. One critical purpose of legal sanctions is to deter misconduct by making the costs of such conduct outweigh its benefits (Brown 2001; Chambliss 1967; Dau-Schmidt 1990; Posner 1985). However, if there is no significant risk of liability, then such liability has very little deterrent value (Paternoster & Simpson 1996; Coffee 2002). Consequently, the near-complete failure to impose legal sanctions on independent directors means that such directors may not be properly motivated to carry out their responsibilities.

**Liability in the Civil Context**

With respect to civil liability, Professors Black, Cheffins, and Klausner (2006) conducted an extensive investigation of outside director liability. The investigation revealed that while there are thousands of suits involving corporate- or securities-law violations filed each year, those suits rarely name independent directors as defendants. Even when such directors are named defendants, they rarely face trial. Professor Black and his co-authors only discovered eight securities trials and twelve direct shareholder suits where independent directors were defendants when the trial commenced.

Even when they go to trial, independent directors are rarely found liable and that liability almost never results in out-of-pocket damages. Professor Black and his co-author's research only found one case where outside directors paid damages after trial. That case, *Smith v. Van Gorkom*, is well known in corporate circles as the one major example of independent directors being held liable for breaching their fiduciary duties (Roe 2002). Independent directors' near-complete absence from the liability regime results primarily from a combination of insurance, indemnification, and statutory protections that make it nearly impossible to extract monetary damages from independent directors (Black, Cheffins & Klausner 2006). Those statutory protections (including the legislative response to Van Gorkom allowing exculpation of directors for breaches of the duty of care) ensure that a *Van Gorkom*-type action will no longer result in out-of-pocket liability. Other studies confirm this pattern. A five-year study of SEC enforcement actions found that while the SEC had filed over 500 actions against some 700 corporate defendants, none of those defendants were independent directors (Sale 2006).

Independent director liability resulting from settlements is also extremely rare. Most cases do not go to trial but instead result in settlement. However, of the thousands of settled cases over the past 25 years, only twelve cases involved independent directors. In most of those

---

[19]   *See Stone v. Ritter*, 911 A.2d 362, 370 (Del. 2006).

cases, the settlements involved nominal amounts. Most of the cases involving significant amounts were also the most recent and the most infamous, including Tyco, WorldCom, and Enron. According to Professor Black and his co-authors, the circumstances that made liability possible in those cases are unlikely to reoccur. Hence, despite such cases, they concluded that directors would continue to have a low risk of liability for money damages in settlements (Black et al. 2006).

## Liability in the Criminal Context

A similar pattern emerges with respect to criminal prosecutions. Historically, very few actions have been brought against white-collar criminals. Moreover, even if such actions are brought, corporate actors rarely face trial and seldom face any significant criminal penalties or jail time (Fairfax 2005). After the corporate scandals of 2002, criminal prosecutions and convictions involving corporate actors rose dramatically. However, none of those actions have involved independent directors. For example, the five-year anniversary report from the Department of Justice Corporate Fraud Task Force revealed that such Task Force had secured more than 1,200 convictions against various corporate officers, directors, and affiliates.[20] None of these convictions involved independent directors. Hence, even in a climate of enhanced focus on white-collar crime, independent directors have escaped liability.

## A Closer Look at the Connection Between Liability and Effective Monitoring

This lack of liability potentially reduces the effectiveness of independent directors. Indeed, legal liability in the form of criminal and civil sanctions is aimed at assuring an actor's fidelity to her fiduciary obligations, particularly through deterrence (Gordon 2007). The lack of such liability reduces that assurance.

Some corporate scholars are unconcerned about the lack of liability imposed on independent directors because they believe such liability has no impact on their performance. Such scholars point to empirical evidence indicating that legal sanctions have very little deterrent value (Braithwaite & Makkai 1991; Simpson & Koper 1992). They also pinpoint the various legal sanctions that existed before, but apparently failed to deter, the corporate scandals of 2002 (Moohr 2003; Ribstein 2002). In this regard, these scholars question the wisdom of relying on legal sanctions to constrain or deter independent director conduct, and are unconcerned with the virtual absence of such sanctions.

This lack of concern is misguided. There are studies revealing the importance of legal sanctions in curbing misconduct (Hollinger & Clark 1983; Klepper & Nagin 1989; Paternoster & Simpson 1996). Such studies suggest that legal sanctions are generally ineffective in deterring improper conduct when there is decreased certainty regarding their implementation. That suggestion may explain why our current liability regime has failed to deter corporate misconduct.

---

[20]   *See* Press Release, US Department of Justice, Fact Sheet: President's Corporate Fraud Task Force Marks Five Years of Ensuring Corporate Integrity (July 17, 2007), available at http://www.justice.gov/opa/pr/2007/July/07_odag_507.html (last accessed October 2011).

Other scholars insist that legal sanctions are unnecessary to curtail director misconduct or otherwise ensure that directors pay heed to their responsibilities because other mechanisms exist that ensure director compliance. As an initial matter, these scholars argue that reliance on legal sanctions could have decidedly negative consequences, including making directors risk-averse, and thereby reducing optimal decision-making (Phillips 1984; Ribstein 2002). Thus, such scholars contend that we should rely on other mechanisms, notably the capital markets and reputational sanctions. First, these scholars insist that capital markets adequately regulate director behavior, deterring directors from taking actions that would harm the corporation because those actions would have a negative impact on stock price (Fischel 1982; Griffith 2003; Phillips 1984). That impact jeopardizes both the corporation and independent directors. In this respect, the markets encourage directors to effectively monitor. However, widespread corporate scandals reflect examples of market failure (Ribstein 2002). Liability regimes are necessary precisely because of the potential for such failure, encouraging managers to act faithfully when such failure occurs (Bainbridge 1993). Hence, it is incorrect to believe that markets can fully shape director behavior.

Second, scholars insist that reputational sanctions sufficiently encourage independent directors' fidelity to their monitoring duties. This rationale points out that independent directors are enmeshed in the business community. Their desire to protect their reputation in that community ensures their compliance with their responsibilities (Barnard 1999). Yet studies have found reputational sanctions to be ineffective in altering director behavior (Fich & Shivdasani 2007; Helland 2006). Moreover, it is likely that such sanctions need the support of legal liability to be most effective.

### Concluding Thoughts on Liability

Because independent directors rarely face liability for their actions, the focus on independent directors means that the corporate-monitoring system depends upon the least accountable actors in the corporate regime. While some contend that markets and reputational sanctions can ensure that independent directors are accountable for their actions (or lack thereof), this contention is flawed. Still others suggest that liability risks cannot encourage directors to adhere to their responsibilities, but studies contradict that suggestion. Hence, the failure to ensure that independent directors face some credible risk of liability means we may have no serious accountability process for those directors. This makes reliance on such directors particularly problematic.

## 8.   THE MIXED EMPIRICAL EVIDENCE

The empirical evidence on the benefits associated with director independence is mixed at best. First, the weight of the empirical evidence tilts against the proposition that independent directors enhance overall corporate performance. Some empirical studies support the notion that independent directors improve corporate performance (Prentice & Spence 2007). But many more contradict that notion, suggesting that there is no correlation between corporate performance and the percentage of independent directors on the board (Bhagat & Black 1999; Fogel & Geier 2007; Klein 1998). Second, the overall evidence with respect to discrete tasks fails to demonstrate a strong correlation between independent directors and improved corporate performance in particular areas. Hence, while some studies find that independent directors perform better at particular tasks, such as firing a poorly performing CEO (Weisbach 1988) or detecting fraud (Uzun et al. 2004), others refute those results (Bhagat & Black 1999; Fich & White 2003; Kesner et al. 1986; Bebchuk et al. 2007). Studies also indicate that independent directors are not more effective at monitoring companies in financial distress or curtailing CEO compensation (Bhagat & Black 1999). A similar pattern emerges with respect to the presence of independent directors on particular committees. Some studies reveal that greater independence on the audit committee improves financial reporting (Prentice & Spence 2007). By contrast, a study of nominating, audit, and compensation committees found little evidence that total independence on those committees positively impacted a company's performance (Klein 1998). Then too, no study exists supporting the proposition that better performance will emerge if boards are comprised of a supermajority of independent directors (Bhagat & Black 1999, 2002).

Taken together, the empirical evidence at least calls into question the contention that independent directors are more effective monitors than insiders. An article by Professors Bhagat and Black (1999) comprehensively surveyed the available empirical data on independent directors to determine whether the trend toward enhanced independence rested on 'sound empirical footing', and concluded that it did not. When Professors Bhagat and Black (2002) performed a follow-up study, their conclusion remained unchanged. They did, however, consider that one reason why empirical evidence did not demonstrate the value of having more independent directors on boards might be that we do not know how to properly measure independence. Nevertheless, the conclusion regarding the relative unsoundness of the empirical evidence in this area was consistent with their own study, which found that companies with more independent directors on their boards do not perform better than others. While other scholars disagree with respect to the weight that should be given to various studies, they nevertheless acknowledge that the empirical evidence on the ability of independent directors to sufficiently perform their monitoring functions is mixed, if not 'weak at best' (Gordon 2007, 500).

In fact, a few studies indicate that independent directors may perform worse than their inside counterparts (Romano 2005). Those studies reveal that inside directors may outperform independent directors both with respect to overall corporate performance and with respect to certain discrete tasks. Thus, some studies found a negative correlation between the presence of independent directors and corporate performance (Bhagat & Black 1999). Others revealed that having inside directors on particular committees correlated with improved performance (Klein 1988). Still others found a negative correlation between outside directors and fraud detection (Klein 1988). These studies collectively suggest that inside directors may have a positive influence on corporate affairs in general, as well as within specific committees or otherwise with respect to areas of particular concern to the public.

Taken as a whole, the empirical evidence does not convincingly prove that independent directors necessarily lead to more effective and efficient monitoring. That lack of proof is consistent with the hypothesis that such directors may be constrained in their ability to perform their functions with the requisite rigor. Moreover, it sets the stage for further exploration of an enhanced role for inside directors within the corporate arena.

## 9.   CONCLUSION: THE UNEASY CASE FOR THE INSIDE DIRECTOR

The fact that independent and inside directors are both significantly constrained in their ability to be objective undermines the rationale for favoring one category of director over the other. Moreover, inside directors may possess some important advantages over independent directors. Unlike independent directors, who require additional methods for incentivizing their commitment to the corporation, inside directors are extremely motivated to act in ways that benefit the corporation. Inside directors can add value to the board because they are better informed and more knowledgeable than independent directors. Empirical evidence appears to support the theory that inside directors make valuable contributions to the board (Klein 1988). Studies also confirm that having board members with intimate knowledge of the business may generate better informed decision-making (Olson & Adams 2004; Sonnenfeld 2002). Increasing the presence of inside directors on the board also may enable corporations to increase board diversity because women and people of color are better represented in managerial positions than they are in the chief-executive level positions typically considered for board membership. Thus, such groups should benefit from corporate recruitment of more inside directors who presumably will come from the managerial ranks.

The primary concern with insiders as monitors centers around the possibility that they will use their inside advantage to enrich themselves, and thereby engage in self-dealing transactions. As indicated in previous sections, this concern creates a corporate governance challenge. One potential response is to reinvigorate the role of external regulations, at least with respect to conflicts of interest and other high-risk transactions.

Another concern is that inside directors may be less likely to detect and prevent fraud. Some scholars contend that the studies related to independent directors reveal strong support for the proposition that independent directors do a better job of detecting and preventing fraud, particularly financial fraud (Prentice & Spence 2007). Indeed, several studies find a negative correlation between financial-reporting fraud and the presence of independent directors (Beasely et al. 1999; Uzun et al. 2004). In particular, recent studies show that director independence on the audit committee correlates with improved financial reporting and fewer earnings restatements (Prentice & Spence 2007).

However, the evidence with respect to financial fraud remains mixed. Hence, some studies find no correlation between director independence and the detection of financial fraud (Bhagat & Black 1999; Kesner et al. 1986). Others find a positive correlation between the two, indicating that in some cases, independent directors may increase the potential for fraud (Tosi et al. 2003). Still others indicate that independent directors may have acquiesced in, and benefited from, such fraud (Bebchuk et al. 2007).

Moreover, the correlation between director independence and enhanced fraud detection may be explained by factors unconnected to a director's status as independent. First, it could be that the empirical results reflect the impact of enhanced rules surrounding auditors, rather than the effect of director independence. Second, the empirical results could reflect the effectiveness of the additional requirements imposed on audit committee members. In fact, the strongest and most robust evidence indicating that directors have a positive impact on reducing fraud has emerged in the context of such directors' role on the audit committee (Prentice & Spence 2007). Nevertheless, the concern regarding financial fraud suggests that we must devote attention to this issue when seeking to increase the number of inside directors on the board.

Another concern associated with inside directors is the potential that such directors, particularly those subordinate to other directors with whom they may serve, may feel beholden to their superiors in a way that undermines their ability to be objective. However, there may be ways in which this phenomenon can be mitigated, e.g. by having inside directors with similar levels of seniority, avoiding having directors who are direct subordinates of other directors, and decreasing the role of the CEO.

Importantly, some of our concerns with inside directors may be alleviated by reinvigorating the role of external regulation, particularly with respect to judicial oversight of high risk transactions. As compared to independent directors, inside directors are more likely to face liability for overreaching and thus breaching their fiduciary obligations (Sale 2006). Thus, imposing liability on inside directors may be a more realistic solution. To be sure, external regulation is not a panacea. Moreover, this chapter does not seek to prove that we should supplant boards dominated by independent directors with those dominated by insiders. Instead, it suggests a need to reconsider the optimal mix of directors in light of the drawbacks associated with independent directors and the potential benefits of inside directors.

The insights of this chapter clearly have implications for corporate governance. First, they demonstrate that independence is not an inherent value and thus should not drive the debate about the appropriate model for board oversight. Second, the chapter highlights the importance of external regulation. In fact, our fears that such regulation could discourage directors from seeking board seats or otherwise stifle appropriate risk-taking have blinded us to the important role that regulation plays in ensuring an effective accountability system. Moreover, our over-reliance on director independence has lulled us into accepting a governance system with very little external oversight. To be sure, we may have reservations about the case for the inside director. However, critically examining the inside directors' role on the board may prompt us to have a broader and more realistic conversation about directors, corporate boards, and the development of more appropriate structures for enhancing corporate monitoring.

# REFERENCES

Abramowicz, Michael & M. Todd Henderson (2007), 'Prediction Markets for Corporate Governance', *Notre Dame Law Review*, 82, 1343–1414.

Agrawal, Anup, Jeffrey Jaffe & Jonathan M. Karpoff (1999), 'Management Turnover and Governance Changes Following the Revelation of Fraud', *Journal of Law and Economics*, 42, 309–42.

Allen, William T., Jack. B. Jacobs and Leo Strine, Jr. (2001), 'Function over Form: A Reassessment of Standards of Review in Delaware Corporation Law', *Delaware Journal of Corporate Law*, 26, 859–95.

Bainbridge, Stephen M. (1993), 'Independent Directors and the ALI Corporate Governance Project', *George Washington Law Review*, 61, 1034–83.

Bancroft, Margaret A. (2006), 'Knowledge Is Power: What Went Wrong in the Mutual Fund Industry', *Journal of Business and Technology Law*, 1, 145–56.

Barnard, Jayne W. (1990), 'Shareholder Access to the Proxy Revisited', *Catholic University Law Review*, 40, 37–105.

Barnard, Jayne W. (1999), 'Reintegrative Shaming in Corporate Sentencing', *Southern California Law Review*, 72, 959–1007.

Baysinger, Barry D. & Henry N. Butler, (1985), 'Corporate Governance and the Board of Directors: Performance Effects of Changes in Board Composition', *Journal of Law, Economics and Organization*, 1, 101–24.

Beasley, Mark S., Joseph V. Carcello & Dana R. Hermanson (1999), 'Comm. of Sponsoring Orgs. of the Treadway Comm'n, Fraudulent Financial Reporting: 1987–1997: An Analysis of U.S. Public Companies 4', available at http://www.coso.org/publications/FFR_1987_1997.pdf (last accessed October 2011).

Bebchuk, Lucian Arye (2005), 'The Case for Increasing Shareholder Power', *Harvard Law Review*, 118, 833–914.
Bebchuk, Lucian Arye, Yaniv Grinstein & Urs Peyer (2007), 'Lucky CEOs and Lucky Directors', *Journal of Finance*, 56, 2363.
Berle, Adolf A. & Gardiner C. Means (1932), *The Modern Corporation and Private Property*, New York: Commerce Clearing House, Inc.
Bhagat, Sanjai & Bernard Black (1999), 'The Uncertain Relationship Between Board Composition and Firm Performance', *The Business Lawyer*, 54, 921–63.
Bhagat, Sanjai & Bernard Black (2002), 'The Non-Correlation Between Board Independence and Long-Term Firm Performance', *Journal of Corporation Law*, 27, 231–73.
Black, Fischer (1986), 'Noise', *Journal of Finance*, 41, 529–43.
Black, Bernard, Brian Cheffins & Michael Klausner (2006), 'Outside Director Liability', *Stanford Law Review*, 58, 1055–1159.
Blair, Margaret M. & Lynn A. Stout (1999), 'A Team Production Theory of Corporate Law', *Virginia Law Review*, 85, 247–328.
Borowski, Irwin (1984), 'Corporate Accountability: The Role of the Independent Director', *Journal of Corporation Law*, 455–71.
Braithwaite, John & Toni Makkai (1991), 'Testing an Expected Utility Model of Corporate Deterrence', *Law and Society Review*, 25, 7–40.
Bratton, William W. (2001), 'Berle and Means Reconsidered at the Century's Turn', *Journal of Corporation Law*, 26, 737–70.
Breeden, Richard C. (2003), 'Restoring Trust: Report to the Hon. Jed S. Rakoff on Corporate Governance for the Future of MCI, Inc.', available at http://law.du.edu/images/uploads/restoring-trust.pdf (last accessed October 2011).
Brown, Darryl K. (2001), 'Street Crime, Corporate Crime, and the Contingency of Criminal Liability', *University of Pennsylvania Law Review*, 149, 1295–1360.
Brudney, Victor (1982), 'The Independent Director – Heavenly City or Potemkin Village?', *Harvard Law Review*, 95, 597–659.
Chambliss, William J. (1967), 'Types of Deviance and the Effectiveness of Legal Sanctions', *Wisconsin Law Review*, 1967, 703–19.
Chandler III, William B. (1999), 'On the Instructiveness of Insiders, Independents, and Institutional Investors', *University of Cincinnati Law Review*, 67, 1083–97.
Clarke, Donald C. (2007), 'Three Concepts of the Independent Director', *Delaware Journal of Corporate Law*, 32, 73–111.
Coffee, John C. Jr. (2002), 'Penalties for White Collar Crime: Are We Really Getting Tough on Crime?', Hearing before the S. Comm. on the Judiciary, 107th Cong. (2002), available at http://judiciary.senate.gov/hearings/testi-mony.cfm?id=4f1e0899533f7680e78d03281fe1f24c&wit_id=4f1e0899533f7680e78d03281fe1f24c-2-1 (last accessed October 2011).
Coffee, Jr. John C. (2004), 'Gatekeeper Failure and Reform: The Challenge of Fashioning Relevant Reforms', *Boston University Law Review*, 84, 301–64.
Cosenza, Elizabeth (2007), 'The Holy Grail of Corporate Governance Reform: Independence or Democracy?', *BYU Law Review*, 2007, 1–54.
Cox, James D. (2003), 'Managing and Monitoring Conflicts of Interests: Empowering the Outside Directors with Independent Counsel', *Villanova Law Review*, 48, 1077–95.
Cox, James D. & Harry L. Munsinger (1985), 'Bias in the Boardroom: Psychological Foundations and Legal Implications of Corporate Cohesion', *Law and Contemporary Problems*, 48, 83–135.
Cunningham, Lawrence A. (2004), 'Choosing Gatekeepers: The Financial Statement Insurance Alternative to Auditor Liability', *UCLA Law Review*, 52, 413–75.
Cunningham, Lawrence A. (2007), 'Beyond Liability: Rewarding Effective Gatekeepers', *Minnesota Law Review*, 92, 323–86.
Dau-Schmidt, Kenneth G. (1990), 'An Economic Analysis of the Criminal Law as Preference-Shaping Policy', *Duke Law Journal*, 1990, 1–38.
Eisenberg, Melvin Aron (1970), 'Access to the Corporate Proxy Machinery', *Harvard Law Review*, 83, 1489–1526.
Eisenberg, Melvin Aron (1975), 'Legal Models of Management Structure in the Modern Corporation: Officers, Directors and Accountants', *California Law Review*, 63, 375–439.
Elson, Charles M. & Christopher J. Gyves (2003), 'The Enron Failure and Corporate Governance Reform', *Wake Forest Law Review*, 38, 855–84.
Fairfax, Lisa M. (2005), 'Sarbanes-Oxley, Corporate Federalism, and the Declining Significance of Federal Reforms on State Director Independence Standards', *Ohio Northern University Law Review*, 31, 381–415.
Fairfax, Lisa M. (2010), 'The Uneasy Case for the Inside Director', *Iowa Law Review*, 96, 127–93.
Fich, Eliezer M. & Lawrence J. White (2003), 'CEO Compensation and Turnover: The Effects of Mutually Interlocked Boards', *Wake Forest Law Review*, 38, 933–59.

Fich, Eliezer M. & Anil Shivdasani (2007), 'Financial Fraud, Director Reputation, and Shareholder Wealth', *Journal of Financial Economics*, 86, 306–36.
Fisch, Jill E. (1993), 'From Legitimacy to Logic: Reconstructing Proxy Regulation', *Vanderbilt Law Review*, 46, 1129–99.
Fischel, Daniel R. (1982), 'The Corporate Governance Movement', *Vanderbilt Law Review*, 1259, 35, 1263–92.
Fogel, Eric M. & Andrew M. Geier (2007), 'Strangers in the House: Rethinking Sarbanes-Oxley and the Independent Board of Directors', *Delaware Journal of Corporate Law*, 32, 33–72.
Forelle, Charles & James Bandler (2006), 'How Did UnitedHealth's McGuire Get Same Options Twice?', *Wall Street Journal*, October 20, 2006, B1.
Gerding, Erik F. (2006), 'The Next Epidemic: Bubbles and the Growth and Decay of Securities Regulation', *Connecticut Law Review*, 38, 393–453.
Gordon, Jeffrey N. (2007), 'The Rise of Independent Directors in the United States, 1950–2005: Of Shareholder Value and Stock Market Prices', *Stanford Law Review*, 59, 1465–1568.
Gorga, Érica & Michael Halberstam (2007), 'Knowledge Inputs, Legal Institutions and Firm Structure: Towards a Knowledge-Based Theory of the Firm', *Northwestern University Law Review*, 101, 1123–1206.
Griffith, Sean J. (2003), 'Deal Protection Provisions in the Last Period of Play', *Fordham Law Review*, 71, 1899–1970.
Helland, Eric (2006), 'Reputational Penalties and the Merits of Class-Action Securities Litigation' *Journal of Law and Economics*, 49, 365–95.
Holdcroft, James P. & Jonathan R. Macey (1997), 'Flexibility in Determining the Role of the Board of Directors in the Age of Information', *Cardozo Law Review*, 19, 291–320.
Hollinger, Richard C. & John P. Clark (1983), 'Deterrence in the Workplace: Perceived Certainty, Perceived Severity, and Employee Theft', *Social Forces*, 62, 398–418.
Institutional Shareholder Services (2006), '2006 Postseason Report: Spotlight on Executive Pay and Board Accountability', available at http://www.riskmetrics.com/system/files/private/2006PostSeasonReportFINAL.pdf (hard copy held by author).
Jehn, Karen A. & Priti Pradhan Shah (1997), 'Interpersonal Relationships and Task Performance: An Examination of Mediating Processes in Friendship and Acquaintance Groups', *Journal of Personality & Social Psychology*, 72 , 775–90.
Jensen, Michael & William Meckling (1976), 'Theory of the Firm: Managerial Behavior, Agency Costs, and Ownership Structure', *Journal of Financial Economics*, 3, 305–60.
Johnson, Lyman (2000), 'The Modest Business Judgment Rule', *The Business Lawyer*, 55, 625–52.
Kesner, Idale F., Bart Victor & Bruce T. Lamont (1986), 'Board Composition and the Commission of Illegal Acts: An Investigation of Fortune 500 Companies', *Academic Management Journal*, 29, 789–99.
Klein, April (1998), 'Firm Performance and Board Committee Structure', *Journal of Law and Economics*, 41, 275–304.
Korn/Ferry Int'l (2004), *31st Annual Board of Directors Study*.
Korn/Ferry Int'l (2008), *34th Annual Board of Directors Study*.
Klepper, Steven & Daniel Nagin (1989), 'Tax Compliance and Perceptions of the Risks of Detection and Criminal Prosecution', *Law and Society Review*, 23, 209–40.
Langevoort, Donald C. (1992), 'Theories, Assumptions and Securities Regulation: Market Efficiency Revisited', *University of Pennsylvania Law Review*, 140, 851–920.
Langevoort, Donald C. (2001), 'The Human Nature of Corporate Boards: Law, Norms, and the Unintended Consequences of Independence and Accountability', *Georgetown Law Journal*, 89, 797–832.
Lin, Laura (1996), 'The Effectiveness of Outside Directors as a Corporate Governance Mechanism: Theories and Evidence', *Northwestern University Law Review*, 90, 898–976.
Millstein, Ira M. (1993), 'The Evolution of the Certifying Board', *The Business Lawyer*, 48, 1485–97.
Mitchell, Lawrence E. (2005a), 'The Trouble with Boards', George Washington University Law School Public Law and Legal Theory Research Papers Series, Paper No. 159.
Mitchell, Lawrence E. (2005b), 'Structural Holes, CEOs, and Informational Monopolies: The Missing Link in Corporate Governance', *Brooklyn Law Review*, 70, 1313–68.
Moohr, Geraldine Szott (2003), 'An Enron Lesson: The Modest Role of Criminal Law in Preventing Corporate Crime', *Florida Law Review*, 55, 937–75.
Nahapiet, Janine & Sumantra Ghoshal (1998), 'Social Capital, Intellectual Capital, and the Organizational Advantage', *Academic Management Review*, 23, 242–66.
Nelson, Reed (1989), 'The Strength of Strong Ties: Social Networks and Intergroup Conflict in Organizations', *Academic Management Journal*, 32, 377–401.
O'Connor, Marleen A. (2003), 'The Enron Board: The Perils of Groupthink', *University of Cincinnati Law Review*, 71, 1233–1320.
Olson, John F. & Michael T. Adams (2004), 'Composing a Balanced and Effective Board to Meet New Governance Mandates', *The Business Lawyer*, 59, 421–52.

Paternoster, Raymond & Sally Simpson (1996), 'Sanction Threats and Appeals to Morality: Testing A Rational Choice Model of Corporate Crime', *Law and Society Review*, 30, 549–84.

Phillips, David M. (1984), 'Principles of Corporate Governance: A Critique of Part IV', *George Washington Law Review*, 52, 653–704.

Posner, Richard A. (1985), 'An Economic Theory of the Criminal Law,' *Columbia Law Review*, 85, 1193–1231.

Prentice, Robert A. & David B. Spence (2007), 'Sarbanes-Oxley as Quack Corporate Governance: How Wise is the Received Wisdom?', *Georgetown Law Journal*, 95, 1843–1909.

Ribstein, Larry E. (2002), 'Market vs. Regulatory Responses to Corporate Fraud: A Critique of the Sarbanes-Oxley Act of 2002', *Journal of Corporation Law*, 28, 1–67.

Rodrigues, Usha (2008), 'The Fetishization of Independence', *Journal of Corporate Law*, 33, 447–95.

Roe, Mark J. (2002), 'Corporate Law's Limits', *Journal of Legal Studies*, 31, 233–71.

Romano, Roberta (2005), 'The Sarbanes-Oxley Act and the Making of Quack Corporate Governance', *Yale Law Journal*, 114, 1521–1611.

Sale, Hillary A. (2006), 'Independent Directors as Securities Monitors', *The Business Lawyer*, 61, 1375–1412.

SharkRepellent (2008), *Study of Activists Campaigns* (hard copy held by author).

Simpson, Sally S. & Christopher S. Koper (1992), 'Deterring Corporate Crime', *Criminology*, 30, 347–76.

Sonnenfeld, Jeffrey (2002), 'What Makes Great Boards Great', *Harvard Business Review*, September.

Stout, Lynn A. (1995), 'Are Stock Markets Costly Casinos?: Disagreement, Market Failure, and Securities Regulation', *Virginia Law Review*, 81, 611–72.

Stuart, Spencer (2009), 2009 Spencer Stuart Board Index, available at http://content.spencerstuart.com/sswebsite/pdf/lib/SSBI2009.pdf (last accessed October 2011).

Tosi, Henry L., Wei Shen & Richard J. Gentry (2003), 'Why Outsiders on Boards Can't Solve the Corporate Governance Problem', *Organizational Dynamics*, 32, 180–92.

Uzun, Hatice, Samuel H. Szewczyk & Raj Varma (2004), 'Board Composition and Corporate Fraud', *Financial Analysts Journal*, May–June 2004, 33–43.

Veasey, E. Norman (1997), 'The Defining Tension in Corporate Governance in America', *The Business Lawyer*, 52, 393–406.

Veasey, E. Norman (2001), 'Should Corporation Law Inform Aspirations for Good Corporate Governance Practices – Or Vice Versa?', *University of Pennsylvania Law Review*, 149, 2179–91.

Velasco, Julian (2004), 'Structural Bias and the Need for Substantive Review', *Washington University Law Quarterly*, 82, 821–917.

Weisbach, Michael S. (1988), 'Outside Directors and CEO Turnover', *Journal of Financial Economics*, 20, 431–60.

Westpahl, James D. & Edward J. Zajac (1997), 'Defections from the Inner Circle: Social Exchange, Reciprocity and the Diffusion of Board Independence in U.S. Corporations', *Administrative Science Quarterly*, 42, 161–83.

Wilmarth, Jr., Arthur E. (2007), 'Conflicts of Interests and Corporate Governance Failures at Universal Banks during the Stock Market Boom of the 1990s: The Cases of Enron and WorldCom', in Benton E. Gup (ed.) *Corporate Governance in Banking: A Global Perspective*, Cheltenham: Edward Elgar Publishing Ltd, 97–133.

# 11. 'Low-cost' shareholder activism: A review of the evidence

*Fabrizio Ferri*

## 1. INTRODUCTION

Over the last decade, a series of corporate governance scandals have given rise to an intense wave of shareholder activism. In this chapter, I focus on two particular tools of shareholder activism, namely shareholder proposals filed under Rule 14a-8 and shareholder votes on uncontested director elections. These tools share an appealing feature. Their cost is quite modest and they do not require a significant equity stake in the company – hence, they are referred to as 'low-cost' tools of activism. But their easy accessibility comes at a price. Both shareholder proposals and shareholder votes on director elections are essentially non-binding on the target firm, casting doubts on their effectiveness as a driver of change.

Low-cost activism can be contrasted with 'activism via large ownership' where the power to influence the firm derives from the (costly) acquisition of a significant equity stake. This equity stake can then be used to press for changes in governance and strategy (through the threat of 'exit' or the threat of gaining control). This power may be quietly exerted behind the scenes (large shareholder activism) or in a more confrontational and public manner (e.g. proxy fights, hedge funds activism).[1] In the case of low-cost activism, the power to influence the firm is predicated upon the ability of the activist to build consensus among a broad spectrum of shareholders – crystallized in a symbolic, non-binding vote – and the assumption that boards will respond because 'symbols have consequences' (Grundfest 1993), for example, in terms of reputation costs.

In view of these differences, it is important to understand the effectiveness of low-cost activism tools since 'activism via large ownership' is not an option for a large class of investors (e.g. diversified funds) and it is prohibitively costly to implement in large firms.[2] The evidence indicates that until a decade ago the answer was clear: with rare exceptions, low-cost activism was also 'low-impact' (Gillan & Starks 2007). Activists were rarely able to rally significant voting support around their initiatives and, even when successful, were largely ignored by boards. However, following a series of high profile accounting scandals in 2001–2002 (e.g. Enron and Worldcom), the quality of corporate governance has become a central concern for institutional investors and low-cost activism seems to have gained more steam.

---

[1]   For a review of the literature on hedge fund activism, see Brav et al. (2009). The literature on the effect of large shareholders is extensive; for a recent study and references, see Cronqvist and Fahlenbrach (2009). For a recent study on proxy fights (and references to earlier studies), see Listokin (2009) and Alexander et al. (2010).

[2]   Targets of proxy fights and hedge fund activism tend to be small firms (Bebchuk 2007; Brav et al. 2009), while low-cost activism usually targets large S&P 500 firms.

In this chapter I review a recent body of research that (re)examines low-cost activism in the post-Enron period and offer suggestions for future studies.[3] Collectively, these studies suggest that low-cost activism has become a more powerful tool, capable of driving governance changes at target firms, promoting market-wide adoption of governance practices, and influencing key policy reforms. They provide insights into the reasons for this enhanced effectiveness and shed light on specific settings. Future research should be directed at understanding whether, when, and how low-cost activism results in value creation and improved performance – a question of utmost importance as recent reforms further empower shareholders (e.g. 'say on pay').

## 2.   DIRECTOR ELECTIONS

Boards play a central role in the legal structure of the modern publicly traded corporation with dispersed ownership, selecting top management and its compensation, advising on strategy, monitoring performance, and deliberating on major corporate decisions. In doing so, boards are supposed to ensure that the firm is run in the best interest of shareholders. For this board-centric corporate governance system to function well, shareholder power to remove directors is a key requisite. The threat of replacement is intended to lead to the selection of directors with the appropriate skills and to keep these directors accountable to the shareholders who elected them. The notion that shareholders can resort to replacing the board when dissatisfied with its performance underlies the legal system's choice to insulate the merits of directors' decisions from judicial review.

In practice, however, a rival team seeking to replace incumbents faces significant impediments (Bebchuk 2007). Perhaps the major one is that while challengers incur the full cost of a proxy contest (regardless of the outcome), they only receive a fraction of the expected benefits – a classic 'free rider' problem. Proxy contests are even costlier when the target firm has a staggered board, because challengers need to win two elections held at least one year apart (in a typical three-class staggered board), not to mention the difficulty of winning other shareholders' support when victory of the challenger implies one year with a divided board and significant uncertainty. These impediments may explain the paucity of electoral challenges,[4] which, in turn, means that almost all director elections are uncontested.

In addition, until recently (see below), under the default arrangements established by state law, the outcome of director elections was determined according to a *plurality voting* standard: that is, the candidate with the most votes 'for' is elected, a system that helps avoid the disruptive effects of failed elections. In uncontested elections, the plurality voting standard

---

[3]   The chapter only reviews research related to shareholder proposals and uncontested director elections (with a focus on the work I am more familiar with, including my own). A related form of low-cost activism is shareholder voting on *management-initiated* proposals. Examples of studies on this topic are Morgan and Poulsen (2001), Martin and Thomas (2005), Listokin (2008) and Bebchuk and Kamar (2010), among others.

[4]   Citing data compiled by Georgeson Shareholders, Bebchuk (2007) reports that the number of proxy contests aimed at replacing the director team at the helm of the company (i.e. aside from takeover-related proxy contests) averaged only 12 per year between 1996 and 2005 (14 between 2001 and 2005), mostly targeting small firms and resulting in the challengers' victory only in one third of the cases. Proxy contests were similarly rare in earlier periods (Grundfest 1993).

means that each nominee will always be elected as long as she receives one vote 'for', no matter the number of votes 'withheld' (under SEC rule 14a-4(b) shareholders cannot vote 'against' a director nominee, they can only vote 'for' or 'withhold' support).

The paucity of contested elections, combined with the plurality voting standard, has led to the following observation: 'corporate democracy in America has most often been a lot like Soviet democracy: the votes didn't really matter, because only one candidate was on the ballot and was assured of winning, whatever the voters thought' (Norris 2004).[5]

However, in a 1990 speech to the Council of Institutional Investors, former SEC commissioner Joseph Grundfest argued that a high percentage of votes withheld from the board in uncontested elections, while unlikely to affect the outcome of the election under plurality voting, could have economic consequences and act as a catalyst for governance and operating changes (Grundfest 1990). Faced with a formal expression of shareholders' discontent (or just the mere threat of it), directors concerned with their reputational capital would stand up to powerful CEOs and become more responsive to shareholders' interests. Hence, Grundfest proposed a new shareholder activism tool – 'just vote no' campaigns – organized efforts to persuade other shareholders to withhold votes from directors up for election in an effort to communicate shareholder dissatisfaction to the board.[6]

### Determinants of Votes Withheld from Directors and the Role of Proxy Advisors

Cai, Garner and Walkling (2009) examine the determinants of the percentage of votes withheld from directors in a sample of 13,384 uncontested director elections (corresponding to almost 2,488 meetings) between 2003 and 2005. The study presents two major findings. First, the vast majority of directors are elected with almost unanimous support (mean and median votes 'for' are 94% and 97%, respectively) – hence, opposition to directors is relatively rare, though increasing over time.[7] Second, essentially only three factors appear to have an economically significant effect on the percentage of votes withheld: a 'withhold' recommendation issued by the influential proxy advisory firm Institutional Shareholder Services (ISS) (resulting in 19% more votes withheld), the presence of a vote-no campaign (7% more votes withheld), and poor attendance at board meetings (14% more votes withheld). All the other factors analyzed, even when statistically significant, have little economic impact (1–2% change in votes withheld). Hence, to understand the determinants of shareholder votes on director elections we need to understand the determinants of vote-no campaigns and withhold (WH) recommendations (poor attendance at board meetings is one of the triggers of WH recommendations). Two studies shed light on this issue.

---

5    In almost every circumstance, (the few) directors failing to win a majority vote do not lose their seat (Lublin 2009).

6    In a follow-up article, Grundfest (1993) noted that their modest costs, combined with the significant potential benefits, made vote-no campaigns perhaps the most cost-effective means for exercising responsible shareholder voice, 'without the *sturm und drang* of tender offers and proxy contests'. By then, some institutional investors, like CalPERS, had begun using vote-no campaigns, often triggering a response from the board.

7    Georgeson (2010) reports that from 2006 to 2009 the number of directors of S&P 1,500 firms receiving greater than 15% votes withheld increased steadily from 385 (at 189 firms) to 1,027 (at 378 firms).

Del Guercio, Seery and Woidtke (2008) analyze a sample of 112 vote-no campaigns between 1990 and 2003 and find that they typically target large, poorly performing firms. The campaigns are staged by institutional investors – mostly public pension funds (54% of the sample) – and are usually motivated by broad concerns with the firm's strategy and performance (60% of the sample), with the other campaigns focusing on specific corporate governance issues (e.g. excess CEO pay or board's lack of responsiveness to shareholder proposals). Three-fourths of the campaigns target the whole board, with the remaining 25% targeting individual directors or committees (e.g. the compensation committee).

Choi, Fisch and Kahan (2009) analyze the determinants of recommendations on director elections issued in 2005 and 2006 by four proxy voting firms: ISS (ISS), Glass Lewis & Company (GL), Egan-Jones Proxy (EJ), and Proxy Governance (PG). Four findings are noteworthy. First, proxy advisors significantly differ in the propensity to issue WH recommendations, ranging from 3.7% of directors for PG to 18.8% for GL, with ISS at 6.6% and EJ at 11.0%. Second, a set of common factors affects the likelihood of a WH recommendation across most or all proxy advisors. For example, all proxy advisors are more likely to issue a WH recommendation for directors with poor attendance at board meetings or with many other directorships, for outside directors with linkages to the firm (non 'independent'), for directors in firms ranking high in terms of abnormal CEO pay, and (relatedly) for compensation committee members. Also, most proxy advisors are likely to exempt new directors from a WH recommendation. However, the weight given to these factors varies dramatically across proxy advisors. For example, attendance at less than 75% of the meetings increases the probability of a WH recommendation from GL by 56.7%, but one from PG by only 6.4%. Third, there are factors emphasized only by one or two proxy advisors. A noteworthy example is that if directors ignore a shareholder proposal supported by a majority of the votes cast, the probability of a WH recommendation from ISS increases by 42.2%, while the probability of a WH recommendation from PG and EJ is unaffected. Finally, there are some factors – namely, the presence of anti-takeover provisions (classified board, poison pill) – which generally do not affect the recommendation of any proxy advisor. Overall, Choi et al. (2009) conclude from their analysis that ISS seems to focus on board-related factors, PG on compensation-related factors, GL on audit-disclosure factors, and EJ on an eclectic mix of factors. These findings may be interpreted as evidence of a competitive market, where new entrants are challenging ISS's dominant position by developing a specific expertise and catering to clients focused on certain issues.

Another interesting finding in Choi et al. (2009) is that proxy advisors pay attention to relative accountability within the board. For example, proxy advisors issuing WH recommendations for directors of firms with abnormally high CEO pay tend to do so only for compensation committee members,[8] while those issuing a WH recommendation from directors of firms experiencing a restatement tend to do so only for audit committee members. Ertimur, Ferri and Maber (2010a) provide further (and more direct) evidence of relative accountability. In their analysis of ISS recommendations on director elections at firms involved in the option backdating scandal, they find that proxy advisors (and voting shareholders) mostly penalized directors sitting on the compensation committee at the time when backdating took place (in most cases, 5–10 years preceding its public discovery).

---

[8]   Accordingly, Cai et al. (2009) find that directors sitting on the compensation committee receive significantly lower votes in firms with excess CEO compensation.

Finally, a puzzling result in Choi et al. (2009) is that proxy advisors do not seem to take into account the conduct that led to a withhold recommendation for a director at firm A in issuing a recommendation for the same director at the annual meeting of firm B. Consistent with this result, Ertimur et al. (2010a) report that none of the directors of firms involved in the backdating scandal received a WH recommendation from ISS when up for election at another firm (and they were not penalized in terms of votes withheld), even when ISS recommended to withhold votes from them at the backdating firm. If proxy advisors and shareholders do not take into account directors' conduct at other firms when, respectively, issuing recommendations and casting votes, then the reputation penalties for monitoring failures are limited. In turn, this implies that *ex ante* incentives to prevent those failures from occurring are reduced. A better understanding of how shareholders view (or should view) directors' actions at one firm when assessing the ability of that director to serve at another firm is an important question for future research.[9]

In addition to calling for a better understanding of proxy voting recommendations, the evidence of a strong correlation between 'withhold' recommendations and shareholder votes also raises a more subtle question about the direction of causality: are shareholders blindly following these recommendations? Or do proxy advisors simply aggregate independently formed shareholder views? Establishing the incremental effect of ISS recommendations is difficult, since ISS forms its voting policies after seeking shareholder input through a yearly survey of its subscribers.

To tackle this question, Choi, Fisch and Kahan (2010) note that observable factors affecting shareholder votes on director elections (*after* controlling for ISS WH recommendations) are similar to those affecting ISS WH recommendations.[10] Hence, they reason, it is likely that unobservable factors affecting both will also be similar. If so, the coefficient on the ISS WH recommendations might be a proxy for unobservable factors independently used by voting shareholders rather than capturing the incremental effect of ISS on the voting outcome – as assumed in prior studies. To estimate such an effect, Choi et al. (2010) suggest an alternative methodology: interact the ISS WH indicator with the percentage ownership by institutional investors and the percentage ownership by individual investors and look at the difference. Under the assumption that institutional investors would vote the same way as the individual investors (i.e. based on the same factors) in absence of ISS and that individual investors do not have access to ISS recommendations, this difference would capture the 'true' independent effect of ISS recommendations on shareholder votes. Choi et al. (2010) estimate this difference to range between 6% and 10% and conclude that the 20% ISS effect reported in prior studies is likely to be overstated.

Ertimur et al. (2010a) explore the question of whether shareholders mechanically follow proxy advisors' recommendations by comparing the voting response to WH recommenda-

---

[9]   In informal conversations, ISS officials confirmed that their policy does not call for automatic carry-over of negative recommendations to a director's other boards, on the ground that, except in the most egregious cases, it is not reasonable to penalize a director for unacceptable actions arising at another company. This policy has been generally supported by ISS's clients (institutional investors). In recent years, as requested by some clients, any issue relevant to a director's qualifications is mentioned in the research reports, even though it does not imply a negative recommendation.

[10]   For example, as discussed earlier, poor attendance at board meetings affects both shareholder votes (Cai et al. 2009) and ISS recommendations (Choi et al. 2009).

tions triggered by different events. In particular, they first compare the effect of backdating-related and non-backdating-related ISS WH recommendations and find that the former is significantly larger (27.1% vs. 18.2%). Then, they examine whether, *within* the set of back-dating-related ISS WH recommendations, the response in terms of shareholder votes varies depending upon the specific reasons for the recommendation and find supporting evidence. They find that a substantial number of shareholders following a backdating-related recom-mendation to withhold votes from directors who sat on the compensation committee during the backdating period ('blamed' by ISS for their failure to prevent or detect backdating) did not follow an identical, backdating-related recommendation when issued against current compensation committee members who did not sit on the board during the backdating period (but nonetheless 'blamed' by ISS for not responding properly to revelations of backdating). These results are not driven by cross-sectional differences in shareholder composition across firms. That is, it appears that the *same* shareholders (and a significant fraction of them) responded differently to ISS WH recommendations depending on their rationale. The authors also present anecdotal evidence of backdating directors experiencing high votes withheld in spite of a 'for' ISS recommendation – further evidence that shareholders do not mechanically follow proxy voting recommendations.

Understanding the role of proxy advisors remains a priority for future research. Reforms empowering shareholders (see below) are likely to increase the influence of proxy advisors and magnify the concerns expressed by many critics with respect to their incentives, poten-tial conflicts of interest, limited transparency and accountability (Choi et al. 2009; Gordon 2009). Tellingly, the role of proxy advisors and whether they should be subject to enhanced regulatory oversight is one of the topics that the SEC is soliciting comments upon in its recent 'proxy plumbing' initiative (see below).

## Consequences of Vote-no Campaigns and Votes Withheld from Directors

Anecdotal evidence suggests that, through their 'power to embarrass' (Norris 2004), vote-no campaigns and 'withhold' votes have become a powerful tool of shareholder activism, with significant economic consequences.[11] A number of recent studies analyze these consequences in large-sample settings. Del Guercio et al. (2008) report improvements in firm operating performance and greater disciplinary CEO turnover in their sample of 112 vote-no campaigns.[12] The effects are stronger when the vote-no campaign is motivated by concerns with overall strategy and performance (rather than specific governance issues). For a subset of 54 cases where the campaign made specific requests, the board implemented 22% of proponents' specific requests completely (and an additional 15% partially), with a higher rate of full implementation (37%) in firms with a larger showing of withheld votes at the annual

---

[11]   Perhaps the event that best represents the increased relevance of this form of activism is the 43% votes withheld from the powerful Disney CEO and Chairman Michael Eisner in 2004 (Norris 2004). Immediately after the vote, the board decided to split the Chairman and CEO role and give the chairmanship to another board member. The annual meeting vote marked the beginning of a crisis that eventually led Eisner to resign the CEO position a year later, ahead of the expiration of his contract.

[12]   For example, the rate of forced CEO turnover at target firms is three times higher than for a size- and performance-matched sample of control firms. Also, the market reacts favorably to the announcements of these CEO turnovers.

meeting.[13] Ertimur, Ferri and Muslu (2011b) focus on a more recent sample of vote-no campaigns driven by compensation-related concerns and report a significant decrease in abnormal CEO pay subsequent to the campaign in target firms characterized by abnormal CEO pay before the campaign. Both studies conclude that vote-no campaigns appear more effective than shareholder proposals – consistent with directors being more responsive to the direct criticism implicit in a vote-no campaign.

Cai et al. (2009) focus on the effect of the percentage of votes withheld. While subsequent firm performance is not affected, they find: (i) a significant decrease in abnormal CEO pay in firms with positive abnormal CEO pay where more votes are withheld from the compensation committee members; (ii) a higher probability of CEO replacement with an outsider in firms where more votes are withheld from outside directors; and (iii) a higher likelihood of subsequent removal of anti-takeover provisions in firms where more votes are withheld from governance committee members. In a similar vein, using a sample of S&P 500 firms between 2000 and 2004, Fischer, Gramlich, Miller and White (2009) find that higher votes withheld from board nominees are followed by greater CEO turnover, more positive price reaction to CEO turnover (particularly when the firm hires an outside CEO), lower abnormal CEO pay, fewer and better-received acquisitions, and more and better-received divestitures.

In brief, all these studies suggest that shareholder dissatisfaction expressed through director elections is followed by value-enhancing choices and a reduction in agency costs. The causality interpretation of these findings is subject to the usual caveats concerning correlated omitted variables. The studies cited above try to control for other observable forms of shareholder pressure and employ useful econometric techniques (e.g. matched sample, propensity score), but ultimately recognize that unobservable forms of shareholder pressure (e.g. behind the scene negotiations) may explain some of their findings (ultimately, withheld votes indicate shareholder dissatisfaction, hence it is likely that dissatisfied shareholders will use multiple channels to push for change).[14] Strengthening the causality interpretation of the above results remains an important challenge and objective for future research.

A puzzling 'no-result' in Cai et al. (2009) is that the percentage of votes withheld from a director is not related to the likelihood she will lose her seat or to the number of other seats held in the future,[15] in contrast with numerous studies documenting loss of directorships in cases of poor monitoring and poor performance (e.g. Coles & Hoi 2003; Yermack 2004; Srinivasan 2005; Fich & Shivdasani 2007; Ertimur et al. 2010b). If directors do not experience any penalty in the director labor market as a result of being the target of shareholder dissatisfaction, why would they take the actions that all these studies document (e.g. reducing CEO pay or changing governance provisions)? One possibility is that shareholders view casting votes and removing directors as substitute mechanisms, resorting to the latter approach only in the most extreme cases. Another, related possibility is that withheld votes

---

    13    As a benchmark, Ertimur, Ferri and Stubben (2010b) report an implementation rate of 31% of shareholder proposals receiving a majority vote between 1997 and 2004. Brav et al. (2008) report an implementation rate of 45% for governance changes requested by activist hedge funds.
    14    Fischer et al. (2009) emphasize that these findings are at least evidence that withheld votes are an informative measure of investors' perceptions of board performance. As such, they may be used in future research to complement other measures.
    15    However, Fischer et al. (2009) document a positive association between the average votes withheld at the *firm-level* and subsequent board turnover.

act as a warning and are followed by a stronger penalty (loss of seat) only when the warning goes unnoticed.[16] Alternatively, it is possible that boards respond to vote-no campaigns and votes withheld not to protect their directorships, but to avoid damaging their public image and their social standing among their peers (Grundfest 1993; Dyck & Zingales 2002). Future research may shed more light on these questions.

### The Move Toward a Majority Voting Standard

In October 2003, in the aftermath of the accounting scandals of 2001–2002, the SEC proposed the introduction of a proxy access rule, that is, a procedure to allow shareholders (under certain conditions) the ability to put their nominees on the proxy ballot along with the board's nominees – a proposal aimed at increasing board accountability to shareholders.[17] The SEC proposal was abandoned amidst strong opposition from the business community, but changing the director election system remained a priority for activists. In 2004 union pension funds began to push for the adoption of a *majority voting* standard, under which a director would not be elected (even in uncontested elections) unless the majority of votes are cast in her favor. Between 2004 and 2007 hundreds of firms were targeted by shareholder proposals requesting the adoption of a majority voting standard. Most of these proposals received substantial shareholder voting support and firms began to adopt this new practice. In 2006 the Delaware Code and the Model Business Corporation Act, while preserving the plurality voting as the default system, were amended to facilitate the adoption of majority voting by corporations. By the end of 2007, two-thirds of S&P 500 firms had adopted some form of majority voting (Allen 2007).

Sjostrom and Kim (2007) study a sample of 371 firms adopting majority voting and conclude that the versions of majority voting adopted in practice did not result in true shareholder veto power over candidates. About 60% of the sample firms, following the example of Pfizer, introduced a 'plurality plus' standard (plurality plus mandatory resignation). Under this system, the plurality standard is maintained and, thus, a director failing to win a majority vote is still elected, but must resign and the board will decide whether to accept her resignation. The other firms, following the example of Intel, adopted a 'majority plus' standard (majority plus mandatory resignation). Under this system, a director failing to win a majority vote is not elected and must also tender her resignation – else, a statutory holdover rule would still leave the director on the board until the next meeting – which the board may or may not accept. Sjostrom and Kim (2007) argue that in the end, under both versions of majority voting, discretion is left to the board, and if the board does not accept the resignation the director remains in office. Hence, they argue that majority voting, as put into practice, is 'little more than smoke and mirrors' since the election outcome ultimately is a board decision (protected by the business judgment rule).[18] Under this view, the rapid spreading of majority

---

[16]   In a similar spirit, Ertimur et al. (2010b) find that directors failing to implement shareholder proposals approved by a majority of votes cast suffer higher risk of losing their seat as well as other seats.

[17]   Security Holder Director Nominations, Release No. 34-48626 (Oct. 15, 2003).

[18]   In a recent decision, the Delaware Supreme Court indicated that the refusal of a board of directors to accept the resignation of a director who fails to obtain a majority vote under a plurality-plus standard is largely immune from judicial review. *City of Westland Police and Fire Retirement System v. Axcelis Technologies, Inc.* 2010 WL 3157145 (Del. 2010).

voting may have been a low-cost means for firms to appease shareholders and, perhaps, avoid more threatening regulatory reforms (e.g. proxy access). In support of their thesis, Sjostrom and Kim (2007) find no market reaction around the announcements of adoptions of majority voting, regardless of the version adopted and also regardless of whether adopted through bylaw amendments (more binding) or through changes in the corporate governance guidelines. Using a similar sample, Cai, Garner and Walkling (2007) also find no market reaction around the announcements of adoptions of majority voting. They also find that majority voting adopters tend to have poor performance, more independent boards and weak shareholder rights – consistent with boards adopting majority voting to appease shareholders.

Overall, these two studies cast doubt on whether investors view the majority voting standard (at least as adopted in practice) as value enhancing. Ertimur and Ferri (2011a), however, re-examine this question using a regression discontinuity design, essentially comparing the stock price reaction to shareholder proposals to adopt majority voting that pass by a small margin to those that fail by a small margin, and find that the passing of the proposal generates a 1.43–1.60% abnormal return. They also find evidence of greater board turnover in response to high votes withheld at firms adopting majority voting, consistent with the notion that the threat of a tougher election system makes boards more responsive to shareholder preferences.

**The Future of Director Elections: Proxy Access and Broker Votes**

On July 21, 2010 President Obama signed into law the Dodd-Frank Wall Street Reform and Consumer Protection Act (henceforth, the Dodd-Frank Act), a wide-ranging set of financial market reforms. One of the provisions of the Dodd-Frank Act[19] explicitly authorizes the SEC to introduce a proxy access rule, which the SEC did on August 25.[20] Under the new rule (SEC Rule 14a-11), a shareholder, or a group of shareholders, who owns – and has owned continually for at least the prior three years – at least 3% of the company's voting stock could put its nominees on the proxy ballot along with the board's nominees (borrowed shares do not count toward the 3% threshold). These shareholders were limited to nominating candidates for no more than 25% of a company's board seats and would not be able to use proxy access for the purpose of changing control of the company. Smaller reporting companies (public float below $75 million) were exempt from complying with the rule for three years (as the SEC monitors its implementation at large firms). The SEC also amended Rule 14a-8 to enable shareholders to submit proposals related to election and nomination procedures, hence removing elections of directors from the reasons for exclusion of a shareholder proposal.[21] The rule was intended to go into effect on November 15, 2010 (in time for the 2011 proxy season). However, on September 29 the Business Roundtable and the U.S. Chamber of Commerce filed a petition challenging the new rule in court. On October 4, the SEC announced that it would delay implementation of the rule until the challenge was resolved.

---

[19]  Pub. L. 111-203, H.R. 4173, § 971.

[20]  Facilitating Shareholder Director Nominations, Release No. 33-9136 (Aug. 25, 2010).

[21]  The new rule also allows shareholders to adopt, through either a management recommendation or Rule 14a-8 shareholder proposal, access rules that provide for greater access – but they cannot limit the new proxy access rule. For details, see: http://sec.gov/rules/final/2010/33-9136.pdf (last accessed October 2011).

On July 22, 2011, the U.S. Court of Appeals for the D.C. Circuit vacated the proxy access rule (Rule 14a-11), essentially on the ground that the SEC had not performed an adequate cost-benefit analysis of the new rule. The SEC decided not to appeal the court's decision and it is unclear whether it will restart a new rulemaking process. However, it also confirmed the amendment of Rule 14a-8 allowing for shareholder proposals on proxy access (which was not subject to the litigation above). Hence, it is likely that some firms will be targeted by proposals to adopt proxy access in the 2012 proxy season.

Proxy access has been the subject of a long and intense debate, which is likely to continue. Much of this debate has taken place in absence of direct empirical evidence, as often happens for untested reforms (Coates 2009). The regulatory events detailed above have given researchers the opportunity to examine the stock market reaction around them.[22] Akyol, Lim and Verwijmeren (2010) find negative (positive) market returns around events that increase (decrease) the probability of passage of proxy access legislation between 2007 and 2009. Larcker, Ormazabal and Taylor (2011) present similar results. Both studies cast doubts on the value of greater shareholder involvement in the director nomination process.

However, these findings need to be interpreted carefully. In addition to the usual concerns with event studies (e.g. contaminated events, signaling), a particular challenge with multi-event studies of regulation is the identification and interpretation of the relevant events. For example, both studies treat as an increase in the likelihood of a proxy access rule the April 2007 SEC announcement of a roundtable on proxy access and the subsequent June 2007 SEC release of a proxy access proposal. But the April 2007 decision by a (then Republican-controlled) SEC to re-open the proxy access debate was 'forced' by a court decision in a case brought by AFSCME (a union pension fund) against AIG. As for the July 2007 event, it should be noted that, along with the proxy access proposal, the SEC released a proposal that would allow companies to exclude from proxy statements shareholder proposals requesting proxy access (the issue debated in the AFSCME-AIG case). A reasonable interpretation of the July 2007 SEC action is that it made a proxy access rule *less* likely (indeed in November 2007 the SEC voted to explicitly allow companies to exclude proxy access shareholder proposals from proxy statements, while dropping the proxy access proposal). To further complicate

---

[22] As discussed above, in 2003 the SEC introduced a proxy access proposal (for a discussion, see Bebchuk 2003a and 2003b). After the proposal was abandoned, activists began to file shareholder proposals at a few firms requesting the introduction of a proxy access provision. The SEC allowed firms to exclude these proposals because they are related to the election of directors – one of the grounds for exclusion under Rule 14a-8. In 2006, though, a court ruling in *CA, Inc. v. AFSCME Employees Pension Plan*, 953 A.2d 227 (Del. 2008) called into question the SEC's long-held view and essentially forced the SEC to clarify the interpretation of Rule 14a-8. On November 28, 2007, the SEC voted to let companies reject shareowner proposals that relate to board nominations or elections, while committing to reconsider a proxy access rule in the future. In April 2009, after Democratic victories in both the legislative and executive branches of government, the proxy access issue was revived. In April 2009, the Delaware code was amended, adding Section 112 to allow corporations to voluntarily adopt bylaws permitting shareholder proxy access. In May 2009, under the leadership of a new chair (Mary Schapiro) the SEC released a new proxy access proposal as well as a proposal allowing shareholders to submit (binding or advisory) proposals on proxy access under Rule 14a-8. The SEC proposals received a record number of comment letters and in December 2009 the SEC reopened the comment period for another 30 days, largely to ask for comments on the idea of a 'private ordering' approach to proxy access, in which companies and/or shareholders would be able to opt out of a federal access rule (for a discussion, see Bebchuk and Hirst 2010a and 2010b).

things, the market reaction to proxy access proposals reflects not only the perceived value of greater shareholder involvement in the director nomination process, but also (perhaps, only) the perceived value of the specific proxy access proposal. For example, the Council for Institutional Investors, while supporting proxy access, strongly opposed the version proposed by the SEC in July 2007 because it was too restrictive (further indication that the July 2007 SEC action did not increase the likelihood of proxy access legislation).[23]

To circumvent these problems, Becker et al. (2010) focus instead on the market reaction to the October 4, 2010, SEC announcement of the suspension of the proxy access rule, calling it a 'move that surprised most observers'. They find that the stock price of firms that would have been most exposed to proxy access (based on the level and type of institutional ownership) declined significantly compared to the stock price of firms that would have been most insulated from proxy access, consistent with the market perceiving the SEC-proposed proxy access rule as a value-creating mechanism. Cohn, Gillan and Hartzell (2011) also focus on legislative events occurring in 2010 (Senator Dodd's proposal to include a proxy access rule in the Financial Reform Bill on June 16, 2010, and its modification on June 24, 2010), exploiting the fact that these events unexpectedly modified the hurdles for using proxy access. They also partition firms based on the likelihood that their current investors would use proxy access, based on their record as activists, the ownership and holding requirements under each proposal, and firm size thresholds. Overall, they find that increased hurdles to proxy access are associated with losses in shareholder value for firms owned by institutional investors who are likely to use proxy access.

While useful, event studies may be misleading in that they assume that investors are able to correctly estimate the value effect of a new, untested mechanism, whose impact is likely to depend on hard-to-predict responses of the interested parties. Kahan and Rock (2010) present a comprehensive analysis of the likely effects of proxy access and conclude that it will have a marginal impact, if any. They argue that the entities most often engaged in activism (hedge funds and union-related funds) usually do not satisfy ownership and holding requirements of the proxy access rule; that the benefits of proxy access are limited (e.g. limited number of board seats) and the cost savings relative to proxy contests are overstated. In other words, they predict that proxy access will be rarely used, rarely successful (in terms of electing a dissident nominee) when used and of marginal effect when successful.

A second regulatory development with important implications for director elections is the June 2009 SEC decision to eliminate so-called 'broker votes' for director elections (thus approving a NYSE proposal first advanced in 2006). Most shareholders (known as beneficial

---

[23]    Another controversial event is Delaware's decision in 2009 to explicitly authorize proxy access bylaws. Both studies consider this event as decreasing the probability of proxy access *legislation*, on the ground that it was viewed by some observers as an attempt to prevent a federal proxy access regulation or at least to affect the SEC's design of a new rule. A positive market reaction around Delaware's decision is thus interpreted as investors reacting positively to the reduced likelihood of mandatory proxy access. Another interpretation is that investors reacted positively to the news that in the future they could submit proposals requesting proxy access bylaws which would have eventually created momentum for widespread adoption of proxy access. Indeed, some observers thought that the Delaware action gave *proxy access* 'a dramatic boost' (Choi et al. 2010). There are also some questions as to what is the 'right' event of interest regarding the Delaware decision (the vote of the Corporate Law section of the Delaware Bar Association vis-à-vis the introduction of the bill in the Delaware House of Representatives; see Becker, Bergstresser and Subramaniam 2010 for a discussion).

owners) hold shares through brokers in street name rather than in their own names (registered owners) (Dixon & Thomas 1998). Prior to this rule change, if brokers had not received voting instruction by the tenth day prior to the annual meeting, they were permitted to exercise discretionary voting authority with respect to these 'uninstructed' shares on 'routine' matters (which included uncontested director elections) – a provision put in place to increase the probability of achieving the required quorum. Historically, brokers have cast these votes in favor of the board's nominees. Previous studies estimate these broker votes to average 13% of outstanding shares and to have the potential to swing the outcome of some routine propos-als (Bethel & Gillan 2002). In their sample of uncontested director elections, Cai et al. (2009) estimate that excluding the broker votes would have increased the percent of withheld votes by an average of 2.5% (with an impact greater than 10% on 10% of the director elections). In some cases, the effect may be much more significant. Choi et al. (2010) report that broker votes comprised 46% of the votes cast at the Citigroup 2009 annual meeting and that two nominees would not have won re-election without the broker vote.

Combined with the use of majority voting and the potential introduction of proxy access, the elimination of broker votes may have a significant impact on director elections.

In view of all these developments, director elections are likely to become a central focus of future research in corporate governance.

## 3.   SHAREHOLDER PROPOSALS UNDER RULE 14A-8

Under Rule 14a-8, promulgated under the Securities Exchange Act of 1934, any shareholder continuously holding shares worth $2,000 (or 1% of the market value of equity) for at least one year is allowed to include one (and only one) proposal with a 500-word supporting state-ment in the proxy distributed by the company prior to its annual shareholder meeting. These proposals request a vote on a particular issue from all shareholders and must be submitted at least 120 days before the proxy is mailed to shareholders. The company may ask the SEC to exclude a proposal if it violates certain conditions[24] or may persuade the proponent to with-draw it (e.g. by agreeing to it). Among other reasons, the proposals can be excluded if it is considered improper under the company's state laws. For a long time proposals that would be binding on the board have been regarded as improper because inconsistent with Section 141 of the Delaware General Corporation Law (and similar provisions of corporate law in other jurisdictions) which vests the board of directors with the power to manage the business and affairs of a corporation. In recent years, the SEC and courts have allowed shareholder propos-als in the form of binding bylaw amendments, under certain conditions (Goodman & Olson 2007). These proposals remain rare, though, and the vast majority of shareholder proposals are written in the form of a non-binding recommendation, regardless of the voting outcome.

Using data from the 1980s and 1990s, a number of studies conclude that shareholder proposals have been a weak governance mechanism.[25] Most proposals were filed by individ-uals (so-called gadflies), few won a majority vote, and even those were often ignored by

---

[24]   *See* Rule 14a-8(i).
[25]   Comprehensive reviews of the evidence are Black (1998), Gillan and Starks (1998, 2007), Karpoff (2001), and Romano (2001).

boards, given their advisory nature.[26] Not surprisingly, then, generally firms targeted by this type of activism did not experience performance improvements, and their stock price did not move around the time these proposals were filed or voted upon.

During the last decade, though, in the aftermath of Enron-type scandals, corporate governance has become a central theme for many institutional investors, giving rise to an intense wave of shareholder activism, symbolized by hedge funds' aggressive strategies. The landscape for shareholder proposals has changed accordingly, with a rise in the number of shareholder proposals, an increasing role of union pension funds, and the emergence of new types of proposals gaining widespread support among many institutional investors. Faced with this new governance-oriented environment, boards have been under greater pressure to respond to shareholder requests. These changes have spurred a series of studies re-examining the effectiveness of shareholder proposals as a governance mechanism.

**Characteristics of Targeted Firms and the Motives of Union Pension Funds**

Similar to earlier periods, recent studies conclude that in general targeted firms continue to be large, poorly performing firms, with weaker governance structures (Thomas & Cotter 2007; Ertimur et al. 2010b), with other characteristics depending on the specific type of proposal (e.g. the level of CEO pay for compensation-related proposals, Ertimur et al. 2011b).

The increased activism by union pension funds has generated interest in whether their targeting criteria reflect a conflict of interest between their dual role as shareholders (the union pension fund) and as representatives of labor in collective bargaining negotiations (the unions) – as suggested by some highly publicized examples (e.g. the governance campaign of AFL-CIO at Safeway during labor negotiations). Ertimur et al. (2011b) examine this question in a sample of about 1,200 compensation-related shareholder proposals between 1997 and 2007, concluding that: (i) relative to other sponsors of shareholder proposals, union pension funds are *not* more likely to target unionized firms; (ii) among unionized firms, union pension funds are not more likely to target unionized firms with a higher percentage of unionized employees, involved in renegotiating their collective bargaining agreements or in labor-related disputes.

While Ertimur et al. (2011b) do not detect labor-related motives in the *targeting* criteria of union pension funds, Agrawal (2008) finds that these motives play a role in their *voting* decisions.[27] Understanding activists' motives and conflicts of interest remains a central question as new regulations empower minority shareholders (Anabtawi & Stout 2008). Translating these motives in large sample analyses is not trivial. In-depth case studies and surveys may be used to complement those analyses.

---

[26]   At Bristol-Myers Squibb, for example, a proposal to declassify the board was ignored despite obtaining a majority vote for six consecutive years (Business Week 2002).

[27]   Agrawal (2008) uses the 2005 AFL-CIO breakup as a source of exogenous variation in the union affiliations of workers across firms and finds that AFL-CIO affiliated shareholders are less likely to vote against director nominees once the AFL-CIO no longer represents workers. He also documents that AFL-CIO funds are more likely to vote against directors of firms with greater frequency of plant-level conflict between labor unions and management during collective bargaining and union member recruiting, but less so once the AFL-CIO no longer represents workers.

### Determinants of Voting Outcome and Voting Patterns of Mutual Funds

As the number of shareholder proposals increased, the percentage of votes in favor of these proposals also went up over time, with the fraction of proposals winning a majority increasing from 10% in 1997 to over 30% in 2003–2004 (Ertimur et al. 2010b).[28] The type of proposal remains the key determinant of shareholder votes, with proposals to remove-anti-takeover defenses continuing to receive the highest support and a number of new types of proposals achieving high approval rates, e.g. proposals to expense stock options (Ferri & Sandino 2009); to adopt majority voting (Cai et al. 2007); and to adopt a say on pay vote (Burns & Minnick 2010; Cai & Walkling 2011). Proxy advisors' recommendations continue to be a major factor in 'determining' the voting outcome (the discussion above applies to shareholder proposals as well).

One interpretation of this evidence is that, by and large, aggregate shareholder votes tend to support value-enhancing proposals, or at least proposals with a reasonable potential to create value. For example, between 2005 and 2009 proposals to declassify the board have averaged between 60% and 70% votes in favor (Georgeson 2010), consistent with a large body of research suggesting that staggered boards are associated with lower firm value (Bebchuk & Cohen 2005; Bebchuk et al. 2009). Another example is the voting outcome for compensation-related proposals. Ertimur et al. (2011b) find significant voting support for proposals aimed at affecting the pay setting *process* (e.g., proposals requesting shareholder approval of large severance payments), lower support for proposals aimed at micromanaging pay (e.g. proposals to adopt specific levels and structure of pay) and almost no support for more 'radical' proposals arguably reflecting objectives other than shareholder value (e.g., proposals to link executive pay to social criteria or to abolish incentive pay).

While this evidence may suggest that aggregate shareholder votes exhibit a certain degree of sophistication, more research is required to determine to what extent or under what circumstances we can interpret the degree of voting support for a proposal as a reasonable proxy for its effect on value.[29]

Another major challenge in the analysis of shareholder votes is that for a long time shareholders were not required to disclose how they actually cast their votes. In 2003, however, the SEC mandated that one class of investors – mutual funds – disclose, on an annual basis, their voting policies as well as how they voted on each item on the ballot at the annual meeting.[30] The new requirement – opposed unanimously by the mutual fund industry – was driven by the concern that mutual funds were not voting their proxies in the best interest of shareholders, due to their potential conflicts of interests (business ties with the firm; e.g. managing employee benefit plans). The availability of these new data has spurred a significant amount of research on the voting behavior of mutual funds – the largest shareholder category in US

---

[28]   The percentage has oscillated above 30% in most of the subsequent years, leveling off at 32% in 2009 (Georgeson 2010).

[29]   Listokin (2009) argues that if the median voting shareholder and the price-setting shareholder share similar information, then close proxy contest outcomes should have no systematic effect on stock prices. Since stock prices instead move around victories of dissidents or management in such contests, Listokin (2009) concludes that voting and market pricing aggregate information in a very different way. While the study relies on a number of assumptions that need further analysis, it represents a novel attempt to examine the relation between shareholder votes and shareholder value.

[30]   Proxy Voting by Investment Advisers, Release No. IA-2106 (Jan. 31, 2003).

public markets, holding 28.9% of all publicly-traded equity securities as of 2008 (Cotter et al. 2010).

A first group of studies has focused on whether potential or actual business ties with the firm affect mutual funds' voting decisions – the premise of the SEC disclosure rule. Rothberg and Lilien (2006) compare the voting records of fund companies that are primarily mutual funds (i.e., non-conflicted), to the voting records of fund companies that are a small part of larger financial services companies (and, thus, potentially conflicted because the funds' parents' business is principally the provision of financial services) and do not find a difference in how often they vote against management, inconsistent with a conflict of interest hypothesis. Ashraf, Jayaraman and Ryan (2009) focus on shareholder proposals related to executive compensation and find no relation between mutual fund votes and pension-related business ties between the mutual fund and the firm (nor between votes and fees for mutual funds with pension-related business ties). Consistent with these results, Davis and Kim (2007) find that funds are no more likely to vote with management of client firms than management of non-clients. However, they also find that aggregate votes at the fund family level indicate a positive relation between business ties and propensity to vote with management, at least for some shareholder proposals.[31] The authors conjecture that the mandatory disclosure may have led fund families with a larger client base to adopt pro-management voting policies at all firms, to avoid the appearance of voting based on client relationships. This would be an ironic effect of the SEC disclosure rule, since its proponents argued that disclosure of votes would force mutual funds with conflicts of interests to exert their monitoring role and, thus, vote more often in support of shareholder proposals. In the absence of data on mutual funds' votes pre-2003, to test whether mutual funds' voting behavior was affected by the 2003 rule, Cremers and Romano (2010, 2011) analyze the relation between voting outcome and mutual fund ownership before and after the rule change for firms facing similar proposals in both periods, and conclude that mutual funds' voting support for management did not decrease after the new disclosure requirement (and actually increased for management proposals related to executive pay plans).

A number of other studies have focused on understanding other determinants of mutual funds' voting behavior, concluding that type of proposal and ISS recommendations are the key determinant of mutual funds' votes, as for shareholder votes in aggregate.[32] However, they also show that both firms' characteristics (governance, ownership, performance) and funds' characteristics (investing style and horizon, size, performance, expense ratio, holdings, own governance, geographical proximity to management) matter (Rothberg & Lilien 2006; Ashraf & Jayaraman 2007; Chou et al. 2007; Das 2007; Ng, Wang & Zaiats 2007; Morgan et al. 2011; Cotter et al. 2010).

Collectively, these studies lead to the following inferences regarding mutual funds' voting behavior. First, mutual funds vote depending on the proposal type (i.e. they do not follow a mechanical rule such as 'vote always with management'), with much greater support for governance-related shareholder proposals over social and environmental issues. Second,

---

[31]   In a related vein, Taub (2009) finds that voting support for shareholder proposals at large fund families is negatively related to the amount of defined contribution assets under management.

[32]   Morgan et al. (2011) report that in their sample of about 1,300 funds, 349 always vote with ISS. Cotter et al. (2010) document that mutual funds tend to vote consistently with ISS more often than all other shareholders on average.

funds differ significantly in terms of which governance-related shareholder proposals to support, with the exception of proposals to remove anti-takeover defenses, supported by most mutual funds.[33] Third, while some funds always support or oppose a type of proposal across all firms where they vote, for some types of proposals the votes of a given fund differ across firms. Fourth, while for a given proposal most large fund families vote their funds as a block – often as a policy – there is some variation across individual funds within a fund family, particularly on certain topics (e.g. poison pills). Overall, these studies reveal a complex and nuanced voting process.

As discussed later, new vote disclosure requirements may allow for an equally careful examination of the voting decisions of other classes of institutional shareholders.

**Economic Consequences of Shareholder Proposals**

A number of studies analyze the economic consequences of shareholder proposals, either by focusing on a specific proposal or across a broad set of proposals. Essentially, they yield three main insights. First, shareholder proposals have become an effective activism tool in prompting firms to modify their governance practices. Firms are more likely to expense stock options (Ferri & Sandino 2009), declassify boards (Guo et al. 2008; Cai et al. 2009), and remove poison pills (Akyol & Carroll 2006; Cai et al. 2009) after receiving a shareholder proposal requesting these actions. Second, the impact of shareholder proposals crucially depends on the degree of voting support they receive. Across a broad set of proposals between 1997 and 2004, Ertimur et al. (2010b) report an implementation rate of 31% for proposals winning a majority vote and only 3% for proposals receiving between 30% and 50% of the votes cast.[34] Within proposals winning a majority vote, the likelihood of implementation increases with the percentage of votes cast for the proposal (as well as other measures of shareholder pressure, e.g. proponents' ownership).[35] The third finding is a marked increase in the rate of implementation of shareholder proposals receiving a majority vote in the post-Enron period (Akyol & Carroll 2006; Thomas & Cotter 2007; Morgan et al. 2011). For example, Ertimur et al. (2010b) report a rate of implementation of 40%–42% in 2003–2004 versus 16%–24% in 1997–2002.

These data are likely to understate the impact of shareholder proposals on governance practices, for three reasons. First, they focus on proposals voted upon at the annual meetings. Many proposals are withdrawn before the meeting because the company agrees to implement them (though there may be other reasons; e.g. the issue becomes moot due to changes in regulation or the firm agrees to other concessions). For example, numerous shareholder proposals to adopt a majority voting standard in 2006–2008 were withdrawn because the firm agreed to adopt majority voting (Sjostrom & Kim 2007). Expanding the

---

[33]    The widespread support for anti-takeover proposals among mutual funds is generally interpreted as an indication that mutual funds tend to support wealth increasing proposals (Ashraf & Jayaraman 2007; Davis & Kim 2007; Morgan et al. 2011).

[34]    Similarly, in a sample of shareholder proposals related to executive pay, Ertimur et al. (2011b) report an implementation of 40.3% (3.8%) for proposals winning (failing to win) a majority vote. Ferri and Sandino (2009) find that a majority vote on a proposal to expense stock options increases the likelihood of its adoption.

[35]    Morgan et al. (2011) find that greater voting support by mutual funds also increases the likelihood of implementation.

analysis to withdrawn proposals (as well as proposals excluded from the proxy because in violation of Rule 14a-8) may be a fruitful endeavor for future studies.

Second, most studies on shareholder proposals focus on their impact on targeted firms. However, another objective of activism is to generate spillover effects on non-targeted firms.[36] Recent studies suggest that these effects may be at work. Ferri and Sandino (2009) find that non-targeted firms were more likely to expense stock options if a peer firm was targeted by a shareholder proposal requesting the expensing of stock options. Ertimur et al. (2010b) find that firms are more likely to implement a shareholder proposal supported by a majority vote if a peer firm implemented a similar proposal. Cai et al. (2007) find that firms are more likely to adopt a majority voting standard if their directors sit on another firm which has already adopted majority voting – consistent with evidence that overlapping directors contribute to the spreading of governance practices (Bouwman 2008).

Third, shareholder proposals are increasingly being used as a lobbying mechanism to influence regulatory reforms – beyond any immediate effect on targeted firms. Ferri and Sandino (2009) note that activists used shareholder proposals to expense stock options as a means to influence standard setters. Arguably, shareholder proposals to adopt a majority voting standard for director elections (Sjostrom & Kim 2007) and proposals requesting a say on pay vote (Cai & Walkling 2011) also aimed at influencing the policy debate. As more of these initiatives develop, future research may shed light on the characteristics of this form of 'reform-oriented' activism, which is likely to have different traits.

Further indirect evidence of the growing influence of shareholder votes is the existence of an active market for votes within the U.S equity loan market, as documented by Christoffersen et al. (2007), who show that vote trading corresponds to support for shareholder proposals and opposition to management proposals;[37] and the emergence of low-cost, low-transparency techniques that allow the decoupling of economic ownership from voting rights, resulting for example in the possibility of holding more votes than shares – so-called 'empty voting' (Hu & Black 2007).

In view of all the above evidence, there is little doubt that shareholder proposals and shareholder votes have become a more effective tool in the post-Enron period (see also above), with boards listening to shareholder 'voice' more than ever before. However, two fundamental questions remain unanswered and call for more research. The first is why boards have become more responsive. Is it because the cost of ignoring shareholder requests has increased?[38] Or because activists have become more sophisticated in identifying value-

---

[36]    Black (1990) argues indeed that activists should focus on systemic market-wide issues with a potential for spillover effects, so as to increase the benefits and limit the cost of their initiatives. Spillover effects are particularly important for indexed funds (Del Guercio & Hawkins 1999). Union pension funds tend to be indeed highly diversified (Schwab & Thomas 1998; Agrawal 2008) and claim that a goal of their activism is to generate market-wide adoption of best practices (Ferri & Weber 2009).

[37]    Bethel et al. (2009) show that institutional investors buy shares and hence voting rights before merger record dates, and that such trading is positively related to voting turnout and negatively related to shareholder support of merger proposals.

[38]    A number of factors may have increased the cost of ignoring shareholders' requests: the underlying threat of hedge funds' activism and vote-no campaigns, the desire to prevent regulatory intervention, greater reputation penalties for unresponsive directors in the director labor market (Ertimur et al. 2010b), the emergence of governance ratings and proxy advisors, greater scrutiny and influence of the media (Dyck et al. 2008; Joe et al. 2009; Kuhnen & Niessen 2010).

enhancing governance changes, causing boards to become more willing to adopt the proposed changes? This leads me to the second and arguably most important unanswered question: is shareholder activism through Rule 14a-8 ultimately associated with value creation?

As mentioned earlier, studies from the 1980s and 1990s largely concluded that shareholder proposals had no effect on shareholder value. While this result was consistent with the fact that most proposals received low voting support and were rarely implemented, it was not clear that the methodologies adopted would have detected any effect on value even if there was such an effect. For example, event studies around proxy filing dates or annual meetings have been recognized to be plagued by numerous problems, making them ill-suited to address the question of the value impact of shareholder proposals (Gillan & Starks 2007).

In a recent study Cuñat, Gine and Guadalupe (2010) adopt a novel approach to address this question. As discussed earlier, there is a large difference in implementation rates depending on whether or not a proposal achieves a majority vote (Ertimur et al. 2010b). Cuñat et al. (2010) note that such difference in implementation rates persists if one compares proposals winning a majority vote by a small margin to proposals failing by a small margin. For these 'close-call' proposals, it is reasonable to assume that there were similar expectations about the likelihood of passage. If so, the passage of some but not others should contain significant information (akin to an exogenous shock). Applying a regression discontinuity technique to a sample of all shareholder proposals between 1997 and 2007, Cuñat et al. (2010) find that approved shareholder proposals yield an abnormal return of 1.3% over the ones not approved, with a more pronounced price reaction for proposals related to anti-takeover provisions (consistent with the evidence on the value relevance of such provisions). They also try to estimate the full value of the proposal taking into account its likelihood of implementation, concluding that adopting a governance proposal increases value by 2.8%. Finally, they find evidence of superior long-term performance after the passage of those proposals. While the authors view these results as supporting the notion that better governance creates value, their findings also (perhaps, mainly) speak to the value of shareholder activism, in that they indicate that, in aggregate, shareholder votes tend to support value-creating proposals. More research is needed, though, to strengthen this conclusion.

### Recent Regulatory Developments: Mandatory Say on Pay Votes

The Dodd-Frank Act mandates that publicly traded firms must let shareholders have an up-or-down non-binding vote on executive pay – known as a 'say on pay' vote – at least once every three years[39] (the SEC has the authority to exempt firms based on size or other criteria).[40] A similar, non-binding vote must be held to approve any golden parachute triggered in connection with mergers and acquisitions (separate from the vote on the transaction itself) and not already subject of a say on pay vote. The Act also extends the prohibition of broker votes for uninstructed shares (recently approved by the SEC for director elections; see above) to say on pay and golden parachute votes. Finally, the Act requires institutional investors to disclose how they voted their shares on say on pay and golden parachutes matters.

---

[39]  Pub. L. 111-203, H.R. 4173, § 951.
[40]  At their first meeting, firms also must let shareholders vote on whether to hold the say on pay vote every one, two or three years.

The first country to mandate an annual non-binding say on pay vote was the UK in 2002. Ferri and Maber (2009) find that the regulation's announcement triggered a positive stock price reaction at firms with weak penalties for poor performance, consistent with the view that shareholders regard say on pay as a value-creating mechanism. Ferri and Maber (2009) also analyze observable changes to compensation contracts and then estimate unobservable changes through a regression of CEO pay on its economic determinants. Across both sets of analyses, they find that say on pay resulted in greater penalties for poor performance. In particular, the analysis of explicit contractual changes in response to the first say on pay votes shows that a high fraction of firms facing high voting dissent responded by removing or modifying controversial provisions that investors viewed as 'rewards for failure' (e.g. large severance contracts, provisions allowing the retesting of unmet performance conditions in equity grants), often in response to institutional investors' explicit requests. These actions do not appear to reflect a general trend but rather the effect of say on pay votes, since their frequency among 'high dissent' firms after the vote is significantly higher than before the vote and also significantly higher than among 'low dissent' firms after the vote. Notably, a substantial number of 'low dissent' firms took similar actions ahead of the say on pay vote, suggesting that proactive changes helped firms avoid voting dissent. Consistent with this conjecture, the authors also find that the 'high dissent' firms that removed controversial provisions experienced a substantial decrease in voting dissent at the second say on pay vote. The study also concludes that the (*ex ante* and *ex post*) effect of say on pay votes differed across different compensation provisions, suggesting that concerns with say on pay votes being used to promote 'one-size-fits-all' compensation practices may be overstated (Gordon 2009).

The UK experience with say on pay soon captured the attention of US activists, who between 2006 and 2008 filed more than 150 shareholder proposals requesting the adoption of say on pay at large US firms, often winning significant voting support. While few firms agreed to adopt say on pay, legislators took notice. In April 2007, the US House of Representatives approved a bill seeking to mandate say on pay. Shortly thereafter, an analogous bill was introduced in the Senate by then Senator Barack Obama. Cai and Walkling (2011) study the market reaction around the passage of the say on pay bill in the House and document positive returns for firms with excessive CEO pay and lower pay-for-performance. Larcker et al. (2011), however, find no significant effect around a broader set of legislative and regulatory events related to say on pay between 2007 and 2009. As noted earlier, event studies around regulatory actions need to be interpreted with caution. The introduction of say on pay will offer an opportunity for more direct research into its costs and benefits for US firms as well as into the role of proxy advisors' recommendations.

The requirement that institutional investors disclose their votes on say on pay and golden parachutes matters will offer an opportunity to examine the voting decisions of institutional investors other than mutual funds (see above). Absent a (not immediately obvious) rationale for limiting the disclosure requirement to these two compensation matters, this provision may eventually lead to a broader disclosure requirement for all institutional investors' votes on any matter voted upon at the annual meetings (e.g. director elections, shareholder proposals, approval of option plans, etc.). Availability of such data would allow researchers to substantially deepen our understanding of how different types of institutional investors use 'exit' and 'voice' strategies.

Finally, another important regulatory development is the SEC issuance in July 2010 of a concept release seeking public comment on the US proxy voting system, the first step of a project aimed at revamping and modernizing an outdated proxy voting infrastructure –

loosely referred to as the 'proxy plumbing' project.[41] The concept release focuses on three broad categories: accuracy, transparency, and efficiency of the voting process (e.g. imbalances in broker votes leading to over-voting and under-voting); communications with shareholders and shareholder participation (e.g. means to facilitate retail investor participation), and the relationship between voting power and economic interest (e.g. 'empty' voting practices, the role of proxy advisors).[42] The broad scope of the project is a further example of the importance assumed by shareholder votes over the last decade.

## 4.   BEYOND THE EMPIRICAL EVIDENCE

The empirical evidence on the enhanced impact of low-cost activism – summarized in this chapter – calls for more analytical work to model and better understand this phenomenon. An important step in this direction is Levit and Malenko (2011). Motivated by the evidence on management's responsiveness to non-binding shareholder proposals and building on prior work in economics and political sciences on the efficiency of binding voting mechanisms, Levit and Malenko (2011) examine under what conditions *non-binding* votes are effective in conveying shareholder expectations. Their model shows that in the most basic setting – when the preferences of shareholders and managers are not aligned (the interesting case) and management suffers no consequences from ignoring majority votes – non-binding votes fail to convey shareholder expectations and are rationally ignored by management. The presence of an activist investor (a proxy for disciplinary mechanisms) improves information aggregation, but only when the activists' interests are in conflict with those of the other shareholders. The model also shows that non-binding votes are often superior to a binding vote mechanism in terms of ability to aggregate shareholders' information. These insights offer a series of testable predictions for future empirical work on the effects of non-binding votes as well as a starting point for other analytical studies.

## 5.   CONCLUSION

Over the last decade, low-cost, non-binding tools of shareholder activism – such as shareholder proposals and shareholder votes on director elections – have proven increasingly effective at influencing firms' governance practices as well as the policy debate. In this chapter, I reviewed the growing body of research that documents this enhanced effectiveness. Recent regulatory reforms that expand shareholder rights (via say on pay, elimination of broker votes on certain matters, and greater disclosure of shareholder votes), combined with the trend toward majority voting and de-classified boards and the potential introduction of proxy access, are likely to further increase the effectiveness of these tools. Whether low-cost activism ultimately results in value creation and improved performance remains an open question and one of utmost importance in view of these reforms.

---

[41]   For details, see http://www.sec.gov/rules/concept/2010/34-62495.pdf (last accessed October 2011).

[42]   For a description of the system of shareholder voting in the US and its problems, see Kahan and Rock (2008).

# REFERENCES

Agrawal, Ashwini K. (2008), 'Corporate Governance Objectives of Labor Union Shareholders: Evidence from Proxy Voting', *Review of Financial Studies,* forthcoming.

Akyol, Ali C. & Carolyn Carroll (2006), 'Removing Poison Pills: A Case of Shareholder Activism', Working Paper, University of Melbourne, available at SSRN: http://ssrn.com/abstract=935950 (last accessed October 2011).

Akyol, Ali C., Lim Wei Fen & Patrick Verwijmeren (2010), 'Shareholders the Boardroom: Wealth Effects of the SEC's Proposal to Facilitate Director Nominations', Working Paper, University of Melbourne, available at SSRN: http://ssrn.com/abstract=1526081 (last accessed October 2011).

Alexander, Cindy R., Mark A. Chen, Duane J. Seppi & Chester S. Spatt (2010), 'Interim News and the Role of Proxy Voting Advice', *The Review of Financial Studies*, 23(12), 4419–54.

Allen, Claudia H. (2007), 'Study of Majority Voting in Director Elections', Neal, Gerber & Eisenberger LLP, available at http://www.ngelaw.com/files/upload/majoritystudy111207.pdf (last accessed October 2011).

Anabtawi, Iman & Lynn A. Stout, (2008), 'Fiduciary Duties for Activist Shareholders', *Stanford Law Review*, 60(5), 1255–1308.

Ashraf, Rasha & Narayanan Jayaraman (2007), 'Determinants and consequences of proxy voting by mutual funds on shareholder proposals', Working Paper, Georgia Institute of Technology available at SSRN: http://ssrn.com/abstract=962126 (last accessed October 2011).

Ashraf, Rasha, Narayanan Jayaraman & Harley E. Ryan (2009), 'Do Pension-Related Business Ties Influence Mutual Fund Proxy Voting? Evidence from Shareholder Proposals on Executive Compensation', Working Paper, Georgia Institute of Technology, available at SSRN: http://ssrn.com/abstract=1351966 (last accessed October 2011).

Associated Press (2007), 'Administration opposes "say on pay" bill', April 19, available at http://www.msnbc.msn.com/id/18203381/ (last accessed October 2011).

Bebchuk, Lucian A. (2003a), 'The Case for Shareholder Access to the Ballot', *The Business Lawyer*, 59, 43–66.

Bebchuk, Lucian A. (2003b), 'Symposium on Corporate Elections. Harvard Law and Economics', Discussion Paper No. 448, 2003, available at SSRN: http://ssrn.com/abstract=471640 (last accessed October 2011).

Bebchuk, Lucian A. (2007), 'The Myth of the Shareholder Franchise', *Virginia Law Review*, 93, 675–732.

Bebchuk, Lucian A. & Alma Cohen (2005), 'The costs of entrenched boards', *Journal of Financial Economics*, 78, 409–33.

Bebchuk, Lucian A., Alma Cohen & Allen Ferrell (2009), 'What Matters in Corporate Governance?', *Review of Financial Studies*, 22, 783–827.

Bebchuk, Lucian A. & Ehud Kamar (2010), 'Bundling and Entrenchment', *Harvard Law Review*, 123(7), 1551–95.

Bebchuk, Lucian A. & Scott Hirst (2010a), 'Private Ordering and the Proxy Access Debate', *The Business Lawyer*, 65(2), 329–60.

Bebchuk, Lucian A. & Scott Hirst (2010b), 'The Harvard Law School Proxy Access Roundtable (January 1, 2010)', Harvard Law and Economics Discussion Paper No. 661, available at SSRN: http://ssrn.com/abstract=1539027 (last accessed October 2011).

Becker, Bo, Daniel Bergstresser & Guhan Subramaniam (2010), 'Does Shareholder Proxy Access Improve Firm Value? Evidence from the Business Roundtable Challenge', Working Paper, Harvard University, available at SSRN: http://ssrn.com/abstract=1695666 (last accessed October 2011).

Bethel, Jennifer E. & Stuart Gillan (2002), 'The Impact of the Institutional and Regulatory Environment on Shareholder Voting', *Financial Management*, 31(4), 29–54.

Bethel, Jennifer E., Gang Hu & Qinghai Wang (2009), 'The Market for Shareholder Voting Rights around Mergers and Acquisitions: Evidence from Institutional Daily Trading and Voting', *Journal of Corporate Finance*, 15, 129–45.

Black, Bernard S. (1990), 'Shareholder Passivity Reexamined', *Michigan Law Review*, 89, 520–608.

Black, Bernard S. (1998), 'Shareholder Activism and Corporate Governance in the United States', in Peter Newman (ed.) *The New Palgrave Dictionary of Economics and the Law*, New York: Stockton Press.

Bouwman, Christa H.S. (2008), 'Corporate Governance Contagion Through Overlapping Directors', Working Paper, Case Western Reserve University, available at SSRN: http://ssrn.com/abstract=1304151 (last accessed October 2011).

Brav, Alon, Wei Jiang, Frank Partnoy & Randall S. Thomas (2008), 'Hedge Fund Activism, Corporate Governance, and Firm Performance', *The Journal of Finance*, 63, 1729–75.

Brav, Alon, Wei Jiang & Kim Hyunseob (2009), 'Hedge Fund Activism: A Review', *Foundations and Trends in Finance*, 4, 185–246.

Burns, Natasha & Kristina Minnick (2010), 'Does Say on Pay Matter? Evidence in the U.S.', Working Paper, The University of Texas at San Antonio, available at SSRN: http://ssrn.com/abstract=1558435 (last accessed October 2011).

Business Week (2002), 'How shareholder votes are legally rigged', May 20.

Cai Jie, Jacqueline L. Garner & Ralph A. Walkling, (2007), 'Democracy or Disruption: an Empirical Analysis of Majority Elections', Working Paper, Drexel University, available at SSRN: http://ssrn.com/abstract=1491627 (last accessed October 2011).

Cai, Jie, Jacqueline L. Garner & Ralph A. Walkling (2009), 'Electing Directors', *Journal of Finance*, 64(5), 2387–2419.

Cai, Jie & Ralph A. Walkling (2011), 'Shareholders' Say on Pay: Does It Create Value?', *Journal of Financial and Quantitative Analysis*, 46, 299–339.

Choi, Stephen J., Jill E. Fisch & Marcel Kahan (2009), 'Director elections and the role of proxy advisors', *Southern California Law Review*, 82, 649–702.

Choi, Stphephen J., Jill E. Fisch & Marcel Kahan, (2010), 'The power of proxy advisors: myth or reality?', *Emory Law Journal*, 59, 869–918.

Chou, Wen-Hsiu, Ng, Lilian K. & Qinghai Wang (2007), 'Do governance mechanisms matter for mutual funds?', Working Paper, University of Wisconsin-Milwaukee, available at SSRN: http://ssrn.com/abstract=972235 (last accessed October 2011).

Christoffersen, Susan K., Christopher Geczy, David K. Musto & Adam V. Reed (2007), 'Vote Trading and Information Aggregation', *Journal of Finance*, 62, 2897–2929.

Coates IV, John C. (2009), 'Testimony before the Subcommittee on Securities, Insurance, and Investment of the Committee on Banking, Housing, and Urban Affairs, United States Senate, July 29, 2009', available at http://papers.ssrn.com/sol3/papers.cfm?abstract_id=1475355 (last accessed October 2011).

Cohn, Jonathan B., S. Gillan & Jay C. Hartzell (2011), 'On Enhancing Shareholder Control: A (Dodd-) Frank Assessment of Proxy Access', Working Paper, University of Texas at Austin, available at SSRN: http://papers.ssrn.com/sol3/papers.cfm?abstract_id=1742506 (last accessed October 2011).

Coles, Jeffrey L. & Chun Keung Hoi (2003), 'New evidence on the market for directors: Board membership and Pennsylvania Senate Bill 1310', *Journal of Finance*, 58, 197–230.

Cotter, James F., Alan R. Palmiter & Randall S. Thomas (2010), 'The Effect of ISS Recommendations on Mutual Fund Voting', *Villanova Law Review*, 55, 1–56.

Cremers, Martijn & Roberta Romano (2010), 'Institutional Investors and Proxy Voting on Compensation Plans: The Impact of the 2003 Mutual Fund Voting Disclosure Regulation', Working Paper, Yale School of Management, available at SSRN: http://ssrn.com/abstract=1498950 (last accessed October 2011).

Cremers, Martijn & Roberta Romano (2011), 'Institutional Investors and Proxy Voting: The Impact of the 2003 Mutual Fund Voting Disclosure Regulation', *American Law and Economics Review*, 13, 220–268.

Cronqvist, Henrik & Rudiger Fahlenbrach (2009), 'Large Shareholders and Corporate Policies', *Review of Financial Studies*, 22, 3941–3976.

Cuñat, Vicente, Mieria Gine & Maria Guadalupe (2010), 'The Vote is Cast: The Effect of Corporate Governance on Shareholder Value', *Journal of Finance*, forthcoming.

Das, Praveen K. (2007), 'Geographical proximity and mutual funds' voting behavior', Working Paper, University of Wisconsin-Milwaukee.

Davis Gerald F. & E. Han. Kim (2007), 'Business ties and proxy voting by mutual funds', *Journal of Financial Economics*, 85, 552–70.

Del Guercio, Diane & Jennifer Hawkins (1999), 'The Motivation and Impact of Pension Fund Activism', *Journal of Financial Economics*, 52, 293–340.

Del Guercio, Diane, Laura Seery & Tracie Woidtke (2008), 'Do Boards Pay Attention When Institutional Investors "Just Vote No"?', *Journal of Financial Economics*, 90, 84–103.

Dixon, C. & Randall S. Thomas (1998), *Aranow & Einhorn on Proxy Contests for Corporate Control*, 3rd ed., New York, NY, Aspen Law & Business.

Dyck, Alexander I.J. & Luigi Zingales (2002), 'The Corporate Governance Role of the Media', in R. Islam (ed.) *The right to tell: The role of the Media in Development*, The World Bank, Washington DC.

Dyck, Alexander I.J., Natalya Volchkova & Luigi Zingales (2008), 'The Corporate Governance Role of the Media: Evidence from Russia', *Journal of Finance*, 63(3), 1093–1135.

Ertimur, Yonca, Fabrizio Ferri & David Maber (2010a), 'Reputation Penalties for Poor Monitoring of Executive Pay: Evidence from Option Backdating', *Journal of Financial Economics*, forthcoming.

Ertimur, Yonca, Fabrizio Ferri & Stephen Stubben (2010b), 'Board of Directors' Responsiveness to Shareholders: Evidence from Shareholder Proposals', *Journal of Corporate Finance*, 16(1), 53–72.

Ertimur, Yonca & Fabrizio Ferri (2011a), 'Does the Director Election System Matter? Evidence from Majority Voting', Working Paper, Duke University, available at SSRN: http://papers.ssrn.com/sol3/papers.cfm?abstract_id=1880974 (last accessed October 2011).

Ertimur, Yonca, Fabrizio Ferri & Volkan Muslu (2011b), 'Shareholder Activism and CEO Pay', *Review of Financial Studies*, forthcoming.

Ferri, Fabrizio & David Maber (2009), 'Say on Pay Votes and CEO Compensation: Evidence from the UK', *Review of Finance*, forthcoming.

Ferri, Fabrizio & Tatiana Sandino (2009), 'The Impact of Shareholder Activism on Financial Reporting and Compensation: The Case of Employee Stock Options Expensing', *The Accounting Review*, 84(2).

Ferri, Fabrizio & James Weber (2009), 'AFSCME vs. Mozilo ... and "Say on Pay" for All (A)', Harvard Business School Case 109-009.

Fich, Eliezer M. & Anil Shivdasani (2007), 'Financial Fraud, Director Reputation, and Shareholder Wealth', *Journal of Financial Economics*, 86, 306–36.

Fischer, Paul E., Jeffrey D. Gramlich, Brian P. Miller & Hal D. White (2009), 'Investor Perceptions of Board Performance: Evidence from Uncontested Director Elections', *Journal of Accounting and Economics*, 48, 172–89.

Georgeson (2010) '2010 Annual Corporate Governance Review', available at http://www.georgeson.com/usa/acgr.php (last accessed October 2011).

Gillan, Stuart & Laura T. Starks (1998), 'A Survey of Shareholder Activism: Motivation and Empirical Evidence', Working Paper, available at SSRN: http://ssrn.com/abstract=663523 (last accessed October 2011).

Gillan, Stuart & Laura T. Starks (2007), 'The Evolution of Shareholder Activism in the United States', *Journal of Applied Corporate Finance* 19, 55–73.

Goodman, Amy L. & John F. Olson (2007), *A Practical Guide to SEC Proxy and Compensation Rules*, 4th ed., USA: Aspen Publishers.

Gordon, Jeffrey N. (2009), '"Say on Pay": Cautionary Notes on the UK Experience and the Case for Shareholders Opt-In', *Harvard Journal on Legislation*, 46, 323–67.

Grundfest, Joseph A. (1990), 'Just Vote No or Just Don't Vote: Minimalist Strategies for Dealing with Barbarians Inside the Gates', Presentation before the Fall Meeting of the Council of Institutional Investors (November 7, 1990).

Grundfest, Joseph. A. (1993), 'Just Vote-No: A Minimalist Strategy for Dealing with Barbarians Inside the Gates', *Stanford Law Review*, 45, 857–937.

Guo, Re, Timothy A. Kruse & Tom Nohel (2008), 'Undoing the Powerful Anti-takeover Force of Staggered Boards', *Journal of Corporate Finance*, 14, 274–88.

Hu, Henry T.C. & Bernard S. Black (2007), 'Hedge Funds, Insiders and the Decoupling of Economic and Voting Ownership: Empty Voting and Hidden (Morphable) Ownership', *Journal of Corporate Finance*, 13, 343–67.

Joe, J., H. Louis & D. Robinson (2009), 'Managers' and investors' responses to media exposure of board ineffectiveness', *Journal of Financial and Quantitative Analysis*, 44 (3), 579–605.

Kahan, Marcel & Edward B. Rock (2008), 'The Hanging Chads of Corporate Voting', *Georgetown Law Journal*, 96, 1227–81.

Karpoff, Jonathan M. (2001), 'The Impact of Shareholder Activism on Target Companies: A Survey of Empirical Findings', Working Paper, available at SSRN: http://ssrn.com/abstract=885365 (last accessed October 2011).

Kuhnen, Camelia M. & Alexandra Niessen (2010), 'Public opinion and executive compensation', Working Paper, Northwestern University.

Larcker, David F., Gaizka Ormazabal & Daniel J. Taylor (2011), 'The Market Reaction to Corporate Governance Regulation', *Journal of Financial Economics*, 101, 431–448.

Levit, Doron & Nadia Malenko (2011), 'Non-binding Voting for Shareholder Proposals', *Journal of Finance*, 66, 1579–1614

Listokin, Yair (2008), 'Management Always Wins the Close Ones', *American Law and Economics Review*, 10(2), 159–84.

Listokin, Yair (2009), 'Corporate Voting versus Market Price Setting', *American Law and Economics Review*, 11(2), 608–35.

Lublin, Joann S. (2009), 'Directors Lose Elections, But Not Seats; Staying Power of Board Member Raises Questions about Democracy', *Wall Street Journal*, September 28.

Martin, Kenneth J. & Randall S. Thomas (2005), 'When is enough, enough? Market reaction to highly dilutive stock option plans and the subsequent impact on CEO compensation', *Journal of Corporate Finance*, 11(1–2), 61–83.

Morgan, Angela & Annette B. Poulsen (2001), 'Linking pay to performance – compensation proposals in the S&P 500', *Journal of Financial Economics*, 62(3), 489–523.

Morgan, Angela, Annette B. Poulsen, Jack G. Wolf & Tina Yang (2011), 'Mutual funds as monitors: evidence from mutual fund voting', *Journal of Corporate Finance*, 17, 914–928.

Ng, Lilian, Qinghai Wang & Nataliya Zaiats (2007), 'Do mutual funds vote responsibly? Evidence from proxy voting', Working Paper, University of Wisconsin, available at SSRN: http://ssrn.com/abstract=1431072 (last accessed October 2011).

Norris, Floyd (2004), 'Corporate democracy and the power to embarrass', *New York Times*, March 4.

Romano, Roberta (2001), 'Less is More: Making Institutional Investor Activism a Valuable Mechanism of Corporate Governance', *Yale Journal on Regulation*, 18, 174–251.

Rothberg, Burton & Steven B. Lilien (2006), 'Mutual Funds and Proxy Voting: New Evidence on Corporate Governance', *Journal of Business & Technology Law*, 1(1), 157–84.

Schwab, Stewart J. & Randall S. Thomas (1998), 'Realigning Corporate Governance: Shareholder Activism by Labor Unions', *Michigan Law Review*, 96, 1018–94.

Sjostrom, William K. & Young Sang Kim (2007), 'Majority Voting for the Election of Directors', *Connecticut Law Review*, 40, 459–510.

Srinivasan, Suraj (2005), 'Consequences of Financial Reporting Failure for Outside Directors: Evidence from Accounting Restatements and Audit Committee Members', *Journal of Accounting Research*, 43, 291–334.

Taub, Jennifer S. (2009), 'Able But Not Willing: The Failure of Mutual Fund Advisers to Advocate for Shareholders' Rights', *Journal of Corporation Law*, 34(3), 103–151.

Thomas, Randall S. & James F. Cotter (2007), 'Shareholder Proposals in the New Millennium: Shareholder Support, Board Response and Market Reaction', *Journal of Corporate Finance*, 13, 368–91.

Yermack, David (2004), 'Remuneration, Retention, and Reputation Incentives for Outside Directors', *Journal of Finance*, 59, 2281–2308.

# 12. Takeover theory and the law and economics movement
*Steven M. Davidoff*

## 1. INTRODUCTION

The legendary Henry Manne can be credited with the first significant application of law and economics scholarship to takeover theory. In his short ten-page article *Mergers and the Market for Corporate Control* (Manne 1965), Manne set forth a theory of the market for corporate control. The takeover market serves as a monitor for managers in public corporate entities. If these managers fail to efficiently run the corporate enterprise or otherwise seek their own private benefits to the detriment of the corporation, the takeover market serves as a monitor. The value of the corporate enterprise will decline relative to shares in similarly situated corporations. This will attract third parties to bid for control of the company, actors who will otherwise operate it more efficiently and without such detriment. Though Manne recognized that various takeover forms could have differing costs, Manne's article was an implicit endorsement of an unconstrained takeover market, one where acquirers could freely bid for companies. This would produce net social gains by allocating resources more efficiently; it would also force managers to operate their companies more capably or otherwise be replaced, itself a net social gain.

Manne's article was framed as primarily about the proper scope of antitrust enforcement and the desirability of horizontal mergers, but its true influence was its implicit support for a free market for corporate control as well as the assignment of a value on corporate control. Manne's theory would shape repeated debates over the subsequent forty years about the proper regulation of the takeover market itself as well as target boards and their discretion in agreeing or opposing a takeover offer (Easterbrook & Fischel 1981; Gilson 1981; Bebchuk 1982; Coffee 1984; Gordon 1997b; Lipton & Rowe 2002; Bainbridge 2006). In the years after Manne first published his article, takeover scholarship would borrow deeply from the law and economics movement in these debates. This was particularly true during the 1980s, a time when the most influential law and economics articles on the proper scope of takeover regulation were written.

Manne's idea and subsequent scholarship based on his thesis proved quite influential in academic circles, but failed to substantively influence legal doctrine. Instead, in the 1980s, both the federal and state governments adopted a patchwork of overlapping takeover regulation allowing for board-adopted anti-takeover defenses. Delaware and other courts also accorded considerable deference to boards' discretion in considering (and often, rejecting) takeovers. This approach was contrary to the law and economics scholarship on the matter, which largely supported an unconstrained market for corporate control and limitations on target boards' ability to reject takeover proposals in favor of shareholder choice.

Thereafter, like the faithful grappling with a lost god, law and economics scholarship would largely attempt to rationalize this doctrinal rejection. The response would split into three strands of theory. The first was a political economy approach: a number of scholars attempted to explain states' and courts' rejection of academic law and economic theory as a consequence of jurisdictional competition. Borrowing from scholarship on the race to the bottom/race to the top debate from the 1970s, scholars theorized that state legislatures and courts, particularly Delaware courts, were catering to the managers who make the incorporation decision rather than adopting wealth-maximizing takeover rules (Bebchuk et al. 2001). Second, legal scholars began to turn from theoretical writing to empirical analysis to assess the effects of this new takeover regime (Bebchuk et al. 2002). Though in large part they found anti-takeover devices to be value-reducing, these analyses had little influence on Delaware's corporate doctrine or were substantively disputed. The third strand was theoretical, but more constrained than the broad-reaching articles and theories of the 1980s. It attempted only piecemeal modification or doctrinal work-arounds (Gordon 1997b). This third strand of scholarship was heavily influenced by the corporate governance movement and its sometime focus on resituating the allocation of authority from directors to shareholders.

We now live in a world of institutional shareholders, proxy ratings agencies, activist hedge funds, cross-border takeovers, more complex and complete debt and equity markets and a renewed emphasis on corporate governance and independent directors. The takeover landscape of the 1980s, when much of the bedrock law and economics scholarship on takeovers was written, is transformed. The world is much more complicated and intricate than it was 30 years ago. Law and economics now encompasses many strands, including 'neoclassical', 'empirical', and 'behavioral'. But while law and economics remains a useful and predominant tool for theoretical takeover analysis, it is also only one among many academic approaches. This creates an opportunity for a reassessment of law and economics takeover theory to take into account this revolution. The first 40 years of scholarship on this topic have set a foundation, but it is a foundation in need of fine-tuning to incorporate the modern financial marketplace and financial theory. This chapter is about the events leading up to that time; it is a survey history of the law and economics field as applied to takeovers. It is also about possible new directions and topics for this field and its future use in structuring and analyzing takeover theory.

## 2. THE 1960S: THE WILLIAMS ACT AND THE TENDER OFFER PROBLEM

Manne's theory was immediately challenged, not by academics but by legislation designed to make tender offers more difficult. In the mid-1960s, there was a sharp rise in unsolicited or 'hostile' takeover attempts by third party bidders. These unsolicited bidders typically preferred to structure their transactions so that they were not subject to the federal and state regulatory apparatus applicable to proxy contests and instead, often made their takeover attempts via cash tender offer. The rise of the tender offer is evidenced numerically: in 1966, there were over 100 tender offers involving companies listed on national securities exchanges. In comparison, there were just eight tender offers in 1960 (Davidoff 2007).

There was a sharp outcry that these tender offers were abusive and coercive. The Securities and Exchange Commission (SEC), led by its Chairman, Manuel F. Cohen, began a vocal campaign in favor of tender offer regulation. The first fruits of the SEC's labor were reaped in 1965, when Senator Harrison A. Williams introduced a bill to regulate tender offers. This response was met by protest that this regulation would 'chill' tender offers and result in a less active takeover market. Stanley F. Reed, the editor of *Mergers and Acquisitions*, testified that the Williams Act 'could cause positive harm to shareholder interests by eliminating what Professor Manne calls the "free market in corporate control"' (Johnson & Millon 1989, 1893 n. 126).

The debate for and against the Williams Act was largely set along these lines. Henry Manne wrote in opposition, as did Robert Mundheim and Arthur Fleischer (Fleischer & Mundheim 1967). The latter two, along with William H. Painter, based their arguments on the lack of empirical evidence supporting the 'corporate raider thesis' as well as the need to preserve Manne's 'market for corporate control'. The empirical evidence was based on the only study of the matter, by Samuel Hayes and Russell Taussig (1967). The authors found that tender offers were not primarily the work of corporate raiders bent on liquidating the corporation's assets.

Largely because of this opposition, in 1967 Senator Williams introduced a revised, more neutral bill. One of its stated main purposes was 'to avoid tipping the balance of regulation either in favor of management or in favor of the person making the takeover bid'. The final bill, signed into law on July 29, 1968, was the Williams Act.[1]

Theoretical articles written after the Williams Act largely accepted the Act as a relatively benign measure necessary to prevent coercive tender offers. But some research found harmful effects. Jarrell and Bradley (1980) concluded that the Williams Act lowered the net gains from takeovers. The Act reallocated surplus to target shareholders; cash tender premiums increased from an average of 32% before the Act to 53% after its enactment. This surplus was, however, offset by a decrease in bidding rates due to the deterrence effect that the Williams Act had on hostile offers. In other words, the reallocation of surplus may, at least according to one study, have come at the expense of aggregate social welfare, as value increasing offers were not made.

## 3.   THE 1970S: GOING-PRIVATE TRANSACTIONS

The debate about the Williams Act gave way in the 1970s to a debate on going-private transactions. In the wake of the market-downturn in the early 1970s a wave of such transactions occurred. These were largely 'take 'em public high – buy 'em out low' affairs: affiliates of corporations who had only recently engaged in initial public offerings when stock market prices were substantially higher offered to buy out their own publicly held stock at markedly lower prices. Because there was an inherently coercive element in these transactions due to the majority shareholders' ability to force through the acquisition, and the opportune timing was at the affiliates' discretion, these purchases engendered cries of fraud and unjust enrichment. The states' response was, at least initially, relatively sluggish, and the SEC again took the wheel, maintaining its role as the nation's primary takeover regulator at the time. Numerous academic articles decried these takeovers and called for heightened regulation.

---

[1]   Pub. L. No. 90-439, 82 Stat. 454 (1968).

Perhaps the most notable of these articles was by Victor Brudney and Marvin Chirelstein. In a 1974 article in the *Harvard Law Review*, the two argued 'that fairness requires recognition and sharing of gains from mergers and that, at least in parent-subsidiary mergers, the most appropriate basis for a sharing formula by which to measure fairness is an equal return on the contribution made to the merger by each set of stockholders' (Brudney & Chirelstein 1974, 345).

Their article was notable in failing to substantively include or even address law and economics theory. Indeed, Brudney and Chirelstein prefaced their article with the following qualifier: '[b]y way of limitation, we emphasize that our aim is to explore investor protection schemes – that is, to examine and reformulate certain aspects of the corporate law of merger – and not to decide whether corporate combinations are desirable from an antitrust standpoint or whether consumers and others are well served by the creation of ever larger financial aggregates' (Brudney & Chirelstein 1974, 299). This was a direct response to Manne's thesis that corporate combinations among competitors could be a net social benefit. Brudney and Chirelstein instead argued that notions of fairness should shape and drive the debate over regulation of going-private transactions.

Some scholarly attempts were made to outline solutions based on mimicking arms-length bargaining (Hazen 1977), a law and economics solution to address the potential for self-dealing inherent in going-private transactions. But the 'fairness' strain dominated the scholarship on the issue, dealing with the scope of any heightened regulation, not whether or not there should be any regulation. Law and economics solutions to the problems inherent in going-private transactions would not become significant until the 2000s, when Delaware sought to liberalize its going-private regulations. This was in part due to the dearth of law and economics scholars during this 1970s time period, but was also due to the intellectual atmosphere of the time, which was more focused on substantive and doctrinal rather than economic solutions to corporate issues of the day. This was about to change.

## 4. THE 1980S: THE DOMINANCE OF LAW AND ECONOMICS TAKEOVER THEORY

The 1980s takeover wave transformed the capital markets and was marked by a surge in hostile and unsolicited takeover offers. It spurred a heated legislative, judicial and academic debate over the proper regulation of these offers. The academic debate was heavily influenced by three law and economics articles written in the early 1980s. While these articles continue to shape takeover theory through today, their influence on courts and legislatures has been less significant.

The first of these papers was published by Frank Easterbrook and Daniel Fischel in the *Harvard Law Review* in 1981 (Easterbrook & Fischel 1981); it was entitled 'The Proper Role of a Target's Management in Responding to a Takeover'. In this article, Easterbrook and Fischel argued that a defensive response by management to a hostile takeover offer decreases shareholder welfare. This conclusion was predicated on the efficiency of the stock market and the influence of the market on any takeover bid premium, making any bid that was above the stock price a wealth maximizing one for shareholders. Easterbrook and Fischel stated:

[w]e can conclude … that a tender offer at a price higher than the prevailing one also exceeds the value of the stock. True, the target's managers may know something about the firm's prospects not yet incorporated into the price of the shares. But the disparity between price and worth could not last long. If a bidder tried to steal the target by capitalizing on its special information, the target's managers could defeat the offer by disclosing the information to the public. The price would adjust to reflect the new information, and the offer would succeed only if it were higher than the new price. Tender offers at a premium thus must benefit the target's shareholders. (Easterbrook & Fischel 1981, 1167–8)

Since any premium would benefit the stockholders and the price was self-adjusting, the proper response of a target board was passivity. Any target board defense would only forestall social welfare enhancing bids and chill takeover activity, such bids and takeover activity being desirable as encouraging the market for corporate control. As a corollary to this conclusion, Easterbrook and Fischel posited that bidding competitions for targets should be discouraged as they would diminish search returns and reduce takeover activity.

Lucian Bebchuk, then still a graduate student at Harvard Law School, responded in an article a year later entitled 'The Case for Facilitating Competing Tender Offers' (Bebchuk 1982). Bebchuk noted that there were 'strong reasons' to restrict defensive tactics since they would entrench management as well as remove shareholders as the primary decision-maker in the takeover decision. However, in contrast to Easterbrook and Fischel, Bebchuk argued for an auctioneering rule: boards should be allowed to adopt defensive tactics in order to facilitate auctions. He concluded that bidders for a company were driven by the prospect of synergies and improved management; to the extent they were successful these transactions should increase social welfare. In response to Easterbrook and Fischel, Bebchuk also argued that auctions would not increase search costs unduly, as significant motivational forces would remain which would still incentivize bidders to make an offer. An auctioneering rule would increase premiums to, and maximize economic welfare for, target shareholders, without decreasing bidding rates.

In between the publication of these two articles, Ronald Gilson published 'A Structural Approach to Corporations: The Case Against Defensive Tactics in Tender Offers' (Gilson 1981). Gilson examined the structure of the corporation and the role of management in light of Michael Jensen and William Meckling's theory of the firm (Jensen & Meckling 1976). Like Manne, Gilson posited that management was likely to rent-seek to its own benefit. Gilson argued that 'the tender offer is centrally important to the structure of the corporation because it is the key displacement mechanism through which the market for corporate control constrains management behavior and because it is a critical safety valve against management's misuse of its controlling role in all other displacement mechanisms' (Gilson 1981, 875). According to Gilson, the tender offer was the key to the market for corporate control; the structure of the corporation necessitated barring defensive tactics by corporate boards and placing the corporate control decision with shareholders. A rule forbidding management from interfering with shareholder ability to accept offers was appropriate.

Though the details and rationale were different, each of the three articles placed the decision to accept or decline a tender offer with shareholders. This would enable the market for corporate control to effectively function in the manner Manne theorized. There were detractors: Marty Lipton argued that directors were best positioned to make the takeover decision and that takeover defenses were appropriate (Lipton 1979). Louis Lowenstein famously argued that the stock market was too inefficient for the disciplining force of the market for corporate control to work (Lowenstein 1983). But the words of John Coffee in 1984 high-lighted the continuing influence of Manne's theory. Coffee wrote that 'the claim that hostile takeovers generate a disciplinary force that constrains managerial behavior cannot seriously be disputed' (Coffee 1984, 1294). This idea (and these articles) would shape the takeover debate through the 1980s and 1990s. 1970s notions of fairness no longer came to the fore; instead, economics and Manne's theory were the start of any takeover regulation analysis.

As the 1980s progressed, this debate would become more complex as others built upon the theories put forth in these three articles. Coffee was notable in expanding the framework of this debate and noting its limitations. In that same 1984 article referred to above, Coffee asserted that 'this view both overstates the potential of the market for control and understates the potential efficacy of other modes of corporate accountability – such as independent boards or intra-corporate litigation' (Coffee 1984, 1153). Coffee postulated that other mechanisms might increase social welfare more than the market for corporate control. Coffee was arguing that these issues were far more complicated than the early literature suggested and that caution was therefore necessary.

While the academic battle raged, the political and judicial one also continued. The battle over the proper regulation of targets and takeovers took place in Congress, the state legisla-tures and the Delaware judiciary. In all three instances, the advocates of a free market for corporate control eventually lost. Second-generation state anti-takeover laws were struck down by the Supreme Court in *Edgar v. Mite*[2] but the states proceeded to enact third gener-ation laws which the Supreme Court upheld in *CTS Corp. v. Dynamics Corp.*[3] In the wake of *CTS*, even Delaware passed a mild form of business combination statute. Congress, despite a number of proposed bills, largely failed to act other than to limit golden parachutes and green-mail.

The Delaware judiciary itself in *Unocal v. Mesa Petroleum*[4] set forth a standard of review for a board decision to adopt takeover defenses. A year after *Unocal*, the Delaware Supreme Court in *Revlon, Inc. v. MacAndrews & Forbes Holdings, Inc.*[5] also adopted a rule requiring that a target board accept the highest price reasonably available upon a decision to sell the company. The *Unocal* and *Revlon* decisions were notable for restricting the use of takeover and transaction defenses, and for doing so on the basis of the inherent conflict between management and shareholders in the takeover context. These decisions posited a judicial review function to ensure that this conflict was mitigated in the market for corporate control. However, in later decisions such as *Paramount Communications, Inc. v. Time, Inc.*[6] the Delaware Supreme Court took a more restrictive view of the scope of both the *Unocal* and *Revlon* standards, significantly cutting back their potential impact on the market for corporate control. None of these decisions relied on the law and economics literature as the basis for their rulings.

Practitioners adapted. When Coffee wrote in 1984 that most tender offers succeeded, this was before the advent of the shareholder rights plan, more commonly known as the poison pill. But by 1986 the poison pill had been validated in Delaware and in statutes in many state

---

[2]    457 U.S. 624 (1982).
[3]    481 U.S. 69 (1987).
[4]    493 A.2d 946 (Del. 1985).
[5]    506 A.2d 173 (Del. 1986).
[6]    571 A.2d 1140 (Del. 1989).

legislatures. The tide had turned. Companies' ability to resist takeovers increased as the decade wore on: practitioners invented new defensive tactics, and legal doctrine and state legislatures increasingly permitted board defensive action.

The law and economics literature at the time decried these developments. For the remainder of the decade, it was largely devoted to arguing against law that permitted targets to adopt defensive measures. This became particularly true when the Delaware Supreme Court decided the *Unocal* case. The case allocated takeover decisions largely to boards, with the possibility of judicial oversight. The nature of that oversight, though, was uncertain; the Delaware Chancery court would spend the rest of the decade exploring the scope of judicial scrutiny under *Unocal*.

Ronald Gilson again entered the debate. Writing with Reinier Kraakman in 1989 in 'Delaware's Intermediate Standard for Defensive Tactics: Is There Substance to Proportionality Review?' (Gilson & Kraakman 1989), the two would begin their article by confining its scope, writing that 'taking Delaware's adoption of proportionality review as given, we seek to facilitate the informed development of this standard as rapidly, and with as little ambiguity, as possible' (Gilson & Kraakman 1989, 248). Gilson and Kraakman then proceeded to analyze the judicial proportionality review of board action embedded in the *Unocal* test. They posited that substantive coercion should be at the heart of any proportionality standard. Given that management has superior information or may be acting to entrench themselves and therefore refusing to disclose relevant information, management should have to justify its defensive actions as being in the interests of shareholders.

Gilson and Kraakman's article constituted a second-line defense in the battle over the proper regulation of takeovers and a dip into doctrine by law and economics scholars. If an unconstrained takeover market was not the legal norm, the literature could still channel its rules towards effective substitutes. Gilson and Kraakman's mode of argument was typical of the literature in the late 1980s, as it came to accept that it had lost the regulatory wars of that time. The literature instead focused on doctrinal matters, and on alleviating the effects of pro-takeover defense rulings and statutes.

## 5.   THE 1990S: THE QUIET PERIOD

The 1990s were a quiet time for takeovers generally; it was also a quiet time for literature on takeovers. There were, however, two important decisions by the Delaware Supreme Court during this time period further allocating decision-making authority (and according deference) to the board of directors with respect to takeovers and the decision to adopt takeover defenses. In *Paramount Communications, Inc. v. QVC Network, Inc.*[7] and *Unitrin, Inc. v. American General Corp.*[8] the Delaware Supreme Court again cut back on the applicability of *Revlon* and the scope of *Unocal* proportionality review. In doing so, the court once again rejected academic writings taking contrary positions (Prentice & Langmore 1990; Gordon 1991). The court's decisions also firmly established the proxy contest as the preferred takeover structure over the tender offer, a development which would come to

---

[7]   637 A.2d 34 (Del. 1994).
[8]   651 A.2d 1361 (Del. 1995).

influence later academic writing in the 2000s focusing on shareholder decision-making authority.

While the 1990s were a quiet time for legal academic writing on takeovers, academics continued their empirical exploration of the new takeover defenses (Romano 1992). A number of studies examined state anti-takeover laws and the wealth effects of the second generation anti-takeover statutes. These studies generally found a corresponding reduction in shareholder and bondholder value in the wake of their enactment (Karpoff & Malatesta 1989). Similar findings followed the post-CTS adoptions of manager-favoring anti-takeover statues in Ohio, Pennsylvania and Massachusetts (Ryngaert & Netter 1988; Szewczyk & Tsetsekos1992; Karpoff & Malatesta 1990, 1995; Swartz 1998). Other studies found a corresponding decline in takeover activity and tender offers (Hackl & Testani 1988) following passage of second generation anti-takeover laws. These studies built upon earlier studies by Aranow et al. (1977) and Jarrell and Bradley (1980), which found shareholder wealth decreasing as a result of first generation anti-takeover statutes.

Early studies of poison pills and shark-repellent amendments also generally concluded that these provisions resulted in shareholder wealth reductions. For example Paul Milgrom and John Roberts surveyed a number of event studies in 1992 and concluded that 'adopting a poison pill typically reduces the firm's share value' (Milgrom & Roberts 1992, 182–3). Similar acknowledgements appear throughout the finance literature in the 1990s.

Nonetheless, despite the general view that takeover defenses were wealth destroying, a number of economists in the 1990s took a contrary position. They argued that certain types of short-term takeover and transaction defenses could produce shareholder wealth. Rene Stulz (1990) argued that boards' use of defensive measures to combat takeovers could increase their bargaining power and thereby enhance shareholder wealth. Giammarino et al. (1997) argued that pre-planned takeover defenses could limit management's incentive to underinvest in the corporate enterprise in anticipation of a hostile takeover and loss of their employment. Others argued that transaction defenses which favored one bidder over another could improve shareholder welfare by enhancing bidding and outcomes. And as early as 1983, significant studies were published questioning whether shareholders lost wealth from takeover defenses (Bradley et al.1983; Jensen & Ruback 1983). In a similar vein, some financial economists supported takeover defenses, arguing that takeovers were harmful since shareholders' gains were often merely redistributed from other stakeholders (such as creditors) (Shleifer & Summers 1989). Some legal literature also took this position. That being said, the majority consensus of the law and economics and finance literatures at the end of 1990s was still that takeover defenses were undesirable.

## 6.   THE 2000S: GRAPPLING WITH REJECTED THEORY AND NEW APPROACHES

In 2001, Robert Thompson and Gordon Smith published 'Toward a New Theory of the Shareholder Role: "Sacred Space" in Corporate Takeovers'. Thompson and Smith noted that *Unocal* had been applied sparingly and that for all effective purposes it was 'dead'. Highlighting the recent increase in shareholder activism, the pair called for 'sacred space' in takeovers which permitted shareholders to decide and vote on a sale decision (Smith & Thompson 2001, 261). Their argument was premised on Ronald Coase's theory of the firm and the incomplete contracts which necessitated the firm. In the takeover realm, the result of contractual incompleteness had been to delegate oversight of the board takeover defense and decision to judges. But this oversight was, they argued, better allocated to shareholders: a governance solution was preferable to a judicial one (Paredes 2003).

Smith and Thompson's article marked a new doctrinal strain in the analysis of takeover defenses and board discretion. This new academic writing supported empowering shareholders and therefore limiting board discretion. The market for corporate control was a pillar of the law and economics movement. But the defeats in Delaware left scholars struggling to reconcile judicial doctrine with the importance of Manne's thesis. The result was a turn away from Manne. The new millennium battles would not be couched in terms of Manne's thesis; rather, they would emphasize shareholder choice and corporate governance. They would be about whether shareholders should have decision-making rights over managers in what many, including Thompson and Smith, theorized was a zero sum game between the two. This was an important and subtle distinction from the debate in the 1980s and earlier, which stressed oversight as the basis for allocating power within a corporation. In this regard, the 1980s literature had championed the tender offer, while the new millennium issue focused more on the availability of the ballot-box for shareholders.

Jeffrey Gordon anticipated this development in an earlier 1997 article '"Just Say Never?" Poison Pills, Deadhand Pills, and Shareholder-Adopted Bylaws: An Essay for Warren Buffet'. Published at a time just before the Delaware Supreme Court was about to consider more extreme forms of poison pills known as dead-hand and no hand pills, Gordon argued that Delaware takeover law had become too 'formalistic' and decried the 'increasingly managerialist stance of the Delaware Supreme Court' (Gordon 1997b, 515). Gordon wrote that:

> The growing restrictiveness of legal rules was, however, in significant measure offset by the rise of institutional investor activism, where stock price performance played a significant role in decisions by institutions to intervene against incumbent CEOs, to criticize complaisant boards, and to support premium takeover bids. Thus, the evolving ownership structure of large public corporations is a critical element in the overall governance regime and can play a crucial role in assuring the necessary managerial responsiveness to capital market signals. (Gordon 1997b, 514)

In other words, the vision of Manne was still viable; the takeover market as a monitoring force should be preserved. Recognizing that the Delaware courts would not go so far as to fully deregulate the takeover market, Gordon concluded that a 'just say no defense' should not be permitted under Delaware law, at least until the next election of directors. He argued for a shareholder choice model which would leverage the rise of institutional and more powerful shareholders and encourage boards and shareholders to converse about the 'shape of governance mechanisms' (Gordon 1997b, 551). Subsequent to Gordon's article the Delaware courts in *Carmody v. Toll Brothers*[9] and *Quickturn Design Systems, Inc. v. Shapiro*[10] would strike down the use of both no-hand and dead-hand poison pills, respectively, on *Unocal* and statutory grounds, providing shareholders a vote which could replace a board and ultimately decide whether a takeover attempt would succeed.

---

[9]    723 A.2d 1180 (1998).
[10]   721 A.2d 1281 (Del. 1998).

The Delaware Supreme Court's 1998 decision in *Quickturn Design Systems* to strike down a no-hand poison pill also implicated another academic debate occurring at the time: the viability of shareholder by-laws providing for the mandatory redemption of the poison pill. The decision further fueled the narrow debate over whether shareholders should be permitted to adopt by-laws to repeal or regulate poison pills. This debate was typical of the time: it was focused on the rights of shareholders but also on the minutiae of doctrine and the proper regulatory role of courts vis-à-vis shareholders. The emphasis was on shareholder power in a new economic order where institutional investors and other modern actors exerted their own monitoring force on the corporation. It also strengthened the related argument that diminishing the market for corporate control would also reduce the power of shareholders to influence the corporation (Gordon 1997a). These notions were expressed in a series of articles both before and after the *Quickturn* decision; in these articles a number of academics put forth strong doctrinal arguments for why Delaware law should (or should not) allow shareholder by-laws which restricted poison pills or other takeover defenses (Coffee 1997; Gordon 1997b; Hamermesh 1998; Coates 2001; McDonnell 2005).

This doctrinal turn was accompanied by an empirical one: law and economics academics began to apply empirical analysis to takeovers. Thus, in the late 1990s and onward a number of academics published empirical studies of anti-takeover laws, staggered boards, and lock-ups (Coates & Subramanian, 2000; Bebchuk et al. 2002). This work continued the empirical studies of the 1980s and 1990s and marked a turn from theory to an attempt to sway takeover doctrine through empirical study. In perhaps the most fitting example of the increasing connection between the corporate governance movement, the proper regulation of takeovers and the empirical turn in corporate academics, Lucian Bebchuk and Allen Ferrell published a paper in 2004 describing what they termed an E-index. This index built on the corporate governance measurement index, the G-Index, of Gompers et al. (2003). The E-index focused on six entrenching devices, including the poison pill and the staggered board, and measured their use in public corporations across an extended period of time from 1990–2007. The authors found that firm performance was positively correlated with a lower E-index (or decreased entrenching defenses). Both the E-Index and G-Index studies were criticized on several grounds, including endogeneity and omitted variable bias. As to the former, results seeming to indicate that takeover defenses caused poor performance might instead indicate that poorly performing companies were more apt to choose takeover defenses. Whatever may be the substantive validity of these studies, they did make the tie between takeover defenses and corporate governance explicit.

Some scholars continued to advocate fundamental change. Lucian Bebchuk and Allen Ferrell also published a series of articles asserting that the state model of takeover law was too protective of managers in the takeover decision. In 'A New Approach to Takeover Law and Regulatory Competition' (2001), they argued that a federal opt-in takeover regime should be established. This new federal regulatory regime would be less protective of managers and provide shareholders with the power to elect their own directors. Bebchuk's and Ferrell's article was a marker that some scholars had lost faith in state control over corporate law; federal intervention was necessary. To support their arguments, Bebchuk and Ferrell instead turned to a new strand of literature which had arisen in response to Delaware's anti-takeover turn in the 1980s.

This literature was built out of the old Cary/Winter debate about whether Delaware was racing to the top or bottom in its corporate law – that is, whether its law was catering to shareholders or to the self-interest of managers. Roberta Romano had written eloquently on this subject during the 1980s; she had postulated that the race between the states generally resulted in economically superior regulation, except perhaps in the context of takeovers (Romano 1987). In the turn of the millennium this view was extended and reaffirmed. A number of academics empirically examined the subject and concluded that Delaware was not racing against any other state: it had no competition as a venue for incorporation (Daines 2002; Kahan 2006). This meant that it was effectively impossible to know if Delaware was racing to the top, with law meant to cater to the corporation's principals, the shareholders, or the bottom, catering to the self-interest of managers making the incorporation decision. The true issue was who Delaware was catering to if it was not competing with other states. In two related papers, Mark Roe examined this question (Roe 2003, 2005). He theorized that Delaware was fighting a battle to forestall federal intervention consistent with preserving its franchise, a modified race to the bottom. However, as Steven Davidoff (2007) later wrote, the federal government had long since ceased regulating, removing this force from the takeover market. Moreover, in light of Delaware's victory and the inaction of the federal government, things remained unchanged from the 1980s and takeover regulation remained political, as judges catered to the managers who made the incorporation decision. The consequence was that while academics generally agreed on the political nature of takeover regulation their solution – the federal government – appeared uninterested in intervening. Bebchuk's and Ferrell's solution lay in a distant future at best.

New theoretical views also came to the forefront which called into question or refined Manne's theory. This scholarship raised Coffee's argument made in 1984, that other market forces, such as institutional shareholders, could be superior monitoring mechanisms. Stephen Bainbridge strongly expounded a theory of director primacy and the desirability of having boards at the center of corporate decision-making based on organization theory (Bainbridge 2006; McDonnell 2009). Jennifer Arlen and Eric Talley theorized that shareholders might rationally restrict shareholder choice because it is more costly than a system which permits board discretion to make decisions about takeovers (Arlen & Talley 2003). Delaware judges wrote repeatedly in the new millennium about the need to allow for board discretion (Allen et al. 2001). Well-known takeover lawyer Marty Lipton continued to advocate a board-centered decision-making regime for takeovers; he was responding to an opposing piece by Gilson at a symposium marking the 20th anniversary of *Unocal* (Lipton & Rowe 2002) in which Gilson had argued 'that Unocal ultimately has developed into an unexplained and … inexplicable preference that control contests be resolved through elections rather than market transactions' (Gilson 2001, 492). New conceptions of the firm, such as Margaret Blair's and Lynn Stout's team production theory, raised the issue of whether shareholder wealth was the primary consideration in setting takeover rules (Blair & Stout 1999). Progressive law scholars continued to write in opposition to the law and economics movement (Mitchell 2009).

The efficient market hypothesis, a cornerstone of Manne's theory, reached its apogee in the late 1980s. But thereafter, academics in finance and law increasingly questioned the efficiency of the stock market casting doubt on Manne's thesis. This trend accelerated in the wake of the technology bubble. Behavioral economics theories began to gain in popularity, and many commentators came to believe stock markets were not semi-strong efficient in part due to shareholders' behavioral biases and their heterogeneous expectations. These biases mitigated against stockholders mediating a contest for corporate control (Stout 2005; Langevoort 2010 and Ch. 23 this volume).

Even those who believed in Manne's thesis and the need for a takeover market accommodated or partly accepted the Delaware regime. Marcel Kahan and Edward Rock (2002) wrote about the adaptability of corporate law. They theorized that even if companies' use of takeover devices was severely restricted, corporations and practitioners would manage to circumvent those restrictions. The markets could create their own monitoring devices to substitute for a more restricted takeover market, such as independent directors and institutional shareholders.

Manne's theory was also challenged by the new prism of shareholder rights, corporate governance and its focus on independent directors. The focus on corporate governance could have helped restore Manne's vision, empowering shareholders over directors with respect to the corporate control decision. However, the corporate governance movement also created a second monitoring force, independent directors. Ironically, the rise of independent directors and the increasingly held view that shareholders could be shortsighted and heterogeneous led to arguments that shareholders should not be the ones making the takeover decision. Independent directors acting in good faith were better situated to assess a takeover offer and determine if it enhanced shareholder value in the long term.

This argument acquired the force of law with Chancellor Chandler's recent decision in *Air Products & Chemicals, Inc. v. Airgas, Inc.*[11] Chancellor Chandler wrote a 158 page opinion in which he agreed with the views of Gilson & Kraakman (1989) that when price was the only factor, shareholders should be the authority on whether or not to accept a takeover offer. However, since Gilson & Kraakman's view was not the law in Delaware, he still ruled against the hostile bidder. Chancellor Chandler was bound by precedent to conclude that independent directors acting in good faith had the power to implement and maintain a poison pill in the face of a hostile offer. Marty Lipton had won the judicial battle if not the theoretical one.

The debate in the 2000s showed that academic theory on the proper scope of takeover regulation was increasingly fractured. Arguments for permitting director discretion were hotly debated. The financial revolution and more developed capital markets provided other disciplining forces on firms. Furthermore, shareholders' ability to make takeover decisions was further brought into question as retail investors increasingly fled the market, institutional investors remained complacent, private equity firms were accused of being in cahoots with management, and hedge funds and large institutional shareholders were accused of self-interest and short-termism. Law and economics' focus shifted from bigger issues such as the scope of regulation to more nuanced ones such as defining doctrine and empirical analysis. The discipline had become part of the broader debate about corporate governance and shareholder rights, proxy access and the proper allocation of managerial authority in the firm rather than about Manne's monitoring theory.

Throughout this debate, the law and economics movement as a discipline and analytical technique remained influential. This was particularly true in the scholarship responding to *In re Siliconix, Inc. Shareholders Litigation,*[12] and other Delaware decisions liberalizing the regulation of freeze-outs. The 1970s literature was dominated by notions of fairness, but in the new millennium the most influential papers on this topic argued for either arms-length bargaining to approximate market mechanisms (Gilson & Gordon 2003), a deregulated

---

[11] 2011 WL 519735 (Del. Ch. Feb. 15, 2011).
[12] 2001 WL 716787 (Del. Ch. June 19, 2001).

approach under which the market would self-correct for the problem by *ex ante* pricing in these transactions (Pritchard 2004), or an empirically informed solution of regulation (Subramanian 2005). This line of Delaware case law illustrates another influence of law and economics theory on Delaware takeover regulation: an increasing judicial preference for takeover rules which allow for private ordering over broad standards such as 'entire fairness', which require thorough judicial review. Thus, while differing theories and approaches were utilized, law and economics maintained its position as one of the primary analytical tools through which to view takeovers. Today, corporate law scholarship regularly references or uses economic analysis. Law and economics remains a dominant, indeed pervasive, tool, but there are other tools available; some can be used alongside law and economics, but others reject it.

## 7.   CONCLUSION

After its judicial defeats, law and economics' influence over takeover scholarship has lessened, although it is still ubiquitous. Takeover theory has become more complex as competing disciplines and modes of thought influence the debate. None of this is surprising: law and economics, like all theory, has evolved, becoming more nuanced as its assumptions and conclusions are refined and in some cases challenged. Commendably, law and economics has become much less rigid and more diverse in its techniques than in its early days.

Law and economics has thus moved beyond Manne's central theory to accommodate the corporate governance movement and its increasing emphasis on shareholder authority in decision-making. Manne's theory is still influential, but there is vigorous debate about whether other conceptions of the firm or different monitoring mechanisms should substitute as a disciplining force on directors and officers. Some law and economics scholars now argue that a target's decision to accept or reject a takeover is *ab initio* better allocated to shareholders – that shareholders should have a deciding voice in corporate takeovers.

The other controlling forces Coffee cited in the 1980s may now also exist, insofar as shareholders such as hedge funds or institutional investors advised by proxy advisory services serve as a check on director behavior. But shareholders and institutions can have their own interests, which can be contrary to those of other shareholders and the corporation. The present debate often focuses on corporate governance more directly, and in particular, when and how should shareholders decide materially economic corporate decisions. The champion of the pro-shareholder movement is Lucian Bebchuk, who has steadfastly argued against antitakeover devices and for shareholder choice over the past 30 years. But he stands in contrast to others whose theories now favor an allocation of that authority in some measure to boards, independent directors or other constituencies (Kahan & Rock 2003; Stout 2005; Bainbridge 2006).

Fundamental questions thus remain as to whether shareholders should be the ones to decide on takeovers. Theoretical and empirical work in this area should continue; comparative work may be particularly useful. In this regard, some other countries' takeover legislation restricts the use of takeover defenses. For instance, in the UK the use of takeover defenses is quite limited. There has been considerable comparative work, but much more can profitably be done (Armour et al. 2011).

Davidoff (2009) theorizes that the takeover market has come to a basic equilibrium whereby shareholder activism and corporate governance provide a force in conjunction with the 'light' touch of Delaware to counteract management. Despite the judicial losses, Manne's idea of a monitor has triumphed through other means. The market may have further adapted by adopting substitute monitoring mechanisms such as proxy advisory services. In this light, the law and economics movement would also do well to theoretically re-engage with and reassess specific questions of takeover regulation, including the validity and scope of the Williams Act. The merger of corporate governance and takeover theory may have muddied the waters. Present-day theoreticians should recast the grand law and economics theories of the 1980s for more complex times, in more complete capital markets and with less certainty about the ability of any single structural force to effectively monitor and discipline directors and management. The markets have adapted to the Delaware decisions of the 1980s and beyond.

## REFERENCES

Allen, William T., Jack B. Jacobs & Leo E. Strine, Jr. (2002), 'The Great Takeover Debate: A Meditation on Bridging the Conceptual Divide', *University of Chicago Law Review*, 69, 1067–1100.

Aranow, Edward Ross, Herbert A. Einhorn & George Berlstein (1977), *Developments in Tender Offers for Corporate Control*, New York: Columbia University Press.

Arlen, Jennifer & Eric Talley (2003), 'Unregulable Defenses and the Perils of Shareholder Choice', *University of Pennsylvania Law Review*, 152, 577–666.

Armour, John, Jack B. Jacobs & Curtis J. Milhaupt (2011), 'The Evolution of Hostile Takeover Regimes in Developed and Emerging Markets: An Analytical Framework', *Harvard International Law Journal*, 52, 219–85.

Bainbridge, Stephen M. (2006), 'Unocal at 20: Director Primacy in Corporate Takeovers', *Delaware Journal of Corporate Law*, 31(3), 769–862.

Bebchuk, Lucian A. (1982), 'The Case for Facilitating Tender Offers', *Harvard Law Review*, 95, 1028–56.

Bebchuk, Lucian (2005), 'The Case for Increasing Shareholder Power', *Harvard Law Review*, 118, 833–914.

Bebchuk, Lucian A. & Allen A. Ferrell (2001), 'A New Approach to Takeover Law and Regulatory Competition', *Virginia Law Review*, 87, 111–64.

Bebchuk, Lucian A., John C. Coates IV & Guhan Subramanian (2002), 'The Powerful Antitakeover Force of Staggered Boards: Theory, Evidence, and Policy', *Stanford Law Review*, 54, 887–951.

Bebchuk, Lucian A. & Alma Cohen (2003), 'Firms' Decisions Where to Incorporate', *Journal of Law and Economics*, 46, 383–425.

Bebchuk, Lucian A., Alma Cohen & Allen Ferrell (2004), 'What Matters in Corporate Governance?', *Review of Financial Studies*, 22(2), 783–827.

Berkovitch, Elazar (1990), 'How Target Shareholders Benefit from Value-Reducing Defensive Strategies in Takeovers', *Journal of Finance*, 45(1), 137–56.

Berle, Adolf A. & Gardiner C. Means (1932), *The Modern Corporation and Private Property*, New York: Macmillan Publishing Co.

Blair, Margaret M. & Lynn A. Stout (1999), 'A Team Production Theory of Corporate Law', *Virginia Law Review*, 85, 247–328.

Bradley, Michael, Anand Desai & E. Han Kim (1983), 'The Rationale Behind Interfirm Tender Offers: Information or Synergy?', *Journal of Financial Economics*, 11, 183–206.

Brudney, Victor & Marvin Chirelstein (1974), 'Fair Shares in corporate Mergers and Takeovers', *Harvard Law Review*, 88, 297–346.

Coates, John C. IV (2000), 'Empirical Evidence on Structural Takeover Defenses: Where Do We Stand?', *University of Miami Law Review*, 54, 783–97.

Coates, John C. IV (2001), 'Explaining Variation in Takeover Defenses: Blame the Lawyers', *California Law Review*, 89, 1301–86.

Coates, John C. IV and Guhan Subramanian (2000), 'A Buy-Side Model of Lockups: Theory and Evidence', *Stanford Law Review*, 53, 307–96.

Coates, John C. IV & Bradley C. Faris (2001), 'Second-Generation Shareholder Bylaws: Post-Quickturn Alternatives', *The Business Lawyer*, 56, 1323–79.

Coffee, John C., Jr. (1997), 'The Bylaw Battlefield: Can Institutions Change the Outcome of Corporate Control Contests?', *University of Miami Law Review*, 51, 605–21.

Coffee, John C. (1984), 'Regulating the Market for Corporate Control: A Critical Assessment of the Tender Offer's Role in Corporate Governance', *Columbia Law Review*, 84, 1145–1296.

Daines, Robert M. (2002), 'The Incorporation Choices of IPO Firms (Initial Public Offerings)', *New York University Law Review*, 77, 1559–1611.

Davidoff, Steven M. (2007), 'The SEC and the Failure of Federal Takeover Regulation', *Florida State University Law Review*, 34, 211–69.

Davidoff, Steven M. (2009), *Gods at War: Shotgun Takeovers, Government by Deal, and the Private Equity Implosion*, New Jersey: John Wiley & Sons, Inc.

Easterbrook, Frank & Daniel Fischel (1981), 'The Proper Role of a Target's Management in Responding to a Tender Offer', *Harvard Law Review*, 94, 1161–1204.

Fama, Eugene F. & Michael C. Jensen (1985), 'Organizational Forms and Investment Decisions', *Journal of Financial Economics*, 14(1), 101–19.

Fleischer, Arthur, Jr. & Robert Mundheim (1967), 'Corporate Acquisition by Tender Offer', *University of Pennsylvania Law Review*, 115, 317–70.

Giammarino, Ronald, Robert Heinkel & Burton Hollifield (1997), 'Defensive Mechanisms and Managerial Discretion', *Journal of Finance*, 52(4), 1467–93.

Gilson, Ronald J. (1981), 'A Structural Approach to Corporations: The Case Against Defensive Tactics in Tender Offers', *Stanford Law Review*, 33, 819–91.

Gilson, Ronald J. (1982), 'Seeking Competitive Bids Versus Pure Passivity in Tender Offer Defense', *Stanford Law Review*, 35, 51–67.

Gilson, Ronald J. (2001), 'Unocal Fifteen Years Later (And What We Can Do About It)', *Delaware Journal of Corporate Law*, 26, 491–513.

Gilson, Ronald J. & Reinier Kraakman (1989), 'Delaware's Intermediate Standard for Defensive Tactics: Is There Substance to Proportionality', *The Business Lawyer*, 44, 247–74.

Gilson, Ronald J. and Jeffrey N. Gordon (2003), 'Controlling Controlling Shareholders', *University of Pennsylvania Law Review*, 152, 785–843.

Gompers, Paul A., Joy L. Ishii & Andrew Metrick (2003), 'Corporate Governance and Equity Prices', *Quarterly Journal of Economics*, 118(1),107–55.

Gordon, Jeffrey N. (1991), 'Corporations, Markets, and Courts', *Columbia Law Review*, 91, 1931–88.

Gordon, Jeffrey N. (1997a), 'The Shaping Force of Corporate Law in the New Economic Order', *University of Richmond Law Review*, 31, 1473–99.

Gordon, Jeffrey N. (1997b), '"Just Say Never?" Poison Pills, Deadhand Pills, and Shareholder-Adopted Bylaws: An Essay for Warren Buffet', *Cardozo Law Review*, 19, 511–52.

Hackl, Jo Watson & Rosa Anna Testani (1988), 'Second Generation State Takeover Statutes and Shareholder Wealth: An Empirical Study', *Yale Law Journal*, 97, 1193–1231.

Hamermesh, Lawrence A. (1998), 'Corporate Democracy and Stockholder-Adopted By-Laws: Taking Back the Street?', *Tulane Law Review*, 73, 409–93.

Hannes, Sharon (2006), 'A Demand-Side Theory of Antitakeover Defenses', *Journal of Legal Studies*, 35, 475–520.

Hayes, Samuel L. & Russell A. Taussig (1967), 'Tactics of Cash Takeover Bids', *Harvard Business Review*,135–48.

Hazen, Thomas L. (1977), 'Transfers of Corporate Control and Duties of Controlling Shareholders. Common Law, Tender Offers, Investment Companies and a Proposal for Reform', *University of Pennsylvania Law Review*, 125, 1023–67.

Jarrell, Gregg A. & Michael Bradley (1980), 'The Economic Effects of Federal and State Regulations of Cash Tender Offers', *Journal of Law and Economics*, 23(2), 371–407.

Michael C. Jensen & William H. Meckling (1976), 'Theory of the Firm: Managerial Behavior, Agency Costs and Ownership', *Structure Journal of Financial Economics*, October, 3(4), 305–60.

Jensen, Michael C. & Richard S. Ruback (1983), 'The Market for Corporate Control: The Scientific Evidence', *Journal of Financial Economy*, 11, 5–50.

Johnson, Lyman & David Millon (1989), 'Misreading the Williams Act', *Michigan Law Review*, 87, 1862–1923.

Kahan, Marcel (2006), 'The Demand for Corporate Law: Statutory Flexibility, Judicial Quality, or Takeover Protection?', *The Journal of Law, Economics, and Organization*, 22(2), 340–65.

Kahan, Marcel & Edward B. Rock (2002), 'How I Learned to Stop Worrying and Love the Pill: Adaptive Responses to Takeover Law', *University of Chicago Law Review*, 69, 871–915.

Kahan, Marcel & Edward B. Rock (2003), 'Corporate Constitutionalism: Antitakeover Charter Provisions as Precommitment', *University of Pennsylvania Law Review*, 152, 473–522.

Kaplan, Steven N. & Per Strömberg (2009), 'Leveraged Buyouts and Private Equity'. *Journal of Economic Perspectives*, 23(1), 121–46.

Karpoff, Jonathan M. & Paul H. Malatesta (1989), 'The Wealth Effects of Second-Generation State Takeover Legislation', *Journal of Financial Economics*, 25(2), 291–322.

Karpoff, Jonathan M. & Paul H. Malatesta (1990), 'PA Law: State Antitakeover Laws and Stock Prices', *Financial Analysts Journal*, 46(4), 8–10.

Karpoff, Jonathan M. and Paul H. Malatesta (1995), 'State Takeover Legislation and Share Values: The Wealth Effects of Pennsylvania's Act 36', *Journal of Corporate Finance*, 1(3–4), 367–82.

Langevoort, Donald C. (2010), 'The Behavioral Economics of Mergers and Acquisitions', Georgetown Law and Economics Research Paper Nos 10–17.

Lipton, Martin (1979), 'Takeover Bids in the Target's Boardroom', *The Business Lawyer*, 35, 101–34.

Lipton, Martin & Paul K. Rowe (2002), 'Pills, Polls and Professors: A Reply to Professor Gilson', *Delaware Journal of Corporate Law*, 27, 1–35.

Lowenstein, Louis (1983), 'Pruning Deadwood in Hostile Takeovers: A Proposal for Legislation', *Columbia Law Review*, 83, 249–334.

Manne, Henry G. (1965), 'Mergers and the Market for Corporate Control', *Journal of Political Economy*, 73(2), 110–120.

Manne, Henry G. (1966), 'Tender Offers and the Free Market', *Mergers & Acquisitions*, 2, 91.

Manne, Henry G. (1967), 'Cash Tender Offers for Shares: A Reply to Chairman Cohen', *Duke Law Journal*, 1967, 231–53.

McDonnell, Brett H. (2005), 'Shareholder Bylaws, Shareholder Nominations and Poison Pills', *Berkeley Business Law Journal*, 3, 205–64.

McDonnell, Brett H. (2009), 'Professor Bainbridge and the Arrowian Moment: A Review of the New Corporate Governance in Theory and Practice', *Delaware Journal of Corporate Law*, 34, 139–90.

Milgrom, Paul & John Roberts (1992), *Economics, Organization and Management*, New Jersey: Prentice Hall.

Mitchell, Dalia Tsuk (2009), 'The End of Corporate Law', *Wake Forest Law Review*, 44, 703–29.

Mundheim, Robert (1967), 'Why the Bill on Tender Offers Should Not Be Passed', *Institutional Investor*, 1(24).

Paredes, Troy A. (2003), 'The Firm and the Nature of Control: Toward a Theory of Takeover Law', *Journal of Corporate Law*, 29, 103–78.

Prentice, Robert A. & John H. Langmore (1990), 'Hostile Tender Offers and the "Nancy Reagan Defense": May Target Boards "Just Say No"? Should They Be Allowed To?' *Delaware Journal of Corporate Law*, 15, 377–481.

Pritchard, A.C. (2004), 'Tender Offers by Controlling Shareholders: The Specter of Coercion and Fair Price', *Berkeley Business Law Journal*, 1, 83–112.

Roe, Mark J. (2003), 'Delaware's Competition', *Harvard Law Review*, 117, 588–646.

Roe, Mark J. (2005), 'Delaware's Politics', *Harvard Law Review*, 118, 2491–543.

Romano, Roberta (1987), 'The Political Economy of Takeover Statutes', *Virginia Law Review*, 73, 111–99.

Romano, Roberta (1992), 'A Guide to Takeovers: Theory Evidence and Regulation', *Yale Journal on Regulation*, 9, 119–78.

Ryngaert, Michael (1988), 'The Effect of Poison Pill Securities on Shareholder Wealth', *Journal of Financial Economics*, 20(1–2), 377–417.

Rynegaert, Michael & Jeffrey M. Netter (1988), 'Shareholder Wealth Effects of the Ohio Antitakeover Law', *Journal of Law, Economics, and Organization*, 4(2), 373–83.

Shleifer, Andrei & Lawrence H. Summers (1988), 'Breach of Trust in Hostile Takeovers', in Alan J. Auerbach (ed.) *Corporate Takeovers: Causes and Consequences*, University of Chicago Press, 33–68.

Smiley, Robert (1981), 'The Effect of State Securities Statutes on Tender Offer Activity', *Economic Inquiry*, 19(3), 426–35.

Stout, Lynn A. (2005), 'Takeovers in the Ivory Tower: How Academics Are Learning Martin Lipton May Be Right', *The Business Lawyer*, 60, 1435–54.

Stulz, Rene (1990), 'Managerial Discretion and Optimal Financing Policies', *Journal of Financial Economics*, 26(1), 3–27.

Subramanian, Guhan (2002), 'The Influence of Antitakeover Statutes on Incorporation Choice: Evidence on the "Race" Debate and Antitakeover Overreaching', *University of Pennsylvania Law Review*, 150, 1795–1873.

Subramanian, Guhan (2005), 'Fixing Freezeouts', *Yale Law Journal*, 115, 2–70.

Swartz, L. Mick (1998), 'The Massachusetts Classified Board Law', *Journal of Economics and Finance*, 22(1), 29–36.

Szewczyk, Samuel H. & George P. Tsetsekos (1992), 'State Intervention in the Market for Corporate Control: The Case of Pennsylvania Senate Bill 1310', *Journal of Financial Economics*, 31(1), 3–23.

Thompson, Robert B. & Gordon D. Smith (2001), 'Toward a New Theory of the Shareholder Role: "Sacred Space" in Corporate Takeovers', *Texas Law Review*, 80, 261–326.

# 13. The law and economics of executive compensation: Theory and evidence

*David I. Walker*

## 1. INTRODUCTION

It is difficult to imagine a corporate law topic that has generated as much consternation, or as much academic research, over the last 20 years as public company executive compensation. In a seminal article on executive pay written in the late 1990s, Kevin Murphy noted that the academic research on the topic 'had exploded' (Murphy 1999), but surely the journal pages devoted to the topic in the 1990s are dwarfed by those produced since. The enterprise was and is highly interdisciplinary, with important contributions emanating from law, economics, corporate finance, and accounting, among other fields. This continuing academic interest is not surprising given the level and salience of executive pay and ongoing debate concerning the extent to which pay practices are consonant with corporate or shareholder interests.

This chapter is intended to provide an overview of the theory and evidence regarding public company executive compensation. It is not comprehensive in either the choice of topics or the coverage of those topics, but is meant to provide the reader with an entryway into the literature on a select group of topics. Priority has been afforded to the most central issues in executive pay, to issues that implicate law more or less directly, and to issues that have been the primary focus of research in the last decade.

The chapter is organized as follows. The next section briefly outlines three broad theoretical perspectives on the pay-setting process and the objectives of compensation: the optimal contracting theory, the managerial power theory, and the team production theory. This chapter does not attempt to declare a winner among these theories. Indeed, they are to a large extent complementary. They are useful frameworks to bear in mind, however, as one considers the more detailed theory and evidence that follows.

The following section focuses on the law, theory, and evidence regarding two aspects of executive pay that have generated much of the economic research – the growth in US executive pay and compensation design. Equity compensation is particularly complex, and one goal of this section is to explain the mechanics and risk and incentive properties of these arrangements.

Next we consider several areas of regulatory intervention into pay processes – board and compensation committee independence, mandatory disclosure, compensation consultants, and shareholder advisory voting on executive pay. The objective here is to understand what the theory and evidence tell us about the efficacy and unintended consequences of such intervention.[1]

---

[1]  In aggregate, the central three sections consider the role that compensation plays in corporate governance as well as the role that law and governance play in setting compensation.

The final section concludes with some brief thoughts regarding the direction of executive pay regulation and research.

Many interesting topics are omitted from this survey, including some relatively narrow topics, such as 'clawbacks' of incentive compensation from executives in the wake of financial restatement. International comparisons are largely neglected, as is consideration of compensation of executives in the financial industry.[2] The focus instead is on the law and economics of executive pay as it applies to US public companies generally.

As noted, one consideration in prioritizing the material for this survey is the extent to which the topic implicates law.[3] Therefore, before turning to the theory of executive pay in the following section, a general word regarding the 'law' of executive pay is in order.

The law of executive compensation arises from a variety of sources. State corporate law has surprisingly little impact on public company pay arrangements. The Delaware corporate law statute is all but silent on the issue.[4] Executive pay decisions necessarily implicate officer and director duties of loyalty under corporate law, but while fiduciary duties may constrain pay processes, they do not seriously constrain the amount or form of executive pay (Barris 1992; Thomas & Martin 2001).[5] Similarly, stock exchange listing requirements impose procedural constraints on pay, requiring, for example, shareholder approval of stock option plans.[6]

Historically, governmental regulation of executive compensation consisted largely of SEC disclosure requirements, federal tax rules, and accounting requirements. The influence of these rules on executive pay is discussed in the third section. In the wake of the debacles at Enron, WorldCom, and other firms and the financial crisis of 2007, federal regulatory intervention has increased, but these interventions have been narrowly focused. The Sarbanes-Oxley Act banned loans to executives. Companies participating in financial bailout programs have faced limitations on executive pay overseen by 'pay czar' Kenneth Feinberg. As a result of the Dodd-Frank Act, public companies now face mandatory advisory shareholder voting on senior executive pay.[7] Although prompted by specific crises, the increased appetite for federal intervention has been influenced by the theoretical and empirical research on executive pay to which this chapter now turns.

---

[2]   Recent contributions to this emerging literature include Bebchuk and Spamann (2010), Fahlenbrach and Stulz (2011), and Tung and Wang (2011).

[3]   Several good surveys are available that focus solely on the economics of executive pay including Murphy (1999), Core et al. (2003), and Frydman and Jenter (2010).

[4]   DGCL § 141(h) simply states as a default rule that 'the board of directors shall have the authority to fix the compensation of directors'.

[5]   For a brief shining moment, it appeared that the Delaware courts might be prepared to hold that the directors of Walt Disney Co. had violated their duty to act in good faith with regard to the compensation and severance of former Disney number two executive, Michael Ovitz. *In re Walt Disney Co. Derivative Litig.*, 825 A.2d 275 (Del. Ch. 2003). Ultimately, however, the Chancery Court determined that the directors had not 'consciously disregarded' their duties, and, hence, had not acted in bad faith. *In re Walt Disney Co. Derivative Litig.*, 907 A.2d 693 (Del. Ch. 2006), aff'd, *In re Walt Disney Co. Derivative Litig.*, 906 A.2d 27 (Del. 2006). Moreover, recent cases suggest that the Delaware courts may be moving in the direction of an even less expansive reading of 'good faith' (Hill & McDonnell 2009).

[6]   New York Stock Exchange Listed Company Manual § 303A.08; NASDAQ Manual § 4350(i).

[7]   Shareholder 'say on pay' is discussed below.

## 2.   THEORETICAL PERSPECTIVES ON THE COMPENSATION-SETTING PROCESS

Managerial agency costs lie at the heart of executive compensation theory. Arising from separation of ownership and control (Jensen & Meckling 1976), these costs reflect the divergence between share-value-maximizing actions of managers and managers' actual actions, plus the monitoring and bonding expenditures (including contracting costs) undertaken to reduce that divergence. Some degree of agency cost is unavoidable in the modern, widely-held corporation.

### Optimal Contracting Theory

The classic economic theory of executive compensation posits that pay arrangements are selected to minimize managerial agency costs and maximize shareholder value (Core et al. 2003). Such value-increasing pay arrangements might result from vigorous bargaining by outside directors attempting to maximize share value or might arise indirectly in response to pressures produced by competitive markets for capital, products, labor or corporate control. Most of the theoretical and empirical literature on executive pay proceeds from the assumption that these arrangements are selected to minimize agency costs and maximize shareholder value.

### Managerial Power Theory

Many observed features of executive compensation appear to be inconsistent with a share value maximizing model (Bebchuk et al. 2002). An alternative view is based on the idea that executive pay practices do not uniformly reflect vigorous bargaining, and that executives exert more influence over the terms of their pay than would be expected in an arm's length bargaining situation. Under this view, executive pay arrangements reflect agency costs as well as combat them.

Under this managerial power view of the compensation setting process, the threat or reality of investor and financial press outrage play an important role in disciplining compensation. As a result, executives seek out low salience channels of pay and other means of camouflaging their compensation to minimize outrage. The managerial power view of executive pay and the optimal contracting view may co-exist, providing relatively more or less explanatory power at particular firms.

### Team Production Theory

A third view is that corporate law issues are better characterized as team production problems rather than traditional principal-agent problems (Blair & Stout 1999). Under the team production view, the board of directors serves as a mediating hierarch between stakeholders (executives, employees, creditors, and shareholders) who make firm-specific investments in the company. This theory predicts that compensation arrangements would not be designed to maximize shareholder value, but to balance the interests of the stakeholders.

## 3. EXECUTIVE PAY GROWTH AND DESIGN: THEORY AND EVIDENCE

Historically, sensitivity of pay to firm performance and other aspects of compensation design were the principal focus of the economic literature on executive pay. Recently, attention has turned to explaining the rapid growth in pay. This section explores the theory, evidence, and law on these topics. The totality of the evidence does not support any single theoretical framework regarding executive compensation, although much work remains to be done.

### Amount and Growth of Executive Pay

Over the last 30 years, the average compensation of the CEOs of large US public companies has increased in real terms by 500% (Gabaix & Landier 2008) or more (Frydman & Saks 2010).[8] The compensation of other senior executives also has risen rapidly, much more rapidly than the compensation of rank and file workers, but has not kept pace with CEO pay (Frydman & Jenter 2010).[9]

No positive law directly limits the level of executive compensation in the US. Disclosure requirements and mandatory shareholder advisory voting on executive pay, which are discussed below, may have an indirect impact on the amount of pay. IRC § 162(m), which limits the deductibility of certain senior executive pay to $1 million per executive per year, might be thought to have a more direct effect on executive pay, but given an exception allowing unlimited amounts of deductible 'performance-based' compensation, § 162(m) likely has more impact on the design than the amount of executive pay.

Analysts have struggled to explain the rapid growth in US CEO pay. Equity compensation, which did not become significant until the 1980s, accounts for almost all of the growth (Frydman & Jenter 2010). Holmström and Kaplan (2001, 2003) argue that the addition of this risky pay necessitated an overall increase in compensation of risk averse executives.[10] Taking the managerial power view, Bebchuk and Grinstein (2005) suggest that the bull market of the 1990s weakened the outrage constraint, allowing boards to increase executive pay, and that the design of equity compensation reduced the salience of this pay, permitting transfers of value that would have been inconceivable if paid in cash. In a similar vein, Murphy (2003)

---

[8]   According to a recent report, the median total direct compensation of CEOs of 200 large US public companies was $6.95 million in 2009 (Hay Group 2010). Median salary was $1 million; median annual bonus was $1.5 million; median value of long-term incentives was over $5 million. Although perquisites continue to attract press coverage, they are now fairly trivial economically, with a median value granted in 2009 of $144,000. Not included in total direct compensation was a median increase in value of executive pensions of $1.3 million. The components of executive pay are discussed in more detail below.

[9]   Leslie and Oyer (2009) and Jackson (2008) compare compensation of public company CEOs with that of CEOs of portfolio companies held by private equity funds. Private equity portfolio company executives face stronger incentives, but there is no evidence of a statistically significant difference in total compensation. However, this evidence does not eliminate the possibility that public company executives are overpaid. Private equity funds may compete with public companies for executive talent and be 'price takers' with respect to compensation levels.

[10]   This view is in line with Jensen and Murphy (1990a) who had argued that improving executive incentives would necessitate paying executives more.

and Jensen, Murphy, and Wruck (2004) argue that the favorable accounting treatment of options in the 1990s led boards to systematically undervalue and over-issue this form of compensation.

Frydman (2007) and Murphy and Zábojník (2004, 2007) explain the growth in CEO pay as following from a shift in the requisite skill set. Formerly, firm-specific skills dominated, limiting outside opportunities, but increasingly general management skills dominate, which leads to greater competition for talent and to managers capturing greater rents. Recently, Gabaix and Landier (2008) proposed a model involving competitive matching of CEO talent and firms. The model predicts that average compensation should vary with firm size, and the model explains the increase in pay over time, as well as cross-industry and cross-country pay observations.[11] The authors find very little dispersion in CEO talent at the largest firms, but given the tremendous amount of assets under management and a multiplier effect, the model can explain large pay differentials. The idea that small differences in talent are consistent with large differences in pay was also explored by Himmelberg and Hubbard (2000).

## Compensation Design[12]

Broadly speaking, executive pay provides both compensation and incentives. In order to attract and retain effective managers, companies must provide a competitive package in terms of both the amount of pay and the type of pay. Given the difficulty of directly monitoring the executives, however, the incentives created by executive pay are extremely important in mitigating agency costs. Of course, pay is not the sole source of incentives within the executive suite. The risk of firing and loss of reputation also influence managerial performance, and some executives, often company founders, hold so much company equity that annual pay incentives can be dispensed with, but for most executives pay design plays an important role in creating incentives.

These goals create a tradeoff. On the one hand, directors want to provide high-powered incentives to encourage executives to work hard and to take on risky projects.[13] On the other hand, pay packages have to be mutually acceptable, and non-diversified executives apply large discounts to risky, high powered incentive arrangements, creating a gap between their cost to shareholders and their value to the executives (Hall & Murphy 2002; Core et al. 2003).

A voluminous theoretical and empirical literature explores these design issues, most of it adopting an optimal contracting perspective.[14] This section will briefly and selectively explore this literature and highlight current issues and puzzles.

### Compensation elements
Public company executive pay is comprised of the following elements: annual salary, short-

---

[11]   Bebchuk and Grinstein (2005) analyzed increases in executive pay over a shorter period (1993–2003) and found that the growth in pay could not be explained by changes in firm size, performance, and industry mix.

[12]   This section draws heavily from Walker (2011).

[13]   All else being equal, executives and other employees whose financial and human capital generally is over-invested in their companies tend to disfavor risky projects relative to diversified shareholders (Hall 2003).

[14]   For a more exhaustive discussion of executive pay design issues and the economic literature on this topic, the reader should see Murphy (1999), Core et al. (2003), and Frydman and Jenter (2010).

term bonus opportunities, long-term incentives including equity compensation, pension contributions and earnings, and perquisites. The design of each element is remarkably uniform. As discussed below, tax and accounting rules contribute to this uniformity. Nonetheless, even given uniform building blocks, firms can create compensation packages that vary widely in their incentive and risk properties.

Although each element of executive pay plays a role within the optimal contracting theory, equity compensation (stock and options) has been the particular focus of much of the theoretical and empirical research in this area. There are two reasons for this. First, equity compensation accounts for well over half of the aggregate *ex ante* value of executive pay at large public companies.[15] Second, equity compensation is viewed as particularly important in aligning managerial and shareholder incentives.

Both restricted stock and options tie pay to stock price performance. Restricted stock does so in a linear fashion. Paradigmatically, restricted stock is granted to an executive at no explicit cost, but the stock cannot be sold or otherwise transferred until it 'vests' in a certain number of years. If the executive's employment terminates prior to vesting, the stock typically must be returned. Assuming that the stock will ultimately vest, in the interim, the value of this restricted stock moves dollar for dollar with the firm's share price.[16]

Options provide the holder with a right, but no obligation, to purchase shares of stock at a pre-determined exercise price.[17] Thus, the defining feature of an option is that the payoff is based on the positive difference, if any, between the share price at exercise or settlement and the exercise price of the instrument. If the share price on a potential exercise date fails to exceed the exercise price, the option provides zero payout. Compensatory stock options typically are granted with an exercise price equal to the market price of the underlying stock on the date of the grant, and like restricted stock, options typically vest and become exercisable several years following grant.

The value of an option increases and decreases with the value of the underlying shares, but the relationship is not linear, it is convex.[18] An option that is far out of the money, i.e., with exercise price far in excess of the value of the underlying shares, has a very low value and a value that is relatively insensitive to small changes in the price of the underlying shares. The value of an option that is far in the money, i.e., with exercise price far below the value of the underlying shares, approaches the current share price less the exercise price, and that value moves dollar for dollar with small changes in the price of the underlying shares.

The sensitivity of an option's value to small changes in the underlying share price is known as the option's delta, and delta is simply the slope of the curve that plots the value of

---

[15]   It has done so since the mid-1990s (Walker 2011).

[16]   Some firms predicate vesting of restricted stock on satisfaction of performance criteria as well as the passage of time, and some firms utilize 'performance share' plans that are the non-equity, economic equivalent of performance vested restricted stock. However, each of these instruments links pay to stock price performance in a linear fashion.

[17]   The exercise price of employee stock options is almost always a fixed price specified at grant, and almost always equal to the fair market value of the stock at grant. A few firms have experimented with indexing exercise prices to a basket of competing stocks or to a broad measure of the stock market, such as the S&P 500, with the idea of focusing the option payout on firm-specific performance rather than market movements generally (Rappaport 1999).

[18]   When graphed, a convex relationship presents a 'u' shaped curve. The relationship between option value and the price of the underlying shares tracks the right half of the 'u'.

the option against the value of the underlying stock.[19] Compared with a share of restricted stock, an at-the-money option on a single share of stock is both less expensive to grant and less sensitive to share price movement. However, *per dollar of compensation expense*, options produce more high powered incentives than restricted stock. For example, an at-the-money option on a single share of stock might have a value that is 40% of the value of a share of restricted stock, but a delta that is 75% of the delta of a share of restricted stock, yielding almost twice the sensitivity to share price per dollar of compensation expense.[20]

At the time of the grant, the sensitivity of option value to stock price depends on the exercise price of the option. Although restricted stock and options are often discussed as separate categories, economically, they are different in degree, not in kind. Economists view restricted stock as a zero exercise price option, an option with zero convexity.

In addition to increasing the sensitivity of pay to share price performance, adding options to compensation packages increases the sensitivity of pay to the *volatility* of share prices. Economists use the term 'vega' to denote the sensitivity of option value to share price volatility. The value of shares is not directly affected by increases or decreases in volatility, and thus stock has vega of zero. However, the value of an option increases with increasing volatility, and thus options have positive vega. The sensitivity of pay to stock price volatility is important in assessing the effect of compensation design on the willingness of executives to take on risky projects.

### Impact of tax and accounting rules on compensation design

As noted, there is little direct regulation of executive pay design. Some potential compensation devices, such as insider trading and executive loans, are precluded under federal law. Mandatory disclosure and shareholder 'say on pay' may influence design, and are given separate treatment below. This subsection will consider the substantial influence of tax and accounting rules on the design of executive pay packages.

*Accounting rules*    Through 2005, US financial accounting rules favored conventional non-discounted options over other forms of equity pay. Under the accounting standard in force at the time, companies were required to recognize as compensation expense at the grant date the intrinsic value of stock or options issued to employees.[21] (The intrinsic value of an option, also known as the option spread, is the positive difference, if any, between the value of the underlying stock and the option exercise price.) The expense was accrued ratably over the vesting period of the instrument, and at that point the accounting books were closed. There was no requirement to update the expense for an option grant as its intrinsic value fluctuated over time. As a result, no expense was recorded at any point for options with a fixed exercise price issued at or out of the money, because, by definition, these options had zero intrinsic value on the date of grant. By contrast, restricted stock grants resulted in an accounting expense equal to the full fair market value of the underlying stock at grant (less any amount

---

[19]    For example, an option delta of .75 means that when the price of the underlying shares changes by a small amount, the value of the option changes by 75% of that amount.

[20]    Per dollar of compensation expense, the option would have a delta that was 1.9 times (.75/.4) the delta of the stock.

[21]    The applicable rule was Accounting Principles Board, Opinion No. 25, Accounting for Stock Issued to Employees (1972).

paid for the stock), despite the restrictions on transfer. Discounted or in-the-money options resulted in an accounting expense equal to the 'spread' at grant. The accounting treatment of options carrying an indexed exercise price was even more complicated. These options generally resulted in a charge against earnings, and the charge had to be updated on a regular basis until the exercise price ultimately was fixed.

In 2004, the Financial Accounting Standards Board (FASB) issued a new standard, requiring firms to determine the grant date fair value of all equity compensation and to recognize the expense over the vesting period of the stock or option.[22] For option compensation, this rule requires firms to calculate a grant date value using an option pricing model. The new standard largely eliminates the previous accounting-induced distortions between stock and option compensation, between discounted and non-discounted options, and between conventional fixed exercise price options and options with exercise prices linked to a market index.[23]

The accounting treatment of options has no effect on cash flows, but Murphy (2003) argues that the perception that options represented inexpensive compensation under the prior accounting regime contributed to the dramatic increase in their use in the 1990s. Option use has declined in the wake of the FASB's rationalization of equity compensation accounting. Option grants accounted for 60% of the *ex ante* value of S&P 500 senior executive compensation in aggregate in 2000. By 2008, the aggregate contribution had declined to about 25%, largely through the substitution of restricted stock and similar instruments for options (Walker 2011). Although a number of factors may have contributed to substitution of restricted stock for options, Brown and Lee (2007) and Carter, Lynch, and Tuna (2007) provide evidence that the shift in emphasis in equity compensation plans relates, at least in part, to FASB's mandate that firms expense stock option compensation.

*Tax rules*   Several tax rules have had significant influence on executive compensation design. IRC § 162(m), enacted in 1993, limits the deductibility of non-performance based compensation issued to certain senior executives to $1 million per year. Although firms increasingly treat the $1 million 'cap' as simply one consideration, and not a limitation on non-performance based pay, the enactment of § 162(m) likely contributed to the shift to option compensation in the 1990s (Hall & Liebman 2000; Polsky 2007).

Current US tax rules essentially limit the equity compensation menu to restricted stock (and economically similar instruments such as performance shares) and non-discounted, fixed exercise price stock options (Walker 2009). IRC § 409A all but precludes firms from issuing explicitly discounted stock options, i.e., options with exercise prices less than the fair market value of the underlying stock at grant, or indexed options. Under regular US tax rules, compensation arising from a non-discounted option is not taxed until the option is exercised,[24] but

---

22   FASB, Statement of Financial Accounting Standards No. 123 (revised 2004).

23   Some potential for distortion remains. The fair value of an option is determined using the Black-Scholes or binomial model and is manipulable. Thus, options provide some accounting flexibility that stock compensation does not. Walker and Fleischer (2009) discuss the potential for option expense manipulation.

24   The discussion in this and the following paragraph assumes that options are non-qualified options, i.e., are not incentive stock options (ISOs) as defined in IRC § 422. The tax rules applying to ISOs differ, but ISOs account for an economically trivial portion of executive equity compensation (Hall & Liebman 2000).

under IRC § 409A, enacted in 2004, compensation income arising from a discounted or indexed option would be taxed at vesting, rather than at exercise, and would be subjected to an additional 20% penalty tax.

Compensating executives with restricted stock or non-qualified stock options creates a modest global (i.e., employer plus employee) tax advantage in comparison to a cash compensation alternative (Knoll 2004; Walker 2004). The advantage arises from the deferral of taxation until the stock vests or the options are exercised. However, the advantage of deferring gains is to some extent offset by the disadvantage of deferring losses in situations in which the equity falls in value. The extent of the *ex ante* tax advantage depends on, inter alia, the impact of capital loss limitations (Walker 2004; Yale 2009).

### Theoretical and empirical evidence on compensation design

*Pay for performance sensitivity (delta)*   Much of the early empirical work on executive compensation design focused on the sensitivity of executive wealth to changes in shareholder value. The incentive effects of existing equity holdings often swamp those created by current year compensation (Core et al. 2003). Thus, both must be considered in analyzing sensitivity of pay to performance. Jensen and Murphy (1990b) reported that between 1974 and 1986 the median CEO of 1,300 companies included in a Forbes' survey experienced a change in wealth of $3.25 for each $1,000 change in shareholder value. The bulk of this sensitivity reflected the delta of executive stockholdings. The remainder reflected option delta as well as the authors' calculation of the increased risk of dismissal associated with a decrease in shareholder wealth. Although the results were statistically significant, Jensen and Murphy concluded that the link between pay and performance was insufficient to constrain executives from, for example, consuming excessive perquisites.

Other commentators noted that even the relatively small delta found by Jensen and Murphy might be adequate to align managerial and shareholder incentives with respect to certain decisions, such as the decision to resist a hostile takeover, since the absolute value of the executives' incentives would be more important than the fraction of the firm 'owned' by the executives (Hall & Liebman 2000; Baker & Hall 2004).[25] Moreover, Jensen and Murphy's data reflected the state of executive pay existing prior to the stock option boom of the 1990s. Even as firms continued to grow, pay for performance sensitivity increased in the 1990s and 2000s as executive stock and option holdings multiplied. Hall and Liebman (1998) reported that the Jensen and Murphy statistic doubled by 1994 and quadrupled on a size-adjusted basis.

Brick et al. (2010) find that average pay for performance sensitivity for CEOs included in Standard & Poor's ExecuComp database doubled between the 1992 to 1994 period and the 2002 to 2004 period. In fact, Brick, Palmon, and Wald suggest that some executives may be bearing too much firm-specific risk. They find that greater pay for performance sensitivity is related to lower future stock returns, which could reflect, in part, flight from risk.

Other agency cost explanations have been put forward to explain observed pay-for-performance sensitivities that are lower than expected at first blush. Reduced delta may mitigate executive incentives to maintain inefficiently high levels of investment (Benmelech et al.

---

[25]   The idea is that in deciding whether to take a perk, an executive would consider the fraction of the cost that she would bear directly, whereas in deciding whether to oppose a hostile takeover, she would consider the magnitude of the payout she would receive on exit.

2010) or mitigate executive incentives to manipulate stock prices (Peng & Röell 2008; Goldman & Slezak 2006). Under the team production theory, pay-for-performance sensitivity that is less than optimal from the perspective of maximizing shareholder value could be an appropriate accommodation to more risk averse corporate constituents, such as creditors and employees.

*Equity portfolio convexity*   Since 2004 there has been no significant regulatory bias favoring stock options or restricted stock, and we have observed greater variety from firm to firm in the mix of equity compensation granted to executives (Walker 2011). How is the equity mix determined?

Under an optimal contracting model, the efficient mix, or convexity, of equity compensation would depend on employee, firm, and market characteristics. At the firm level, theoretical models suggest that greater growth opportunities should result in more option-heavy or convex executive pay contracts that increase the incentives to exploit those opportunities (Core & Qian 2001). To some extent, as growth opportunities increase, the benefit of encouraging executives to take on risk and maximize firm value more than offsets the discount the executives apply to risky compensation. In the same vein, optimal convexity increases with the desired riskiness of projects (Choe 2001, 2003), but decreases with firm risk generally and with firm leverage, which increases the risk of an option contract (Choe 2003). The overall market environment affects optimal convexity in a similar fashion, i.e., market volatility should be negatively correlated with convexity (Lambert & Larcker 2004). Finally, optimal convexity increases with the marginal productivity of executive effort at the firm (Lambert & Larcker 2004).

Of the employee characteristics modeled by corporate finance researchers, risk aversion appears to be the most important, and certainly the most frequently modeled, individual trait affecting optimal sensitivity (Hall & Murphy 2000; Feltham & Wu 2001; Tian 2001, 2004; Lambert & Larcker 2004; Dittmann & Maug 2007).[26] A highly risk averse executive will more greatly discount options with more remote payoff prospects. Thus, as risk aversion increases, the optimal design shifts in the direction of stock (Tian 2001; Hall 2003).

Depending on firm and employee characteristics (and on model specifications), researchers have concluded that optimal equity compensation design ranges from far in-the-money options (i.e., restricted stock) (Hall & Murphy 2002; Dittmann & Maug 2007) to at-the-money options (Dittmann & Yu 2010)[27] to far out-of-the-money options (Lambert & Larcker 2004). Optimal equity compensation design is quite sensitive to model specification, but even within a given model, optimal sensitivity can be highly dependent on the assumptions listed above. Tian (2001) finds that at-the-money options are nearly optimal for executives who exhibit relatively low risk aversion; in-the-money options are optimal for those with somewhat greater risk aversion; and for executives who are highly risk averse, restricted stock is optimal.

---

26   Other characteristics that have been modeled include loss aversion (Dodonova & Khoroshilov 2006), effort aversion (Palmon et al. 2008; Tian 2001; Dittmann & Maug 2007; Feltham & Wu 2001), overall wealth (Tian 2001), firm equity held (Tian 2001), and outside investment opportunities (Tian 2001).

27   Dittmann and Yu's model indicates that most options should be granted in the money but that the incremental benefit is less than the tax cost of granting in-the-money options.

*Cross-sectional variation*   Some of the foregoing theoretical predictions are supported by cross-sectional data. Core and Guay (1999) find that firms actively manage the level of new CEO equity incentives in response to deviations between existing incentives and optimal incentives associated with economic determinants such as firm size, growth opportunities, and monitoring costs. Guay (1999) finds a positive association between the sensitivity of CEO wealth to firm risk and investment opportunities.

On the other hand, a great deal of uniformity in equity pay design persists even after the relaxation of accounting rules favoring option compensation. Walker (2011) demonstrates that the mix of stock and options granted to senior executives in the late 2000s is not uniformly or normally distributed from firm to firm but is clustered, with most firms granting options only, stock only, or a 50/50 mix by *ex ante* value. He also finds that the mix of stock and options tends to be consistent within executive suites, casting doubt on the extent to which firms adjust equity mix to optimize incentives.

## Compensation design puzzles for the optimal contracting model

*Relative performance evaluation*   According to theoretical predictions (Holmström 1982), executive compensation arrangements should employ relative performance measures in order to filter out the noise of industry or market movements over which executives have no control. Instead of basing an annual bonus on total shareholder return, for example, a firm could base the bonus on the return relative to the average return of a peer group of companies. In practice, relative performance evaluation is rarely observed (Core et al. 2003).

The value of equity compensation is particularly sensitive to market movements over which executives have no control. Rappaport (1999) and others have proposed that the exercise price of options be indexed to filter out market swings, but indexed options have been used by only a handful of companies. Unfavorable accounting treatment might account for the dearth of indexed options before 2004, and current tax rules would complicate their use today. However, these rules do not explain the failure of firms to condition restricted stock vesting or performance share awards on relative firm performance. However, as Core et al. (2003) explain, the lack of *explicit* relative performance evaluation in executive pay arrangements does not mean that executives do not adjust their own portfolios in order to manage their exposure to the broader market.[28]

*Stock option backdating*   In March 2006, the *Wall Street Journal* offered evidence suggesting highly suspicious timing and pricing of stock options issued by some companies in the late 1990s and early 2000s (Forelle & Bandler 2006). Almost all options are issued with an exercise price equal to the fair market value of the company's stock on the date of the grant. The evidence indicated that the grant dates of some stock options had been selected with hindsight. By 'backdating' option grants to low stock price dates, these firms had effectively granted options that were 'in the money' from the start.

Further research revealed that the practice of backdating was quite widespread. Heron and Lie (2007) estimated that about 30% of firms participated in backdating during this period.

---

[28]   A related puzzling strand of research suggests that executives often are rewarded for good luck – felicitous occurrences outside their control – but are not penalized for bad luck (Bertrand & Mullainathan 2001; Garvey & Milbourn 2006).

Bebchuk et al. (2010) found that 9% of CEO options granted between 1996 and 2005 were manipulated to achieve exercise prices equal to one of the three lowest prices of the month.

Although stock option backdating was not in itself illegal, firms that backdated options ran afoul of both accounting and tax rules (Walker 2007). Numerous firms were required to restate their financials to properly account for the backdated options. The SEC investigated option grant practices at over one hundred companies and filed civil and/or criminal charges against executives of a handful of firms.

The backdating episode remains something of a mystery. The reputational and financial cost to firms and executives that engaged in the practice (and were discovered) was great, and the payoff to the recipients of backdated options was often less than one might expect. Efficiency explanations for backdating are unpersuasive. In some cases, backdating may have been inadvertent or, though purposeful, an innocent mistake (Fleischer 2007). In many cases, however, backdating yielded stealth compensation, which calls into question the capacity or motivation of boards to oversee executive compensation.

## 4.   REGULATORY INTERVENTION AND EXECUTIVE PAY: SELECTED TOPICS

This section considers four aspects of the executive compensation process in which regulatory intervention has occurred or is in the offing – board and compensation committee independence, disclosure, use of compensation consultants, and shareholder 'say on pay'. These topics have in themselves generated considerable research. This section considers that research and what it tells us about the efficacy and unintended consequences of such intervention.

### Impact of Board Structure on Executive Pay

There is a widespread view that board of director independence should lead to improved corporate governance, including more responsible executive pay practices. Public company boards and compensation committees, which are principally responsible for determining senior executive pay, have become more independent over the last 20 years in response to various regulatory initiatives.

Since 1993, companies that seek to take advantage of the performance-based-pay exception to the limit on the deductibility of senior executive pay under IRC § 162(m) have been required to limit compensation committee membership to 'outside' directors, i.e., directors who are not and have not been employees or executives of the company. Stock exchange rules adopted in 2003 require listed companies to have compensation committees composed entirely of 'independent' directors, i.e., directors with no material ties to the listed company aside from their service as directors. Stock exchange rules also require that a majority of board members be independent directors. Complete compensation committee independence was federally mandated in 2010 under the Dodd-Frank Act.[29]

---

[29]   Pub. 111–203, § 952.

The evidence regarding the relationship between board or compensation committee independence and the quality of executive pay is mixed (O'Reilly & Main 2005). For example, Core et al. (1999) find a positive association between CEO pay and the fraction of outside directors on the board appointed by the CEO. They also find a positive association between outside directors who serve on multiple boards, and presumably have their attention more divided, and CEO pay. On the other hand, Anderson and Bizjak (2003) find little evidence that greater compensation committee independence affects executive compensation.

There are reasons to be both more and less optimistic about the ability of high quality boards and compensation committees to effectively manage executive pay than these studies suggest. While most studies have focused on the amount of executive pay or pay for performance sensitivity, Sun et al. (2009) examine the relationship between compensation committee quality and the quality of equity grants. They find that options issued to executives by firms with higher quality compensation committees generate greater future operating income.

On the other hand, Singh (2006) provides a theoretical model that undermines the simplistic view that entrusting executive compensation to more independent directors is necessarily in the interest of shareholders. He employs a signaling model to demonstrate that independent directors with career concerns might provide pay packages with inefficiently high incentives if such incentives are generally associated with good governance.

Other research questions the extent to which we should rely on nominally independent directors to effectively manage executive compensation. In a series of papers, Main et al. have stressed the importance of social and psychological forces on boards. As in any situation involving small group decision making, norms of reciprocity and social influence affect outcomes. Nominally independent directors may feel beholden to the CEO even if the CEO was not a member of the nominating committee that appointed them to the board. Independent directors who are demographically similar to their CEOs tend to award their CEOs greater compensation (Main et al. 1995).

Moreover, while stock exchange rules and legislative proposals focus on first order relationships between companies and board members, Larcker et al. (2005) demonstrate that more attenuated connections between inside and outside directors can affect executive pay. They calculate the distance, *à la* 'Six Degrees of Separation'[30] between each member of the boards of over 3,000 firms, ignoring, of course, the link created by serving on the same board. They find that a relatively short 'backdoor' distance between the CEO and the members of the compensation committee and between inside and outside directors is associated with greater CEO pay.

A related structural issue is whether the CEO also serves as board chairman. Splitting these roles is common abroad and is becoming more common in the US. In 2009, 36% of S&P 500 companies split the CEO and Chairman roles, up from 22% in 2002 (Millstein 2009). As in the case of outside director independence, some researchers have found a positive relationship between CEO pay and CEO/Chairman 'duality' (O'Reilly & Main 2007). Earlier studies are cited in O'Reilly and Main (2005).

In sum, support for the intuition that increased board and compensation committee independence leads to more shareholder-friendly executive pay practices is mixed, at best. In fact,

---

[30]   In his 1990 play, 'Six Degrees of Separation,' and the subsequent film, John Guare popularized the notion that everyone on the planet is connected to everyone else by a chain of no more than six people.

some observers question whether the premise is well founded to begin with. As Holmström (2005) and Core et al. (2005) observe, outside directors serve other important roles in addition to policing executive pay. Their primary value may lie in advising management on strategic decisions and in succession planning. The individuals who would best perform these roles and the attitudes and processes they would adopt vis-à-vis management in doing so might be different than the individuals and policies adopted by executive pay cops. In other words, the optimal board membership and processes would maximize share value, but would not necessarily minimize managerial agency costs.

**Compensation Disclosure**

Mandatory periodic disclosure of executive pay dates back to the Securities Exchange Act of 1934. Two efficiency explanations for mandatory disclosure might apply particularly to executive compensation. Easterbrook and Fischel (1984) argue that voluntary production of information would be suboptimal from a social perspective in cases in which the disclosure creates a positive externality. Bizjak, Lemmon, and Naveen (2008) document that benchmarking of compensation against peer firm pay is pervasive and argue that benchmarking is an efficient means of determining the reservation wage. Of course, if all firms engage in benchmarking, each would have a private incentive to disclose compensation data, at least to compensation consultants who effectively manage the benchmarking process. Thus, the more important rationale for mandatory disclosure of executive compensation is the existence of managerial agency costs (Coffee 1984; Mahoney 1995). Investors rely on mandatory disclosure to monitor managerial self-dealing, including executive compensation.

Given the agency problem, it is important that the mandatory disclosure regime be both comprehensive and transparent. The current SEC disclosure regime largely achieves these objectives. Prior regimes did not and likely led to distortions in pay practices as companies sought to minimize the apparent compensation of executives.

The 'modern' disclosure regime dates from 1992 when the SEC reinstituted tabular disclosure of executive pay and expanded coverage to the CEO plus the four most highly compensated executives other than the CEO. The 1992 disclosure regime required a summary compensation table that detailed the dollar value of salary, annual bonuses, restricted stock awards, payouts from non-equity long-term performance plans, and perks, as well as the number of shares underlying option grants.

Although an improvement over the immediately preceding disclosure regime, the 1992 rules were less than ideal. The summary compensation table did not yield a bottom line dollar value of pay. Some items were included on an *ex ante* basis; others on an *ex post* basis; other items were excluded from the summary table entirely. In addition to stock option value, the value of defined-benefit pension plans was not included in the summary compensation table and pension values have been found to represent a significant fraction of remuneration for CEOs who participate in such plans (Bebchuk & Jackson 2005).

Under the 1992 regime, companies were required to disclose further information on stock option grants in a separate table and were given the choice of reporting the Black-Scholes value of these options or the 'potential realizable value' based on arbitrary assumptions of 5% and 10% annual appreciation in the stock price during the option term. Murphy (1996) provides evidence that firms exploited this choice of methodology to reduce reported compensation.

The lack of comprehensiveness in the disclosure regime raised two concerns. First, investors might not have received an accurate picture of executive pay. Bebchuk and Jackson (2005) suggest that the poorly disclosed defined-benefit pension entitlements led to overestimation of the sensitivity of executive pay to performance. Second, firms may elect to compensate executives through channels that are less transparent, even if less efficient (Bebchuk et al. 2002). Anecdotal evidence indicates that a lack of transparency encouraged some directors to approve enhancements to executive defined-benefit pensions (Bebchuk & Jackson 2005).

Executive compensation disclosure was improved significantly in 2006. The summary compensation table was revised to provide a bottom line figure for the total *ex ante* value of compensation, including the annual increase in the value of defined-benefit pensions. The 2006 rule also eliminated firm choice regarding option valuation. Firms were required to report the amount expensed under Generally Accepted Accounting Principles (GAAP) for stock and options in the summary table. The amount expensed under GAAP is the 'fair value' (essentially the Black-Scholes value) of options pro-rated over the option vesting period. The inclusion in the summary table of pro-rated accounting expense for equity compensation, however, was inconsistent with the goal of providing a bottom line figure for the value of pay provided to an executive within the fiscal year. This deficiency was corrected in 2009. Going forward, firms are required to report the total *ex ante* value of stock and option grants in the year of grant, yielding a reasonably accurate and comparable total compensation figure in the summary table.

Earnings statements prepared in accordance with GAAP are an additional source of compensation disclosure. Although these statements do not focus specifically on senior executives, they do provide an overall tally of compensation expense within the firm. As noted above, stock option compensation was elevated from a footnoted item to a recognized expense in 2004, largely eliminating an accounting bias in favor of options.

Given reasonably accurate and comprehensive compensation disclosure in earnings statements and proxy statements, are there remaining disclosure concerns? Some commentators have suggested enhanced disclosure combined with the ubiquitous practice of benchmarking pay versus that of peer firms leads to upward ratcheting of compensation (Bebchuk et al. 2002). Bizjak et al. (2008) find that the 'vast majority' of firms that engage in benchmarking target pay levels at or above the 50th percentile. Grinstein, Weinbaum, and Yehuda (2011) find that following enhanced disclosure requirements for executive perks in 2006, firms that had granted low levels of perks relative to their peers increased perks, while firms that granted relatively high amounts of perks did not decrease them. Upward ratcheting may result from boards' genuine beliefs that their executives are above average or from an unwillingness to risk undermining investor confidence by admitting, through compensation policy, that management is below average (Elson 2003).

Finally, given the complexity of executive compensation, it is unrealistic to think that no undisclosed benefits are flowing to executives. Firms that backdated stock options in order to reduce exercise prices reported values for these options that were far less than the true fair values of these instruments (Walker 2007). Even without backdating, the ability of executives to exploit information advantages in timing grants and exercises of equity compensation causes the actual expected value of equity pay to exceed that reported to shareholders.

## Compensation Consultants

In 2006, 86% of S&P 1500 firms utilized compensation consultants (Cadman et al. 2010). Consultants can increase the efficiency of compensation processes by providing expert advice on the economic, disclosure, tax, and accounting consequences of very complex pay arrangements and by acting as information intermediaries – collecting confidential pay data and providing summarized, redacted data to their clients. However, many observers question whether consultants serve the interests of investors or of the managers who have traditionally hired them. Objectivity is particularly suspect in situations in which the compensation consultant provides other services, such as actuarial or benefits management services, to the company that engages them for compensation consulting.

Until recently, there was no regulation of the relationship between pay consultants and public companies in the US. In fact, disclosure of the use of compensation consultants was not mandated until 2006. However, the Dodd-Frank Act of 2010 confers upon compensation committees the authority to hire and manage compensation consultants.[31] The act also addresses compensation consultant conflicts of interest, requiring consultants to meet standards of independence established by the SEC.[32]

Do compensation consultants, particularly conflicted consultants, favor management? The evidence, as summarized and augmented in Conyon (2010), is mixed. Some studies have found a positive correlation between the use of compensation consultants and CEO pay, but CEOs of firms utilizing consultants tend to receive pay packages with a greater emphasis on equity. Hence, the correlation found could represent a risk premium (Conyon 2010). Similarly, Walker (2011) reports that firms that do not use compensation consultants tend to grant pay packages with fewer equity compensation elements. But again, the direction of causation is unclear. It may be that consultants complicate pay packages to justify their services or it may be that firms at which complex pay arrangements are optimal are more likely to employ the services of consultants.

Murphy and Sandino (2010) find an association between conflicted consultants and greater CEO pay.[33] However, Cadman et al. (2010) and Conyon et al. (2009) find little or no evidence that consultant conflicts lead to greater CEO pay. Additional evidence provided in Conyon (2010) casts further doubt on the theory that the use of consultants, conflicted or otherwise, leads to greater executive pay.

## Shareholder 'Say on Pay'

The Dodd-Frank Act of 2010 mandates non-binding shareholder voting on executive pay.[34] Over 50 US companies voluntarily adopted shareholder 'say on pay' prior to this legislative mandate, and a majority of shareholders voted to disapprove of pay plans at Motorola and Occidental Petroleum in 2010.[35] Although the vote is precatory, executives will not want to

---

[31]   Pub. 111–203 § 952(c).

[32]   Pub. 111–203 § 952(b).

[33]   Surprisingly, the authors find that CEO pay is higher when compensation consultants are employed by the board rather than management.

[34]   Pub. 111–203 § 951.

[35]   A majority of shareholders also voted against the executive pay plan at KeyCorp in 2010. As

lose shareholder votes on pay and will likely modify pay practices as needed to gain majority approval. The question is whether the effect of 'say on pay' on executive compensation will be salutary.

Although 'say on pay' is new in the US, it has been mandated for UK public companies since 2002. The evidence regarding the UK experience is mixed. Alissa (2009) found a relationship between UK shareholder dissatisfaction, as measured by the percentage of no-votes cast, and greater than expected CEO pay.[36] Ferri and Maber (2011) found no evidence of a change in the level or growth rate of CEO pay after the introduction of 'say on pay' in the UK. They did find a change in compensation design. A significant number of firms increased the sensitivity of pay to poor performance by curtailing highly publicized 'rewards for failure', such as generous severance contracts. The authors found that firms made these changes before shareholder votes as well as after, suggesting that the threat of an adverse vote had an effect on compensation. It is also clear that UK firms have increased consultation with institutional shareholders regarding pay practices.

From a theoretical standpoint, Gordon (2009) argues that mandatory 'say on pay' is likely to inefficiently restrict diversity in pay practices. He suggests that proxy advisory firms, which are already influential in corporate elections, would become more influential under mandatory 'say on pay', and that these firms will reduce search costs by establishing 'close to "one size fits all"' best practice guidelines. Motorola, which suffered a negative shareholder vote on executive pay, has an unusual management structure with co-CEOs, who are highly compensated, but whose compensation is closely linked to performance and to the firm's strategy of splitting into two publicly traded companies. For good or ill, such a strategy might be harder to maintain under mandatory 'say on pay'.

## 5.   EXECUTIVE PAY REGULATION AND RESEARCH: GOING FORWARD

Where are executive pay regulation and research headed? This chapter concludes with brief thoughts on the first question and a suggestion regarding the second.

It appears that mandatory shareholder 'say on pay' will be the most significant, perhaps the only significant, generally applicable executive pay reform to come out of the most recent financial crisis. Other reforms certainly have been advanced. Commentators who blamed the crisis on reckless, short-term behavior by executives whose compensation was inadequately linked to long-term firm performance proposed the elimination of options and/or the imposition of lengthy holding periods on stock grants (Bhagat & Romano 2009; Posner 2009; Samuelson & Stout 2009). The opposing view is that executive compensation is a highly

---

a participant in the Troubled Asset Relief Program (TARP), KeyCorp was required to adopt shareholder 'say on pay' earlier than most public companies.

   36   Just over a month before the negative 'say on pay' vote at Occidental Petroleum, the *Wall Street Journal* reported that Oxy's CEO, Ray Irani, was the highest paid executive in its 2009 survey of 200 large companies, with total direct compensation of over $50 million (Lublin 2010). This figure did not include $96 million that Irani had gained in 2009 from the exercise of options and vesting of restricted stock. Although Oxy's recent financial performance has been outstanding, shareholders may have been targeting Irani's outsized compensation.

complex subject that is not well suited for one-size-fits-all, coercive regulation (Gordon 2009; Walker 2010). Going forward, US public companies will likely face a combination of evolving disclosure and board/committee independence requirements, further congressional hearings, and perhaps some industry-specific (e.g., banking) regulation. Although regulation via 'nudge' is unlikely to result in significant reform, it does minimize unintended consequences and inefficiencies.

The complexity of executive pay has been a central theme of this chapter. The suggestion for future work is that researchers more directly address this complexity and the cognitive limitations faced by executives, boards, and even compensation consultants. How do boards and compensation committees manage technically complex compensation matters such as selecting the optimal mix of stock and options? Do compensation consultants understand and effectively mitigate these complexities? How do holdings of stock and options affect the incentives and risk preferences of executives who often have a naïve grasp of the economics of these instruments? The inherent complexity of executive compensation presents a fundamental challenge for directors. Understanding how the management of complexity translates into pay packages is a key challenge for future compensation research.

# REFERENCES

Alissa, Walid M. (2009), 'Boards' Response to Shareholders' Dissatisfaction: The Case of Shareholders' Say on Pay in the UK', Working Paper, available at http://ssrn.com/abstract=1412880 (last accessed October 2011).

Anderson, Ronald C. & John M. Bizjak (2003), 'An Empirical Examination of the Role of the CEO and the Compensation Committee in Structuring Executive Pay', *Journal of Banking and Finance*, 27, 1323–48.

Baker, George P. & Brian J. Hall (2004), 'CEO Incentives and Firm Size', *Journal of Labor Economics*, 22, 767–98.

Barris, Linda J. (1992), 'The Overcompensation Problem: A Collective Approach to Controlling Executive Pay', *Indiana Law Journal*, 68, 59–100.

Bebchuk, Lucian A. & Yaniv Grinstein (2005), 'The Growth of Executive Pay', *Oxford Review of Economic Policy*, 21, 283–303.

Bebchuk, Lucian A. & Robert J. Jackson, Jr. (2005), 'Executive Pensions', *Journal of Corporation Law*, 30, 823–55.

Bebchuk, Lucian A. & Holger Spamann (2010), 'Regulating Bankers' Pay', *Georgetown Law Journal*, 98, 247–87.

Bebchuk, Lucian, Jesse Fried & David Walker (2002), 'Managerial Power and Rent Extraction in the Design of Executive Compensation', *University of Chicago Law Review*, 69, 751–846.

Bebchuk, Lucian A., Yaniv Grinstein & Urs Peyer (2010), 'Lucky CEOs and Lucky Directors', *Journal of Finance*, 65, 2363–2401.

Benmelech, Effi, Eugene Kandel & Pietro Veronesi (2010), 'Stock–Based Compensation and CEO (Dis)Incentives', *Quarterly Journal of Economics*, 125, 1769–1820.

Bertrand, Marianne & Sendhil Mullainathan (2001), 'Are CEOs Rewarded for Luck? The Ones Without Principles Are', *Quarterly Journal of Economics*, 116, 901–32.

Bhagat, Sanjai & Roberta Romano (2009), 'Reforming Executive Compensation: Focusing and Committing to the Long-term', *Yale Journal on Regulation*, 26, 359–72.

Bizjak, John M., Michael L. Lemmon & Lalitha Naveen (2008), 'Does the Use of Peer Groups Contribute to Higher Pay and Less Efficient Compensation?', *Journal of Financial Economics*, 90, 152–68.

Blair, Margaret M. & Lynn A. Stout (1999), 'A Team Production Theory of Corporate Law', *Virginia Law Review*, 85, 248–328.

Brick, Ivan E., Oded Palmon & John K. Wald (2010), 'Too Much Pay Performance Sensitivity?', Working Paper, available at http://ssrn.com/abstract=1108522 (last accessed October 2011).

Brown, Lawrence D. & Yen-Jung Lee (2007), 'The Impact of SFAS 123R on Changes in Option-Based Compensation', Working Paper, available at http://ssrn.com/abstract=930818 (last accessed October 2011).

Cadman, Brian, Mary Ellen Carter & Stephen Hillegeist (2010), 'The Incentives of Compensation Consultants and CEO Pay', *Journal of Accounting and Economics*, 49, 263–80.

Carter, Mary Ellen, Luann J. Lynch & Irem Tuna (2007), 'The Role of Accounting in the Design of CEO Equity Compensation', *Accounting Review*, 82, 327–57.

Choe, Chongwoo (2001), 'Maturity and Exercise Price of Executive Stock Options', *Review of Financial Economics*, 10, 227–50.

Choe, Chongwoo (2003), 'Leverage, Volatility and Executive Stock Options', *Journal of Corporate Finance*, 9, 591–609.

Coffee Jr., John C. (1984), 'Market Failure and the Economic Case for a Mandatory Disclosure System', *Virginia Law Review*, 70, 717–53.

Conyon, Martin J. (2010), 'Compensation Consultants and CEO Pay', Working Paper on file with author.

Conyon, Martin J., Simon I. Peck & Graham V. Sadler (2009), 'Compensation Consultants and Executive Pay: Evidence from the United States and United Kingdom', *Academy of Management Perspectives*, 23(1), 43–55.

Core, John & Wayne R. Guay (1999), 'The Use of Equity Grants to Manage Optimal Equity Incentive Levels', *Journal of Accounting and Economics*, 28, 151–84.

Core, John E. & Jun Qian (2000), 'Option-like Contracts for Innovation and Production', Working Paper, available at http://ssrn.com/abstract=207968 (last accessed Oct. 30, 2011).

Core, John E., Robert W. Holthausen & David F. Larcker (1999), 'Corporate Governance, Chief Executive Compensation, and Firm Performance', *Journal of Financial Economics*, 51, 371–406.

Core, John E., Wayne R. Guay & David F. Larcker (2003), 'Executive Equity Compensation and Incentives: A Survey', *FRBNY Economic Policy Review*, 9(1), 27–50.

Core, John E., Wayne R. Guay & Randall S. Thomas (2005), 'Is U.S. CEO Compensation Inefficient Pay Without Performance?', *Michigan Law Review*, 103, 1142–85.

Dittmann, Ingolf & Ernst G. Maug (2007), 'Lower Salaries and No Options? On the Optimal Structure of Executive Pay', *Journal of Finance*, 62, 303–43.

Dittmann, Ingolf & Ko-Chia Yu (2010), 'How Important are Risk-Taking Incentives in Executive Compensation?', Working Paper, available at http://ssrn.com/abstract=1176192 (last accessed October 2011).

Dodonova, Anna & Yuri Khoroshilov (2006), 'Optimal Incentive Contracts for Loss-Averse Managers: Stock Options versus Restricted Stock Grants', *Financial Review*, 41, 451–82.

Easterbrook, Frank H. & Daniel R. Fischel (1984), 'Mandatory Disclosure and the Protection of Investors', *Virginia Law Review*, 70, 669–715.

Elson, Charles (2003), 'What's Wrong with Executive Compensation?', *Harvard Business Review*, 81(1), 68–77.

Fahlenbrach, Rüdiger & Rene M. Stulz (2011), 'Bank CEO Incentives and the Credit Crisis', *Journal of Financial Economics*, 99, 11–26.

Feltham, Gerald. A. & Martin Wu (2001), 'Incentive Efficiency of Stock Versus Options', *Review of Accounting Studies*, 6, 7–28.

Ferri, Fabrizio & David A. Maber (2011), 'Say on Pay Votes and CEO Compensation: Evidence from the UK', Working Paper, available at http://ssrn.com/abstract=1420394 (last accessed October 2011).

Fleischer, Victor (2007), 'Options Backdating, Tax Shelters, and Corporate Culture', *Virginia Tax Review*, 26, 1031–64.

Forelle, Charles & James Bandler (2006), 'The Perfect Payday: Some CEOs Reap Millions by Landing Stock Options When They Are Most Valuable', *The Wall Street Journal*, March 18, A-1.

Frydman, Carola (2007), 'Rising through the Ranks: The Evolution of the Market for Corporate Executives, 1936–2003', MIT Sloan School of Management Working Paper, available at http://mitsloan.mit.edu/finance/pdf/frydman–090208.pdf (last accessed October 2011).

Frydman, Carola & Dirk Jenter (2010), 'CEO Compensation', *Annual Review of Financial Economics*, 2, 75–102.

Frydman, Carola & Raven E. Saks (2010), 'Executive Compensation: A New View from a Long-Run Perspective, 1936–2005', *Review of Financial Studies*, 23, 2099–2138.

Gabaix, Xavier & Augustin Landier (2008), 'Why Has CEO Pay Increased so Much?', *Quarterly Journal of Economics*, 123, 49–100.

Garvey, Gerald T. & Todd T. Milbourn (2006), 'Asymmetric Benchmarking in Compensation: Executives are Rewarded for Good Luck but Not Penalized for Bad', *Journal of Financial Economics*, 82, 197–225.

Goldman, Eitan & Steve L. Slezak (2006), 'An Equilibrium Model of Incentive Contracts in the Presence of Information Manipulation', *Journal of Financial Economics*, 80, 603–26.

Gordon, Jeffrey N. (2009), '"Say on Pay": Cautionary Notes on the U.K. Experience and the Case for Shareholder Opt-In', *Harvard Journal on Legislation*, 46, 323–67.

Grinstein, Yaniv, David Weinbaum & Nir Yehuda (2011), 'The Economic Consequences of Perk Disclosure', Johnson School Research Paper Series No. 04-09, available at http://ssrn.com/abstract=1108707 (last accessed October 2011).

Guay, Wayne R. (1999), 'The Sensitivity of CEO Wealth to Equity Risk: An Analysis of the Magnitude and Determinants', *Journal of Financial Economics*, 53, 43–71.

Hall, Brian J. (2003), 'Six Challenges in Designing Equity-Based Pay', *Journal of Applied Corporate Finance*, 15(3), 21–33.

Hall, Brian J. & Jeffrey B. Liebman (1998), 'Are CEOs Really Paid Like Bureaucrats?', *Quarterly Journal of Economics*, 113, 653–91.

Hall, Brian J. & Jeffrey B. Liebman (2000), 'The Taxation of Executive Compensation', in James M. Poterba (ed.) *Tax Policy and the Economy*, National Bureau of Economic Research, 14, 1–44.

Hall, Brian J. & Kevin J. Murphy (2000), 'Optimal Exercise Prices for Executive Stock Options', *The American Economic Review*, 90, 209–14.

Hall, Brian J. & Kevin J. Murphy (2002), 'Stock Options for Undiversified Executives', *Journal of Accounting and Economics*, 33, 3–42.

Hay Group (2010), 'The Wall Street Journal Survey of CEO Compensation', *The Wall Street Journal*, March 31, available at http://graphicsweb.wsj.com/php/CEOPAY10.html (last accessed October 2011).

Heron, Randall A. & Erik Lie (2007), 'Does Backdating Explain the Stock Price Pattern Around Executive Stock Option Grants?', *Journal of Financial Economics*, 83, 271–95.

Hill, Claire & Brett McDonnell (2009), 'Executive Compensation and the Optimal Penumbra of Delaware Corporation Law', *Virginia Law & Business Review*, 4, 333–72.

Himmelberg, Charles P. & Glenn R. Hubbard (2000), 'Incentive Pay and the Market for CEOs: An Analysis of Pay-for-Performance Sensitivity', Working Paper, available at http://ssrn.com/abstract=236089 (last accessed October 2011).

Holmström, Bengt R. (1982), 'Moral Hazard in Teams', *The Bell Journal of Economics*, 13, 324–40.

Holmström, Bengt R. (2005), 'Pay Without Performance and the Managerial Power Hypothesis: A Comment', *Journal of Corporation Law*, 30, 703–16.

Holmström, Bengt R. & Steven Kaplan (2001), 'Corporate Governance and Merger Activity in the U.S.: Making Sense of the 1980s and 1990s', *Journal of Economic Perspectives*, 15(2), 121–44.

Holmström, Bengt R. & Steven Kaplan (2003), 'The State of U.S. Corporate Governance: What's Right and What's Wrong?', *Journal of Applied Corporate Finance*, 15(3), 8–20.

Jackson, Robert J. Jr. (2008), 'Private Equity and Executive Compensation', Working Paper on file with author.

Jensen, Michael C. & William H. Meckling (1976), 'Theory of the Firm: Managerial Behavior, Agency Costs and Ownership Structure', *Journal of Financial Economics*, 3, 305–60.

Jensen, Michael C. & Kevin J. Murphy (1990a), 'CEO Incentives: It's Not How Much You Pay, But How', *Harvard Business Review*, 68(3), 138–53.

Jensen, Michael C. & Kevin J. Murphy (1990b), 'Performance Pay and Top-Management Incentives', *Journal of Political Economy*, 98, 225–64.

Jensen, Michael C., Kevin J. Murphy & Eric Wruck (2004), 'Remuneration: Where We've Been, How We Got to Here, What Are the Problems, and How to Fix Them', Harvard Negotiations, Organizations, and Markets Unit Research Paper Series No. 04-28, available at http://ssrn.com/abstract=72338 (last accessed October 2011).

Knoll, Michael S. (2004), 'The Tax-Efficiency of Stock–Based Compensation', *Tax Notes* 103, 203–14.

Lambert, Richard A. & David F. Larcker (2004), 'Stock Options, Restricted Stock, and Incentives', Working Paper, available at http://ssrn.com/abstract=527822 (last accessed October 2011).

Larcker, David F., Scott A. Richardson, Andrew Seary & A. Irem Tuna (2005), 'Back Door Links Between Directors and Executive Compensation', Working Paper, available at http://ssrn.com/abstract=671063 (last accessed October 2011).

Leslie, Phillip & Paul Oyer (2009), 'Managerial Incentives and Value Creation: Evidence from Private Equity', Working Paper, available at http://ssrn.com/abstract=1341889 (last accessed October 2011).

Lublin, Joann S. (2010), 'Occidental Chief Tops Pay List', *The Wall Street Journal*, April 1, B-1.

Mahoney, Paul G. (1995), 'Mandatory Disclosure as a Solution to Agency Problems', *University of Chicago Law Review*, 62, 1047–1112.

Main, Brian G. M., Charles A. O'Reilly III & James Wade (1995), 'The CEO, the Board of Directors, and Executive Compensation: Economic and Psychological Perspectives', *Industrial and Corporate Change*, 11, 293–332.

Millstein Center for Corporate Governance and Performance (2009), *Chairing the Board: The Case for Independent Leadership in Corporate North America*, Yale School of Management.

Murphy, Kevin J. (1996), 'Reporting Choice and the 1992 Proxy Disclosure Rules', *Journal of Accounting, Auditing, and Finance*, 11, 497–515.

Murphy, Kevin J. (1999), 'Executive Compensation', in Orley Ashenfelter (ed.), *Handbook of Labor Economics*, North Holland: Elsevier, 2485–563.

Murphy, Kevin J. (2003), 'Stock-Based Pay in New Economy Firms', *Journal of Accounting and Economics*, 34, 129–47.

Murphy, Kevin J. & Ján Zábojník (2004), 'CEO Pay and Appointments: A Market-Based Explanation for Recent Trends', *The American Economic Review*, 94(2), 192–96.

Murphy, Kevin J. & Ján Zábojník (2007), 'Managerial Capital and the Market for CEOs', Working Paper, available at http://ssrn.com/abstract=984376 (last accessed October 2011).

Murphy, Kevin J. & Tatiana Sandino (2010), 'Executive Pay and "Independent" Compensation Consultants', *Journal of Accounting and Economics*, 49, 247–62.

O'Reilly III, Charles A. & Brian G. M. Main (2005), 'Setting the CEO's Pay: Economic and Psychological Perspectives', Stanford GSB Research Paper No.1912, available at http://ssrn.com/abstract=804584 (last accessed October 2011).

O'Reilly III, Charles A. & Brian G.M. Main (2007), 'Setting the CEO's Pay: It's More Than Simple Economics', *Organizational Dynamics*, 1–12.

Palmon, Oded , Sasson Bar-Yosef, Ren-Raw Chen & Itzhak Venezia (2008), 'Optimal Strike Prices of Stock Options for Effort-Averse Executives', *Journal of Banking and Finance*, 32, 229–39.

Peng, L. & A. Röell (2008), 'Executive Pay and Shareholder Litigation', *Review of Finance*, 12, 141–84.

Polsky, Gregg D. (2007), 'Controlling Executive Compensation through the Tax Code', *Washington and Lee Law Review*, 64, 877–926.

Posner, Richard A. (2009), 'Are American CEOs Overpaid, and, if so, What if Anything Should be Done About It?', *Duke Law Journal*, 58, 1013–47.

Rappaport, Alfred (1999), 'New Thinking on How to Link Executive Pay with Performance', *Harvard Business Review*, 77(2), 91–101.

Samuelson, Judith F. & Lynn A. Stout (2009), 'Are Executives Paid Too Much?', *The Wall Street Journal*, February 25, A-13.

Singh, Ravi (2006), 'Board Independence and the Design of Executive Compensation', Harvard NOM Working Paper No. 673741, available at http://ssrn.com/abstract=673741 (last accessed October 2011).

Sun, Jerry, Steven F. Cahan & David Emanuel (2009), 'Compensation Committee Governance Quality, Chief Executive Officer Stock Option Grants, and Future Firm Performance', *Journal of Banking and Finance*, 33, 1507–19.

Thomas, Randall S. & Kenneth J. Martin (2001), 'Litigating Challenges to Executive Pay: An Exercise in Futility?', *Washington University Law Quarterly,* 79, 569–614.

Tian, Yisong S. (2001), 'Optimal Contracting, Incentive Effects and the Valuation of Executive Stock Options', Working Paper, available at http://ssrn.com/abstract=268738 (last accessed October 2011).

Tian, Yisong S. (2004), 'Too Much of a Good Incentive? The Case of Executive Stock Options', *Journal of Banking and Finance*, 28, 1225–45.

Tung, Frederick & Xue Wang (2011), 'Bank CEOs, Inside Debt Compensation, and the Financial Crisis', Emory Law and Economics Research Paper No. 10-63, available at http://ssrn.com/abstract=1570161 (last accessed October 2011).

Walker, David I. (2004), 'Is Equity Compensation Tax Advantaged?', *Boston University Law Review*, 84, 695–755.

Walker, David I. (2007), 'Unpacking Backdating: Economic Analysis and Observations on the Stock Option Scandal', *Boston University Law Review*, 87, 561–623.

Walker, David I. (2009), 'The Non-Option: Understanding the Dearth of Discounted Employee Stock Options', *Boston University Law Review*, 89, 1505–63.

Walker, David I. (2010), 'The Challenge of Improving the Long-Term Focus of Executive Pay', *Boston College Law Review*, 51, 435–72.

Walker, David I. (2011), 'Evolving Executive Equity Compensation and the Limits of Optimal Contracting', *Vanderbilt Law Review*, 64, 611–74.

Walker, David I. & Victor Fleischer (2009), 'Book/Tax Conformity and Equity Compensation', *Tax Law Review*, 62, 399–444.

Yale, Ethan (2009), 'Investment Risk is Important When Assessing the Tax Benefit of Deferred Compensation' *Tax Law Review*, 62, 377–98.

# PART III


# GATEKEEPERS

# 14. Transaction cost engineers, loophole engineers or gatekeepers: The role of business lawyers after the financial meltdown

*Richard W. Painter*

## 1. INTRODUCTION

Modern commentators have advanced three competing views of transactional lawyers: the 'transaction cost engineer' model championed by some law and economics commentators in the 1980s and 1990s, the notion that lawyers are 'loophole engineers' in keeping with the longstanding belief that lawyers exploit loopholes in the law for the benefit of clients, and the more paternalistic view that lawyers, along with other professionals such as accountants and investment bankers, are 'gatekeepers' who lend their credibility to clients while at the same time protecting capital markets and broader societal interests from client wrongdoing.

What do lawyers actually do? As discussed in more detail below, the answer is that lawyers do all three. The three roles are also linked, sometimes reinforcing each other and sometimes undermining each other.

The first view, the 'transaction cost engineer' model, centers on lawyers' role in allocating economic risk in business transactions. Most 'transaction cost' savings involve shifting transaction risks from one person to another, a shift that usually adds value when risk is transferred to a party better able to understand the risk and to deal with it through insurance, diversification or a similar strategy. Academic literature promoting the transaction cost engineer model uses relatively simple examples of two or three party transactions – often in the mergers and acquisitions context – where lawyers add value by drafting contracts that overcome information asymmetry or some other impediment to efficiently allocating risk.

Some transactions, however, are more complex than these simple examples and involve opportunities to shift economic risk in multiple directions. Complex transactions combined with shortcomings in investor protection and consumer protection laws ('loopholes') make it possible to shift risk to someone else who does not understand the risk, does not want the risk, and/or may not be able to bear the risk. Sometimes, a transaction participant will end up worse off because lawyers were involved in devising a transaction structure that benefited the other side. In other cases, both transaction participants are better off, but someone else – perhaps a party to a subsequent transaction such as the end investor in a pool of securitized mortgages – is worse off. In these situations legal and other complexities in transactions give lawyers a substantial role in determining who is better off and who is worse off. The transaction cost engineer role can evolve into 'loophole engineering' when lawyers look for ways to allocate risk in a way that the law did not intend. Although loophole engineering is common in many areas of law practice, tax practice being one of the most often mentioned (Hickman & Hill 2010), the focus of discussion here will be on lawyers specializing in the law governing business organizations (e.g. corporate law, banking law, etc.) and disclosure that business organizations make to investors (securities law).

This deflection of risk inherent in loophole engineering is contrary to the gatekeeper function which involves lawyers protecting third parties from their clients. In this gatekeeper model, the more lawyers protect third parties from client wrongdoing the more valuable lawyers become. Loophole engineering at the expense of third parties has the opposite effect.

## 2.   TRANSACTION COST ENGINEER

In the 1980s commentators with an economic perspective on law began asking questions about the role of lawyers in business transactions. How is what lawyers do in business transactions different from what lawyers do in litigation? Do transactional lawyers merely allocate value among parties to a transaction, or do transactional lawyers create additional value that makes their fees more than a deadweight loss for the parties?

Some commentators concluded that lawyers not only help redistribute wealth in transactions toward their clients and away from other parties – a zero sum game – but that that lawyers also increase the total value of transactions by allocating business risks to persons best able to evaluate and bear those risks. Ronald Gilson, one of the commentators to pioneer work in this area, observed that lawyers don't just assist clients in fighting over the size of the pie in business transactions, but help make the pie bigger by assisting clients in more accurately valuing the underlying assets (Gilson 1984). In Gilson's model the lawyer ensures that financial assets are valued accurately according to the Capital Asset Pricing Model (CAPM) which assumes homogeneous information for both parties to a transaction, consistent time horizons for the parties, no transaction costs, and that information acquisition is costless (Gilson 1984). Lawyers do this by designing deals that overcome the parties' incomplete information. Overcoming information asymmetries and costs of acquiring information lies at the heart of what business lawyers do.

One of Gilson's examples is the earn-out provision in a business acquisition agreement (Gilson 1984). The seller thinks the business is worth more than the buyer thinks the business is worth. The seller has some inside information about the business, so perhaps he is in a better position to judge, but the seller also has an incentive to inflate the purported value of the business in order to get a higher purchase price. This mismatch in valuations can cause deals that otherwise should be done not to be done. The lawyer's solution: draft a contract that provides for the business to be sold for a lower amount equal to the buyer's estimate of what the business is worth based on the buyer's earnings projections, plus an additional amount that will be paid later if the business performs better than the buyer's earnings projections. If the business in fact performs in line with the seller's higher earnings projections, the earn-out clause provides for an additional payment from the buyer to the seller. Information asymmetry between the parties that could have prevented the deal from being done at all is overcome by a provision allocating the risk to the party that knows the most about it.

This and most of Gilson's other examples involve lawyers efficiently allocating business risks between the parties to a transaction, usually two parties, sometimes three. Value is created by shifting risk from parties that do not want to bear it to parties that do, provided they are compensated for it.

Gilson's model of the 'transaction cost engineer' is rooted in business acquisitions, venture capital and other transactions for clients with tangible assets. The model is particularly well suited for transactions involving businesses in an early unpredictable stage. The principals in these transactions negotiate against a background of substantial uncertainty and lawyers help them to efficiently deal with the uncertainty. Lawyers allocate risks to persons best able to understand risks, monitor risks and diversify against risks. Lisa Bernstein pointed out the application of Gilson's model to Silicon Valley lawyers in a 1995 issue of the *Oregon Law Review* dedicated to exploring the model in various contexts (L. Bernstein 1995; Gilson & Mnookin 1995). Bernstein and other commentators analyzed the model in contexts such as commercial agreements (E. Bernstein 1995) and underwriting of securities (Okamoto 1995). The risks lawyers allocate in Gilson's examples and in examples used by commentators elaborating on Gilson's model are almost all business risks, not risks from financial instruments bought or sold by lawyers' clients.

By the 1990s, however, the 'transaction cost engineer' model of value creation had found another venue, centered not in Silicon Valley but in New York City. Two Sullivan & Cromwell lawyers published an article on how asset securitization reallocated risk to the benefit of borrowers and investors. They defined securitization as:

> [T]he sale of equity or debt instruments, representing ownership interests in, or secured by, a segregated, income-producing asset or pool of assets, in a transaction structured to reduce or reallocate certain risks inherent in owning or lending against underlying assets and to ensure that such interests are more readily marketable and, thus, more liquid than ownership interests in and loans against the underlying assets. (Schenker & Colletta 1991, 1374–5)

Of principal importance was the greater liquidity achieved through conversion of illiquid mortgages or other loans to securities that could be traded in markets. Other advantages include the signal that securitization gives to the markets that assets are of high quality and other information that securitization provides to investors (Schenker & Colletta 1991; Hill 1996). Lawyers have an important role in this process (Schenker & Colletta 1991). As in Gilson's model, lawyers are reallocating risk, although in the securitization transaction risk is reallocated from the party that knows the most about the asset (the original lender) through an intermediary (an investment bank that is often the lawyer's client) and then ultimately to parties that know the least about the risk (investors). These investors may (or may not) be better positioned to bear the risk than the other parties. Whether or not they are better risk bearers, it is probably not because they know more about the risk than the parties who passed it on to them. In some situations, notably including subprime mortgage securitizations, risks were transferred to people who knew far less about them than they should have (and, in any event, the transferees usually were not better risk bearers). This is the opposite of the type of risk reallocation that occurs in most of Gilson's examples, where the party that ends up bearing the risk knows the most or is for some other reason the best risk bearer.

Securitization transactions also illustrate how some business lawyers create value for their clients not through the relatively simple mergers and acquisitions transactions discussed by Gilson, but instead through highly complex deals that allocate different types of risk among many different parties. Keeping track of the risk in securitization deals can be difficult. The temptation to conceal risk is much stronger than for simpler transactions because it is less likely that concealment will be detected. The temptation is also great to look for ways to shift to other parties more risk than they bargained for. Although securitization deals had been done successfully since the 1970s, by the 2000s significant market volume consisted of securitization of subprime loans and other lower quality assets. The increasingly complex deal structures designed for these transactions by lawyers as well as investment bankers helped conceal the inherent risks.

Finally, an unanswered question in the discussion of value creation by 'transaction cost engineers' is why lawyers are unique in this role. Other professionals, including accountants and investment bankers, can devise mechanisms to allocate risks among the parties to transactions. As Larry Ribstein observes:

> In other words, lawyers are not necessarily the key transaction cost engineers, as argued [by Gilson]. Their historical importance as the 'passkeys' of large transactions may be an artifact of licensing and ethical rules … rather than of the inherent importance of lawyers' legal expertise and other unique skills. (Ribstein 2010, 43 n. 166)

Lawyers have legal training and, because of licensing rules barring non-lawyers from the practice of law, substantially more experience working with the law. This training and experience gives lawyers a unique advantage in using the law to benefit their clients in transactions. The more difficult the law is to understand, particularly in the context of a complex transaction, the greater this advantage should be. The difficulty from a societal perspective is that lawyers can most easily use their training and experience to create value for clients by devising legal – or arguably legal – ways to allocate risk away from their clients and impose that risk instead on other parties to a transaction, third parties or society as a whole. The closer a transaction gets to legal limits on risk taking or concealment of risk the more lawyers are essential to this type of value creation for clients. The risk can be financial risk, environmental risk, safety risk, or any other type of risk that the client wants to impose on others but that the law – or at least the spirit of the law – does not want the client to impose on someone else. This type of risk shifting is not the type of law practice that Gilson had in mind although some subsequent commentators have addressed the interaction of Gilson's model with regulatory arbitrage (Davidson 2009). This is the type of law practice that was embedded in the popular view of the legal profession long before Gilson's concept of the transaction cost engineer was first publicized.

## 3.   LOOPHOLE ENGINEER

There is a more cynical image of the role of transactional lawyers – that of the 'loophole engineer' who helps clients get around the law. This image reflects the reality that lawyers don't just represent clients vis-à-vis other private parties, but also vis-à-vis the state, and the state provides rules that lawyers help their clients, and sometimes both parties to a transaction, circumvent. Whether described as regulatory arbitrage (Fleischer 2010), loophole lawyering, or something else, this aspect of law practice has been with us for a long time.

One of the earlier business law statutes that instigated loophole lawyering was England's Bubble Act of 1720. This statute constrained the sale of transferable shares in limited liability companies in response to the collapse of the South Sea Company in 1720. The South Sea Company, a trading company, had been used as an investment bank to refinance millions of pounds of government debt through the sale of its own stock to investors (Painter 2006). Parliament believed that the combination of limited liability and tradable shares had led to the Company's collapse and sought to address the problem in the Bubble Act. By the mid 1720s, however, London solicitors were hard at work devising ways to get around the Act (Dubois 1971[1938]). Solicitors quickly devised ways to raise capital with transferable shares despite the restrictions of the Act. The *Morning Chronicle* newspaper in England on November 16, 1807 reported:

> All the subterfuges and expedients that have been resorted to by plausible solicitors, of introducing clauses into deeds of settlement by which the partners are not answerable beyond the amounts of their respective subscriptions, are laughed at by real lawyers and would be scouted at by a protecting judge. (French 2010, quoting Hunt 1936 at 28 and McQueen 2009 at 30)

Many lawyers today have forgotten this early history of loophole engineering, although Robert French, Chief Justice of the High Court of Australia in 2010 reminded an audience of Australian business lawyers of their profession's historical role in evading the Bubble Act and pointed out some parallels to what lawyers do today (French 2010).

By the late nineteenth century, the bar in the United States also established a reputation in this area. Philip Jessup, in his biography of Elihu Root, discusses the practice of one of the greatest Wall Street Lawyers at the end of the nineteenth century. According to Jessup (1964 [1938]):

> There was no lawyer practicing at the American Bar in the 1890s who was more sought-after than Elihu Root. It was the heyday of his practice … The Sherman Anti-Trust Act of 1890 had made necessary some reorganizations in big business combinations, but neither the statute nor the early court decisions made large corporate organizations illegal. Nor did the *mores* of the time condemn them. The law had failed to keep pace with all the violent new methods of business. This was partly because the law rarely does; it waits until the evils have roused public opinion. Partly it was because legislatures were too much controlled by corporate wealth …
>
>    Root, as it happened, never actually formed a 'trust.' He did advise on a number of important reorganizations which new laws made necessary …
>
>    There are many forms of the remark, variously attributed to Thomas Fortune Ryan and to William C. Whitney: 'I have had many lawyers who have told me what I cannot do; Mr. Root is the only lawyer who tells me how to do what I want to do.' …
>
>    'Everybody knows,' Root once said, 'that some rules for the conduct of life are matters of right and wrong, substantial, essential, and that other rules for the conduct of life are matters of convenience, of form, of method, desirable but not essential.' Root kept the two categories perfectly distinct in his mind and neither advised nor countenanced what he considered wrong … Root came to realize later that the law had inadequately regulated business practices and he favored changes in the law, but he never doubted that as a lawyer he acted properly in advising clients regarding the rights which they had under the law as it was at the time.

Jessup then describes from a perspective sympathetic to Root some of the particular transactions in which Root's conduct had been called into question by the popular press. Even as Jessup describes the transactions, however they appear to be examples of 'loophole lawyering'.

Several of these transactions involved the State Trust Company of which Root was a director and counsel. The Company apparently made illegal loans for approximately $2 million to Daniel Shea, an office boy in Thomas Fortune Ryan's office, and improper if not illegal loans of $435,000 to Louis F. Payn, the State Superintendent of Insurance. The State Trust Company meanwhile was in control of the same men who controlled the American Surety Company, an insurance company regulated by Payn (Jessup 1964 [1938]).

Of the first of these loans, to Ryan's office boy, Jessup writes:

The $2,000,000 loan to Ryan's office boy, Daniel Shea, came about as follows: Ryan, P.A.B. Widener, Whitney and others, were members of a syndicate engaged in a merger or reorganization of the Electric Vehicle Company. According to the usual business practice of the times, pending the completion of the arrangement for the final transfer of stock, the stock was held in the name of a nominal holder, who in this case was Shea. Shea of course never had any vestige of interest in the stock. Shea signed a formal note to the Trust Company asking it to take up 20,000 shares of the preferred stock of the Electric Vehicle Company at par, and agreeing to reimburse them with interest at four per cent, the stock to be held by the bank until the loan was paid. The stock at the time had just paid an 8% dividend and was selling at 135, a total value of $2,700,000 for securing the loan of $2,000,000. In addition, Whitney and Widener signed a guarantee of the loan. As part of the same transaction, an additional loan of the same amount was extended and repaid in cash within a short time. The arrangement also provided that a substantial part of the loan was to remain on deposit with the Trust Company. When the cash balance fell just below one million dollars, additional collateral was deposited in the form of 20,000 shares of New York Gas, Light, Heat & Power Company, which shortly produced $2,000,000 Debenture Bonds of the Consolidated Gas Company. Moreover, other companies involved in the plans of the syndicate opened accounts at the Trust Company so that during the entire time the Trust Company had on deposit from these sources more than the face amount of the loan.

The transactions involved two technical violations of the banking law of the state: the law forbade any single secured loan in excess of fifty per cent of the paid-in capital and surplus of the banking institution. The law was so much of a dead letter that the President of the State Trust Company did not even know of its existence until this case was aired. He pointed out in a letter to Root that if they had known of the law, it would have been a simple matter to distribute the loan among the six members of the syndicate, any one of whom could have paid off the whole two million without embarrassment. The second legal provision, of which the President of the State Trust Company was also ignorant and which he considered entirely ridiculous, forbade loans to any director. The Shea loan was in part at least a loan to Ryan who was a director; Widener, his co-guarantor, was not even a stockholder. Since the business practice of the time considered such transactions perfectly proper, the transaction could have been made entirely in Widener's name had they considered such a course necessary. The legal technicalities are relatively unimportant; it is significant that this transaction was of such a usual type in those days that the admittedly able and diligent bank examiner, who had in routine course examined the State Trust Company a little while before, had made no comment on either the size of the loan or the fact that a director was involved. Superintendent of Banking Kilburn, in parts of his report which the *World* reproduced in fine print, indicated a belief in the general soundness and good management of the Trust Company. (Jessup 1964 [1938])

In sum a $2 million loan was made by a bank to one of its own directors although the law forbade the practice. To get around the law, which the bank President thought of as 'ridiculous', Root structured the deal so the loan was made to the director's office boy instead. The loan also exceeded the maximum amount the bank was allowed to lend, but the bank examiners were not enforcing that law. Jessup does not discuss why the bank examiners were not enforcing the law, although he had already pointed out that the same bank was making loans to the state's top insurance regulator.

The factors Jessup identifies here are all too familiar over 100 years later: aggressive business promoters; regulators who cannot keep up with rapidly changing business practices; laws that business promoters and their lawyers see as ridiculous or a mere technicality; and brilliant lawyers who help businesses get around these laws (Katz 1996).

Not all lawyer interaction with the regulatory system has involved taking advantage of loopholes in the law; legitimate reduction in regulatory costs is still an important part of what lawyers do. Surveys of clients show that transactional lawyers add value primarily by reducing regulatory costs (Schwarcz 2007). This is particularly true when regulation exceeds its purpose because as applied it has a broader reach than intended. Lawyers thus can help their clients avoid costly overregulation while still conducting their businesses in a manner that respects both the letter and the spirit of the law. Avoiding regulation that was not intended to apply to a particular type of transaction creates value both for the client and for society by avoiding regulatory compliance costs in situations where there is unlikely to be any commensurate societal benefit.

There are also, however, situations where lawyers or their clients, or lawyers and their clients, convince themselves that a regulation that was intended to apply to their business should not apply, or simply decide that they do not want to follow the regulation. There is no attempt to follow the spirit of the law, and the letter of the law is stretched as far as possible to meet the client's objectives. Through exploiting loopholes in the law and structuring transactions to avoid the law, lawyers create value for clients, but at the expense of third parties and society as a whole.

In the late 1990s, Enron's lawyers designed special purposes entities (SPEs) and other complex corporate structures that were used to conceal the company's true financial condition. Admittedly, the lawyers involved may not have been aware of the extent of the loophole they were exploiting or the impending consequences. Part of Enron's strategy was to use a large number of lawyers and limit the scope of each lawyer's representation. This approach made it less likely that any one lawyer would understand the full implications of what that lawyer was asked to do. Even when concerns were raised by a whistleblower and Enron hired outside counsel to investigate these concerns, limitations were placed on the scope of the investigation.

Even if these lawyers did not know everything that was going on, perhaps they should have asked. Former SEC Chairman David Ruder later raised this issue shortly after the Enron scandal broke:

> Should the Texas outside lawyers have acquiesced in the limited scope of their internal investigation? Should they have brought to management, to the Enron Board, or to the Enron Audit Committee any concerns they might have had about matters not covered by the investigation, including possible concerns about the SPEs?
>
> Even if Enron's lawyers did not know that fraud was occurring, should they nevertheless have engaged in investigation of the underlying facts? Should they have expressed concerns about Enron's business practices to the Enron Board and the Enron Audit Committee? (Ruder 2002, 19)

Because they acquiesced to the limited scope of their engagements, some of Enron's lawyers may have thought they were exploiting little loopholes in the law with relatively insignificant consequences, oblivious to the fact that combined the little loopholes became big loopholes. Other lawyers may not have been aware they were exploiting loopholes at all. Even lawyers investigating alleged wrongdoing investigated only the matters they were asked to investigate, meaning the investigation was not genuine but instead a means of providing necessary cover so Enron's management could continue to do what it wanted to do. In many of these engagements, the lawyers probably thought they had the deniability they needed to do the work they were asked to do and get paid without running afoul of prohibitions on lawyer assistance of client fraud.[1] The fact that Enron's limitations on the

---

[1]    See ABA Model Rule of Professional Conduct, Rule 1.2(d): 'A lawyer shall not counsel a client to engage, or assist a client, in conduct that the lawyer knows is criminal or fraudulent, but a

scope of representation may have been unreasonable[2] apparently was not considered until it was too late.

Loophole lawyering came back into the public eye with the financial crisis of 2008. As pointed out above, many of the complex mortgage-backed securities and other securitized products that helped create the financial crisis were created by lawyers. Many of these lawyers worked for investment banks that sold these products and carried them as assets on their balance sheets. Most of the products themselves were legal. As in the Enron situation, however, a broader look might have revealed that the products were created in a process that involved concealing information from investors, including the investment banks' own stockholders and creditors. Then, when investment banks' balance sheets became overloaded with bad assets, lawyers actively helped move the assets off balance sheets so investors would not notice them.

One of the most notorious transactions was Lehman Brothers' Repo 105. In this maneuver lawyers assisted Lehman with its efforts to conceal $50 billion in debt on its quarterly balance sheets through temporary sales of Lehman's bad assets to other financial institutions in return for cash that Lehman used to pay down debt temporarily at the end of each quarter. Even though Lehman and the counterparty agreed that the transaction would be unwound a few days later, English law apparently allowed it to be treated as a 'sale' if the assets were valued at 105% or more of the cash 'paid' for them. It did not matter that the parties contemplated that substantially equivalent assets would be transferred back to Lehman and the cash returned a few days later. Lehman could not find New York lawyers who would agree to characterize the transaction as a sale under United States law, but Linklaters in London was willing to opine that the sale coupled with a repurchase agreement was a true sale under English law (Valukas 2010). To accomplish this, Lehman had to transfer the securities involved to London (this transaction no doubt was done with the knowledge if not the assistance of United States lawyers). In London, the transaction would be executed through LBIE, Lehman's European broker-dealer in London (Valukas 2010). It was reported back to Lehman's auditors in the United States as a true sale under English law and recorded as such on Lehman's consolidated balance sheet for its quarterly report. After the transaction was unwound, it could be repeated at the end of the next quarter and so on. Substantial fees were paid to the counter party each time, all for only one apparent purpose: dressing up Lehman's quarterly balance sheet to look better than it actually was.

---

lawyer may discuss the legal consequences of any proposed course of conduct with a client and may counsel or assist a client to make a good faith effort to determine the validity, scope, meaning or application of the law'. For loophole lawyers, the language after the word 'but' in this rule is sufficiently broad that it is an exception that negates the rule. Comment [9] to the rule goes on to provide the loophole lawyer with even more apparent cover: '[9] Paragraph (d) prohibits a lawyer from knowingly counseling or assisting a client to commit a crime or fraud. This prohibition, however, does not preclude the lawyer from giving an honest opinion about the actual consequences that appear likely to result from a client's conduct. Nor does the fact that a client uses advice in a course of action that is criminal or fraudulent of itself make a lawyer a party to the course of action. There is a critical distinction between presenting an analysis of legal aspects of questionable conduct and recommending the means by which a crime or fraud might be committed with impunity.'

2    See ABA Model Rule of Professional Conduct, Rule 1.2(c): 'A lawyer may limit the scope of the representation if the limitation is reasonable under the circumstances and the client gives informed consent.' Whether limitations on scope of representations are reasonable if they deny lawyers critical information is discussed further below in the context of the lawyer gatekeeping function.

A close reading of the Linklaters opinion reveals how artfully lawyers can navigate around the law. First the opinion discusses its overall purpose, stating that at the same time as the transaction for the sale of certain Purchased Securities the parties will enter into an agreement whereby the Buyer will sell to the Seller (Lehman Brothers) securities that are 'equivalent' to the Purchased Securities on an agreed upon Repurchase Date, and that '[t]he purpose of this opinion is to advise you about whether the transfer of the Purchased Securities to the Buyer for the Purchase Price, may under English law, be classified as a sale involving the disposition off the Seller's entire proprietary interest in the Purchased Securities, as opposed to a charge' (Linklaters 2006, 1.4–1.5). Next the opinion goes into substantial detail on the legal distinction between a 'sale' and a 'charge' (Linklaters 2006, 2.2). The opinion then identifies the controlling factor as being the fact that under Lehman's master repurchase agreement the counterparty is not obligated to return the same assets to Lehman when the transaction is unwound a few days later, only substantially equivalent assets. If the parties had agreed that the same assets would be returned, it would be a charge rather than a true sale (Linklaters 2006, 2.2), but it would instead be a true sale if the parties agreed to return of virtually identical assets with the same CUSIP numbers (CUSIP is a numerical code analogous to a DNA code for identifying the essential characteristics of securities). 'The mere fact that the securities which are to be delivered have the same CUSIP numbers as the ones that the transferee originally received would not prevent them from being regarded as equivalent assets rather than the very assets that were originally delivered' (Linklaters 2006, 2.2).

After discussing a wide range of issues largely irrelevant to what was going on in the transaction, the opinion finally warns against a 'sham' transaction such as one where the parties have a side agreement orally or in writing that equivalent securities would not in fact be transferred or that otherwise alters the terms of the Master Agreement (Linklaters 2006, 2.6). The lawyers who have successfully exploited a loophole thus recite in their opinion those things that the client should not do and that the client apparently did not want to do anyway. There is no mention in the opinion of the reason why Lehman wanted to do the transaction or of the fact that the Master Agreement itself was intended to be a sham. The Linklaters opinion reeks of form over substance, the glue that binds the reasoning of a loophole engineer.

Loophole lawyering of this sort is made possible by the fact that the consequences are often externalities imposed on someone other than the lawyers or their clients. Furthermore, agency costs within organizational clients may mean that officers and other agents for clients do not act in the best interests of the clients, yet it is these agents who instruct the lawyers. Finally, whoever is hurt by loophole lawyering – whether third parties or lawyers' own clients or their shareholders – may not realize what is happening until it is too late.

## 4. GATEKEEPER

A third perspective focuses on lawyers' gatekeeping role. Lawyers – in a manner similar to underwriters, accountants, rating agencies and other professionals – certify their clients as being suitable for business interaction with other people. Most discussion of the gatekeeper role focuses on public securities markets, with lawyers and other professionals providing or denying the certification that issuers need to gain access to investors' capital (Kraakman 1986; Jackson 1993; Coffee 2006).

Effective gatekeeping turns on there being appropriate incentives for gatekeepers to do their job, incentives sufficiently strong to overcome the fact that a client who seeks to enter the gateway is paying the gatekeeper. Underwriters, for example, certify which issuers are and are not of sufficient quality to deserve a major Wall Street investment bank's name on their prospectuses. For years underwriters claimed that their own reputational incentives overcame incentives to cave into the demands of issuers who were paying them, but time after time it did not work out that way. Finally, after the Wall Street crash of 1929 the federal government decided to regulate this process. A key provision of the federal securities laws – Section 11 of the 1933 Securities Act – was intended to give underwriter firms an additional stake in their gatekeeper role by making them liable if registration statements for securities they underwrote were materially misleading and the underwriters could not affirmatively prove that they had tried to be good gatekeepers – e.g. their due diligence defense. Through the 1970s most of the leading underwriter firms were general partnerships, with the investment bankers, personally liable for firm debts, and the threat of Section 11 liability for deficient gatekeepers may have successfully deterred many investment bankers from excessively risky underwritings (Hill & Painter 2010). Although auditors of issuer financial statements are also subject to Section 11 liability, the law has been more lenient with respect to other gatekeepers. Rating agencies, for example, until recently escaped extensive scrutiny (Manns 2009) and in most situations it is difficult to characterize rating agencies as underwriters for purposes of imposing Section 11 liability. Lawyers, unless they submit an opinion letter to be included in a registration statement, are not directly covered by Section 11.

Presumably lawyers could be sued by investors if their gatekeeping was so deficient that they aided and abetted a client in committing securities fraud, but this deterrent has been removed by the Supreme Court's ruling that only primary violators, not aiders and abettors, can be sued by private plaintiffs under the securities fraud statutes.[3] The bar on private suits even extends to suits against persons who participate in a conspiracy to violate the securities laws.[4] Lawyer gatekeepers may have to worry about liability to their corporate clients but the securities laws give them relatively little reason to worry about their own liability to investors.

Yet another problem is that effective gatekeeping is undermined by the same 'divide and conquer' strategy that clients sometimes use to induce even reluctant lawyers into playing the role of loophole engineer. Lawyers, accountants, underwriters, rating agencies and other gatekeepers are parceled out particular assignments, and each gatekeeper conditions its seal of approval on the approval of one or more other gatekeepers (for example, Lehman Brothers' US accountants conditioned their accounting treatment of Repo 105 on the UK lawyers' opinion that it was a true 'sale'). As mentioned above, Enron split its legal work up among many different lawyers. Multiple engagements make it easier for clients to hide the big picture – and fraud – from all of the gatekeepers, particularly if these gatekeepers don't ask questions about the broader picture. Lawyers may not appropriately consider whether limitations placed by corporate clients on the scope of their engagements are reasonable (under ABA Model Rule 1.2 such limitations on scope must be reasonable).

Finally, lawyers sometimes limit the scope of their own gatekeeping engagement by drawing the line at addressing only conduct they know to be illegal, while ignoring facts that they find suspicious. These lawyers ignore the advice of former SEC Chairman David Ruder:

---

    3    *Central Bank of Denver, N.A. v. First Interstate Bank of Denver, N.A.,*114 S. Ct. 1439 (1994).
    4    *Stoneridge Investment Partners, Llc v. Scientific-Atlanta, Inc.,* 552 U.S. 148 (2008).

I believe lawyers who become suspicious about corporate conduct should caution both management and the board about potential legal hazards known to them even if these hazards are not sufficiently certain to create an obligation to do so. In that sense, lawyers should serve as monitors of management conduct. (Ruder 2002, 19)

A genuine gatekeeper not only complies with SEC rules and other applicable law, but communicates regularly with persons at the appropriate level of authority in a client organization – including where appropriate the board of directors – about legal risk. The problem is that this often is not a comfortable task, and it is one that may cost the lawyer the client.

Congress in the 1990s began the process of more specifically addressing the gatekeeping role of professionals – chiefly accountants – in securities transactions. Ironically, the vehicle for doing so was the Private Securities Litigation Reform Act of 1995 (PSLRA),[5] a largely pro-defendant law designed to curtail private plaintiffs' class-action litigation, including litigation against accountants, underwriters and other gatekeepers. As a whole, this legislation probably lessened this deterrent against gatekeeper malfeasance. Section 104 of PSLRA, however, amended Section 20 of the 1934 Exchange Act[6] to expressly grant the Commission authority to prosecute persons who aid and abet violations of the securities laws. This includes attorneys who aid and abet securities fraud, although attorneys are not specifically mentioned in the Act.

Congress also affirmed the longstanding view that auditors have a heightened obligation to prevent client fraud both by 'reporting up' within client organizations, to the full board of directors if necessary, and by 'reporting out' to the SEC if issuers still refuse to follow the law. Section 301 of PSLRA thus requires accountants to follow specified procedures when confronted with client fraud. The Act amends the Securities Exchange Act of 1934 by inserting a Section 10A providing that each audit performed pursuant to the securities laws must include procedures designed to discover illegal acts having a material effect on financial statements. In addition, the Act requires accountants who discover information indicating that an illegal act may have occurred to report the illegal act to the appropriate level of management. If the accountant does make a report to management, and the accountant is unsatisfied that management has remedied the problem, then the accountant must go to the full board of directors. The statute then requires the board within one day of the accountant's report to disclose the problem to the SEC; if the board does not, the statute requires disclosure by the accountant to the SEC.

Some commentators asked at the time whether Congress should have imposed similar rules on securities lawyers. Even if the 'reporting out' provision requiring accountants to notify the SEC was inappropriate for lawyers, the 'reporting up' provision requiring notification of the full board of directors arguably should have been applied to lawyers as well as accountants. Although lawyers do not generally make representations about a client to the public the way auditors do, and thus should be subject to different rules for 'reporting out', lawyers do have a duty to communicate with their clients. Congress should have mandated that a securities lawyer report ongoing illegal acts to the client's full board of directors if management will not take appropriate remedial measures (Painter & Duggan 1996). Congress, however, did not do so. This issue of lawyer regulation presumably remained

---

5   Pub. L. 104-67, 109 Stat. §737 (codified as amended in scattered sections of 15 U.S.C.).
6   Securities Exchange Act of 1934, Section 20 (15 U.S.C. §78t).

where it had traditionally been handled, in the states where lawyers are licensed to practice law.

State ethics rules are based in large part on the ABA Model Rules of Professional Conduct. The ABA in turn has been hesitant to envision a stringent gate-keeping role for lawyers, particularly one that is imposed on lawyers. The ABA continued to resist requiring 'reporting up' even in situations where a lawyer knew there was ongoing securities fraud. For example, in the aftermath of litigation by the Office of Thrift Supervision against the Kaye, Scholer law firm over its representation of Lincoln Savings and Loan in the early 1990s, an ABA working group stated that among the Office of Thrift Supervision's 'novel theories of professional responsibility' in that case was the notion that lawyers have an obligation to report misconduct to superiors, going 'all the way to the client's board of directors'.[7] In 2000, the ABA Ethics 2000 Commission considered a proposal that would more explicitly require a lawyer for an organizational client to report prospective or ongoing illegal acts by the client to its full board of directors.[8] The Commission, however, rejected the proposal and decided to leave Model Rule 1.13 essentially unchanged until 2003.

Reporting 'out' was even more strenuously rejected as an option by the ABA because it breached client confidences (ABA Model Rule 1.6 prior to 2003 prohibited disclosure of client confidences, even if necessary to prevent client fraud).

Then in 2002 Enron and WorldCom went bust and lawyers were attributed part of the blame (Cramton 2002; Powers 2002). Congress began drafting the Sarbanes-Oxley Act of 2002. The Act required public companies to have audit committees of independent directors, established a new government board, the Public Company Accounting Oversight Board (PCAOB), to regulate accounting firms that audited public companies and provided for detailed regulation of auditors.

Congressman John Edwards (D. N.C.) noticed that the role of lawyers as gatekeepers had been the topic of an exchange of letters between a group of law professors and the SEC in the spring of 2002. The law professors had asked the SEC to impose a 'reporting up' requirement on lawyers.[9] The SEC had declined to do so, citing prior proposals that such a reform should be imposed by Congress.[10]

> As you noted in the 1996 SMU Law Review article which you enclosed, there may be reasons to prefer having one uniform nation-wide rule governing lawyers who participate in nation-wide securities law practices; but there are also good reasons why consideration of such a significant change in established practice should be undertaken in the context of Congressional legislation, as opposed to agency rulemaking. As I understand it, your 1996 article concludes that any such changes to the rules governing lawyers should be the result of Congressional changes to the securities laws, analogous to Section 10A's rules for accountants.

---

[7]   Working Group on Lawyers' Representation of Regulated Clients, ABA Report to the House of Delegates 2 (1993).

[8]   See Painter (1998).

[9]   Letter from 28 law professors to Harvey Pitt, Chairman of the Securities Exchange Commission March 7, 2002 (urging the SEC to adopt a rule mandating that securities lawyers for issuers report known securities fraud up the ladder to senior management and, if necessary, boards of directors).

[10]   Letter from David Becker, General Counsel of the Securities Exchange Commission to Richard W. Painter, March 28, 2002 (citing Painter & Duggan 1996).

Senator Edwards, himself a lawyer and running for President, read this exchange of letters and decided to add lawyers to the list of gatekeepers who would be regulated under Sarbanes-Oxley. Edwards – along with Senators John Corzine (D. N.J.), the former chairman of Goldman Sachs & Co., and Mike Enzi (R. W.Y.) who formerly had been an accountant – introduced a two paragraph amendment that became Section 307 of the Act:

> Not later than 180 days after the date of enactment of this Act, the Commission shall issue rules, in the public interest and for the protection of investors, setting forth minimum standards of professional conduct for attorneys appearing and practicing before the Commission in any way in the representation of issuers, including a rule–
>
> 1   requiring an attorney to report evidence of a material violation of securities law or breach of fiduciary duty or similar violation by the company or any agent thereof, to the chief legal counsel or the chief executive officer of the company (or the equivalent thereof); and
> 2   if the counsel or officer does not appropriately respond to the evidence (adopting, as necessary, appropriate remedial measures or sanctions with respect to the violation), requiring the attorney to report the evidence to the audit committee of the board of directors of the issuer or to another committee of the board of directors comprised solely of directors not employed directly or indirectly by the issuer, or to the board of directors.[11]

This short provision established a sea change in the regulation of lawyers' gatekeeping role, not only in imposing the 'reporting up' obligation the ABA had resisted but in putting regulation of securities lawyers firmly within the hands of the SEC. The SEC promulgated its rules under Section 307 shortly thereafter.[12] The SEC even sought to impose a requirement of 'noisy withdrawal' from representing a client if the board refused to take remedial action.[13] The SEC, however, eventually dropped this version of mandatory 'reporting out' in the final rule. Most important, however, the SEC now had unquestioned authority to regulate lawyers as gatekeepers. State bar ethics rules would no longer be the exclusive or even the primary source of regulation for lawyers representing public companies.

The ABA lobbied strenuously against Section 307 (Glater 2002), but to no avail. The ABA moved quickly in the summer of 2002 to begin the process of amending Model Rule 1.13 to impose a 'reporting up' obligation, but it was too late to avoid enactment of Section 307. A substantial portion of the bar, and one of the most lucrative areas of law practice, had come under federal regulation.

The SEC rules under Section 307 contain pages of detailed provisions addressing such questions as how much evidence of a violation is required to trigger the 'reporting up' obligation, what type of remedial action needs to be taken for the lawyer not to have to report

---

[11]   July 30, 2002, 107 P.L. 204, Title III, § 307, 116 Stat. 745.

[12]   17 CFR Part 205, Implementation of Standards of Professional Conduct for Attorneys [Release Nos. 33-8185; 34-47276; IC-25919; File No. S7-45-02], January 29, 2003.

[13]   See Proposed Rule under Section 307 of the Sarbanes-Oxley Act of 2002, Implementation of Standards of Professional Conduct for Attorneys [Release Nos. 33-8150, 34-46868, IC 25829, File No. S7-45-02], Nov. 21, 2002 ('Where the material violation at issue is ongoing or has yet to occur, Section 205.3(d)(1) of the proposed rule would require an outside attorney appearing and practicing before the Commission in the representation of the issuer to give notice to the Commission of the issuer's inappropriate response to the reported evidence through the "signal" or "flag waving" of "noisy withdrawal" that has long been recognized as a compromise between silent withdrawal and disclosure of specific confidential information').

further up the ladder, and when the lawyer has the option to disclose information to the SEC if reporting up has been to no avail. On this last question the SEC specifically stated that, in circumstances where the rule allowed the lawyer to report information to the SEC, the rule preempted state bar ethics rules to the contrary. The SEC rule also provided that an issuer could, if it wanted, opt out of up-the-ladder reporting to its full board of directors and instead designate a Qualified Legal Compliance Committee (QLCC) of independent directors to which the report could be made instead. The possibility of Congress or the SEC allowing an issuer to arrange *ex ante* for lawyers to report violations to a committee of the board of directors instead of to the full board had been discussed in proposals for federally mandated up-the-ladder reporting (Painter & Duggan 1996) but it was uncertain at the time these SEC rules were promulgated in 2003 whether this was an alternative that client companies would seriously consider.

How effective has SOX Section 307 been? Few if any enforcement actions have been brought against lawyers under the rules. Occasionally the SOX rules have been cited as a reason for lawyers reporting conduct to a client's board of directors, for example when TV Azteca's lawyers at Akin Gump Strauss Hauer & Feld in New York apparently reported evidence of securities law violations to the company's board (McGeehan 2003). In most instances, however, the fact that lawyers reported up the ladder and to whom they reported remains confidential as the SEC rules contemplate, particularly if the board takes appropriate remedial measures and there is no reporting out (reporting out to the SEC is optional under the final SEC rules). The Qualified Legal Compliance Committee (QLCC) provision apparently has not been widely used, probably because few directors want to serve on a QLCC and because QLCCs have high potential costs relative to their modest benefits (Fisch & Gentile 2003). Furthermore in most instances where reporting is required under the rules the full board of directors presumably would want to know the information. A crucial data point for determining whether SOX Section 307 has made a difference would be how many lawyers have been sued before SOX and how many lawyers have been sued after SOX for not going to the full board of directors of a client or taking other remedial action. The difficulty for researchers is that almost all such suits are settled, the settlements are secret, and lawyer liability insurance companies keep the information secret. Absent a Congressional subpoena of this information, which is unlikely unless there is a high profile investigation of lawyer conduct in this area, the information is likely to remain confidential.

Enron, WorldCom and the response in the Sarbanes-Oxley Act sparked a renewed interest by commentators on the role of lawyers as gatekeepers (Gordon 2002). John Coffee in particular has written extensively on the ways in which accountants, lawyers, rating agencies, and securities analysts failed to do their jobs because of changing corporate cultures and poor professional standards, conflicts of interest, and lack of competition (Coffee 2002, 2004, 2006; Gordon 2002). This renewed focus on gatekeeper roles, reinforced by the Sarbanes-Oxley Act provisions on lawyers and accountants, may have made gatekeepers more vigilant for certain types of problems, particularly problems directly related to clients' compliance with the law.

After the financial crisis of 2008, attention turned to broader definitions of gatekeeping going beyond legal risk. Should gatekeepers, including lawyers, be obligated to monitor for and disclose to clients risks even if those risks do not on the surface involve illegal conduct? Should gatekeepers be personally liable when they fail to detect these risks and alert appropriate persons within a client organization?

For director gatekeepers, the answer from the Delaware courts in a case brought against Citicorp's directors appeared to be that there is no duty to monitor for excessive risk.[14] The answer from Congress in the Dodd-Frank Act, however, is different. The Act requires financial services firms to establish risk committees of the board[15] to monitor for the types of risks that almost brought down Citicorp and did bring down some other Wall Street firms. In view of Dodd-Frank's mandate for a risk committee in some public companies, it is not certain whether Delaware courts will continue to hold that directors under state corporate law do not have a duty to monitor for risk. Knowing failure by directors to comply with this or any other Dodd-Frank provision presumably would violate the directors' fiduciary duties to the company.[16] If so, lawyers who represent the company would presumably be responsible for assisting the board in monitoring for risk at least to the extent required by the law.

The 2008 financial crisis thus adds to the things 'gatekeepers' may be expected to look for. Before the 2008 financial crisis, the focus was on discreet conduct in specific companies such as Enron's SPEs, not overall business risk or the dependence of companies on other companies. The events of 2008, however, showed that otherwise independent failures can combine to facilitate systemic shocks. There were at least two types of failures to see correlations:

(i) the failure to see, or at least to fully appreciate, correlations between the risk of low probability events (such as unlikely declines in collateral value) and institutional integrity; (ii) the failure to see or fully appreciate correlations in financial institution interrelatedness – viewing the term 'institution' broadly to include both firms and markets. (Schwarcz 2010, citing Schwarcz & Anabtawi 2010)

The collapse of the insurance giant American International Group (AIG) affected Goldman Sachs and others owed billions of dollars by AIG; what happened at Lehman Brothers affected just about everybody. Financial institutions in particular live in an interdependent world. To what extent should gatekeepers be responsible for monitoring how dependent their clients are upon the creditworthiness of counterparties or otherwise closely tied to the fortunes of other companies? When gatekeepers discover a problem what should they do about it?

It is debatable how much of the duty to monitor for these types of failures is the responsibility of lawyers, as opposed to other gatekeepers, including directors, rating agencies, and auditors. Still, when public companies are involved, these types of risks are likely to be material to financial disclosure, and may need to be emphasized in the 'risk factors' section toward the beginning of a registration statement. The fact that a low probability event such as illiquidity in the commercial paper market could be devastating for a company might be material to the company's investors who would want to know about it to make an investment decision. The fact that the well-being, or even the solvency, of one financial institution is heavily dependent upon another also could be material. Failure to adequately disclose material risk violates securities laws, and preventing such violations is the core mission of a securities lawyer. So is making sure that important risks are discussed in the 'risk factors' section of a

---

[14] *See In re Citigroup Inc. Shareholder Derivative Litigation*, No. 3338-CC, 2009 WL 481906 (Del. Ch. Feb. 24, 2009).

[15] Dodd-Frank Act, Pub. L. No. 111-203, § 165(h) (2010).

[16] *See In Re Caremark Derivative Litigation*, 698 A.2d 959 (Del. Ch. 1996), and *Stone v. Ritter*, 911 A.2d 362, 370 (Del. 2006) (upholding a duty to monitor for illegal conduct in some instances).

securities filing and not minimized or relegated to boilerplate text buried amidst relatively useless disclosure of marginally material information. Advising clients on how to detect such risks and how to discuss such risks in securities disclosure documents is a part of the gate-keeper profile for lawyers representing public companies.

One difficulty with an expanded view of gatekeeping, and indeed with any version of the gatekeeper role, is that economic incentives sometimes point in another direction. Effective gatekeeping generates benefits for lawyers, but many of these benefits accrue as reputational capital which belongs to law firms as well as to individual lawyers who frequently switch firms. For a short time at least, lawyers can abandon gatekeeping and switch to loophole engi-neering, yet still take advantage of trust earned through the reputation that they and their firms acquired over many years of effective gatekeeping. The temptation thus to 'cash in' on repu-tational capital arises whenever doing so could generate a substantial payout from clients who want to take advantage of their lawyers' reputation and ingenuity. This temptation to switch from effective gatekeeping to loophole engineering is particularly strong in a 'boom' econ-omy where the monetary value of transactions temporarily but dramatically increases. In such times officers of organizational clients also may be tempted to cash in on their own good reputations, and effective lawyer gatekeeping will be under severe stress. Recognizing this challenge, and being willing to deal with it through stricter ethics rules, professional training or other mechanisms, will be an important part of the legal profession proving itself capable of effective gatekeeping in good times as well as in bad.

## 5.   CONCLUSION

Lawyers can create value for clients by allocating risk in transactions to persons best able to bear that risk at the lowest cost. 'Transaction cost engineering' is a genuine contribution of economic value by the legal profession. Danger arises, however, when lawyers transfer risk from their clients to other parties to a transaction who are not in a position to evaluate that risk or who have no incentive to evaluate risk because they are investing other people's money, or to other third parties such as investors who are only tangentially part of the trans-action or who are not represented in the negotiation at all. Danger also arises when lawyers assist agents of their clients in foisting upon the client entities high levels of risk that inure principally to the benefit of the agents but not the clients. The more complex the mechanisms of risk allocation become, the greater the risk that they will be abused.

Lawyers also can create value for their clients, at least temporarily, with loophole engi-neering. Much of the value turns out to be ephemeral, particularly when the loopholes allow companies to conceal their own financial condition or to engage in risky business practices. The loophole lawyering may benefit the senior managers of the lawyers' clients but often not the client entities and their shareholders, and certainly not the general public.[17] Philip Jessup's account of Elihu Root's law practice demonstrates that loophole lawyering is noth-

---

[17]   Arguably, in some contexts such as tax, corporations and their shareholders may benefit if a loophole is used and not successfully challenged by the government, or if the cost of defending against government challenges is relatively modest. Once a client successfully uses loophole lawyering, however, both the client and the lawyer may be emboldened to use loopholes in a manner that yields government challenges that are very costly for the client.

ing new. Then as now some commentators were worried about the impact of loophole lawyering on the general standard of ethics in business and the economy as a whole, and others such as Jessup sought to justify what these lawyers do.

The next wave of research on transactional lawyers will probably rely less on generalizations and stylized models of lawyers' role, including all three of the models discussed in this chapter, and look closely at what lawyers actually do in particular types of transactions. Commentators have begun to explore in depth precisely what lawyers did – and did not do – for clients involved in the 2008 mortgage meltdown (Schwarcz 2010). The financial crisis will provide a wealth of materials to examine. The attorney-client privilege, often a hindrance to researchers in this area, in some instances will be waived by bankruptcy trustees, the government after a bailout or by the corporate clients themselves. Once it is determined what lawyers did and did not do in particular types of transactions, the next question is whether they should have a legal responsibility – and a moral responsibility – to have done something else (Painter 1994).

Commentators long ago abandoned the unrealistic assumption that the role of a transactional lawyer is similar to that of a litigator who usually has no responsibility for his client's conduct. Transactional lawyers are intimately involved in client conduct, and in some instances a 'but for' cause of client conduct (Painter 1994). Lawyers are responsible for that conduct in situations where they helped make it happen and could have prevented it.

## REFERENCES

Bernstein, Edward A. (1995), 'Law & Economics and the Structure of Value Adding Contracts: A Contract Lawyer's View of the Law & Economics Literature', *Oregon Law Review*, 74, 189–237.
Bernstein, Lisa (1995), 'Silicon Valley Lawyer as Transaction Cost Engineer', *Oregon Law Review*, 74, 239–55.
Coffee, John C. Jr. (2002), 'Understanding Enron, It's About the Gatekeepers, Stupid', Columbia Law & Economics Working Paper No. 207, available at SSRN: http://ssrn.com/abstract=325240 or doi:10.2139/ssrn.325240 (last accessed November 2011).
Coffee, John C. Jr. (2004), 'Gatekeeper Failure and Reform: The Challenge of Fashioning Relevant Reforms', *Boston University Law Review*, 84, 301–64.
Coffee, John C. Jr. (2006), *Gatekeepers: The Role of the Professions and Corporate Governance*, New York: Oxford University Press.
Cramton, Roger C. (2002), 'Enron and the Corporate Lawyer: A Primer on Legal and Ethical Issues', *Business Lawyer*, 58, 143–87.
Davidson, Nestor M. (2009), 'Values and Value Creation in Public-Private Transactions', *Iowa Law Review*, 94, 937–85.
Dubois, A. (1971 [1938]), *The English Business Company After the Bubble Act 1720–1800*, New York: Octagon Books.
Fisch, Jill E. & Caroline M. Gentile (2003), 'The Qualified Legal Compliance Committee: Using the Attorney Conduct Rules to Restructure the Board of Directors', *Duke Law Journal*, 53, 517–84.
Fleischer, Victor (2010), 'Regulatory Arbitrage', *Texas Law Review*, 89, 227–89.
French, Robert (2010), 'A Complicated Brief: The Corporations Law Advisor', dinner speech for the Business Law Section, Law Council of Australia, July 31, Canberra, Australia, available at http://www.hcourt.gov.au/speeches/frenchcj/frenchcj31july10.pdf (last accessed November 2011).
Gilson, Ronald J. (1984), 'Value Creation by Business Lawyers: Legal Skills and Asset Pricing', *Yale Law Journal*, 94, 239–313.
Gilson, Ronald J. & Robert H. Mnookin (1995), 'Foreword: Business Lawyers and Value Creation for Clients', *Oregon Law Review*, 74, 1–14.
Glater, Jonathan D. (2002), 'Round Up the Usual Suspects. Lawyers, Too?', New York Times, August 4, 2002, 3–4.
Gordon, Jeffrey N. (2002), 'What Enron Means for the Management and Control of the Modern Business Corporation: Some Initial Reflections', *University of Chicago Law Review*, 69, 1233–50.
Hickman, Kristin E. & Claire A. Hill (2010), 'Concepts, Categories, and Compliance in the Regulatory State' *Minnesota Law Review*, 94, 1151–1201.

Hill, Claire (1996), 'Securitization: A Low-Cost Sweetener for Lemons', *Washington University Law Quarterly*, 74, 1061–1126.
Hill, Claire & Richard Painter (2010), 'Berle's Vision Beyond Shareholder Interests: Why Investment Bankers Should Have (Some) Personal Liability', *Seattle Law Review*, 33, 1173–99.
Hunt, Bishop Carleton (1936), *The Development of the Business Corporation in England 1800–1867*, Cambridge: Harvard University Press.
Jackson, Howell E. (1993), 'Reflections on Kaye, Scholer: Enlisting Lawyers to Improve the Regulation of Financial Institutions', *Southern California Law Review*, 66, 1019–74.
Jessup, Philip C. (1964 [1938]), 'The Clients of Elihu Root', Vol. 1, Chapter X.
Katz, Leo (1996), *Ill-Gotten Gains: Evasion, Blackmail, Fraud, and Kindred Puzzles of the Law*, Chicago: University of Chicago Press.
Kraakman, Reinier H. (1986), 'Gatekeepers: The Anatomy of a Third-Party Strategy', *Journal of Law, Economics, and Organization*, 2, 53–104.
Linklaters (2006), Letter of 31 May 2006 to Lehman Brothers International (Europe), available at http://www.scribd.com/doc/28247093/Linklaters-Letter-to-Lehman-Brothers-re-Repo-105 (last accessed November 2011).
Manns, Jeffrey (2009), 'Rating Risk After the Subprime Mortgage Crisis: A User Fee Approach for Rating Agency Accountability', *North Carolina Law Review*, 87, 1011–89.
McGeehan, Patrick (2003), 'Lawyers Take Suspicions on TV Azteca to its Board', *New York Times*, December 24, 2003, C1.
McQueen, Rob (2009), *A Social History of Company Law – Great Britain and the Australian Colonies 1854–1920*, Aldershot: Ashgate Publishing Limited.
Okamoto, Karl S. (1995), 'Reputation and the Value of Lawyers', *Oregon Law Review*, 74, 15–55.
Painter, Richard W. (1994), 'The Moral Interdependence of Corporate Lawyers and Their Clients', *Southern California Law Review*, 67.
Painter, Richard W. (1998), 'Proposal to the ABA Ethics 2000 Commission for Amendment of Model Rule 1.13 (organization as client)', *The Professional Lawyer (ABA)*, Spring, 10.
Painter, Richard W. (2006), 'Ethics and Corruption in Business and Government: Lessons from the South Sea Bubble and the Bank of the United States', 2006 Maurice and Muriel Fulton Lecture in Legal History published by the University of Chicago Law School, available at www.ssrn.com (last accessed November 2011).
Painter, Richard W. & Jennifer E. Duggan (1996), 'Lawyer Disclosure of Corporate Fraud: Establishing a Firm Foundation', *SMU Law Review*, 50, 225–76.
Powers, William C. (2002), Report of Investigation by the Special Investigative Committee of the Board of Directors of Enron Corp., February 1, 2002, available at http://news.findlaw.com/hdocs/docs/enron/sicreport/ (last accessed November 2011).
Ribstein, Larry E. (2010), 'The Death of Big Law', *Wisconsin Law Review*, 2010(3), 749–815.
Ruder, David (2002), 'Lessons from Enron: Director and Lawyer Monitoring Responsibilities', paper prepared for the 41st Annual Corporate Counsel Institute, Chicago, Illinois, October 10, 2002, sponsored by Northwestern University School of Law.
Schenker, Joseph C. & Anthony J. Colletta (1991), 'Asset Securitization: Evolution, Current. Issues and New Frontiers', *Texas Law Review*, 69, 1369–1429.
Schwarcz, Steven L. (2007), 'Explaining the Value of Transactional Lawyering', *Stanford Journal of Law, Business & Finance*, 12, 486–535.
Schwarcz, Steven L. (2010), 'The Role of Lawyers in the Global Financial Crisis', Keynote Address, *Australian Journal of Corporate Law*.
Schwarcz, Steven L. & Iman Anabtawi (2010), 'Regulating Systemic Risk', Duke Law Working Papers. Paper 45, available at http://scholarship.law.duke.edu/working_papers/45 (last accessed November 2011).
Valukas, Anton R. (2010), Examiner's Report in re Lehman Bros. Holdings Inc., No. 08-13555, US Bankruptcy Court in the Southern District of New York, March 11, 2010.

# 15. Credit rating agencies and regulatory reform
## Aline Darbellay and Frank Partnoy

## 1. INTRODUCTION

The law and economics of credit ratings has been a topic of increasing importance and interest. A decade ago, few scholars were interested in the study of ratings from either a theoretical or empirical perspective. Yet in recent years, research in the area has become prolific. One reason for this increase in interest was the prominent role credit rating agencies played in the recent financial crisis (Crouhy et al. 2008; Mathis et al. 2009; White 2009; Griffin & Tang 2009; Hill 2010a). In particular, various commentators have raised questions about the role of rating agencies in the proliferation of structured finance products (Alexander et al. 2007; Hunt 2009).

One important area of research has addressed the unusual hybrid gatekeeper role played by the rating agencies as a cross between government and private providers of rating services. Historically, ratings issued by Nationally Recognized Statistical Rating Organizations (NRSROs) have been part of a wide range of regulatory and contractual requirements in the United States and abroad.[1] As legal requirements for ratings have proliferated, some have argued that the rating agencies have evolved from information providers to purveyors of 'regulatory licenses' (Partnoy 1999). As this argument goes, NRSROs profit from providing ratings that unlock access to the markets, regardless of the accuracy of their ratings.

Moreover, behavioral reliance on ratings reinforces regulatory reliance (Partnoy 2009b; Hill 2010b). The most intriguing example of behavioral reliance is the extensive use of ratings in private contracting. Ratings are widely used as a contractual signal of a borrower's creditworthiness. Rating triggers can give counterparties the right to require the posting of collateral based upon a rating downgrade (IOSCO 2003). Contractual clauses can accelerate the repayment of an outstanding loan if the rating falls below a certain level. As a consequence, a rating downgrade can cause a company to default under the terms of its debt covenants (Macey 2002).

In this chapter we describe some of the leading research and ideas related to credit ratings, and we assess several related regulatory proposals. Some of these proposals are new; others are not. We include proposals that became law on July 21, 2010, when President Obama signed the Dodd-Frank Wall Street Reform and Consumer Protection Act[2] (Dodd-Frank Act). Policymakers in the United States and abroad continue to consider measures to make rating agencies more accountable and rating processes more transparent. Proposals to overhaul

---

[1]    Ratings dictate the net capital requirements of banks and broker-dealers, the securities money market funds may hold, and the investment options of pension funds. On a global scale, the Basel II and III Accords explicitly recognize rating agencies, and the standardized approach assigns a prominent role to ratings to measure bank capital requirements (Weber & Darbellay 2008; Alexander et al. 2010).
[2]    Pub. L. 111–203 (2010).

credit rating agency regulation run the gamut, from increased disclosure requirements to removing references to ratings in rules and regulations. Lawmakers in the European Union have developed a new European credit rating agency regulatory authority (Regulation (EC) No. 1060/2009 of the European Parliament and of the Council on Credit Rating Agencies). In the aftermath of the financial crisis, credit rating agency regulation has also been considered as an important topic by financial market regulators in Japan, Hong Kong, Australia, Mexico and Canada (Rousseau 2009; IOSCO 2010). One theme, reflected in Section 931 of the Dodd-Frank Act, has been that the 'gatekeeper' role of rating agencies justifies a similar level of public oversight and accountability as the role played by other gatekeepers such as securities analysts and auditors.

Two leading sets of regulatory ideas cover oversight and accountability. First, with respect to oversight, one proposal, partially advanced by the Dodd-Frank Act, is to create a new regulatory body with the power to regulate rating agency practices, including disclosure, conflicts of interest, and rating methodologies. We describe and assess the advantages and disadvantages of such an approach. Second, with respect to accountability, the regulatory approaches have largely involved deference to the judiciary in a relatively small number of lawsuits involving the rating agencies. The Dodd-Frank Act includes some limited provisions that would make rating agencies more accountable by treating them the same as bankers, accountants, securities analysts and lawyers with respect to Section 11 of the Securities Act of 1933. The legislation also requires the removal of many rating-based regulations, and thus encourages a reduction in reliance on ratings for both regulatory and behavioral purposes. We describe some potential alternatives to ratings that have emerged in scholarly discussion about decreasing regulatory reliance on ratings.

These legislative reforms are the beginning, not the end, of the regulatory debate. Many of them require additional study or regulation. As a result, the future roadmap for rating agency regulation remains uncertain. Ratings regulation also will remain an important area for scholarly debate about policy. It is not clear what role the NRSROs will play, as compared to non-NRSROs, once regulatory references to ratings are withdrawn. Nor is it obvious how new oversight authority will affect the structure of the rating industry or the reliability of ratings. The success of the Dodd-Frank Act will depend on the interpretation and implementation of the new rules, with the Securities and Exchange Commission (SEC) and, potentially, a proposed new Office of Credit Ratings playing a crucial role.

This chapter proceeds as follows. The next section provides some background, explaining why ratings and rating agencies are so important even though they are often so unreliable. The following two sections address two major areas of reform: oversight and accountability. The final section concludes.

## 2.   BACKGROUND

Three players have long dominated the rating business: Moody's, Standard & Poor's and Fitch.[3] According to Egan (2008), the rating industry is a US$5–6 billion market. Despite the presence of seven additional NRSROs, the three leading rating agencies are responsible for

---

3    Fitch's market share, however, is significantly smaller than the share of its two main rivals.

98% of all outstanding ratings and collect 90% of the total rating revenue (Shorter & Seitzinger 2009). This leading trio has wielded immense, quasi-governmental power.

NRSROs have been the subject of intense criticism because of the part they played in the financial crisis. The three leading rating agencies gave high ratings to eleven large financial institutions that later faltered or failed. They rated AIG in the double-A category. Lehman Brothers retained its investment-grade rating until a few days prior to collapsing.[4] Until the subprime mortgage crisis began in 2007, the three leading rating agencies maintained triple-A ratings on thousands of subprime-related instruments that proved nearly worthless (Moloney 2008; McVea 2010). Moody's, for instance, was practically a triple-A ratings factory; from 2000 through 2007, Moody's gave its triple-A rating to 42,625 residential mortgage-backed securities (RMBSs) (Angelides 2010). In 2006, US$869 billion worth of mortgage-related securities were rated triple-A by Moody's and 83% went on to be downgraded within six months (Angelides 2010; Morgenson & Story 2010). Standard & Poor's had ratings coverage of a similar magnitude and similar ratings; Fitch's share of the ratings market was smaller, but still substantial (Hill 2010b).

In June 2008, the SEC reported that its examination of the three dominant agencies had uncovered serious deficiencies in their ratings and rating processes. Most infamously, one Standard & Poor's analyst expressed concern that the firm's model did not capture 'half' of a deal's risk, and that '[w]e rate every deal … it could be structured by cows and we would rate it' (SEC 2008b). Legislators have held hearings criticizing the agencies, and regulators recommended reforms. However, the SEC released only a handful of e-mails and little evidence from its investigation. Most of the evidence uncovered during this investigative process has remained inaccessible to researchers and the public.

**From Information Intermediaries to Regulatory Licensors**

Rating agencies began as information intermediaries, entities that step in to assess product quality when sellers cannot credibly make claims about product quality themselves.[5] Information intermediaries function best when they have reputational capital at stake and will suffer a loss if their assessments are biased, negligent, or false.

Over time, however, rating agencies have shifted from selling information to selling 'regulatory licenses', keys that unlock the financial markets. This shift began after the 1929 crash, when regulators turned to the rating agencies – primarily Moody's and Standard & Poor's – for measures of bond quality in banking and insurance guidelines. Federal Reserve examiners proposed a system for weighting the value of a bank's portfolio based on ratings. Bank and insurance regulators expressed the 'safety' or 'desirability' of portfolios in letter ratings, and used such ratings in bank capital requirements and bank and insurance company investment

---

[4]    Lehman Brothers was downgraded to junk status on September 12, 2008; on September 15, 2008, this investment bank filed for bankruptcy.

[5]    In the early debt markets, rating agencies helped to bridge information gaps between bond buyers and sellers. In 1909, John Moody published his first *Manual of Railroad Securities*, in which he rated 200 railroads companies and their securities. Moody's insight was that he could profit by selling to the public a synthesis of complex bond data in the form of single letter ratings: Aaa, Aa, A, Baa, Ba, B, Caa, Ca, C, in declining order of credit quality. These letter ratings were a rough compilation of disparate information about bonds that investors found difficult or costly to assess on their own.

guidelines. States relied on rating agencies to determine which bonds were 'legal' for insurance companies to hold. The Comptroller of the Currency made similar determinations for federally chartered banks.

The SEC's introduction of the NRSRO concept in the mid-1970s further encouraged regulators to increase their reliance on ratings.[6] During that same period, the NRSROs stopped selling ratings to investors and began charging the companies that issue the debt they rate. The issuer-pay model introduced significant new conflicts of interest – chiefly, the challenge for credit raters of impartially rating securities of companies that generate their revenues.

Beginning in the 1970s, regulators dramatically expanded their use of ratings in financial market regulations. As a result, financial markets regulators effectively mandated that institutions of all types pay heed to NRSRO ratings as a necessary step for regulatory compliance. Some rules required that certain investors could only buy bonds with high ratings. Other rules reduced capital requirements for institutions that purchased highly rated bonds. Without high ratings, bond issuers could not access certain markets because they did not have a 'license' from the NRSROs to comply with NRSRO-dependent regulations.

Regulatory dependence on ratings created higher demand for ratings and increasingly higher profits for NRSROs, even when their ratings proved spectacularly inaccurate. Too often, rating changes lagged the revelation of public information about rated issuers and instruments. Even before the recent financial crisis, prominent examples included California's Orange County and Enron Corp., both of which received high ratings until just before they filed for bankruptcy protection (Hill 2004, 2009; Flood 2005).[7] More recently, the obligations of major financial institutions, such as Bear Stearns and Lehman Brothers, received high single-A ratings just before they collapsed, and thousands of subprime mortgage-related structured finance instruments similarly received high investment grade ratings. Beginning in 2007, there were massive and sudden rating downgrades, surprising many investors and market participants who had relied on the expertise of the leading rating agencies.

During recent years, rating agencies had begun rating substantially greater numbers of borrowers and increasingly complex instruments. At the same time, the resources expended per rating declined. Specifically, as the rating agencies expanded ratings to cover large numbers of structured finance products, including tranches of various collateralized debt obligations (CDOs), some NRSROs neglected to divert resources to update rating models and methodologies or recruit additional staff needed to keep pace with financial innovation (Hill 2004). Evidence suggests the agencies were not sufficiently concerned about allocating adequate resources to rate complex deals (Kolchinsky 2010; Froeba 2010). As a senior analytical manager at one of the big three rating agencies put it in a February 2007 e-mail, '[w]e do not have the resources to support what we are doing now' (SEC 2008b).

---

[6]   More precisely, the regulatory dependence on ratings began in 1973, when the SEC proposed amending broker-dealer 'haircut' requirements, which set forth the percentage of a financial asset's market value a broker-dealer was required to deduct for the purpose of calculating its net capital requirement. Rule 15c3-1, promulgated two years later, required a different 'haircut' based on the ratings assigned by NRSROs. *See* 17 C.F.R. 240.15c3-1. Since the mid-1970s, statutes and regulations increasingly have come to depend explicitly on NRSRO ratings.

[7]   See Macey (2002).

Interestingly, even as ratings became less accurate rating agencies maintained their role as powerful and important financial market participants. Rating agencies protected their franchises, and defended themselves against liability. Historically, their success in avoiding liability has been due to legislative policy and also a handful of judicial decisions characterizing their ratings as free speech. With rare exceptions, rating agencies historically have not suffered damages from litigation even when they were negligent or reckless in issuing overly optimistic ratings. More recently, courts have expressed skepticism about the rating agencies' free speech claims. Moreover, the Dodd-Frank Act marks a turning point by removing the special treatment for rating agencies, which we address in the penultimate section.

Overall, the lack of accountability has impeded the ability and willingness of rating agencies to effectively function as information intermediaries because they do not – indeed they cannot – credibly pledge reputational and economic capital in the event they fail to perform their core function. Rating agencies that are insulated from liability have a more profitable, dominant franchise, but do not play an effective gatekeeping role.

## The Paradox of Credit Ratings

The leading NRSROs have become more profitable even as the quality of their ratings has declined. Operating margins for some agencies in recent years topped 50%. From 2000 to 2007, Moody's documents reported operating margins averaging 53%; in contrast, Microsoft and Exxon respectively had margins of 36% and 17% in 2007 (Levin & Coburn 2010). Moody's market capitalization was nearly US$20 billion at its peak; Standard & Poor's was similarly profitable and large. The companies that owned NRSROs drew savvy investors, looking to profit from the reliable returns associated with the sale of 'regulatory licenses'.[8]

Some evidence suggests that recent fundamental changes in the leading rating agencies reflect an increasingly short-term focus. For example, some commentators have suggested that Moody's culture suffered a deleterious change after that company's initial public offering in 2000 (Jones 2008). Others argue that the primary impetus driving changes in ratings practice was economic, and that rating quality and reputational capital became secondary to market share, particularly with respect to structured finance ratings, where maintaining and increasing market share was particularly important (Kolchinsky 2010).

Whatever the cause, it is apparent that the leading rating agencies compromised their standards in order to capture higher fees from increasingly complex deals (CGFS 2008). The leading rating agencies were overwhelmed by the huge volume of new structured finance deals that they were being asked to rate: one Moody's analyst even recalls rating a US$1 billion structured deal in 90 minutes (Jones 2008). The leading rating agencies also experienced pressure from clients, issuers, and arrangers of these instruments, and junior employees have said they felt pressured by more senior managers (SEC 2008b; Hill 2010a). Consider as one example the following testimony from Mark Froeba (2010), a former Moody's employee: '[Moody's senior management] used intimidation to create a docile population of analysts afraid to upset investment bankers and ready to cooperate to the maximum extent possible.'

---

[8]    For instance, Warren Buffet's Berkshire Hathaway, Inc. has owned more than 20% of Moody's outstanding common shares in recent years, and retained more than 12% of Moody's shares as of June 2011.

As the structured finance market grew, rating agencies increasingly focused on more complex, higher-margin deals. Complex financial instruments generated a significant source of revenues for rating agencies. Coval et al. (2008) report that, in 2006, 44% of Moody's revenue came from rating structured finance products, surpassing the 32% of revenue from corporate bonds. According to Levin and Coburn (2010), from 2002 to 2007, the three leading agencies doubled their revenues, from approximately US$3 billion to US$6 billion per year. Froeba (2010) contends that rating agencies were attracted by significant profits and were not deterred from rating complex financial instruments by reputational constraints.

Moreover, market forces penalized rating agencies for issuing quality ratings by awarding rating mandates based on the lowest credit enhancement needed for the highest rating (Wutkowsky & Younglai 2008).[9] In fact, the leading rating agencies faced a dilemma to maintain both market share and rating quality (Wutkowsky & Younglai 2008). They opted for market share as competitive pressures incentivized them to loosen their rating standards in order to get more issuers' fees.

To make matters worse, if a rating agency said no to a transaction, investment bankers could easily take their business to another one and obtain the desired triple-A rating (Kolchinsky 2010). Evidence from former employees suggests that the threat of losing deals was significant (SEC 2008b). Ratings could be inflated without an effective reputational constraint: rating agencies did not suffer long-term economic consequences because of the deterioration of their reputations.[10] Again, paradoxically, the value of ratings declined, even as rating agencies' profits rose.

This paradox is partly explained by over-reliance on ratings. As noted above, over-reliance on ratings has been not merely regulatory but also behavioral. Regulatory reliance on ratings implies that profits from the sale of 'regulatory licenses' do not depend greatly on the informational value of ratings. Behavioral reliance describes the fact that market participants – such as institutional investors – base decisions on ratings. If regulators and private actors defer to private standard setters, those private standard setters will earn profits from that deference even if their standards are not useful.

Accordingly, the paradox of credit ratings has persisted during the recent financial crisis. Even though ratings have plummeted in informational value, portions of the US government rescue efforts relied on them. Thus, ratings became even more important. For example, the Federal Reserve's US$1 trillion Term Auction Lending Facility (TALF) plan, which loaned money to investors to purchase new securities backed by consumer debt, mandated that only securities rated investment grade by two or more major NRSROs were eligible for government support.

Likewise, when government officials anticipated the potential negative impact of AIG's announcement of quarterly earnings in March 2009, they implemented a fourth rescue package for the insurer. They consulted privately with representatives of the dominant NRSROs to be sure the plan would be attractive enough to avoid a downgrade of AIG, because a downgrade would have killed the company. Both regulators and investors were in a ratings trap.

---

9    *See also* 'Wall Street and the Financial Crisis: The Role of Credit Rating Agencies, Exhibits', 2010. Hearing Before the Permanent Subcommittee on Investigations of the Senate Committee on Homeland Security and Governmental Affairs, April 23.

10    House of Lords, Select Committee on Economic Affairs (2009) 'Banking Supervision and Regulation', London: The Stationery Office Limited, June.

## 3. OVERSIGHT

### Research

Scholars have advocated overhaul of the credit rating industry and process for more than a decade. There were prominent calls for ratings reform in the aftermath of the Enron debacle (Hill 2004). More recently, since the financial crisis of 2007, lawmakers and regulators around the world have acknowledged that the architecture of rating agency regulatory oversight needs reform (Schapiro 2009; IOSCO 2010). Even the President's Working Group on Financial Markets (2008), long a champion of deregulation and financial innovation, sharply criticized the flaws in the rating agencies' assessments of complex products and called them a 'principal underlying cause' of the crisis. Lawmakers in the European Union have continued to push for the development of a new European credit rating agency regulatory authority.

Research has shown that necessary improvements would require both a change in regulatory structure and new regulatory powers. Like other areas of financial regulation, regulating ratings has been piecemeal and is spread throughout numerous state and federal governing bodies, including securities, banking, and insurance. A more uniform regulatory structure would consolidate ratings regulation within one umbrella organization with additional responsibilities and new powers. The Dodd-Frank Act includes several attempts to follow this approach.

Some scholars are skeptical of proposals expanding oversight of rating agencies to a great extent. White (2009) contends that some recent regulatory reform is misguided and would make incumbents even more important (Segal 2009). Hill (2010b) argues that regulators would not be able to detect rating inaccuracies better than market participants such as the self-interested money managers who failed to discipline the rating agencies.

The following discussion appraises several regulatory approaches. The next Section discusses the approach actually taken in the recently-enacted Dodd-Frank Act.

### Regulatory structure

One approach would be to create a single independent Credit Rating Agency Oversight Board (CRAOB), with a structure and mission similar to that of the Public Company Accounting Oversight Board (PCAOB). It could be a free-standing entity created by statute to oversee registration, inspections, standards, and enforcement actions related to NRSROs, just as the PCAOB oversees audit firms (Partnoy 2009a; Smith 2009a). The board could also encourage and facilitate the development of alternatives to NRSRO ratings among market participants.

Two alternatives to that approach would be to establish an office within the SEC strictly dedicated to the regulation of NRSROs, with enhanced powers, or to house oversight of rating agencies within the PCAOB (Partnoy 2009a; Smith 2009a). The Dodd-Frank Act opted for the former approach, creating a new SEC Office of Credit Ratings, although the SEC had delayed implementing this new office as of 2011. In either approach, the functions and duties of a rating agency overseer would be somewhat consistent with the mandate of the PCAOB, which was created to protect investors and the public interest by promoting informative, fair, and independent audit reports. Nevertheless, integrating credit rating agency oversight duties into the PCAOB would present organizational and legislative challenges.

Ideally, a consolidated rating agency overseer would have two overriding characteristics: independence and specialized expertise. A free-standing board would require independent funding so that it would not depend on Congress or other agencies for frequent funding or decision-making.[11] Securing reliable funding would be particularly important in order to offer salaries sufficient to attract high caliber board members. Board members should have specific expertise in assessing credit risk and, more generally, an understanding of financial markets, asset pricing, and alternative information sources and intermediaries. Members of the board should be independent and appointed for limited terms. The appointment process should be designed to limit the potential for influence by the rating agencies, and board members should not be permitted to join NRSROs after their service.

The Dodd-Frank Act follows the approach of giving the SEC increased oversight of the rating business. Some critics argued that this approach would be suboptimal, because the SEC has been reluctant to strengthen accountability and disclosure rules in the past (Partnoy 2009a). In fact, the SEC's Office of Credit Ratings remains unstaffed and inactive a year after the passage of the Dodd-Frank Act.

Critics of a free-standing rating agency oversight board counter that more fragmentation of financial regulation would add more layers to the already complex web of financial market regulation in the United States. They also believe that the SEC already has the staff, expertise, and contacts to regulate rating agencies; they say it simply needs greater authority and resources from Congress (Manns 2009; Smith 2009b). In any event, the future of the SEC's new Office of Credit Ratings remains unclear.

### Scope of regulatory authority
Below we briefly highlight a few areas related to the scope of regulatory authority, some of which have generated scholarly interest. The SEC's regulatory authority in particular is in flux. Although the SEC adopted new rules for credit ratings pursuant to the Credit Rating Agency Reform Act of 2006, the scope of that legislative authority was limited.[12] The Dodd-Frank Act expanded the SEC's regulatory authority, and the SEC continues to promulgate new rules in the area. We anticipate that these areas will be of scholarly interest in the future.

*Disclosure of rating actions*   One open question is whether a rating agency overseer should have the statutory authority to require significantly more extensive NRSRO disclosure, including a complete record of rating history, such as initial rating, upgrades, downgrades, placements on watch for upgrade or downgrade, and withdrawals.

---

[11]   Initial funding could be in the form of an endowment; alternatively, funding could be provided through required, periodic NRSRO user fees or transaction fees.

[12]   While the Credit Rating Agency Reform Act of 2006 standardized the process for NRSRO registration and gave the SEC new oversight powers, it prohibited the SEC from regulating 'the substance of credit ratings or the procedures and methodologies by which any [NRSRO] determines credit ratings'. The Act also stated that it 'creates no private right of action'. The rating agencies supported this Act, in part because its scope was so narrowly circumscribed. In June 2008, the SEC released a report outlining serious deficiencies in the rating process. It subsequently adopted new rules designed to increase the transparency of NRSRO rating methodologies, strengthen NRSRO disclosures of rating performance, prohibit certain conflicted NRSRO practices, enhance NRSRO recordkeeping, and eliminate certain regulatory references to ratings.

Disclosure proposals were previously more limited, in part due to the scope of regulatory authority granted by the Credit Rating Agency Reform Act of 2006 (Bai 2010). For example, the SEC finalized new rules in February 2009 that require NRSROs to make available to the commission individual records for each of their outstanding ratings showing all rating actions. In addition, the rules require NRSROs to publicly disclose rating action histories in eXtensible Business Reporting Language (XBRL) format. However, they can delay disclosures for six months and must disclose rating action histories only for a randomly selected 10% of issuer-paid ratings. Similarly, in February, the SEC proposed requiring disclosure, on a 12-month delay, of all issuer-paid ratings issued on or after June 26, 2007. Under the rules adopted in February and proposals still pending, unsolicited ratings and subscriber-paid ratings are exempt from disclosure.

Congress could authorize the board to require that NRSROs disclose complete records to the public, not merely to the regulator.[13] In addition, disclosure could extend to unsolicited ratings and subscriber-paid ratings. Current rules do not provide investors with the level of information necessary to assess and compare ratings and rating agencies. Securities included in one NRSRO's 10% disclosure pool are not necessarily included in other NRSROs' pools, thus making a true comparison between rating agencies impossible. Moreover, excluding unsolicited and subscriber-paid ratings from public analysis eliminates valuable data from market scrutiny. Therefore, effective oversight of the rating business must include market oversight, which requires that investors have access to complete data regarding ratings. Critics, however, argue that requiring full disclosure for subscriber-paid ratings would undermine the business model of agencies that issue them.

*Symbology* Regulating the use of rating symbols is a contentious topic. Although an oversight board might assess different categories of ratings and require NRSROs to use alternative symbology (e.g., numbers instead of letters, or letter subscripts) for ratings in different categories, it arguably should be cautious in exercising that power. The regulation of rating symbols might generate substantial benefits, but potentially could intrude into rating agencies' practices of assessing borrowers and debt instruments.[14]

In June 2008, the SEC proposed amendments to current regulations to require NRSROs to distinguish ratings on structured products by either (i) attaching a report to the rating itself describing the unique rating methodologies used in establishing the rating and how the security's risk characteristics differ from others (i.e. corporate bonds); or (ii) using symbols unique to structured products only (i.e. numbers rather than letters). The SEC's intent was to spur investors to perform more rigorous internal risk analysis on structured products, thereby reducing undue reliance on ratings in making investment decisions. In November 2009, the European Union adopted Regulation (EC) No. 1060/2009 on Credit Rating Agencies, requiring that rating agencies identify ratings on structured products, as well as unsolicited ratings, by different symbols (preamble (21) and (40), art. 10 para. 3 and 5).

Alternative symbology could benefit investors in a number of ways (SEC 2008b). Particular letter ratings mean different things when applied to structured finance issuers as

---

[13] The Dodd-Frank Act has addressed this. See below.
[14] The Dodd-Frank Act has partially addressed this. See note 29 and accompanying text.

opposed to corporate issuers or municipal issuers.[15] Different symbols for structured products could help differentiate risk for investors, signaling that the securities' risk characteristics are more volatile than those of other securities.

On the other hand, if NRSROs were required to use different symbols to rate different categories of securities, the investing public might be more confused than informed. The rating agencies also contend that mandating different nomenclature for different classes of securities would violate their First Amendment protection, although they have not succeeded with this particular free speech argument in any venue. In any case, symbology regulation is a sensitive area in which both proponents and opponents have strong views about the benefits and costs.

*Methodologies*   Some scholars have argued that flawed methodologies were a core reason NRSROs gave overly high ratings to complex structured finance instruments (Manns 2009; Lewis 2010). Allowing investors the opportunity to analyze rating agencies' methodologies could serve as a vital market-based quality check (IOSCO 2008).[16]

Previous SEC registration rules required minimal disclosure of methodologies. Rating agencies' registrations were stale, and their descriptions of methodologies and procedures were opaque (SEC 2008b). It has not been helpful for investors for rating agencies to release their general statistical methods and models without also specifying the assumptions in those models.

Arguably, regulation should focus on disclosures that would enable investors to assess key underlying variables, such as expected probability of default (Smith 2009b). Letter ratings alone are not particularly helpful in this assessment. Indeed, the rating agencies admit that letter ratings are ordinal, not cardinal, in that they rank issues in order of relative credit risk, but do not specify any particular expected default (Partnoy 2009a). Yet the rating agencies use default probabilities in their models, and ratings reflect implied default probabilities, which can vary substantially from those implied by market prices.

On the other hand, rating agencies contend that their methodologies are proprietary and that requiring detailed disclosure of their methodologies would promote free-riding, remove incentives for innovation, and leave the market with a smaller number of similarly derived ratings rather than a larger pool of ratings based on different methods of analysis.

Certain rating methodologies might be systemically important enough to the global market to warrant regulation notwithstanding the agencies' concerns (Smith 2009b). For example, an oversight board might sanction rating agencies whose ratings consistently failed to meet or exceed an acceptable level of accuracy. The board could bar NRSROs from issuing ratings on new types of securities for which there is little historical data. It also could require NRSROs to use third-party due diligence services to ensure the accuracy of data used to establish ratings on complex securities. Such powers should be exercised cautiously and only after the regulator has investigated the potential costs and benefits.

---

[15]   At a basic level, different symbols for different classes of securities would notify users that the agencies used different methodologies to generate the ratings.

[16]   The Dodd-Frank Act has addressed disclosure of methodologies. See note 31 and accompanying text.

*Conflicts of interest*  Even before the Dodd-Frank Act, Section 15E(h)(1) of the Securities Exchange Act of 1934 required NRSROs to establish, maintain, and enforce policies and procedures reasonably designed to address and manage conflicts of interest (Bai 2010). Congress directed the SEC in 2006 to issue final rules to prohibit or require the management and disclosure of conflicts of interest. However, the SEC was reluctant to, and did not, take full advantage of its power.

Although Congress and regulators have criticized the conflicts of interest between issuers and rating agencies, scholars have responded that a shift to an investor-pay business model is not viable given the public good nature of ratings and the minimal incentives for investors to pay for credit ratings (Grundfest & Hochenberg 2009). Forcing rating agencies to rely exclusively on investors to generate rating fees would result in a lack of financial resources and therefore a decreasing production of financial information (Bai 2010). Further, subscriber-paid NRSROs are not exempt from conflicts of interest. They are subject to potential pressure from clients to slide ratings one way or another. For example, institutions that can only invest in highly rated instruments might pressure a rater to guarantee that a particular security receives an investment-grade rating. Others might press the rating agencies for lower ratings in hopes of receiving higher returns.

An alternative to a blanket prohibition of the issuer-pay business model would be to require disclosure of business relationships and to prohibit NRSROs from engaging in business activities other than issuing ratings. Auditors face similar restrictions. Both the SEC and the rating agencies recognize that conflicts of interest are endemic in the rating process, and the SEC (2008a) stated that 'NRSROs that are compensated by subscribers appear less likely to be susceptible to "rating shopping" or reducing quality for initial ratings to induce revenues'. Increased disclosure rules and prohibitions on ancillary business activities arguably should apply equally to all NRSROs.[17]

*Fees*  Not surprisingly, the disclosure of rating agency fees and compensation has been a controversial issue. The rationale for requiring disclosure of rating agency fees and compensation is similar to that requiring disclosure of executive compensation more generally: disclosure reduces agency costs and enables investors to determine whether the incentives of the rating agency are sufficiently well aligned with their own to warrant investing. Many commentators believe the overseer should require rating agencies to disclose their fees; they also call for a re-examination of the compensation structure of NRSROs (SEC 2008b; Bai 2010).

Requiring public disclosure of fee schedules and individual rating fees for every rated deal could increase incentives for ratings accuracy by creating a new method of competition in the rating business.[18] 'Rating shopping' based on fee levels would not present the same conflicts and challenges as 'rating shopping' based on rating standards. Moreover, such disclosure could also reveal potential conflicts of interest arising from an issuer's heavy use of one particular agency.

---

[17]  The Dodd-Frank Act addresses conflicts of interest at several points, but only weakly. See note 33 and accompanying text.

[18]  The rating agencies previously disclosed only summary information regarding fees, and they did not make data available for fees on individual deals.

Alternative pay structures, and the power to reform those structures, might also be considered. Some critics have suggested that issuers could pay a small percentage of any fees upfront, with the remaining fee being 'earned out' in the following years, until the maturity of the rated instrument (Partnoy 2009a; Smith 2009b). In order to motivate NRSROs to update their outstanding ratings regularly, fees could depend on certain contingencies or milestones, and might even be related to the accuracy of the rating, as assessed by comparison to other measures of credit risk, including market measures. Over time, such performance-based compensation could discipline NRSROs to strive for greater accuracy (Manns 2009).[19] However, these fee structures could create perverse incentives if rating agencies became reluctant to downgrade borrowers or debt instruments for fear of causing further deteriorations that would lead to further downgrades (Hill 2004).

*Access to inside information*   In 2000 the SEC implemented Regulation Full Disclosure – or Regulation FD – in order to eliminate the selective disclosure of material information to a few privileged interested parties (Jorion et al. 2005). For years rating agencies enjoyed an exemption from Regulation FD,[20] thereby allowing them to receive inside information from issuers that is not shared with the market. Therefore, rating agencies often had access to information denied to analysts and investors (Flood 2005). The agencies contend that the exemption is needed in order to fully evaluate credit risk.

However, a strong case can be made that this exemption was unjustified (Partnoy 2009b). The Regulation FD exemption gave to rating agencies an unfair privilege as compared with other market participants in need of financial information (Jorion et al 2005). Further, it has not been apparent that rating agencies incorporated inside information in their ratings. Most notoriously, even though Enron made non-public rating agency presentations, information about the risks described in those presentations was not reflected in Enron's ratings. The same has been true of structured finance ratings.[21]

Regulators also could set governance standards for NRSROs more broadly. It is worth noting that federal overseers have become more involved in governance of other financial institutions as the government's interest in those institutions has increased during the financial crisis. Rating agencies, too, played a key role in the debacle, and their quasi-governmental powers arguably require stronger checks and balances.

### Summary of the Dodd-Frank Act and Open Questions

### Summary of the Dodd-Frank Act

The Dodd-Frank Act sets up a new regulatory structure for rating agencies, increasing authority to supervise the rating industry. As noted above, Section 932(a)(8) enhances oversight of the rating industry through the creation of a new authority within the SEC: the Office of Credit Ratings.[22] Ultimately, the Office of Credit Ratings is to have staff and a director who

---

[19]   Alternatively, rating agencies might be required to hold stakes in certain instruments that they rate highly.

[20]   17 C.F.R. 243.100-243.103

[21]   The Dodd-Frank Act requires the SEC to remove the Regulation FD exemption. See note 32 and accompanying text.

[22]   15 U.S.C. 78o-7(p); see above.

will police the rules of rating agencies and file an annual report to the public.[23] These supervisory rules result from the realization that rating agencies are fundamentally commercial, thereby implying that they have to be subject to stricter regulatory standards similar to other gatekeepers such as auditors and securities analysts. The Dodd-Frank Act expressly acknowledges the systemic importance of ratings.[24]

The Dodd-Frank Act gives regulators increased powers to set standards in the rating industry. The emphasis is on transparency; rating agencies are required to disclose a significant amount of information.[25] The intent is to provide regulators and investors with more information about NRSRO ratings (Dallas 2011). NRSROs have to file reports with the SEC and these reports must be made available to the public as well.

The statute gives the SEC the ability to bar NRSROs in case of serious shortcomings in how they rate. Under Section 932(a)(3)(I), the SEC has the ability to revoke the registration of a NRSRO with respect to a particular class of securities.[26] There are new governance rules. NRSROs have to establish effective internal control structures. Internal controls govern the implementation of the policies, procedures and methodologies for determining ratings.[27]

The law also provides that the SEC must implement rules requiring that NRSROs disclose their rating performance. Disclosure requirements under Section 932(a)(8) aim at allowing users to evaluate the accuracy of ratings and compare the performance of ratings by different NRSROs.[28]

Section 938(a)(2-3) requires NRSROs to (i) define the meaning of any rating symbols and (ii) apply any symbols consistently.[29] NRSROs can use the same symbols across different categories of financial instruments if their symbols are used in a consistent manner. A triple-A rating in structured finance should have the same meaning as a triple-A rating in corporate or sovereign debt. Otherwise, rating agencies have to use symbols that differentiate between different rating categories. Rating agencies will likely have to add new symbols in the structured finance segment. Thus, these provisions appear to have recognized the controversial nature of symbology reform, discussed above, and follow a middle ground approach.

The Dodd-Frank Act establishes new regulation of rating procedures and methodologies: NRSROs must create a form to accompany the publication of each credit rating that discloses information on rating methodologies.[30] Investors are given access to information regarding the assumptions underlying the ratings such as the correlation of defaults. Rating agencies must determine and publicize which five assumptions would have the greatest impact on their ratings if they were false. This provision also is responsive to prior research on rating agencies: if this information had been available with respect to the subprime mortgage market, investors might have better understood that CDO ratings were heavily dependent on variables such as default correlations and home price appreciation, and they might have been able to

---

[23] With the new Office of Credit Ratings and the many supervisory rules, the Dodd-Frank Act goes further than what most scholars were asking for.
[24] Section 931(1).
[25] See above.
[26] 15 U.S.C. 78o-7(d)(2)(A).
[27] 15 U.S.C. 78o-7(c)(3)(A).
[28] 15 U.S.C. 78o-7(q)(1).
[29] See note 14 and accompanying text.
[30] 15 U.S.C. 78o-7(s)(1).

assess more completely the risk that CDO ratings would have been rapidly downgraded with increasing default correlations and/or declining house prices.[31]

The qualifications of analysts will now fall under regulatory scrutiny. Section 936 includes requirements for standards governing rating agencies' analysts. A new training process will be supervised by the government. Regulators will have a role to play with respect to whether analysts hired by rating agencies have sufficient skills.

With respect to access to inside information, Section 939B requires the SEC to remove the exemption for rating agencies from Regulation FD. As noted above,[32] this exemption allowed issuers to give material non-public information to rating agencies for the purposes of determining or monitoring ratings. The Dodd-Frank Act acknowledged that there is no justified reason to privilege rating agencies in access to financial information.

Finally, legislators were not able to agree on mandatory rules to resolve conflicts of interest in the rating industry.[33] Section 931(4) of the Dodd-Frank Act merely acknowledges that rating agencies face conflicts of interest that need to be addressed. Pursuant to Section 932(a)(8), the Office of Credit Ratings is charged to ensure that NRSROs ratings are not unduly influenced by conflicts of interest.[34] A few governance rules require rating agencies to monitor conflicts of interest. For instance, the board of directors of the NRSROs has a duty to address conflicts of interests.[35]

These modest governance reforms arguably are directed at symptoms, not causes. For those who believe that conflicts of interest arise primarily out of the issuer-pay business model, the most effective solution would consist of reverting to subscriber-paid ratings. However, that kind of dramatic change was too difficult and controversial for Congress. Instead, the Dodd-Frank Act called for various governmental bodies to undertake studies to analyze how to address the conflict-of-interest issue. Sections 939C-E contemplate three studies: an SEC study on strengthening credit rating agency independence, a Government Accountability Office study on alternative business models, and an SEC study (and rulemaking) on assigned credit ratings.

## Open questions
The Dodd-Frank Act provides for credit rating agency oversight similar to oversight of other gatekeepers. Yet the Act provides regulators with significant room for interpretation and implementation. It is not clear to what extent and in what direction the SEC will use its enhanced regulatory powers. Moreover, the question arises as to whether the Office of Credit Ratings will take full advantage of its new regulatory authority. In comparison to the previous regulatory regime, the rules will be more stringent.

---

[31]   See note 16 and accompanying text.
[32]   See note 21 and accompanying text.
[33]   See note 17 and accompanying text. Senator Al Franken championed a proposal that would end the practice of issuers choosing the rating agencies. The Franken amendment would have created a board, overseen by the SEC, which would have assigned rating agencies to provide ratings in order to eliminate conflicts of interest. However, the House of Representatives did not accept the proposed solution and Congress had to strip the Franken amendment out of the financial reform bill (Sorkin 2010). A similar proposal came from Mathis et al (2009), suggesting that a central platform could organize the rating process by acting as an independent intermediary between rating agencies and issuers.
[34]   15 U.S.C. 78o-7(p)(1)(A)(iii).
[35]   15 U.S.C. 78o-7(t)(3)(B).

Concern has already been raised that the new bureaucracy might reinforce the rating oligopoly. Altman et al. (2010) suggest that too much oversight would undermine competition in the rating industry by raising regulatory barriers to entry. The oversight framework may make it difficult for competitors of Moody's, Standard & Poor's, and Fitch to comply with all the regulatory requirements. It will be easier for leading rating agencies to hire qualified analysts under the new training process. It will be crucial to monitor these issues since the purpose of the Dodd-Frank Act is not only to enhance the regulatory oversight but also to promote competitive incentives in the rating industry. Moreover, behavioral 'stickiness' such as described by Hill (2010b) may keep issuers and investors turning on the same rating agencies. The positive effect of the Dodd-Frank Act consists of reducing over-reliance on the credit ratings of the leaders in the rating industry. The agency reform would, however, be counterproductive if it raises additional barriers to entry.

Removing the exemption from Regulation FD is a significant change, but its effects will depend substantially on how issuers react. Will they disclose more information to the public? Or, as some commentators have stated, will they enter into confidentiality agreements under Rule 100(b)(2)(ii) of Regulation FD, or perhaps some new SEC rule, which would enable them to disclose material non-public information to rating agencies (Quinlivan 2010)?[36] Moreover, the effects of removing the Regulation FD exemption will depend on regulatory interpretations and SEC rulemaking. The changes will have little impact if the rating agencies are deemed not to be investment advisers, or do not otherwise fall within the definition of enumerated entities under Rule 100(b)(1) of Regulation FD (Quinlivan 2010).

The Dodd-Frank Act seeks to address concerns about the systemic risks posed by ratings; it mentions this issue in the first sentence of its section on credit rating agency reform. However, Congress has not taken any direct measures specifically designed to address systemic problems in the rating industry.[37] Only a few research articles have focused on these problems. One example is a paper discussing the necessity of macroprudential regulation in addressing the systemic risks inherent to ratings (Sy 2009). The systemic risk question should be increasingly taken into account by regulators and researchers.

Last but not least, Dodd-Frank leaves open the question of conflicts of interest in the rating industry. As noted above, the few governance rules address the symptoms of the problem but not the causes. The government studies might offer innovative solutions, or they might leave in place the issuer-pay business model.

---

[36] It is unclear what regulatory treatment applies to ratings based on inside information subject to confidentiality agreements: if the resulting ratings are disclosed to the public, rating agencies may be accused of infringing the confidentiality agreements; if the resulting ratings are selectively disclosed to subscribers, rating agencies may be accused of violating Regulation FD.

[37] Even though the Dodd-Frank Act did not explicitly address the systemic risk issue, certain regulatory measures such as the enhanced agency oversight and the removal of regulatory references to ratings may play a role. The removal of regulatory references to ratings may help decrease systemic risks in the rating industry by reducing over-reliance on ratings.

## 4.   ACCOUNTABILITY

### Research

Research on the accountability of rating agencies has focused on two threats to rating agencies as gatekeepers: liability and competition. A credible threat of civil liability could force rating agencies to be more vigilant in guarding against negligent, reckless, and fraudulent practices. A credible threat that both regulators and market actors will switch to alternatives to ratings could force rating agencies to behave more like information intermediaries than providers of 'regulatory licenses'.

### Eliminating the rating agency exemption from liability

Historically, the threat of liability has been an effective tool in encouraging gatekeeper accountability. In general, gatekeepers are less likely to engage in negligent, reckless, or fraudulent behavior if they are subject to a risk of liability. As rational economic actors, gatekeepers factor in the expected costs of litigation, including the cost of defending lawsuits as well as any damage awards or settlements.

Although most financial market gatekeepers have been subject to serious litigation threats, rating agencies have not been constrained by civil liability; they have been sued relatively infrequently, and rarely have been held liable (Partnoy 2006). Given the litigation track record, the fact that the rating agencies have published unreasonably high ratings should not be surprising. Some market observers believe that, with appropriate changes in policy, litigation could become a viable tool for ensuring NRSRO accountability. Hunt (2009) argues that a mechanism to deter rating agencies from issuing low-quality ratings is especially needed for novel product ratings, because reputational constraints fail to work for novel products.

Litigation against the rating agencies was often deterred by statutory provisions and judicial precedents that limited the liability of NRSROs. A handful of judicial decisions accepted the rating agencies' assertion that ratings are merely 'opinions,' which, under the First Amendment, should be afforded the same free speech privileges as opinions of publishers. Moreover, some securities laws explicitly exempted rating agencies from liability. NRSROs were immune from liability for misstatements in a registration statement under Section 11 of the Securities Act of 1933. Rule 436(g) – recently repealed by the Dodd-Frank Act – provided that NRSROs were exempt from expert liability under Section 11. The Credit Rating Agency Reform Act of 2006 also included some limitations on private rights of action.

The threat of NRSRO liability also was limited by judicial precedent in the area (Partnoy 2002). Rating agencies were sued following a number of defaults, including class action litigation related to the Washington Public Power Supply System default in 1983; claims related to the Executive Life bankruptcy in 1991; a suit by the Jefferson County, Colorado, School District against Moody's in 1995; and claims by Orange County, California, based on professional negligence, against Standard & Poor's in 1996. However, the only common element in these cases was that the rating agencies won (Partnoy 2002). The suits were dismissed or settled on favorable terms to the rating agencies.[38]

---

[38]   For instance, Orange County's US$2 billion lawsuit against Standard & Poor's netted a paltry settlement of US$140,000, roughly 0.007% of the claimed damages.

A recent example was the portion of the consolidated Enron litigation involving claims brought by the Connecticut Resources Recovery Authority.[39] The Enron court, like some other courts, extended a qualified First Amendment protection to rating agencies. Ironically, in doing so, the judicial decision cited the Senate Committee on Governmental Affairs report, 'Financial Oversight of Enron: The SEC and Private-Sector Watchdogs' (2002) and its statement that 'It is difficult not to wonder whether lack of accountability – the agencies' practical immunity to lawsuits and nonexistent regulatory oversight – is a major problem.'

More recently, a few courts have expressed skepticism about judicial protection of rating agencies from liability. One plaintiff has had success alleging that Moody's made misrepresentations regarding its independence and rating methodologies.[40] Another court indicated skepticism of the rating agency's First Amendment argument in the context of private placements, where the rating is not published generally to the public.[41] With respect to other cases related to the financial crisis, courts have denied motions to dismiss claims against the rating agencies, so these claims likely will be adjudicated in the near future. As one example, the California Public Employees' Retirement System (Calpers) won an early court decision against the three leading rating agencies (Morse 2010). The pension fund claims that it lost about US$1 billion U.S. dollars due to inaccurate ratings.

This judicial pushback against the rating agencies' free speech assertions is strongly rooted in the economics of ratings, and the fact that rating agencies are compensated for their 'opinions' by the same issuers they are opining about. Rating agencies' profit margins have exceeded 50%, whereas more traditional publishing companies' profit margins have been less than 10%. Given the high profile nature of the problems with rating agencies and the continuing profitability of the rating business, rating agencies hardly act like publishers, something courts are finally recognizing.

In order to make NRSROs properly accountable, critics contend, there must be a real threat of liability (Partnoy 2006). Many believe that Congress should amend Section 11 of the Securities Act of 1933 to add NRSROs as potential defendants. Further, they say lawmakers also should adopt legislation indicating that NRSROs are subject to private rights of action under the anti-fraud provisions of the securities laws. That legislation should include a description of the pleading standard for cases against rating agencies, to indicate that it would be sufficient for a plaintiff to plead the required state of mind by stating that the rating agency failed to conduct a reasonable investigation of the rated security or to have obtained reasonable verification from other sources independent of the issuer.[42]

One final advantage to imposing accountability on rating agencies through liability is that it would obviate the need for regulators to provide parameters upfront governing when NRSROs have satisfied their responsibilities as part of the oversight process. In other words, *ex ante* oversight does not need to be as specific or draconian if regulators and investors can rely on *ex post* adjudication of rating agency negligence, recklessness, and fraud. Through an evolutionary approach, judges and private litigants could develop a common law understanding of appropriate rating agency behavior.

---

[39]   *Newby v. Enron Corporation*, 511 F. Supp. 2d 741 (S.D. Tex. Feb. 16, 2005).
[40]   *In re Moody's Corporation Securities Litigation*, 2009 U.S. Dist. LEXIS 13894 (S.D.N.Y. Feb. 23, 2009).
[41]   *In re National Century Financial Enterprises, Inc., Investment Litigation*, 580 F. Supp. 2d 630 (S.D. Ohio. Jul. 22, 2008).
[42]   The Dodd-Frank Act has introduced a liability regime for rating agencies. See below.

As discussed below, the Dodd-Frank Act somewhat encourages litigation against credit rating agencies. It remains unclear whether either future decisions in financial crisis cases or decisions based on future conduct under the new Dodd-Frank standards will lead to substantially increased litigation exposure for credit rating agencies.

### Enhancing accountability through competition and reduced reliance on ratings

Many critics contend that competition in the rating business has not been effective. White (2009) argues that rating-based regulations created a substantial barrier to entering the rating industry. Opp et al. (2010) argue that regulatory references to ratings distort incentives in the rating industry. Some say the problem is due to insufficient industry competition and that the solution is to designate more NRSROs (SEC 2003; Cinquegrana 2009). Consistent with this view, the Credit Rating Agency Reform Act of 2006 was seeking to enhance competition in the rating industry by opening the NRSRO designation process to make sure that smaller rating agencies could compete with Moody's, Standard & Poor's and Fitch. However, merely increasing the number of NRSROs failed to change the fundamental feature of the rating business, which is that ratings are driven by 'regulatory licenses'.

Moreover, competition among NRSROs may lead to a 'race to the bottom' if NRSROs compete on lowering their standards to attract more business instead of competing on quality ratings (Coffee 2009). Rosner (2009) argues that so long as credit ratings are used in regulations, increasing the number of NRSROs may actually result in an ill-conceived competition to inflate ratings. Macey (2008) suggests that issuers may have hired the NRSROs that were the most malleable and the most liberal with the investment-grade rating. According to these arguments, competitive incentives in the rating industry can be restored only after eliminating the regulatory use of credit ratings (Darbellay 2011).

Ratings became an important tool for regulators, and sometimes a mandated tool for many categories of market participants.[43] The withdrawal of rating-based regulations is necessary (Partnoy 1999; Weber & Darbellay 2008; Casey & Partnoy 2010).[44] It would remove many of the incentives that led banks and rating agencies to create a huge market for mortgage-related securities (Casey & Partnoy 2010). However, critics contend that if 'regulatory licenses' were what was keeping market participants from using other rating agencies, diminution of the leading rating agencies' market share should have been expected after the designation in the mid 2000s of more NRSROs by the SEC (Hill 2010b). An open question suggested by this criticism is whether behavioral reliance by investors, which remains prevalent and is not directly addressed by regulation, might be the key factor driving the dominant rating agencies' market share.

In any event, removing the regulatory use of ratings will force regulators and investors to find substitutes. A variety of alternative measures may be used to evaluate credit risk and supplement or even replace ratings. They include:

---

[43]   Today, references to ratings are incorporated in investment guidelines, swap documentation, loan agreements, collateral triggers, and other important documents and provisions. Regulatory and behavioral reliance on ratings has become excessive over the past decades. However, most institutional investors do not rely exclusively on ratings. While ratings are part of the mosaic of information considered as part of the investment process, they are generally not an appropriate sole source for making decisions.

[44]   The Dodd-Frank Act seeks to remove regulatory references to credit ratings. See below.

(a)    Using the variables underlying ratings, such as expected probability of default, recovery in the event of default, and default correlation, when relevant. For example, an investor might amend its investment guidelines to state it would only purchase bonds with an expectation probability of default of 1% or less during maturity. The decision about expected probability of default then could be made based on a wide range of information.

A 'first cut' filter might be based on the market-wide expectation of default, as reflected in a bond's price. Most bond underwriters can provide this information for a range of issues.[45] Professor Edward Altman also has published extensive data in this area. In addition, credit default swap (CDS) data is available from services, such as Markit, for numerous fixed income issues. Even though CDSs have been criticized in various ways, abundant evidence suggests that CDS spreads reflect underlying credit risks more accurately than ratings (Flannery et al. 2010).

(b)    Using the default probability implied by a bond's price, not only at the time of purchase but over time, as part of their portfolio management process. Many services provide such information. Indeed, NRSROs increasingly incorporate such market measures into their own ratings, though on a lagged basis. Investors concerned about the volatility of market prices could use 30-day or 90-day rolling averages.

Rolling averages of market prices at least potentially reflect a wider range of available information than ratings, and may be a more timely and accurate measure of credit risk. Rolling averages also more accurately reflect available information than ratings and are not likely to be subject to manipulation or abuse.

(c)    Investors might revise their guidelines to reflect a blended standard of information sources used to make investment decisions based in part on professional judgment. For example, investors might rely on: (i) private information obtained through due diligence, (ii) publicly available 'soft' information, and (iii) market-based measures and prices. The blended information might include ratings.

(d)    Investors and regulators might look to the size and liquidity of an issue. The SEC recently proposed replacing reliance on ratings for Forms S-3 and F-3 and related forms and rules with provisions designed to determine whether issuers are widely followed in the market.[46]

Liquidity risk is also becoming a more important part of investment decision making. NRSRO ratings do not cover liquidity risk. As a result, the market for information about liquidity risk does not suffer from the same 'regulatory license' distortions as the market for credit risk. Many relatively new information intermediaries, such as Markit, Kamakura Corp., and some investor-paid NRSROs, have developed competing analytic systems for assessing both credit and liquidity risk.

---

[45]    Moreover, relatively inexpensive information services, such as Bloomberg and Reuters, also provide such information.

[46]    The SEC solicited comments on this proposal on February 9, 2011. See http://www.sec.gov/news/press/2011/2011-41.htm (last accessed October 2011).

## Summary of the Dodd-Frank Act and Open Questions

### Summary of the Dodd-Frank Act

The Dodd-Frank Act addresses both legal liability for rating agencies and the regulatory over-reliance on ratings.

The Act is intended to remove the rating agencies' relative immunity.[47] Section 933(a) specifies that rating agencies should be as liable for misconduct as other gatekeepers such as accounting firms or securities analysts.[48] Eliminating the exemption from liability threats makes it easier to sue the rating agencies in various ways.

The state of mind standard of the Securities and Exchange Act of 1934 potentially offers an easier path for those who sue rating agencies. Previous cases might have been decided differently under the new standard.[49] In private actions, Section 933(b)(2) makes it sufficient to prove that rating agencies knowingly or recklessly failed to conduct a reasonable investigation or to obtain reasonable verification of factual elements relied upon by their methodology.[50]

Further, Section 939G of the Dodd-Frank Act changes the impact of Section 11 of the Securities Act of 1933. The repeal of Rule 436(g) – even though not yet implemented by the SEC, as noted below – implies that rating agencies will be deemed to be experts under Section 11. The rule had shielded rating agencies from expert liability with respect to the disclosure of ratings in registration statements. Disclosure rules require the filing of written consents by experts. Since rating agencies will be considered experts under Section 11, issuers will have to seek their written consent if they want to use ratings in registration statements. If rating agencies deliver their consent, they are potentially liable as an expert under Section 11.[51]

The Dodd-Frank Act seeks to remove regulatory references to ratings in many regulations, statutes and other rules.[52] First and foremost, Section 939(a-f) has expressly removed statutory references to ratings. Even though Congress included the most important references to ratings into the amendment, such as all banking and securities references, Congress did not remove every statutory reference to ratings.[53] Pursuant to Section 939A, every Federal agency had one year to remove regulatory reliance on ratings. References to ratings thus have to be removed from every type of governmental rule.

Further, although Congress did not require the private sector to eliminate references to ratings, the agency reform should be interpreted as an important message coming from Congress. Every market participant with investment guidelines or other internal rules should understand that such guidelines or rules should not refer to ratings. The culture and practice should change: If institutional investors continue to rely on ratings after one year, their own reputational risks or even litigation risks may arise.

---

47   See above.

48   15 U.S.C. 78o-7(m)(1).

49   For instance, the Enron claims would probably have gone forward.

50   15 U.S.C. 78u-4(b)(2)(B).

51   See further below.

52   See above.

53   For instance, the Dodd-Frank Act has not removed statutory references to ratings in several provisions: title 20 with respect to student loans, title 23 with respect to highways and infrastructure finance, title 47 with respect to telephone media rules and loan guaranties. It is not clear whether Congress simply forgot some of the statutory references to ratings or whether it is a consequence of the rating agencies lobbying against the amendment.

The withdrawal of 'regulatory licenses' will fully take effect within two years. In the meantime, interested parties have to work on finding alternatives to ratings. Congress does not propose substitutes but merely requires that regulators have to come up with substitutes. As noted above, there are numerous viable substitutes for ratings.

**Open questions**

The Dodd-Frank Act has shown how to enhance accountability in the rating industry. Still, many issues remain unresolved.

One of the main changes regards the prospect of lawsuits. Courts will have to interpret the new legislation. The state of mind rule might be deemed to have limited scope. It remains unclear whether plaintiffs will be able to establish that rating agencies knowingly or recklessly failed to conduct a reasonable investigation, or precisely how courts will apply this standard.

A more difficult issue relates to the repeal of Rule 436(g). The intent was to establish a regime where rating agencies are subject to expert liability. However, major rating agencies responded to the requirement by refusing to consent to the inclusion of their ratings in certain transaction documents (Ishmael 2010). In response, on July 22, 2010, the SEC has published a no-action letter to avoid enforcement actions so long as the amendment could not be effectively implemented.[54] Moreover, on November 23, 2010, the SEC extended its no-action position pending further notice.

It remains unclear how this impasse will be resolved. One possibility is that the rating agencies will give their consent only if they are able to charge a higher fee to cover possible litigation costs. Another is that the rating agencies will persuade the SEC to act in a manner that is contrary to the mandate of the Dodd-Frank Law with respect to Rule 436(g). At this stage, it is unclear whether the rating agencies will be subject to expert liability. Since the purpose of the provision is to hold rating agencies more accountable for their ratings, industry and the SEC will have to work together towards a solution that does not undermine the intent of the financial reform.

Regarding the removal of regulatory reliance on ratings, the challenge consists of finding appropriate substitutes for ratings. The SEC seems receptive to market-based measures. Governmental agencies and market participants will have to work on finding the solutions that are most appropriate for their own needs. In order to reduce private reliance on ratings, credible alternatives and substitutes must be developed, particularly for institutions that lack the resources to assess independently the huge number of available fixed income instruments.

The purpose of any measure of risk is to get the best estimates possible of three variables: probability of default, expected recovery in the event of default, and – for investments with multiple assets – correlation of defaults. There are two potential categories of substitutes for ratings: quantitative and qualitative substitutes. Quantitative substitutes are market measures of risk. The market reflects a great deal of information. Market-based measures have historically been more accurate than ratings. As noted above, they can involve credit spreads (Partnoy 1999) or CDS spreads (Flannery et al. 2010).[55] A method

---

[54]   See above.

[55]   However, regulation based on market-based measures has the potential to distort the market overall in the same way that regulation based on credit ratings distorted ratings. If these distortions became sufficiently large, then market-based measures might no longer provide a superior indication of

that warrants consideration is to take into account lagged market-based measures, for instance 30-day or 90-day rolling averages. The advantage would be to remove the volatility arising out of a day-to-day basis measure. It will in any event be important to go beyond a simple letter rating of risk.

Once regulatory reliance on ratings is eliminated, it is not clear why the NRSRO designation should persist (Altman et al. 2010). The Dodd-Frank Act concentrates its regulatory efforts on NRSROs even though it seeks the withdrawal of rating-based regulations. After a transition period, privileges with respect to the NRSRO status are expected to disappear. Eventually, NRSRO status may merely remain as a sort of registration process instead of a certification process.

## 5.   CONCLUSION

Until recently, rating agencies had thrived from the dysfunctional approach to financial market regulation. They were largely exempt from liability and oversight, yet they benefited from regulations that required the use of ratings. That regime ended when evidence emerged of the rating agencies' prominent role in the recent financial crisis, and Congress attempted to impose a new liability and oversight regime, while eliminating regulatory reliance on ratings.

However, it remains unclear how the removal of credit rating references from regulation will affect the markets. The central question is how much investors will stop relying on ratings, and whether a healthy and competitive market for ratings will emerge. Market over-reliance on ratings will not disappear when references to ratings are removed from regulation. Behavioral reliance on ratings has deeply been anchored in the financial markets. It will take a certain period of time in order to find the appropriate substitutes for ratings. Alternatives are emerging but may be out of reach for some investors for some time. Ultimately, as institutional investors become more comfortable with alternative sources of credit information, competitive pressure could spur rating agencies to improve their performance and accountability. During this transition period, NRSROs, or at least the leading rating agencies, will still enjoy a certain privilege in comparison to other rating agencies. Meanwhile, more vigorous oversight and accountability measures can improve the performance of NRSROs.

In sum, Dodd-Frank introduces at least as many questions as it answers. What will be the effects of increased liability for rating agencies? How will rating agencies deal with issuers without an exemption from Regulation FD? What will regulators and investors use as substitutes for ratings in their own regulations and guidelines? These questions present an interesting and important agenda for future research.

---

credit risk. The key question is whether market participants could manipulate a market-based measure in the same way they have manipulated ratings (for example, by buying or selling in order to trigger a regulatory consequence). If the markets that regulators are relying on are sufficiently deep, and the time period of the rolling average is sufficiently long, that degree of manipulation is unlikely.

# REFERENCES

Alexander, Kern, John Eatwell, Avinash Persaud & Robert Reoch (2007), 'Financial Supervision and Crisis Management in the EU', available at http://www.europarl.europa.eu/document/activities/cont/201108/20110818ATT25070/20110818ATT25070EN.pdf (last accessed October 2011).

Alexander, Kern, Lord Eatwell, Avinash Persaud & Robert Reoch (2010), 'Crisis Management, Burden Sharing and Solidarity Mechanisms in the EU', available at http://www-cfap.jbs.cam.ac.uk/publications/downloads/2010_alexander__eatwell_persaud_reoch_crisis.pdf (last accessed October 2011).

Altman, Edward I., Sabri Oncu, Anjolein Schmeits & Lawrence J. White (2010), 'What Should Be Done about the Credit Rating Agencies?', NYU Stern Regulating Wall Street Blog, April 6, available at http://w4.stern.nyu.edu/blogs/regulatingwallstreet/credit-markets/regulation-of-rating-agencies (last accessed October 2011).

Angelides, Phil (2010), Opening Remarks before the Financial Crisis Inquiry Commission (FCIC), Hearings & Testimony, Credibility of Credit Ratings, the Investment Decisions Made Based on those Ratings, and the Financial Crisis, June 2, available at http://fcic-static.law.stanford.edu/cdn_media/fcic-testimony/2010-0602-Angelides.pdf (last accessed October 2011).

Bai, Lynn (2010), 'On Regulating Conflicts of Interest in the Credit Rating Industry', *New York University Journal of Legislation and Public Policy*, 13, 253–313.

BCBS (Basel Committee on Banking Supervision (2004), 'International Convergence of Capital Measurement and Capital Standards, A Revised Framework', Basel II, June, available at http://www.bis.org/publ/bcbs118.pdf (last accessed October 2011).

Casey, Kathleen & Frank Partnoy (2010), 'Downgrade the Ratings Agencies', *New York Times*. June, 4.

CGFS (Committee on the Global Financial System) (2008), 'Ratings in structured finance: what went wrong and what can be done to address shortcomings', CGFS Papers, No. 32, available at http://www.bis.org/publ/cgfs32.pdf (last accessed October 2011).

Cinquegrana, Piero (2009), 'The Reform of the Credit Rating Agencies: A Comparative Perspective', ECMI Policy Brief, No. 12, 1–11, February, available at http://www.ceps.be/book/reform-credit-rating-agencies-comparative-perspective (last accessed October 2011).

Coffee, John C. (2009), 'What Went Wrong? An Initial Inquiry into the Causes of the 2008 Financial Crisis', *Journal of Corporate Law Studies*, 9, 1–22.

Coval, Joshua D., Jakob Jurek & Erik Stafford (2008), 'The Economics of Structured Finance', Harvard Business School Finance Working Paper, No. 09-060, 1–36.

Crouhy, Michel G., Robert A. Jarrow & Stuart M. Turnbull (2008), 'The Subprime Credit Crisis of 07', available at http://papers.ssrn.com/sol3/papers.cfm?abstract_id=1112467 (last accessed October 2011).

Dallas, Lynne (2011), 'Short-Termism, the Financial Crisis and Corporate Governance', University of San Diego Legal Studies Research Paper Series, No. 11-052, 1–115.

Darbellay, Aline (2011), *Regulating Ratings, The Credit Rating Agency Oligopoly from a Regulatory Perspective*, in Dieter Zobl, Mario Giovanoli & Rolf H. Weber (eds), *Schweizer Schriften zum Finanzmarktrecht*, Zurich: Schulthess Verlag.

Egan, Sean (2008), Statement before the House Committee on Oversight and Government Reform, 'Credit Rating Agencies and the Financial Crisis', 110th Cong. 2nd Sess., H.R. Serial No. 110–155.

Flannery, Mark J., Joel F. Houston & Frank Partnoy (2010), 'Credit Default Swap Spreads As Viable Substitutes for Credit Ratings', *University of Pennsylvania Law Review*,158, 2085–2123.

Flood, John (2005), 'Rating, Dating, and the Informal Regulation and the Formal Ordering of Financial Transactions: Securitisations and Credit Rating Agencies', in Michael B. Likosky (ed.), *Privatising Development: Transnational Law, Infrastructure and Human Rights*, Leiden: Martinus Nijhoff Publishers.

Froeba, Mark (2010), Testimony before the Financial Crisis Inquiry Commission (FCIC), Hearings & Testimony, 'Credibility of Credit Ratings, the Investment Decisions Made Based on those Ratings, and the Financial Crisis', June 2, available at http://fcic-static.law.stanford.edu/cdn_media/fcic-testimony/2010-0602-Froeba.pdf (last accessed October 2011).

Griffin, John M. & Dragon Yongjun Tang (2009), 'Did Subjectivity Play a Role in CDO Credit Ratings?', available at http://papers.ssrn.com/sol3/papers.cfm?abstract_id=1364933 (last accessed October 2011).

Grundfest Joseph A. & Evgeniya E. Hochenberg (2009), 'Investor Owned and Controlled Rating Agencies: A Summary Introduction', Rock Center for Corporate Governance Working Paper Serices, No. 66, and Stanford University Law School Law & Economics Olin Working Paper Series, No. 391, 1–12.

Hill, Claire A. (2004), 'Regulating the Rating Agencies', *Washington University Law Quarterly*, 82, 43–94.

Hill, Claire A. (2009), 'Why Did Anyone Listen to the Rating Agencies after Enron?', *Journal of Business & Technology Law*, 4, 283–94.

Hill, Claire A. (2010a), 'Who Were the Villains in the Subprime Crisis, and Why it Matters', *Entrepreneurial Business Law Journal*, 4, 323–50.

Hill, Claire A. (2010b), 'Why Did Rating Agencies Do Such a Bad Job Rating Subprime Securities?', *University of Pittsburgh Law Review*, 71, 1–24.

Hunt, John Patrick (2009), 'Credit Rating Agencies and the "Worldwide Credit Crisis": The Limits of Reputation, the Insufficiency of Reform, and a Proposal for Improvement', *Columbia Business Law Review*, 2009, 109–209.

IOSCO (International Organization of Securities Commissions) (2003), 'Report on the Activities of Credit Rating Agencies', September, available at http://www.iosco.org/library/pubdocs/pdf/IOSCOPD153.pdf (last accessed October 2011).

IOSCO (International Organization of Securities Commissions) (2008), 'The Role of Credit Rating Agencies in Structured Finance Markets', Final Report, May, available at http://www.iosco.org/library/pubdocs/pdf/IOSCOPD270.pdf (last accessed October 2011).

IOSCO (International Organization of Securities Commissions) (2010), 'Regulatory Implementation of the Statement of Principles Regarding the Activities of Credit Rating Agencies', Consultation Report, May, available at http://www.iosco.org/library/pubdocs/pdf/IOSCOPD319.pdf (last accessed October 2011).

Ishmael, Stacy-Marie (2010), 'What's the SEC to do about 436(g)? Call a time out', *FT Alphaville*, July 22.

Jones, Sam (2008), 'When Junk was Gold', *Financial Times*, October 17.

Jorion, Philippe, Zhu Liu & Charles Shi (2005), 'Informational effects of regulation FD: evidence from rating agencies', *Journal of Financial Economics*, 76, 309–30.

Kolchinsky, Eric (2010), Testimony before the FCIC, Hearings & Testimony, 'Credibility of Credit Ratings, the Investment Decisions Made Based on those Ratings, and the Financial Crisis', June 2, available at http://fcic-static.law.stanford.edu/cdn_media/fcic-testimony/2010-0602-Kolchinsky.pdf (last accessed October 2011).

Levin, Carl, Senator & Senator Tom Coburn (2010), Memorandum before the Permanent Subcommittee on Investigations of the Senate Committee on Homeland Security and Governmental Affairs. 'Wall Street and the Financial Crisis: The Role of Credit Rating Agencies', April 23, available at http://hsgac.senate.gov/public/_files/Financial_Crisis/042310Exhibits.pdf (last accessed October 2011).

Lewis, Michael (2010), *The Big Short, Inside the Doomsday Machine*, New York, NY: W.W. Norton & Company.

Macey, Jonathan R. (2002), Testimony before the Senate Committee on Governmental Affairs, Hearing on 'Rating the Raters: Enron and the Credit Rating Agencies', 107th Cong. 2nd Sess., S. Hrg.107–471, Washington, D.C.: US Government Printing Office.

Macey, Jonathan R. (2008), *Corporate Governance: Promises kept, Promises Broken*, Princeton, NJ: Princeton University Press.

Manns, Jeffrey (2009), 'Rating Risk after the Subprime Mortgage Crisis: A User Fee Approach for Rating Agency Accountability', *North Carolina Law Review*, 87, 1011–89.

Mathis, Jérôme, James McAndrews & Jean-Charles Rochet (2009), 'Rating the raters: Are reputation concerns powerful enough to discipline rating agencies?', *Journal of Monetary Economics*, 56, 657–74.

McVea, Harry (2010), 'Credit Rating Agencies, the Subprime Mortgage Debacle and Global Governance: the EU Strikes Back', *International and Comparative Law Quarterly*, 59, 701–30.

Moloney, Niamh (2008), *EC Securities Regulation*, 2nd ed., Oxford: Oxford University Press.

Morgenson, Gretchen & Louise Story (2010), 'Rating Agency Data Aided Wall Street in Deals', *New York Times*, April 23.

Morse, Andrew (2010), 'Calpers Ratings Case Can Go Forward', *Wall Street Journal*, May 4.

Opp, Christian C., Marcus M. Opp & Milton Harris (2010), 'Rating Agencies in the Face of Regulation, Rating Inflation and Rating Arbitrage', available at http://papers.ssrn.com/sol3/papers.cfm?abstract_id=1540099 (last accessed October 2011).

Partnoy, Frank (1999), 'The Siskel and Ebert of Financial Markets?: Two Thumbs Down for the Credit Rating Agencies', *Washington University Law Quarterly*, 77, 619–715.

Partnoy, Frank (2002), 'The Paradox of Credit Ratings', in Richard M. Levich, Giovanni Majnoni & Carmen M. Reinhart (eds), *Ratings, Rating Agencies and the Global Financial System*, Boston, MA: Kluwer Academic Publishers.

Partnoy, Frank (2006), 'How and Why Credit Rating Agencies Are Not Like Other Gatekeepers', University of San Diego Legal Studies Research Paper Series, No. 07-46, 59–102.

Partnoy, Frank (2009a), 'Rethinking Regulation of Credit Rating Agencies: An Institutional Investor Perspective', Council of Institutional Investors White Paper, April 2009, available at http://www.cii.org/UserFiles/file/CRAWhitePaper04-14-09.pdf (last accessed October 2011).

Partnoy, Frank (2009b), 'Overdependence on Credit Ratings was a Primary Cause of the Crisis', University of San Diego Legal Studies Research Paper Series, No. 09-015.

Quinlivan, Steve (2010), 'Dealing with Rating Agencies after Regulation FD Change', October 10, available at http://dodd-frank.com/dealing-with-rating-agencies-after-regulation-fd-change (last accessed October 2011).

Rosner, Joshua (2009), 'Toward an Understanding: NRSRO Failings in Structured Ratings and Discreet Recommendations to Address Agency Conflicts', *Journal of Structured Finance*, 14, Issue 4, 7–22.

Rousseau, Stéphane (2009), 'Regulating Credit Rating Agencies after the Financial Crisis: The Long and Winding Road Toward Accountability', available at http://papers.ssrn.com/sol3/papers.cfm?abstract_id=1456708 (last accessed October 2011).

Schapiro, Mary L. (2009) 'Address to Practising Law Institute's "SEC Speaks in 2009" Program', February 6, available at http://www.sec.gov/news/speech/2009/spch020609mls.htm (last accessed October 2011).

SEC (Securities and Exchange Commission) (2003), 'Report on the Role and Function of Credit Rating Agencies in the Operation of the Securities Markets: As Required by Section 702(b) of the Sarbanes-Oxley Act of 2002', January, available at http://www.sec.gov/news/studies/credratingreport0103.pdf (last accessed October 2011).

SEC (Securities and Exchange Commission) (2008a), 'Annual Report on Nationally Recognized Statistical Rating Organizations, As Required by Section 6 of the Credit Rating Agency Reform Act of 2006', June, available at http://www.sec.gov/divisions/marketreg/ratingagency/nrsroannrep0608.pdf (last accessed October 2011).

SEC (Securities and Exchange Commission) (2008b), 'Summary Report of Issues Identified in the Commission Staff's Examinations of Select Credit Rating Agencies', July, available at http://www.sec.gov/news/studies/2008/craexamination070808.pdf (last accessed October 2011).

Segal, David (2009), 'Debt Raters Avoid Overhaul After Crisis', *New York Times*, December 8.

Shorter, Gary & Michael V. Seitzinger (2009), 'Credit Rating Agencies and Their Regulation', Congressional Research Service, September 3.

Smith, Gregory W. (2009a), 'Roundtable to Examine Oversight of Credit Rating Agencies', statement before the SEC, April 8, available at http://www.sec.gov/comments/4-579/4579-5.pdf (last accessed October 2011).

Smith, Gregory W. (2009b), 'Approaches to Improving Credit Rating Agency Regulation', testimony before the Subcommittee on Capital Markets, Insurance, and Government Sponsored Enterprises of the House Committee on Financial Services, May 19, available at http://www.house.gov/apps/list/hearing/financialsvcs_dem/gregory_w__smith_testimony.pdf (last accessed October 2011).

Sorkin, Andrew Ross (2010), 'Congress Drops Changes for Credit-Rating Agencies', *New York Times DealBook*, June 16.

Sy, Amadou N.R. (2009), 'The Systemic Regulation of Credit Rating Agencies and Rated Markets', IMF Working Paper, No. 09/129, available at http://www.imf.org/external/pubs/ft/wp/2009/wp09129.pdf (last accessed October 2011).

The President's Working Group on Financial Markets (2008), 'Policy Statement on Financial Market Developments', March, available at http://www.treasury.gov/resource-center/fin-mkts/Documents/pwgpolicystatemktturmoil_03122008.pdf (last accessed October 2011).

Weber, Rolf H. & Aline Darbellay (2008), 'The Regulatory Use of Credit Ratings in Bank Capital Requirement Regulations', *Journal of Banking Regulation*, 10, 1–16.

White, Lawrence J. (2009), 'Financial Regulation and the Current Crisis: A Guide for the Antitrust Community', available at http://papers.ssrn.com/sol3/papers.cfm?abstract_id=1426188 (last accessed October 2011).

Wutkowsky, Karey & Rachelle Younglai (2008), 'Lawmakers, former execs blast creditraters', *Reuters*, October 22.

# 16. The influence of law and economics on law and accounting: Two steps forward, one step back

*Lawrence A. Cunningham*

## 1. THEORY

### Models and their Limits

Under agency theory, shareholders are treated as principals and corporate managers as agents. The theory, elaborated since the 1970s, notes how interests of principals and agents diverge. The cost of controlling that divergence and the cost of the part that cannot be controlled are called agency costs (Jensen & Meckling 1976; Tirole 2006). Agency costs are limited by various markets, especially capital and corporate control markets. In the law and accounting context, divergence of interests between managers and shareholders can be further reduced by investing in monitoring devices, such as internal controls, board oversight, and independent auditing, and bonding devices, principally transparent accounting and financial disclosure.

To evaluate agency costs and ways to reduce them, scholars sought a proxy to express the shareholder interest and manager actions in relation to it. They found it in the efficient capital market hypothesis (ECMH), cornerstone of modern finance theory. For centuries, shareholders were seen to be interested in maximization of profits and managerial performance was measured in those terms. Beginning in the 1960s, theorists saw stock market price as a proxy for the shareholder interest. They developed the ECMH, a hypothesis that stock price incorporates all public information about a firm, including accounting measures of profits, and supplies a measure of value. The ECMH thus also suggests that stock price incorporated agency costs: companies with higher stock prices are better managed, posing lower agency costs, than those with lower prices (all other things being equal) (Fama 1970; Gilson & Kraakman 1984).

To assess the meaning of price within the ECMH requires a separate model, called the capital asset pricing model (CAPM). Dating to the 1960s, CAPM assumes investors are risk averse and hold rational expectations about expected returns (meaning expected return is the risk-free rate of return plus compensation for an investment's systematic risk). The latter is measured by the degree of variability of the individual investment versus the market, designated *beta*. Beta measures relative risk (higher ones signaling greater risk and lower ones lesser risk). CAPM and beta spawned many models to measure the value of a wide variety of capital market assets, beyond equity shares of a corporation, including options and other financial derivatives (Ross 1976; Roll 1977).

These pillars of modern finance theory have been subjected to voluminous empirical testing for generations. Tests tend to support the models, though constrained by methodological limits, and subject to qualifications that continue to result in considerable debate about their significance and policy implications (Black 1986). The most dramatic limit is the joint hypothesis problem: tests of the ECMH assume CAPM's validity while tests of CAPM assume ECMH's validity. Even so, consensus was reached on two polar forms of the ECMH: most agree that old price histories yield no useful trading information (the weak form) and most reject that inside information lacked value (the strong form). Robust debate concerns whether other public information is reflected in prices, and if so, how quickly, accurately, and meaningfully (the semi-strong form).[1]

Of particular relevance to law and accounting, tests examine the utility of accounting information and the significance of alternative approaches to identical accounting matters. (Griffin 1982; Holthausen & Leftwich 1983). At issue is whether markets are influenced by accounting forms or pierce them, reducing the importance of particular requirements of generally accepted accounting principles (GAAP). Many tests tend to support modern finance theory: market prices did not appear to be influenced by choices among accounting conventions, such as alternative ways to measure inventory or depreciation (Sunder 1975). But modern finance theory has not been proven with scientific certitude and many tests leave questions about its descriptive validity. As early as the 1980s, studies showed there is too much securities price volatility for the ECMH to hold (Shiller 1989). Anomalies have always plagued the hypothesis (DeBondt & Thaler 1985). An accounting example is how highly-priced stocks, measured by accounting metrics like the market-to-book ratio, tend to achieve lower average future returns than lower-priced stocks.

Regarding accounting in particular, research studies and the literature also generally carefully emphasize that modern finance theory's implications are limited to the importance of accounting to markets, investors outside the firm. Accounting remains vital within the firm, especially to managers whose performance and compensation is determined by accounting results. This distinction's importance is amplified in positive accounting theory, which helps explain why managers care about accounting measures, despite any stock market indifference, including how debt covenants often are tied to accounting measures (Watts & Zimmerman 1990; Walker 2006). Positive accounting theory underscores the persistence of agency costs, though capital markets can limit them.

Compounding debate are periodic market convulsions that seem to defy ECMH's proposition that price changes are due to information changes so that non-events should not induce price changes (Shleifer 2000; Shiller 2000). Examples include incidents of dramatic market swings lacking justifying cause, such as the stock market crash of 1987, the stock prices of many companies and market indexes amid the technology bubble of the late 1990s and early 2000s, and even the 'flash crash' of May 6, 2010 when stock market indexes plunged 10% in half an hour only to regain half of that by day's end. A spectacular illustration of the limits of CAPM appeared in the 1997 failure of the global hedge fund, Long Term Capital Management, managed by modern finance theory pioneers using its risk models that turned out to be less reliable in practice than in theory. Vast accounting frauds, particularly those at Enron, WorldCom, and other companies in the early 2000s, suggest outer limits of modern finance theory's assumptions and implications (Gordon 2002).

---

[1]   For a discussion of the ECMH in the wake of the recent financial crisis, see Gilson and Kraakman (Ch. 24).

Challenges to modern finance theory long questioned its assumption of investor rationality.[2] Skeptics, dating to the 1970s and 1980s, consider how investors do not always use information or probabilities but often rely on inferences and hunches (Kahneman & Riepe 1988). Proponents responded that an economic model's assumptions are irrelevant so long as it enables reliable prediction. But even this as-if rationality may not hold when deviations from expected behavior are systematic rather than random or when it is too costly for other participants to correct the misperceptions (Cunningham 2002a).

Examples of systematic departures from rationality include biases like loss aversion, manifested in greater reluctance to sell losing rather than winning stocks (Odean 1998; Kahneman et al. 1990; Benartzi & Thaler 1995). Of particular relevance to law and accounting is the concept of frame dependence, a bias that leads people to comprehend information differently according to its form of presentation (Tversky & Kahneman 1981). Frame dependence suggests that accounting conventions matter to investors, markets and pricing, including how forward-looking information is presented, the use of pro forma information, what prominence cash flow presentations are given, and whether assets are recorded at historical cost or fair value.

These systemic biases even plague professional money managers. Sophisticated arbitrageurs cannot eliminate them since there are not always good substitutes for mispriced securities and there is no assurance that market errors will be corrected before an arbitrage position must be closed out. The upshot is recurring sustained deviations between stock price and business value. Thus, the ECMH may correctly predict 'information efficiency', that price impounds public information, while not speaking to whether price is or best approximates value, a notion of 'fundamental efficiency' (Gordon & Kornhauser 1985; Stout 2003). The significance of trading based on information unrelated to fundamental value but which price nevertheless reflects, termed noise trading, remains hotly debated and related policy implications for law and accounting contestable.

**Theory into Policy**

As with most theories, the literature on both agency theory and modern finance theory cautions that these models are depictions of ideal conditions, not necessarily descriptions of real world activity (Tirole 2006). It is well known that even the best-designed monitoring or bonding devices are both costly and porous. The most well-intentioned corporate boards cannot provide comprehensive oversight, internal controls can be evaded, and even the clearest accounting principles can be manipulated and used to obfuscate financial disclosure. Capital market prices are proxies, sometimes imperfect, and there can be sustained deviations between stock prices and underlying business value. Cautious scholars are thus continually alert to two vital matters.

First, scholars seek to refine theories or assumptions to render them more plausible. Second, they are conscious that theory-reality deviations are inherent in economic modeling – no abstract economic model can perfectly accurately describe or capture reality. Aware of this, people take care to avoid invoking theory overzealously in support of normative policy prescriptions (Rock 1992). Despite caution, policy makers can miss subtleties and advance

---

[2]   For a discussion of behavioral finance and its implications for law, see Langevoort (Ch. 23).

policy by invoking theories that should not be taken literally as describing the real world. It is even possible for theorists, charting new terrain, to draw stronger conclusions from early research that later generations of researchers find requires important qualifications. The arc of efficient market research suggests a degree of such evolution. Neither point prevents the models from having substantial explanatory power, but do require reconsideration of normative policy implications (Langevoort 1992; Cunningham 1994).

Ensuing discussion illustrates using a paired example within each of four subjects, securities regulation, standard setting, corporate law, and financial auditing. The first example in each pair exhibits substantial congruence between agency theory and modern finance theory and substantial fidelity in how modern finance theory was used compared to its assumptions and limits. Hence forward-looking disclosure, mandatory cash flow statements, discounted cash flow valuation in appraisal proceedings, and the reputation model of auditing all tend to be supported by both theories, though in varying degrees and with qualifications. The second example in each pair shows considerable divergence and infidelity. Paired illustrations of these more problematic topics are pro forma reporting, fair value measures, the stock market exception to the appraisal remedy, and allowing auditors to discharge duties merely by technical compliance with GAAP.

Before turning to policy implications, it should be noted that those discussed evolved as they did amid debate and development of these theories but this is not to say that theories alone drove the changes. Many factors – economic, historical, political, ideological, and otherwise – affect policy development and adjustment. That said, there were express invocations of these theories and related literature during debate about policy development (Lowenstein 1994). That warrants recognizing them as a factor driving results, even if those results could be justified and achieved absent that set of ideas.

## 2.  FEDERAL SECURITIES REGULATION

**Forward-looking Disclosure**

Probably the most sweeping policy effect of agency theory and modern finance theory for law and accounting was the adoption of a forward-looking disclosure system by the Securities and Exchange Commission. Through the 1970s, federal securities disclosure laws focused on historical information and generally barred prospective information (Heller 1961). This policy stance reflected how traditional accounting deals with numerical history. Modern finance theory reoriented attention towards prognostication. If historical accounting information is quickly reflected in stock price and rapidly becomes valueless, what was seen to have value was information that could be used to forecast future financial performance (Cunningham 2005).

Forward-looking disclosure would transform inside information into public information, enabling it to be priced. In terms of the three forms of the ECMH, this meant exposing related information to the semi-strong form, where public information is incorporated into price, instead of its strong form, where non-public information is not incorporated into price. Congruently, to the extent that managerial disclosure of forward-looking information constrains discretion, by effectively compelling managers to share internally-generated forecasts and plans, such a regime may contribute to agency cost reduction (Burton 1974; Kripke 1970).

Despite this compelling combination of theory, considerable controversy accompanied the movement towards a forward-looking disclosure regime and, despite ultimate adoption, the issues remain real. Three arguments justify opposing forward-looking disclosure, then and now: (1) since no one can know the future, financial forecasts are inherently unreliable and misleading *per se*; (2) investors are inclined to rely on information that management supplies; and (3) since it is about the unknown future in stories told by management, it is much easier to manipulate than accounting histories. The primary argument favoring forward-looking disclosure is an underlying premise of modern finance theory about which there is little controversy: investment decisions and valuation judgments are about the future.

The fighting issue is whether investors or managers are better positioned to conduct prognostication. The traditional view, opposing forward-looking disclosure, asserted that management is better at preparing financial information and investors better at interpreting it. Proponents implied the opposite, effectively asserting that managers were better at both preparing and interpreting historical information and suggesting that forward-looking disclosure can reduce agency costs by binding managers to a degree. Proponents also redefined disclosure's target audience, from ordinary to sophisticated investors, a move partially deflecting opponents' argument (2) about propensity to vest managerial forecasts with unwarranted credence. Addressing objection (3), proponents argued that manipulation risk could be neutralized by imposing good faith disclosure duties on managers, an argument likewise supported by agency theory.

Victory in the debate gradually shifted from opponents to proponents, the latter first getting a series of modest SEC endorsements for voluntary forward-looking disclosure and ultimately a variety of mandatory items (Seligman 1982). Sub-victories concerned target investors. For nearly two decades, managers targeted forward-looking disclosure to institutional investors, including by giving analysts favored information not always given to the public at large. By the late 1990s, however, this practice came to be viewed as pernicious and was outlawed by Regulation FD, requiring that financial forecasting and guidance provided to one investor must be provided to all.[3] Regulatory resolution of the debate over forward-looking information thus strongly endorsed forecasts, often requiring them, and making them available to all. In addition, good faith duties were imposed, requiring reasonable grounds for predictions and presentation in a suitable format (Langevoort 1994).

The primary outstanding issue, in the early debate and today, is the reliability of forward-looking information (Cunningham 2005). Almost immediately after implementation, the forward-looking disclosure system led to disclosure that was inherently unreliable. Management forecasts routinely were overly optimistic. Such managerial optimism invariably appears during periods of economic exuberance, and the appearance of bubbles that eventually burst (Cunningham 2003a). Contemporary examples include the early 2000s technology bubble and housing and financial bubbles later that decade. Such phenomena retrospectively showed some prudence in the SEC's early resistance to allowing forward-looking disclosure. In response to the early period's observed optimism, a series of legal devices were designed to regulate resulting litigation, seeking to distinguish the merely unreliable from the intentionally manipulative. The chief legal tools are safe harbors (statutory, judicial and regu-

---

[3]    Selective Disclosure and Insider Trading, Federal Register 65, 51716 (Regulation FD).

latory) insulating some information from litigation review, primarily those accompanied by cautionary language about their inherent unreliability (Coffee & Sale 2011).

It is difficult to measure the net value of the forward-looking disclosure regime, though it is almost certainly positive. There is evidence that the regime enhanced information quality, increasing the value and relevance of information investors find useful. The cost of that enhancement is some earnings estimates that are overly optimistic but create market-wide expectations that pressure managers to meet them. Pressure can increase managerial propensity to manipulate accounting reports to meet previous forecasts.

A forward-looking disclosure regime can in some cases increase the risk and frequency of accounting fraud, a form of agency cost. Some interpretations of modern finance theory may discount the significance of the latter costs when asserting that markets are not fooled by forecasts. But when that assumption fails, results include distorted capital allocation and long-run investor losses. On balance, however, the forward-looking disclosure system reduced agency costs generally by generating public information incorporated into price, though at some agency cost in accounting manipulation.

## Pro Forma Reporting

A more undesirable byproduct of the forward-looking disclosure system, however, was the expansion of pro forma reporting by management. This refers to financial statement presentations that depart from required accounting conventions. This practice proliferated during the market bubble of the late 1990s and early 2000s, supported by what may have been excessively optimistic interpretations of modern finance theory and failing to emphasize agency costs sufficiently. Experience generally suggested that the practice raised rather than lowered agency costs and the practice was eventually curtailed.

Pro forma reporting was a product of the forward-looking disclosure regime because pro forma reporting was positioned in the context of how management is thinking about its business, past and future. Pro forma reporting depicts historical accounting information but in ways that depart from GAAP. It then uses that information as the basis of generating financial forecasts. It is typically less reliable than GAAP figures such as net income (Nichols et al. 2005; Fields 1988). Proponents seeking to defend it in terms of modern finance theory would have to rely upon fairly aggressive interpretations of that theory, such as that investors and markets are not fooled by alternative forms of presenting historical financial information.

The theory itself does not necessarily support such bold assertions, however. It does not say pro forma reports omitting categories of expenses that appear in a GAAP-compliant financial statement will not mislead investors. Such information could fairly be regarded as mere noise and, in theory, be ignored and not affect price, if investors can determine actual costs despite pro forma reports omitting them. But pro forma information does influence price, as the reporting that pervaded the Enron era showed, when extensive use of pro forma reporting was correlated with accounting manipulation and financial fraud (Cunningham 2003a; Gordon 2002). The result was misallocations of capital as well as enormous agency costs. If modern finance theory and the ECMH were held to deny that such price-value discrepancies could exist due to pro forma reports, then this episode provides strong evidence against them.

In response to the Enron era's pro forma calamities, the SEC adopted Regulation G to restrict the permissible scope of pro forma reporting, including by requiring any such assertions to be accompanied by the parallel results GAAP would show.[4] On the other hand, later SEC staff interpretations suggested relaxation of those restrictions.[5] To the degree that this relaxation is based on faith that efficient markets mean investors are not collectively fooled by pro forma reporting, the position is difficult to defend. Only if markets and investors really do pierce through such formal information to identify substantive reality can one have confidence in condoning its dissemination. It does not seem responsible to invoke modern finance theory to support such assertions of faith in efficient markets, and associated agency costs warrant doubting them.

## 3.   ACCOUNTING STANDARDS

### Cash Flow Statement

Both modern finance theory and agency theory supported the development within accounting of requiring a separate statement of cash flows to augment the traditional balance sheet and income statement. Modern finance theory puts future cash flows at the center of valuation exercises and agency theory supports a cash flow statement because it discourages earnings management. Insofar as using modern finance theory to promote the cash flow statement succeeded in generating additional useful information for investors and markets, it was a resounding success, though some interpretations seemed to go further to elevate cash flows and demote other accounting information.

Accounting's traditional accrual system allocates economic events to discrete fiscal periods based on links to underlying business activity. The accrual system's matching principle implements the links by burdening the income statement with expenses of the period to which they contribute revenue generation (or earlier if this cannot be determined) (Cox 1980). This focus links the income statement with specific managerial stewardship. The accrual system obscures cash flows, something modern finance theory considers central, and the theory's rise drove accounting standard setters in 1987 to require an additional statement, of cash flows, to make cash flows more transparent.[6] Using cash flow statements along with the income statement and balance sheet can be useful for detecting earnings management, by comparing reports of accrual income with reports of cash flows (Krishnan & Largay 2000). The effect is to discourage managerial accounting manipulations, a way to reduce agency costs.

Modern finance theory and agency theory both thus point to the same policy implication and, generally, there was considerable coherence between modern finance theory's theoretical support of a cash flow statement and the practical achievement of requiring one. But some proponents of modern finance theory pushed its utility a bit further, certainly more boldly than in promoting forward-looking disclosure. In this view, cash became more important than earnings or other accounting metrics as a benchmark of corporate performance and valuation.

---

[4]   Securities and Exchange Commission, Regulation G, 17 C.F.R. pt. 244 (2005).

[5]   Securities and Exchange Commission, Compliance & Disclosure Interpretations: Non-GAAP Financial Measures (Jan. 15, 2010), available at www.sec.gov/divisions/corpfin/guidance/nongaapinterp. htm (last accessed November 2011).

[6]   Financial Accounting Standards Board (1987), 'Statement of Cash Flows', Statement of Financial Accounting Standards No. 95.

The assertion that cash, not earnings, moves stock market prices suggests investors pierce accounting conventions that influence reported earnings with laser focus on expected cash flows.

Whatever its plausibility, a troubling consequence of this 'cash as king' viewpoint is how it undercuts traditional accounting functions, especially to allocate costs to multiple time periods, like depreciation, inventory accounting, even accounting for stock options. If modern finance theory says market prices result from cash flows, not earnings, this suggests managers lack capital market incentives to manipulate accounting results like earnings. Though this allows for the possibility of managerial manipulation incentives from other sources, like their own contracts and bonuses, it removes an important basis and payoff to accounting scholarship and policy invested in promoting accounting to discourage manipulation. Attention, especially in the academic literature, shifted to positive accounting theory, to explain how managers consider accounting important mainly in terms of compliance with debt and other contracts.

Modern finance theory may not overtly state that managers lack incentives for accounting manipulation, but some interpret it to mean that manipulation will not fool markets, because enough investors pierce accounting conventions to unearth business and economic reality. Yet managerial accounting manipulation does fool markets, whether based on relatively simple matters like whether a telecom company expenses or capitalizes disbursements for line costs (the WorldCom case) or more complex matters like recognizing revenue on contract formation based on forecasted cash flows from an energy-exchange derivative contract (the Enron case). It is therefore imprudent to accept interpretations of modern finance theory that make cash and cash flow the end-all and be-all of corporate financial reporting. At its best, the cash flow statement provides additional useful information and adds a tool to detect for and thus discourage earnings management, reducing agency costs, but should not be exalted. Within those limits, both agency theory and modern finance theory helpfully supported mandatory cash flow statements.

**Fair Value Measures**

The tools and ideas central to modern finance theory contributed significantly to expanded use of fair value measures in accounting rather than using its traditional cost method, though agency theory may have warranted caution in this expansion. Accounting's traditional measure for most assets is historical cost, justified as observable, objective, and reliable – though its relevance may decline with the passage of time. For certain classes of assets, current market value may be superior to historical cost for both reliability and relevance. Accounting standards have long recognized that possibility in many contexts, such as receivables/payables, the lower of cost or market principle applied to inventory, and pushdown accounting for acquired subsidiaries.

Beginning in the 1980s and accelerating rapidly during the 1990s, a strong trend began toward making fair value the preferred measure for an increasing variety of assets, a trend strongly influenced by the rising influence and expanding interpretations of modern finance theory (Siegel 1996). This refers to an elevation of references to market-based prices for capital assets, especially bonds and derivative financial instruments, whose values could increasingly be estimated by tools that trace their roots to modern finance theory's capital asset pricing model. These measures, whether based on actual market prices or implied valuations from models, were increasingly seen not only as more relevant but also potentially more reliable and objective than cost.[7] Yet markets sometimes freeze, as occurred during the financial crisis of 2008, and valuation models repose considerable discretion in managers. Both points indicate some degree of agency costs associated with fair value accounting that must be compared to agency costs incurred under traditional historical cost accounting.

The choice of asset measurement is vital both for the balance sheet, where the asset is listed, and the income statement, as it can affect both revenue or gains and expenses or losses. A good example concerns fluctuations in the prevailing fair value of marketable securities, including financial instruments and derivatives. Gains and losses are recorded on an ongoing basis, though the securities are not sold. When market prices are rising, managers may find using fair value measures appealing. But when market prices are falling, they may feel the opposite way.

In the years preceding the financial crisis that began in 2008, managers of financial institutions generally tended to favor using fair value measures for instruments like these. But as that crisis unfolded, and as markets for such instruments froze and values accordingly plummeted, they sought changes in applicable accounting standards. That turnabout raised valid questions about agency costs. True, fair value accounting in a broadly collapsing market can magnify the problem into a downward spiral. But the lack of information poses at least some cost to investors. The net balance may not be obvious but caution rather than exuberance should be used when considering the appeal of fair value accounting. More vivid support for this warning appeared in Enron's case. Enron used fair value measures to record revenue on long-term contracts when formed, shredding basic cost-based accounting traditions in favor of predictions, supported by some interpretations of modern finance theory, that misled markets and investors to allocate substantial capital to the fraudulent enterprise (Cunningham 2003a; Gordon 2002). Agency costs were enormous.

## 4.   STATE CORPORATION LAW

**Measurements in Appraisal Proceedings**

The rise of modern finance theory drove and corresponded with the broad trend in corporate law towards promoting shareholder value, measured by stock price. Within law and accounting, the trend manifested in a move towards modern finance theory techniques applied in valuation disputes, especially corporate appraisal proceedings. This involved a shift from traditional accounting measurements towards discounted cash flow analysis with reference to CAPM's beta to establish risk (Thompson 1996). In general, agency theory had little to contribute directly to this development. But insights it produces when applied to contexts like forward-looking disclosure and the cash flow statement tend to reinforce the utility of accounting information and to discourage exalting cash flow or analysis of it above traditional accounting information and analysis.

---

[7]   Financial Accounting Standards Board (2000) 'Using Cash Flow Information and Present Value in Accounting Measurements', Statement of Financial Accounting Concepts No. 7.

By statute in most states, stockholders who vote against certain transactions are entitled to a judicial appraisal of the fair value of their shares exchanged in the transaction. Before the 1980s, cases tended to estimate value by weighting accounting measures like earnings and assets, along with market price and dividend-based calculations. Beginning in 1983, in *Weinberger v. UOP, Inc.*,[8] discounted cash flow became the fashionable valuation tool, with some courts relegating accounting's traditional tools, based on earnings or assets, to the sidelines. On the other hand, the move to modern finance theory in appraisal proceedings has never been universal or complete: some courts do not adopt it in any measure and courts that do adopt it rarely use it to the exclusion of traditional valuation methods (Campbell 2003).

During this process of change, the old method came routinely to be described as the 'Delaware block method', a term that, interestingly, appears in the cases only after 1983, with each reference to it used for historical explanation only, rather than application. It refers to the exercise of estimating alternative measures of value based on earnings, assets, and market prices and then weighting them according to their relative reliability in particular cases to pinpoint value. The incremental move towards beta-based discounted cash flow valuation reflected dissatisfaction with traditional accounting approaches to valuation (Fischel 1983; Schaefer 1982). The elements used in the block method were not always reliable indicators of value. The traditional technique ultimately involved a weighting of components that seemed arbitrary, often based on intuitions about how reliable the particular numerical expressions were, rather than whether they were good indicators of value.

As a result, while proponents applaud the judicial trend to adopt modern finance theory, some lament that too few judges do so and even judges who adopt it fail to apply it in a thorough, laser-focused fashion. Thus courts give experts too much leeway and hear evidence that modern finance theory deems irrelevant. They allow debates over whether to use future versus past cash flows, whether to estimate cash flows based on past accounting earnings or some other metric, and allow the discount rate to be set either by reference to modern finance theory or using old-fashioned price-earnings ratios. Yet the virtues of modern finance theory compared to traditional methods should not be overstated. After all, the tools of modern finance theory are susceptible to the same or similar critiques leveled against the traditional block method. They require estimating future cash flows and modeling a terminal value at the estimation period's end, which can be speculative propositions. They also require identifying a group of comparable businesses and extracting their betas, a notoriously judgment-laden process.

It should be unsurprising, then, that few judges in appraisal proceedings limit inquiry solely to predicting cash flows and discounting them to present value using modern finance theory tools like beta. Assets and earnings can and often do matter and analyzing them can and often does illuminate value estimates. At least traditional analysis relies on historical realities, measures of assets and earnings, whereas modern finance theory analysis relies on finance forecasts, predicted cash flows over long time horizons using highly-contestable discount rates. If modern finance theory's contribution to valuation in appraisal proceedings were to replace traditional analysis with forecasted cash flows discounted using beta, the net effect would have been negative, not positive. Instead it contributes additional tools judges use flexibly and contextually. To that extent, properly received with judicious caution, modern finance theory has contributed a useful tool to appraisal proceedings.

---

[8]  457 A.2d 701 (Del. 1983).

## The Stock Market Exception to the Appraisal Remedy

Though appraisal remedy rights date to the nineteenth century, a stock market exception to them emerged in the late 1960s, inspired by the rise of modern finance theory, especially the ECMH. The exception, which has generated considerable debate, can be defended on two different grounds, depending in turn on the remedy's purpose (Manning 1962). If the remedy is to provide dissenting stockholders with liquidity, then the existence of a public market for shares does that adequately. But this rationale for the remedy, though once endorsed, no longer commands wide assent (Wertheimer 1998). The other, now dominant, rationale for the appraisal remedy is to deliver fair value to dissenting shareholders. The stock market exception can be justified in these terms only if market price is a reliable estimate of fair value, as modern finance theory supposes, at least compared to judicial proceedings (Seligman 1984). Agency theory may caution against expansive invocation of the exception, however, when those in control of the corporation can manipulate the timing of a transaction to extract rents from other shareholders.

Today, the stock market exception exists in nearly half the states, including Delaware, dominant domicile of large corporations. It is narrowly tailored to deny the appraisal remedy only to certain kinds of transactions involving certain kinds of publicly-traded securities. It is not embraced in the American Bar Association's Model Business Corporation Act, the statutory law in a majority of states, or in the American Law Institute's influential treatise, Principles of Corporate Governance. The Model Act flirted with the exception, adopting it in 1969 but abandoning it in 1978. Participants attributed the 1969 adoption in part to modern finance theory's assertions of capital market valuation prowess and partly to the then-accepted liquidity rationale of appraisal proceedings (Scott 1968). The 1978 version of the Model Act removed it with an oblique explanation that suggested doubt about both the efficiency theory of markets and the liquidity rationale for the remedy.

As a matter of positive law, then, modern finance theory's influence on the stock market exception to the appraisal remedy has been mixed. It has received an equally mixed reception in related legal scholarship. Some scholars enthusiastically endorse the exception as part of a general dim view of the appraisal remedy itself (Manning 1962; Fischel 1983). Others equally enthusiastically and generally endorse the remedy and reject the exception, directly challenging modern finance theory's assertions that market prices are good or best value estimates, denying that market prices protect investors (Eisenberg 1976; Stout 1990). In between are those opposed to invoking the exception when addressing conflict-of-interest transactions, a recognition of the role of agency theory (Thompson 1995; Seligman 1984). This middle stance appears to be defensible without regard to whether markets are efficient, at least if market prices do not reveal the value effects of self-dealing by managers or controlling shareholders. It is an agency cost problem not solved by modern finance theory.

But any serious limitations on the ECMH would warrant more strenuous objections to the stock market exception to the appraisal remedy and, more generally, skepticism about the weight courts should give to market prices in any event. Several factors would warrant judicial subordination of market price to a substantive valuation inquiry. First, cash-out mergers, the most frequent transaction leading to the appraisal remedy, often are effected at a premium to prevailing market price. Some scholars say this raises doubt about market efficiency as a fundamental matter, though this could reflect the distinction between the value of a single share and the value of corporate control (Wertheimer 1998). Second, market price volatility is significant, so determining at what point price is a good or best estimate of value can be difficult. But an appraisal proceeding requires selecting a particular point. Law may rightly be skeptical of relying on market price at the date of a transaction, since the deal's proponents choose that date and may choose a date they know or believe to represent a low point for the stock, not a high point.

Ultimately, the ECMH has had only a narrow and limited impact on the availability of appraisal proceedings to dissenting stockholders, and agency theory makes an important contribution to explaining why. The stock market exception is only recognized in about half the states, although they are states in which large numbers of large corporations are incorporated. Within those, there are statutory limits on the transactions to which it applies. Scholars, and courts, remain cautious about jettisoning the valuation inquiry simply in favor of market price, recognizing inherent problems arising from conflicts of interest, stock market pricing volatility, and insider power to determine the timing of transactions otherwise triggering appraisal rights. Accordingly, while modern finance theory spawns considerable discussion and debate about the appraisal remedy and valuation, an intellectual plus, it has more modest influence on the law governing the availability of this remedy, in part a reflection of offsetting concerns agency theory identifies.

## 5. FINANCIAL AUDITING

### A Reputation Model

Agency theory and modern finance theory both contributed perspectives on financial auditing in what may be called the reputation model of auditing (Gilson & Kraakman 1984). Despite theoretical congruity, however, the role of agency costs may have been subordinated to the perceived power of modern finance theory, requiring related policy adjustments. The model supposes that enterprises hire auditors as a device to reduce agency costs. Auditors attest to financial statements in large part based on the auditors' reputation for thoroughness and veracity. Thorough and honest gatekeepers enjoy more credibility, a valuable trait. The more valuable it is, the greater is the risk of reputation loss so that, at some point, no additional incentives are necessary. In addition, the more frequently firms are employed to serve as such gatekeepers, and the larger the number of repeat occasions in which they expect to play these roles, the greater the value. Enterprises pay fees for this credence. Market participants are assumed to appreciate these as valuable signals (Goldberg 1988; Fischel 1987).

When operating effectively, such agency cost management can contribute to a market where securities prices tend to converge accurately toward the fundamental value of the related enterprise. They are mechanisms of market efficiency within the modern finance theory framework. Despite considerable theoretical appeal, some of the policy implications drawn from this model remain contestable, particularly concerning the scope of auditor legal liability (Cunningham 2007). Auditors long have been exposed to legal liability under various state and federal claims, SEC administrative sanctions, and criminal law. Scholars endlessly debate and policy analysts endlessly tinker with the numerous intricacies of this framework to seek its optimal structure. The exact ambit of legal liability may be shaped according to one's views about the role that reputation plays in inducing reliable performance and the importance of auditing to investors and markets – to which agency theory and modern finance theory can contribute.

During the decades of modern finance theory's ascendance, the role of an external agent's reputation and market efficiency assumed greater significance, resulting in a contraction of the ambit of auditor liability risk, by statutes like the 1995 Private Securities Litigation Reform Act (PSLRA) and in Supreme Court opinions.[9] Alas, financial bubbles and calamities, especially those of the early twenty-first century, revealed some of the limits of the reputation model of auditing (Bratton 2003). Many diagnoses have been offered. Some systemic accounts strike at the heart of modern finance theory while revealing the important role of agency costs.

Critiques of efficient market theory gave several examples of widely-known information about agency costs that Enron's stock price ignored – misaligned auditor-firm incentives, extensive audit firm cross-selling of auditing and consulting services, and weak auditor internal controls (Gordon 2002; Cunningham 2007). More generally, clients pay auditor fees and the auditing industry severely concentrated during the 1990s as a result of firm mergers, which weakens the reputation constraint and yields inferior audit quality (Cunningham 2004, 2006). But share prices did not reflect any of these publicly-known facts about agency costs.

Accordingly, that episode showed limits of modern finance theory. Even so, the reputation model of auditing, drawing on agency theory, suggested how auditing can promote reliable market pricing. The enduring issue is how to use these models to inform the optimal level of auditor liability, something that has eluded the best theories for many generations. An important response to the Enron period's revelations was the Sarbanes-Oxley Act of 2002, containing provisions targeted at the agency costs of auditing, including provisions committed to promoting the independence of auditors and audits. While a controversial piece of legislation in many ways, those provisions at least reflected the insights of agency theory and the limits of modern finance theory.

## Fairly Presents and GAAP Conformity

It would be a mistake to assume that agency theory and modern finance theory warrant substantially curtailed auditor duties or related legal liabilities, a proposition that appears in an important area of the law governing auditor liability. It concerns the longstanding issue of whether conformity with GAAP is a defense to an assertion that financial statements did not fairly present an enterprise's financial condition and results. Auditors sign opinions saying that financial statements both fairly present an enterprise's condition and results and are prepared in conformity with GAAP. The joint opinion has long stimulated question about whether one of these assertions should be privileged. That is, if it is true that financial statements are in conformity with GAAP, should that discharge an auditor's duties, even if the statements do not fairly present condition or results? Judge Henry Friendly famously answered that question years before the birth of agency theory and modern finance theory, announcing in *United States v. Simon*[10] that conformity with GAAP is no defense to assertions of auditor negligence liability if statements do not fairly present.

---

[9]   For example, *Central Bank of Denver v. First Interstate Bank of Denver*, 511 U.S. 164 (1994); *Stoneridge Investment Partners v. Scientific-Atlanta, Inc.*, 552 U.S. 148 (2008).

[10]   425 F.2d 796 (2d Cir. 1969) (Friendly, J.), *cert. denied*, 397 U.S. 1006 (1970).

As agency theory and modern finance theory developed, experts began to wonder about the durability of that legal ruling. During a remarkable period of quiescence on the issue, the SEC and other authorities made some implicit suggestions that it was more important for financial statements to conform with GAAP than to assure a fair presentation (Cunningham 2003b). These suggestions seemed to address concern that auditor opinions on financial statements that departed from GAAP would more likely amount to a violation of auditor duties. Amid the Enron-era's crisis in financial reporting and auditing, the SEC clarified its position, emphatically denying that conformity with GAAP by itself discharged an auditor's duties.

In a case arising from that period's scandals, concerning WorldCom, the Second Circuit Court of Appeals, the same court for which Friendly wrote, updated *Simon* and endorsed it in whole.[11] The case involved a corporate executive's assertions that a criminal indictment was flawed because it did not allege that the asserted accounting was improper under GAAP, arguing that it was necessary for the government to prove violations of GAAP at trial. The court, in an opinion written by Judge Ralph Winter, said a similar argument was made and rejected in *Simon* and that it saw 'no reason to depart from *Simon*'. It acknowledged that GAAP compliance may be relevant to issues of good faith or probative of intent to deceive. But conformity notwithstanding, the applicable statute contemplates only proof of intentionally misleading material statements. Intentionally and materially false financial statement assertions can violate that statute even if in conformity with GAAP.

The court gave an example of how a revenue allocation decision may not have violated GAAP, but if the allocation decision was made deliberately to increase revenue, that could constitute a statutory violation despite GAAP compliance. The financial statements, in other words, might still not fairly present the company's condition or performance. Similarly, some decisions concerning capitalization of line costs were not based on examining the underlying terms of the exchange but on the imperative to meet stated financial targets for the express purpose of 'artificially inflating its stock price'. This acknowledges that accounting and financial machinations can cause a stock price to depart from fundamental value, despite modern finance theory. Agency theory suggests that auditing can help reduce agency costs but also that auditing itself presents agency costs and it is probably irresponsible to interpret modern finance theory to mean that either of these can be wholly eliminated.

## 6.  CONCLUDING NOTE

Ongoing debate about the significance and scope of agency costs and modern finance theory continues to have important implications for legal scholarship and education, particularly concerning the resources devoted to corporate finance compared to law and accounting. The development of agency theory and its application to law did not alter the resource commitment much, though it reshaped much of the content of many courses, including corporations and securities regulation. But the arrival of modern finance theory induced a dramatic reduction in the academy's resource investment in law and accounting and concomitant increased allocation to corporate finance. That shift began in the mid-1970s and accelerated through ensuing decades, with a slight rejuvenation of investment in law and accounting inspired by

---

[11]    *United States v. Ebbers*, 485 F.3d 110 (2d Cir. 2006) (Winter, J.).

the Enron-era fiascos (Bratton 1985; Cunningham 2002b; Fiflis 1993; Weiss 1997; Zeff 1971).

These trends seem to elevate the theoretical power and influence of modern finance theory above the practical reality of corporate life and practice. Agency theory and positive accounting theory make clear the vitality of reliably-audited accounting information that some enthusiastic interpretations of modern finance theory tend to discount. The relative shift in the legal academy's commitment to corporate finance compared to law and accounting suggests it mirrors the phenomena captured in the second of each pair of examples in this chapter, instances presenting divergence between prescriptions of agency theory compared to modern finance theory and of overstatements of the latter's reliability and scope of its conclusions. On this telling, the influence of law and economics on law and accounting can be approximated by the hoary trope, two steps forward one step backward, though the dance is far from complete.

# REFERENCES

Benartzi, Shlomo & Richard H. Thaler (1995), 'Myopic Loss Aversion and the Equity Risk Premium Puzzle', *Quarterly Journal of Economics*, 110, 73–92.
Black, Fischer (1986), 'Noise', *Journal of Finance*, 41, 529–43.
Bratton, Jr., William W. (1985), 'Corporate Finance in the Law School Curriculum', *Duke Law Journal*, 1985, 237–60.
Bratton, Jr., William W. (2003), 'Shareholder Value and Auditor Independence', *Duke Law Journal*, 53, 439–89.
Burton, John C. (1974), 'Elephants, Flexibility and the Financial Accounting Standards Board', *Business Lawyer*, 29, 151–4.
Campbell, Jr., Rutheford B. (2003), 'The Impact of Modern Finance Theory in Acquisition Cases', *Syracuse Law Review*, 53, 1–48.
Coffee, Jr., John C. & Hillary A. Sale (2011), *Securities Regulation*, 11th ed., New York: Foundation Press.
Cox, James D. (1980), *Financial Information, Accounting and the Law*, Boston: Little, Brown.
Cunningham, Lawrence A. (1994), 'From Random Walks to Chaotic Crashes: The Linear Genealogy of the Efficient Capital Market Hypothesis', *George Washington Law Review*, 62, 546–608.
Cunningham, Lawrence A. (2002a), 'Behavioral Finance and Investor Governance', *Washington & Lee Law Review*, 59, 767–837.
Cunningham, Lawrence A. (2002b), 'Sharing Accounting's Burden: Business Lawyers in Enron's Dark Shadows', *Business Lawyer*, 57, 1421–62.
Cunningham, Lawrence A. (2003a), 'The Sarbanes-Oxley Yawn: Heavy Rhetoric, Light Reform (And It Might Just Work)', *Connecticut Law Review*, 35, 915–88.
Cunningham, Lawrence A. (2003b), 'Semiotics, Hermeneutics and Cash: An Essay on the True and Fair View', *North Carolina Journal of International Law and Commercial Regulation*, 28, 893–933.
Cunningham, Lawrence A. (2004), 'Choosing Gatekeepers: The Financial Statement Insurance Alternative to Auditor Liability', *UCLA Law Review*, 52, 413–75.
Cunningham, Lawrence A. (2005), 'Finance Theory and Accounting Fraud: Fantastic Futures versus Conservative Histories', *Buffalo Law Review*, 53, 789–813.
Cunningham, Lawrence A. (2006), 'Too Big to Fail: Moral Hazard in Auditing and the Need to Restructure the Industry before it Unravels', *Columbia Law Review*, 106, 1698–1748.
Cunningham, Lawrence A. (2007), 'Beyond Liability: Rewarding Effective Gatekeepers', *Minnesota Law Review*, 92, 323–86.
DeBondt, Warner & Richard H. Thaler (1985), 'Does the Stock Market Overreact', *Journal of Finance*, 40, 793–805.
Eisenberg, Melvin A. (1989), 'The Structure of Corporation Law', *Columbia Law Review*, 89, 1461–1525.
Fama, Eugene F. (1970), 'Efficient Capital Markets: A Review of Theory and Empirical Work', *Journal of Finance*, 25, 383–417.
Fields, Thomas D., Srinivasan Rangan & S. Ramu Thiagarajan (1988), 'An Empirical Evaluation of the Usefulness of Non-GAAP Accounting Measures in the Real Estate Investment Trust Industry', *Review of Accounting Studies*, 3, 103–30.
Fiflis, Ted J. (1993), 'Thoughts Provoked by "Accounting and the New Corporate Law"', *Washington and Lee Law Review*, 50, 959–76.

Fischel, Daniel R. (1983), 'The Appraisal Remedy in Corporate Law', *American Bar Foundation Research Journal*, 193, 875–902.

Fischel, Daniel R. (1987), 'The Regulation of Accounting: Some Economic Issues', *Brooklyn Law Review*, 52, 1051–6.

Gilson, Ronald & Renier Kraakman (1984), 'The Mechanisms of Market Efficiency', *Virginia Law Review*, 70, 549–644.

Goldberg, Victor (1988), 'Accountable Accountants: Is Third-Party Liability Necessary?', *Journal of Legal Studies*, 17, 295–312.

Gordon, Jeffrey N. (2002), 'What Enron Means for the Management and Control of the Modern Business Corporation: Some Initial Reflections', *University of Chicago Law Review*, 69, 1233–50.

Gordon, Jeffrey N. & Lewis A. Kornhauser (1985), 'Efficient Markets, Costly Information, and Securities Research', *NYU Law*, 60, 761–849.

Griffin, Paul A. (1982), 'Usefulness to Investors and Creditors of Information Provided by Financial Reporting: A Review of Empirical Accounting Research', *FASB Research Report*, Norwalk, C.T., 196–207.

Heller, Harry (1961), 'Disclosure Requirements Under Federal Securities Regulation', *Business Lawyer*, 16, 300–320.

Holthausen, Robert W. & Richard W. Leftwich (1983), 'The Economic Consequences of Accounting Choice', *Journal of Accounting and Economics*, 5, 77–117.

Jensen, Michael C. & William H. Meckling (1976), 'Theory of the Firm: Managerial Behavior, Agency Costs and Ownership Structure', *Journal of Financial Economics*, 3, 305–60.

Kahneman, Daniel & Mark W. Riepe (1988), 'Aspects of Investor Psychology', *Journal of Portfolio Management*, 24, 52–65.

Kahneman, Daniel, Jason L. Knetsch & Richard H. Thaler (1990) 'Experimental Tests of the Endowment Effect and the Coase Theorem', *Journal of Political Economy*, 98, 132–48.

Kripke, Homer (1970), 'The SEC, the Accountants, Some Myths and Some Realities', *NYU Law Review*, 45, 1151–1205.

Krishnan, Gopal V. & James A. Largay III (2000), 'The Predictive Ability of Direct Method Cash Flow Information', *Journal of Business, Finance and Accounting*, 27, 215–45.

Langevoort, Donald C. (1992), 'Theories, Assumptions and Securities Regulation: Efficient Markets Revisited', *University of Pennsylvania Law Review*, 140, 851–920.

Langevoort, Donald C. (1994), 'Disclosures that "Bespeak Caution"', *Business Lawyer*, 49, 481–503.

Lowenstein, Louis (1994), 'Efficient Market Theory: Let the Punishment Fit the Crime', *Washington & Lee Law Review*, 51, 925–44.

Manning, Bayless (1962), 'The Shareholder's Appraisal Remedy: An Essay for Frank Coker', *Yale Law Journal*, 72, 223–65.

Nichols, Nancy B., Donna L. Street & Sidney J. Gray (2005), 'Pro Forma Adjustments to Earnings: Bias, Materiality, and SEC Action', *Research in Accounting Regulation*, 18, 29–52.

Odean, Terrance (1998), 'Are Investors Reluctant to Realize Their Losses?', *Journal of Finance*, 53, 1775–98.

Rock, Edward B. (1992), 'Preaching to Managers', *Journal of Corporation Law*, 17, 605–714.

Roll, Richard, A. (1977), 'Critique of the Asset Pricing Theory's Tests', *Journal of Financial Economics*, 4, 129–76.

Ross, Richard (1976), 'The Arbitrage Theory of Capital Asset Pricing', *Journal of Economic Theory*, 13, 341–60.

Schaefer, Elmer J. (1982), 'The Fallacy of Weighting Assets Value and Earnings Value in the Appraisal of Corporate Stock', *Southern California Law Review*, 55, 1031–96.

Scott, Willard P. (1968), 'Changes in the Model Business Corporation Act', *Business Lawyer*, 24, 291–304.

Seligman, Joel (1982), *Transformation of Wall Street*, Boston: Houghton Mifflin.

Seligman, Joel (1984), 'Reappraising the Appraisal Remedy', *George Washington Law Review*, 52, 829–71.

Shiller, Robert J. (1989), *Market Volatility*, Cambridge, Mass.: MIT Press.

Shiller, Robert J. (2000), *Irrational Exuberance*, Princeton, NJ: Princeton University Press.

Shleifer, Andrei (2000), *Inefficient Markets*, Oxford: Oxford University Press.

Siegel, Stanley (1996), 'The Coming Revolution in Accounting: The Emergence of The Fair Value as the Fundamental Principle of GAAP', *Wayne Law Review*, 42, 1839–62.

Stout, Lynn A. (1990), 'Are Takeover Premiums Really Premiums? Market Price, Fair Value, and Corporate Law', *Yale Law Journal*, 99, 1235–96.

Stout, Lynn A. (2003), 'The Mechanisms of Market Inefficiency: An Introduction to the New Finance', *Journal of Corporation Law*, 28, 635–69.

Sunder, Shyam (1975), 'Stock Price and Risk Related to Accounting Changes in Inventory Valuation', *Accounting Review*, 50, 1305–15.

Thompson, Robert B. (1995), 'Exit, Liquidity, and Majority Rule: Appraisal's Role in Corporate Law', *Georgetown Law Journal* 84, 1–60

Thompson, Jr., Samuel C. (1996), 'A Lawyer's Guide to Modern Valuation Techniques in Mergers and Acquisitions', *Journal of Corporation Law*, 21, 457–540.

Tirole, Jean (2006), *The Theory of Corporate Finance*, Princeton, NJ: Princeton University Press.
Tversky, Amos & Daniel Kahneman (1981), 'The Framing of Decisions and the Psychology of Choice', *Science*, 211, 453–58.
Walker, David I. (2006), 'Financial Accounting and Corporate Behavior', *Washington and Lee Law Review*, 64, 927–1009.
Watts, Ross L. & Jerold L. Zimmerman (1990), 'Positive Accounting Theory: A Ten Year Perspective', *Accounting Review*, 65, 131–56.
Weiss, Elliott J. (1997), 'Teaching Accounting and Valuation in the Basic Corporation Law Course', *Cardozo Law Review*, 19, 679–95.
Wertheimer, Barry M. (1998), 'The Shareholders' Appraisal Remedy and How Courts Determine Fair Value', *Duke Law Journal*, 47, 613–715.
Zeff, Stephen A. (1971), 'Accounting for Business Lawyers', *Tulane Law Review*, 46, 358–62.

# 17. The role and regulation of the research analyst
*Jill E. Fisch*

## 1. INTRODUCTION

The role of the research analyst (also known as an equity analyst or a securities analyst) is to provide information to the marketplace. Analysts enhance capital market efficiency by enabling stock prices to reflect information and by reducing the need for each investor individually to gather and analyze that information. As the United States Supreme Court explained in *Dirks*,[1] 'The value to the entire market of these efforts cannot be gainsaid; market efficiency in pricing is significantly enhanced by such initiatives to ferret out and analyze information, and thus the analyst's work redounds to the benefit of all investors.'

Developments in the structure of the capital markets as well as the accessibility of firm-specific information led to substantial growth in the research industry. At the same time, the industry faced a continual challenge with respect to the cost of producing quality research and the difficulties involved in exploiting that information profitably. This challenge, in the 1990s, led the major Wall Street Investment Banks to fund their research through investment banking revenues, creating the subsidization structure underlying the conflicts of interest and ensuing scandals revealed by then New York Attorney General Eliot Spitzer in 2002.

The scandals led to the Global Research Settlement between ten Wall Street investment banks and the Securities and Exchange Commission (SEC), the New York State Attorney General, the North American Securities Administrators Association, the National Association of Securities Dealers and the New York Stock Exchange. They also led to regulatory reforms. At the time, commentators mourned the failure of research analysts to uncover massive corporate frauds at companies like Enron, WorldCom and HealthSouth (Coffee 2004). Greater independence, they argued, would make research analysts more effective gatekeepers. Both the Research Settlement and Sarbanes-Oxley included explicit mandates for increased analyst independence.

It is unclear whether the reforms will live up to their promise. Although the terms of the Research Settlement were designed to increase marketplace competition, few of the research firms that entered the market were able to compete with the Wall Street investment banks. More recently, economic forces required many firms to reduce their research budgets, leading to declines in coverage. Empirical studies showed that, while the reforms appeared to lead to less optimistic analyst recommendations, analyst information also became less informative. At the same time, developments in internet technology make it increasingly difficult for firms to exploit the value of their research through commissions (D'Avolio et al. 2001). These developments have increased the pressure to remove the information barriers between

---

[1]  *Dirks v SEC*, 463 U.S. 646, 659 n. 17 (1983), quoting *In re Dirks*, 21 S.E.C. Docket 1401, 1406 (1981).

research and investment banking. More generally, they raise questions about the continued viability of the research industry under a mandate of independence.

## 2.   THE DEVELOPMENT OF THE RESEARCH INDUSTRY

The research industry has its roots in the traditional full service brokerage firms that, until 1975, served as intermediaries for virtually all securities transactions. Before the 1960s, Wall Street firms did not have formal research departments and few, if any, brokers engaged in substantial research. The emergence and rapid growth of institutional investors in the 1960s created both a demand for research, however, and the financial resources to pay for that research (Coffee 1984). Early institutional investors competed on the basis of performance and valued the research provided by brokerage firms in enhancing their performance. Brokers, in turn, used research in part to compete for institutional customers and developed reputations based on the quality of their research.[2]

Because trading commissions were fixed and uniform across firms, brokers could not compete for investor business on the basis of price.[3] The inability of competitors to discount their commissions provided protection for a firm's research services because a customer had no incentive to execute its trades elsewhere. In addition, the margins provided by fixed commission rates at supra-competitive levels offered a mechanism for financing the costs of providing research.

Raymond Dirks – perhaps the best-known research analyst of his time as a result of the SEC's decision to sanction him for insider trading violations – typified the original analyst model. In 1973, Dirks was a securities analyst at a Wall Street brokerage firm where he specialized in covering insurance stocks for institutional clients. Dirks' research generated customer loyalty, and those customers in turn directed their substantial trading business to Dirks' firm. In addition to his base salary, Dirks received a commission for the securities transactions, above a certain amount, that his clients directed through his employer.[4]

Brokers also used research to compete for retail customers. E.F. Hutton's rapid growth in the 1970s and 1980s was due to its aggressive effort to cultivate retail customers, based in part on its reputation for making knowledgeable recommendations (Fromson 1988). As its famous advertising slogan stated: 'When E.F. Hutton talks, people listen.' By 1980, the firm had revenues of $1.1 billion (Fromson 1988).

---

[2]   Brokers also competed through the provision of other services such as block trading.

[3]   The New York Stock Exchange adopted fixed and uniform commissions for all member firms as part of the original Buttonwood Agreement in 1792. When Congress adopted the Federal Securities Laws in 1933 and 1934, it essentially incorporated fixed commissions into the federal regulatory scheme.

[4]   In the insider trading case for which the SEC sanctioned Dirks, Dirks revealed information to at least six institutional clients who collectively sold almost $20 million worth of stock. *Dirks v. SEC, Brief of Securities and Exchange Commission in Opposition to Petition for Writ of Certiorari*, 1982 U.S. S. Ct. Briefs LEXIS 754, *9, Oct. 19, 1982. The parties stipulated, in the litigation, however, that neither Dirks nor his firm received any commission or other remuneration from any person to whom Dirks provided information about EFA. *Dirks v. SEC*, Stipulation 13, Joint Appendix, Volume II of II, 1982 U.S. S. Ct. Briefs LEXIS 756, *6, Dec. 30, 1982.

The SEC's decision, in 1975, to eliminate fixed commissions, upset the business model by which Wall Street financed its research operations (Choi & Fisch 2003). Within a few years, discount brokerage firms emerged – offering investors the opportunity to execute their trades at dramatically lower costs.[5] As the number of discount brokers grew, brokers could no longer profit from the value of the research they provided because investors could obtain research from a full service broker and then execute their trades at lower cost through a discount broker. At the time, commentators predicted that these developments would result in the disappearance of the research industry. Instead, the industry evolved, incorporating analysts into the growing investment banking operations of Wall Street firms, a development that will be considered in more detail below.

## 3.   THE ROLE OF THE RESEARCH ANALYST

Research analysts collect information about specific firms and the overall market. They then package that information for use by investors in trading decisions. Most media, regulatory and academic attention focuses on the sell side analyst. Sell side analysts are typically employed by the research department of a full service financial firm such as an investment bank or broker-dealer and provide their research to firm's clients, which may include both institutional and retail investors. Importantly, sell side analysts also commonly make their research available to the public at large, although the public may receive more limited information and on a less timely basis. Buy side analysts, in contrast, are generally employed by an institutional investor, such as a mutual fund or hedge fund, and produce their research exclusively for the benefit of their employer. A third category of analysts, sometimes described as independent analysts, are not affiliated with investment banks or broker dealers, and provide fee-based research services.

The first and arguably most important component of the analyst's product is coverage. The analyst's decision to cover a company increases the company's visibility to potential investors. In addition, coverage independently conveys information – the decision to initiate coverage is often a positive signal of issuer quality, and the decision to terminate coverage is generally a negative signal.[6]

Analyst coverage varies dramatically among publicly traded companies – some companies are followed by multiple analysts and some, particularly mid and small cap companies, have no coverage at all (Fisch 2007a).[7] Coverage increases the efficiency of market prices, and studies show that the quantity and quality of analyst coverage has a substantial effect on a company's cost of capital (Bowen et al. 2008). Higher levels of analyst coverage are

---

[5]   As it happens, Charles Schwab created his brokerage firm, Charles Schwab & Co., Inc. just a few years before the elimination of fixed commissions. As a result, Schwab was well positioned to benefit from the regulatory change (Kador 2002). In addition, although most full service brokerage firms reacted to the elimination of fixed commissions by lowering commissions for their institutional clients and raising commissions for retail investors, Schwab targeted retail investor clients, a decision that enabled it to become, today, one of the largest financial firms (Entrepreneur.com n.d.).

[6]   Termination of coverage was commonly used as an alternative to a downgrade during the 1990s when sell recommendations were infrequent (Fisch 2007a).

[7]   One study of analyst coverage during the 1994–2001 time period reported that the average company studied was covered by 6.1 analysts (O'Brien et al. 2005).

correlated with 'higher market valuation, better performance, and lower level[s] of discretionary accruals' (Yu 2008).

Analysts provide coverage by producing research reports. The Securities and Exchange Commission defines a research report as 'a written communication (including an electronic communication) that includes an analysis of a security or an issuer and provides information reasonably sufficient upon which to base an investment decision'.[8] Analysts typically specialize in a particular industry and/or geographic region and engage in a range of activities to gather the information that they use to create their reports, including building relationships with sources of information, tracking industry and broader economic trends, and financial modeling.

In addition to qualitative and quantitative analysis, a research report contains several components that reflect that analyst's conclusions, including a recommendation, earnings estimates and/or a price target. Analyst recommendations or ratings, which were the focus of the scandals leading to the Global Research Settlement, purport to evaluate each covered security in terms of its relative attractiveness. Recommendations are usually based on a three to five point scale ranging from the most positive rating of strong buy or buy to the most negative rating of sell or strong sell. Following the adoption of new analyst regulations in 2002, the majority of firms migrated to a three point rating system, and one study found that 75% of ratings issued between January 2002 and December 2004 used a three point system (Kadan et al. 2009).

Earnings estimates are the component of the report that purportedly has the greatest impact on stock price (Chan et al. 2007). Based on their analysis, analysts predict the earnings that a company will announce in the future. Commentators suggest that earnings estimates impose pressure on corporate managers and find that the market reacts negatively to companies that fail to meet consensus estimates (Koh et al. 2008).[9]

Earnings estimates are often a factor used by the analyst to develop a price target. The price target indicates the analyst's opinion about the price level at which the stock is expected to trade in the subsequent 6–12 month period (Huang et al. 2009). Studies have shown that target prices have investment value in addition to that provided by the recommendation (Huang et al. 2009; Da & Schaumburg 2011).

A major Wall Street firm may issue hundreds of research reports in a single day.[10] Most of those reports are not expected to generate immediate trading activity. Some reports, however, are likely to result in immediate trading and frequently have a direct impact on stock price. The information contained in these reports is highly time sensitive. Terming such reports 'actionable reports', Judge Cote explained that they include those 'that upgrade or downgrade a security; begin research coverage of a company's security (an event known as an "initiation"); or predict a change in the security's target price'.[11] Historically, the challenge to the business model of the research industry is the public good problem (Coffee 1984). The distinguishing feature of a public good is non-excludability, meaning that consumption of the good by one user does not reduce its availability to others. Securities

---

8    Regulation Analyst Certification, 17 C.F.R. § 242.500 (2005).
9    This market reaction may have diminished subsequent to the analyst scandals and regulatory reforms. See Koh et al. (2008) (providing evidence of changes in market reactions).
10    *Barclays Capital Inc. v. Theflyonthewall.com,* 700 F. Supp. 2d 310 (S.D.N.Y. 2010).
11    *Ibid.,* 316.

research is a classic public good – once it is disseminated to some investors, it is easily transmitted to others. Information rapidly leaks into the marketplace, and those investors who purchase information have an incentive to transmit that information to others once they have acted upon it. As a result, although the production of quality information is costly, analysts have a limited opportunity to sell their research before the information becomes publicly available (Choi & Fisch 2003).

Firms take aggressive measures to control access to time-sensitive research which is often prepared and distributed within a short time period before the markets open.[12] This research is distributed to specific institutional clients based on the level of revenue they generate for the firm. Firms control the distribution through a variety of measures including password protected systems, limitations on distribution platforms and licensees and prohibitions on distribution to unauthorized recipients.[13] In recent years, firms have also restricted press access to their research, in an effort to prevent media disclosures from reducing their ability to generate trading revenues from the information.

With the growth of the internet, cell phones and other forms of electronic communication, the public good problem has become more serious. Research information rapidly appears on on-line sites such as social networks and chat-rooms. Various internet services collect and publish securities information, including Wall Street proprietary research and recommendations, often on a subscription basis. Although a recent district court decision found theflyonthewall.com liable for 'hot-news misappropriation' based on its 'systematic ... gathering and selling the Firms' Recommendations to investors',[14] a firm's ability to control the dissemination of its research is, as a practical matter, quite limited.

Once information leaks into the market, it is incorporated into stock prices, and its value to subsequent users dissipates rapidly. As a result, despite extensive measures to safeguard the confidentiality of time-sensitive research, it is difficult for firms to recoup the full cost of analyst research through direct sales. Instead, financial firms have traditionally subsidized their research costs through their other business operations (Choi & Fisch 2003).

The value of analyst research is based, in large part, on the quality of information possessed by the analyst. Analysts rely heavily on issuers to obtain company information, and the degree to which an analyst has access to company officials may influence the quality of the analyst's research. At the same time, those company officials who control analyst access to information have an incentive to reward favorable coverage and to limit the information they provide to analysts who are critical of company policies. The result of these incentives, for a long time, was a practice of selective disclosure, in which company officials rewarded analysts for favorable coverage by providing them with superior access to information (Fisch 2007a).

This practice was problematic for two reasons. First, it had the potential to bias analyst recommendations. An analyst who issued a report that was critical of an issuer risked being frozen out of future access (Fisch & Sale 2003). The media reported frequent examples in

---

[12]  *See ibid.* (describing majority of time-sensitive reports as being released between midnight and 7 am).

[13]  *See ibid.*

[14]  *See ibid*, 63. The appellate court reversed this decision, finding that the misappropriation claim was preempted by federal copyright law. *Barclays Capital Inc. v. Theflyonthewall.com, Inc.*, 650 F.3d 876 (2d Cir. 2011).

which corporate officials responded to criticism by refusing to take analyst phone calls, barring them from conferences and prohibiting employees from speaking with them. Some issuers went further and retaliated by pressuring firms to fire analysts who issued negative coverage or by initiating litigation.

The second problem with selective disclosure was its similarity to illegal insider trading. Favored analysts were able to provide their clients with a systemic trading advantage through access to information that was not generally available to the market. The SEC has consistently viewed this practice as unfair and illegal. During the 1970s, the SEC brought a number of enforcement actions against analysts and their clients for trading on the basis of information selectively disclosed by corporate officials. The best known of these cases is *Dirks v. SEC*, in which the SEC attempted to censure Raymond Dirks for communicating information to his clients about a massive fraud at Equity Funding of America.[15]

The Supreme Court ultimately rejected the SEC's contention that Dirks had aided and abetted his clients' commission of securities fraud.[16] In response, the SEC adopted Regulation FD, which banned the practice of selective disclosure.[17] Although critics warned that Regulation FD would decrease the quality of information, studies of its impact indicate that it has largely leveled the playing field and improved investor access to information. Research also shows that, post-Regulation FD, analyst forecasts are less optimistic, suggesting that the rule has reduced analyst incentives to inflate their estimates in order to maintain access to issuer information (Hovakimian & Saenyasiri 2009). A byproduct of the regulation has been improved media access to issuer information by facilitating reporters' ability to participate in company conference calls and encouraging website disclosures.

## 4.   COUPLING RESEARCH WITH INVESTMENT BANKING

The industry's response to the elimination of fixed commissions was to identify an alternative source for subsidizing research – investment banking revenues. Most Wall Street firms with substantial equity research departments also engaged in investment banking. During the 1990s, investment banking business grew dramatically. By the late 1990s, investment banking business was responsible for the majority of the revenues of the Wall Street firms (Fisch & Sale 2003). In contrast, brokerage commissions, which had represented more than half of firm revenues in the 1960s, had fallen to less than 20%.

Firms found that analysts could play a valuable role in enhancing their investment banking operations. Analysts' clients were institutional investors who could serve as a customer base for the firm's underwriting efforts. A firm's access to a customer base enhanced its competitiveness in attracting underwriting business. A strong and reputable research department strengthened the firm's ability to sell newly issued securities, and the promise of contin-

---

[15]   *In re Dirks*, 21 S.E.C. Docket 1401 (1981).

[16]   *Dirks v. SEC*, 463 U.S. 646 (1983).

[17]   17 C.F.R. §§243.100–103 (2006). In its proposing release, the SEC explained that 'many have viewed *Dirks* as affording considerable protection to insiders who make selective disclosures to analysts, and to the analysts (and their clients) who receive selectively disclosed information'. Regulation FD, Regulation FD, Proposed Rule, Selective Disclosure and Insider Trading, Securities Act Release No. 33-7787, 1999 SEC LEXIS 2696 (Dec. 20, 1999).

ued analyst coverage provided comfort to purchasers, particularly of smaller companies, of ongoing price efficiency and liquidity. Interactions with analysts increased the information available to investment bankers, enabling them to evaluate issuer quality and set offering prices more accurately (Mehran & Stutz 2007). Access to investment banking operations was also valuable for analysts, providing them with new sources of information about covered companies, the market and the industry.

These synergies led investment banks increasingly to draw analysts into their underwriting operations. It was common, during the 1990s, for investment banks to use analysts to vet prospective offerings, to analyze the financial structure of deals, and to help sell the securities to investors. Banks sent their analysts, along with their investment bankers, on road shows to assist in marketing and to maintain continued interest in the securities of the bank's underwriting clients. Top analysts became integral parts of their firms' underwriting operations, and the prestige of a firm's research department contributed to its success as an underwriter. As Krigman et al. found, 'issuers place value on incremental and perceived high-quality research coverage by sell-side analysts. They allocate their resources, in the form of underwriting fees, to increase and improve this coverage' (Krigman et al. 2001, 278).

As a result of the growing relationship between research and investment banking, the compensation of sell side analysts began to reflect their contribution to the firm's investment banking business. One of the most prominent analysts of the era was Jack Grubman, who covered telecommunications for Salomon Brothers. Grubman's reputation was based, in part, on his key role in facilitating Salomon's underwriting of telecommunications securities. During the late 1990s, when Grubman's research dominated the industry, Salomon earned almost $1 billion from underwriting and advising in connection with telecommunications firms. Grubman testified before Congress that his compensation during this time period averaged $20 million per year.[18] Compensation of other top analysts was similar. Morgan Stanley analyst Mary Meeker, once termed the 'Queen of the Internet', reportedly earned $15 million in 1999 (Gasparino & Craig 2003). The following year, internet stocks plummeted. Yet Meeker's contributions to Morgan's investment banking operations 'more than doubled to $425.1 million, [and] her pay rose by $8.7 million' (Smith 2003).

## 5. THE RESEARCH ANALYST SCANDALS

The tie between investment banking and research led ultimately to the research analyst scandals of the late 1990s. On April 8, 2002, New York State Attorney General Eliot Spitzer announced that an investigation by his office revealed widespread abuse in the research industry. In particular, Spitzer disclosed, through public filings, that Wall Street research was tainted by conflicts of interest, knowingly misleading, and deliberately over-optimistic. Spitzer's court papers cited numerous examples of analysts maintaining positive recommendations on securities while privately describing those securities as 'dogs' and 'junk' (Fisch 2007b).

---

[18]   *NASD Department of Enforcement v. Jack Grubman*, No. CAF 020042, Sept. 23, 2002, ¶ 6, available at http://fl1.findlaw.com/news.findlaw.com/hdocs/docs/ssb/nasdgrubman92302cmp.pdf (last accessed October 2011).

The concerns raised by Spitzer's investigation were not limited to particular examples of explicit misrepresentations. Favorable analyst coverage sold securities. Wall Street firms could use the strength of their research departments to attract lucrative underwriting business. This role, however, created an incentive for analysts to provide favorable coverage for current and prospective underwriting clients – leading to so-called biased coverage.[19] The need to maintain stock prices for previously sold securities, both to further the interests of the firm's underwriting clients and its institutional investor clients, generated pressure to maintain positive recommendations even if a company's prospects deteriorated. These forces led analysts to become cheerleaders for the companies they covered (Ackman 2001). As the tech bubble expanded in the late 1990s, an increasing percentage of the covered companies had no profits and limited revenue. As Forbes Magazine wrote, 'until the bubble burst, everyone was happy' (Ackman 2001). When it burst, investors blamed the cheerleaders.

The scandal was exacerbated by revelations of corruption and self-dealing by some of the highest profile analysts. Merrill Lynch analyst Henry Blodget, in particular, was singled out in Spitzer's investigation for issuing recommendations that were inconsistent with his personal assessments of the companies (Fisch & Sale 2003).

The revelations about Grubman were even more damaging. Spitzer's filings indicated that Jack Grubman had issued a buy recommendation on AT&T stock in an effort to get his children admitted to a prestigious private nursery school.[20] Grubman also reportedly coached WorldCom CEO Bernard Ebbers on his disclosures to the market, assisting him in putting a positive spin on the company's financial condition despite the fact that it was rapidly approaching bankruptcy (Scianni 2004).[21] Suspicions emerged about Grubman's other recommendations as, by 2001, four of the companies on which he issued buy recommendations were bankrupt, and over half traded at less than $5 per share (Morgenson 2001).

Spitzer's investigation was later joined by the SEC as well as the NASD and the New York Stock Exchange. In April 2003, Spitzer, the SEC and the self-regulatory organizations (SROs) resolved the litigation by entering into the Global Research Settlement with ten Wall Street banks.[22] The Settlement rejected the previously-existing business model in which research was financed by investment banking. Instead, the Settlement mandated a formal separation between research and investment banking.[23] Under the Settlement, the banks agreed that their research and investment banking operations would be both physically separated and subject to information barriers. Investment bankers were prohibited from communicating with analysts except on specified topics, and all communications were to take place

---

[19]   *See* Krigman et al. (2001) (showing that firms switch underwriter post IPO to purchase increased analyst coverage); Chan et al. (2007) (describing effect of investment banking boom and tech bubble).

[20]   *SEC v. Grubman*, 03-CV-2938, Complaint (S.D.N.Y. 2003), available at http://www.sec.gov/litigation/complaints/comp1811b.htm (last accessed October 2011); Norris (2003).

[21]   *Ibid.* Grubman issued a bullish report and reiterated his 'strong buy' recommendation on WorldCom's stock just five months before the company filed for bankruptcy.

[22]   The settling banks included Bear Stearns, Credit Suisse First Boston, Goldman Sachs, Lehman Brothers, J.P. Morgan, Merrill Lynch, Morgan Stanley, Citigroup, UBS Warburg and Piper Jaffray (SEC 2003b). Subsequently two additional investment banks, Deutsche Bank and Thomas Weisel Partners, agreed to be bound by the Settlement (SEC 2004).

[23]   The Settlement also required the defendant banks to pay $875 million in civil penalties and disgorgement (SEC 2003a).

in the presence of a chaperone. Investment bankers were barred from determining which companies an analyst would cover, from attempting to influence the content of an analyst's report and from evaluating an analyst's performance. In turn, analysts were prohibited from participating in efforts to obtain investment banking business.

The Global Settlement contained several additional provisions designed to improve investor access to quality research. The defendant banks agreed to provide their customers with independent research in addition to their proprietary research for five years following the Settlement. The banks agreed to purchase this independent research, at a cost of $432.5 million, under the supervision of an independent consultant (SEC 2003a). The banks also contributed an additional $80 million for investor education.

In addition to the structural reforms and other regulatory components, the Global Settlement required the defendant banks to pay penalties and disgorgement totaling more than $800 million. Jack Grubman and Henry Blodget were required to pay $15 million and $4 million respectively, and each was permanently barred from the securities industry.

Spitzer's revelations also generated private litigation. Investors filed numerous suits alleging that they had been misled by recommendations that were overly optimistic, inconsistent with the analyst's personal opinions, and tainted by investment banking conflicts of interest (Olazabal 2004). Courts dismissed many of these cases. Southern District Judge Milton Pollack, for example, dismissed a number of high profile cases, finding that the bursting of the technology bubble and investor speculation caused the plaintiffs' losses rather than analyst misconduct (Thomas 2003b). Nonetheless, many other courts upheld investor claims, particularly when the complaints alleged sufficiently specific and egregious misconduct.[24] The Second Circuit issued a significant opinion holding that the presumption of reliance that the U.S. Supreme Court had previously adopted in *Basic, Inc. v. Levinson*[25] applies to analyst (and other third party) statements communicated to the market, so long as those statements are material and impact the market price of the securities to which they relate.[26]

A substantial number of investors also filed arbitration claims against their brokers in connection with the purchases of companies that were the subject of 'tainted research' (Karp 2003).[27] As with the litigated cases, the results of these claims varied. One commentator reported that arbitrators awarded damages in less than one-third of the cases filed (SIFMA 2007). Some arbitrations resulted in substantial recoveries, however. One panel, for example, awarded investors over $1 million, including punitive damages, on their claim against Merrill Lynch. The panel found that there was 'clear and convincing evidence that [Merrill's] employees were guilty of intentional misconduct' in maintaining the 'skewed rating system' upon which the investors relied.[28]

---

[24]   *See, e.g., In re WorldCom, Inc. Sec. Litig.*, 294 F. Supp. 2d 392, 429-30 (S.D.N.Y. 2003); *Swack v. Credit Suisse First Boston*, 383 F. Supp. 2d 223 (D. Mass. 2004).

[25]   485 U.S. 224 (1988).

[26]   The Second Circuit had previously failed to reach this issue in *Hevesi v. Citigroup, Inc.*, 366 F.3d 70, 79 (2d Cir. 2004).

[27]   *See also* SIFMA (2007) (describing arbitration claims in connection with analyst scandals).

[28]   *Friedman v. Merrill Lynch*, NASD Dispute Resolution Award, Case No. 03-06176, Feb. 17, 2005, available at www.secatty.com/pearce-investor-awards-1.pdf (last accessed October 2011).

## 6. EMPIRICAL STUDIES OF ANALYST RESEARCH

Spitzer's revelations generated widespread concern that analyst ties to investment banking 'corrupted' the quality of the resulting research. The existing empirical literature offered only modest support for this conclusion, however. Studies confirmed that recommendations and earnings estimates during the late 1990s were overly optimistic (Dugar & Nathan 1995). The overwhelming majority of analyst recommendations consisted of 'buy' and 'strong buy' recommendations; 'sell' recommendations were extremely rare. In 2000, for example, one study found that analysts issued buy recommendations on 74% of covered companies while maintaining sell recommendations on only 2% (Barber et al. 2006). An SEC survey in 2000 reported that less than 1% of all recommendations were sell recommendations (Fisch & Sale 2003). In addition, there was evidence that analysts affiliated with investment banking firms issued more optimistic recommendations than unaffiliated analysts (Michaely & Womack 1999; Dugar & Nathan 1995; Agrawal & Chen 2005) and that this optimism was most pronounced with respect to issuers that had underwriting relationships with the analysts' firms (Michaely & Womack 1999).[29]

Some research demonstrated that earnings forecasts and price targets were also overly optimistic (Bradshaw et al. 2003; Agrawal & Chen 2005). One study found that earnings estimates were biased by an average of 2% of the stock price from 1984–2006 (Hovakimian & Saenyasiri 2009). On the other hand, a Thomson Reuters study found that analyst earnings forecasts from 1999 to 2010 have typically been pessimistic – 64% of companies, on average, beat analysts' forecasts in any given quarter (Denning 2010). That reported earnings might 'beat the Street' is unsurprising; issuers actively seek to 'manage' analyst expectations in order to avoid missing their numbers, an event that often triggers an adverse market reaction.

Commentators have identified a number of explanations for optimistic analyst recommendations (Fisch 2007a). Buy recommendations have a larger target audience than sell recommendations – the entire universe of investors as opposed to current shareholders – and therefore offer greater potential to generate brokerage commissions. Analysts have an incentive to maintain good relationships with issuers in order to maximize their access to information. In some cases, analysts who produced unfavorable research have faced retaliation from issuers or their own employers. And, of course, positive analyst coverage makes it easier for investment banks to attract and retain underwriting business.

At the same time, however, studies show that analyst research was both accurate and influential prior to the Settlement and associated regulatory reforms. Indeed, several studies revealed that, although investment bank affiliated analysts issued more buy recommendations, their earnings forecasts were generally more accurate than those issued by independent analysts (Clarke et al. 2004; Jacob et al. 2003) or buy side analysts (Groysberg et al. 2008). Similarly, studies indicated that the market responded to the release of analyst research (Ryan & Taffler 2004; Busse & Green 2002), that the market reacted to analyst forecast revisions in the predicted direction (Gleason & Lee 2003; Ivkovic & Jegadeesh 2004), that early access

---

[29]  *But see* Agrawal & Chen (2005) (finding that brokerage conflicts of interest have a greater influence on analyst forecasts than investment banking conflicts).

to recommendations had investment value (Green 2004), and that analyst-recommended stocks outperformed the market (Howe et al. 2007; Boni & Womack 2006).[30]

These studies suggest that analyst reports were conveying valuable information to the market. They also seemed to indicate that institutional investors, at least, adjusted for potential analyst bias and were not misled by the analysts' buy recommendations within the context of the full research report (Boni & Womack 2006). In a review of 29 empirical studies of analyst bias, Mehran and Stultz found that, although the majority of the study found evidence of bias, there was no consensus that this bias had an adverse impact on customers (Mehran & Stultz 2007). Studies seem to indicate, however, that analyst recommendations misled retail investors (Malmendier & Shanthikumar 2007).

## 7.   REGULATORY CHANGES

Spitzer's announcement of the analyst scandals occurred just months before Congress adopted the Sarbanes-Oxley Act in July 2002. In response to the concerns identified by Spitzer, the Act contained, among its many components, a provision requiring the SEC and the SROs to adopt measures to address analyst conflicts of interest. In response to this statutory mandate, the SEC adopted Regulation Analyst Certification or AC in February 2003.[31] The stated goal of Regulation AC is to 'promote the integrity of research reports and investor confidence in the reports'.[32] Regulation AC requires that analysts provide, as part of their research reports, a certification indicating that the report accurately reflects their personal views. Analysts are also required to disclose any compensation received in connection with the recommendations or views in the report.

The SROs also changed their rules to address analyst conflicts of interest. As Congress was considering adopting Sarbanes-Oxley, in May 2002, the SEC approved SRO rule changes[33] that, in the words of then-Chairman Harvey Pitt, implemented 'groundbreaking reforms to minimize and disclose conflicts of interest facing research analysts' (Pitt 2002). Subsequently, in July 2003, the SEC approved a second set of rule changes.[34]

Both sets of rule changes focused specifically on investment banking conflicts and implemented a combination of structural safeguards, prohibitions of specified practices, and increased disclosure requirements. The structural changes increased the formal separation of research from investment banking. Investment bankers were prohibited from supervising research analysts or approving their reports, and banks were required to adopt mechanisms, such as compensation committees, to insulate analyst compensation from investment banking influence. Analysts were also subjected to registration, qualification and continuing education requirements.

---

[30]   *But see* Barber et al. (2003) (finding that analyst picks in 2000 and 2001 dramatically underperformed the market); Altinkilic et al. (2009) (reporting findings that analyst forecast revisions are not informative).

[31]   Regulation AC – Analyst Certification, 17 C.F.R. §§ 242.500–.505 (2006).

[32]   17 CFR § 242.500 *et seq.*

[33]   Research Analyst Conflicts of Interest, 67 Fed. Reg. 34,968, 34,969 (May 10, 2002).

[34]   Research Analyst Conflicts of Interest, 68 Fed. Reg. 45,875 (July 29, 2003).

The rules prohibited a variety of practices – they limited analyst participation in the solicitation of investment banking business and the use of booster shots, and established quiet periods during the underwriting process during which participating investment banks are prohibited from issuing research reports. The rules also limited personal trading by research analysts. Analysts were forbidden from engaging in personal trading during a period surrounding their release of a research report and from receiving pre-IPO securities.

Finally, the SRO rules mandated increased disclosure. Analysts were required to disclose a variety of actual and potential conflicts of interest, and their firms were required to provide information about the firm's rating system, including the meaning of the ratings, the percentage of securities subject to each rating, and the circumstances surrounding a ratings change. Analysts were required to disclose whether a covered company was a client of the analyst's firm and, if so, the types of services provided to the company. Analysts were also required to provide notice to customers of all terminations in coverage, including, where possible, a final recommendation.

Importantly, neither of the SRO rule changes extended the provisions of the Global Research Settlement to investment banks that were not parties to the Settlement. In addition, because the rules were implemented by the SROs pursuant to their regulatory authority over member firms, they applied only to analysts employed by broker-dealers. In particular, the rules did not apply to research-only firms and their employees, despite the fact that even so-called independent analysts may have business relationships such as affiliated mutual funds or hedge funds that create potential conflicts of interest (Fisch 2007a).

## 8.   THE EFFECT OF THE REGULATORY CHANGES

The full effect of the regulatory changes remains unclear. Initially, the requirement that firms sever the ties between research and investment banking led to reductions in the size of Wall Street research departments (Sorkin 2008; Thomas 2003a) and to cuts in analyst compensation (Munk 2003). Many top analysts from investment banks left sell side research (Guan et al. 2009). Some moved to the buy side, working in-house for hedge funds, private equity firms or venture capital firms (Sorkin 2008), and some moved across the Chinese wall to investment banking (Guan et al. 2009).

Investment banks also began to shift the nature of their research departments, focusing primarily, if not exclusively, on institutional customers (Fisch 2007a). This shift was due to a number of factors, including the willingness of institutional (but not retail) clients to bear the increased cost of unsubsidized research and the desire by firms to reduce the liability exposure that might result from providing research to retail customers (Fisch 2007a). The resulting segmentation of the research market reduced retail investor access to information. Firms also began to develop specialized research services for institutional clients including customized research and direct access to industry executives (Fisch 2007a; O'Hara 2010). One report estimated that institutional investors 'with deep pockets' spent almost $2 billion in 2008 for exclusive research services that included collecting field data and surveys as well as specialized forensic accounting (Cowan & Welsch 2009).

Perhaps most significantly, the overall level of research coverage decreased dramatically.[35] Large firms cut their research staffs, often to the point where they lacked analyst coverage in entire industry sectors. The ten defendants in the Global Research Settlement reduced their coverage by almost 20% in the two years from 2001 to 2003 (Boni 2006).

The reductions in coverage affected small issuers most dramatically. The Advisory Committee on Smaller Public Companies reported to the SEC in 2006 that 'approximately 1,200 of 3,200 NASDAQ-listed companies and 35% of all public companies, receive no analyst coverage at all'.[36] Reuters reported that from 2002 to 2005, 691 companies lost all coverage (Craig 2005). With respect to the IPO market, analyst coverage became far more difficult for issuers to obtain, and virtually all analyst coverage 'comes from the investment banking team ... despite the intentions of the Global Research Settlement' (Weild & Kim 2009).[37]

The precarious financial condition of many major Wall Street banks in connection with the Financial Crisis of 2008 led to further cuts in coverage (Opdyke & Lobb 2009). For example, in 2008, Citigroup cut the number of companies covered by its research department by 7% (Wilchins 2008). These reductions in coverage, especially a firm's total loss of analyst coverage, are costly, affect liquidity and trading volume and increase the likelihood of delisting (Khorana et al. 2007; Kecskés & Womack 2008).

Notably, the overall reduction in coverage occurred in spite of the Global Research Settlement's subsidy for independent research. As indicated above, the Global Research Settlement required the defendant banks to spend $432.5 million to purchase independent research for their customers. The prospect of receiving funding as a result of this subsidy led a number of new research firms to begin operations, but the media has issued mixed reports on their success. Banks purchased the majority of the subsidized research from a few large firms such as Standard & Poors and Morningstar, and only a small percentage of the independent firms received Settlement money (Fisch 2007a; O'Hara 2009). In addition, brokerage customers made little use of the subsidized research (Kim 2009; Peek 2008). As the Settlement provision expired in July 2009, several banks explicitly announced that they would no longer purchase independent coverage for their customers (Kim 2009).

What about the effect of the regulatory changes on analyst bias? In response to the Spitzer investigation and regulatory changes, the majority of investment banks moved from a five-tier to a three-tier rating system (Kadan et al. 2009).[38] Their recommendations also became more balanced. Studies found dramatic reductions in the number of strong buy and buy recommendations, particularly at the end of 2002 (Barber et al. 2006). As of 2009, *Time Magazine* reported that sell ratings ranged from 15–20% of covered companies, as compared to 1–2% in the late 1990s (Kiviat 2009). These effects were much greater at the large investment banks that were subject to the Global Settlement. A Thomson study in 2004 found that, following the Settlement, the analyst recommendations from the large investment banks were substantially more balanced than those at the smaller firms such as Jefferies and A.G. Edwards.[39]

---

[35]    *But see* Kolasinski (2006) (finding that the restrictions on cooperation between analysts and investment bankers did not reduce issuer coverage).

[36]    SEC (2006, 72, n. 144).

[37]    *See also* Freeman (2008) (quoting Novak Biddle co-founder Jack Biddle as stating that 'if banking cannot subsidize research, there will be no research, and therefore no institutional buyers or liquidity for small cap companies').

[38]    A substantial number changed their rating systems in 2002.

[39]    Craig (2004) (reporting findings of Thomson study).

In addition, studies have found that optimism and forecast bias were reduced following the regulatory changes (Hovakinian & Saenyasiri 2009). One study reported that analyst recommendations were more strongly related to fundamental value after the regulatory changes (Agrawal et al. 2006). The Wall Street Journal reported that, following the recession, analyst earnings estimates displayed a pessimistic bias (Denning 2010). On the other hand, a study by McKinsey and Co. found that analyst forecasts have been overly optimistic – almost 100% too high – both over the past 25 years, and subsequent to the regulatory reforms (Stuart 2010).

At the same time, empirical studies generally found that analyst research became less informative (Kadan et al. 2009; Clarke et al. 2004). Analyst forecasts were less precise (Agrawal et al. 2006; Gintschel & Markov 2004) and the amount of dispersion increased (Bailey et al. 2003). Stock price reactions to the release of analyst research also decreased, suggesting that the information value of this research decreased (Cornett et al. 2005).

## 9.   RECENT DEVELOPMENTS IN THE RESEARCH INDUSTRY

The research industry continues to evolve in response to regulatory developments, technological changes, and market shifts. In particular, the industry has struggled to develop a business model by which to finance quality research in the absence of investment banking ties or other so-called conflicts of interest. This concern has intensified with the end of the subsidies provided by the Global Research Settlement for independent research.

### Issuer and Exchange Financed Research

One response has been the emergence of issuer-financed research coverage. Approximately a dozen research firms such as Spelman Research, Investrend and Dutton Associates, now provide fee-based research to issuers (Fisch 2007a; Kirk 2008). Fee-based research offers a mechanism for small issuers to purchase some level of coverage at a fairly low cost – typically $25,000–$50,000 for services ranging from the preparation and distribution of a single report to a year's worth of coverage (Fisch 2007a). An initial study of the industry finds 'an increase in liquidity, institutional investor holding, and sell side analyst following after the initiation of paid-for coverage' (Kirk 2008, 29). The study also finds that issuer-financed research has information value, although it is more optimistic and less accurate than sell side coverage.

A related development is the introduction of exchange-sponsored research. In May 2009, the NYSE Euronext initiated a project through which Virtua Research would provide independent research for a group of NYSE listed companies (NYSE Euronext 2009). In June 2009, NASDAQ-OMX announced a similar agreement providing for Morningstar to furnish research reports on over 3,600 NASDAQ-OMX listed companies (NASDAQ 2009). It is too early to assess the impact of these projects. Significantly, however, unlike traditional sell side research, neither project will offer investors a buy/sell/hold recommendation.

Both issuer-financed research and exchange-sponsored research are variations on an academic article proposing voucher financing for analysts (and other securities intermediaries) as a solution to the financing problem (Choi & Fisch 2003). As the article observed, issuer financing of research is logical because research benefits covered companies, resulting in more efficient prices, a lower cost of capital and increased liquidity. To overcome concerns about analyst conflicts of interest and/or bias, the article argued that investors, rather than company management, should allocate financing among research firms. To facilitate investors' evaluation of analyst quality, another academic article proposed regulations to require increased disclosure of analyst research through a public database that would enable investors to track analyst performance and to identify potential sources of bias (Fisch 2007a). As this article argued, and empirical data suggests, investors can evaluate the quality of research provided by analysts with so-called conflicts of interest, and disclosure rather than prohibition of such conflicts enables analysts to retain the subsidies and, in some cases, the synergies, resulting from related business activities.

**Recent Litigation Involving Analyst Research**

Research departments also face challenges posed by the public good problem in light of the internet and its capacity for increasing the ability of market players to capture and transmit information cheaply and rapidly. In particular, the internet has given rise to a variety of financial news aggregators and packagers that offer rapid access to financial and market developments on a subscription basis.[40] These services offer, inter alia, information about Wall Street research including recommendations and sometimes the underlying analysis.[41] Streetaccount.com, for example, states that it provides investors with analyst upgrades and downgrades (StreetAccount 2010). Analyst research is also available on internet chat rooms. As Judge Cote explained, 'there is a crowded marketplace with small internet companies and major news organizations reporting [sell side analyst] recommendations before and after the market opens'.[42] The presence of these companies threatens the business model of traditional research departments.

In 2006, Lehman, Merrill Lynch and Morgan Stanley[43] sued theflyonthewall.com ('the Fly'), alleging copyright infringement and hot news misappropriation of their research. In a controversial decision, Judge Cote enjoined the Fly from publishing the plaintiffs' recommendations, finding that the Fly's conduct 'substantially threatened' the continued viability of the plaintiffs' research business.[44] Recognizing, however, that 'the practice of posting the [plaintiffs'] recommendations had become a widespread phenomenon', Judge Cote held that the court would modify or vacate the injunction unless the plaintiffs took reasonable steps to restrain the use of their recommendations by the Fly's competitors.[45]

At the same time that research firms struggle to limit access to their research, they continue to face pressure to produce optimistic research. In some cases, issuers that have been the targets of negative analyst coverage have even brought suit. BankAtlantic sued Richard ('Dick') Bove, a high-profile banking analyst, in 2008, after Bove published a report that

---

[40]   Currently these firms include theflyonthewall.com, Tradethenews.com, streetaccount.com, briefing.com and others (*Barclays, supra* note 10, 35).

[41]   *Ibid.*

[42]   *Ibid*, 326–7.

[43]   Barclays Capital subsequently acquired Lehman's equity research operations and was substituted as a plaintiff.

[44]   *Barclays, supra* note 10, 341.

[45]   *Ibid*, 347. Judge Cotes' decision was reversed in part by the Second Circuit. *Barclays Capital Inc. v. Theflyonthewall.com, Inc.*, 650 F.3d 876 (2d Cir. 2011).

included BankAtlantic among 24 banks that might fail (Gaffen 2008; Pettersson 2008). The case, which reportedly cost Bove nearly $800,000 in legal fees, was settled in June 2010 without any payment by Bove to BankAtlantic (Martin & Story, 2010). The risk of a lawsuit appears highest for independent research firms who publish negative information and provide that information to hedge fund clients who rely on that information to sell short. In addition to litigation initiated by the targets of their negative coverage, analysts have also been the subject of regulator investigations (Sasseen 2006; Fisch 2007a). Bove, for example, was investigated by FINRA, although he was never sanctioned (Martin & Story 2010).

Litigation against Gradient Analytics, an independent research firm, offers another example.[46] In 2006, two issuers, Biovail and Overstock.com, filed racketeering lawsuits alleging that Gradient had conspired with its hedge fund clients to produce false research in an effort to drive down stock prices (Anderson 2006). Gradient settled the lawsuit with Overstock.com in 2008, retracting its negative statements about Overstock.com and issuing a public apology (Sage 2008). A court dismissed Biovail's claims against Gradient and its co-defendants in 2009, finding it lacked personal jurisdiction over Gradient.[47] Gradient subsequently filed suit against Biovail, alleging that the 2006 lawsuit constituted malicious prosecution (News-Medical.Net 2010).

### The Global Research Settlement

Although the SEC and other regulators touted the value of the Global Research Settlement, implementing many of the Settlement's provisions proved to be challenging. As indicated above, retail investors did not appear to make substantial use of the subsidized independent research. The Settlement fund, which was to be used to compensate injured investors, was criticized as inadequate, and the distribution process was slow (Schack 2005). The SEC also struggled with the distribution methodology.[48] As Judge Pauley stated, in frustration with the ongoing and ineffective distribution efforts, 'while the SEC professed its interest in restitution, it did not focus its considerable analytical resources on the identification of relevant securities, time frames and potential claims before presenting the distribution plans to this Court.'[49]

At the end of almost five years, the parties were unable to distribute $79 million of Settlement funds, and on June 10, 2009, Judge Pauley ordered the funds to be distributed to the US Treasury. Similar problems occurred with respect to the funds earmarked for investor education. The final judgment allocated $55 million that was originally directed to 'an investor education foundation to fund worthy and cost-effective programs designed to provide investors with the knowledge and skills necessary to make informed investment decisions'.[50] The SEC subsequently abandoned the plan to create the new entity because of 'organizational issues'. The SEC then requested and received court approval to transfer the funds

---

[46]   See also Blodget (2009) (reporting that issuer Fairfax Holdings sued a Wall Street analyst and a hedge fund claiming that they colluded to drive down its stock price).

[47]   *Biovail Corp. v. S.A.C. Capital Mgmt.*, Docket Number ESX-L-1583-06, Opinion Dated Aug. 20, 2009.

[48]   *SEC v. Bear, Stearns & Co.*, 626 F. Supp. 2d 402 (S.D.N.Y. 2009).

[49]   *Ibid*, 411.

[50]   *Ibid*, 418.

to the NASD Foundation, an existing investor education entity.[51] As Judge Pauley noted in 2009, for the three years ending September 30, 2008, the foundation had distributed only $6.5 million of the $55 million allocation.[52]

More recently, the defendant investment banks asked Judge Pauley to modify the terms of the Global Research Settlement. In particular, the banks sought to weaken the firewall between research and investment banking by allowing research and investment banking personnel to communicate with each other about market or industry trends outside the presence of legal or compliance staff (Cleary Gottlieb 2009).[53] Although the SEC, somewhat surprisingly, joined in the banks' request (Cleary Gottlieb 2009; Craig & Scannell 2010), Judge Pauley refused to approve this modification, finding that 'it would be inconsistent with the Final Judgments and contrary to the public interest'.[54] The banks' request and the SEC's acquiescence in that request show a disturbing lack of sensitivity to the concerns reflected in the Settlement about potential conflicts of interest.

The Dodd-Frank Act[55] requires the Comptroller General of the United States to conduct a study of analyst conflicts of interest. The study is to include an assessment of the undertakings to which the defendant firms agreed as part of the Global Research Settlement and an evaluation of whether these undertakings should be codified and applied more broadly.[56] As this book goes to publication, the Government Accountability Office is in the process of conducting this study (Singletary 2010).

## 10.   THE FUTURE OF THE RESEARCH INDUSTRY

The Global Research Settlement and heightened regulation of research analysts have created changes in the research industry, but the market for investment information continues to evolve. The market volatility and economic developments of recent years highlight a continuing need for quality research, and as the economy recovers, new businesses will have a particular need for coverage to facilitate their access to capital. The extent to which this coverage will be financed by traditional sell side firms, independent analysts, exchanges, issuers, or investors themselves, remains unclear. Technological developments create challenges for traditional methods of producing and distributing financial information, but are also reshaping the industry (Schaefer 2009).

The extent to which media attention and regulatory changes have increased the independence of analyst research is similarly unclear. Rightly or wrongly, Wall Street firms do not appear to have internalized the concern that analysts be free from potential conflicts of interest. The industry's recent effort to dismantle the information barriers instituted by the Global Research Settlement is a visible example, and the effort is likely to reflect a pervasive attitude in the industry.

---

[51]   The NASD Foundation is now known as the FINRA Investor Education Foundation. See FINRA (2010).

[52]   *SEC v. Bear, Stearns & Co., supra* n. 48 at 418.

[53]   *SEC v. Bear, Sterns & Co.*, 03 Civ. 2949 (WHP) (S.D.N.Y.), Order dated March 15, 2010.

[54]   *Bear Sterns* Order dated March 15, 2010, at 3.

[55]   The Dodd-Frank Wall Street Reform and Consumer Protection Act of 2010, Pub. L. 111-203, 124 Stat. 376 (2010).

[56]   *Ibid.* Sec. 919A(b)(1).

Consider, for example, the actions of Jennifer Jordan. In 2005, Jordan, the lead Wells Fargo analyst for Cadence Design Systems, issued three reports on the company. At the same time that Jordan was issuing these reports, she was negotiating for employment with Cadence. Prior to issuing the third report, she accepted a job offer from Cadence, the terms of which included an award of Cadence stock and options to purchase additional stock. None of her reports disclosed this conflict of interest (Norris 2007; FINRA 2007). In addition, despite knowing that Jordan had accepted Cadence's offer of employment, the Wells Fargo director of research approved the release of the third report without requiring disclosure of the conflict.

Wells Fargo and its director of research settled the charges that Jordan's reports violated FINRA rules by failing to disclose Jordan's material conflicts of interest (FINRA 2007). Jordan, however, maintained that she had done nothing wrong (Norris 2007). In 2008, a FINRA Hearing Panel found that, while Jordan had violated the disclosure rules, she lacked culpable intent, and imposed a fine of $12,500 (FINRA 2009).

The National Adjudicatory Council took a different view of the significance of Jordan's conduct than the Hearing Panel, Wells Fargo and Jordan herself. On appeal of the Hearing Panel's decision, the Council found that Jordon 'failed to disclose actual, material conflicts of interest in all three research reports at issue, in violation of NASD Rules' (FINRA 2009, 6). As the Council stated, Jordan's ongoing employment discussions gave her 'incentives to skew her research reports to improve or avoid damaging her chances of obtaining an offer from Cadence Design' (FINRA 2009, 7). The Council described Jordan's entire course of conduct as reckless and increased the sanctions to a fine of $20,000 and a two-year suspension from the industry. Most importantly, the Council warned that the Hearing Panel's modest sanctions sent 'the dangerous message that the rule provisions that FINRA adopted in the wake of the research scandals of just a few years ago are ones that FINRA no longer takes seriously' (FINRA 2009, 21). Although the benefits of mandated analyst independence may be overstated (Fisch 2007a), going forward, investors would do well to remain skeptical about whether FINRA, the Wall Street investment banks, and the analysts themselves take those rules seriously.

# REFERENCES

Ackman, Dan (2001), 'Management & Trends: Analyst Lawsuits: Blaming the Cheerleader', Forbes.com, August 8, available at http://www.forbes.com/2001/08/08/0808lawsuits.html (last accessed October 2011).

Agrawal, Anup & Mark A. Chen (2005), 'Analyst conflicts and research quality', Working Paper, University of Alabama and University of Maryland.

Agrawal, Anup & Mark A. Chen (2008), 'Do Analyst Conflicts Matter? Evidence from Stock Recommendations', *Journal of Law and Economics*, 51, 503–37.

Agrawal, Anup, Sahiba Chadha & Mark A. Chen (2006), 'Who Is Afraid of Reg FD? The Behavior and Performance of Sell-Side Analysts Following the SEC's Fair Disclosure Rules', *Journal of Business*, 79, 2811–34.

Altinkilic, Oya, Vadim S. Balashov & Robert S. Hansen (2009), 'Evidence that Analysts are not important information Intermediaries', Working Paper, available at http://papers.ssrn.com/sol3/papers.cfm?abstract_id=1364859 (last accessed October 2011).

Anderson, Jenny (2006), 'True or False: A Hedge Fund Plotted to Hurt a Drug Maker?', *New York Times*, March 26.

Bailey, Warren, Connie X. Mao & Rui Zhong (2003), 'Regulation fair disclosure and earnings information: market, analyst, and corporate responses', *Journal of Finance*, 58, 2487–2514.

Barber, Brad, Reuven Lehavy, Maureen McNichols & Brett Trueman (2003), 'Reassessing the Returns to Analysts' Stock Recommendations', *Financial Analysts Journal*, 59, 88–96.

Barber, Brad M., Reuven Lehavy, Maureen McNichols & Brett Trueman (2006), 'Buys, holds, and sells: The distribution of investment banks' stock ratings and the implications for the profitability of analysts' recommendations', *Journal of Accounting and Economics*, 41, 87–117.

Blodget, Henry (2009), 'Jim Chanos, SAC Snared In Wall Street Research Scandal Business Insider', Clusterstock, February 13, available at http://in.reuters.com/article/2008/10/13/overstock-settlement-idINN134638432008 1013 (last accessed October 2011).

Boni, Leslie (2006), 'Analyzing the Analysts After the Global Settlement', in Robert E. Litan and Yasuyuki Fuchita (eds) *Financial Gatekeepers: Can They Protect Investors?*, Washington, DC: Brookings Institution Press and the Nomura Institute of Capital Markets Research.

Boni, Leslie & Kent L. Womack (2002), 'Wall Street's Credibility Problem: Misaligned Incentives and Dubious Fixes?', Working Paper, The Brookings-Wharton Papers in Financial Services, available at http://fic.wharton.upenn.edu/fic/papers/02/0204.pdf (last accessed October 2011).

Boni, Leslie & Kent L. Womack (2006), 'Analysts, Industries and Price Momentum', *Journal of Financial and Quantitative Analysis*, 41, 85–109.

Bowen, Robert, Xia Chen & Qiang Cheng (2008), 'Analyst Coverage and the Cost of Raising Equity Capital: Evidence from Underpricing of Seasoned Equity Offerings', *Contemporary Accounting Research*, 25, 657–99.

Bradshaw, Mark T., Scott A. Richardson & Richard G. Sloan (2003), 'Pump and Dump: An Empirical Analysis of the Relation Between Corporate Financing Activities and Sell-side Analyst Research', Working Paper, available at http://ssrn.com/abstract=410521 (last accessed October 2011) or doi:10.2139/ssrn.410521.

Busse, Jeffrey A. & T. Clifton Green (2002), 'Market Efficiency in Real Time', *Journal of Financial Economics*, 65, 415–37.

Chan, Louis K.C., Jason J. Karceski & Josef Lakonishok (2007), 'Analysts' Conflict of Interest and Biases in Earnings Forecasts', *Journal of Financial and Quantitative Analysis*, 42, 893–913.

Chen, Chih-Yeng & Peter Chen (2009), 'NASD Rule 2711 and Changes in Analysts' Independence in Making Stock Recommendations', *Accounting Review*, 84, 1041.

Choi, Stephen J. & Jill E. Fisch (2003), 'How To Fix Wall Street: A Voucher Financing Proposal for Securities Intermediaries', *Yale Law Journal*, 113, 269–346.

Clarke, Jonathan, Ajay Khorana, Raghu Rau & Ajay Patel (2004), 'The good, the bad and the ugly? Differences in analyst behavior at investment banks, brokerages, and independent research firms', Working Paper unpublished, Purdue University.

Coffee, John C. Jr. (1984), 'Market Failure and the Economic Case for a Mandatory Disclosure System', *Virginia Law Review*, 70, 717.

Coffee, John C. Jr. (2004), 'Gatekeeper Failure and Reform', *Boston University Law Review*, 84, 301.

Cornett, Marcia Millon, Hassan Tehranianb & Atakan Yalçın (2005), 'Regulation Fair Disclosure and the Market's Reaction to Analyst Investment Recommendation Changes', Working Paper unpublished, Boston College.

Cowan, Lynn & Ed Welsch (2009), 'Investors, Research Firms Brace For Settlement's End', *Dow Jones News*, May 27, available at http://www.thelion.com/bin/forum.cgi?tf=wall_street_pit&msg=1634559&cmd=r&t= (last accessed October 2011).

Cowan, Lynn and Ed Welsch (2009), 'Investors, Research Firms Brace For Settlement's End,' NASDAQ, May 27, http://www.nasdaq.com/aspx/company-news-story.aspx?storyid=200905121151dowjonesdjonline000521.

Craig, Susanne (2004), 'Research Rules Trickle Down To Small Firms', *Wall Street Journal*, January 19.

Craig, Susanne (2005), 'Moving the Market: Firm to Research Stock "Orphans,"' *Wall Street Journal*, June 7.

Craig, Susanne and Kara Scannell (2010), 'SEC Tried to Ease Curbs,' *Wall Street Journal*, March 17.

D'Avolio, Gene, Efi Gildor & Andrei Shleifer (2001), 'Technology, Information Production, and Market Efficiency', Working Paper, Harvard Institute of Economic Research, Discussion Paper Number 19292001, available at www.economics.harvard.edu/pub/hier/2001/HIER1929.pdf (last accessed October 2011).

Da, Zhi & Ernst Schaumburg (2011), 'Relative Valuation and Analyst Target Price Forecasts', *Journal of Financial Markets*, 14, 161.

Denning, Liam (2010), 'Wall Street's Not-So-Great Expectations', *Wall Street Journal*, April 26.

Dugar, Amitabh & Siva Nathan (1995), 'The Effect of Investment Banking Relationships on Financial Analysts' Earnings Forecasts and Investment Recommendations', *Contemporary Accounting Research*, 12, 131–60.

Entrepreneur.com (n.d.), 'Charles Schwab: Budget Broker', available at http://www.entrepreneur.com/growyour-business/radicalsandvisionaries/article197694.html (last accessed October 2011).

FINRA (2007), 'FINRA News Release: NASD Fines Wells Fargo Securities $250,000 for Failing to Disclose Analyst's Employment with Covered Company in Research Report', June 27, available at http://www.finra.org/Newsroom/NewsReleases/2007/P019344 (last accessed October 2011).

FINRA (2010), FINRA Home Page, available at http://www.finrafoundation.org/ (last accessed October 2011).

Fisch, Jill E. (2007a), 'Does Analyst Independence Sell Investors Short?', *UCLA Law Review*, 55, 39.

Fisch, Jill E. (2007b), 'Fiduciary Duties and the Analyst Scandals', *Alabama Law Review*, 58, 1083.

Fisch, Jill E. & Hillary A. Sale (2003), 'The Securities Analyst as Agent: Rethinking the Regulation of Analysts', *Iowa Law Review*, 88, 1035.

Freeman, James (2008), 'Who's Going to Fund the Next Steve Jobs?', *Wall Street Journal*, July 18.

Fromson, Brett Duval (1988), 'The Slow Death of E.F. Hutton', *Fortune Magazine*, February 29, available at http://money.cnn.com/magazines/fortune/fortune_archive/1988/02/29/70241/index.htm (last accessed October 2011).

Gaffen, David (2008), 'MarketBeat: Bank Analyst Sued by Bank', Wall Street Journal.com, July 21, available at http://blogs.wsj.com/marketbeat/2008/07/21/bank-analyst-sued-by-bank/ (last accessed October 2011).

Gasparino, Charles & Susanne Craig (2003), 'Meeker Won't Face Securities Law Charges', *Wall Street Journal*, April 2.

Gintschela, Andreas & Stanimir Markov (2004), 'The Effectiveness of Regulation FD', *Journal of Accounting and Economics*, 37, 293–314.

Gleason, Kristi & Charles M.C. Lee (2003), 'Analyst Forecast Revisions and Market Price Discovery', *The Accounting Review*, 78, 193–225.

Gottlieb Cleary (2009), Letter to Judge Pauley, August 3, available at http://blogs.law.harvard.edu/corpgov/files/2010/03/Request-to-modify-2003-settlement.pdf (last accessed October 2011).

Green, T. Clifton (2004), 'The Value of Client Access to Analyst Recommendations', Working Paper, available at http://elvis.sob.tulane.edu/Documents/Gmgt626/CGreen.pdf (last accessed October 2011).

Groysberg, Boris, Paul Healy & Craig Chapman (2008), 'Buy-Side vs. Sell-Side Analysts' Earnings Forecasts', *Financial Analysts Journal*, 64 , 25–39.

Guan, Yuyan, Hai Lu & M.H. Franco Wong (2009), 'Global Settlement and Star Analysts' Career Choices', Working Paper, available at http://www.nd.edu/~carecob/Workshops/09-10%20Workshops/Wong%20Paper.pdf (last accessed October 2011).

Hovakimian, Armen G. & Ekkachai Saenyasiri (2009), 'Conflicts of Interest and Analyst Behavior: Evidence from Recent Changes in Regulation', Working Paper, available at http://papers.ssrn.com/sol3/papers.cfm?abstract_id=1133102 (last accessed October 2011).

Howe, John S., Emre Unlu & Xuemin (Sterling) Yan (2007), 'The Predictive Content of Aggregate Analyst Recommendations', Working Paper, available at http://business.missouri.edu/yanx/research/AggRec.pdf (last accessed October 2011).

Huang, Joshua, G. Mujtaba Mianb & Srinivasan Sankaraguruswamy (2009), 'The value of combining the information content of analyst recommendations and target prices', *Journal of Financial Markets*, 12, 754–77.

Ivkovic, Zoran & Narasimham Jagadeesh (2004), 'The timing and value of forecast and recommendation revisions', *Journal of Financial Economics*, 73, 433–63.

Jacob, John, Steve Rock & David P. Weber (2003), 'Do analysts at independent research firms make better earnings forecasts?', Working Paper, available at http://ssrn.com/abstract=434702 (last accessed October 2011).

Kadan, Ohad, Leonardo Madureira, Rong Wang & Tzachi Zach (2009), 'Conflicts of Interest and Stock Recommendations: The Effects of the Global Settlement and Related Regulations', *Review of Financial Studies*, 22, 4189–4217.

Kador, John (2002), *Charles Schwab: How One Company Beat Wall Street and Reinvented the Brokerage Industry*, Hoboken, N.J.: John Wiley & Sons, Inc.

Karp, Richard (2003), 'Hardball: Securities Arbitration Cases are Surging and Turning Nasty', *Barrons*, October 20.

Kecskés, Ambrus & Kent L. Womack (2008), 'Adds and drops of coverage by equity research analysts', Working Paper, available at http://papers.ssrn.com/sol3/papers.cfm?abstract_id=960501 (last accessed October 2011).

Khorana, Ajay, Simona Mola & Raghavendra Rau (2007), 'Is There Life after Loss of Analyst Coverage?', Working Paper, available at http://graphics8.nytimes.com/images/blogs/dealbook/AnalystCoverageStudy.pdf (last accessed October 2011).

Kim, Jane (2009), 'Stock-Research Reform to Die?', *Wall Street Journal*, June 9.

Kirk, Marcus (2008), 'Can Companies Buy Credible Analyst Research?', Working Paper, available at http://www.scribd.com/doc/17241615/Can-Companies-Buy-Credible-Analyst-Research-by-Marcus-Kirk (last accessed October 2011).

Kiviat, Barbara (2009), 'Wall Street Stock Research: Soon, Less Independent', *Time Magazine*, April 25.

Koh, Kevin, Dawn A. Matsumoto & Shivaram Rajgopal (2008), 'Meeting or Beating Analyst Expectations in the Post-Scandals World: Changes in Stock Market Rewards and Managerial Actions', *Contemporary Accounting Research*, 25, 1067–98.

Kolasinski, Adam (2006), 'Is the Chinese Wall too High? Investigating the Costs of New Restrictions on Cooperation Between Analysts and Investment Bankers', Working Paper, available at http://papers.ssrn.com/sol3/papers.cfm?abstract_id=895365 (last accessed October 2011).

Krigman, Laurie, Wayne H. Shaw & Kent L. Womack (2001), 'Why do firms switch underwriters?', *Journal of Financial Economics*, 60, 245–84.

MacDonald, Larry (2009), 'On Small Cap Research', *Seeking Alpha*, January 26, available at http://seekingalpha.com/article/116520-on-small-cap-research (last accessed October 2011).

Malmendier, Ulrike & Devin Shanthikumar (2007), 'Are small investors naive about incentives?', *Journal of Financial Economics*, 85, 457–89.

Martin, Andrew & Louise Story (2010), 'The Loneliest Analyst', *New York Times*, September 11, http://www.nytimes.com/2010/09/12/business/12suit.html?r=1 (last accessed October 2011).

Mehran, Hamid & René M. Stulz (2007), 'The economics of conflicts of interest in financial institutions', *Journal of Financial Economics*, 85, 267–96.

Michaely, Roni & Kent L. Womack (1999), 'Conflict of Interest and the Credibility of Underwriter Analyst Recommendations', *Review of Financial Studies*, 12, 653–86.

Morgenson, Gretchen (2001), 'Telecom's Pied Piper', New York University, Stern School of Business, November 18, available at http://pages.stern.nyu.edu/~adamodar/New_Home_Page/articles/GrubmanFalls.htm (last accessed October 2011).

Munk, Cheryl Winokur (2003), 'Split of Research From Banking Means Still-Lower Analyst Pay', *Wall Street Journal*, May 14.

NASDAQ (2009), 'NASDAQ OMX Selects Morningstar to Provide Equity Research Profile Reports On All NASDAQ-Listed Companies', NASDAQ OMX, June 8, available at http://ir.nasdaq.com/releasedetail.cfm?releaseid=388459 (last accessed October 2011).

News-Medical.Net (2010), 'Separate Complaints filed against Biovail by S.A.C. Capital Advisors and Gradient Analytics', The Medical News from News-Medical.Net, February 21, available at http://www.news-medical.net/news/20100221/Separate-Complaints-filed-against-Biovail-by-SAC-Capital-Advisors-and-Gradient-Analytics.aspx (last accessed October 2011).

Norris, Floyd (2003), 'A Climb to Riches, One Merger at a Time', *New York Times*, July 17.

Norris, Floyd (2007), 'Wells Fargo and Ex-Analyst Are Fined', *New York Times*, June 28.

NYSE Euronext (2009), 'News Releases: NYSE Euronext, Virtua Research Initiate Project to Boost Independent Research Coverage of Listed Issuers', available at http://www.nyse.com/press/1243505663215.html (last accessed October 2011).

O'Brien, Patricia C., Maureen F. McNichols & Hsiou-wei Lin (2005), 'Analyst Impartiality and Investment Banking Relationships', Working Paper, available at http://ssrn.com/abstract=709201 (last accessed October 2011).

O'Hara, Neal A. (2010), 'Independent Research: Salvation in the Middle Market', *The Finance Professional's Post*, available at http://www.theinvestmentprofessional.com/vol_2_no_4/indep-research.html (last accessed October 2011).

Olazabal, Ann Morales (2004), 'Analyst and Broker-Dealer Liability under 10(b) for Biased Stock Recommendations', *New York University Journal of Law and Business*, 1, 1.

Opdyke, Jeff & Annelena Lobb (2009), 'MIA Analysts Give Companies Worries', *Wall Street Journal*, May 26.

Peek, Liz (2008), 'Spitzer's Legacy Haunts Bear Stearns', *The New York Sun*, March 18.

Pettersson, Edvard (2008), 'BankAtlantic Sues Firm, Analyst Bove for Defamation', *Bloomberg*, July 21, available at http://preview.bloomberg.com/apps/news?pid=newsarchive_en10&sid=aKq4yHbl1Ejk (last accessed October 2011).

Pitt, Harvey L. (2002), 'Statement by SEC Chairman: Proposal of Regulation AC', US Securities and Exchange Commission, available at http://www.sec.gov/news/speech/spch578.htm (last accessed October 2011).

Ryan, Paul & Richard J. Taffler (2004), 'Are Economically Significant Stock Returns and Trading Volumes Driven by Firm-Specific News Releases?', *Journal of Business Finance and Accounting*, 31, 49–82.

Sage, Alexandria (2008), 'Overstock says settled claims against Gradient', Reuters.com, October 13, available at http://in.reuters.com/article/2008/10/13/overstock-settlement-idINN1346384320081013 (last accessed October 2011).

Sasseen, Jane (2006), 'The Secret Lives Of Short-Sellers', *Businessweek*, April 10.

Schack, Justin (2005), 'Settling for Nothing, Institutional Investors', *Institutional Investor*, 39, 26–36.

Schaefer, Steve (2009), 'Research Industry Heads For A Makeover', Forbes.com, May 8, available at http://www.forbes.com/2009/05/08/best-analysts-brokerages-zacks-brokerage-analysts-09-research.html (last accessed October 2011).

Scianni, Gina N. (2004), 'Note: From Behind the Corporate Veil: The Outing of Wall Street's Investment Banking Scandals – Why Recent Regulations May Not Mean the Dawn of a New Day', *Fordham Journal of Corporate & Financial Law*, 9, 257–94.

SEC (Securities and Exchange Commission) (2003a), 'SEC Fact Sheet on Global Analyst Research Settlements', available at http://www.sec.gov/news/speech/factsheet.htm (last accessed October 2011).

SEC (Securities and Exchange Commission) (2003b), 'Ten of Nation's Top Investment Firms Settle Enforcement Actions Involving Conflicts of Interest Between Research and Investment Banking', available at http://www.sec.gov/news/press/2003-54.htm (last accessed October 2011).

SEC (Securities and Exchange Commission) (2004), 'Deutsche Bank Securities Inc. and Thomas Weisel Partners LLC Settle Enforcement Actions Involving Conflicts of Interest Between Research and Investment Banking', Press Release, available at http://www.sec.gov/news/press/2004-120.htm (last accessed October 2011).

SEC (Securities and Exchange Commission) (2006), 'Final Report of the Advisory Committee on Smaller Public Companies to the U.S. Securities and Exchange Commission', available at www.sec.gov/info/smallbus/acspc/acspc-finalreport.pdf (last accessed October 2011).

SIFMA (Securities Industry and Financial Markets Association) (2007), 'White Paper on Arbitration in the Securities Industry', October, available at www.sifma.org/workarea/downloadasset.aspx?id=21334 (last accessed October 2011).

Singletary, Michelle (2010), 'Insecure about securities? Lawmakers hope studies will teach otherwise', *The Washington Post*, August 5.

Smith, Randall (2003), 'The Stock-Research Pact: Morgan Stanley Stock-Research Tactics Are Criticized in Pact', *The Wall Street Journal*, May 5.

Sorkin, Andrew Ross (2008), 'Dealbook: Analyzing Wall Street's Research', *New York Times*, August 11, available at http://www.nytimes.com/2008/08/12/business/12sorkin.html (last accessed October 2011).

StreetAccount (2010), 'Products & Services', available at https://www.streetaccount.com/v2/productsServices.aspx (last accessed October 2011).

Stuart, Alix (2010), 'Forecast Perpetually Sunny, for Analysts', CFO.com, May 13, available at http://www.cfo.com/article.cfm/14497484 (last accessed October 2011).

Thomas, Landon (2003a), 'Changed Smith Barney Is Thin on Analysts', *New York Times*, June 13.

Thomas, Landon (2003b), 'Judges Reject Suits Blaming Analysts For Losses', *New York Times*, July 2.

Weild, David & Edward Kim (2009), 'The Slow Degradation of the IPO Market', *Mergers & Acquisitions*, 44, 54.

Wilchins, Dan (2008), 'Citi cuts global equity research coverage', Reuters, October 15, available at http://www.reuters.com/article/idUSTRE49E96820081015 (last accessed October 2011).

Yu, Fang (Frank) (2008), 'Analyst coverage and earnings management', *Journal of Financial Economics*, 88, 245–71.

# 18. D&O insurance and the ability of shareholder litigation to deter
*Sean J. Griffith*

## 1. SHAREHOLDER LITIGATION AND DETERRENCE

Deterrence is widely recognized by legal scholars as the principal policy justification for shareholder litigation. Arguments in favor of the alternative, the compensation rationale, have been more or less dispatched, at least as regards the paradigmatic form of shareholder litigation, the 10b-5 class action, on the basis that damages awards provide meager compensation relative to investor loss and, from the perspective of diversified shareholders, amount to mere pocket-shifting.[1] Instead, much shareholder litigation is justified wholly by its ability to cause corporate officers and directors, out of fear of being held liable to their shareholders, to foreswear bad acts – by its ability, that is, to deter.

A significant problem with the deterrence rationale, however, lies in the fact that individual directors and officers are almost never made to pay for the consequences of their actions (Black et al. 2006). Nor, indeed, are the corporations they manage. Instead, an insurance policy typically steps in to fund losses arising from shareholder litigation. This form of insurance – Directors' and Officers' Liability Insurance or, simply, 'D&O' insurance – is purchased by virtually all public corporations in the United States in amounts sufficient to fund the vast majority of shareholder settlements. Moreover, most D&O policies cover individual directors and officers as well as the corporate entity they manage.

D&O insurance thus transfers the risk of shareholder litigation from corporate defendants to a third party insurer. But, following the familiar logic of moral hazard, a party that is no longer liable for the costs of their actions can no longer be expected to minimize the costs of their actions. In the corporate context, managers who are no longer personally at risk for investor losses may take less care to avoid them, and corporations that are no longer at risk of loss from shareholder litigation may expend less effort in monitoring the conduct of their managers. D&O insurance thus threatens to destroy the deterrence effect of shareholder litigation and, with it, the very justification for its continued existence.

Unless, that is, the insurer does something to avoid this outcome. Insurers, after all, are unlikely to favor an arrangement that fails to prevent or, worse, encourages conduct that will lead to covered losses. Moreover, in taking action to avoid this outcome, insurers may effectively deter the conduct most likely to give rise to losses from shareholder litigation. Insurers, in other words, may preserve rather than subvert the deterrence function of shareholder liti-

---

[1]  See 17 C.F.R. § 240.10b-5 (codifying Rule 10b-5). The consensus opinion and arguments refuting the compensation rationale are nicely summarized in Rose (2008). Prominent academic lawyers writing from the consensus perspective include Alexander (1996); Coffee (2006); Easterbrook & Fischel (1985); Langevoort (1996); and Pritchard (1999).

gation. There are at least three opportunities in the typical insurance arrangement for the insurer to exert this constraining influence. First, in underwriting the insurance, D&O carriers may seek to price their product to the expected risk of loss and, by doing so, provide the insureds with an incentive, in the form of lower D&O premiums, to design governance arrangements to minimize the risk of costly shareholder litigation. Second, during the course of the insurance relationship, insurers may monitor the conduct of their insureds and seek to improve corporate governance practices in an effort to minimize the risk of shareholder litigation. Third, insurers may engage in the selective payment of claims, either by refusing to settle nuisance litigation or by seeking to avoid coverage obligations in light of evidence of wrongdoing on the part of the insured, thereby leaving worse-governed firms with a larger share of each claim, thus providing an incentive to reform.

Whether and how insurers in fact do any of this is, of course, an empirical question, and it is one that I set out to answer with my co-author and co-investigator, Tom Baker. We spent several years researching the D&O insurance industry, conducting in-depth interviews with over 100 people involved in D&O insurance and securities litigation in various capacities.[2] In addition, we immersed ourselves in the industry literature and participated in numerous industry conferences (Griffith 2006; Baker & Griffith 2007a, 2007b, 2009).

What did we find? The short answer is that insurers no longer invest any effort in monitoring their insureds during the life of the policy. Any past attempts to do so ended in failure. Nevertheless, D&O insurers do indeed seek to price their coverage to risk and do indeed exert influence in the settlement of claims. The question remains, however: do these practices of D&O insurers succeed in preserving the deterrence function of shareholder litigation?

In this chapter I will seek to sketch an overview of our research on this point. I will first describe how D&O insurance arrangements typically work. Then I will summarize some of our key findings on how well or poorly D&O insurers do in fact preserve the deterrence function of shareholder litigation. Finally, I will allude to our recommendations for improving the situation. Space constraints have forced me to abbreviate much of this discussion, which is described in much greater length and in much greater detail in our book, *Ensuring Corporate Misconduct: How Liability Insurance Undermines Shareholder Litigation* (Baker & Griffith 2010).

## 2.   A BRIEF INTRODUCTION TO D&O INSURANCE

Directors' and Officers' liability insurance was invented by Lloyd's of London in the 1950s and has been widely used by US corporations since the mid-1960s. As noted above, it is now purchased by the virtually all public companies in the United States. One source reports that 100% of public company respondents purchased coverage (Towers Perrin 2006).[3]

---

[2]   Interviewees included: D&O underwriters, D&O claims managers, securities defense lawyers, plaintiffs' lawyers specializing in shareholder litigation, the monitoring or coverage counsel providing outsider representation to insurance companies, insurance brokers, actuaries, risk managers, damages experts, and mediators.

[3]   We did hear of the rare exception – Berkshire-Hathaway, for example, was sometimes claimed not to purchase coverage, but this is indeed the exception to the rule. D&O Insurance is also available for privately held and not-for-profit corporations. In that context, however, employment-related claims

D&O insurance protects officers and directors from liability-related costs arising out of any wrongful acts allegedly committed in the course of their duties. Typical policy language offers coverage against 'any actual breach of duty, neglect, error, misstatement, misleading statement, omission or act ... by such Executive in his or her capacity as such or any matter claimed against such Executive solely by reason of his or her status as such ...' (AIG Specimen Policy 2000, § 2(z)). For public companies, the predominant source of risk under these policies is shareholder litigation, specifically 10b-5 class actions and, to a considerably lesser extent, derivative suits. Covered losses under a D&O policy include compensatory damages, settlement amounts, and defense costs.

Contemporary D&O policies protect more than the individual directors and officers who may be named as defendants in a shareholder suit, extending coverage to the corporation's own losses resulting from shareholder litigation. I will refer to D&O coverage of the corporate entity as 'entity-level coverage'. Entity level coverage is typically triggered by the corporation's own losses in a securities lawsuit or, alternatively, by the corporation's indemnification obligations to its officers and directors arising as a result of shareholder litigation. Individual level coverage is typically triggered only when directors and officers suffer losses for which the corporation cannot indemnify them, as for example, when the corporation is insolvent or when loss arises from the settlement of derivative litigation which, in Delaware at least, is not indemnifiable.[4]

### Exclusions

D&O policies contain four principal exclusions: (1) the 'Fraud' exclusion for claims involving fraud or personal enrichment; (2) a set of 'timing' exclusions that seek to assign claims to the proper policy period; (3) the 'Insured v. Insured' exclusion for litigation between insured persons; and (4) 'market segmentation' exclusions that carve out coverage from those losses for which other forms of insurance are available – such as environmental claims, ERISA claims, and claims alleging bodily injury or emotional distress – thus leaving shareholder litigation as the principal covered risk. Of these, only the Fraud exclusion has a significant impact on claims.

The potential relevance of the Fraud exclusion is perhaps most clear upon consideration of 10b-5 litigation, which after all, involves a type of fraud. The Fraud exclusion bars coverage for any 'dishonest or fraudulent act or omission or any criminal act or omission or any willful violation of any statute, rule or law'.[5] Were it to operate as written, it would seem to exclude 10b-5 claims by definition. However, most shareholder suits avoid the Fraud exclusion on the basis of the plaintiffs' attorneys' artful pleading and by settling before the adjudication of any actual wrongdoing.

In our interviews, plaintiffs' lawyers regularly reported that the Fraud exclusion leads them to plead strategically, crafting their pleadings to avoid coming within the exclusion. In

---

are the most common source of D&O liabilities. Because we were most interested in the interaction of D&O insurance with shareholder litigation, the dominant source of risk for public companies, our research focused exclusively on the public company D&O market.

[4]   Delaware permits indemnification for defense costs but not amounts paid to settle derivative claims. See 8 Del. Code Ann. §145(a).

[5]   Executive Risk Indemnity, Inc., *Executive Liability Policy*, III.A.3. Similar language appears in the AIG and Chubb policies.

the context of a 10b-5 class action, for example, where the state of mind requirement can be met by showing either intent to defraud or recklessness, plaintiffs' lawyers will plead recklessness since, in the words of one, 'why would you want to plead yourself into a coverage denial?' Similarly, another plaintiffs' lawyer remarked, 'we make sure that we don't use words like "you intentionally cooked the books" or "you did this" or "you did that". We don't want to provide any sort of out for the insurance carriers. We are careful to emphasize that recklessness can prove scienter and that is not intentional.' Pleading intentional fraud would give the D&O insurers a bargaining chip that they could use in settlement negotiations either to reduce their obligation to fund settlement or, potentially, to avoid the claim altogether. As a result, it is now standard practice for plaintiffs' lawyers to construct their cases around allegations of reckless conduct, in order to avoid jeopardizing the defendant's D&O coverage.

### Limits and Towers of Coverage

The amount of D&O insurance purchased correlates to the market capitalization of the corporate buyer, a fact that is unsurprising considering that a company's exposure to loss from shareholder litigation is correlated to the company's market capitalization. According to the Towers Perrin survey, in 2007, small-cap companies purchased an average of $26.41 million in D&O coverage limits.[6] Mid-cap companies purchased an average of $42.8 million in limits. And large-cap companies purchased an average of $168.65 million in D&O coverage. Deductibles seem to vary in proportion to total coverage.[7] In 2007, the average public company deductible was $1.5 million and the highest reported deductible was approximately $5.5 million (Towers Perrin 2008, 29–30).

The largest coverage limit available to any single corporation, according to the participants in our study, was $300 million. And, in general, insurers prefer not to underwrite the entire limit purchased by any one corporation, especially for the high-limit policies purchased by large- and mid-cap companies, and seek to limit their risk on any one account to no more than $25 million. As a result of these constraints, corporations must purchase several D&O policies in order to reach the aggregate amount of insurance they desire. D&O insurance packages are thus said to come in 'towers' – that is, separate layers of insurance policies stacked to reach a desired total amount of coverage.

The bottom layer of a D&O tower is called the 'primary policy' and the insurance company offering that policy is the 'primary insurer'. Because the primary insurer's policy is the first to respond to a covered loss and therefore is the most likely to incur a payment obligation, the primary insurer is most closely involved in the underwriting process and receives a higher premium than those higher up in the tower of coverage to compensate for their greater risk. The market for primary insurance was dominated by a small number of companies

---

    6    Here I treat those companies with market capitalizations between $400 million and $1 billion as 'small cap companies'. 'Mid-cap companies' are those with market capitalizations between $1 billion and $10 billion, and 'large cap companies' are those exceeding $10 billion in market capitalization. Limits are reported in Towers Perrin (2008, 34).
    7    Technically, D&O policies have retentions, which are similar to, but not the same as, deductibles. Deductibles typically reduce policy limits while retentions, by contrast, do not. Also, it is worth noting that in general only the entity-coverage portion of a D&O policy carries any retention.

during the period of our research, most significantly AIG and Chubb.[8] After the primary policy is used up ('exhausted' in the language of the trade), excess insurers – those higher up in the coverage tower – become responsible for covered losses on a layer-by-layer basis as the limits of each underlying policy are successively exhausted by the payment of losses. As a result, the total premium that a corporate insured pays for its D&O coverage will be a blended amount of several distinct premiums paid to separate insurance companies, and the higher the limits a corporation buys, the more companies that are likely to make up the tower of coverage. This structure gives rise, among other complications, to a coordination problem among insurers in settling claims.

## 3.   DETERRENCE THROUGH THE PRICING OF THE POLICY

D&O insurers may preserve the deterrence function of shareholder litigation through the pricing of the policy. During underwriting, insurers decide which risks to cover and how much to charge for that coverage. If D&O insurers use a prospective insured's risk of incurring shareholder litigation to decide whom to insure and how much to charge for coverage, then these decisions will, in turn, have an effect on prospective insureds. If, for example, insurers charge higher premiums to higher risk firms, then those firms must either alter their practices or face higher insurance costs. If insurers engage in this form of selective underwriting, then firms would seem to have a natural incentive to minimize the risk of shareholder litigation in order to avoid paying high D&O premiums. Through underwriting, the insurer would thus preserve the deterrence function of shareholder litigation.

### Evaluating and Pricing D&O Risk

Our interviews uncovered ample evidence that D&O insurers do indeed seek to price to risk. Every underwriter we talked to stressed individual risk selection, each seeking to 'out-select [its] peers'. Likewise, each underwriter had its own method of assessing D&O risk, with wide variation in their pricing methods. Some underwriters are driven by mathematical models and others by much less formal discussions around a conference table. In the words of one underwriter, '[D&O underwriting is not like] auto insurance or these other lines of insurance where an underwriter can actually plug numbers into an actuarial model. We didn't do that. We literally sat at a round table and, just based on the experience of the more senior folks, we would say this is a great number. We threw a number out of the hat.'

In assessing risk, underwriters reported that they start with publicly available information, such as news reports, analyst estimates, SEC filings, as well as corporate governance reviews and accounting studies. This is much the same information that would be available to any investor. Additionally, however, insurers take information from prospective insureds in the form of applications and questionnaires and at underwriting meetings.

---

8   In 2005 AIG and Chubb together controlled 53% of the total U.S. market measured by premium volume and 36% of the total US market by policy count (Towers Perrin 2006, 86, figures 36 and 37).

D&O applications typically elicit general information on the background and experience of officers and directors as well as a description of the claims history of the corporation itself. Additionally, the D&O application inquires into the prospective insured's plans to make acquisitions or issue securities and into whether the prospective insured has knowledge of conduct likely to give rise to a claim. Beyond the application, insurers are given private access to officers and directors of the prospective insured in Underwriters' Meetings, often involving the prospective insured's Chief Financial Officer or Treasurer as well as members of the accounting and legal departments. The executives of prospective insureds typically present information about their business model, strategies, and risks, while underwriters ask questions and gather further information. In gathering this information, underwriters clearly are looking to gauge the prospective insured's risk. What is D&O risk? Underwriters described looking at two broad features of the prospective insured. First, financial factors, and second, corporate governance.

When evaluating a prospective insured's financial risk factors, D&O underwriters focus on the probability and the likely magnitude of losses to investors. In arriving at this estimation, underwriters described taking into account numerous factors, including the prospective insured's industry and maturity, and various accounting ratios. Above all, however, they seemed to be most interested in the prospective insured's share price volatility and its market capitalization. Share price volatility was treated as a clear indicator of the probability of loss while market capitalization, because it signals how far the company's value might fall, was seen to indicate the possible magnitude of loss.

In terms of corporate governance factors, underwriters described being most interested in soft governance variables such as the personal 'character' of top managers as well as the system of incentives and constraints operating within the organization, which our respondents often described as 'culture'. In evaluating these factors, underwriters investigate who reports to whom and inquire into the actual practices underlying formal policies. As one risk manager described, underwriters ask not only whether there is a process of controls in place, 'but how are you exercising the process and what evidence do you have to support your controllership process ... [A]ll the questions are around that subject.' To inquire further into a corporation's internal controls, underwriters reported that they also retain forensic accounting consultants to detect inadequacies in internal controls.

All of these factors, our participants reported, are ultimately used to generate a price for the risk. Underwriters described the pricing process as starting from a formal algorithm, then employing a highly discretionary system of credits and debits to arrive at the ultimate price. Financial factors and other easily observable factors play a prominent role in most algorithms, with culture and character variables forming the basis for the discretionary credits and debits.

Discretionary discounts result in pricing that varies widely from actuarially determined rates. Some insurers described a formal approach to discounting that limits the maximum credit for particular variables. For example, one underwriter described using a model where, 'if you are in a certain industry class, you are going to get debited between 5–10% or credited between 5–10%. If you have got a very poor board score, you are going to pay anywhere from 10–20% more.' Other underwriters, by contrast, employed much less rigid methods in arriving at the ultimate price. As described by one such underwriter: 'An underwriter ultimately consciously or unconsciously formulates an opinion about a risk, and that opinion leads him to make a certain decision' about price. Insurers often subject these opinions to additional layers of consultation and approval, depending upon the size of risk, with ultimate authority typically residing in a small group of experienced D&O underwriters.

**Pricing and Deterrence**

Having thus uncovered evidence that underwriters do indeed seek to estimate and price the risk of each individual D&O policy, the question remains: do these efforts of D&O insurers serve to preserve the deterrence function of shareholder litigation? More specifically, by pricing D&O premiums to risk, do insurers thereby induce firms to improve their corporate governance practices in order to reduce the cost of their D&O policies? On this point, there remains reason for doubt. In spite of the insurers' best efforts, D&O premiums may not succeed in accomplishing effective deterrence, either because the price is not right or because the marginal difference in price is not enough to stimulate corporate reform.

First, deterrence may fail because premium prices may not correlate to actual risk. This may be so because underwriters make mistakes and are influenced more by individual career incentives – for example, to bring in as much underwriting business as possible – than by long term company interests, that is, to avoid bad risks. Many of our respondents mentioned this possibility. Moreover, underwriters operate in a highly cyclical market in which insurance premiums are significantly influenced by underwriting capacity, which contracts with large losses to reserve accounts and expands with new entrants into the market, resulting in fluctuations to underwriting premiums that have nothing to do with the underlying risk. While each of these sources of error is undoubtedly present in the D&O market, it is not clear that these factors alone will lead to systematic mispricing. First, as far as errors and individual career incentives are concerned, while every insurance company faces these problems, every insurance company also has competitive incentives to address them, and although such problems may well lead to the mispricing of the occasional account, it is unlikely considering the law of large numbers that such mispricings occur systematically throughout the market. Second, regarding the cyclical nature of the market, while these fluctuations may indeed lead to unusual prices, all underwriters operate in the same market at the same time. The market, in other words, is hard or soft for everyone at once, with the result that at any given time, pricing is likely to be competitive, and all that is required for effective deterrence is that prices for higher risk insureds be high relative to lower risk insureds, not that prices be high or low vis-à-vis some absolute standard.

The bigger problem with pricing and deterrence arises in light of the possibility that the difference in price between high risk and low risk companies may not be sufficiently large to induce reform. Simply put, D&O expenses may not be large enough to change corporate behavior. This could be so either because D&O expenses are an insignificant portion of a large corporation's total costs or because the marginal difference in D&O expense between good firms and bad firms may not be large enough to induce bad firms to change their ways.

First, D&O insurance expenses might be so small, given a corporation's overall costs and cash flows, that companies do not consider them as a significant source of cost savings. Although D&O premiums are non-trivial and quite possibly large enough to affect some firms' behavior – small cap companies typically pay half a million dollars a year, mid-cap companies pay between $1 million and $2 million, and large cap companies may pay in excess of $2 million or $3 million in annual D&O premium – it may well be the case that taking into account a public corporation's overall budget, D&O premiums simply may not be large enough to induce insureds to change their behavior. In the words of one underwriter, 'it seems to me that however high D&O premiums climb, they are not going to climb high enough to get the companies to really pay attention ...'.

Second, even if D&O expenses are nontrivial and therefore noticeable to corporations, the difference between the premiums paid by good and bad firms may not be sufficiently large to force bad firms to improve. Good firms might pay too much while bad firms pay too little. This could be because underwriters, aware of their own fallibility, hesitate to give large price discounts to low-risk firms or, alternately, because the liability system allows the cost of shareholder litigation to fall too evenly on both good firms and bad firms. As a result of either or both of these possibilities, good firms may cross-subsidize bad firms to some degree, thus blunting the deterrence effect of D&O pricing.

In sum, although D&O insurers do indeed attempt to price corporate governance risk, their efforts may not be sufficient to reintroduce the deterrence function of shareholder litigation. If there is not much difference in the price paid by these two categories of firms, then there will be little incentive for the worse-governed firms to improve. Instead, all firms will simply pay their D&O premiums, whatever they are, and continue with business as usual. This is perhaps the most serious obstacle to the ability of D&O insurers to reintroduce deterrence through pricing, since it suggests that however carefully the underwriter works to understand the risk, the paltry difference in price charged to good versus bad firms will not deter misconduct in the same way that shareholder litigation might in a world without insurance.

## 4.   DETERRENCE THROUGH THE SELECTIVE PAYMENT OF CLAIMS

If pricing alone fails to preserve deterrence, insurers could nevertheless accomplish deterrence through the selective payment of claims. First, insurers could use their control over the defense and settlement of claims to insist that insureds refuse to settle nuisance claims. Second, in the event that genuine corporate wrongdoing is uncovered, insurers could seek to avoid their payments obligations under the policy, on the basis either of a policy exclusion or by rescinding the policy. As described in the sections that follow, however, the insurer's ability to pursue either of these tactics is significantly constrained. D&O insurers in fact have relatively little control over defense and settlement, and are similarly limited in their ability to avoid the payment of claims.

### The Insurer's Control over Defense and Settlement

Traditionally, liability insurance policies are written on a 'duty to defend' basis. Automobile policies, for example, are 'duty to defend' policies, which allocate to the insurer control over the defense and settlement of claims. [9] D&O policies, by contrast, are 'indemnity' policies, obliging the insurer to reimburse the insured for amounts spent in defense and settlement. Although D&O policies provide the insurance company with the right to 'associate' in the defense of the claim – meaning that the insurer is entitled to receive information about the defense of the claim and to provide input to the defense lawyers – the clear understanding and practice is that the policyholder, not the insurance company, controls the defense of the claim. Moreover, D&O insurance policies do not give the insurance company the traditional control

---

[9]   The history of defense coverage in liability policies is described in Abraham (2008).

over settlement reflected in the standard 'discretion to settle' provision in other liability insurance policies. Rather, D&O insurance policies put the policyholder in charge, but obligate the policyholder to obtain the insurance company's *consent* before settling a case. In shareholder litigation, in other words, the policyholder is in charge, subject only to the need to obtain the insurers' consent to settlement. Why is the arrangement structured in this way? As a senior lawyer in the general counsel's office of a Fortune 100 company pointedly asked: 'Would you trust an insurance company to defend you?' For him, at least, the answer was an emphatic 'No'.

With this lack of control over strategic decisions, our participants reported, goes an inability to control the costs of defense, which by all accounts are substantial. Excluding claims that were closed with no payment to the claimant, the median and mean defense costs in shareholder litigation in 2006 were $800,000 and $3,042,159 per claim (Towers Perrin 2007). Compared to the median and mean settlement amounts reported in the same survey ($1.6 million and $26.5 million), this suggests that defense costs fluctuate between 50% and 11% of the cost of paid claims, declining in percentage terms as the settlement amount increases. Our respondents confirmed this back-of-the-envelope estimate. One senior underwriter reported that defense costs commonly rise to 25% to 35% of the settlement amount, and sometimes go as high as 50%.

Nevertheless, the D&O insurer's authority to approve or reject settlements might give them the necessary leverage to fight nuisance suits and insist on greater contribution to settlement from genuine wrongdoers. However, our respondents emphasized that the insurer's authority at settlement is circumscribed by a principle of insurance law that holds insurers liable for the entire resulting judgment if they are deemed to have acted unreasonably in refusing to settle (Syverud 1990). In other words, by rejecting offers that are within an established norm for shareholder litigation, D&O insurers put themselves at risk for the entire resulting judgment, even in excess of the limits of the D&O policy. Given the potentially large damages at stake in a securities class action, and the small size of any individual D&O policy in relation to those damages, the duty to settle places considerable pressure on D&O insurers.

Indeed, plaintiffs' lawyers confirmed that they craft their settlement offers precisely to put this kind of pressure on insurers: 'it is great to [make a demand to settle within limits] because then you put the insurers in a bad faith posture potentially'. Defense counsel, in turn, are apt to emphasize that an insurer's failure to settle at an amount that his or her client considers fair might expose the insurer to a bad faith claim. As one defense lawyer described the situation, 'if you are a defendant, you want a policy limits demand because that is what puts you in a position to say [to the insurers], "You can now settle this case without hurting me, and I demand you do it"'. Another defense lawyer was still more direct on this point: 'When I'm talking to coverage counsel, I always use little terms to remind them [about bad faith].'

In sum, what these observations suggest is that the insurer's most powerful means of creating leverage at settlement – the power to refuse to consent to proffered settlements – is constrained by the risks associated with refusing a reasonable settlement. This leads insurers to consent to settlements that are viewed as falling within a normal range, that is, settling by reference to settlements in similar suits. Accordingly, our participants emphasized the importance of comparable settlements in deciding whether to approve settlement offers.

**Coverage Defenses**

If it is difficult to refuse consent to settle, D&O insurers may still preserve deterrence by seeking to avoid their policy obligations when there is evidence of actual wrongdoing on the part of the insured. Such efforts could preserve the deterrence effect of shareholder litigation by creating an incentive on the part of the insureds to monitor their officers and directors more closely in order to prevent the sorts of misconduct that might cause the corporation to lose coverage. One way that a corporation can effectively lose coverage is through the policy's Fraud exclusion, which as noted above is nevertheless rarely applicable, due in large part to the plaintiffs' artful pleading. An additional means by which the insurer might seek to avoid coverage, however, is through rescission of the policy.

In seeking to rescind the policy, insurers typically employ a version of the basic fraud-in-the-inducement defense to contract. In the D&O context, their argument typically will turn on false information supplied in connection with the application for insurance. The insurers seeking to void coverage will argue that any such misstatements are material and that they relied on these material misstatements in entering into the insurance contract. Insurers who can establish these elements may either terminate coverage by simply cancelling the policy and returning any premiums paid by the policyholder or they may sue to have the policy declared *void ab initio* in a rescission action. Intent to deceive is not required. And an insurer's right to rescind on the basis of misrepresentations is typically buttressed by policy language that requires the policyholder to acknowledge that all information submitted to underwriters forms a part of the application on which the decision to insure is based and that all such information is true.

Financial misrepresentations, in particular, are a common basis of rescission actions. Because D&O insurers base their risk-assessments in large part on the financial condition of prospective policyholders, misstatements of financial information are frequently material to insurer's underwriting decisions. Such misstatements may be made in the application itself or in attached documents expressly incorporated into the policy application, such as a corporation's annual report to shareholders.

It is thus not uncommon for the same misstatement to be the basis both for the plaintiffs' 10b-5 claim and the insurer's rescission action. This close relationship between an insurer's rescission action and a shareholder's underlying claim suggests that insurers will have a plausible rescission argument for much shareholder litigation. Indeed, the most common basis for the proto-typical 10b-5 class action is a financial misrepresentation in a public disclosure document which, as long as it is also provided to the insurer in connection with the policy application or a renewal application, will also provide a strong basis for a rescission claim. Because the same conduct provides the basis for both claims, it would seem that insurers will often have a plausible rescission argument and an ability to at least threaten to deny coverage to the basic shareholder cause of action.

Furthermore, because the insurer's coverage defenses and the shareholders' claim are often based on the same underlying facts, the strength of insurers' rescission argument should correlate to the strength of the underlying shareholder claim. The participants in our study confirmed this relationship. Roughly speaking, the bigger the fraud and the easier it is to prove, the stronger the insurers' rescission or fraud defenses will likely be. It is thus not surprising that insurers litigated coverage defenses in each of the major frauds from the previous round of corporate scandals – including Enron, Worldcom, Tyco, and Adelphia.

## Cashing in the Coverage Defense

As a result of their ability to seek to rescind on the basis of the insured's misrepresentations, D&O insurers will often have a coverage defense to a given claim, at least as to some of the defendants.[10] Nevertheless, our participants emphasized that rescission actions are something of a rarity. Nor, they suggested, do insurers typically try to stretch available exclusions to avoid coverage in cases where they are arguably applicable. There are exceptions, of course, but most potential rescission claims are, as practitioners sometimes put it, dogs that don't bark.

The rarity of rescission or outright denial of coverage can be explained in large part by the adverse market impact that attends a carrier with a reputation for rescinding or denying coverage. Our respondents repeatedly emphasized that, in particular, a rescission action can have immediate negative consequences for an insurance carrier. Not only does it make other policyholders worry that the carrier will seek to rescind their policies, it also substantially harms the community of insurance brokers who assured their clients when placing their coverage that the carrier would be there to cover any liabilities that might subsequently arise. And brokers react, according to our respondents, by no longer bringing the carrier business.[11] Market discipline, in other words, accounts for the relative rarity of rescission actions.

But the rarity of full blown rescission actions should not be taken to imply that insurers do not make use of their potential coverage defenses. Instead insurers extract value from their coverage defenses by insisting on concessions in settlement from their policyholders. Most often, our respondents said, insurers trade any applicable coverage defenses, promising not to pursue them, in exchange for greater contributions from their policyholder to settlement amounts that the insurers otherwise would be obligated to pay. Insurers, in other words, use their coverage defenses to threaten not to pay, a threat that is more or less credible depending upon the strength of their argument for rescission and which is, in any event, taken seriously by both plaintiffs and defendants alike. As described by a plaintiffs' lawyer in the following colloquy:

Q   Do you feel like [insurers] use [coverage defenses] in settlement negotiations?
A   Oh, yes.
Q   Because they say, 'Hey, we have this good coverage defense.' Is that meaningful to you?
A   Absolutely, because I mean it's a credible threat.

Coverage defenses thus are rarely used to avoid payment altogether but are more often used to reduce the amount that insurers must ultimately pay at settlement.[12]

---

[10]   Some, not all defendants if the policy contains a 'severability' provision – that is, a term which expressly provides that actions taken by one or more covered persons cannot be imputed to other covered persons not themselves involved in the same conduct.

[11]   The point was also made anecdotally. As related by the head of claims at a major insurance carrier: 'Genesis successfully rescinded Cutter & Buck. That was a huge nail in their coffin ... Brokers talked about that endlessly ... They pulled accounts from them and wouldn't put new business with them.' *See also Cutter & Buck, Inc. v. Genesis Ins. Co.,* 144 Fed. App. 600, 601, 602 (9th Cir. 2005).

[12]   It may seem curious that although insurers (almost) never rescind, they are nevertheless able to use the threat of rescission to extract settlement contributions from corporate defendants. Likewise, if such threats are indeed credible, how do they not damage the insurer's reputation in the market for insurance? The answer, again, may lie with insurance brokers who accept some such leverage in the give-and-take of settlement while reacting more strongly against genuine efforts to rescind.

As a result of this negotiating dynamic, it would seem that the worse a defendant's conduct, the more the defendant firm contributes to settlement. The defendants' share of a settlement, relative to the available limits, could thus be seen as a proxy for the seriousness of the misconduct. Unfortunately, the data necessary to test this relationship – that is, firm-specific information on D&O policy limits and deductibles as well as information on how settlements are funded – are not publicly available.

In any event, our respondents reported that insurers do indeed make use of their coverage defenses by bargaining with the policyholder and, if the policyholder is in poor financial condition, with the plaintiffs' lawyers as well, effectively cashing in their grounds for rescission in exchange for a discount on their contribution to settlement. This finding is directly relevant to the question of deterrence. If, as our respondents suggested, the strength of a policyholder's coverage defense is proportional to the strength of the underlying shareholder claim – or, to paraphrase one of our respondents, the larger the fraud, the bigger the discount – then by forcing policyholders to make additional contributions to settlement on the basis of their coverage defenses, insurers effectively offer less coverage for worse frauds. In this way they increase the cost of shareholder litigation for worse-governed firms. If worse-governed firms pay more in connection with shareholder litigation, then the deterrence function of shareholder litigation would seem to survive the distorting effect of insurance.

Still, there is good cause to doubt the strength of the deterrence offered under this arrangement if the amount of coverage effectively lost by poorly governed firms is not materially different from the amount preserved for well-governed firms. The problem, in other words, is akin to that described above in the context of pricing where doubt was raised that the marginal savings in premium allocated to well-governed firms would be sufficiently material to induce a change in firm behavior on the part of worse-governed firms. Here, the loss of coverage suffered by poorly governed firms, since it is after all only a discount on the insurer's contribution and not outright rescission, may be insufficient to create an incentive for such firms to change their ways. Although it is impossible to draw a strong conclusion on this point without the firm-specific and settlement-specific data to test this relationship, the insurers' cashing-in of coverage defenses would nevertheless seem to be a thin reed on which to base one's hope for deterrence.

## 5.   POLICY IMPLICATIONS

In light of these considerations, it seems likely, at the very least, that D&O insurance significantly weakens the ability of shareholder litigation to deter. This, of course, does not mean that bad acts on the parts of corporations and their managers are utterly undeterred since there may, after all, be other mechanisms, ranging from market reactions to SEC enforcement actions and even criminal liability, that serve to constrain fraud and bad acts. What it does suggest, however, is that shareholder litigation is not in fact doing the job it is supposed to do. If shareholder litigation fails to deter and is not supported by another equally compelling policy justification, then it is difficult to justify its continued existence. Indeed, it appears essentially as waste, a means by which plaintiffs' and defense attorneys enrich themselves at the expense of the shareholders of defendant corporations. Legal reformers would thus seem to be right to call for its abolition or, alternately, for the abolition of D&O insurance.

Before going this far, however, it is worth pausing to consider whether there are any features of the current system that can be reformed to reinvigorate the deterrence function of shareholder litigation in the presence of liability insurance. The simplest reform involves disclosure. The securities laws could be amended to require public corporations to disclose, first, certain details concerning their D&O coverage – including limits, premium, and the structure of coverage – and second, certain details concerning the settlement of shareholder litigation, including, principally, how settlement and defense costs were funded. In a vigorous capital market, this additional public information would be used by professional investors to adjust their valuations of firms, thus changing the market value of the insured's securities and thereby recreating the effect of deterrence through capital market pricing mechanisms. In other words, worse-governed firms will have an additional incentive, due to the disclosure of this new information, to improve their corporate governance in order to increase the value of their securities on the market.

**Disclosure of D&O Policy Details**

The cost and structure of a firm's D&O coverage package encodes important information about its governance quality. Most basically, the more a corporation pays for its D&O coverage, other things being equal, the greater the shareholder liability risk it poses. Because a significant component of the risk assessment of D&O professionals is governance quality – including the variables focusing on firm culture and character – the resulting premiums should reflect differences in these variables. Moreover, the D&O insurer's assessment of governance quality is uniquely credible because the insurer bears the costs, in the form of payout obligations, of any mistakes. Furthermore, a company's D&O insurance premium is based upon information that is uniquely available to the insurer – the private underwriters' meetings with management – which therefore may not already be in the market, making it particularly valuable to investors and other market participants. A company's D&O insurance premium would thus seem to be a valuable proxy for information that is not otherwise available.

Of course, as noted above, a company's insurance premium is not based purely on corporate governance factors but contains a number of basic financial factors as well, such as market capitalization and share price volatility. However, investment professionals could easily back these factors out of the premium number, thus turning a company's insurance premium into a measure of governance quality. The necessary adjustments are relatively simple. First, because insurance premiums depend in part on the coverage limits and the firm's retention, premium data must be adjusted for effective coverage amounts. This, however, would be a relatively easy adjustment to make, given data that included each company's insurance premiums, limits, and retentions. Second, in addition to these features of the insurance policy itself, insurance premiums may correlate to other features of the corporation or its business. For example, firms within a particular industry may be subject to systematically higher D&O rates than firms in other lines of business with less industry-wide risk of shareholder litigation. However, this distortion too could be corrected by comparing D&O insurance pricing across a set of firms within a specific industry in order to identify norms and outliers. Finally, the distortion introduced by market capitalizations and measures of volatility can be eliminated by controlling for those factors. Thus, in spite of the noise in insurance prices, with a few simple adjustments a firm's premium for D&O insurance should convey important information concerning the firm's corporate governance. Most basically, the more a firm pays, other things being equal, the worse its governance.

Understanding this proxy for governance quality, fund managers, arbitrageurs, and other professional investors can be expected to build these signals into their models of firm value. And, once incorporated into pricing models, this information would recreate the deterrence function of shareholder litigation. If a D&O insurance policy reveals negative information – for example, unusually high premiums – traders' pricing models would likely discount the company's share price in capital markets. Firms would have an incentive to improve governance practices in order to avoid this discount to their share price. In this way, mandating disclosure of D&O policy details would breathe new life into the deterrence function of shareholder litigation. All that is needed is a rule mandating disclosure of D&O policy details – including limits, premiums, and coverage structures – and the market will do the rest.

**Disclosure of Settlement Details**

In addition to the disclosure of D&O policy details, the disclosure of settlement details would serve to reinvigorate the deterrence function of shareholder litigation. Currently, although settlement *amounts* are matters of public record and indeed are carefully tracked by industry sources, there is no systematic information about *how* settlements are funded. Perhaps most importantly, we cannot be sure, based on publicly available information, what percentage of any given settlement is funded by insurance versus funded by the corporation itself. We also do not know what additional amounts, beyond the total settlement, were spent in defense of the claim. This is useful information and should be disclosed.

Information on how settlements and defense costs are funded – that is, what percentage of the total settlement is paid for by insurance versus by the corporation itself – would prove most useful when interacted with information on the amount and structure of coverage. First, these two pieces of information together could yield valuable insight into the 'cashing in' of coverage defenses – the bargain in which the insurer agrees to drop potential coverage defenses in exchange for a larger contribution to settlement from the corporate defendant. This is particularly valuable because the practice of cashing in coverage defenses, which our participants reported takes place with some frequency in the give and take of settlement, may shed light on the question of merit in any given claim. Claims where insurers are able to cash in substantial amounts seem likely, on the whole, to be more meritorious claims for two basic reasons. First, some of the insurer's strongest coverage defenses – such as the threat to rescind on the basis of fraud in the application – are implicitly based on the underlying merits of the claim. Second, the more realistic the possibility of a plaintiffs' verdict in excess of the policy limits, the more willing defendants will be to contribute to a within-limits settlement. As a result, a claim in which an insurer is able to cash in its coverage defenses, should be, on average, a claim of greater underlying merit.

This dynamic would be exposed if insurance limits and structure could be compared to how settlements and defense costs are funded. A strong inference of merit could thus be drawn concerning those cases where a corporation has contributed substantial amounts to a settlement and/or defense costs when the total settlement is nevertheless within the limits of the corporation's D&O coverage. The more a corporation contributes in such cases – after taking into account, of course, deductibles and coinsurance and other possible reasons for an insurance shortfall – the more likely there is to be actual fraud underlying the plaintiffs' claim. Exposing such bargains in the settlement process would thus uncover another proxy for merit, which would alert market professionals that something did in fact go awry in the corporate governance of the insured that, unless corrected, could recur. Following the logic sketched above, professional investors would thus build this new information into their pricing models for the defendant's securities, causing a change in market price, which itself might create an incentive for corporate reform.

## 6. CONCLUSION

Ultimately, if shareholder litigation fails to deter corporate misconduct, then it is little more than waste. Moreover, D&O insurance is at the very least an obstacle to this deterrence. Insurers, it would seem, are not sufficiently able to avail themselves of the mechanisms at their disposal – such as pricing and control over settlement – to preserve the deterrence function of shareholder litigation. Nevertheless, disclosure – both of D&O policy details and settlement details – holds promise as a means of reinvigorating the essential function of deterrence without the dislocating effects of more radical solutions, such as the abolition of shareholder litigation or prohibitions on the purchase of D&O insurance. Policymakers ought to consider mandating these additional disclosures if the deterrence function of shareholder litigation is to be preserved.

## REFERENCES

Abraham, Kenneth S. (2008), *The Liability Century: Insurance And Tort Law From The Progressive Era To 9/11*, Cambridge, MA: Harvard University Press.
Alexander, Janet Cooper (1996), 'Rethinking Damages in Securities Class Actions', *Stanford Law Review*, 48, 1487–1537.
Baker, Tom & Sean J. Griffith (2007a), 'Predicting Corporate Governance Risk: Evidence from the Directors' & Officers' Liability Insurance Market', *University Of Chicago Law Review* 74, 487–544.
Baker, Tom & Sean J. Griffith (2007b), 'The Missing Monitor in Corporate Governance: The Directors' & Officers' Liability Insurer', *Georgetown Law Journal*, 95, 1795–1842.
Baker, Tom & Sean J. Griffith (2009), 'How the Merits Matter: D&O Insurance and Securities Settlements', *University Of Pennsylvania Law Review*, 157, 755–832.
Baker, Tom & Sean J. Griffith (2010), *Ensuring Corporate Misconduct: How Liability Insurance Undermines Shareholder Litigation*, Chicago, IL: University of Chicago Press.
Black, Bernard S., Brian Cheffins & Michael Klausner (2006), 'Outside Director Liability' *Stanford Law Review* 58, 1055–1159.
Coffee, John C. (2006), 'Reforming the Securities Class Action: An Essay on Deterrence and its Implementation', *Columbia Law Review*, 106, 1534–86.
Easterbrook Frank H. & Daniel R. Fischel (1985), 'Optimal Damages in Securities Cases', *University of Chicago Law Review*, 52, 611–52.
Griffith, Sean J. (2006), 'Uncovering a Gatekeeper: Why the SEC Should Mandate Disclosure of Details Concerning Directors' & Officers' Liability Insurance Policies', *University Of Pennsylvania Law Review*, 154, 1147–1208.
Langevoort, Donald C. (1996), 'Capping Damages For Open-Market Securities Fraud', *Arizona Law Review*, 38, 639–64.
Pritchard, A.C. (1999), 'Markets as Monitors: A Proposal to Replace Securities Class Actions with Exchanges as Securities Fraud Enforcers', *Virginia Law Review*, 85, 925–1020.
Rose, Amanda (2008), 'Reforming Securities Litigation Reform: A Proposal for Restructuring the Relationship Between Public and Private Enforcement of Rule 10b-5', *Columbia Law Review*, 108, 1301–64.
Syverud, Kent D. (1990), 'The Duty to Settle,' *Virginia Law Review*, 76, 1113–1209.
Towers Perrin (2006), 'Directors and Officers Liability Survey'.
Towers Perrin (2007), 'Directors and Officers Liability Survey'.
Towers Perrin (2008), 'Directors and Officers Liability Survey'.

# 19. The influence of investment banks on corporate governance

*Tamar Frankel*

This chapter analyses the influence of investment banks on corporate governance. In this chapter, 'corporate governance' or 'governance' generally means the part of the institutional structure that vests the power to control the operations and direction of a corporation. This part consists of the board of directors and top management.

The first part of the chapter defines 'corporate governance' and 'management'. The second part examines the role of finance in shaping corporate management and their strategies. The third part describes investment bankers and what investment bankers currently do. The fourth part examines the parallel rise of the importance of finance and the influence of investment bankers on corporate management. It evaluates the role that investment banks play in corporate governance and the benefits and disadvantages of such influence to the corporate enterprise and its investors. The fifth part concludes by comparing past and present practices. Like most cases, there is a slippery slope in which the good could turn into bad, and life-giving could turn toxic. Therefore, the more difficult question is when and how does the influence of investment bankers over corporate governance begin to turn from good to bad and what warning signals show that the beneficial influence of investment bankers on corporate governance turns or might turn sour. The answer to this question is related to the role that financing plays in management of large corporations. As the financing role rises, so does the influence of investment bankers.

## 1. CORPORATE GOVERNANCE: THE MANAGEMENT

'Governance' derives from the source word 'government'. The two are similar yet different. 'Governance' denotes supremacy, domination, power, authority and control, as well as management. The synonyms of 'government' include not only control, supervision, command, leadership and rule, but also direction, administration, management, and regime. Both 'government' and 'governance' include the concept of management.[1] Those who occupy government and governance positions are the holders of power to determine the 'range of feasible actions' in the organizations that they control (Rajan & Zingales 2001). Governance and government differ with respect to the source of their power and purposes of the power, as well as its extent and its means of enforcement. Corporate governance represents private power over pooled resources for the purpose of production. Government represents political power over a population in a defined area for the purpose of keeping the peace and enhancing the benefits of a civil society. The allocation of power and its limitations are

---

[1]    For a broad and informed discussion of corporate governance see Davis (2005).

important because, among other things, they affect the power holders' incentives and the incentives of those subject to the holders' exercise of their power.

Corporate governance has been defined in a number of ways, such as 'the structures, processes, and institutions within and around organizations that allocate power and resource control' (Davis 2005, 143). Under the nexus-of-contracts model, the corporation 'serves as a nexus for contracting relationships' (Jensen & Meckling 1976, 311). Some scholars believe that under this view, 'markets will lead managers to adopt optimal governance' (Baysinger & Butler 1987, 129).

Among others, governance represents two concepts: the institutional structure that bestows power on the holders, and the particular individuals that fill the power position (e.g., the boards of directors and top management). In this chapter both meanings will be covered in the word 'management'. As a noun management denotes corporate governance structure as well as the people that occupy the positions in the structure. As a verb to manage denotes broadly what directors and top management of corporations do.

'The American system of corporate governance is regarded as the prototype market-oriented system of arms-length transactions organized around impersonal financial markets' (Davis 2005, 157). 'Market participants are aware of the theories used by the stock market to evaluate companies and can be quite savvy in playing to them' (Davis 2005, 157).

Another interesting development reflecting the world view as a market was the emergence of governance as a commodity. Governance was discussed in terms of the 'market for corporate control'. Similarly, there emerged a 'market for corporate law' which became more market-like after it was named by law and economics scholars (although the notion of states competing for incorporation fees appears in practice to apply mostly to Delaware).

A flurry of research beginning in the mid-1990s sought to understand the functioning of corporate governance in various institutions, sometimes drawing explicitly on sociological theory, and generally taking the American system of corporate governance as the base case.

Mark Roe's *Strong Managers, Weak Owners* (1994) concluded that fragmented ownership was the result of politics, causing a shift of power from owners to managers. Modigliani & Perrotti (2000) claimed that the value of securities to dispersed owners is based largely on the legal framework.

## 2. THE RISING IMPORTANCE OF FINANCE

This section recounts the history of modern corporate finance. In 1890, fewer than ten manufacturing companies' securities were traded on the major stock exchanges, but by 1983 the aggregate capital in publicly traded manufacturing companies was over $7 billion (Roy 1997, 4–5).[2]

Since then the importance of finance for corporations and their management has been rising. That has been especially so during the past 20 years. Today's management focuses on finance both for the corporations' benefit, and management's personal benefits.

---

[2]    Roy (1997) discusses the changes between 1890 and 1905, from a society with few large manufacturing firms to one dominated by large firms. Fligstein (1990) discusses the changes in corporate control from 1880 to 1980.

Corporations have increased their borrowing. In 2004 corporations' leverage had increased dramatically. Arguably leverage was made possible by a change in the regulation of the Securities and Exchange Commission (SEC) relating to investment bankers. The change relaxed the net capital requirements applicable to investment banks. It allowed investment banks to opt out of the restrictions, which required specific ratios of debt to equity (Rhee 2010). Thus, the bankers could lend more, and they did. This issue was viewed as among the 'consequences of the deregulation and the collapse of the investment banks' (Coffee 2009, 413) with reference to the Consolidated Supervised Entity Program (CSE)[3] of the SEC in 2004, which exempted the big five investment banks from the SEC's traditional Net Capital Rule (Coffee 2009).[4] The exemption allowed these investment banks to design their own individualized credit model (Coffee 2009).[5]

Thus, in the past 20–30 years, technology, regulation, and institutional changes have facilitated the expansion of the financial system, facilitated the creation and pricing of complex instruments, and provided means of spreading risk. Arguably, deregulation opened the door to increasing competition among financial institutions which enhanced the impact of finance on corporate management. Some called the changes a 'financial revolution'. This revolution transformed the power of management and the influence of financial intermediaries, including investment bankers (Rajan & Zingales 2001). While personal power vanishes with the person, money power can be transferred and depends on who holds the money at the particular time. Human capital cannot be controlled the same way as money. Clients might follow a talented employee, and the enterprise that loses such an employee might be less productive. But money is fungible. Control over money can vest far more power than control over productive employees. Control over machinery is also less powerful as machinery becomes obsolete, unless the obsolescence is backed up by money.

This section considers some changes to the nature of corporations and management resulting from changes in finance and investment banking.

Beginning in 1890 Congress passed antitrust legislation, including the Sherman Antitrust Act to prohibit cartels formed in restraint of trade (Fligstein 1990, 23), the Clayton Act of 1914 to prohibit certain purchases of competitors' stock, tying arrangements and predatory pricing (Fligstein 1990, 25), and the Celler-Kefauver Act of 1950, to prevent horizontal and vertical mergers (Fligstein 1990, 29).

The Celler-Kefauver Act had the effect of encouraging mergers with firms in unrelated industries (Fligstein 1990, 222). By 1980 firms had adopted a 'firm as portfolio' model and most large industrial firms were multi-industry (Davis 1994, 547). Under the 'finance

---

   [3]   Alternative Net Capital Requirements for Broker-Dealers That Are Part of Consolidated Supervised Entities, 69 Fed. Reg. 34,428 (June 21, 2004).
   [4]   Net Capital Requirements for Brokers or Dealers, 17 C.F.R. § 240.15c3-1 (2008).
   [5]   The CSE was a reaction to the European Union Financial Conglomerate Directive of 2002. Council Directive 2002/87, 2003 O.J. (L 35) 1 (EC). The directive provided that the regulator has to review the parent company's financials and evaluate the conglomerate as a whole from a top-down perspective (Coffee 2009). European regulators were fearful that 'the parent company could take actions that would jeopardize the solvency of the regulated entity'. The investment banks, for their part, feared the examination by the European regulators and urged the SEC to regulate them in order to apply an exemption clause within the European Union Directive. The SEC followed this request with the CSE Program intending to finally oversee the five investment banks, but fatally failed to oversee the credit model of each investment bank (Coffee 2009).

conception of the modern corporation', firms are considered 'collections of assets earning different rates of return' rather than members of a certain industry. Strategies are finance-based, include mergers and divestments, 'financial ploys to increase the stock price', and 'financial controls to make decisions about the internal application of capital' (Fligstein 1990, 15).[6]

The move towards finance and its utilization has greatly influenced corporate business models. If growth signifies success, then sales should increase. An effective way to increase sales of assets is to finance the buyers. Moreover, available capital renders real assets less important. Capital enables employees to leave and start on their own by acquiring the real assets they need (or newer ones). For the firm, financial resources have become more critical to survive competition. 'From the owner's perspective, these resources – people, ideas, strategies – are harder to control directly. In particular, some of the "glue" holding these other resources to the organization in the past was their dependence on it for financing' (Rajan & Zingales 2001, 3–4).

Financing enables management to expand and grow the corporation by acquisition rather than by internal growth. For the same reason mutual fund managers focus on the sale of fund shares in order to increase their fees rather than on growing the assets by performance. They seek as much financing as possible to pay brokers to sell fund shares (Rajan & Zingales 2001).[7]

The emphasis and attention to the corporate stock prices and the financial situation of the corporation has been based on three assumptions. One is that the stock prices reflect the performance of the corporations and their management. The higher the prices are the more successful the corporation and management. The second assumption is that the higher stock prices enhance the shareholders' value (Davis 2005). The third assumption regarding stock prices is that the higher the prices the higher the management's compensation should be (Davis 2005).[8]

Indeed, the link between managements' benefits and the share prices of corporations has increased the self-interest of management to raise their corporations' share prices. This incentive is related to and sometimes identical to the interests of investment bankers. Both would seek to raise corporate financial activities. The stock prices affect the companies' businesses. The market evaluators and analysts directed the companies' holdings. For example, diversified firms are likely to de-diversify when there is a mismatch with their identity among analysts (Zuckerman 2000). Biotechnology firms that partner with prominent firms, including prestigious investment banks, attain higher share values at initial public offering (Stuart et al. 1999). Boards sharing directors with other boards are better perceived by analysts (Davis & Robbins 2004, 308). Firms announce stock repurchase programs that they do not implement in response to external pressures (Westphal & Zajac 2001).

---

[6]    Since 1995 sociological governance studies focused on the impact of interlocking boards of directors, in which individual directors serve on two or more boards at one time, and showed that directors with experience in changes reflecting greater board control over management were more attractive to companies with high board control and less attractive to companies with low board control (Zajac & Westphal 1996, 524).

[7]    The authors note that other changes have occurred. Real assets are less unique, intellectual property is more important, information technology has developed, helping owners and top management to monitor and control large, global businesses (Rajan & Zingales 2001).

[8]    Citing Westphal & Zajac (1998).

Managements' desires to continue in their positions could be threatened by takeovers – takeovers that could be financed by investment banks, using a variety of then-novel financial instruments. Takeovers also affected corporate structures by the design of 'poison pills'. Lawyers offered management tools to protect itself against takeover through poison pills. More important is the network of interlocking managements which helped to pass information. For example, firms are more likely to adopt poison pills as a defense against takeovers if their boards are influenced by contacts, such as directors of firms in similar sectors (Davis & Greve 1997, 29). In addition, firms with board members from financial institutions are more likely to borrow (Mizruchi & Stearns 1994, 97).

## 3.   WHAT DO INVESTMENT BANKS DO?

What makes investment bankers thrive? There is a connection between the size of businesses and industrial corporations and the size and the degree of their employment of investment banks. Arguably investment bankers emerge only when there are a sufficient number of large corporations seeking their services (Anand & Galetovic 2001). A number of studies find that active securities markets help increase economic growth (Demirgüç-Kunt & Maksimovic 1998; Levine & Zervos 1998; Obstfeld 1994; Rajan & Zingales 1998).

To succeed, investment bankers establish and develop long-term relationships with business firms that generate a large enough volume of deals as issuers and investors. 'Finance follows industry' (Anand & Galetovic 2001, 1). Investment banks seek ongoing and repeated business relationships with the same large issuers. The banks are familiar with their corporate clients and assure the high quality of the corporate securities that they underwrite, as the banks do repeat business with the firms and have the incentive to maintain their reputations.

Investment banking can be divided by 'prestige' or reputation (Carter & Manaster 1990) into 'bulge bracket' investment banks – the truly large ones – and the rest (Rhee 2010). Between 1987 and 1998, 'the average size of an M&A deal by a firm [that] did two or more of such deals' was 'about three times larger than the average deal size of a firm that did only one M&A deal' (Anand & Galetovic 2001, 13). In the IPO market 'major bracket' investment firms were involved in IPOs with gross proceeds of $10 million or more, whereas the rest were committed to IPOs with gross proceeds of $2 million or less (Anand & Galetovic 2001). Therefore, 'bulge bracket' investment banks underwrite and distribute primarily for bigger corporations, while other investment banks conduct business with smaller corporations.

Most bulge brackets did not own retail distribution organizations. They distributed securities through a network of independent retail brokers (*The Economist* 1985). Yet the elimination of the Glass-Steagall Act may not have put investment bankers at a disadvantage because pools of small investors' savings have grown. Investment bankers have become experts in acquiring and securitizing consumer and mortgage loans, enabling clients to lend more to consumers (Park 1996). General Motors has enhanced the sale of its cars by creating a financing entity (GMAC), which received the auto buyers' obligations, and securitized them to cash the buyers' notes (Plank 2004, 1657, n. 4). Goldman Sachs had a large securitization department,[9] as did Citibank (Gumbel 2004).[10]

---

[9]   *Wall Street and the Financial Crisis: The Role of Investment Banks: Hearing Before the Subcomm. on Investigations of the S. Comm. on Homeland Security and Governmental Affairs,* 111th

Investment banks today engage in four kinds of activities: (i) investment banking services, such as underwriting (Sher 2006),[11] (ii) trading and restructuring, (iii) asset management and securities services (Wilhelm & Downing 2001; Rhee 2010), and (iv) the creation of securities based on securities (Galbraith 1979, 46–51).

**Investment Banking Services**

Historically, investment bankers raised money for clients, including corporations, by underwriting securities. When commercial banks functioned as investment banks as well, investment banks offered corporations financing by both loans and services of underwriting corporate securities and the services of creating markets for trading in these securities. These functions could include wholesale and retail marketing. After the passage of the Glass-Steagall Act in 1933,[12] commercial banking was separated from investment banking. The separation reduced the number of investment bankers' competitors and facilitated the growth of the few. Investment bankers established other investment pools (e.g., investment companies and pension funds), and drew clients from the banks. Bank regulators 'pushed the envelope' of the Glass-Steagall Act to protect the banks' hegemony and in 1999 Congress eliminated the prohibitions of the Glass-Steagall Act.[13] Since the late 1970s, the size and variety of the markets for financial assets have expanded, and with this expansion the role and services of investment bankers has enlarged.

Investment bankers offer advisory services to management in connection with mergers and acquisitions – 'fairness opinion letters' – the investment bankers' judgment regarding the financial fairness of the terms of the transaction (Giuffra 1986). 'In theory, such opinions should protect shareholder interests' (Giuffra 1986, 120).[14] The fairness opinion states that a transaction 'meets a threshold level of fairness from a financial perspective' (Davidoff 2006, 1558). Providing these opinions is lucrative for investment banks (Kisgen et al. 2009; Bowers 2002). However, the letters are 'prone to subjectivity' and frequently are prepared by utilizing methodologies that follow best practice, as well as by conflicts of interest (Davidoff 2006). Conflicts arise for a number of reasons (Sorkin 2004; Morgenson 2005). First, compensation for a fairness opinion and advice depends on the completion of the deal (Davidoff 2006). An investment banker has a strong incentive to ensure 'that the contemplated transaction for which it will issue a fairness opinion progresses to completion' (Davidoff 2006, 1586–7). Second, the close relationship between investment bank and management can induce the investment bank to find a transaction fair and avoid displeasing

Cong. (2010), Fed. News Serv., Apr. 27, 2010, LEXIS, News Library, Curnws File; Complaint, *SEC v. Goldman Sachs & Co.*, No. 10 CV 3229 (Apr. 15, 2010), available at http://www.sec.gov/litigation/complaints/2010/comp21489.pdf (last accessed October 2011).

<sup>10</sup> Noting the involvement of Citibank in the Parmalat securitization. The Parmalat fraud was described as the 'biggest' in European history (Gumbel 2004, 44).

<sup>11</sup> Citing Gilson & Kraakman (1984, 613–21).

<sup>12</sup> Banking Act of 1933 (Glass-Steagall Act), Pub. L. No. 73-65, 48 Stat. 162 (codified as amended in scattered sections of 12 U.S.C.).

<sup>13</sup> Gramm-Leach-Bliley Act, Pub. L. No. 106-102, § 101, 113 Stat. 1338, 1341 (1999) (repealing 12 U.S.C. §§ 78, 377).

<sup>14</sup> Pointing out that '[w]hen rendering fairness opinions, investment bankers can serve as "gatekeepers"', explaining that '[g]atekeepers are third parties who can obstruct misconduct by withholding a specialized good or service', citing Kraakman (1984, 1986).

management, who stand to benefit from the transaction (Davidoff 2006).[15] Third, investment banks 'often maintain business interests that extend to both sides of a corporate control transaction and beyond their own opinion' (Davidoff 2006, 1587–8),[16] such as stapled financing. Stapled financing means that the investment bank arranges for the potential buyer's financing. Therefore, the buyer, in theory, need not seek additional financing to purchase the target because its bankers have already 'stapled' the necessary financing contracts to the purchase agreement.

Because the directors have fiduciary duties to the corporations that they advise, hiring investment bankers allows directors to essentially delegate their functions and cover their fiduciary duty of care (Giuffra 1986). Management may then 'rely on incomplete or misleading fairness opinions to pursue takeovers that could damage shareholders' interests or oppose transactions benefiting shareholders' (Giuffra 1986, 121). Similar to the correlation between corporations' size and investment banks' employment, investment banks choose large firms for establishing long-term relationships.

Arguably, services of investment bankers are likely to involve conflicts of interest. Critics note that their opinions and their assumptions tend to be subjective, failing to be grounded in best practices (Davidoff 2006). And yet, in 2006 at least, fairness opinions 'survive … and thrive … earning investment banks millions, if not billions, of dollars annually' (Davidoff 2006, 1561).

Investment bankers offer advisory opinions on mergers and acquisitions (M&A). In a study of financial conglomerates' M&As advised by affiliated investment banks, researchers argue that advisers 'take positions in the targets before M&A announcements'. Investment bankers are more likely to vote with management than with unaffiliated blockholders. The advisers obtain the information about the bids and the deals, and real high profits. 'The advisory stake is positively related to the likelihood of deal completion and to the termination fees. However, these deals are not wealth-creating: there is a negative relation between the advisory stake and the viability of the deal' (Bodnaruk et al. 2009, 4989). 'These results provide new insights into the conflicts of interests affecting financial intermediaries that simultaneously advise on deals and invest in the equity market' (Bodnaruk et al. 2009, 5025). The attitude to antitakeover amendments is more uniform while activist shareholders vary in their reactions (Borokhovich et al. 2006).

## Trading

Investment banking has 'evolved significantly' from 1996 to 2008 from a 'balanced' mix of trading, asset management, and investment banking services, to 'trading overshadowing the other product lines' (Rhee 2010, 6). The business model of five major investment banks before the current financial crisis evolved increasingly to trading during the period 2003–2007 (Rhee 2010). They played a key role in the ensuing financial crisis (Weinstein 2009).

Investment bankers have been raising venture capital. They developed venture capital divisions through which they invested in venture capital on their own account (Fisch & Sale 2003).

---

[15]   Citing e.g. O'Brien (2005).
[16]   See also Foulds (2009); Steele & Verret (2007, 208).

Arguably, investment banks have steered their business away from providing client services. Instead they became intermediaries in the capital markets (Morrison & Wilhelm 2007). The traditional segment of investment banking became 'ancillary activities' (Rhee 2010). Investment banks became similar to 'publicly traded hedge funds taking massive proprietary bets on the market' (Rhee 2010).

**Asset Management and Securities Services**

For their significant clients, investment banks have traditionally provided detailed reports about particular corporations (Fisch & Sale 2003). This analysis is valuable to market investors generally, and some investment banks have used their analysts to offer mass-produced analysis of particular corporations. The research of large investment banks includes monitoring of corporations. Not surprisingly this research serves as monitors to advisers and managers of securities pools (mutual funds and pension funds). Corporate governance of such pools may be affected by these services.

Investment bankers hold equity securities as nominees, as well as equity for their own account. These banks:

> also manage substantial mutual fund and pension assets. British investment banks have been more active in corporate governance than their almost completely passive American counterparts … [S]ome merchant banks participate in institutional coalitions and occasionally lead them. But, at the same time, British investment banks play a much less prominent role than insurers. As with commercial banks, multiple factors … interact to explain the degree of interest shown by investment banks in corporate governance. (Black & Coffee 1994, 2017)

However, in the recent information about Goldman Sachs it seems that this investment bank created securities based on financial assets that it purchased, packaged, and sold to investors on the one hand while shorting some of the same type of investment on the other hand, and helping a hedge fund that bet on the decline of market price of these securities as well.[17]

Large investment bankers manage dark pools. These are in fact, securities exchanges. The numbers and volume of trades in these exchanges have increased dramatically throughout the years (Roane 2007). 'These pools are basically [investment banks'] internal systems for trading stocks privately, off of public exchanges and out of the public eye. They are growing rapidly, both in number and in volume of trades' (Roane 2007). Traders are 'large hedge funds and institutional investors that want to build and liquidate large stock positions at lower costs, while also being shielded from those who might profit by knowing their intentions' (Roane 2007). However, sellers in dark pools cannot discover whether they are getting the best price. Dark pools lack transparency. Often neither of the parties knows the identity of the other. This lack of transparency eliminates possible pressures that information of their identity could raise (e.g., if the seller is in financial difficulties or the buyer intends to launch a

---

[17]    *Wall Street and the Financial Crisis: The Role of Investment Banks: Hearing Before the Subcomm. on Investigations of the S. Comm. on Homeland Security and Governmental Affairs,* 111th Cong. (2010), Fed. News Serv., Apr. 27, 2010, LEXIS, News Library, Curnws File; Complaint, SEC v. Goldman Sachs & Co., No. 10 CV 3229 (Apr. 15, 2010), available at http://www.sec.gov/litigation/complaints/2010/comp21489.pdf (last accessed October 2011).

takeover).[18] Required information is not helpful, especially if brokers match the orders with orders of other clients, as they are permitted to do (Peek 2007). This system might attract large clients but may harm small investors by reducing liquidity and transparency in the marketplace (Peek 2007); yet dark pools have remained unregulated (Peek 2007).

Such exchanges have not arisen in the past perhaps because managing such pools was not profitable. The volume of the pools was too low. The costs of management were too high. However, managing the dark pools may have become profitable in the 2000s. The volumes traded have risen significantly because traditional public exchanges no longer met the traders' needs. In addition:

> [r]apid advances in technology have permitted innovative participants in the financial markets to offer traditional services in new and more efficient ways, including by permitting electronic order-matching and trade execution outside the confines of the physical trading floor of a stock exchange … Through online connections, proprietary software or terminals, subscribers may access and execute orders through ATSs, both domestically and in multiple foreign jurisdictions. (Collins 2002, 481–2)

Dark pools may be attractive to corporate management, interested in sheltering the price of corporate shares (too high or too low) (Aite Group 2007). 'As has long been the case, the old boys really do like to operate behind closed doors' (Fitz-Gerald 2008). Management may be interested in issuing and buying back large numbers of corporate securities in a less public manner.

### Creation of Securities Based on Securities

Investment bankers structure securitizations of various types of obligations as well as synthetic securities. The April 2010 hearings before a congressional subcommittee concerning Goldman Sachs's securitization activities,[19] and the claim against the firm by the Securities and Exchange Commission,[20] highlighted the role of investment banks in structuring, composing portfolios, selling securities or financial instruments issued by entities so designed, and trading for their own account in instruments issued by entities so designed. Thus, this investment bank acted as indirect issuer, dealer, adviser, underwriter, and commission broker in these and other instruments.

In sum, investment bankers offer varied financial services. These include advice on asset allocation, and mergers and acquisitions; financing by loans and marketing debt and equity securities in the capital markets. They manage pools of securities through closed-end mutual

---

[18]   It should be noted that making markets in particular securities was usually developed by broker dealers who desired to offer clients liquidity when none existed in the markets. Dark exchanges, however, seem to have emerged when the stock exchanges could not fulfill the promise of secrecy. A similar issue arises concerning settlements among plaintiffs and defendants in court cases. Parties are allowed to include confidentiality clauses in their settlements, and these clauses are honored by courts, with rare exceptions, such as information concerning public safety hazards (Moss 2007, 869–70).

[19]   *Wall Street and the Financial Crisis: The Role of Investment Banks: Hearing Before the Subcomm. on Investigations of the S. Comm. on Homeland Security and Governmental Affairs,* 111th Cong. (2010), Fed. News Serv., Apr. 27, 2010, LEXIS, News Library, Curnws File.

[20]   Complaint, SEC v. Goldman Sachs & Co., No. 10 CV 3229 (Apr. 15, 2010), available at http://www.sec.gov/litigation/complaints/2010/comp21489.pdf (last accessed October 2011).

funds, private equity funds, and a variety of other such pools. They create financial assets by securitization and derivatives. They offer clearing services, brokerage-dealer transactions, including prime brokerage, and securities lending programs. And they provide local and global financial research.

## 4.   THE PARALLEL RISE OF FINANCE AND THE INFLUENCE OF INVESTMENT BANKERS ON CORPORATE GOVERNANCE AND MANAGEMENT

With the financial revolution the value of investment bankers' services as well as the variety of the services rose. In parallel, each of the services that investment banks offer to the corporations carries with it the ability to influence management in different ways. Being intermediaries for financing, investment banks can either lend to corporations or underwrite the corporations' securities or both. The influence which they might exert depends on (1) the importance of the service to the corporation and the management; (2) the extent to which management is itself an expert and can closely monitor the service; (3) the extent the corporation or management needs the services; and (4) the extent of the corporation's involvement in M & A activity.

### The Importance of Financing to the Corporation and Management

During the past 20 years the importance of financing for publicly held corporations has risen. Their managements became more interested in growth through acquisitions and takeovers in addition to internal growth (Pare & De Llosa 1994). Stock prices became more important to management as bonuses and stock option values were linked to stock prices (Day 2002). Institutional and other investors pressed management to show 'share price performance' (McMurdy 2000). Securities market prices are measured mostly by corporate earnings and less by corporate assets and liabilities. Hence, increasing liabilities by financing acquisition and raising the earnings was the way to go. Finally, managements were interested in increasing the consumers' abilities to buy the corporations' products. That increase could come from financing the consumers and securitizing the consumers' debt so as to receive cash almost immediately rather than wait for the consumers to pay their loans. Investment banks have helped corporate management establish financing mechanisms for the consumers of their products. These services were valuable to corporate management. These raised the corporations' sales, the revenues, and the stock prices as well as the size of the corporations and the rewards to the top management. The prestige of an investment banker is positively related to the performance of IPO firms and, according to one study, announcement-period returns for firms conducting seasoned equity offerings (McLaughlin et al. 2000).

### The Extent to which Management are Expert Financiers

Management needs the advice of investment bankers. Relatively few corporate directors are expert financiers and relatively few are investment bankers. According to one examination, 'Less than 11% of Directors are Investment Professionals' (Association for Investment

Management and Research 2003). The United States was higher than the global average, with 17%. 'Only an estimated one in 10 directors on corporate boards at top public companies around the world are investment professionals, by even the broadest definition of the term, according to the global Association for Investment Management and Research' (Association for Investment Management and Research 2003).

Whether the managements or the investment bankers seek participation on boards is unclear. One way in which investment bank competitors could have gained an advantage could have been by investment bankers seeking to be on potential clients' boards. This could have gained for the bank more timely information about the clients' situation and an ability to influence the client to engage in activities that might benefit and profit the investment banker. According to one study corporations that included investment bankers on their board of directors are likely to engage in more takeover activities than corporations that did not have investment bankers on their boards (Güner et al. 2008).

However, there are reasons for investment bankers to avoid seats on corporate boards. They might lose the ability to independently advise on M&As, underwriting and other financial activities. Therefore, the percentage of investment bankers on corporate boards is relatively small, although it is higher than the percentage in other countries. It seems that the influence of investment bankers is not grounded in board membership. In addition, it seems that relatively few corporate directors are experts in financial matters. They are more often experts in the business of the corporations. The obvious and expected exception is in boards of financial institutions. However, even though the percentage is higher than in other industries, most US financial institutions have few independent directors with financial industry experience (Lorsch 2010; Horwood 2008).

**The Extent to which the Corporation needs Financial Services**

Financing services are valuable to management and profitable to investment bankers. Investment bankers' research analysis is a valuable service for managers and directors. Favorable analysis for public consumption enhances the distribution or trading of corporate stock.

A favorable but inaccurate analysis may mislead corporate clients and be harmful long-term. Client corporate management may press for a positive analysis, even if in the long run these positive analyses may not benefit the corporations either (Fisch 2006). Thus, '[s]tar analysts Henry Blodgett and Mary Meeker were sued over their propensity to tout stocks of companies they groused about in private as "such a piece of crap" or "a dog"' (Boland et al. 2003). In *Adelphia Communications Corporation v. Bank of America, N.A.*,[21] for example, the Creditors' Committee of a bankrupt company argued that investment banks which participated in offering the bankrupt corporation borrowing arrangements did not provide value to the corporation and were 'motivated by the much greater profitability of the investment banking side of the transactions'. '[A]pproximately 24 investment banks [were] alleged to be affiliated, or under common control, with the [lending] banks.' The defendants retorted, among other things, 'that the Defendants provided reasonably equivalent (or, indeed, full) value (and that the use of the loan proceeds was the Debtors' problem, not the bank lenders')'. While the court rejected these allegations, the court wrote:

---

[21]   365 B.R. 24 (Bankr. S.D.N.Y. 2007).

This claim, then, asserts that the Agent Banks and Investment Banks *themselves* owed fiduciary duties to the Debtors ... As relied on by the Creditors' Committee in its brief, they include allegations that the Debtors 'placed their trust and confidence' in the Agent Banks and Investment Banks 'to use their superior expertise in complex financial transactions to devise, structure, and execute the type of bundled financial transactions involved here in a manner that would benefit the Debtors;' and that '[b]y accepting the obligation to provide expert advice to the Debtors on how to structure and conduct these transactions, the [Agent Banks and Investment Banks] entered into a fiduciary relationship that required them to provide that advice and to perform their duties properly'.[22]

With respect to investment banks another court noted that '[b]reach of fiduciary duty is a tort, and in the absence of contractual agreement establishing the existence or nonexistence of the underlying fiduciary duty, the Court believes conflicts of law principles applicable to torts should apply'. Further:

Research analysts become experts in a particular industry; their job is to collect information about the companies that comprise that industry and develop recommendations to investors based on that information. Analyst reports will often include a variety of information, including historical and projected financials, news of corporate events, and purchase recommendations or rankings. In addition, analyst reports also contain a stock price target, which is the analysts' prediction of the market price of that company's stock at some time in the future ... Analyst recommendations to purchase RSL stock while RSL's financials were deteriorating could be expected to significantly alter the total mix of information available to investors. The content of these reports was therefore certainly material.[23]

### The Extent of the Corporation's Involvement in M & A Activity

Investment banks are involved in monitoring corporate performance and that affects corporate management, including the management's decisions concerning M&A activity. Investment managers monitoring management presents problems in this context. Monitoring of management's performance raises 'a fundamental tradeoff' by the monitors (Boot & Macey 2004). 'Each monitor within a corporate governance system must choose a role that features one of these characteristics or the other; a monitor cannot exhibit both proximity and objectivity' (Boot & Macey 2004, 358). A monitor can be 'captured', and adopt the perspective of the supervised management (Boot & Macey 2004). Further, 'there is a tradeoff between proximity and objectivity that makes it impossible for a particular monitor within a corporate governance system to provide both proximate and objective monitoring' (Boot & Macey 2004, 360). 'This raises a difficult question: how should the corporate governance system be arranged to best protect shareholder interests? The basic tradeoff between proximity and objectivity exists regardless of whether the monitors act on behalf of residual claimants or some other, more complex constellation of constituents' (Boot & Macey 2004, 362). 'The United States is an example of a corporate governance system in which the entities that monitor and discipline may lack information, but enjoy objectivity' (Boot & Macey 2004, 379).

Investment banks are involved in the 'market for corporate control'. A study of 'holdings in merger and acquisition (M&A) targets by financial conglomerates in which affiliated investment banks advise the bidders' has shown 'that advisors take positions in the targets

---

22   365 B.R. at 32, 33, 36, 62.
23   *Fogarazzo v Lehman Bros., Inc.*, 263 F.R.D. 90 103 (S.D.N.Y. 2009), footnotes omitted.

before M&A announcements. These stakes are positively related to the probability of observing the bid and to the target premium' (Bodnaruk et al. 2009, 4989). '[A]dvisors[,] ... privy to important information about the deal, invest ... in the target in the expectation of its price increasing' (Bodnaruk et al. 2009, 4989). The study documents 'the high profits of this strategy' (Bodnaruk et al. 2009, 4989) as well as 'a positive relationship between [the] advisory stake and [the] deal characteristics' (Bodnaruk et al. 2009, 5024). 'The advisory stake is positively related to the likelihood of deal completion and to the termination fees. However, these deals are not wealth-creating: there is a negative relation between the advisory stake and the viability of the deal' (Bodnaruk et al. 2009, 4989). 'These results provide new insights into the conflicts of interests affecting financial intermediaries that simultaneously advise on deals and invest in the equity market' (Bodnaruk et al. 2009, 5025).

The study also suggests that if advisers to a corporation hold a large stake in a corporation it is more likely that the corporations will become a takeover target. This conclusion was based on 'a strategy long in the actual positions of the advising investment banks and short in the positions of the non-advisory banks' (Bodnaruk et al. 2009, 4990). The researchers found that the strategy 'delivers 1.40% per month (adjusted for risk), providing evidence of information embodied in the advisor holdings' (Bodnaruk et al. 2009, 4990–91). Further, 'if the advisory bank holds a stake in the target firm, the target's premium is ... higher than when the advisory bank holds no such stake. Moreover, deals in which the advisory bank holds a stake in the target are more likely to [succeed] ... [T]arget firms in which the advisory bank holds a stake tend to be overvalued by more than 10% compared with targets in deals in which the advisor does not hold a stake' (Bodnaruk et al. 2009, 4991). '[A]dvisors take advantage of their privileged position, not only by acquiring positions in the targets in the deals on which they advise, but also by directly affecting the outcome of the deal in order to realize higher capital gains from their positions' (Bodnaruk et al. 2009, 4991).

When bankers sit on boards, they affect various practices. As noted earlier, firms with board members from financial institutions are more likely to borrow (Mizruchi & Stearns 1994, 134). More generally, interlocking boards can have an effect on takeovers, presumably to information flow. For example, in the wave of corporate acquisitions in the 1960s, firms with outside directors also sitting on boards of commercial banks were less likely to be acquired in predatory acquisitions (Palmer et al. 1995, 489), although in the 1980s, among Fortune 500 firms, firms with heavily interlocked boards did not have a lower risk of takeover (Davis & Stout 1992, 627). In addition, states with more local interlocks among boards of directors were earlier adopters of antitakeover statutes between 1982 and 1990 (Vogus & Davis 2005, 118).

A recent article seems to show a similar phenomenon among commercial banks. Commercial banks also facilitate takeovers of firms in which they hold a stake – a debt position – by 'transmission of ... private information [about firms] to potential acquirers'. 'Greater bank lending intensity to a firm results in a higher likelihood that it will receive a takeover bid ... The role of bank lending intensity in predicting takeover attempts is stronger for those takeovers in which the target and acquirer have a relationship *with the same bank*' (Ivashina et al. 2009, 22–3). The study suggests that a bank's motive for such information transmission is to reduce default risk by transferring loans from 'bad' to 'good' borrowers; i.e., 'where a target firm's credit quality is low, a relationship bank has a greater incentive to transfer information to a potential acquirer and thus increase the probability of a target firm's takeover' (Ivashina et al. 2009, 71–2). In sum, management needs and depends on investment banks. Investment banks influence management. The effect of the banks' influence on management can be positive or negative.

In his letter to his shareholders in 2010 Warren Buffett made a telling statement:

> I have been in dozens of board meetings in which acquisitions have been deliberated, often with the directors being instructed by high-priced investment bankers (are there any other kind?). Invariably, the bankers give the board a detailed assessment of the value of the company being purchased, with emphasis on why it is worth far more than its market price. In more than fifty years of board memberships, however, never have I [seen] the investment bankers (or management!) discuss the true value of what is being *given*. When a deal involves the issuance of the acquirer's stock, they simply used market value to measure the cost. *They did this even though they would have argued that the acquirer's stock price was woefully inadequate – absolutely no indicator of its real value – had a takeover bid for the acquirer instead been the subject up for discussion.*
>
> When stock is the currency being contemplated in an acquisition and when directors are hearing from an advisor, it appears to me that there is only one way to get a rational and balanced discussion. Directors should hire a second advisor to make the case *against* the proposed acquisition, with its fee contingent on the deal *not* going through. Absent this drastic remedy, our recommendation in respect to the use of advisors remains: 'Don't ask the barber whether you need a haircut.' (Buffett 2010)

## 5.   THE PAST REVISITED AND COMPARED TO THE PRESENT

The influence of investment banks on management and its decision-making has increased significantly in the last 30 years. The influence is remindful of the influence that was exerted by J.P. Morgan before the Pecora Hearings[24] before the passage of the Glass-Steagall Act in 1933. Unlike the current scene, however, during that period, persons who worked for, or were connected to, J.P. Morgan sat on each board of the large corporations.[25] J.P. Morgan believed that by controlling corporate America he would enhance the economy of America. One can understand his approach in light of the fact that the financial center of the world was not the US but the United Kingdom (Peet 1992).

The fees and power of investment banks have risen since the 1980s. Investment banks provide many different types of services; one way to show the rise in their fees is to use data from their fees in reorganizations. A 2008 study has shown that in large, public company reorganizations financial advisers collected the largest part of the fees.

> [M]ore than 80% of court-awarded fees and expenses were paid for representation of, or advice to, the debtor-in-possession (DIP). Nearly all of the remaining fees, about 19%, were paid for representation of, or advice to, unsecured creditors ... Thus, the debtors' managers – who have the exclusive right to control the DIP's professionals – have considerably greater power than the unsecured creditors or shareholders. (LoPucki & Doherty 2008, 142)

The banks' power is also shown in the division of fees.

---

[24]   *Stock Exchange Practices: Hearings Before the Sen. Comm. on Banking and Currency,* 73d Cong. (1933–1934).

[25]   *Stock Exchange Practices: Hearings Before the Sen. Comm. on Banking and Currency,* pt. 2, 73d Cong., at 604–46 (1933), available at http://fraser.stlouisfed.org/publications/sensep/issue/3912/download/59484/19330526_sensep_pt02.pdf (last accessed October 2011).

The division of fee and expense awards among the professions is also important because it reflects the nature of the reorganization process. The fees awarded to financial advisors have been rising much faster than the fees awarded to attorneys, and the change seems to have been going on for a long time. Financial advisors – principally investment banks and turnaround managers – were bit players in the large public company bankruptcies of the 1980s. During the period this study covers – plans confirmed in 1998 through 2003 – attorneys still took the largest piece of the pie. Courts awarded 54% of fees and expenses to attorneys and 41% to financial advisors. Accountants received nearly all of the remaining 5%. But during this period, the fees of financial advisors grew at the rate of about 25% per year, whereas professional fees and expenses as a whole grew only about 9% per year. We conclude that since the 1980s, the nature of the restructuring process has changed. A greater proportion of professional efforts is now directed to the financial aspects of restructuring, a smaller proportion to the legal aspects. (LoPucki & Doherty 2008, 142)

To what extent do investment bankers influence corporate governance? The question can be partially answered by an analogous question: to what extent do physicians influence patients? Some patients seek doctors' advice when they truly feel sick and whatever they tried to heal themselves was ineffective. Some patients become addicted to seeking the physicians' advice whenever they believe that they might be ill or become ill. Many of the patients' attitudes depend on the surrounding culture. A 'network effect' can dominate the drive to seek physicians' advice or avoid it. Managements are no different. Whoever started the cycle of focusing on finance is not as important as the phenomenon of the changing emphasis in corporate governance, from focusing on production to focusing on finance.

Both corporate management and investment bankers share an important feature: Both exercise entrusted power and deal with other people's money (Frankel 2010). While the opinions of numerous shareholders may differ, the corporations' obligations to the country and communities may differ, corporate management is entrusted with power and discretion to determine these issues. The more varied the purposes of entrustment, the more varied the ways in which the general purposes can be achieved, the more discretion management can exercise. Investment bankers are guided by their own objectives. They command discretion and influence, derived from the clients' reliance on the bankers' expertise and discretion. When one group commanding entrusted power – the management – interacts with another group commanding entrusted power – investment bankers – they might either compete or support each other. Because the power source, range of discretion, and purpose of each group differ significantly, they cannot, and in fact do not, wish to compete. In such circumstances there is a high probability that they will cooperate and support each other.

Do investment bankers influence corporate governance, and if so, how? The answer to this question may depend on a number of factors. First, the influence of investment bankers and management may change with the relationship. At the outset, investment bankers may seek to be hired, and management may have a choice of bankers – although not an extremely rich choice. However, the shoe may be on the other foot. Managements of smaller corporations might seek to hire certain investment bankers, and the bankers may hesitate whether to accept them as clients.

Similarly, once hired, some investment bankers are likely to exercise great influence over corporate governance, especially in supporting management's objectives (whether in the service of the corporations or in the service of management's own interests). And yet, there are situations in which investment bankers may succumb to the pressure of management and change their advice to accommodate management's desires.

Because finance is complex management depends on investment bankers and advisers

(Bodnaruk et al. 2009). How else can management deal in global foreign exchange issues? While management must resort to investment banks' services, it should be aware of its own as well as the banks' conflicts of interest. When these conflicts become blatant and costly, there should be mechanisms to help management verify the reliability of their investment bankers. Law interferes to limit the conflicts by corporate governance principles, allowing and even encouraging the use of investment bankers but preventing their abuse. As anything else, investment banking influence on corporate governance is both good and destructive. One solution may be to recruit a number of board members who have expertise, but are not currently engaged, in finance and investment banking.

However, regardless of these pressures, once investment bankers are hired, and if they exercise independent judgment, they are likely to influence the decisions of management with respect to the subject of their advice, M&As, issuance, distribution and repurchase of corporate securities and opinion letters relating to some of the transactions and to the evaluations of other financial matters. Whether they concede or deny, investment bankers are fiduciaries. They are experts who acquire the power of discretion over other people's decisions and money. Management is unable to evaluate the bankers' advice and must rely on it. Hence to this extent, and barring counter powers of management, investment bankers influence management in the area of the bankers' expertise. So long as finance influences management, investment bankers will influence corporate management as well.

# REFERENCES

Aite Group (2007), 'Rise of Dark Pools and Rebirth of ECNs: Death to Exchanges?', available at http://www.aitegroup.com/Reports/ReportDetail.aspx?recordItemID=358 (last accessed October 2011).

Anand, Bharat N. & Alexander P. Galetovic (2001), *Investment Banking and Security Market Development: Does Finance Follow Industry?*, Washington D.C.: International Monetary Fund.

Association for Investment Management and Research (2003), 'To Become More Investor-Focused, World's Corporate Boards Should Have More Investment Managers, AIMR Says', PR Newswire, May 12.

Baysinger, Harry D. & Henry N. Butler (1987), 'Modes of Discourse in the Corporate Law Literature: A Reply to Professor Eisenberg', *Delaware Journal of Corporate Law*, 12, 107–33.

Black, Bernard & John Coffee Jr. (1994), 'Hail Britannia?: Institutional Investor Behavior Under Limited Regulation', *Michigan Law Review*, 92, 1997–2087.

Bodnaruk, Andriy, Massimo Massa & Andrei Simonov (2009), 'Investment Banks as Insiders and the Market for Corporate Control', *Review of Financial Studies*, 22, 4989–5026.

Boland, Beth I.Z., Megan N. Gates & Daniel B. Trinkle (2003), 'State Regulation Of Corporate Governance in the Wake Of Sarbanes-Oxley: Is Even More Reform on the Horizon?', *Metropolitan Corporate Counsel* (Mid-Atlantic edition), January, 8.

Boot, Arnoud W.A. & Jonathan R. Macey (2004), 'Monitoring Corporate Performance: The Role of Objectivity, Proximity, and Adaptability in Corporate Governance', *Cornell Law Review*, 89, 356–93.

Borokhovich, Kenneth A., Kelly Brunarski, Yvette S. Harman & Robert Parrino (2006), 'Variation in the Monitoring Incentives of Outside Blockholders', *Journal of Law and Economics*, 49, 651–80.

Bowers, Helen M. (2002), 'Fairness Opinions and the Business Judgment Rule: An Empirical Investigation of Target Firms' Use of Fairness Opinions', *Northwestern University Law Review*, 96, 567–78.

Buffett, Warren (2010), Letter to Berkshire Hathaway, Inc. Shareholders, available at http://www.berkshirehathaway.com/letters/2009ltr.pdf (last accessed October 2011).

Carter, Richard & Steven Manaster (1990), 'Initial Public Offerings and Underwriter Reputation', *Journal of Finance*, 45, 1045–67.

Coffee, John C. Jr. (2009), 'What Went Wrong – A Tragedy in Three Acts', *University of St. Thomas Law Journal*, 6, 403–520.

Collins, Alexis L. (2002), 'Regulation of Alternative Trading Systems: Evolving Regulatory Models and Prospects for Increased Regulatory Coordination and Convergence', *Law and Policy in International Business*, 33, 481–506.

Davidoff, Steven M. (2006), 'Fairness Opinions', *American University Law Review*, 55, 1557–1625.

Davidson, Kenneth M. (1985), *Megamergers: Corporate America's Billion-Dollar Takeovers*, Pensacola, Fla.: Ballinger Publishing Company.

Davis, Gerald F. (2005), 'New Directions in Corporate Governance', *American Review of Sociology*, 31, 143–62.

Davis, Gerald F. & Suzanne K. Stout (1992), 'Organization Theory and the Market for Corporate Control: A Dynamic Analysis of the Characteristics of Large Takeover Targets, 1980–1990', *Administrative Science Quarterly*, 37, 605–33.

Davis, Gerald F., Kristina A. Diekmann & Catherine H. Tinsley (1994), 'The Decline and Fall of the Conglomerate Firm in the 1980s: the Deinstitutionalization of an Organizational Form', *American Sociological Review*, 59, 547–70.

Davis, Gerald F. & Henrich R. Greve (1997), 'Corporate Elite Networks and Governance Changes in the 1980s', *The American Journal of Sociology*, 103, 1–37.

Davis, Gerald F. & G.E. Robbins (2004), 'Nothing but Net? Networks and Status in Corporate Governance', in Karin Knorr-Cetina & Alex Preda (eds), *The Sociology of Financial Markets*, Oxford: Oxford University Press, 290–311.

Day, Kathleen (2002), 'After High-Profile Corporate Busts, Governance Consulting Booms', *Washington Post*, December 27, E01.

Demirgüç-Kunt, Asli & Vojislav Maksimovic (1998), 'Law, Finance, and Firm Growth', *Journal of Finance*, 53, 2107–37.

Fisch, Jill E. (2006), 'Regulatory Responses to Investor Irrationality: The Case of the Research Analyst', *Lewis and Clark Law Review*, 10, 57–83.

Fisch, Jill E. & Hillary A. Sale (2003), 'The Securities Analyst as Agent: Rethinking the Regulation of Analysts', *Iowa Law Review*, 88, 1035–98.

Fitz-Gerald, Keith (2008), 'Are "Dark Pools" Destined to be the Capital Markets' Next Black Hole?', *Money Morning*, available at www.moneymorning.com/2008/07/10/dark-pools (last accessed October 2011).

Fligstein, Neil (1990), *The Transformation of Corporate Control*, Cambridge, Mass.: Harvard University Press.

Foulds, Christopher (2009), 'My Banker's Conflicted and I Couldn't be Happier: the Curious Durability of Staple Financing', *Delaware Journal of Corporate Law*, 34, 519–41.

Frankel, Tamar (2010), *Fiduciary Law*, Oxford: Oxford University Press, Chapter 1.

Galbraith, John Kenneth & James K. Galbraith (FRW) (1979), *The Great Crash 1929*, Boston, Mass.: Houghton Mifflin.

Gilson, Ronald J. & Reinier H. Kraakman (1984), 'The Mechanisms of Market Efficiency', *Virginia Law Review*, 70, 549–644.

Giuffra, Robert J. Jr. (1986), 'Investment Bankers' Fairness Opinions in Corporate Control Transactions', *Yale Law Journal*, 96, 119–41.

Gumbel, Peter (2004), 'How It All Went So Sour: The Inside Story of Parmalat, the Biggest, Most Brazen Corporate Fraud in European History', *Time*, November 21.

Güner, A. Burak, Ulrike Malmendier & Geoffrey Tate (2008), 'Financial Expertise of Directors', *Journal of Financial Economics*, 88, 323–54.

Horwood, Clive (2008), 'Board Stupid', *Euro Money*, 39, February, 74–9.

Ivashina, Victoria, Vinay B. Nair, Anthony Saunders, Nadia Massoud & Rogert Stover (2009), 'Bank Debt and Corporate Governance', *Review of Financial Studies*, 22, 41–77.

Jensen, Michael C. & William H. Meckling (1976), 'Theory of the Firm: Managerial Behavior, Agency Costs, and Ownership Structure', *Journal of Financial Economics*, 3, 305–60.

Kisgen, D.J., Jun Qing 'QJ' & Weihong Song (2009), 'Are Fairness Opinions Fair? The Case of Mergers and Acquisitions', *Journal of Financial Economics*, 91, 179–207.

Kraakman, Reinier (1984), 'Corporate Liability Stategies and the Costs of Legal Controls', *Yale Law Journal*, 93, 857–98.

Kraakman, Reinier (1986), 'Gatekeepers: The Anatomy of a Third-Party Enforcement Strategy', *Journal of Law, Economics, and Organization*, 2, 53–104.

Levine, Ross & Sara Zervos (1998), 'Capital Control Liberalization and Stock Market Development', *World Development*, 26, 1169–83.

LoPucki, Lynn M. & Joseph W. Doherty (2008), 'Professional Overcharging in Large Bankruptcy Reorganization Cases', *Journal of Empirical Legal Studies*, 5, 983–1017.

Lorsch, Jay W. (2010), 'Lessons from the Crisis about Governing Financial Institutions', *Executive Counsel*, 7(1), February–March, 18–22.

McLaughlin, Robyn, Assem Safieddine & Gopala K. Vasudevan (2000), 'Investment Banker Reputation and the Performance of Seasoned Equity Issuers', *Financial Management*, 29, 96–110.

McMurdy, Deirdre (2000), 'Making Mergers Work', *Maclean's*, January 17, 54.

Mizruchi, Mark S. & Linda Brewster Stearns (1994), 'A Longitudinal Study of Borrowing by Large American Corporations', *Administrative Science Quarterly*, 39, 118–40.

Modigliani, Franco & Enrico Perotti (2000), 'Security Markets Versus Bank Finance: Legal Enforcement and Investor Protection', *International Review of Finance*, 1, 81–96.

Morgenson, Gretchen (2005), 'Mirror, Mirror, Who is the Unfairest', *New York Times*, May 29, C31.

Morrison, Alan & William Wilhelm (2007), *Investment Banking: Institutions, Politics, and Law*, New York, N.Y.: Oxford University Press.

Moss, Scott A. (2007), 'Illuminating Secrecy: A New Economic Analysis of Confidential Settlements', *Michigan Law Review*, 105, 867–912.

O'Brien, Timothy L. (2005), 'The Man With the Golden Slingshot', *New York Times*, June 5, C1.

Obstfeld, Maurice (1994), 'Are Industrial-Country Consumption Risks Globally Diversified?', *National Bureau of Economics Research Working Papers* 4308.

Palmer, Donald A., Brad M, Barber, Zhou Xueguang & Yasamin Soysal (1995), 'The Friendly and Predatory Acquisition of Large U.S. Corporations in the 1960s: the Other Contested Terrain', *American Sociological Review*, 60, 469–99.

Pare, Terence & Patty De Llosa (1994), 'The New Merger Boom: New Combinations are Reshaping America's Largest Industries, with Consequences for All. Shareholders Could be Big Losers', *Fortune*, November 28, 130, 61–8.

Park, Edward (1996), 'Allowing Japanese Banks to Engage in Securitization: Potential Benefits, Regulatory Obstacles, and Theories for Reform', *University of Pennsylvania Journal of International Economics*, 17, 723–52.

Peek, Liz (2007), 'Dark Pools Threaten Wall Street', *The New York Sun*, October 16.

Peet, C. (1992), 'Declining Hegemony and Rising International Trade: Moving beyond Hegemonic Stability Theory', *International Interactions*, 18, 101–27.

Plank, Thomas E. (2004), 'The Security of Securitization and the Future of Security', *Cardozo Law Review*, 25, 1655–1742.

Rajan, Raghuram G. & Luigi Zingales (1998), 'Power in a Theory of the Firm', *CEPR Discussion Papers* 1777.

Rajan, Raghuram G. & Luigi Zingales (2001), 'The Great Reversals: The Politics of Financial Development in the 20th Century', *CEPR Discussion Papers*, 2783.

Rhee, Robert J. (2010), 'The Decline of Investment Banking: Preliminary Thoughts on the Evolution of the Industry 1996–2008', *Journal of Business & Technology Law*, 5, 75–98.

Roane, Kit (2007), 'Will Dark Pools Swallow Wall Street?', *Portfolio.com*, available at http://www.portfolio.com/news-markets/national-news/portfolio/2007/07/06/Dark-Pools-Grow-Scrutiny-Does-Not/ (last accessed October 2011).

Roe, Mark J. (1996), *Strong Managers, Weak Owners*, Princeton, NJ: Princeton University Press.

Roy, William G. (1997), *Socializing Capital: The Rise of the Large Industrial Corporation in America*, Princeton, NJ: Princeton University Press.

Sher, Noam (2006), 'Negligence Versus Strict Liability: The Case of Underwriter Liability in IPOs', *DePaul Business and Commercial Law Journal*, 4, 451–96.

Sorkin, Andrew Ross (2004), 'Good Deals for Banks, Both Coming and Going', *New York Times* (Late Edition, East Coast), September 5, 3.6.

Steele, Myron T. & J.W. Verret (2007), 'Delaware's Guidance: Ensuring Equity for the Modern Witenagemot', *Virginia Law and Business Review*, 2, 189–219.

Stuart, Toby E., Ha Hoang & Ralph C. Hybels (1999), 'Interorganizational Endorsements and the Performance of Entrepreneurial Ventures', *Administrative Science Quarterly*, 44, 315–49.

*The Economist* (1985), 'Keys to Success: Only a Few Will Hold Them', March 16, Issue 7381(28), 33–4.

Vogus, Timothy J. & Gerald F. Davis (2005), 'Elite Mobilizations for Antitakeover Legislation, 1982–1990', in Gerald F. Davis, Doug McAdam, W. Richard Scott & Mayer N. Zald (eds) *Social Movements and Organization Theory*, New York, N.Y.: Cambridge University Press, 96–121.

Weinstein, Alan C. (2009), 'Current and Future Challenges to Local Government Posed by the Housing and Credit Crisis', *Albany Government Law Review*, 2, 259–76.

Westphal, James D. & Edward J. Zajac (1998), 'The Symbolic Management of Stockholders: Corporate Governance Reforms and Shareholder Reactions', *Administrative Science Quarterly*, 43, 127–53.

Westphal, James D. & Edward J. Zajac (2001), 'Decoupling Policy from Practice: The Case of Stock Repurchase Programs', *Administrative Science Quarterly*, 46, 202–55.

Wilhelm, William J. Jr. & Joseph Downing (2001), *Information Markets: What Businesses Can Learn from Financial Innovation*, Boston, Mass.: Harvard Business Press.

Zajac, Edward J. & James D. Westphal (1996), 'Director Reputation, CEO-Board Power, and the Dynamics of Board Interlocks', *Administrative Science Quarterly*, 41, 507–29.

Zuckerman Ezra W. (1999), 'The Categorical Imperative: Securities Analysts and the Illegitimacy Discount', *American Journal of Sociology*, 104, 1398–438.

Zuckerman, Ezra W. (2000), 'Focusing the Corporate Product: Securities Analysts and Dediversification', *Administrative Science Quarterly*, 45, 591–619.

# PART IV


# JURISDICTION

# 20. Varieties of corporate law-making: Competition, preemption, and federalism

*Robert B. Ahdieh*

## 1. INTRODUCTION

In few areas have legal scholars focused more closely on the sources of law than in the study of corporate governance.[1] Questions of institutional design thus pervade the literature of corporate law. Is the scope of directors' and managers' fiduciary obligations best determined *ex ante*, by means of positive law, or *ex post*, in the context of individual disputes (Coffee 1989; Fisch 2000)? If the former, should relevant legislative committees or specialized administrative agencies akin to the Securities and Exchange Commission lead the way (Letsou 2009)? If the latter, are such case-by-case assessments best made by courts of general jurisdiction or judges expert in corporate law (Holland 2009; Sullivan & Conlon 1997)? What is the appropriate role of self-regulatory entities in corporate law, including exchanges, associations of broker-dealers, and various standard-setting organizations (Karmel 2008; Roe 2003)? And what are we to make of hybrid public-private entities such as the Public Company Accounting Oversight Board (Nagy 2010; Pildes 2009; Romano 2009)?

Most prominent among the questions of institutional design in corporate law, however, have been those surrounding the allocation of law-making authority as between federal and state authorities: what is the dynamic by which corporate law will be generated at the state level, absent federal intervention? What is the normative quality of the resulting rules? When might a federal role be advisable, if not essential, in the regulation of public corporations? What form ought any such intervention take, and what distortions might it be expected to introduce into our traditionally state-based regime of corporate law?

There has been much debate over these questions, of course, to which the literature of law and economics has contributed mightily.[2] To a striking degree, however, scholars have come to embrace – at least in broad terms – a common view on these questions (Ahdieh 2009b; Choi & Guzman 2001; Klausner 1995). In this standard account, sub-national rules of corporate governance are to be preferred. State law – and the dynamic of state competition that arises from it – generates (at least some) efficiency gains, helping to reduce agency costs, as between shareholders and managers. Even if not a *race* to the top, state rules move us in the right direction, in addressing what has been the core challenge of corporate law since Berle and Means: achieving an optimal allocation of wealth and authority as between owners of the modern public corporation and those who manage it for their benefit.

---

[1] The natural polestar might be constitutional law. Given the relatively substantial attention devoted to the substance of the latter as well, however, the proportion of source to substance may be still greater in corporate law.

[2] Beyond contract theory, corporate governance may be the area over which law and economics has had greatest influence.

For these and other reasons, the law and economics literature admonishes, the scope of federal law in an optimal regime of corporate governance should be limited (Bainbridge 2003; Choi & Guzman 2001; Ribstein 2002). Federal rules may have a role in imposing mandatory disclosure obligations, regulating aspects of the issuance and trading of corporate securities, and in selected other circumstances, but not more generally. For many scholars of law and economics, in fact, even these limited federal interventions are superfluous – if not harmful.

In what follows, I suggest that this account of corporate law, widely accepted as it has become in the law and economics literature, deserves a closer look. As to what might be thought of as its horizontal and vertical axes – the perception of (horizontal) state competition as beneficial for shareholder-managerial relations, and the notion of (vertical) federal preemption as properly limited – the meaning and implications of the conventional account turn out to be more ambiguous.[3] A careful analysis thus highlights critical limitations of each of these claims, and offers a more complex picture of the optimal sources of corporate law.[4] Ultimately, a closer analysis of the horizontal dimension of state-to-state interaction and the vertical dimension of potential federal intervention points us to the same result in institutional design: a more mixed architecture of corporate law-making.[5]

## 2.   THE HORIZONTAL AXIS OF LAW-MAKING IN CORPORATE LAW

In its origins, the corporate literature's story of competition among states to provide rules of corporate governance can be famously traced to the work of William Cary (1974). In 1974, Cary joined others – including Ralph Nader, Donald Schwartz, and Joel Seligman – in calling for some federal preemption of state corporate law. What distinguished Cary's account, however, was his particular account of the regulatory dynamic that demanded such intervention. Cary highlighted what he saw – including while chair of the Securities and Exchange Commission – as a pattern of destructive competition among states to attract corporate charters. In Cary's telling, this competition – led by Delaware, 'a pygmy among … states' – was driving a 'race for the bottom' in the level of shareholder protection provided under state law (Cary 1974, 666, 701).

With this, Cary drew an indelible link between state competition and the challenges of corporate governance. He thus tied what has been the core concern of corporate law since Berle and Means' seminal study of the modern public corporation – shareholder-managerial

---

[3]     Among other reasons, this conclusion matters because of the substantial influence that stories of efficient competition in corporate law have had in other areas, including environmental, antitrust, bankruptcy, and even family and criminal law (Butler & Macey 1996; Guzman 2002).

[4]     My argument, it bears noting, goes beyond that of work by Bebchuk and Hamdani, and Kahan and Kamar suggesting the lack of any competition among states for corporate charters (Bebchuk & Hamdani 2002; Kahan & Kamar 2002). My claim is not that there is not competition, but that any such competition leads us to an entirely different place than we have commonly assumed.

[5]     I have advanced the arguments I outline herein across a number of previous articles – both in corporate and securities law, and beyond (Ahdieh 2004a, 2004b, 2005, 2006, 2009a, 2009b) – and my discussion of them herein borrows substantially from that prior work.

relations and the separation of ownership and control – with its core institutional characteristic: the dynamic of interstate competition for charters.[6] At least as applied in the conventional
law and economics account of corporate law, however, that linkage is lacking.

In Cary's telling, states – motivated by the promise of increased franchise tax revenue and
increased business for in-state lawyers – compete for the charters of public companies (Cary
1974). To succeed in this competition, states focus on the interests of managers, the functional decision-makers in determining place of incorporation (Cary 1974; Hadfield & Talley
2006). States thus offer packages of rules, institutions, and taxes designed to meet managerial demand. In particular, they compete to reduce the operative constraints on managers – and
hence the level of shareholder protection – producing the infamous 'race for the bottom'
(Cary 1974, 666).[7]

For the most part, Cary's analysis was greeted with enthusiasm. This was not, however,
the universal view. Perhaps most significant was the rejoinder of then-professor Ralph
Winter, who responded with one of the seminal early works of the law and economics literature (Winter 1977). As with other famous works cited more often than they are read, however,
we do well to give Winter's analysis another look (Ellickson 1989; Rock 1996).

Contrary to standard accounts of his argument, Winter agreed with Cary on far more than
he disagreed.[8] Winter did not dispute the pattern of state competition described by Cary, as
either a theoretical or empirical matter. Nor did he question Cary's assertions that managers
were the critical decision-makers in determining place of incorporation, or that states could
consequently be expected to cater to managerial demand. In fact, Winter did not even dispute
Cary's observation of declining levels of shareholder protection.

Cary's error did not lie in any of his observations about *state* competition, thus, but in his
inattention to a distinct pattern of competition: one among managers, to meet the demands of
shareholders (Winter 1977). Channeling earlier work of Henry Manne (Manne 1965, 1967),
Winter's argument was simple and compelling: If managers are to secure scarce investment
capital – and to survive in the market for corporate control – they would be ill-advised to
behave in ways contrary to shareholder interests. By driving up their cost of capital, and
increasing the prospect of takeover and arbitrage, such behavior would undermine managers'
long-term interests, whatever its potential to generate short-term returns.

Correct as Cary may have been as to each of his premises, then, his ultimate conclusion
could – in Winter's view – be dismissed. Given the distinct pattern of *managerial* competition

---

6   'Ever since Berle and Means, the central issue of corporate law has been how to create a legal
structure that monitors management' (Romano 1993, xii). And as Winter puts it: 'With a few exceptions, the legal literature is single-mindedly concerned with the discretion corporate management can
exercise as a result of the "separation of ownership and control" popularized by Berle and Means'
(Winter 1977, 262). *See also* Bainbridge (2002); Bratton (2001); Cary (1974): Fischel (1982); Kahn
(1997).

7   A decline of shareholder protection, it bears emphasizing, does not necessarily signify a race
to the bottom. In Winter's account, thus, the progressive reduction of constraints on managerial discretion is fully consistent with an *increase* in shareholder welfare – given the potential utility in trading
diminished protection for increased returns (Winter 1977).

8   Some of the perception of sharp disagreement can be traced to the tenor of Winter's piece,
which was sharply dismissive of Cary and other critics of Delaware law (Winter 1977, 257) ('That the
impact of a legal system on investors would be known only to law professors and Mr. Nader seems a
rather tenuous proposition').

for capital (and job security), *state* competition ought not be expected to produce any race to the bottom in shareholder welfare.[9] More broadly, agency costs attendant to the separation of ownership and control – the motivating project of corporate law (Berle & Means 1932; Blair & Stout 1999; Jensen & Meckling 1976) – need not be a worry.

Critically for present purposes – and contrary to the standard account of Winter's argument – the latter required no endorsement of state competition.[10] To the contrary, state competition was irrelevant to it. Winter's story was not about federalism, it turns out, but about the distinct dynamic of managerial competition.[11]

In the law and economics analysis of corporate governance that followed, however, this point was lost. Winter's response came to be seen as echoing Cary's linkage of state competition and shareholder-managerial relations – but simply with the obverse normative result. Where Cary had posited a race to the bottom, Winter was seen as champion of the opposite view: a race to the top.

According to the conventional wisdom, then, Winter laid the foundation for the since-prevailing view of state competition as beneficial for shareholder-managerial relations.[12] As Roberta Romano eloquently states it, federalism and resulting state competition are 'the genius of American corporate law' – critical determinants of 'the relations between a firm's shareholders and managers' (Romano 1993: 1).[13]

When we appreciate that Winter's argument was not about state competition, but about a distinct pattern of *managerial* competition, however, the conventional view – widely accepted as it has come to be in the corporate literature – requires reconsideration. Unto itself, state competition will not supply rules that are substantively efficient, as determined by some extrinsic standard of optimal corporate governance. To the contrary, if managers demand substantively *inefficient* rules of corporate governance, state competition can be expected to supply them. It will do so, however, *in an efficient fashion*. State competition may thus help us generate *effective* rules of corporate governance – i.e., rules that effectively advance whatever ends we choose to pursue in corporate governance. It does nothing, however, to ensure that those ends are efficient.[14]

---

[9]    To reiterate, Winter did not dispute that charter competition had reduced the level of legal protection of shareholders. In his eyes, however, this was not 'the bottom'. Rather, such declines should be seen as evidence of shareholders' willingness to grant managers wider discretion, in hope of securing greater returns.

[10]    To be sure, some suggestion of an embrace of federalism can be found in Winter's original article (Winter 1977). In later work, moreover, he was even more explicit, invoking (for the first time) the rhetoric of a 'race to the top' in corporate law (Winter 1982). Subsequently, however, he would step back from that claim: 'I am far more confident that Professor Cary's argument about the race to the bottom is wrong than I am that my argument that Delaware is leading a race to the top is right' (Winter 1989, 1528). At best, he suggested, state competition might motivate a 'leisurely walk' to the top (Winter 1989, 1529).

[11]    Winter's claim was not that federalism was *good*, thus, but simply that it was *not bad* (Winter 1977; *see also* Easterbrook & Fischel 1991).

[12]    Abramowicz thus notes 'the increasing scholarly consensus that competition improves corporate law' (Abramowicz 2003, 139–41).

[13]    Examples of such linkage of state competition to shareholder-managerial relations abound (Bebchuk 1992; Butler & Ribstein 1990; Choi & Guzman 2001; Fischel 1982; Romano 1985; Thompson 1999).

[14]    Stating it differently, managerial competition may generate efficient rules; state competition, by contrast, simply generates rules efficiently.

Winter's account thus turns out to be no less relevant to a purely federal regime of corporate chartering, than a competitive state regime. Consider, for example, the need to choose between mandatory versus enabling rules of corporate governance, at the national level (Easterbrook & Fischel 1989; Eisenberg 1989; Gordon 1989). How might Winter respond to the possibility of mandatory federal rules? No need for them, he would surely advise. Why? 'See my famous article.'

Managers, Winter would remind us, must effectively navigate both the capital markets and the market for corporate control. Given as much, they can largely be expected to behave in shareholders' best interest – even in the face of merely enabling federal rules. Markets work, so law need not get in the way (Winter 1977).

This, of course, is precisely the same response that Winter offered to Cary's recommendation that state competition be partially preempted, by a baseline of federal standards. Yet it applies equally to the choice between mandatory and enabling rules *in the absence of state competition*. Even as to the question of whether to regulate at all – as opposed to the particular source or nature of relevant rules – Winter's rejoinder would remain unchanged: No need to worry, as efficient capital markets and resulting managerial competition will deal with it. Winter's account, then, plays out identically at the federal or state level, as to the choice of regulatory form, and as to any question of law. Why? Because Winter's dynamic of managerial competition is not, ultimately, a question of federalism, state competition, or sources of law at all.[15]

The heavy lifting in determining the substantive quality of corporate governance, then, is done not by state competition, but by efficient capital markets – and by the managerial competition that Winter identified as arising out of them. Consider the caliber of corporate governance that we would expect to emerge out of state competition, thus, as we move from strong-form efficiency in the capital markets, to a somewhat efficient market and, ultimately, an inefficient market. In the first case, state competition is likely to be associated with a fairly efficient equilibrium of shareholder-managerial relations. In the second, the latter would be relatively less efficient. In the last, finally, the quality of corporate governance is likely to be sub-optimal. The 'genius' at work in shaping American corporate governance, this suggests, is not the federalist organization of corporate law, but rather the operation of efficient markets.[16]

In sum, state competition is only as good as the managerial competition on which it relies. If efficient capital markets are disciplining managers to optimally promote shareholder interests, state competition can help us achieve that result. If they are not, then it will not.[17] If the concern of corporate law is the separation of ownership and control, then, it is on managerial – rather than state – competition that we must rely.

---

[15]    Framed as such, the analysis herein can be read to echo Bernie Black's assertion of the triviality of corporate law (Black 1990).

[16]    The question, to be clear, is not whether state competition is beneficial for the modern public corporation. As I will suggest below, it likely is. Rather, the question is whether state competition can improve on the allocation of decision-making authority and resources (as between shareholders and managers) that is dictated by the capital markets and resulting managerial competition. Can state competition, unto itself, advance the core project of corporate law: redressing the separation of ownership and control? Contrary to our common rhetoric to that effect, it cannot.

[17]    The basic claim I advance might thus be framed as follows: State competition may better align legal rules with managerial demand – but it does nothing to alter that demand. Rather, it takes managerial preferences as it finds them.

Even if the foregoing is correct, and state competition does not *directly* increase efficiency in shareholder-managerial relations, might it be understood to do so indirectly? Most robustly, might we see state competition as an essential prerequisite to managerial competition's minimization of agency costs? More modestly, might state competition help to *reinforce* the impact of managerial competition? State competition might thus help to undercut rules that insulate managers from managerial competition, including anti-takeover statutes, rules regarding their ability to draw on retained earnings (rather than the capital markets) for financing, and others.[18] Under national-level rules of corporate governance, by comparison, such rules might be more likely to persist. Even these narrower claims for federalism and state competition, however, ultimately fall short.

A plausible account of the political economy at work, to begin, might question whether managers are significantly insulated by such rules in any case. Most corporate law, of course, consists of default rules (Easterbrook & Fischel 1989; Eisenberg 1989; Gordon 1989). Given as much, managers motivated to maximize shareholder value can waive inefficient corporate governance rules in favor of value-maximizing charter terms – even in a purely federal system. But they need not even go that far. Even if their charters permit them to adopt policies adverse to shareholder interests, managers can simply decline to do so – if capital market-driven managerial competition counsels as much. That managers of a given firm *may* invoke a given anti-takeover device, thus, does not mean they *must* do so.

This is only true, of course, if the enabling character of corporate governance rules is independent of whether they are enacted at the state or federal level. In a national-level regime of corporate law, however, perhaps the contrary assumption of *mandatory* rules – and even of rules that serve to insulate managers from capital market-driven competition – might be more appropriate.[19] It is at least not obvious, however, why this should be so.

Consider, to begin, the case in which capital market-driven competition among managers is already at work. In the presence of such competition, the latter can be expected to seek enabling federal rules consistent with shareholder interests. With managerial and shareholder preferences aligned in this fashion, the persistence of enabling rules – even at the federal level – would seem a plausible assumption.

This assumes, however, that the relevant interest group politics are not substantially distinct at the federal level, such that other interests – public employee or labor union pension funds, or public interest associations, for example – would not regularly overcome the orientation of both managers and (majority) shareholders to enabling rules (Bainbridge 2011; Grundfest 2010). As Mark Roe has highlighted, some – even significant – differences seem likely at the federal versus state level (Hill & McDonnell 2007; Roe 2003, 2005). An array of groups ill-positioned – or inadequately incentivized, given the relative ease of re-incorporation – to engage Delaware corporate law might thus be expected to participate in corporate law-making at the federal level (Grundfest 2010).[20]

---

[18]   Such rules might be seen as the converse of the 'market perfecting' rules that Easterbrook describes as welcome in the marketplace of corporate law (Easterbrook 1984).

[19]   Most law and economics analysis of corporate law can be read to embrace this assumption, whether explicitly or implicitly (Carney 1997; Choi & Guzman 2001; Gordon 1994; Note 2005). In a sense, it can be understood as a strong-form claim about federalism's nexus with the separation of ownership and control. Here, the claim is not that federalism can help to generate the efficient rules dictated by managerial competition, but rather that federalism *alone* can achieve that result.

[20]   This tendency may be aggravated, Roe suggests, given differences in federal versus state insti-

The critical question remains whether such interests should be expected to overcome, with any regularity, the basic equilibrium of corporate law that emerges from the aligned preferences of the two most proximately interested actors – managers and shareholders.[21] And, more particularly for present purposes, whether one can imagine an interest group dynamic that generates not simply rules that are broadly detrimental to the firm, but specifically rules that favor managerial entrenchment, at the expense of shareholders (Bebchuk 2001). While such a possibility cannot be excluded, it is at least not obvious that it should be expected, even at the federal level (Roe 2005, 2502 ('It's not that these outside groups could readily beat a tight managerial-investor alliance. Ordinarily, they cannot because they're too weak'); Romano 1998).[22]

This expectation holds, moreover, even absent a baseline assumption of capital market-driven competition among managers of US public corporations. Even without the latter, state competition may not be necessary to avoid mandatory rules that insulate managers from competition for capital and the market for corporate control. To begin, it is not easy to imagine what federal mandatory rules of this sort would even look like. Rules *mandating* the exercise of anti-takeover protections or the use of retained earnings thus seem implausible on their face. However peculiar they might appear, though, might managers freed from the demands of state competition not seek such rules at the federal level? Once again, we do well to recall what Winter actually said.

Winter's story of competition for capital operates not only among US public corporations, but across the entire universe of potential investment opportunities (Winter 1977). Managers who accede to mandatory federal rules that reduce shareholder value may not lose capital to other publicly-held US corporations, which will be subject to the same (mandatory) rules. As Winter counseled, however, they will lose it to 'stock in companies incorporated in … other countries, bonds, bank accounts, certificates of deposit, partnerships (general or limited), individual proprietorships, joint ventures, present consumption, etc' (Winter 1977, 257). Even if US capital markets did not discourage the collusion of managers to enact national rules eliminating competition among themselves (e.g., by mandating that all managers of US public corporations *must* act to prevent a takeover), competition for capital with the other investment targets enumerated by Winter would limit their incentive to do so.[23]

---

tutional structures – in particular, the greater role of administrative agencies at the federal level (Roe 2005). Such agencies bring their own interests into the dynamics of corporate law-making. Further, they serve as a more ready – or at least an additional – entry-point for interest groups besides managers and shareholders.

[21] It is telling, in this regard, that Roe's hypothetical examples of cases in which interest group politics at the federal level could generate distinct outcomes involve partnerships of either managers or shareholders with outside interests – contrary to the baseline assumption of aligned managerial and shareholder interests (Roe 2005).

[22] A separate question is whether a 'monopolist' federal regulator may favor mandatory rules – and perhaps even ones designed to insulate managers – more so than state regulators, given greater competitive pressures on the latter. I will return to this question below. For the moment, though, two points bear emphasizing: First, federal regulators are not entirely insulated from competitive pressures – perhaps especially in corporate and securities law (Brummer 2008; Gadinis 2008; Langevoort 2008; Licht 2001). More importantly, my argument does not dispute the capacity of state competition to contribute to the constraint of *regulatory* behavior. My point is simply that, by contrast with managerial competition, state competition is not determinative of managers' treatment of shareholders – at least in the prevailing law and economics account of the latter.

[23] As to overseas beneficiaries of such flight capital, the potential universe is even greater today than when Winter wrote. The rise of derivatives and a wide array of synthetic financial products, meanwhile, has strengthened the force of Winter's argument yet further.

To be sure, reliance on competition with other investment opportunities alone would generate some slack in the disincentive of managers to pursue mandatory federal rules protective of their incumbency. Given the difficulty of imagining the form such rules would take, and the need for at least some (perhaps significant) subset of managers to compete actively with other investment opportunities, however, a robust story of managerial collusion to enact federal mandatory rules remains more difficult to tell than has been commonly acknowledged. In any case, if we expect managers to seek mandatory rules that favor their interests over those of shareholders in the absence of efficient capital markets, there is nothing that state corporate law (and resulting state competition) can do about it. In that scenario, states can be expected to give managers what they want – perhaps especially if there's competition.

Federalism, then, neither *directly* advances efficiency in shareholder-managerial relations, as the standard law and economics account of the genius of American corporate law would have it, nor does so *indirectly*, as a necessary reinforcement to managerial competition's promotion of those ends. But perhaps we can construct an even more modest account of state competition's contribution to addressing the separation of ownership and control, in which it is not *necessary* for managerial competition, but simply reduces the cost associated with the latter.

State competition effectively fosters, in this telling, the production of off-the-rack charter terms consistent with an optimal balance of shareholder and managerial power. Rather than relying on promoters or managers to modify inefficient default rules in order to achieve the equilibrium dictated by the capital markets – let alone expecting them to draft contracts from scratch or seek the modification of mandatory rules through the political process – state competition offers efficiency up on a plate.

Important as such a cost-savings function for state competition might be, however, it is not clear that it can be reconciled with the law and economics literature's enthusiastic embrace of federalism in corporate law. In the rhetoric of the literature, thus, state competition is 'the genius of American corporate law'. In a purely cost-savings account, by contrast, it is valuable – perhaps even immensely so – but not essential. However much it may accelerate our journey to an efficient result, is not necessary to get there. In due course, we would get there regardless.

Equally important, such a cost-savings account of the role of state competition is in no way unique to shareholder-managerial relations, the separation of ownership and control, or agency costs. Rather, it applies equally to any set of rules, in any area, governing anything. It is, simply put, the story of federalism generally.[24]

This does not, to reiterate, make the cost-savings function of state competition any less significant. Over the length and breadth of incorporations, the provision of default charter terms likely generates substantial transaction cost savings. If we count the capacity for *ex post* elaboration of such rules by way of specialized courts as part of the relevant cost-savings, this is only more true (Fisch 2000; Klausner 1995; Romano 1985).[25] Even integrating the latter,

---

[24]    Of course, to the extent one conceives corporate governance as *entirely* contractarian, one might minimally see federalism and state competition as more palatable in this arena of regulation, than in others (Butler & Ribstein 1990), *but see* note 42 and accompanying text.

[25]    One might question whether this aspect of corporate law's institutional architecture is properly credited to state competition. Romano's 'credible commitment' account of Delaware's competitive advantage, however, offers a particularly strong argument that it is (Romano 1985).

however, one is left with state competition as less striking an achievement in corporate law than the literature's wholehearted embrace of it would seem to suggest.

Even if talk of corporate law's 'genius' amounts to nothing more than a story of cost-savings, however, this cannot rescue the literature's common linkage of state competition to efficiency in shareholder-managerial relations. To the contrary, it points us back to where we started – the twin competitions we have commonly overlooked in Cary and Winter's original call-and-response. A purely cost-savings account of the role of state competition in corporate law is thus best understood as turning on the operative ends of state versus managerial competition.

To appreciate as much, it is useful to recall the distinct origins of corporate scholars' study of these distinct patterns of competition. At base, Berle and Means's account of the separation of ownership and control was motivated by fears that managers would act against shareholder interests – a possibility they saw as the critical challenge facing the modern public corporation (Berle & Means 1932). To address this danger, Berle and Means offered a prescription well suited to their times. As committed New Dealers, writing on the cusp of the explosive growth of the administrative state, Berle and Means saw *regulation* as the answer (Berle & Means 1932).[26] Heightened regulation of the corporation, in their eyes, was essential to protect shareholders against managerial depredations.

Forty-five years later, Winter spoke to that same fear – now under the rubric of agency costs. When it came to solutions, however, Winter found them not in regulation, but in the capital markets and their promotion of a salutary competition among managers. By way of such managerial competition, Winter argued, the separation of ownership and control would be effectively policed. In the years since, the literature of law and economics has largely concurred – though with an important strand of dissent, including in the work of those who would dispute the underlying assumption of efficiency in the capital markets.[27]

State competition is, quite literally, a different story, with distinct origins – and entirely distinct ends. In its genesis, scholarly enthusiasm about state competition can be traced to public choice critiques of the regulatory state in the 1960s – more than three decades after publication of Berle and Means's New Deal-era call for increased regulation. With the work of James Buchanan and Gordon Tullock, Anthony Downs, Mancur Olson, George Stigler, and others, scholars began to challenge public interest accounts of regulation akin to that of Berle and Means (Buchanan & Tullock 1962; Olson 1965; Stigler 1971). Corporate and securities law scholars – including Bill Carney, Jonathan Macey and David Haddock, Henry Manne, and Susan Phillips and Richard Zecher – joined the fray, focusing their attention on questions including SEC capture, the role of in-state interest groups in jurisdictional competition, and the utility of the securities laws' mandatory disclosure regime (Carney 1997; Easterbrook & Fischel 1984; Macey & Haddock 1985; Manne 1974; Phillips & Zecher 1981).

---

[26] '*Time* magazine called *The Modern Corporation and Private Property* "the economic Bible of the Roosevelt administration"' (Hovenkamp 1988, 1685).

[27] Notably, for the important minority of law and economics scholars who question the capacity of capital markets to align managers' preferences with shareholder interests (Bebchuk 1992; Partnoy 2000), the linkage of state competition to shareholder-managerial relations – which I resist above – is valid. Absent efficient capital markets, thus, Cary turns out to have been right. Without some alternative check, state competition may well provide a ready avenue for managerial abuse.

With this, students of corporate law came to see threats to the public corporation as arising not only in the interaction of shareholders and managers – the concern that motivated Berle and Means – but likewise in the firm's interaction with its state of incorporation and other regulators as well. Rent extractions by state actors came to be considered as likely – if not more likely – to impact shareholders' bottom line, as managerial extractions (Carney 1997; Easterbrook 1994; Romano 1993). Minimizing such regulatory costs, in turn, emerged as a distinct project – as a distinct set of ends – of corporate law.

Properly understood, it is in the pursuit of this project that we find the true 'genius' of American corporate *law*. So long as re-incorporation is a viable option (Black 1990; Bratton 2000; Romano 1985), federalism and resulting state competition can serve both as an impetus for effective regulation and as a check on regulatory abuse – 'cost-savings' of the very broadest sort (Qian & Weingast 1997). Thus, states that enact indeterminate rules or fail to innovate efficiently – whether because of the self-interested choices of relevant bureaucrats or the influence of special interest shareholders – can be expected to face both a decline in new incorporations and re-incorporations out of state. Conversely, states that align their rules with the needs of relevant corporations – and their franchise taxes with the value of the services they provide – can be expected to thrive. In this way, a regime of state competition has the potential to produce a non-zero-sum enhancement of both state *and* corporate welfare. Minimally – and perhaps more commonly – it can be expected to foster a shift of surplus from the state of incorporation (and its interest groups) to the firm.[28]

Critically for present purposes, however, these salutary benefits of federalism and state competition do not speak to managerial failure and the relationship between shareholders and managers – the separation of ownership and control that has been the central project of corporate law since Berle and Means. Rather, they are directed to the interaction between the corporation *as a whole* and its state of incorporation, and to the distinct project of minimizing regulatory failure in that relationship.

Putting it differently, corporate federalism does not speak – at least in any analytically relevant way – to the allocation of corporate surplus as between shareholders and managers within the firm. Rather, it speaks to the size of the surplus that the firm manages to capture from without. It is not about shareholders versus managers' share of the corporate pie, thus, but about how big a pie they have to share.[29]

---

[28]   It is important, in this vein, to recognize the distinct nature of any purported 'efficiency' in state versus managerial competition. There is little or no normative complexity to the efficiency gains from managerial competition. By comparison, a state competition-driven reallocation of surplus as between state and firm is more ambiguous in its normative implications. In some cases, federalism and resulting state competition may encourage regulatory initiatives that broadly enhance the efficiency of the relevant legal regime. This might be the case, for example, where state competition fosters an appropriate balance of innovation and continuity in relevant regulatory rules, or where it minimizes corruption or shirking among state regulators. In these cases, the gains accrue to both state and firm. More commonly, however, state competition might be expected to produce not an *increase* in the available surplus, but simply its shift from state to firm. This, most obviously, occurs when charter competition drives marginal franchise tax rates to zero – by matching relevant rates with the cost of services provided. This result – by contrast with managerial competition's minimization of shareholder-managerial agency costs – is normatively ambiguous. It eliminates, of course, the redistributive effects of corporate tax policy. But there is nothing inherently 'efficient' about this result. We consequently do well to be cautious in speaking of the 'efficiency' of state competition in corporate law.

[29]   Notably, this framing of the potential role of corporate federalism aligns most closely with

In assessing law and economics' analysis of corporate law, thus, we do well to think of a pair of distinct projects at work in the governance and regulation of the modern public corporation – projects advanced by respective dynamics of competition among managers and among states. Too often, these patterns of competition are collapsed in the corporate literature, in ways that obscure the independent nature and distinct normative ends of each. The older, and more traditional, focus of corporate law has been the relationship of shareholder and manager, internal to the corporation. As to this dynamic, the motivating project – assertedly advanced by the structure of American corporate *finance*, by efficient capital markets, and by resulting managerial competition (*but see* notes 27 & 33) – is to minimize agency costs attendant to the separation of ownership and control. In this way, it is hoped, the surplus available to the modern public corporation may be most efficiently allocated between shareholders and managers.

At least since the 1970s, however, there has been a distinct project at work as well. Here, the aim is to enhance the surplus available to the entire firm – and, in the most hopeful scenario, to both firm *and* state – without regard to its distribution between shareholders and managers. It is in the pursuit of this distinct project that American corporate *law* – and the federalism and state competition at the heart of its institutional design – may reveal a certain genius. The prevailing law and economics account of state competition as driving a race to the top in corporate law may thus be true; it is mistaken, however, as to spoils of victory.

## 3.   THE VERTICAL AXIS OF LAW-MAKING IN CORPORATE LAW

At one level, the vertical axis of the institutional architecture of American corporate law might be seen as simply the corollary of the horizontal axis of interstate competition. It is the lack of federal preemption of corporate law, thus, that allows competition among states to play itself out (Bebchuk & Hamdani 2002; Bratton & McCahery 1995; Roe 2003). The reality, however, is more complex.

At least since the adoption of federal securities rules in the 1930s, the federal government has played a significant role in shaping governance of the modern public corporation. Over the last century, this role has progressively expanded, reaching a new high-water mark with the Sarbanes-Oxley Act and Dodd-Frank Act, of 2002 and 2010, respectively. With the latter and former, the substantial impact of federal law on corporate governance – already evident to those prepared to admit it – became crystal clear.

The federal role in corporate governance has commonly been critiqued, however, in the law and economics literature (Bainbridge 2003; Choi & Guzman 2001; Engledow 2002; Ribstein 2002). Much of this critique can be traced to the asserted existence of some doctrinal distinction between *state* corporate law and *federal* securities regulation – a division of labor naturally disturbed by federal rules of corporate governance (Cary 1974; Kahan & Rock 2005). Beyond the latter, criticisms of federal intervention have often relied on the invocation

---

Tiebout's influential work on sub-national regulation. Tiebout was interested in the capacity of a decentralized political system to efficiently align the production of public goods with public demand (Tiebout 1956). In that analysis, the dependent variable of interest – as in the project of corporate law to which I would describe charter competition as being directed – is state behavior. Tiebout's analogous metric of efficiency thus lay in the alignment of public regulation with the demands of a mobile citizenry.

of federalism. On one or both of these grounds, law and economics scholars have commonly concluded, federal rules of corporate governance should be deemed presumptively sub-optimal.

Upon closer reflection, however, these critiques of federal intervention prove problematic. Corporate law and securities regulation are less distinct than commonly assumed. Invocations of federalism in corporate law, meanwhile, are better understood as being about something else.

The asserted boundary between federal and state law in regulating the modern public corporation, to begin, is far more meandering – and permeable – than standard accounts might be read to suggest (Moyer 1997).[30] Some traditional emphasis of federal law on disclosure and fraud, on the regulation of securities issuances, and on secondary trading, and of state law on corporate governance, is beyond dispute. But the rigor and resilience of this tradition are far less than commonly acknowledged (Roe 2003).

Two lines of doctrinal segregation are most commonly suggested in the literature: To begin, there is the notion of corporate law as *private* in nature – by contrast with *public* securities law. Further, there is the framing of corporate law as the regulation of *substance*, with securities law speaking to *process*.

Corporate law undoubtedly possesses many of the features of private law (Licht 2001). The public character of state-chartered corporations has been stripped of any operational meaning, including through the rise of federal securities law and its more direct association with protection of the public interest. Contractarian theories of the firm have further solidified our conception of corporations as private in nature – and of corporate law as private law. The predominant articulation of corporate law in primary legislation rather than regulation, its enabling character, and its retrospective enforcement by courts are yet further indicia of the private nature of corporate law.

A converse set of factors, however, counsel a more public conception of corporate law. Naturally, this begins with the original conception of corporations as public in nature – and the resurgence of interest in that approach in recent years.[31] Bert Westbrook, for example, has drawn on the collapse of Enron to suggest a conception of corporate law as policing not only the relationship between managers and shareholders, but also the emphatically *public* interaction of managers and shareholders collectively – as 'owners' of the firm – with the outside world of 'non-owners' (Westbrook 2003, 108–10). Even broader in scope have been claims of the private as the necessary medium of the public interest, in a market-driven state.[32] The array of pre-Sarbanes-Oxley federal mandatory interventions in corporate governance – including the impact of federal proxy rules on corporate voting, the regulation of fundamental changes in corporate structure, and the prohibition against insider trading (Karmel 2005; Licht 2001; Roe 2003) – likewise cut against a purely private account of corporate law's char-

---

[30]    In proposing to extend corporate law's market model to securities regulation, Roberta Romano and other advocates of issuer choice (Romano 1998) might be read to acknowledge the overlap across these spheres.

[31]    Less famously than their other observations, Berle and Means also embraced a public conception of the corporation (Berle & Means 1932).

[32]    The literature of progressive corporate law might also be noted more generally (Bradley et al. 1999; Mitchell 1995; Westbrook 2003).

acter.[33] To be sure, such public dimensions of corporate law's character do not obviate its many private characteristics. They do, however, undercut claims of a bright line distinction between federal/public versus state/private regulation of the modern public corporation.

The same is true of the differentiation of state corporate law (from federal securities law) as the regulation of *substance* versus *process* – as Judge Frank Easterbrook has described, in contrasting federal proxy rules from state rules directed to the internal affairs of the corporation.[34] And likewise of the notion of federal law as being solely about disclosure (Berg 1992). As with the public-private distinction, it cannot be disputed that federal regulation in the corporate arena has *largely* been directed to procedural requirements, or that state law offers the lion's share of substantive rules of corporate governance – even if only in enabling form. As even Judge Easterbrook acknowledges, however, significant ambiguity attends the substance-process distinction in corporate law.[35] Regulation of proxy solicitation is suggestive: while nominally directed to questions of process, relevant federal rules go – for all practical purposes – to the heart of the corporation's internal affairs (Roe 2003). To similar effect, one might ask whether the Sarbanes-Oxley Act's regulation of audit committee membership and certification requirement are purely questions of 'process', or speak to the substance of corporate governance.

Doctrinal demarcations, then, offer weak support – at best – for the law and economics literature's widespread objection to a federal role in corporate governance. Beyond doctrine, such resistance has also been framed, unsurprisingly, as a question of federalism. Upon closer examination, however, invocations of 'federalism' in analysis of the vertical allocation of corporate law-making power turn out to be about something different.

To appreciate as much, it is useful to recall the core arguments that have commonly been advanced in favor of federalism (Schapiro 2005). At the center of the latter stand claims about the value of placing authority in proximity to relevant constituencies – given both the inherent value of autonomy and the correlation of increased responsiveness with such proximity. Of similar vintage, though a degree less central than the latter arguments, are assertions of the benefits of permitting diverse policy choices across multiple sub-national jurisdictions. More recently, a second generation of arguments for federalism has emerged. Reflecting a stronger emphasis on efficiency, these claims highlight the benefits of state and local experimentation, and the related possibility of salutary competition among relevant jurisdictions.

Each of these arguments for federalism turns out to be problematic, however, in its application to corporate law. As to the earliest claims for federalism – grounded in local autonomy, effective representation, and policy diversity – federalism in corporate law is an awkward fit. Such arguments resonate far less clearly as to public corporations than as to individuals, and perhaps even other forms of collective association. Even after the Supreme

---

[33] The potential for market failure in corporate governance and the securities markets may also suggest a place for the public in regulation of the modern public corporation. In recent years, scholars have explored a variety of potential inefficiencies in corporate and securities law, including the potential for network externalities to constrain efficient innovation and variation (Ahdieh 2003; Klausner 1995), patterns of inertia (Korobkin 1998), and informational inefficiencies suggested by recurrent market breaks (Partnoy 2000).

[34] *Amanda Acquisition Corp. v. Universal Foods Corp.*, 877 F.2d 496, 503 (7th Cir. 1989); *see also* Bainbridge (2011).

[35] *See ibid.*

Court's decision in *Citizens United*, the notion that we should worry about the effective representation of corporations in the political process must necessarily prompt a chuckle.

Even greater difficulty, meanwhile, characterizes the attempt to apply local autonomy and policy diversity arguments to corporate law. Both the theory of state competition in corporate law and the empirical reality thereof thus cut against those arguments. At the heart of claims of efficiency in state competition for corporate charters stands the ability of state legislatures to incorporate efficient innovations undertaken by competing states. The basic assumption of corporate law, as such, is not that state corporate rules will diverge to capture distinct tastes and morays – whether geographic or substantive. Rather, it assumes some significant convergence in said rules (Easterbrook & Fischel 1991; Hansmann & Kraakman 2001). The empirical reality, of course, bears this out. Delaware enjoys an overwhelming share of (out-of-state) incorporation business (Bebchuk & Hamdani 2002). With defined exceptions, meanwhile, the law of competing jurisdictions tracks significant features of Delaware law (Carney 1998).[36] For better or worse, then, corporate law sits uneasily with autonomy and diversity theories of federalism.

Similar difficulties attend the application of more recent experimentation and competition arguments for federalism.[37] Law and economics critics of federal corporate law undoubtedly do see value in experimentation by and competition among local regulators. State-level corporate law permits relevant authorities to implement innovative legal technologies they consider likely to offer competitive advantage. If they are right, such innovations can be expected to take root, both in the first-moving state and among its competitors. Even if flawed rules persist in certain jurisdictions, meanwhile, their harm is necessarily contained. Universally applicable federal rules, by comparison, would stifle experimentation and innovation – hallmarks of an efficient market (Carney 1998; Romano 1985).

As above, though, the story proves problematic both in practice and theory. It is not clear, to begin, that experimentation and competition are especially vibrant in corporate law. Michael Abramowicz points to externalities in corporate law innovation as allowing only a 'crawl' to the top (Abramowicz 2003). Marcel Kahan and Ehud Kamar identify barriers to entry and the political economy of charter competition as constraints on active competition (Kahan & Kamar 2002). Other analysts concur (Bebchuk et al. 2002), *but see* Romano (2005).

Beyond the limited degree of experimentation and competition in reality, a state regime of corporate law turns out to be less crucial to fostering such experimentation and competition than conventionally assumed. What is essential is not state versus federal law, but rather the ability to avoid the sub-optimal rules of a given jurisdiction. This only becomes an issue of *federalism* (i.e., of the choice between state and federal law) because of the traditionally mandatory nature of relevant federal rules, and the enabling nature of state rules. Were federal rules of corporate law enabling, by contrast, federal law would be unobjectionable as a matter

---

[36]   It bears noting, in this vein, that Delaware is usually not the first mover when it comes to innovations in corporate law. Where Delaware has proven adept, instead, is in its ability to quickly identify and embrace desirable innovations of its competitors (Carney 1998).

[37]   As suggested above, arguments premised on local experimentation and interstate competition were not at the heart of most early American analyses of federalism. Among other reasons, this might be traced to relatively greater limits on geographic mobility.

of experimentation and competition.[38] If state rules were mandatory, conversely, federalism would lose much of its charm for traditional law and economics analyses of corporate law.

Consider the latter possibility more concretely: Imagine that California were to make its corporate default rules *effectively* mandatory (Bebchuk 1992). What if, for example, it were to require local incorporation by all firms for which California was the primary – or perhaps merely a significant – place of business? Less invasively, but no less aggressively, what if it were to impose certain minimum standards of corporate governance on all entities that do business in the state? It does not take much further imagination to guess the likely reaction, from the conventional law and economics perspective – for it would surely track the response to federal interventions in corporate governance.[39]

Law and economics critiques of federal corporate law, then, are only incidentally concerned with federalism – with the choice of state versus federal law-making. Relevant critics harbor no greater affection for state law that is unwaivable and unavoidable, than they do for federal law. The critical objection, this suggests, is not jurisdictional, but regulatory. Federal rules are not questioned because they're federal – or even wrong – but simply because they're rules (Bebchuk 1992).

To be clear, I do not doubt that critics of federal corporate law truly do bewail the potential loss of experimentation and competition attendant to the federalization of corporate law. The critical loss they fear, however, is not efficient (versus inefficient) regulation. Nor is it default (versus mandatory) rules. Rather, it is the ability of relevant consumers – in this case, public corporations – to determine their own rules of governance (Roe 2005). In broadest terms, it is the status quo reliance on market forces, rather than the law, to define the nature and obligations of corporate governance that they hope to preserve.

In today's world of default rules negotiated via regulatory competition, thus, the motivating force behind regulatory design is not (even asserted) public interest, but private incentive.[40] If a given default rule comports with private preferences, it persists; if not, it is waived. To similar effect, if a state's corporate law regime (including both its default rules and its trivial mandatory rules) effectively advances private interests, it is embraced via incorporation; if not, it is abandoned.

This is not to suggest that state corporate law amounts to nothing more than a contract law regime. Corporate entities do not literally write their own ticket. Common law fiduciary duties, to begin, offer a layer of extra-contractual constraints on corporate governance.[41] The regulatory preferences of corporate entities are codified through political mechanisms, meanwhile,

---

[38] On the possibility of federal enabling rules of corporate governance, see the preceding section. One caveat, however, arises from the fact that federal default rules might have disproportionately strong focal power, by comparison with state default rules (*cf.* Ahdieh 2010; Schelling 1980).

[39] Of course, the above scenario need not be imagined. California's relatively aggressive outreach statute, in Section 2115 of its Corporations Code, Cal. Corp. Code § 2115, imposes a number of the state's corporate governance rules on corporations primarily doing business in the state. Enthusiasts of charter competition, unsurprisingly, find that provision lamentable.

[40] In stating as much, I do not mean to suggest any necessary normative critique of this state of affairs. The interplay of private incentives – absent relevant externalities or other market failures – will often maximize social welfare. Whether the end result is efficient or otherwise, however, one might hesitate to characterize this dynamic as 'regulation'.

[41] That said, one might plausibly conceive of the body of common law applicable to corporate governance – including its fiduciary duty standards in particular – as an über-default rule of sorts.

introducing some potential 'imperfection' into the market for corporate law. Given the ultimate grounding of the process in private incentives, however, corporate law – at least in the idealized form predicted in the law and economics literature – does not stray all that far from a contract regime (Ribstein 2002; Roe 2003; Romano 2005). Few scholars have been explicit in their embrace of such complete reductionism, but their underlying theory of corporate law can be understood to assume it.[42]

The law and economics literature's 'federalism' objection to federal corporate law, then, turns out not to be about the choice between state versus federal regulation. Rather, it is about the imposition of public regulation where private incentives had previously played out in a market dynamic. It is not *federal* law that law and economics invocations of federalism critique; it is *law* – or at least law in any prescriptive or regulatory sense.

## 4.   LEGAL PLURALISM, INTERSYSTEMIC GOVERNANCE, AND CORPORATE LAW

Where does all this leave law and economics analyses of the sources of law in corporate law? Given reasons to doubt the efficacy of both competition and regulation, as well as the self-evident (if still gradual) growth in the federal role in corporate governance, what can law and economics contribute to our thinking about the institutional architecture of corporate law?

The respective analyses offered above – of the horizontal and vertical dimensions of institutional design in corporate law – ultimately lead us to the same place. Neither account can be reconciled with a single-minded orientation to state law. Nor do they counsel a far-reaching program of federal preemption. Rather, I would argue, both counsel to a species of legal pluralism – a pattern I have explored under the rubric of 'intersystemic governance' – in corporate law. Consider each dimension in turn.

Once we appreciate the distinct nature, implications, and normative ends of state and managerial competition, law and economics' strong presumption in favor of state law becomes difficult to defend. In corporate law's pursuit of reduced agency costs – in its response to the separation of ownership and control – there is nothing *per se* optimal about state law, nor any categorical ground for dismissing federal intervention as the work of regulatory 'monopolists' (Kahan & Kamar 2002, 747). State law need not, as such, be the necessary default rule in corporate law. Rather, as to any particular question or category of questions, we must ask whether the political economy of state regulation is preferable to federal regulation – or vice-versa (Bebchuk 1992). In any given case, considering the specific dynamic at work, is a state or a federal rule likely to generate optimal results?

More precisely, I would suggest, we need to assess the appropriate *balance* of state and federal law as to any given issue. In light of the operative political economy in the relevant sphere, what mix of state competition and federal regulation is likely to yield efficient outcomes in corporate governance (Bratton & McCahery 1995; Kahan & Kamar 2002; McConnell 1987)? An optimal regime of corporate law might not, as such, be easily characterized as either federal or state (Ahdieh 2005, 2007). It may be far more effective in advan-

---

[42]   Henry Manne, perhaps unsurprisingly, is the exception (Manne 2003). Even Easterbrook and Fischel, by contrast, acknowledge at least some role for mandatory rules (Bebchuk 1992).

cing the distinct projects of managerial and regulatory efficiency described above, however, for that very reason.

The benefits of overlap and pluralism in corporate law follow even more clearly from our analysis of the *vertical* dimensions of corporate law's institutional design. We have seen that there is no doctrinal basis for categorically excluding federal regulators from corporate law-making. Arguments from federalism fare no better in dictating a purely state law regime. More importantly, such federalism claims help to reveal the true dynamic at work. Where federal interventions in corporate law are critiqued, it turns out, the issue is again one of balance: What is the appropriate balance of market dynamics and public regulation, as to any given question of governance in the modern public corporation?

More affirmative arguments for overlap and pluralism in the regulation of corporate governance – for a mix of federal and state rules – might also be offered. These begin with the 'conservative' claim that we should favor the status quo. A mix of rules – public, mandatory, and federal, as well as private, enabling, and state – characterize corporate law today. Lending dynamism to this mix, regulatory competition is pervasive. This includes, as highlighted by Mark Roe, competition not only among states, but between federal and state regulators as well (Roe 2003). In Roe's account, thus, Delaware carefully calibrates its choices in corporate law – otherwise motivated by interstate competition – with the distinct values, interest group politics, and priorities of the federal government. The relative longevity of this pattern of what I have termed 'intersystemic governance' might be seen, then, to suggest its wisdom.

For those not moved by such claims from the status quo, other arguments for intersystemic governance might also be advanced. A mixed regime of corporate law, to begin, might better comport with the nature of the firm. As suggested above, the modern public corporation – and corporate law itself – clearly integrates some mix of public and private elements. The private elements are obvious. But recall its public features as well. These include the origins of the 'public' corporation as a creature of public law; the significant external consequences of many internal governance decisions (including not only those traditionally highlighted, such as decisions related to takeovers, but also corporate decisions more generally, given the increasingly wide dispersion of (indirect) equity ownership); and the necessary role of the state in supporting any 'nexus of contracts' comprising the firm (Bratton 1989; La Porta et al. 1997; Levine 2004; Millon 1990; Westbrook 2003).[43]

Ultimately, however, the argument for overlap and pluralism in corporate law can be conceived even more broadly. Contrary to the conventional preference of legal scholars for clean lines of jurisdiction, there may be significant utility in a regime of corporate law defined by 'jurisdictional redundancy'. Corporate governance, in such a scheme, would at once be subject to conventional, mandatory regulation by federal authorities *and* market-driven, enabling regulation by state authorities (Bebchuk 2001). The respective jurisdictional roles of federal and state government – and, more broadly, the influence of regulation versus the market – would cease to be determinate in any familiar sense. Rather, the regulation of business associations would play out against a backdrop of regulatory competition and coordination, selective delegation, and a baseline orientation to market dynamics (Romano 2005).[44]

---

[43]   Growing evidence of a linkage between strong securities markets and economic growth might likewise counsel a more public conception of corporate regulation (Levine 2004).

[44]   In recent years, a growing number of scholars have described the benefits of shared federal and

Almost 35 years ago, Robert Cover and Alexander Aleinikoff pointed to the overlapping jurisdiction of state criminal courts and federal habeas courts as generating a pattern of 'dialectical federalism' in criminal procedure (Cover & Aleinikoff 1977). In their view, redundancy in the law-making efforts of these courts – and their resulting need to engage one another – offered the promise of a beneficial evolution in legal norms. Echoing that analysis, I have highlighted the potential for a salutary dynamic of inter-systemic governance – or 'dialectical regulation' – to play itself out in the interaction of corporate governance and securities market regulators operating at distinct levels.

The engagement of the US Securities and Exchange Commission and then-Attorney General of New York Eliot Spitzer – and ultimately a broader group of state regulators – a decade ago might be noted by way of example. As in Cover and Aleinikoff's analysis, it was by way of this interaction that an enhanced level of financial market regulation emerged (Ahdieh 2006). The Commission's review of no-action letter requests concerning shareholder petitions for proxy access under Rule 14a-8 might be cited to similar effect (Ahdieh 2007). Especially after Delaware's constitutional amendment in 2007, to permit the Commission to certify questions of law to its Supreme Court, one might imagine development of a significantly more vibrant jurisprudence of Rule 14a-8, with resulting improvements in the efficiency of relevant legal rules, and even corporate governance. From the opposite direction, the potential for salutary overlap might also be seen in growing pressure on the Commission to engage the needs of foreign and transnational securities market regulators – including in the choice of mandatory disclosure standards (Ahdieh 2006).

Overlap and redundancy may thus offer significant utility in the regulation of corporate governance. Most obviously, they may ensure that issues in need of regulatory intervention are not overlooked and that process failures do not stymie optimal regulation (or de-regulation, for that matter) in corporate governance. Such fail-safe mechanisms, however, represent only part of the utility of jurisdictional redundancy. Given charter competition among states, even efficient mandatory rules may be difficult to sustain – at least in the short-run – without jurisdictional redundancy (Bebchuk 1992). This would include rules protecting other stakeholders in the firm – for those who would accept the latter as an appropriate function of corporate law – and rules addressing negative externalities that arise from takeover bids, proxy contests, and other corporate behavior – for those who acknowledge such externalities to exist (Bebchuk 1992; Bebchuk & Kahan 1990). Of course, the stronger one's contractarian assumptions – including the efficiency of the capital markets, the irrelevancy of other stakeholders to corporate law, and the absence of externalities – the less room one would see for such mandates. Anywhere short of the outer bound of those assumptions, though, the recognition of some need for mandatory rules would favor some degree of overlap and redundancy.

The most significant benefit of overlapping jurisdiction over corporate governance, however, may be its potential to encourage desirable innovation. In the interaction of independently constituted regulatory authorities – with distinct ideas, approaches, and constituen-

---

state authority in corporate and securities law, if not within the particular frame of jurisdictional redundancy that I posit (Di Trolio 2004; Jones 2005). Robert Thompson's analysis of 'collaborative' regulation in corporate governance, with its emphasis on the relationship between federal regulation and the body of private rules imposed by self-regulatory organizations, might also be noted in this regard (Thompson 2003).

cies – some heightened capacity for innovation might plausibly be expected (Ahdieh 2004). Clear lines of jurisdictional authority are necessarily effective in minimizing conflict, thus, but also favor stasis – in part for that very reason. Extrinsic shock may be a necessary impetus for systemic change. More modestly, institutional architectures that foster interaction among distinctly situated actors, motivated by distinct incentives, might be expected to create greater opportunities to borrow and learn.

Can this be said of the dynamic at work in the regulation of corporate governance? As noted above, Mark Roe offers an account of corporate law as defined by state responsiveness to federal pressures generated by Congress, the SEC, and even the courts and securities exchanges (Jones 2004; Karmel 2005; Roe 2003). Variously, he suggests, both the *actual* preemption of state corporate law (as to proxy solicitation, the all-holders rule, going-private transactions, and other areas) and even the mere *threat* of it constrain Delaware's autonomy and discretion in corporate law-making.[45]

Yet federal regulation may likewise respond to state interests. Take the seemingly extreme case of the Sarbanes-Oxley Act. Whatever the precise extent of Sarbanes-Oxley's intervention in corporate governance, it surely cannot be construed as an across-the-board preemption of state authority in the area (Ahdieh 2005). No one could credibly argue that corporate law is now federal law. Nor has Congress more generally shown itself prone to dramatic expansions in its regulation of business associations. However forcefully some have criticized the Securities Act of 1933 and the Securities Exchange Act of 1934's interventions into state law, we do well to recall that it is decrees of some 75 years ago that are at issue in such debates.

More concretely, evidence of a dialectical, two-way pattern of interaction between federal and state regulators in corporate governance might be divined from those occasions on which federal regulators have followed a state lead. In such cases, Congress and the SEC can be understood to have borrowed – even learned – from state regulatory authorities. Most broadly, the 1933 Act, which drew its terms from the corpus of existing state securities law, might be conceived in this light. More recently, SEC regulation of mutual fund practices can quite clearly be traced to the enforcement efforts of Eliot Spitzer.

It bears emphasizing that such a pattern of jurisdictional redundancy need not mean that the regulation of corporate governance is indiscriminately shared by federal and state regulators. Borrowing from the aforementioned aspiration to distinguish a *process*-oriented federal securities law from a *substance*-oriented state corporate law, one might imagine a generalized, but not unvarying, orientation of federal corporate law to questions of form. Sarbanes-Oxley's corporate governance provisions, in fact, might plausibly be construed in these terms. The latter require certification of financial statements, for example, but do not prescribe rules for the preparation and review of those statements. Similarly, relevant federal rules do not delve into the content of audits, but simply require their preparation by independent auditors, selected by independent board members. Even given the substantial degree of SEC rulemaking that followed from it, much of Sarbanes-Oxley's implementation was ultimately a

---

[45]    The pattern of jurisdictional redundancy I posit, of course, speaks directly to the story of federal preeminence offered by Roe (2003). I do not dispute the possibility of the hierarchical pattern of engagement that Roe describes – as distinct from the more dialectical pattern of engagement I outline. I am unsure that the history of corporate law, however, is best conceived in so strongly federal a light. By contrast with Roe, thus, I might cast state rules of corporate governance as arising in the *shadow* of federal law, rather than as a product of it.

product of private ordering. Even as substantial a federal intervention as Sarbanes-Oxley, then, leaves significant room for private incentives to play out within its requirements (McDonnell 2004).[46]

## 5.   CONCLUSION

Traditional law and economics analysis of the sources of corporate law have generated a pair of claims, respectively directed to a horizontal axis of state competition for corporate charters, and a vertical axis concerning the federal role in corporate governance. As to the former, law and economics sees a salutary dynamic, in which state competition at least moves shareholder-managerial relations *toward* the top. As to the latter, meanwhile, it sees the appropriate scope of federal intervention in corporate law as limited – at best.

Upon closer reflection, however, each of these stories proves incomplete. Properly understood, the institutional implications of a law and economics analysis of corporate law are not that state competition limits agency costs, or that federal corporate law is sub-optimal. Nor, at the extreme, that either state law or federal law should be the exclusive source of American corporate law. Rather, once we appreciate the respective horizontal and vertical dimensions of the institutional architecture of corporate law, the ideal approach falls somewhere in the middle – a pluralistic regime defined by overlap and redundancy.

An optimal regime of corporate law is thus likely to integrate both state rules born of charter competition, and federal rules generated by way of more conventional political and regulatory processes. The precise nature of this balance will depend on the particular issue at stake. As to one question of corporate governance versus another, it will vary. Wherever the precise boundary falls in any given case, however, the crucial lessons of pluralism, overlap, and redundancy in the sources of corporate law warrant the attention of the law and economics literature.

## REFERENCES

Abramowicz, Michael (2003), 'Speeding Up the Crawl to the Top', *Yale Journal on Regulation*, 20, 139–205.
Ahdieh, Robert B. (2003), 'Making Markets: Network Effects and the Role of Law in the Creation of Strong Securities Markets', *Southern California Law Review*, 76, 277–350.
Ahdieh, Robert B. (2004a), 'Between Dialogue and Decree: International Review of National Courts', *NYU Law Review*, 79, 2029–2163.
Ahdieh, Robert B. (2004b), 'Law's Signal: A Cueing Theory of Law in Market Transition', *Southern California Law Review*, 77, 215–305.
Ahdieh, Robert B. (2005), 'From "Federalization" to "Mixed Governance" in Corporate Law: A Defense of Sarbanes-Oxley', *Buffalo Law Review*, 53, 721–56.
Ahdieh, Robert B. (2006), 'Dialectical Regulation', *Connecticut Law Review*, 38, 863–927.

---

[46]   The process-substance distinction might thus support a prudential emphasis on process, even if it cannot support a bar against *any* federal regulation of substantive corporate law. Some such line of demarcation, in fact, might be seen in other federal interventions into areas of traditional state authority. The No Child Left Behind Act, for example, can be read to prescribe certain institutions in primary and secondary education, but not to mandate the mechanisms of their creation, or the details of their operation.

Ahdieh, Robert B. (2007), 'The Dialectical Regulation of Rule 14a-8: Intersystemic Governance in Corporate Law', *Journal of Business and Technology Law*, 2, 165–84.

Ahdieh, Robert B. (2009a), 'The (Misunderstood) Genius of American Corporate Law', *George Washington Law Review*, 77, 730–39.

Ahdieh, Robert B. (2009b), 'Trapped in a Metaphor: The Limited Implications of Federalism for Corporate Governance', *George Washington Law Review*, 77, 255–307.

Ahdieh, Robert B. (2010), 'The Visible Hand: Coordination Functions of the Regulatory State', *Minnesota Law Review*, 95, 578–649.

Bainbridge, Stephen M. (2002), 'The Board of Directors as Nexus of Contracts', *Iowa Law Review*, 88, 1–34.

Bainbridge, Stephen M. (2003), 'The Creeping Federalization of Corporate Law', *Regulation*, 26, 23–31.

Bainbridge, Stephen M. (2011), 'Dodd-Frank: Quack Federal Corporate Governance Round II', *Minnesota Law Review*, 95, 1779–1821.

Bebchuk, Lucian A. (1992), 'Federalism and the Corporation: The Desirable Limits on State Competition in Corporate Law', *Harvard Law Review*, 105, 1435–1510.

Bebchuk, Lucian A. (2001), 'A New Approach to Takeover Law and Regulatory Competition', *Virginia Law Review*, 87, 111–64.

Bebchuk, Lucian Arye & Assaf Hamdani (2002), 'Vigorous Race or Leisurely Walk: Reconsidering the Competition Over Corporate Charters', *Yale Law Journal*, 112, 553–615.

Bebchuk, Lucian, Alma Cohen & Allen Ferrell (2002), 'Does the Evidence Favor State Competition in Corporate Law?', *California Law Review*, 90, 1775–1821.

Bebchuk, Lucian Arye & Marcel Kahan (1990), 'A Framework for Analyzing Legal Policy Toward Proxy Contests', *California Law Review*, 78, 1071–1135.

Berg, Philip C. (1992), 'The Limits of SEC Authority Under Section 14(a) of the Exchange Act: Where Federal Disclosure Ends and State Corporate Governance Begins', *Journal of Corporation Law*, 17, 311–45.

Berle, Adolf A. & Gardiner C. Means (1932), *The Modern Corporation and Private Property*, New York, N.Y.: MacMillan Co.

Black, Bernard S. (1990), 'Is Corporate Law Trivial?: A Political and Economic Analysis', *Northwestern University Law Review*, 84, 542–97.

Blair, Margaret & Lynn A. Stout (1999), 'A Team Production Theory of Corporate Law', *Virginia Law Review*, 85, 247–328.

Bradley, Michael, Cindy A. Schipani, Anant K. Sundaram & James P. Walsh (1999), 'The Purposes and Accountability of the Corporation in Contemporary Society: Corporate Governance at a Crossroads', *Law and Contemporary Problems*, 62, 9–86.

Bratton, Jr., William W. (1989), 'The "Nexus of Contracts" Corporation: A Critical Appraisal,' *Cornell Law Review*, 74, 407–65.

Bratton, William W. (2000) 'Delaware Law as Applied Public Choice Theory: Bill Cary and the Basic Course After Twenty-Five Years', *Georgia Law Review*, 34, 447–75.

Bratton, William W. (2001) 'Berle and Means Reconsidered at the Century's Turn', *Journal of Corporation Law*, 26, 737–70.

Bratton, William W. & Joseph A. McCahery (1995), 'Regulatory Competition, Regulatory Capture, and Corporate Self-Regulation', *North Carolina Law Review*, 73, 1861–1948.

Brummer, Christopher (2008), 'Stock Exchanges and the New Markets for Securities Law', *University of Chicago Law Review*, 75, 1435–91.

Buchanan, James M. & Gordon Tullock (1962), *The Calculus of Consent: Logical Foundations of Constitutional Democracy*, Ann Arbor, Mich.: University of Michigan Press.

Butler, Henry N. & Larry E. Ribstein (1990), 'Opting Out of Fiduciary Duties: A Response to the Anti-Contractarians', *Washington Law Review*, 65, 1–72.

Butler, Henry N. & Jonathan R. Macey (1996), 'Externalities and the Matching Principle: The Case for Reallocating Environmental Regulatory Authority', *Yale Journal on Regulation*, 14, 23–66.

Carney, William J. (1997), 'The Political Economy of Competition for Corporate Charters', *Journal of Legal Studies*, 26, 303–29.

Carney, William J. (1998), 'The Production of Corporate Law,' *Southern California Law Review*, 71, 715–77.

Cary, William L. (1974), 'Federalism and Corporate Law: Reflections Upon Delaware', *Yale Law Journal*, 83, 663–705.

Choi, Stephen J. & Andrew T. Guzman (2001), 'Choice and Federal Intervention in Corporate Law', *Virginia Law Review*, 87, 961–92.

Coffee, Jr., John C. (1989), 'The Mandatory/Enabling Balance in Corporate Law: An Essay on the Judicial Role', *Columbia Law Review*, 89, 1618–91.

Cover, Robert M. & T. Alexander Aleinikoff (1977), 'Dialectical Federalism: Habeas Corpus and the Court', *Yale Law Journal*, 86, 1035–1102.

Di Trolio, Stefania (2004), 'Public Choice Theory, Federalism, and the Sunny Side to Blue-Sky Laws', *William Mitchell Law Review*, 30, 1279–1314.

Easterbrook, Frank H. (1984), 'Managers' Discretion and Investors' Welfare: Theories and Evidence', *Delaware Journal of Corporate Law*, 9, 540–71.

Easterbrook, Frank H. (1994), 'Federalism and European Business Law', *International Review of Law and Economics*, 14, 125–32.

Easterbrook, Frank H. & Daniel R. Fischel (1984), 'Mandatory Disclosure and the Protection of Investors', *Virginia Law Review*, 70, 669–715.

Easterbrook, Frank H. & Daniel R. Fischel (1989), 'The Corporate Contract', *Columbia Law Review*, 89, 1416–48.

Easterbrook, Frank H. & Daniel R. Fischel (1991), *The Economic Structure of Corporate Law*, Cambridge, Mass.: Harvard University Press.

Eisenberg, Melvin Aron (1989), 'The Structure of Corporation Law', *Columbia Law Review*, 89, 1461–1525.

Ellickson, Robert C. (1989), 'The Case for Coase and Against "Coaseanism"', *Yale Law Journal*, 99, 611–30.

Engledow, Wells M. (2002), 'Handicapping the Corporate Law Race', *Journal of Corporation Law*, 28, 143–77.

Fisch, Jill E. (2000), 'The Peculiar Role of the Delaware Courts in the Competition for Corporate Charters', *University of Cincinnati Law Review*, 68, 1061–1100.

Fischel, Daniel R. (1982), 'The "Race to the Bottom" Revisited: Reflections on Recent Developments in Delaware's Corporation Law', *Northwestern University Law Review*, 76, 913–45.

Gadinis, Stavros (2008), 'The Politics of Competition in International Financial Regulation', *Harvard International Law Journal*, 49, 447–507.

Gordon, Jeffrey N. (1989), 'The Mandatory Structure of Corporate Law', *Columbia Law Review*, 89, 1549–98.

Gordon, Jeffrey N. (1994), 'Institutions as Relational Investors: A New Look at Cumulative Voting', *Columbia Law Review*, 94, 124–80.

Grundfest, Joseph A. (2010), 'The SEC's Proposed Proxy Access Rules: Politics, Economics, and the Law', *Business Lawyer*, 65, 361–94.

Guzman, Andrew T. (2002), 'Choice of Law: New Foundations', *Georgetown Law Journal*, 90, 883–940.

Hadfield, Gillian & Eric Talley (2006), 'On Public versus Private Provision of Corporate Law', *Journal of Law, Economics and Organization*, 22, 414–41.

Hansmann, Henry & Reinier Kraakman (2001), 'The End of History for Corporate Law', *Georgetown Law Journal*, 89, 439–68.

Hill, Claire A. & Brett H. McDonnell (2007), 'Disney, Good Faith, and Structural Bias', *Journal of Corporation Law*, 32, 833–64.

Holland, Randy J. (2009), 'Delaware's Business Courts: Litigation Leadership', *Journal of Corporation Law*, 34, 771–88.

Hovenkamp, Herbert (1988), 'The Classical Corporation in American Legal Thought', *Georgetown Law Journal*, 76, 1593–1689.

Jensen, Michael C. & William H. Meckling (1976), 'Theory of the Firm: Managerial Behavior, Agency Costs, and Ownership Structure', *Journal of Financial Economics*, 3, 305–60.

Jones, Renee M. (2004), 'Rethinking Corporate Federalism in the Era of Corporate Reform', *Journal of Corporation Law*, 29, 625–63.

Jones, Renee M. (2005), 'Dynamic Federalism: Competition, Cooperation and Securities Enforcement', *Connecticut Insurance Law Journal*, 11, 107–31.

Kahn, Faith Stevelman (1997), 'Pandora's Box: Managerial Discretion and the Problem of Corporate Philanthropy', *UCLA Law Review*, 44, 579–76.

Kahan, Marcel & Ehud Kamar (2002), 'The Myth of State Competition in Corporate Law', *Stanford Law Review*, 55, 679–749.

Kahan, Marcel & Edward Rock (2005), 'Symbiotic Federalism and the Structure of Corporate Law', *Vanderbilt Law Review*, 58, 1573–1622.

Karmel, Roberta S. (2005), 'Realizing the Dream of William O. Douglas – The Securities and Exchange Commission Takes Charge of Corporate Governance', *Delaware Journal of Corporate Law*, 30, 79–144.

Karmel, Roberta S. (2008), 'Should Securities Industry Self-Regulatory Organizations be Considered Government Agencies?', *Stanford Journal of Law, Business & Finance*, 14, 151–97.

Klausner, Michael (1995), 'Corporations, Corporate Law, and Networks of Contracts', *Virginia Law Review*, 81, 757–852.

Korobkin, Russell (1998), 'Inertia and Preference in Contract Negotiation: The Psychological Power of Default Rules and Form Terms', *Vanderbilt Law Review*, 51, 1583–1651.

La Porta, Rafael, Florencio Lopez-de-Silanes, Andrei Shleifer & Robert W. Vishny (1997), 'Legal Determinants of External Finance', *Journal of Finance*, 52, 1131–50.

Langevoort, Donald C. (2008), 'U.S. Securities Regulation and Global Competition', *Virginia Law and Business Review*, 3, 191–205.

Letsou, Peter V. (2009), 'The Changing Face of Corporate Governance Regulation in the United States', *Willamette Law Review*, 46, 149–99.

Levine, Ross (2004), 'Finance and Growth: Theory and Evidence', NBER Working Paper No. 10766, available at http://www.nber.org/papers/w10766.pdf (last accessed October 2011).

Licht, Amir N. (2001), 'Stock Exchange Mobility, Unilateral Recognition, and the Privatization of Securities Regulation', *Virginia Journal of International Law*, 41, 583–627.

Macey, Jonathan R. & David D. Haddock (1985), 'Shirking at the SEC: The Failure of the National Market System', *University of Illinois Law Review*, 1985, 315–62.

Manne, Henry G. (1965), 'Mergers and the Market for Corporate Control', *Journal of Political Economy*, 73, 110–20.

Manne, Henry G. (1967), 'Our Two Corporation Systems: Law and Economics', *Virginia Law Review*, 53, 259–84.

Manne, Henry G. (1974), 'Economic Aspects of Required Disclosure Under Federal Securities Laws', in Henry G. Manne and Ezra Solomon (eds), *Wall Street in Transition: The Emerging System and its Impact on the Economy*, New York, N.Y.: New York University Press, 21–110.

Manne, Henry G. (2003), 'A Free Market Model of a Large Corporation System', *Emory Law Journal*, 52, 1381–1400.

McConnell, Michael W. (1987), 'Federalism: Evaluating the Founders' Design', *University of Chicago Law Review*, 54, 1484–1512.

McDonnell, Brett H. (2004), 'Sox Appeals', *Michigan State Law Review*, 2004, 505–39.

Millon, David (1990), 'Theories of the Corporation', *Duke Law Journal*, 1990, 201–62.

Mitchell, Lawrence E. (ed.) (1995), *Progressive Corporate Law*, Boulder, Colo.: Westview Press.

Moyer, Patrick (1997), 'The Regulation of Corporate Law by Securities Regulators: A Comparison of Ontario and the United States', *University of Toronto Faculty of Law Review*, 55, 43–76.

Nagy, Donna M. (2010), 'Is the PCAOB a "Heavily Controlled Component" of the SEC?', *University of Pittsburgh Law Review*, 71, 361–402.

Note (2005), 'The Case for Federal Threats in Corporate Governance', *Harvard Law Review*, 118, 2726–47.

Olson, Mancur (1965), *The Logic of Collective Action*, Cambridge, Mass.: Harvard University Press.

Palmiter, Alan R. (1989), 'Reshaping the Corporate Fiduciary Model: A Director's Duty of Independence', *Texas Law Review*, 67, 1351–1464.

Partnoy, Frank (2000), 'Why Markets Crash and What Law Can Do About It', *University of Pittsburgh Law Review*, 61, 741–817.

Phillips, Susan M. & J. Richard Zecher (1981), *The SEC and the Public Interest*, Cambridge, Mass.: MIT Press.

Pildes, Richard H. (2009), 'Separation of Powers, Independent Agencies, and Financial Regulation: The Case of the Sarbanes-Oxley Act', *NYU Journal of Law and Business*, 5, 485–547.

Qian, Yingyi & Barry R. Weingast (1997), 'Federalism as a Commitment to Preserving Market Incentives', *Journal of Economic Perspectives*, 11, 83–92.

Ribstein, Larry E. (2002), 'Market vs. Regulatory Responses to Corporate Fraud: A Critique of the Sarbanes-Oxley Act of 2002', *Journal of Corporation Law*, 28, 1–67.

Rock, Edward B. (1996), 'America's Shifting Fascination with Comparative Corporate Governance', *Washington University Law Quarterly*, 74, 367–91.

Roe, Mark J. (2003), 'Delaware's Competition', *Harvard Law Review*, 117, 588–646.

Roe, Mark J. (2005), 'Delaware's Politics', *Harvard Law Review*, 118, 2491–2543.

Romano, Roberta (1985), 'Law as a Product: Some Pieces of the Incorporation Puzzle', *Journal of Law, Economics & Organization*, 1, 225–83.

Romano, Roberta (1993), *The Genius of American Corporate Law*, Washington, D.C.: AEI Press.

Romano, Roberta (1998), 'Empowering Investors: A Market Approach to Securities Regulation', *Yale Law Journal*, 107, 2359–2430.

Romano, Roberta (2005), 'Is Regulatory Competition a Problem or Irrelevant for Corporate Governance?', *Oxford Review of Economic Policy*, 21, 212–31.

Romano, Roberta (2009), 'Does the Sarbanes-Oxley Act Have a Future?', *Yale Journal on Regulation*, 26, 229–341.

Schapiro, Robert A. (2005), 'Toward a Theory of Interactive Federalism', *Iowa Law Review*, 91, 243–317.

Schelling, Thomas C. (1980), *The Strategy of Conflict*, Cambridge, Mass.: Harvard University Press.

Stigler, George J. (1971), 'The Theory of Economic Regulation', *Bell Journal of Economics & Management Science*, 2, 3–21.

Sullivan, Daniel P. & Donald E. Conlon (1997), 'Crisis and Transition in Corporate Governance Paradigms: The Role of the Chancery Court of Delaware', *Law and Society Review*, 31, 713–62.

Thompson, Robert B. (1999), 'Preemption and Federalism in Corporate Governance: Protecting Shareholder Rights to Vote, Sell, and Sue', *Law and Contemporary Problems*, 62, 215–42.

Thompson, Robert B. (2003), 'Collaborative Corporate Governance: Listing Standards, State Law, and Federal Regulation', *Wake Forest Law Review*, 38, 961–82.

Tiebout, Charles M. (1956), 'A Pure Theory of Local Expenditures', *Journal of Political Economy*, 64, 416–24.

Westbrook, David A. (2003), 'Corporation Law After Enron: The Possibility of a Capitalist Reimagination', *Georgetown Law Journal*, 92, 61–127.
Winter, Jr., Ralph K. (1977), 'State Law, Shareholder Protection, and the Theory of the Corporation', *Journal of Legal Studies*, 6, 251–92.
Winter, Ralph (1982), 'Private Goals and Competition Among State Legal Systems', *Harvard Journal of Law and Public Policy*, 6, 127–33.
Winter, Ralph K. (1989), 'The "Race for the Top" Revisited: A Comment on Eisenberg', *Columbia Law Review*, 89, 1526–29.

# 21. The past and future of comparative corporate governance

*Donald C. Clarke*[*]

## 1. INTRODUCTION

Recent years have seen the rise of comparative corporate governance (CCG) as an increasingly mainstream approach within the world of corporate governance studies. In part, this stems from a recognition by legal scholars that globalization calls for an increased understanding of how things are done in the rest of the world. And in part, it is a function of an increasingly empirical turn in corporate law scholarship generally. Different practices in other jurisdictions present at least the possibility of natural experiments that attempt to find causal relationships between particular features of a corporate governance regime and real-world outcomes.

What specifically is unique about CCG as an approach to corporate governance studies? What have we learned, and where should we go? These questions are particularly urgent as we enter the second decade of the twenty-first century. The financial crisis has called into question (if it has not yet, perhaps, definitively overturned) many of our traditional ways of thinking about corporate governance and the relationship between business enterprises and the state (Westbrook 2009; Verret 2010; Posner 2009). Are there other countries that do it better?

But there is another economic trend that makes comparative corporate governance research more urgent than ever: the rise of what we might call 'non-traditional' jurisdictions. As this chapter will show, CCG research has dealt extensively and skillfully with Anglo-American jurisdictions, Europe, and Japan. But the last 30 years have seen a startling rise in the economic importance of other countries, particularly China and the rest of non-Japan Asia. Students of business organization simply cannot ignore what is going on in those countries.

With these questions in mind, this chapter reviews where we have come in the last several years and the prospects for the future. The next section examines and clarifies the concepts of corporate governance and comparative corporate governance in order to set the stage for the ensuing discussion. It makes the point that comparative corporate governance has in general – although not without controversy – been focused on agency problems between shareholders and managers. It need not, however, always be so.

The following section looks at the methodology of comparative corporate governance, focusing particularly on the problems of functionalism and empirical studies.

---

[*] Reprinted, with edits and additions, from Clarke (2010b). I wish to thank Larry Ribstein for our many conversations about corporate law and for inspiring me to write this Article, and Barry Naughton for his close reading and helpful suggestions.

Then we review briefly some of the major lessons learned from comparative corporate governance scholarship, while the next section lays out some future directions and challenges for research, focusing particularly on the vexed problem of convergence. The final section offers a brief conclusion.

## 2.   WHAT IS COMPARATIVE CORPORATE GOVERNANCE?

Corporate governance can mean many things to many people, and the definition typically will depend on what the definer cares about. I canvass some definitions below in order to clarify what CCG typically excludes as well as includes.

The simplest definition may be that of the Cadbury Report, which defines corporate governance as 'the system by which companies are directed and controlled' (Financial Reporting Council 1992). Economist Margaret Blair (1995) also supplies a broad definition: 'the whole set of legal, cultural, and institutional arrangements that determine what publicly traded corporations can do, who controls them, how that control is exercised, and how the risks and returns from the activities they undertake are allocated'. Institutional economists favor a narrower definition, focusing on the relationship between the firm and its constituencies: labor, capital (equity and debt), suppliers, customers, the community, and management (Williamson 1985). Some scholars use a quite narrow concept of corporate governance. This concept is concerned with issues of finance and agency cost and has a policy component: the prevention of the exploitation of those who supply the money by those who control it (Jensen & Meckling 1976; Shleifer & Vishny 1997). It centers on the relationship between stockholders, the board of directors, and senior management.

CCG has typically focused on the issues implicated in the approaches of Shleifer and Vishny and of Williamson: (1) agency problems between investors and management – i.e., the narrow definition of corporate governance – and in particular how this is related to ownership patterns; and (2) shareholder versus stakeholder theories – i.e., questions of for whose benefit the corporation should be run (Cioffi 2000; Cunningham 2000; Pinto 2005; Jackson 2000).

Once we have decided what corporate governance is, it would seem to follow that comparative corporate governance involves asking what other jurisdictions do and seeing how they differ. But such inquiries do not take place in a realm of abstract purposelessness; they are invariably driven by some purpose of the inquirer. Thus, the question of 'what is CCG?' can best be answered by asking '*why* do CCG?'

CCG began, and continues, as an approach to corporate governance studies that found inspiration for solutions to problems in one jurisdiction by looking at the practice of other jurisdictions. The policy orientation is explicit (Hopt et al. 1998; Coffee 2006). It has developed into something much richer, however, and now encompasses studies that are less aimed at policy recommendations than at simply attempting to understand, through comparison of different regimes, why certain approaches to common problems work or do not work in different contexts (Hopt et al. 1998; Roe 1997; Gourevitch & Shinn 2005).

These studies have also taken various approaches to comparison. Some studies have been of single countries, in which the explicit comparative lesson, if any, comes tacked on at the end. Thus, we see studies of takeover law in England (Shea 1990) or derivative suits in Japan (West 2001a) or fiduciary duties in China (Howson 2008). Some studies explicitly take a few countries that are similar enough to make comparison worthwhile – for example, they are all advanced economies – but that have differences from which hopefully something can be learned (Armour et al. 2009). These studies examine particular national solutions in great detail.

Then there is the 'LLSV' and LLSV-inspired literature,[1] which codes particular traits of national corporate governance regimes in a large number of countries and then attempts to correlate those traits with other features of a country's economy, such as per capita GDP or capital market development.

In some cases, scholars have used law to explain economic and financial phenomena (La Porta et al. 2008; Roe 1994). At other times, scholars have used economics and finance to explain law (Coffee 2001; Banner 1997).

The 'why' of CCG can perhaps best be explained through its history. Although CCG came into its own in the 1990s, its modern reform-oriented version can be traced back to the 1960s and 1970s. Ever since Berle and Means (1932) published *The Modern Corporation and Private Property*, American corporate law scholarship has been focused on the separation of ownership from control, and on the ways of mitigating the problems created by that separation. But the problems stubbornly persisted, and it seemed impossible that directors could ever truly play a significant role in managing the corporation, given their limitations of time and information. The late 1960s and early 1970s then saw essentially the abandonment of the ideal of the managing board; the board was reconceptualized as a body that *monitored* but did not manage. As part of this shift in thinking, American academics began to look in particular at the German system of a two-tier board (Rock 1996). At the same time, CCG scholarship remained largely doctrinal, focusing on differences in rules (Tunc 1982; Conard 1976; Pinto 2005).

Several events brought gradual changes to this picture. First, as early as 1976, Jensen and Meckling's (1976) seminal article turned the focus of corporate law scholarship in the United States to issues of agency cost and ownership structure. This focus naturally made American scholars interested in ownership structures outside the United States and in the implications of their differences. Second, Mark Roe's (1994) work on the political roots of American corporate ownership patterns and their associated governance institutions suggested that corporate governance might be not just a matter of market-driven evolution toward an optimal set of arrangements, but instead the product of political choices.[2] Other scholarship showed that the lifetime employment system in Japan, explained variously as a venerable tradition or as an effort to encourage workers to invest in human capital, in fact grew out of a postwar political deal (Gilson & Roe 1999; Gilson 2004). What all this meant was that the institutions of any one country were not necessarily the most efficient ones for it, and thus research into alternatives could have real payoffs.

---

[1] 'LLSV literature' refers to a series of studies by the economists Rafael La Porta, Florencio Lopez-de-Silanes, Andrei Shleifer, and Robert Vishny. Representative early works are Shleifer & Vishny (1997); La Porta et al. (1997, 1998, 1999). Three of the group summarize their work in La Porta et al. (2008).

[2] For challenges to Roe's work, *see* Coffee (1999) and Cheffins (2001). The most extended and sophisticated approach to political explanations of corporate governance patterns of which I am aware is Gourevitch & Shinn (2005).

Finally, as globalization made issues of national competitiveness increasingly salient, scholars viewed governance systems as competing in much the same way that products do (Gilson 2004). CCG studies began to proliferate in the 1980s and 1990s. When Japan and Germany were riding high economically in the 1980s, there was great interest in the apparent strengths of German and Japanese models and what was thought to be their contribution to economic performance both at the corporate and at the national level. Some scholars produced studies of the monitoring benefits of the Japanese main bank system (Aoki 1990, 1994; Aoki & Patrick 1994) and *keiretsu* structure (Gilson & Roe 1993; Berglof & Peroti 1994),[3] while others argued that American equity markets forced executives to focus on quarterly results whereas 'the bank centered capital markets of Germany and Japan allowed executives to manage in the long run' (Gilson 2004, 130). In a word, Japan and Germany were going to eat our lunch unless we improved our corporate governance system (Porter 1992; Grundfest 1990).

By later in the 1990s, however, the worm had turned, and the US economy seemed to be outperforming the others. CCG then became, for both Americans and many non-Americans, a study of the superiority of the American system in raising capital and constraining agency costs (Macey & Miller 1995; Milhaupt 1997). The focus changed from importing foreign practices to exporting American ones (Bratton & McCahery 1999). But whoever was viewed as on top, the research agenda of CCG had pretty much crystallized by this time: in the words of two leading scholars in 1999, '[i]n these globalizing times, corporate law's leading question is whether there is a national corporate governance system (or component thereof) that possesses relative competitive advantage' (Bratton & McCahery 1999, 235). The second question that dominated the field was what the future would bring: if one model was indeed better than another, would national corporate governance regimes converge? Or would national differences remain?

There was by then no shortage of excellent and detailed studies (Hopt et al. 1998; Cioffi 2000), but the question of convergence seemed as unsettled as ever. Into this morass of doubt and uncertainty, Hansmann and Kraakman (2001) tossed their bombshell, entitled 'The End of History for Corporate Law': the debate was over, US-style corporate governance had won, convergence had already taken place at the ideological level, and formal convergence was 'only a matter of time'.

## 3.   METHODOLOGIES OF COMPARATIVE CORPORATE GOVERNANCE

### Functionalism and its Problems

The overall methodology of CCG has traditionally been, and remains, functionalism. The scholar identifies a need or a function or a problem that is shared by several jurisdictions, and

---

[3]   Mark Ramseyer and Yoshiro Miwa deny the existence of both the main bank system and the *keiretsu* structure in a series of articles collected in Miwa & Ramseyer (2006). Curtis Milhaupt challenges the challengers in Milhaupt (2002), as do three other Japanese law scholars in Nottage, Wolff & Anderson (2009).

then asks how they address it. The solutions will by definition be functionally equivalent and therefore comparable. This approach is widely used in comparative law generally (Barton et al. 1983). An often-cited example in the CCG field is Gilson (2004). In this paper, Professor Gilson explicitly takes a function-centered approach to CCG in examining various problems, stating, for example, that '[a]ny successful system must find a way to replace poorly performing senior managers' (Gilson 2004, 137) and then showing that different systems manage to do it with similar levels of efficiency despite formally different structures. As noted above, CCG scholarship has traditionally taken the cross-national problem to be that of minimizing agency costs in the shareholder-management relationship.

Although this approach has been praised as 'value-neutral', the injection of values into a study is in fact unavoidable, and can only be managed, not eliminated. First, values enter the picture because there is no objective way of knowing what function or need a particular practice serves. What is a problem in one system may not be a problem (or perceived as one) in another. The very act of deciding what is a problem involves a value judgment. Thus, for example, the separation of ownership and control is perceived as a central problem in American corporate law and is therefore assumed often to be a central problem in other jurisdictions (Gilson & Roe 1993). But it has been embraced as a *solution* in much of Chinese corporate governance discourse (Clarke 2003). While one could argue (as I have) that this discourse misconceives the nature of the problem that separating ownership from control is supposed to solve, the fact remains that a search for Chinese solutions to the 'problem' of this separation is going to yield odd results.

This leads to the second problem: that if the function is exogenously determined, we can always, if we look hard enough, find something that we judge attempts to accomplish it. Consider this passage from Max Gluckman's *The Judicial Process Among the Barotse of Northern Rhodesia (Zambia)*:

> [I]n contract cases the court begins by defining the social positions of the litigants: buyer and seller, lender and borrower, employer and servant, cattle-owner and herder, owner and share-cropper in fishing, partners. These positions are linked by agreement (*tumelano*), in sale (*muleko*) or barter (*musintana*), loan (*kukalimela*), employment (*kusebezisa*), herding (*kufisa*), share-fishing (*munonelo*), or partnership (*kopanyo*). (Gluckman 1955, 315)

It may well be that the Lozi terms in question are the closest one can get to the English term preceding it. And it is of course possible that Lozi society happened to come up with a legal system that also uses abstract definitions such as 'buyer' and 'seller', 'lender' and 'borrower', and so on, and has business organizations like partnerships as we know them. But one cannot escape the suspicion that Gluckman began with the concept from English or Roman-Dutch law, proceeded to look for its equivalent, and inevitably (because the methodology required it) found one.[4]

A third problem with functionalism crops up when starting not with a posited function, but instead coming from the other direction: starting with an institution and attempting to attribute to it a function. In Teemu Ruskola's colorful example:

---

4    See Paul Bohannon's critique of what he calls 'backward translation' in Bohannon (1969, 410).

Explaining in a functionalist framework why the medieval French chose to try rats, for example, would require considerable ingenuity. How would one even begin to frame the inquiry? ('How did the French deal with the problem of criminal rodents in the Middle Ages?' Or, 'How did medieval French law address cross-species disputes?') (Ruskola 2002, 203–04)

Thus, we might see a foreign practice as a response to the 'need' to limit controlling-shareholder exploitation of non-controlling shareholders, whereas in fact it serves some other, quite different social purpose.[5] This risk is admittedly small when we are looking at foreign jurisdictions similar to our own, and where there is considerable cross-communication among scholars, so that we have a good sense of how people in the jurisdiction in question view the practice. But once we move to more unfamiliar and exotic jurisdictions without much of a shared legal tradition, and in particular if we do not go below the surface but simply code the rules on the books, the danger of missing something important is very high.

Finally, functionalism is problematic because it requires one in effect to take for granted the function that is served in the analyst's home jurisdiction. For example, much of the discussion in CCG is over whether there is a single optimal form of corporate governance, and if so, what it is. But although this discussion has resulted in many different views, even to have it requires agreement on what corporate governance is supposed to be optimizing. Although many would say it is or should be about maximizing shareholder returns, there is a sizable dissent from those associated with stakeholder theory and the progressive corporate governance school.

None of this is to condemn functionalism out of hand or to deny its usefulness in some circumstances. Many corporate governance regimes do indeed face common problems. For example, to whom do assets used by the corporation belong, and to whose creditors shall they be made available? Who can act for the corporation, and how shall that actor's performance be monitored and controlled? CCG studies have gotten a great deal of mileage out of the comparative approach by showing how similar results can sometimes be achieved in spite of different formal legal norms (Gilson 2004). Functionalism can also be useful in naturalizing the exotic, as it were; in showing that what seems at first glance to be utterly strange can in fact be reduced to familiar terms. As CCG extends its reach beyond the familiar jurisdictions of the industrialized world to transition and developing economies, this approach may still prove valuable. The key is to be alert to, and avoid, functionalism's tendency to reduce to familiar terms that which truly *is* exotic, thereby hiding precisely what is different and interesting about it.

**Cross-sectional Studies Versus Longitudinal Studies**

A marked feature of CCG in recent years has been its focus on cross-sectional studies. These studies can examine the relative efficiency of given structures at given times and yield policy recommendations, but do not tell us how structures change over time (Bradley et al. 1999). One notable exception is an admirable 2002 study by Katharina Pistor and her colleagues of the evolution of corporate law in several jurisdictions since about the late eighteenth century

---

[5]   Roberta Romano, for example, posits that institutional blockholding in Germany and Japan exists not to minimize agency costs in that particular institutional environment, but to prevent hostile takeovers or to allow the blockholders 'to safeguard or favor their non-shareholder positions at the public shareholders' expense' (Romano 1993, 2033).

(Pistor et al. 2002). Another exception is a 2001 article by Mark West showing how Japanese corporate law began after World War II looking like Illinois corporate law, and then gradually diverged over time (West 2001b). West then uses this phenomenon to develop a theory about the differences between Japanese and US corporate law understood as systems; it is their larger unchanging features that explain the way subsidiary features change over time.

## Empirical Studies Using Standardized Data

The well-known LLSV literature and its progeny are empirical studies using standardized data (La Porta et al. 2008). Particular areas of importance are identified, the relevant rules are found and coded, and then attempts are made to make correlations.

Although one must admire the energy and ambition behind these coding efforts, this genre of literature has been the subject of extensive criticism. First, it is said to focus too much on law on the books, with inadequate attention to whether the law is actually enforced (Rosser 2003; Coffee 2007), and that when it does pay attention to enforcement issues, it again looks at law on the books (Cools 2005; Braendle 2005; Schmidbauer 2006; Spamann 2006). Second, the literature's descriptive account of the law is sometimes simply wrong or inconsistent (Braendle 2005).

Related to the second critique is a third: that the indicia the literature focuses on do not in fact measure something useful. Some of the shareholder rights measured in the literature supply only partial protection to shareholders and are easily circumvented (Coffee 2001). In other cases, bad or good rules can be varied by contractual arrangements. In still other cases, such as shareholders' pre-emptive purchase rights for new issues or cumulative voting rights, it is not clear that shareholders – particularly minority shareholders, who are the main objects of this literature's concern – are better off in a regime that mandates such rights and makes it impossible for shareholders to decide that a different rule might be of greater collective benefit (Pistor et al. 2002; Gordon 1994).

Finally, it has been argued that the correlations this literature finds are spurious and the product of data mining (West 2002).

On the other hand, some of the LLSV literature has shed valuable light on comparative questions. It was the LLSV literature that showed how rare regimes of dispersed ownership actually are around the world (La Porta et al. 1999), suggesting therefore that rules designed for such a regime, where the main agency problem is the vertical one between shareholders and management, are of limited transplantability to countries where the main agency problem is the horizontal one between controlling shareholders and non-controlling shareholders. It also suggested, although not irrefutably, that existing ownership structures are an equilibrium response to domestic legal environments. Controlling shareholders in block holder-dominated systems do not lobby for more protection for minority shareholders, even though that might increase overall firm value, probably because they would lose more than they would gain by it (Bebchuk & Roe 1999).

More generally, the problem pointed out over a decade ago by Jonathan Macey remains:

[T]here are no generally accepted criteria for the appropriate means to *measure* alternative systems of corporate governance. That is to say, there are no formalized, generally accepted criteria for determining whether a particular system of corporate governance is working. Once such criteria are developed, it should be possible to begin serious comparative empirical work in corporate governance. (Macey 1998, 908)

## 4.  LESSONS FROM COMPARATIVE CORPORATE GOVERNANCE

Despite the suspicion that it is somewhat dull work, taxonomy in CCG has been quite illuminating. Scholars have distinguished between insider- and outsider-dominated systems, with the latter relying more heavily on disclosure and markets than the former (Nestor & Thompson 2001), and Hansmann and Kraakman (2001) classify corporate governance systems by their orientation to shareholders, managers, labor, or the state. Gourevitch and Shinn (2005) go further to produce a typology of six political coalitions resulting from different outcomes of alliance and conflict between owners, managers, and workers.

CCG scholarship also led to the discovery that national systems vary dramatically along dimensions of ownership – some countries have large groups of related corporations (for example, *chaebol* in South Korea, holding companies in Europe, *keiretsu* in Japan); others show patterns of family control (for example, Canada, Italy, and Hong Kong); and others show relatively dispersed shareholding (for example, the United States and the United Kingdom). A great deal of CCG scholarship has been about trying to explain cross-country variations in patterns of corporate ownership. Different studies have reached different conclusions, not all of them mutually reconcilable. But it is a sign of the vigor of the field that so many different theories have been raised and discussed, and it is hardly a sign of failure that no consensus on a definitive conclusion has yet been reached.

The simplest hypothesis of the CCG literature is that economics, and only economics, matters. Corporate governance is a technology of business organization, just like lean production or indeed the assembly line itself. Countries faced with similar economic pressures will, over time, adopt similar corporate governance institutions. Evolutionary processes will ensure the elimination of unsuccessful competitors.

CCG research has forced this hypothesis into some major qualifications. Significant differences do persist that are hard to explain as the result of different competitive pressures (Doremus et al. 1999). The response of the 'economics matters' school has essentially been to say that economics matters within the constraints imposed by politics (Easterbrook 1997), which has something of a tautological flavor, or to maintain that economics still matters in the long run; that even though short- or mid-term differences may persist, long-term trends are decided by competitive economic pressures.

A second hypothesis is that law matters. This is essentially the message of the LLSV literature, which finds a correlation between formal law on the one hand and systems of finance and corporate governance, including ownership patterns, on the other. Whether the link is indeed one of cause and effect, and whether the link is more than spurious, can be (and has been) debated. But in any case, the hypothesis is out there, and it has not been decisively refuted.

A third hypothesis is that history and politics matter. This is, of course, the position of Mark Roe, who argues, 'The economic model cannot alone explain foreign structures and their differences with the American structures; it needs a political theory of American corporate finance to provide an adequate explanation' (Roe 1993, 1935). This hypothesis incorporates path dependency (Bebchuk & Roe 1999): different ownership patterns prevail because of previous choices in corporate structures and corporate law itself. Both result in regimes that are costly to change even though if we were starting from scratch we might not choose them.

While the Roe hypothesis is far from unchallenged, it has inspired a number of inquiries into the details of various national corporate governance regimes, and has proven a useful lens through which to view national differences. It is hard to find a work of CCG these days that does not cite Roe's work on path dependency and the importance of history and politics, even if it does not always completely agree with it.

A fourth hypothesis is that culture matters. A traditional concern of comparative law scholarship generally has been that of the transplantability of laws and legal institutions. Will the transplant take? Why or why not? Are there things that need to be considered beyond market pressures and interest-group politics? The 'culture matters' school answers 'Yes', and the argument has been applied in the corporate governance context. The problem with culture as an independent variable is that it is very susceptible to vague cliché-mongering, and often used by vested interests as a reason to oppose change. Amir Licht is probably the scholar most prominently associated with an effort to be more rigorous about looking at the relationship between culture and corporate law (Licht 2001, 2004).

Finally, another effort to get at deep-structure issues can be called the 'property rights matter' approach essayed by Curtis Milhaupt (1998). The hypothesis here is that we need to understand the claims on corporate assets and behavior that can be made by state as well as private actors, and that the security and predictability of property rights in a polity will affect the ownership structure of firms. In particular, the claim is that dispersed ownership is possible only in countries where private property rights are highly secure, and that concentrated ownership is a response to insecure property rights.

## 5.   FUTURE DIRECTIONS AND CHALLENGES

### Comparative Corporate Ecology

One criticism leveled at the LLSV literature is that it mistakes the rules on the books for actual practice. This is so in two ways. First, it neglects enforcement issues. But perhaps more importantly, it neglects the ways in which actors can often negotiate around the rules if they wish, to the extent that Bernard Black has famously called corporate law 'trivial' (Black 1990).[6] A contractarian theory of corporate law would hold that the rules we see applying to participants in the corporate enterprise are all rules that they have in some sense chosen. The LLSV literature in effect rejects by implication this theory of corporate law without ever directly engaging it or even acknowledging its existence.

More broadly, CCG would benefit from a stronger focus on the institutional environment for corporate governance (Clarke 2010a). This means comparing not just rules, no matter how well selected, but also the various institutions that exist to make the rules meaningful, as well as non-legal institutions that may work to accomplish the purposes – for example, the reduction of agency costs – attributed to corporate governance rules. A decade ago, for example, John Cioffi asserted that:

---

[6]   Black does not actually assert that *all* corporate law is trivial in the sense that unwanted rules can be avoided at low cost. He argues that where such rules cannot be avoided, political pressures will be brought to bear to change them.

even under the liberal legal tradition and pluralist political conditions in the United States, fiduciary duties cannot fulfill their governing function unless one assumes the existence of powerful, pervasive, and effective extra-legal social mechanisms of norm internalization. Whatever the moral force and effect of fiduciary duty law, the hypertrophy of the business judgment rule reveals the impracticability of structuring corporate governance through formal rights and judicial enforcement … Economically functional corporate governance regimes thus require alternative or additional legal mechanisms of governance such as disclosure regulations, proxy rules, board structure and operation, and board and/or works council codetermination. Hence, corporate governance regimes and their reform reflect a *politics of institutional mechanisms*. (Cioffi 2000, 523–4)

The last ten years have seen numerous studies of the 'alternative or additional legal mechanisms' noted by Cioffi, plus others not mentioned. A few scholars have produced comparative studies of shareholder derivative actions, for example (West 1994; Grechenig & Sekyra 2007; de Nicola 2007; Mollett 2008–2009). And the CCG community is certainly aware of the importance of institutional context in general. But further comparative research on many specific institutions is needed; surely interesting insights could be gained by studying the role in other countries of the financial press or of gatekeepers such as lawyers and accountants (Coffee 1999).

**The Issue of Convergence**

A key question occupying CCG almost from the beginning has been that of the prospects for convergence. Most of the arguments on convergence – whether it is going to happen, and what pressures exist either for or against it – were already out there in the literature ten years ago (Bebchuk & Roe 1999; Bratton & McCahery 1999; Gilson 2004; Coffee 1999). Yet there was no consensus then and there is none now.

The definition of insanity is said to be doing the same thing over and over and expecting different results.[7] If so many scholars after so many years still cannot get any traction on the problem, perhaps this is a clue that we are asking the wrong question.

The issue of convergence can be divided into three main sub-issues. First, why might it happen? Second, is it happening? Third, is it a good thing?

The CCG literature has proposed several reasons why convergence might happen. Foremost among these explanations is the economic Darwinist one: convergence will occur because one system must necessarily be more efficient than the others, and that system will prevail in economic competition between corporations.

This view sees corporate governance as an organizational technology, and firms must adopt the best available technology to survive (Nestor & Thompson 2001). With the increased flow of information, lack of knowledge about this technology is no longer an obstacle to its diffusion. Countries that fail to adopt efficient rules will suffer; their corporations will be worth less, and will have a harder time raising capital. Business will suffer, or will move elsewhere (Bebchuk & Roe 1999).

To be complete, this explanation must be supplemented by another one setting forth the mechanism by which competitive adaptation takes place. The literature offers a number of suggestions: technological determinism, in which similar problems dictate similar solutions;

---

[7]   The expression is often attributed to Einstein or Franklin, but I have found no specific citation.

emulation, where policymakers consciously imitate the practices of other countries; elite networking, where a cosmopolitan group of experts forms a consensus and then proselytizes it back in the members' home countries; harmonization, where policymakers recognize inter-dependence and the need to avoid unnecessary incompatibilities; and penetration, where states face serious externally imposed costs of some kind for not adopting converging structures (Backer 2002).

Indeed, it is not even undisputed that economic factors will lead to convergence, as argued by the Darwinian view. The 'varieties of capitalism' perspective (Hall & Soskice 2001) holds that:

> an understanding of the foundations of economic performance suggests the persistence of diversity in systems of corporate governance. [This perspective] emphasize[s] the importance of institutional diversity for shaping enterprise behaviour and economic performance. [It] reject[s] the assumption that there is one best way to organize an economy and, in particular, that the free flow of economic resources through 'perfect' capital, labour and product markets will lead to optimal economic outcomes. (O'Sullivan 2003, 27)

Moreover, the argument that firms must adopt international norms in order to attract investment is empirically questionable. The standard view is expressed by Nestor and Thompson (2001, 20), who state that in an era of globalized capital markets, firms know that 'in order to tap this large pool of global financial resources, they need to meet certain governance conditions'.

This argument is not implausible on its face, and may well be true at least at the margin and when all other things are equal. But all other things are never equal, and the question is whether corporate governance survives as a decisive factor when other factors have been taken into account. Particularly in emerging markets with poor and unreliable disclosure, investment decisions are as often driven by predictions about broad economic trends or government policies as they are driven by company-specific matters such as governance. Randall Morck et al. (2000) found a high degree of synchronicity in stock prices in emerging market countries, suggesting that investors in those markets pay more attention to systemic risk factors than to corporation-specific information. Investment in many emerging markets often seems to be driven by a desire simply to be there, with little attention paid to the quality of the company in which the investment is made.

But even if economic pressures do drive firms *toward* a single model, it does not follow that Darwinian selection will actually result in convergence. First, for this result to obtain, selection pressures brought about by corporate governance differences would have to operate quickly and massively. To say that selection pressures push firms toward a particular destination is a different thing from saying that they will actually arrive there, and to show that some structure is efficient in the long run is not to show that at any given moment no inefficient structures can be observed (Elster 1986; Granovetter 1985).[8]

Finally, if the story of selection pressures were true, then not only would we see convergence in corporate governance, but we would long ago have seen convergence in political and

---

8  Miwa and Ramseyer (2002), for example, while sometimes acknowledging that competitive pressures 'drive firms toward' a firm-specific optimum number of outside directors, elsewhere go much further and assert in effect that all firms are always already there.

economic systems. All societies would look the same now. But they do not, and therefore the optimal set of corporate governance rules in each society is likely to be different even if you believe that selection pressures push companies toward optimality.

Are we actually seeing convergence? Despite Hansmann and Kraakman's provocative bombshell, there is no consensus that we are. In the advanced industrial countries, there has been little movement toward convergence. German-style co-determination, for example, has not proven attractive to other countries, but the Germans for their part show little inclination to reject it. In what for CCG studies has traditionally been the key realm of shareholder rights, an extensive recent study concludes that it is 'a mixed picture' (Siems 2008, 358). There has been some convergence in management compensation practices, but no noticeable convergence in the area of defenses against hostile takeovers.

At the same time, we should not overlook some important specific instances of convergence. Over the last several years, Japanese corporate law has undergone 'massive'[9] revisions in what could be called an American direction (Nottage et al. 2009; Keleman & Sibbitt 2002), culminating in the consolidated Company Law of 2005. Most observers, however, maintain that despite revisions to the formal law, the practice of corporate governance in Japan is changing only slowly (Nottage et al. 2009; Haley 2005; Aronson 2009).

The same might be said about China. Given that the People's Republic of China did not even have a general corporate statute for the first four-plus decades of its existence, the very adoption of such a statute in 1993 could be viewed as a formidable example of convergence. More to the point, the 2005 revisions of China's company and securities laws were unquestionably in a direction that brought them closer to, and not further from, the mainstream.[10] Yet the reality of corporate governance practices in China remains very different from what appears in the statute books, and indeed is so opaque that it is difficult to measure reliably where it is, let alone to know in what direction it is moving (Clarke 2010a).

Finally, it is worth considering the question of whether convergence would be desirable even if we had it. Here the argument for cross-national convergence or uniformity seems less compelling than in other areas of the law. While there is general agreement that forum-shopping in areas such as bankruptcy or contract law is a bad thing, there is much less agreement that the corporate law equivalent of forum-shopping – that is, incorporating in the jurisdiction that offers the best form of business entity for one's particular needs – should be discouraged.[11] It has long been allowed in the United States, and is increasingly allowed in Europe following the landmark *Centros* decision.[12] Clearly, there is substantial political as well as intellectual force behind the idea that choice is a good thing. It has even been argued that diversity in corporate governance regimes is per se a good thing, in the same way that bio-

---

[9]    Nottage et al. (2009, 1, 2) *supra* note 3. A table showing the reforms is appended to the article; *see ibid*, 11.

[10]    For an analysis of revisions, see Krause & Quin (2007); Dickinson (2007); Wang & Huang (2006); on the original Securities Law, see Tomasic & Fu (1999); Zhang (1999); Gu & Art (1996); on the original Company Law, see Art & Gu (1995); Huo (1995).

[11]    For discussion in this volume, *see* Ahdieh (Ch. 20).

[12]    Case C-212/97, *Centros Ltd. v. Erhvervs-og Selskabsstyrelsen*, 1999 E.C.R. 11459. For a sample of commentary on the case, see Jankolovits (2004); Ringe (2011).

logical diversity is a good thing: it preserves alternative ways of organizing that may prove superior to current ways if the relevant environment changes (McDonnell 2002).[13]

The whole discussion of convergence in corporate law is, in fact, oddly different from discussions of convergence in other fields of law, because convergence in corporate law does not necessarily mean uniformity. For corporate governance models do not vary only on the substantive rules they apply to business organizations. They vary also on the degree to which they offer and respect choices about which form of organization to use. Convergence on Delaware law, for example, which allows wide scope for creativity in the design of business organizations, is in effect a non-convergent convergence.

Given that the very meaning of convergence is so uncertain, and in view of the failure over so many years to come to any consensus as to whether it is occurring, perhaps it is time to abandon the crystal-ball approach to CCG studies. After all, what purpose is really served by trying to figure out if convergence is inevitable or not? There is value in determining which features of which system do what well and do what badly. If policy advocacy has any real-world effect, then one should advocate what seems to work well, regardless of what direction the rest of the world is going in.

## Breadth of Focus

### Focus on the public corporation
CCG studies have tended to focus on publicly listed corporations. There are probably several reasons for this: they are the type of corporation that law professors tend to know best, and disclosure laws around the world mean that they produce the most numbers for economists to crunch. Furthermore, such companies feature almost by definition the involvement of small, passive shareholders, and thus present public policy questions arguably not present in business entities involving a small number of people who bargain with each other. Finally, if large public corporations dominate the economy, then the value of studying them is self-evident.

Although the focus on public corporations is for all these reasons understandable, it means that a great deal of interesting territory has been left largely unexplored. American corporate law scholarship and teaching has long been moving from a 'corporations' approach to a 'business organizations' approach, and scholars such as Henry Hansmann (1996) and Larry Ribstein (2010) have written extensively about alternative business structures. It is time for CCG to do the same. Non-public-corporation business organizations (NPCBOs) play a major role not just in advanced industrialized economies, but even more in the transition and emerging market economies that have become increasingly important (Nixson & Cook 2005; Green et al. 2006; Weeks 2003; Cook & Nixson 2000; Abdullah 2000; Liedholm & Mead 1999; Anderson 1982). They are major sources of employment, and are an essential stage in the life cycle of the large, successful public corporation. To focus on public corporations without understanding how NPCBOs operate, then, is to overlook a major part of the global economic landscape.

---

[13]    The metaphor is a little strained; a biological species, once gone, is gone for good, at least until *Jurassic Park*-like technology is invented. A species of organization, by contrast, can exist in the minds of human beings even if there are no examples of it on earth, and thus can be resurrected any time someone thinks it might be useful.

What insights might such an approach yield? Perhaps to the extent the current perceived superiority of American over Japanese capitalism can be attributed to differences in corporate governance, we should study the differences not in the governance of large, public corporations – after all, General Motors went bankrupt, not Toyota – but rather in the way innovative start-ups such as Apple and Google could be governed and funded through venture capital.[14]

### Focus on the boundaried firm

As noted earlier in the chapter, the focus of CCG studies, particularly in the United States, has tended to be on the relatively narrow set of issues involving the relationship between shareholders and managers – in other words, on corporate law and securities law. Some voices have urged greater attention to labor issues (Cioffi 2000). But the desirability of broadening CCG's focus goes beyond the familiar shareholder vs. stakeholder conceptions of the corporation. Those competing conceptions still have one important thing in common: a vision of the corporation as a well-defined entity, with insiders and outsiders, employees and non-employees, shareholders and creditors.

But CCG, at least as practiced by legal scholars, needs to come to grips with patterns of industrial organization in which the boundaries of the firm are by no means clear. As William Klein pointed out almost three decades ago, although '[t]he notion that activity is organized either within firms or across markets does seem useful' for some purposes,

> [t]he types of organization people use to accomplish their economic goals, however, vary greatly; one can draw a clear line between firms and nonfirms only by adopting simplistic and unhelpful definitions. More realistically, one should envision a spectrum with varying degrees of 'firmishness' and treat the firm not as an entity, but as an abstraction that facilitates the examination of complex relationships among different actors. (Klein 1982, 1523)

Stephen Cheung (1983, 18) argued that the notion of a firm with boundaries made no sense and that, from an economist's standpoint, 'it is futile to press the issue of what is or is not a firm'. And Ronald Coase himself, in his seminal article (1937, 391), admitted that 'it is not possible to draw a hard fast line which determines whether there is a firm or not'.

So far, however, these insights into the complexities of contracting have not been extensively explored in the CCG literature. What might such an exploration show – that is, what insights might be gained by approaching comparative corporate governance from a 'firmishness' perspective? One reward might be a better understanding of the trade-offs between contractual governance arrangements and hierarchical ownership arrangements, and perhaps even insights into arrangements that are completely outside this duality. For example, vertical integration is often thought of as the solution to excessive contracting costs – costs that include not only negotiation, but also enforcement. In societies where contracts cannot be reliably enforced, we would expect to see a higher degree of vertical integration. But do we? China poses the example of highly specialized production chains involving complex networks of firms not tied together through vertical integration, and yet its courts are generally considered unreliable as contract enforcers. What institutions are performing the governance function, and what do we find in other countries that appear to exhibit the same combination of weak contract enforcement and low levels of vertical integration?

---

[14]   I am grateful to Barry Naughton for suggesting this point.

## Moving beyond the traditional jurisdictions

As the previous point suggests, CCG would benefit by moving to newer and more exotic – but still very important – jurisdictions and truly taking account of foreignness. This means countries like India and China. The challenge is that they are going to look in some respects very familiar, with familiar forms. But in other respects they are quite different, especially China, since at least India shares a common legal tradition with the United States (and, more directly, England). Even that, however, can be misleading. How well can India fit into theories of legal governance designed for the United States or Europe when simple cases can drag on for decades? Both of these countries are going to challenge legal scholars to think about how corporate governance can work when it cannot rely on a reasonably efficient court system. Can gatekeepers and reputation effects do all the work? And if so, does this suggest that a sound court system, even in countries where it exists, is not as important as we might have thought?

## Contingency of problem issues

One of the original insights from CCG was that others are not necessarily concerned with the same problems that we are. This in turn is a lesson about the contingency of our own concerns; maybe there are problems we should be worrying about other than shareholder-management agency costs. Back in 1996, Edward Rock wrote about the comparative scholarship of Richard Buxbaum, for whom the interesting question was not how we can make managers sufficiently accountable to shareholders, but rather 'why society permits the establishment and persistence of massive private concentrations of economic and political power over which the political process exercises relatively little control' (Rock 1996, 389). Comparative scholarship can thus show us that what we think is fundamental may not be so fundamental, and that we may be taking for granted issues that outsiders find of intense interest.

CCG has not really taken up this challenge. By and large it is still interested in the basic issue of convergence or divergence, and the fundamental issue is that of reducing agency costs. The virtues and vices of dispersed ownership versus blockholding are typically discussed in terms of their monitoring capacities, not in terms of, say, their contribution to social cohesion.

But if corporate law is defined more broadly as a kind of business law, then it is clear that we do have a lot of law dealing with these claims, and in different ways (Winkler 2004). Let me be clear: I am not advocating here a stakeholder theory of corporate governance as a normative matter. I want only to make the point that a focus on agency costs is not self-evidently the only way to go in comparative work. Simple and even self-evident though this point may be, it does suggest a new area of research in CCG: the comparative meta-study, as it were, of the key issues in corporate governance *as they are perceived* in different societies. Current research is focused largely on understanding the different ways in which legal systems solve similar problems. But there is much to be gained from understanding the different ways in which societies understand the problems they face. Not only can this alert us to the potential importance of problems we may have overlooked or deemed trivial, but it can also help us understand why transplants go wrong: the adopting jurisdiction may not have understood the problem the transplanted institution was designed to address in the home jurisdiction (Michaels 2006).

## 6.   CONCLUSION

Despite the somewhat undertheorized nature of the comparative project generally, CCG has proven a successful approach to corporate governance scholarship, if success is measured by the ability to generate interesting insights that provoke further scholarship and seem likely to continue to do so. This chapter's call to enlarge the scope of CCG scholarship is not a lamentation of its failures but an appreciation of its accomplishments.

One of CCG's important successes is really an achievement of corporate law scholarship generally, and that is to bring comparative law – an interest in what people in other countries do – into the mainstream of a branch of American legal scholarship. Corporate law scholars who do not do CCG are still likely to be familiar with much of what this chapter has discussed, and to have read at least some of the literature. Much of this popularization of CCG has occurred in the last decade or so. One does not see a pervasive sense of American exceptionalism in the field of corporate law; even those who think we do it better than foreigners have some sense of how foreigners actually do it, and there have been periods in which the mainstream view was that foreigners do it better than we do. Regardless, therefore, of how the debates on convergence or other issues come out, corporate law scholars can indulge in a bit of self-congratulation.

## REFERENCES

Abdullah, Moha Asri (2000), 'Small and Medium Enterprises (SMEs): Some Pertinent Issues', in Moha Asri Abdullah & Mohd. Isa Bin Baker (eds) *Small and Medium Enterprises in Asian Pacific Countries*, Hauppauge, N.Y.: Nova Science Publishers.

Anderson, Dennis (1982), 'Small Industry in Developing Countries: A Discussion of Issues', *World Development*, 10, 913–48.

Aoki, Masahiko (1990), 'Toward an Economic Model of the Japanese Firm', *Journal of Economic Literature*, 27, 1–27.

Aoki, Masahiko (1994), 'The Japanese Firm as a System of Attributes: A Survey and Research Agenda', in Masahiko Aoki & Ronald Dore (eds) *The Japanese Firm: The Sources of Competitive Strength*, Oxford: Clarendon Press.

Aoki, Masahiko & Hugh Patrick (eds) (1994), *The Japanese Main Bank System*, Oxford: Clarendon Press.

Armour, John, Bernard S. Black, Brian R. Cheffins & Richard Nolan (2009), 'Private Enforcement of Corporate Law: An Empirical Comparison of the UK and US', *Journal of Empirical Legal Studies*, 6, 687–722.

Aronson, Bruce E. (2009), 'Changes in the Role of Lawyers and Corporate Governance in Japan – How Do We Measure Whether Legal Reform Leads to Real Change?', *Washington University Global Studies Law Review*, 8, 223–40.

Art, Robert C. & Minkang Gu (1995), 'China Incorporated: The First Corporation Law of the People's Republic of China', *Yale Journal of International Law*, 20, 273–308.

Backer, Larry Catá (2002), *Comparative Corporate Law*, Durham, N.C.: Carolina Academic Press.

Banner, Stuart (1997), 'What Causes New Securities Regulation?: 300 Years of Evidence', *Washington University Law Quarterly*, 75, 849–55.

Barton, John H., James Lowell Gibbs, Jr., Victor H. Li & John Henry Merryman (eds) (1983), *Law in Radically Different Cultures*, St. Paul: West Group.

Bebchuk, Lucien Arye & Mark Roe (1999), 'A Theory of Path Dependence in Corporate Ownership and Governance', *Stanford Law Review*, 52, 127–70.

Berglof, Eric & Enrico Peroti (1994), 'The Governance Structure of the Japanese Financial Keiretsu', *Journal of Financial Economics*, 36, 259–84.

Berle, Adolph A. & Gardiner C. Means (1932), *The Modern Corporation and Private Property*, New York: Harcourt, Brace & World.

Black, Bernard S. (1990), 'Is Corporate Law Trivial?: A Political and Economic Analysis', *Northwestern University Law Review*, 84, 542–97.

Black, Bernard, Reinier Kraakman & Anna Tarassova (2000), 'Russian Privatization and Corporate Governance: What Went Wrong?', *Stanford Law Review*, 52, 1731–1808.

Blair, Margaret M. (1995), *Ownership and Control: Rethinking Corporate Governance for the Twenty-First Century*, Washington, D.C.: Brookings.

Bohannon, Paul (1969), 'Ethnology and Comparison in Legal Anthropology', in Laura Nader (ed.) *Law in Culture and Society*, Berkeley: University of California Press.

Bradley, Michael, Cindy A. Schipani, Anant K. Sundaram & James P. Walsh (1999), 'The Purposes and Accountability of the Corporation in Contemporary Society: Corporate Governance at a Crossroads', *Law & Contemporary Problems*, 62, 9–86.

Braendle, Udo C. (2005), 'Shareholder Protection in the USA and Germany – On the Fallacy of LLSV', Working Paper, University of Manchester School of Law, available at http://ssrn.com/abstract=728403 (last accessed November 2011).

Bratton, William W. & Joseph A. McCahery (1999), 'Comparative Corporate Governance and the Theory of the Firm: The Case Against Global Cross-Reference', *Columbia Journal of Transnational Law*, 38, 213–97.

Cheffins, Brian R. (2001), 'Putting Britain on the Roe Map: The Emergence of the Berle-Means Corporation in the United Kingdom', in Joseph McCahery, Piet Moerland, Theo Raaijmakers & Luke Renneboog (eds) *Corporate Governance Regimes – Convergence and Diversity,* Oxford: Oxford University Press.

Cheung, Stephen N.S. (1983), 'The Contractual Nature of the Firm', *Journal of Law & Economics*, 26, 1–21.

Cioffi, John (2000), 'State of the Art', Review Essay, *American Journal of Comparative Law*, 48, 501–34.

Clarke, Donald C. (2003), 'Corporate Governance in China: An Overview', *China Economic Review* 14, 494–507.

Clarke, Donald C. (2006), 'The Independent Director in Chinese Corporate Governance', *Delaware Journal of Corporate Law*, 31, 125–228.

Clarke, Donald C. (2010a), 'Law Without Order in Chinese Corporate Governance Institutions', *Northwestern Journal of International Law & Business*, 30, 131–99.

Clarke, Donald C. (2010b), '"Nothing But Wind"? The Past and Future of Comparative Corporate Governance', *American Journal of Comparative Law*, 59, 75–110.

Coase, Ronald H. (1937), 'The Nature of the Firm', *Economica*, 4, 386–405.

Coffee, Jr., John C. (1999), 'The Future as History: The Prospects for Global Convergence in Corporate Governance and Its Implications', *Northwestern University Law Review*, 93, 641–707.

Coffee, Jr., John C. (2001), 'The Rise of Dispersed Ownership: The Roles of Law and the State in the Separation of Ownership and Control', *Yale Law Journal*, 111, 1–82.

Coffee, Jr., John C. (2006), 'A Theory of Corporate Scandals: Why the United States and Europe Differ', in Joseph J. Norton, Jonathan Rickford & Jan Kleineman (eds) *Corporate Governance Post-Enron: Comparative and International Perspectives*, London: British Institute of International and Comparative Law.

Coffee, Jr., John C. (2007), 'Law and the Market: The Impact of Enforcement', *University of Pennsylvania Law Review*, 156, 229–311.

Conard, Alfred F. (1976), *Corporations in Perspective*, Mineola, N.Y.: Foundation Press.

Cook, Paul & Frederick Nixson (2000), 'Finance and Small and Medium-Sized Enterprise Development', University of Manchester School of Economic Studies, Finance and Development Research Programme Working Paper Series, Paper No. 14.

Cools, Sofie (2005), 'The Real Difference in Corporate Law Between the United States and Continental Europe: Distribution of Powers', *Delaware Journal of Corporate Law* 30, 697–766.

Cunningham, Lawrence A. (2000), 'Comparative Corporate Governance and Pedagogy', *Georgia Law Review*, 34, 721–43.

de Nicola, Alessandro (2007), *Shareholder Suits: The Roles and Motivations of Minority Shareholders and Directors in Derivative Suits*, Boston, Mass.: Aspatore Books.

Dickinson, Steven M. (2007), 'Introduction to the New Company Law of the People's Republic of China', *Pacific Rim Law & Policy Journal*, 16, 1–11.

Doremus, Paul N., Willam W. Keller, Louis W. Pauly & Simon Reich (1999), *The Myth of the Global Corporation*, New York: Princeton University Press.

Easterbrook, Frank (1997), 'International Corporate Differences: Markets or Law?', *Journal of Applied Corporate Finance*, 9, 23–30.

Elster, Jon (ed.) (1986), *Rational Choice*, New York: NYU Press.

Financial Reporting Council (London Stock Exchange) (1992), *Report of the Committee on the Financial Aspects of Corporate Governance* 2.5, available at http://www.ecgi.org/codes/code.php?code_id=132 (last accessed November 2011).

Gilson, Ronald J. (2004), 'Globalizing Corporate Governance: Convergence of Form or Function', in Jeffrey N. Gordon & Mark J. Roe (eds), *Convergence and Persistence in Corporate Governance*, Cambridge: Cambridge University Press.

Gilson, Ronald J. & Mark J. Roe (1993), 'Understanding the Japanese Keiretsu: Overlaps Between Corporate Governance and Industrial Organization', *Yale Law Journal*, 102, 871–906.

Gilson, Ronald J. & Mark J. Roe (1999), 'Lifetime Employment: Labor Peace and the Evolution of Japanese Corporate Governance', *Columbia Law Review*, 99, 508–40.

Gluckman, Max (1955), *The Judicial Process Among the Barotse of Northern Rhodesia (Zambia)*, Manchester: Manchester University Press.

Gordon, Jeffrey N. (1994), 'Institutions as Relational Investors: A New Look at Cumulative Voting', *Columbia Law Review*, 94, 124–92.

Gourevitch, Peter & James Shinn (2005), *Political Power and Corporate Control: The New Global Politics of Corporate Governance*, Princeton: Princeton University Press.

Granovetter, Mark (1985), 'Economic Action and Social Structure: The Problem of Embeddedness', *American Journal of Sociology*, 91, 481–510.

Grechenig, Kristoffel & Michael Sekyra (2007), 'No Derivative Shareholder Suits in Europe – A Model of Percentage Limits, Collusion and Residual Owners', Columbia University School of Law, Center for Law and Economic Studies, Working Paper No. 312.

Green, Christopher J., Colin H. Kirkpatrick & Victor Murinde (2006), 'Finance for Small Enterprise Growth and Poverty Reduction in Developing Countries', *Journal of International Development*, 18, 1017–30.

Grundfest, Joseph (1990), 'Subordination of American Capital', *Journal of Financial Economics*, 27, 89–114.

Gu, Minkang & Robert C. Art (1996), 'Securitization of State Ownership: Chinese Securities Law', *Michigan Journal of International Law*, 18, 115–39.

Haley, John O. (2005), 'Heisei Renewal or Heisei Transformation: Are Legal Reforms Really Changing Japan?', *Journal of Japanese Law*, 19, 5–18.

Hall, Peter A. & David Soskice (eds) (2001), *Varieties of Capitalism: Institutional Foundations of Comparative Advantage*, Oxford: Oxford University Press.

Hansmann, Henry (1996), *The Ownership of Enterprise*, Boston: Belknap Press.

Hansmann, Henry & Reinier Kraakman (2001), 'The End of History for Corporate Law', *Georgetown Law Journal*, 89, 439–68.

Hopt, Klaus, Hideki Kanda, Mark J. Roe, Eddy Wymeersch & Stefan Prigge (eds) (1998), *Comparative Corporate Governance: The State of the Art and Emerging Research*, Oxford: Oxford University Press.

Howson, Nicholas C. (2008), 'The Doctrine that Dared Not Speak Its Name: Anglo-American Fiduciary Duties in China's 2005 Company Law and Case Law Intimations of Prior Convergence', in Hideki Kanda, Kon-Sik Kim & Curtis J. Milhaupt (eds) *Transforming Corporate Governance in East Asia*, New York: Routledge.

Huo, Sunny (1995), 'The Company Law of the People's Republic of China', *UCLA Pacific Basin Law Journal*, 13, 373–89.

Jackson, Gregory (2000), 'Comparative Corporate Governance: Sociological Perspectives', in John Parkinson, Andrew Gamble & Gavin Kelly (eds) *The Political Economy of the Company*, Oxford: Hart Publishing.

Jankolovits, Laura (2004), 'No Borders. No Boundaries. No Limits. An Analysis of Corporate Law in the European Union After the Centros Decision', *Cardozo Journal of International & Comparative Law*, 11, 973–1005.

Jensen, Michael & William Meckling (1976), 'Theory of the Firm: Managerial Behavior, Agency Costs, and Ownership Structure', *Journal of Financial Economics*, 3, 305–60.

Keleman, R. Daniel & Eric C. Sibbitt (2002), 'The Americanization of Japanese Law', *University of Pennsylvania Journal of International Economic Law*, 23, 269–323.

Klein, William A. (1982), 'The Modern Business Organization: Bargaining Under Constraints', *Yale Law Journal*, 91, 1521–64.

Krause, Nils & Chuan Qin (2007), 'An Overview of China's New Company Law', *Company Law*, 28, 316–20.

Licht, Amir N. (2001), 'The Mother of All Path Dependencies: Toward a Cross-Cultural Theory of Corporate Governance Systems', *Delaware Journal of Corporate Law*, 26, 147–205.

Licht, Amir N. (2004), 'Legal Plug-Ins, Cultural Distance, Cross-Listing, and Corporate Governance Reform', *Berkeley International Law Journal*, 22, 195–239.

La Porta, Rafael, Florencio Lopez-de-Silanes, Andrei Shleifer & Robert Vishny (1997), 'Legal Determinants of External Finance', *Journal of Finance* 52, 1131–50.

La Porta, Rafael, Florencio Lopez-de-Silanes, Andrei Shleifer & Robert Vishny (1998), 'Law and Finance', *Journal of Political Economy*, 106, 1113–55.

La Porta, Rafael, Florencio Lopez-de-Silanes & Andrei Shleifer (1999), 'Corporate Ownership Around the World', *Journal of Finance* 54, 471–517.

La Porta, Rafael, Florencio Lopez-de-Silanes & Andrei Shleifer (2008), 'The Economic Consequences of Legal Origins', *Journal of Economic Literature*, 46, 285–332.

Liedholm, Carl & Donald C. Mead (1999), *Small Enterprises and Economic Development*, New York: Routledge.

Macey, Jonathan R. (1998), 'Institutional Investors and Corporate Monitoring: A Demand-Side Perspective in a Comparative View', in Klaus Hopt, Hideki Kanda, Mark J. Roe, Eddy Wymeersch & Stefan Prigge (eds), *Comparative Corporate Governance: The State of the Art and Emerging Research*, Oxford: Oxford University Press.

Macey, Jonathan & Geoffrey Miller (1995), 'Corporate Governance and Commercial Banking: A Comparative Examination of Germany, Japan, and the United States', *Stanford Law Review*, 48, 73–112.

McDonnell, Brett H. (2002), 'Convergence in Corporate Governance – Possible, But Not Desirable', *Villanova Law Review*, 47, 341–85.

Michaels, Ralf (2006), 'The Functional Method of Comparative Law', in Mathias Reimann & Reinhard Zimmermann (eds) *The Oxford Handbook of Comparative Law*, Oxford: Oxford University Press.

Milhaupt, Curtis (1997), 'The Market for Innovation in the United States and Japan: Venture Capital and the Comparative Corporate Governance Debate', *Northwestern University Law Review*, 91, 865–98.

Milhaupt, Curtis J. (1998), 'Property Rights in Firms', *Virginia Law Review*, 84, 1145–94.

Milhaupt, Curtis J. (2002), 'On the (Fleeting) Existence of the Main Bank System and Other Japanese Economic Institutions', *Law & Social Inquiry*, 27, 425–37.

Miwa, Yoshiro & J. Mark Ramseyer (2002), 'Who Appoints Them, What Do They Do?: Evidence on Outside Directors from Japan', Harvard Law School John M. Olin Center for Law, Economics, and Business, Discussion Paper No. 374, available at www.ssrn.com/abstract=326460 (last accessed November 2011).

Miwa, Yoshiro & J. Mark Ramseyer (2006), *The Fable of the Keiretsu: Urban Legends of the Japanese Economy*, Chicago: Chicago University Press.

Mollett, Scott H. (2008–2009), 'Derivative Suits Outside Their Cultural Context: The Divergent Examples of Italy and Japan', *University of San Francisco Law Review*, 43, 635–70.

Morck, Randall, Bernard Yeung & Wayne Yu (2000), 'The Information Content of Stock Market: Why Do Emerging Markets Have Synchronous Stock Price Movement?', *Journal of Financial Economics*, 58, 215–60.

Nestor, Stilpon & John K. Thompson (2001), 'Corporate Governance Patterns in OECD Economies: Is Convergence Under Way?', in *Organization for Economic Cooperation and Development, Corporate Governance in Asia: A Comparative Perspective*, OECD.

Nixson, Frederick & Paul Cook (2005), 'Small and Medium Sized Enterprises in Developing Countries', in Christopher J. Green, Colin H. Kirkpatrick & Victor Murinde (eds) *Finance And Development: Surveys of Theory, Evidence And Policy*, Northampton: Edward Elgar Publishing.

Nottage, Luke, Leon Wolff & Kent Anderson (2009), 'Japan's Gradual Transformation in Corporate Governance', in Luke Nottage, Leon Wolff & Kent Anderson (eds) *Corporate Governance in the 21st Century: Japan's Gradual Transformation*, Northampton: Edward Elgar Publishing.

O'Sullivan, Mary (2003), 'The Political Economy of Comparative Corporate Governance', *Review of Political Economy*, 10, 23–72.

Pinto, Arthur R. (2005), 'Globalization and the Study of Comparative Corporate Governance', *Wisconsin International Law Journal*, 23, 477–504.

Pistor, Katharina, Yoram Keinan, Jan Kleinheisterkamp & Mark West (2002), 'The Evolution of Corporate Law: A Cross-Country Comparison', *University of Pennsylvania Journal of International Economic Law*, 23, 791–871.

Porter, Michael (1992), 'Capital Disadvantage: America's Failing Capital Investment System', *Harvard Business Review*, September–October.

Posner, Richard A. (2009), *A Failure of Capitalism: The Crisis of '08 and the Descent into Depression*, Cambridge, Mass.: Harvard University Press.

Ribstein, Larry E. (2010), *The Rise of the Uncorporation*, Oxford: Oxford University Press.

Ringe, Wolf-Georg (2011), 'Sparking Regulatory Competition in European Company Law – The Impact of the Centros Line of Case-Law and its Concept of "Abuse of Law"', in R. de la Feria & S. Vogenauer (eds) *Prohibition of Abuse Law – A New General Principle of EU Law*, New York: Hart Publishing.

Rock, Edward C. (1996), 'America's Shifting Fascination with Comparative Corporate Governance', *Washington University Law Quarterly*, 74, 367–91.

Roe, Mark J. (1993), 'Some Differences in Corporate Structure in Germany, Japan, and the United States', *Yale Law Journal*, 102 ,1927–2003.

Roe, Mark J. (1994), *Strong Managers, Weak Owners: The Political Roots of American Corporate Finance*, Princeton: Princeton University Press.

Roe, Mark J. (1997), 'Path Dependence, Political Options, and Governance Systems', in Klaus J. Hopt & Eddy Wymeersch (eds) *Comparative Corporate Governance: Essays and Materials*, Berlin: Walter de Gruyter.

Romano, Roberta (1993), 'A Cautionary Note on Drawing Lessons from Comparative Corporate Law', *Yale Law Journal*, 102, 2021–37.

Rosser, Andrew (2003), 'Coalitions, Convergence and Corporate Governance Reform in Indonesia', *Third World Quarterly*, 24, 319–37.

Ruskola, Teemu (2002), 'Legal Orientalism', *Michigan Law Review* 101,179–234.

Schmidbauer, Robert (2006), 'On the Fallacy of LLSV Revisited – Further Evidence About Shareholder Protection in Austria and the United Kingdom', Working Paper, University of Manchester School of Law, available at http://ssrn.com/abstract=913968 (last accessed November 2011).

Shea, Tony (1990), 'Regulation of Takeovers in the United Kingdom', *Brooklyn Journal of International Law*, 16, 89–110.

Shleifer, Andrei & Robert Vishny (1997), 'A Survey of Corporate Governance', *Journal of Finance*, 52, 737–83.
Siems, Mathias M. (2008), *Convergence in Shareholder Law*, Cambridge: Cambridge University Press.
Spamann, Holger (2006), 'On the Insignificance and/or Endogeneity of La Porta et al.'s "Anti-Director Rights Index" Under Consistent Coding', Harvard Law School John M. Olin Center for Law, Economics, and Business, Fellows' Discussion Paper Series, Discussion Paper No. 7, available at http://www.law.harvard.edu/programs/olin_center/fellows_papers/pdf/Spamann_7.pdf (last accessed November 2011).
Tomasic, Roman & Jian Fu (1999), 'The Securities Law of the People's Republic of China: An Overview', *Australian Journal of Corporate Law*, 10, 268–89.
Tunc, André (1982), 'A French Lawyer Looks at American Corporation Law and Securities Regulation', *University of Pennsylvania Law Review*, 130, 757–74.
Verret, J.W. (2010), 'Treasury Inc.: How the Bailout Reshapes Corporate Theory and Practice', *Yale Journal on Regulation*, 27, 283–350.
Wang, Baoshu & Hui Huang (2006), 'China's New Company Law and Securities Law: An Overview and Assessment', *Australian Journal of Corporate Law*, 19, 229–42.
Weeks, John (2003), 'Small Manufacturing Establishments in Developing Countries: An Empirical Analysis', *International Review of Applied Economics*, 17, 339–59.
West, Mark D. (1994), 'The Pricing of Shareholder Derivative Actions in Japan and the United States', *Northwestern University Law Review*, 88, 1436–1507.
West, Mark D. (2001a), 'Why Shareholders Sue: The Evidence from Japan', *Journal of Legal Studies*, 30, 351–82.
West, Mark (2001b), 'The Puzzling Divergence of Corporate Law: Evidence and Explanations from Japan and the United States', *University of Pennsylvania Law Review*, 150, 527–601.
West, Mark D. (2002), 'Legal Determinants of World Cup Success', University of Michigan Law Sch. John M. Olin Ctr. for Law & Economics, Paper No. 02-009, available at http://ssrn.com/abstract=318940 (last accessed November 2011).
Westbrook, David A. (2009), *After the Crisis: Rethinking Our Capital Markets*, Boulder, Colorado: Paradigm Publishers.
Williamson, Oliver E. (1985), *The Economic Institutions of Capitalism*, New York: Free Press.
Winkler, Adam (2004), 'Corporate Law or the Law of Business?: Stakeholders and Corporate Governance at the End of History', *Law & Contemporary Problems*, 67, 109–33.
Zhang, Xian Chu (1999), 'The Old Problems, the New Law, and the Developing Market – A Preliminary Examination of the First Securities Law of the People's Republic of China', *International Lawyer*, 33, 983–1014.

# PART V

# NEW THEORY

# 22. Self-dealing by corporate insiders: Legal constraints and loopholes

*Vladimir Atanasov, Bernard Black, and Conrad S. Ciccotello*

**Abstract:** Insiders (managers and controlling shareholders) can extract (tunnel) wealth from firms using a variety of methods. This chapter examines the different ways in which US law limits, or fails to limit, three types of self-dealing transactions – cash flow tunneling, asset tunneling, and equity tunneling. We examine how US corporate, securities, bankruptcy, and tax law, accounting rules, and stock exchange rules impact each form of self-dealing, and identify weaknesses in these rules. We argue that a variety of complex asset and equity transactions, as well as equity-based executive compensation, can escape legal constraints. We propose changes in corporate, disclosure, and shareholder approval rules to address the principal gaps that emerge from our analysis.

## 1. INTRODUCTION[1]

Managers and controlling shareholders (insiders) can extract (tunnel) wealth from firms using a variety of self-dealing transactions. Self-dealing occurs across both developed[2] and developing[3] markets. It impacts the value of shares and the premiums paid for corporate control.[4] This chapter studies how effectively US rules limit self dealing by insiders of public companies. We consider three broad types of self-dealing transactions: cash flow tunneling, in which insiders extract some of the firm's current cash flows; asset tunneling, in which insiders buy (sell) assets from (to) the firm at below (above) market prices; and equity tunneling, in which insiders acquire equity at below market price, either from the firm through an equity issuance or from other shareholders, often in a freezeout.

We also examine how a broad set of rules, including corporate, securities, accounting, tax, and creditor protection rules impact each type of tunneling. The prior law-and-finance literature discusses the potential anti-tunneling role of these sources, but not how they affect particular types of tunneling. Also, creditor protection rules have been seen as important only to protect creditors. However, as we develop below, they also have an important role in indirectly protecting minority shareholders. Though beyond the scope of our chapter, creditor contracts can also limit tunneling and thus protect minority shareholders (Harvey et al. 2004; John & Litov 2009).

---

[1]    For an expanded version of this chapter, including case studies illustrating the use of different types of tunneling, see Atanasov et al. (2011b).

[2]    Papers studying the United States include Bates et al. (2006), Ciccotello et al. (2004), and Gordon et al. (2004).

[3]    Examples include Atanasov (2005), and Atanasov et al. (2010) (Bulgaria), Baek et al. (2006) (Korea), Bertrand et al. (2002) (India), Cheung et al. (2006) (Hong Kong), and Djankov et al. (2006) (multicountry). China is a favorite subject of study, see, e.g., Berkman et al. (2007), Deng et al. (2007), Jiang et al. (2010), and Ming & Wong (2003).

[4]    Examples include Barak & Lauterbach (2007) (Israel), Black (2001a) (Russia), Goetzmann et al. (2003) (Russia), Nenova (2003) (multicountry), Dyck & Zingales (2004) (multicountry).

Prior research on the strengths of legal protections against self-dealing in the US is usually limited to a single type of tunneling. For example, a large literature discusses freezeouts (DeAngelo et al. 1984; Subramanian 2007; Bates et al. 2006; Rock 1997); a separate literature discusses executive compensation (Bebchuk & Fried 2004; Crystal 1991; Jensen et al. 2004). Though outside our scope, the weak position of minority shareholders in *private* companies is well understood (O'Neil & Thompson 2004). Gilson and Gordon (2003) discuss generally the problem of limiting the power of controlling shareholders, but focus primarily on freezeouts and sales of control, which are forms of equity tunneling. Most studies, especially in the US, also consider only corporate and securities law.[5] The role of creditor protection laws in protecting minority shareholders against tunneling has not been discussed.

In contrast, this chapter studies how a broad set of rules affects a broad range of self-dealing transactions. This breadth comes at a cost – we delve less into the details of the regulation of any one type of transaction. But this breadth lets us illustrate a major theme which has largely gone unrecognized – US rules do not effectively limit the full range of self-dealing opportunities for insiders. It also lets us explore the role of bankruptcy and other creditor protection rules in protecting minority shareholders as well as creditors.

In this chapter, we discuss the strengths and limits of US rules impacting each major form of tunneling. For cash flow tunneling, for example, entire fairness review under corporate law has some bite. Corporate tax law limits pyramid structures and thus incentives and opportunities for cash-flow tunneling within business groups, but is less effective in limiting cross-border transfers through creative transfer pricing. Securities law and accounting rules ensure some disclosure of related party transactions, but the disclosure can often be generic and leave investors in the dark about transaction fairness. For asset tunneling, disclosure is often limited, and corporate law leaves substantial room for transactions at off-market prices. The principal protection against mispriced transactions is review by independent directors, but if the insiders can fool or co-opt them, shareholders can do little. Bankruptcy law provides some protection against asset tunneling for failing firms. Equity tunneling through freezeouts is relatively well-controlled, but creative insiders can often extract much of a company's value through complex recapitalizations, and can extract a surprising amount of value over time through equity-based executive compensation.

Writ broadly, the prevalent methods of tunneling involve insiders exploiting gaps in current rules. The rules block some brute-force schemes that might succeed in less developed markets, but can sometimes be evaded through more complex schemes. We propose changes in corporate, disclosure, and shareholder approval rules to address the principal gaps that emerge from our analysis.

In this chapter we study only public companies. We do not study special rules that apply to firms in particular industries, such as mutual funds. We also study only US rules. We do not consider tunneling by equity holders at the expense of debt-holders, or vice-versa.[6] However, our taxonomy of tunneling is not limited to the US. Moreover, our analysis of how

---

[5]   Exceptions include Black (2001b), who discusses the legal and market institutions needed to control self-dealing, but focuses on emerging markets, and Desai et al. (2007), who study how tax enforcement can limit cash flow tunneling.

[6]   For discussion of the former, see Akerlof et al. (1993). For a Russian example of the latter, see Lambert-Mogilansky et al. (2003). We do address below the ability of a controlling equity holder to use a creditor position in the firm to engage in equity tunneling.

a broad set of rules, taken together, controls particular forms of tunneling is readily adaptable to other countries.

The chapter proceeds as follows: Section 2 provides a summary of tunneling types. Section 3 examines how accounting rules and tax, corporate, and securities law impact various types of tunneling, and points out the loopholes. Section 4 then provides some recommendations to address the existing loopholes. Section 5 concludes.

## 2.   UNBUNDLING SELF-DEALING

In the law and finance literature the term 'self-dealing' is often interchangeable with 'tunneling'. Simon Johnson and co-authors (2000) define tunneling as the 'transfer of resources out of a company to its controlling shareholder (who is typically also a top manager)'.[7] This definition is appropriate for emerging markets, where most firms have a controlling shareholder. We use here a broader definition that includes transfers to managers who are not controllers, often through executive compensation that exceeds a market rate. We follow the taxonomy of tunneling developed in Atanasov et al. (2009), and divide self-dealing transactions into three basic types: cash flow tunneling, asset tunneling, and equity tunneling. We summarize these here, without pretending to capture all of the creative ways in which insiders can extract value from firms.

*Cash flow tunneling* removes a portion of current year's cash flow, but does not affect the remaining stock of long-term productive assets, and thus does not directly impair the firm's value to all investors, including the controller. Cash flow tunneling can repeat year after year, but the fraction of cash flow which is tunneled can change over time. Often, cash-flow-tunneling transactions are not directly with insiders, but instead with firms that the insiders control (or simply have a larger percentage economic ownership than in the subject firm).

*Asset tunneling* involves the transfer of major long-term (tangible or intangible) assets from (to) the firm for less (more) than market value. It includes overpriced purchases of assets or equity in affiliated firms and underpriced asset sales to affiliated firms. Asset tunneling differs from cash-flow tunneling because the transfer has a permanent effect on the firm's future cash-generating capacity. Transfers out of (into) the firm may also affect the profitability of the firm's other assets, if the transferred assets have positive (negative) synergy with the firm's other assets.

*Equity tunneling* increases the controller's share of the firm's value, at the expense of minority shareholders, but does not directly change the firm's productive assets or cash flows. Examples of equity tunneling are dilutive equity issuances, freeze-outs of minority shareholders, and insider trading.

If one describes a firm as a grove of apple trees, which grow better together than apart, cash flow tunneling can be seen as stealing some of this year's crop of apples, asset tunneling out of the firm involves stealing some of the trees (potentially making the remaining trees less valuable); and equity tunneling steals claims to ownership of the grove.

---

[7]   Johnson et al. (2000). This article offers a simpler tunneling taxonomy than the one developed here. The authors treat what we term cash-flow and asset tunneling as 'self-dealing transactions'.

Asset and equity tunneling principally affect items on the balance sheet, and involve the transfer of the *stock of firm value*. In contrast, cash flow tunneling principally affects the income statement and statement of cash flows, and captures the *flow* of firm value.[8] Equity tunneling often does not affect the firm's financial statements at all. In terms of operational impact, asset tunneling directly affects the company's future operations and profitability, while equity and cash flow tunneling do not.

This section dissects self-dealing transactions into our three main types: cash flow, asset, and equity tunneling. We begin by summarizing which types of transactions and activities fall within each type, and then discuss transactions which do not cleanly fit our typology. Transactions between a firm and related parties can sometimes be intended to benefit the firm – sometimes called propping (Friedman et al. 2003; Cheung et al. 2006). One firm investing in a troubled affiliate is a common example. The transaction both props the affiliate, and is a form of asset tunneling for the investing firm. We do not discuss here the argument that tunneling and propping transactions within business groups can sometimes reflect efficient risk-sharing in an inefficient capital market (Morck & Nakamura 2007).

## Cash Flow Tunneling

Cash flow tunneling can be defined as self-dealing transactions which divert what would otherwise be operating cash flow from the firm to insiders. The central stylized attributes of cash flow tunneling are: (1) it can potentially recur indefinitely, but may or may not recur in fact; (2) it leaves the firm's long-term productive assets unchanged; (3) it leaves ownership claims over the firm's assets unchanged; and (4) if limited in extent, it does not significantly affect the firm's long-term cash-generating ability.

One major form of cash flow tunneling involves transfer pricing, where the firm either sells outputs to insiders for below-market prices, or purchases inputs from insiders at above-market prices. The inputs can be either goods or services.[9] A second major form is above-market current-year executive salaries, bonuses, or perquisites (we treat above-market equity-based compensation as equity tunneling). Cash flow tunneling also includes small-scale sales or purchases of replaceable assets at off-market prices.

Some transactions cannot be neatly classified as a single type of tunneling. For example, loans to insiders involve cash flow tunneling if, as is often the case, the loan is at a below-market interest rate. Loans that are large enough to significantly affect the firm's cash resources, where the firm may have difficulty finding other sources of cash in bad economic times, reflect, in part, asset tunneling. If loans to insiders will not be repaid in bad economic times, as is often the case, they have aspects of equity tunneling – the insider receives a valuable embedded put option or, equivalently, a larger share of firm value in bad times. Guarantees of loans to insiders by third parties can be analyzed similarly to direct loans to insiders.[10]

---

[8]   The stock versus flow analogy is adapted from Gilson and Gordon (2003). They argue, using our terminology, that equity tunneling is more damaging to minority shareholders than cash flow tunneling because it extracts the present value of a stream of income, rather than just this year's flow.

[9]   We are concerned here with transfer pricing that benefits insiders, not the also popular form which transfers profits from a high-corporate-tax jurisdiction such as the US to a lower-tax jurisdiction.

[10]   If an insider's control is strong enough, one can understand him as holding an option to borrow

While cash flow tunneling does not directly affect the firm's expected future cash flows, it can have indirect effects, especially if it occurs on a large scale. If controllers remove enough cash from the firm, this can reduce the internal capital or borrowing capacity the firm needs to purchase productive assets, or raise the firm's cost of capital, thus impacting future profitability.

## Asset Tunneling

Asset tunneling involves self-dealing transactions which either (1) remove significant, productive assets from the firm for less than fair value, for the benefit of insiders (tunneling 'out'); or (2) add overpriced assets to the firm (tunneling 'in').

Asset tunneling can include both tangible and intangible assets, which can be either on or off the balance sheet. Tangible asset tunneling includes sales (purchases) of significant assets, often falling within the property, plant, and equipment (PPE) or investments lines on the balance sheet. One common form, especially outside the U.S., involves investing in an affiliate on terms the affiliate could not obtain from outside investors (Baek et al. 2006). Intangible assets offer fertile ground for tunneling because they are often not directly recorded on a firm's balance sheet, so the tunneling leaves fewer traces. Valuation of intangible assets is often difficult, so it is hard for minority shareholders to prove off-market pricing. Examples include providing trade secrets or other intellectual property to related parties at a discount (buying them from related parties at a premium); and diverting business opportunities to related parties. Investing in a troubled affiliate (propping) is a common form of asset tunneling 'in'. Repurchases of shares from insiders for above market value is also a form of asset tunneling 'in', because the insider gets more cash than their shares are worth.

We treat asset tunneling as separate from cash flow tunneling for several reasons. First, asset tunneling out diverts all future cash flows associated with an asset. In contrast, cash flow tunneling is an ongoing process, which can be modified in the future. For example, an executive might receive an excessive salary in one year, but not the next. Second, if there is synergy between different aspects of a firm's business, diverting productive assets reduces the value of the firm's remaining assets and the firm's overall profitability. In contrast, cash flow and equity tunneling are closer to being purely redistributive – they do not directly affect a firm's future operating performance. Third, asset tunneling and cash flow tunneling affect different aspects of financial performance (as captured by standard financial metrics), and need to be addressed through different legal and accounting rules. One can think of asset tunneling as primarily impacting the balance sheet while cash flow tunneling primarily affects the income statement and statement of cash flows.

The classification of some self-dealing transactions will be unclear. Consider a lease of assets from a related party for more than fair value. If the lease term is short, relative to the life of the asset, the transaction looks like cash flow tunneling. If the lease term is long, relative to asset life, the transaction looks more like asset tunneling. Accounting rules struggle with the distinction between short-term 'operating' leases and long-term 'capital' leases; our

---

money in bad times and not repay it, even if the company currently has lent him no money. Thus, Bernie Ebbers borrowed $341 million from WorldCom on the way down (Solomon & Sandberg 2002). For a more recent example, in which insider borrowing in an economic downturn drove a Russian firm into bankruptcy, see Chazan (2009).

taxonomy will do no better than they do. An assets-for-equity transaction can involve both asset and equity tunneling.

## Equity Tunneling

The core characteristic of equity tunneling is that it increases the insiders' ownership claims over the firm's assets, at the expense of minority shareholders, without directly affecting the firm's operations. Equity tunneling can take a variety of forms, including: dilutive equity offerings (issuance of shares or securities convertible into shares, to insiders for below fair value); freezeouts (transactions in which insiders take the firm private) for less than fair market value; loans from the firm to insiders (which will not be repaid in bad states of the world, and hence act partly as put options); sale of a controlling stake (without an offer to buy minority shares); and insider trading which transfers value from uninformed investors to insiders without directly affecting the firm's operations. A repurchase for more than fair value dilutes the value of the minority shares. Equity-based executive compensation that exceeds a market rate for services is a common form of equity tunneling. Within business groups, equity investments in or loans to affiliates can involve both tunneling from the investing firm and propping the investee firm.

## 3.   PRINCIPAL LAWS AND RULES THAT AFFECT SELF-DEALING

There is broad consensus that better legal rules are associated with stronger financial markets, but much less on which rules matter, or how they matter.[11] Some rules directly control self-dealing transactions; some do so indirectly, some do so incidentally but still importantly. We discuss here the principal laws and rules that are likely to do the bulk of the work in controlling self-dealing ('anti-tunneling rules'), and how effective they are against different forms of tunneling. We build on the taxonomy of tunneling developed in the second section, in order to link specific laws and institutions to specific forms of tunneling.

The tunneler's job is often to find a way through or around the web of anti-tunneling rules. Similar to tax planning, if there are several ways to a given goal, and law blocks only some of them, tunnelers can often follow the path less-regulated. Thus, we attend both to the paths that legal rules block, and those they leave open.

We limit our analysis to US laws, stock exchange rules, and accounting rules. A similar analysis can be applied to other countries, whose rules will have different strengths and weaknesses in controlling tunneling. We consider the following principal sources of law and related rules: corporate law, securities law, bankruptcy law, tax law, accounting rules, and stock exchange listing rules.

To assess which rules affect which types of tunneling, we need a taxonomy of rules that does not depend on the idiosyncratic decision to place a rule of type A in a statute of type B. For example, the boundary between corporate and securities law is indistinct – important

---

[11]   On the finance side of law and finance, see, e.g., La Porta et al. (1997, 1998, 2002), La Porta et al. (2006), and the now large related literature, including Beck et al. (2003a, 2003b); Demirguc-Kunt & Maksimovic 1998); and Levine (1998, 1999). On the law side, see; e.g., Armour et al. (2009); Black (2001a), Berkowitz et al. (2003), Roe (2006), and Spamann (2010).

parts of US securities law address matters that are often thought of as involving internal corporate governance. We will use the following taxonomy:

*Corporate governance rules*: rules that principally regulate the relations among shareholders and between shareholders and managers, including rules that create shareholder rights (such as preemptive and appraisal rights), specify transaction approval requirements, specify internal structure (independent directors, audit committees, and so on), specify procedures for corporate decision making, or, occasionally, ban particular types of transactions. These rules are located primarily in state corporate law, but important parts are also located in securities law (for example, the Securities Exchange Act regulates insider trading, shareholder voting, and corporate takeover bids), the Sarbanes-Oxley Act (which regulates audit committees and bars corporate loans to directors and executive officers) and in stock exchange rules (for example, rules on audit committees and independent directors, and rules requiring firms to have a shareholder vote for a large equity issuance or limiting the issues on which record holders who are not beneficial owners may vote).

*Disclosure rules*: rules that specify the content of the disclosure that public companies must make to shareholders and investors. These are located primarily in securities law and accounting rules, but also partially in corporate law, stock exchange rules (such as rules requiring disclosure of new corporate developments), and other places. We consider here federal securities law, but not state securities law. For accounting rules, we assume US GAAP applies. For stock exchange rules, we consider New York Stock Exchange and NASDAQ listing rules.

*Tax rules*: rules which affect taxes paid by corporations, and by investors on cash flows received from corporations. These rules can indirectly protect minority shareholders against cash flow tunneling, by providing an outside monitor with its own interest in keeping cash flows, and thus taxable profits, within the corporation. Tax rules can also reduce incentives to create pyramid or circular ownership structures, which provide opportunities for self-dealing. We consider here federal income tax law, but not state law.

*Creditor protection rules*: rules that are principally intended to protect creditors against actions by shareholders and managers, but in practice can also protect minority shareholders. Conversely, weak bankruptcy laws can facilitate equity tunneling (Lambert-Mogilansky et al. 2003). These rules are principally located in federal bankruptcy law and state insolvency and fraudulent conveyance law, but also include corporate law rules limiting distributions to shareholders.

## Cash Flow Tunneling

Cash flow tunneling involves potentially recurring 'related party transactions' (RPTs), between a firm and insiders or another firm that the insiders control, at off-market prices. The firm buys inputs (goods or services) for an above-market price, or sells outputs for a below-market price.

*Corporate governance rules*: the principal corporate governance rules affecting self-dealing are those which specify fiduciary duties of corporate officers and directors, specify approval requirements for RPTs, provide an opportunity for shareholder suits challenging particular transactions, and ban particular transactions. Corporate law once narrowly restricted related party transactions (Marsh 1966), but over the course of the twentieth century, largely retreated to a process approach: RPTs are lawful if approved through a proper process. Usually, approval by disinterested directors suffices (Allen et al. 2000). This creates risk to shareholders if the board is co-opted or asleep. Assuming the process meets corporate law requirements, a substantive challenge to fairness is difficult. Save for large, extraordinary transactions (which would involve asset or equity tunneling, rather than cash flow tunneling), such challenges are practically impossible. In practice, challenges are rare, and successful ones, to our knowledge, nonexistent.

The Sarbanes-Oxley Act bans corporate loans to directors and executive officers, previously a common RPT (Gordon et al. 2004). But it does not limit loans to other insiders or affiliated firms.

*Disclosure rules*: the principal disclosure rules affecting RPTs are rules requiring disclosure of these transactions and disclosure of major shareholders, so that outside shareholders know who the insiders are. Disclosure rules require companies to disclose the existence of many cash-flow tunneling RPTs. The principal constraint is the federal proxy rules, which require disclosure of executive compensation, and of transactions between the company and its directors, officers, and affiliates with a low $120,000 threshold.[12] Accounting rules are of little help – they require disclosure only of 'material' RPTs.[13] The principal SEC rule on financial statements, Regulation S-X, also contains a materiality exception.[14] Most cash-flow tunneling RPTs will be well under the materiality threshold.

In practice, executive compensation aside, disclosure of RPTs is often opaque, and gives no guidance to investors as to whether the RPT was in fact on arm's-length terms. Enron is a poster child, with its impenetrable disclosures of transactions with special purpose vehicles (Black 2006). A company that discloses extensive RPTs will likely pay a penalty in its share price, but the penalty may be only loosely related to the degree of self-dealing.

The importance of disclosure in limiting executive compensation is suggested by two examples involving stock options. One involves the option backdating scandals that became public in 2005–2006, in which hundreds of companies issued options at below-market prices, by looking backwards to a date when the price was low, and deeming the option granted at that date. Many option plans permit below-market grants. However, the need to disclose that a grant was below market and record compensation expense, which arose once the SEC required officers to promptly report option grants under Securities Exchange Act § 16, stopped most such grants (Heron & Lie 2007). The second involves an accounting rule change in 2002 which required US firms, beginning in 2005, to report compensation expense more generally for granting at-the-money options to executives. Option grants dropped at firms which were formerly above-norm option granters (Feng & Tian 2009).

*Tax rules*: the government has an interest in ensuring that firms report the profits they earn, in order to collect corporate income taxes (Desai et al. 2007). The tax authorities will be especially interested in transactions that move income off-shore, where it may escape US taxation. But in practice, firms retain substantial latitude. For example, the IRS has never succeeded in charging significant taxes on US subsidiaries of foreign parent firms – the foreign parents seem to be able to arrange sufficient transfer pricing transactions to more or less zero out their US taxable income. As long as the income remains on-shore, the tax

---

[12]   Regulation S-K, Item 404. Item 404 disclosure of RPTs is made annually in a company's proxy statement.

[13]   Statement of Financial Accounting Standards 57 (1982), ¶ 2.

[14]   Regulation S-X, Rule 4-02.

authorities have limited interest in where it lands, given the similarity between corporate and individual income tax rates.

Tax rules do indirectly limit a controller's incentives and opportunities to tunnel cash flow. To oversimplify, under US tax law, intercorporate dividends and transactions are partially taxed unless a parent owns at least 80% of a subsidiary and thus is consolidated with the subsidiary for tax purposes. As Randall Morck (2004) notes, this imposes a substantial penalty on pyramidal and circular ownership structures.[15] These structures are common in other countries and provide both incentives and opportunities for the controller to tunnel profits up to the top level of the pyramid (Bebchuk et al. 2000). For executive compensation, Internal Revenue Code § 162 discourages non-incentive compensation by denying a corporate deduction for compensation over $1 million per year. However, in practice, this limit is fairly readily avoided by shifting compensation to other forms.

*Creditor protection rules*: the principal relevant creditor protection rules are those which limit cash distributions and asset transfers from insolvent companies.[16] Both state fraudulent conveyance law and federal bankruptcy law permit courts to examine RPTs involving insolvent companies, and reverse transactions in which the company does not receive value 'reasonably equivalent' to what it pays.[17] Bankruptcy law also allows the bankruptcy court to retrieve payments by the firm to creditors within three months of the filing (one year if the creditor is an insider).[18] Creditors are the principal beneficiaries of these rules, but minority shareholders will also benefit if the firm retains positive equity value (without the tunneling that would occur without these rules).

Still, on the whole, if the insiders of a solvent firm are so inclined, and can find cooperative outside directors, US law neither strongly limits the power of insiders to tunnel cash flows, nor ensures full disclosure of the transactions that occur. To be sure, US rules and norms tilt strongly toward board independence. Companies without a majority shareholder must have a majority of independent directors under NYSE rules,[19] and Delaware law gives greater deference to decisions by board with a majority of outside directors (Allen et al. 2009). In practice, many large firms have a substantial majority of independent directors. Often, these directors will resist gross self-dealing. But independent directors have been notably lax on executive compensation and more than occasionally lax in other areas. Enron and WorldCom are examples where highly independent boards approved self-dealing. They are scarcely alone.

## Asset Tunneling

Asset tunneling is different from cash flow tunneling in several ways. Asset tunneling involves the transfer of productive assets, as opposed to simply cash. Asset tunneling would

---

[15]   We refer to these rules below as 'anti-pyramid rules'.

[16]   We do not consider here the special rules that govern related party transactions involving investment companies (mutual funds), located in the Investment Company Act of 1940.

[17]   Uniform Fraudulent Transfer Act § 4(a)(2), 5(a); Federal Bankruptcy Act § 548 (one-year lookback period).

[18]   Federal Bankruptcy Act § 547(b).

[19]   New York Stock Exchange, Listed Company Manual § 303A.01 (general rule); 303A.00 (exception for controlled companies).

also tend to involve larger transaction size and be more of a one-time event, as opposed to recurring. Asset tunneling can also go in two directions: tunneling 'out' (sale of assets for below fair value) and tunneling 'in' (purchase of assets for above fair value, loans to insiders, and investments in related firms).[20]

*Corporate governance rules*: other than sale of all or substantially all of a firm's assets aside, the corporate law rules governing approval of RPTs do not depend on transaction size, and thus are the same for cash-flow and asset tunneling, and for asset tunneling in or out. The transaction can be approved by disinterested directors, regardless of size. If so approved, it is nearly immune from shareholder attack. The shareholders would have to persuade a court that the transaction was on terms so grossly unfair that the directors must not have satisfied the notoriously lax business judgment rule.[21]

Shareholder approval is never required for asset tunneling 'in'. It is required for asset tunneling 'out' only if the transaction is so extraordinary that it involves sale of 'all or substantially all assets'. Even then, the interested insider can vote in favor of the transaction, and minority shareholders have no appraisal rights.[22]

*Disclosure rules*: the proxy rules, discussed above for cash-flow tunneling, also apply for asset tunneling, and have similar deficiencies. Additional disclosure is required only if the transaction is material – so much can also be hidden by staying below the materiality threshold.

Even for material RPTs, disclosure is often weak or absent. The principal accounting rule which requires disclosure of 'material' RPTs, SFAS 57, contains a suitably broad definition of what parties are related. But there are exceptions for executive compensation and other 'ordinary course of business' transactions. Moreover, even material RPTs need not be disclosed if they are within a group which is consolidated for accounting purposes (accounting consolidation generally kicks in at 50% ownership).[23] Under Regulation S-X, material RPTs that 'affect the financial statements' should be disclosed, including the transaction amount. This implicitly contains the same exception for transactions within a consolidated group.[24]

When transactions are disclosed, details can be scant or opaque. There is no requirement that the accountants verify that the transaction was on arms-length terms, unless the insiders so claim as part of the RPT disclosure (in which case the accountants must test this claim).[25] Atanasov et al. (2011b) analyze a case involving recurring asset sales by Coca-Cola to its majority owned subsidiary, Coca-Cola Enterprises ('Enterprises'), which totaled $15 billion

---

[20]   For loans to insiders or investments in related firms, one can see the asset acquired as the obligation of the insider to repay, or the securities issued by the related firm.

[21]   The discussion below oversimplifies the rather complex corporate law rules governing such suits, and in particular, collapses the problem of bring a derivative suit in the face of demand requirements with the need to win such a suit on the merits, if it can be brought. For details, see, e.g., Allen et al. (2009, Ch. 8: duty of care and business judgment rule; Chapter 10: demand requirements for derivative suits).

[22]   Delaware General Corporation Law § 271; *Hariton v. Arco Electronics, Inc.*, 182 A.2d 22 (Del. Ch. 1962), affirmed, 188 A.2d (Del. 1963). In contrast, the Model Business Corporation Act, § 13.02(a)(3), does provide appraisal rights in this situation.

[23]   Statement of Financial Accounting Standards 57, ¶ 1 (definition of RPTs); ¶ 2 (exception for transactions which are eliminated in consolidated financial statements).

[24]   Regulation S-X, Rule 4-08(k).

[25]   Statement of Financial Accounting Standards 57 (1982), ¶ 3.

over 1985–2001, largely to pay for intangible franchise rights. By 2001, these rights represented over two-thirds of the book value of Enterprises' assets. There was no disclosure of how the purchase price for the acquired assets was determined, and no outside market that would let shareholders value the franchise rights, and hence no way for shareholders to assess fairness.[26] Similarly, for material investments in affiliates, the fact of the investment will be stated, its amount will often be stated, but interest rates on loans or other measures from which investors could assess fairness will often be absent.

*Tax rules*: for cash flow tunneling, tax law had two potential impacts: tax authorities want to keep income within firms, and tax rules discourage pyramids. The 'anti-pyramid rules' constrain asset tunneling as well. However, tax authorities will have limited interest in asset tunneling as such. For asset tunneling 'out', the tax authorities normally won't care as long as the assets move from one taxable firm to another. They will care if assets move offshore, but much as for cash flow tunneling, have had limited success in policing transactions within a business group. Determining the fair value of a long-lived asset can be complex, especially for intangible assets. Some assets-for-equity transactions will be tax-free, as will all transactions within a tax-consolidated group (80% threshold).

Tax enforcement has even less effect on asset tunneling 'in'. These transactions will lead to higher depreciation and hence lower taxable income by the acquirer, but this will often be offset by higher capital gains taxes paid by the seller, so the net impact on tax revenue is not clear. We are unaware of IRS efforts to challenge transactions for being overpriced.

*Creditor protection rules*: the bankruptcy and fraudulent conveyance rules discussed above for cash-flow tunneling also apply to asset tunneling by insolvent or soon-to-be-insolvent firms. Larger transactions provide greater incentives for challenges by creditors or a bankruptcy trustee. A loan or other transfer to an insider will be treated as a preference and reversed if it occurs less than a year before a bankruptcy filing, but will be hard to challenge after that.[27]

## Equity Tunneling

The effect of legal rules on equity tunneling depends on the type of transactions. We consider here, as non-exhaustive examples, dilutive equity offerings, freezeouts, sales of control, and insider trading.[28]

## Equity Offerings

*Corporate governance rules*: corporate governance rules provide protection against dilutive offerings, but only partial protection. Under corporate law, boards must approve equity

---

[26]   Also see Gordon et al. (2004).
[27]   The one-year lookback period is at 11 U.S.C. § 547(b)(4)B).
[28]   There are a myriad of other forms of equity tunneling. One example, for firms that do not go public with two classes of common stock, involves a midstream 'dual-class recapitalization' in which a company offers to exchange low-voting shares for regular common shares on terms that non-controlling shareholders will find individually attractive, with the effect of increasing the insiders' voting control, although not their economic stake. In the US, stock exchange rules effectively bar dual-class recapitalizations.

offerings, including grants of options or restricted stock to executives. Under NYSE rules, shareholders must approve equity compensation plans, but have no say over individual grants if below the 1% threshold noted below.[29] Votes against option plans are uncommon, but the need to obtain shareholder approval for option plans likely constrains some firms.[30]

In the US, the Dodd-Frank Financial Reform Act and related SEC rules require a shareholder 'say on pay', to begin in 2011.[31] Shareholders will cast a nonbinding advisory vote, once every three years, on the overall compensation of all executive officers, and can decide, every six years, to require more frequent votes (every one or two years). Issues such as how often shareholders will cast no votes, against what levels or types of compensation, and with what responses from companies, are as yet unknown. Experience with 'vote no' and similar campaigns against corporate directors in the US (Ertimur et al. 2011; Cai & Walkling 2011), and with a say-on-executive-pay in the UK (Gordon 2009; Ferri & Maber 2010) suggests that these advisory votes may induce some constraints, but likely not strong ones.

US corporate law, unlike many other countries, does not require companies to provide preemptive rights for share issuances, and companies rarely include these rights in their charters. The maximum number of authorized shares must be stated in a company's charter, and shareholders approve charter amendments, but most charters authorize far more shares than are currently outstanding, so this constraint rarely binds. Many company charters also authorize 'blank check' preferred shares, which can be issued on any terms the board decides.

NYSE rules require shareholder approval if the company issues common shares (or securities convertible into common shares) exceeding 1% of the previously outstanding common shares for issuances to directors and officers, and 5% for issuances at market value to substantial shareholders.[32] For very large offerings, above 20% of the company's previously issued common shares, NYSE and NASDAQ rules require shareholder approval, with exceptions for public offerings for cash and 'bona fide' private offers at market value.[33] However, the rule does not cover preferred stock, even if the shares convey economic and voting rights similar to common stock.[34]

*Disclosure rules*: disclosure is required for most equity transactions between the company and insiders. For common shares (and options or other securities convertible into common shares), insiders must report all transactions, with the company or anyone else, regardless of size, under Exchange Act § 16.[35] Exchange Act § 16 covers only publicly registered classes of shares. But transactions with insiders in unregistered shares must also be disclosed, as part of general disclosure of related party transactions, with a $120,000 threshold.[36]

---

[29]   NYSE Listed Company Manual § 312.03(a).
[30]   Proxy advisory firms typically establish guidelines on when they will recommend that shareholders approve a stock option plan. See, e.g., RiskMetrics Group, 2009 US Proxy Voting Guidelines Summary (Dec. 2008), available at http://www.riskmetrics.com/sites/default/files/ RMG2009Summary GuidelinesUnitedStates.pdf, page 32 (last accessed October 2011).
[31]   Dodd-Frank Wall Street Reform and Consumer Protection Act § 951 (2010); Securities Exchange Act rule 14a-21 (2011).
[32]   NYSE Listed Company Manual § 312.03(b). The threshold for issuance to a substantial security holder with no other affiliation to the company is 5% if the issuance price is at least the greater of book value or market value.
[33]   NYSE Listed Company Manual § 312.03(c).
[34]   NYSE Listed Company Manual § 312.03(c).
[35]   Securities Exchange Act § 16(a); Exchange Act Forms 3–5.
[36]   See discussion of related party disclosure above.

After a long battle with executives over accounting for stock options ended in 2005, the company must treat issuance of options to executives as a compensation expense.[37] There is evidence that this change reduced option grants, especially for executives who previously received larger option grants than executives at similar firms. The drop in option grants is only partly offset by larger grants of restricted shares (Feng & Tian 2009).

While the compensation charge to income is now transparent, there remains a hidden tax cost to the company from using option compensation, relative to cash or restricted stock. Some (for 'nonqualified' options) or all (for 'qualified' options) of the option value becomes capital gain to the executive, with no deduction to the company.[38] The lost deduction increases the company's tax liability, but its effective cost is not separately disclosed.

Equity-based compensation through stock options (or restricted stock awards) also affects a firm's operating cash flow. In the year of grant, there is no cash flow impact. In the year when the restrictions on exercise lapse, the executive recognizes compensation income and the firm gets an offsetting deduction, which reduces tax liability and thus increases after-tax operating cash flow. For some firms, this tax benefit comprises a high percentage of total operating cash flow (Ciccotello et al. 2004).

Many firms offset dilution due to option grants by repurchasing shares. Imagine a firm that routinely offsets its option-based dilution. One can understand the cost of repurchasing shares as reflecting the cash cost of option compensation. But that is not how it is treated under accounting rules. The repurchase is a negative *financing* cash flow in the year of repurchase, but does not offset the positive effect of the compensation deduction on operating cash flow. Thus, a firm which pays executives with options, but offsets the dilution by repurchasing shares, will report higher operating cash flow than a similar firm which pays executives in cash. It is unclear whether investors fully understand how option compensation affects cash flow (Landsmann et al. 2006; Atanasov & O'Brien 2010).

*Tax and creditor protection rules*: tax and bankruptcy law do not directly affect equity issuances to insiders, because equity issuance is not a taxable event. Indirectly, tax law encourages use of equity compensation and limits its form. I.R.C. § 162 effectively limits non-incentive compensation to $1 million per executive; the company can pay more than this but can deduct only $1 million. Restricted stock and stock options are treated as incentive compensation.

With regard to the form of compensation, taxation of stock options and restricted stock grants can be deferred until the restrictions lapse; the executive will then typically sell enough shares to pay the income tax.[39] As noted above, option compensation has a tax cost relative to cash or restricted stock, which is normally not disclosed.

---

[37]   Financial Accounting Standards Board Rule 123R (replacing Accounting Principles Board Opinion No. 25, which allowed companies to report zero expense for options with an exercise price equal to current market value).

[38]   The executive normally pays ordinary income on the value of restricted stock, and (for non-qualified options, the 'in-the-money' value of options, when the restrictions lapse; the company gets a corresponding deduction for compensation expense. The remaining option value is not taxed; any eventual gain to an executive is capital gain, with no deduction to the company. For 'qualified' incentive stock options, the executive pays capital gain when the restrictions lapse, and the company receives no deduction at all.

[39]   I.R.C. § 83.

**Freezeouts**

*Corporate governance rules*: these rules give minority shareholders moderate protection against underpriced freezeouts. Some countries require majority-of-minority approval of the freezeout price (Kraakman et al. 2009), but the US does not (Gilson & Black 1995; Gilson & Gordon 2003). Many controllers behave well, for example by creating a special committee of independent directors, negotiating the freezeout price with the committee (quasi arms-length negotiation), conditioning the freezeout on majority-of-minority approval (or majority-of-minority acceptance of a first-step tender offer) (Bates et al. 2006). But some simply make a buyout offer directly to shareholders, which on average is likely at a lower price than the quasi-arms-length process would produce (Subramanian 2007).[40] Some start by negotiating with a special committee, but switch to a tender offer if the committee insists on a higher price than the controller is willing to pay. And some simply bull ahead, judging that they will do better in court defending the predictable suit by minority shareholders than by paying a higher price up front. The circumstances under which a first-step tender offer faces entire fairness review remain uncertain.[41]

As against a hard-nosed controller, shareholders retain appraisal rights, but these are realistically available only for large shareholders. Moreover, they will be based on observable value after other forms of tunneling. Judges tend to trust market prices unless they are shown to be wrong in a particular case. Thus, appraised value is often heavily dependent on market price. If a controller is tunneling some of the firm's cash flow, is engaging (or expected to engage) in equity tunneling, or simply uses private information about expected future cash flows to conduct the freezeout at an opportune time, these factors will create a gap between market value and no-tunneling value, which minority shareholders are unlikely to recapture through appraisal (Maug 2006; Atanasov et al. 2009; Atanasov et al. 2010a). So will the controller's ability to manipulate its financial reports reduce market value?[42] In some situations, a class action suit will be available, but the effectiveness of this remedy depends on the uncertain vigor of class action counsel.[43]

*Disclosure rules*: freezeouts are affected by general public disclosure as well as freezeout-specific disclosure rules, which require detailed discussion of the freezeout process and the basis for any fairness opinion delivered to the company or the special committee.[44] This disclosure helps to ensure that the market price reflects observable value, but for the reasons noted above, the pre-freezeout price will still likely be below the firm's no-tunneling value. Still, disclosure helps to provide the information on which a lawsuit can be based.

---

[40]   The buyout offer is typically followed by a freezeout merger, but damages are lower if the controller owns over 90% and can complete a short form merger, for which appraisal is the only remedy; and are lower even if the controller holds less than 90% because there are fewer minority shareholders left.

[41]   Compare *In re CNX Gas Corp.* (Del. Ch. 2010) (Laster) with *In re Pure Resources, Inc. Shareholders Litigation*, 808 A.2d 421 (Del. Ch. 2002) (Strine).

[42]   This is the opposite of the known tendency of firms to report unusually high earnings before IPOs (Teoh et al. 1998a, 1998b). There is no comparable study of pre- versus post-freezeout earnings because post-freezeout, firms are private.

[43]   For a recent example of class counsel non-vigor despite strong facts in a case involving Ronald Perelman, who has been a prior abuser of minority shareholders and creditors, see *In re Revlon, Inc. Shareholders Litigation* (Del. Ch., C.A. No. 4578-VCL, 2010).

[44]   The principal regulation of going-private transactions is in Exchange Act Rule 13e-3 and related Schedule 13E-3.

*Tax rules*: freezeout transactions involve a sale of shares by minority shareholders, which accelerates the payment of capital gains tax. They can normally be structured to be tax-free for the controllers. Since freezeouts are typically revenue-positive for the Treasury, they receive no special scrutiny.

*Creditor protection rules*: freezeouts often involve borrowing the funds used to pay the minority. There can be occasional instances in which the company's solvency after the freezeout is in doubt, in which case fraudulent conveyance rules might dissuade lenders from lending, in which case the freezeout will not happen.

A more important concern for a financially troubled firm involves a controller lending funds to the firm, and then using its creditor position to freeze out minority shareholders for little or no consideration. For example, the controller can swap its debt for a high percentage of the firm's post-swap shares (potentially 100%), thus diluting minority shareholders. These 'loan to own' schemes sometimes take place in bankruptcy, sometimes in its shadow. Fairness of price can be very hard to determine (Atanasov & O'Brien 2010; Atanasov et al. 2011a).

Corporate governance rules provide little protection against equity tunneling by controller-creditors. The controller, wearing its debtholder hat, has no fiduciary obligation to anyone.[45] If the non-conflicted directors can be persuaded to approve a debt-for-equity swap outside bankruptcy, a fiduciary duty suit against them is unlikely to succeed. Once in bankruptcy, most bankruptcy judges have little sympathy for equity holders.

**Sales of control**

*Corporate governance rules*: many countries limit the power of a controller to sell control, leaving the minority behind. This reduces the cost of a purchase of control, which can be efficient in some situations, but places the minority at risk of self-dealing by the new controller (Gilson & Gordon 2003; Kraakman et al. 2009; Burkart et al. 1998). Many jurisdictions, including the European Union, require an equal offer to be made to all shareholders. Others, including Bulgaria, require majority of minority approval of the transfer of control. US law does not directly protect minority shareholders against the risk of a sale of control, but does provide some indirect constraints.

The main line first. In general, a controller can sell his shares to whomever he pleases for whatever price the market will bear. If the controller sits on the company's board, he has fiduciary duties in that capacity, but he faces no separate duty as a controlling shareholder, with a narrow exception for sale of control to a known (or reason to know) looter.

However, sale of control at a premium is not so simple in practice. First, Delaware corporate law § 203, adopted to limit hostile takeovers, but supplanted in that function by the poison pill, limits a second step freezeout following acquisition of a 15% stake, unless the acquisition is approved by the target's board or the acquirer obtains over 85% ownership in a single step. This gives the independent directors substantial power. They have a duty to use their § 203 power to negotiate on behalf of the minority, and can refuse to approve the acquisition unless the acquirer offers to buy the minority's shares at the same price. Selling control at a premium is easier if a firm uses dual-class shares, though here too the independent directors can use their § 203 power to limit the premium paid for high-voting shares.

---

[45]  A similar situation arises if the controller holds convertible preferred; the preferred shareholder may have effective control but few or no fiduciary duties (Fried & Ganor 2006).

Second, if the firm has a poison pill in place, it will usually need to be waived to permit the sale of control. Here too, the independent directors can refuse to waive the pill unless the acquirer buys all shares for the same price. For both § 203 and the poison pill, the controller's nominees can often outvote the independent directors, but will face a suit for breach of fiduciary duty that they will likely lose. As with freezeouts, some controllers bull ahead despite the expected lawsuit.[46]

*Disclosure rules*: the sale of control will not be a secret. The acquirer and the controller will each report the sale, including the price paid for the controlling shares. The acquirer will report the acquisition and its future plans on Exchange Act Schedule 13D; the controller must report as part of the general Exchange Act § 16 system for insider reporting of trades in a company's shares; the company will thereafter report the new controller's ownership in its annual proxy statements.

*Tax rules*: no special rules apply.

*Creditor protection rules*: usually, no special rules apply, because the transaction is between two shareholders, and does not directly affect the firm's solvency. However, lenders sometimes negotiate for loan terms which give them the right to be paid on a change of control ('poison put covenants'). If they distrust the new controller, they can demand repayment. More commonly, they will demand some compensation for agreeing to waive the right to repayment.

### Insider trading

Insiders can extract value by using their informational advantages to trade with less-informed investors in public securities markets at advantageous prices. Sometimes, they can manipulate the firm's near term results, or the information available to public investors, to make their trades more profitable. Sometimes they can directly manipulate the trading price. A freezeout at an opportune time, including one made opportune by manipulating performance, disclosure, or trading prices, is an example of these more general problems.

*Corporate governance rules*: insiders and firms are barred from trading on inside information by a general prohibition under Exchange Act § 10(b) on trading while in possession of 'material' inside information. Officers, directors, and 10% shareholders are also subject to 'short swing profit recapture' rules under Exchange Act § 16, which extract any profit the insider earns from offsetting sales and purchases (or purchases and sales) within a six-month period. Both sets of rules are actively enforced. The SEC and the stock exchanges investigate unusual trading before important announcements; violators face triple damages in a civil suit by the SEC, and potential criminal liability as well. Lawyers police the short-swing rules because they can earn fees by bringing suits on the company's behalf to recapture the insider's profits. Insider trading by directors and officers would also violate their fiduciary duties, but in practice, this adds little to the 10(b) and 16(b) rules.[47]

At the same time, there are areas that the insider trading rules do not reach. Insiders can lawfully profit by *not* trading – not selling before good news, nor buying before bad. They can rely on the Rule 10b5-1 safe harbor for pre-arranged sales on a regular schedule – and

---

[46]   See, for example, *In re Digex Inc. Shareholder Litigation*, 789 A.2d 1176 (Del. Ch. 2000).

[47]   For an overview of the insider trading rules, see Allen et al. (2009, Ch. 13). On the potential for insider trading rules and enforcement to affect share prices, see Beny (2008); Bhattacharya & Daouk (2002, 2009).

then cancel a sale if good news is expected (Jagolinzer 2009). An insider who is willing to wait out the six-month short swing period can benefit from soft information that outside investors lack, but which is not material, or not provably so. In general, what insiders can do directly, they can cause their firms to do as well.[48]

*Disclosure rules*: the short-swing profit recapture rules are combined with reporting rules governing all transactions in shares, options, and other equity derivatives. Thus trades by insiders must be either reported or actively concealed. Concealment would provide evidence of intent, and thus raise the risk of criminal prosecution. The company reports quarterly the number of shares outstanding, which is related to whether it has issued or repurchased any shares, but not details of particular transactions.

*Tax rules*: no special rules apply.

*Creditor protection rules*: creditor protection rules don't reach transactions between insiders and other shareholders. They can restrict a corporation from purchasing shares from insiders shortly before bankruptcy; repurchases from insiders within a year of the bankruptcy filing will be reversed.

### An Overview of Gaps in Rules Regulating Self-dealing

We have thus far offered a detailed assessment of how particular rules affect particular forms of tunneling. We now take a step back and offer an overall assessment of how effective US rules are in preventing self-dealing transactions. Table 22.1 (below) contains an overview of our own judgment on the strength of legal protections against different types of tunneling as none, minimal, weak, moderate, or strong. Some cells involve close calls, but the big picture is clear. For many tunneling types, there are significant gaps in legal controls.

This table summarizes the strength of tunneling protections for small-to-moderate transactions. In some cases, additional protections may apply for very large transactions (for example, shareholder approval of large issuances of common shares to insiders, or for sale of 'all or substantially all' assets). We consider creditor protection rules that apply to firms that are in financial distress (or would be after the tunneling); these rules provide essentially no tunneling protection for other firms.

Consider first the columns in Table 22.1. Corporate governance rules have the largest overall effect, but vary in strength, and are minimal or weak in a number of areas. Disclosure rules are strong for equity tunneling and executive compensation, but weak elsewhere. Moreover, many insiders will be willing to line their own pockets if the only constraint is telling shareholders what they have done. This particular disclosure dog is all bark and no bite. The most important effect of tax rules is indirect: they discourage pyramids and thus limit opportunities for intra-group asset tunneling and transfer pricing. Tax rules otherwise have little impact. Creditor protection rules matter for financially distressed firms, but only in some areas.

Consider now the rows of Table 22.1. Where corporate governance rules are weak, there is no assurance that another set of rules will pick up the slack. Controls on equity tunneling are reasonably robust, with the notable exception of executive compensation. In some other

---

[48]   The corporation must comply with rules, notably Exchange Act Rule 10b-18, designed to limit price manipulation. There is also no corporate analogy to a Rule 10b5-1 plan.

*Table 22.1  Law and tunneling*

| | Corporate governance rules | Disclosure rules | Tax rules | Creditor protection rules |
|---|---|---|---|---|
| **Cash flow tunneling** | | | | |
| Transfer Pricing | Weak | Weak | Indirect: discourage pyramids Weak (US to foreign); none (US to US) | Weak |
| Excessive executive compensation | Weak | Strong | Weak | Minimal |
| **Asset tunneling** | | | | |
| Asset sales to related parties | Weak | Weak | Indirect: discourage pyramids | Moderate |
| Asset purchases from related parties | Minimal | | | Rare |
| Investments in affiliates | Weak | | Direct: none or minimal | Rare |
| Divert business opportunities | Minimal | None | | None |
| **Equity tunneling** | | | | |
| Dilution through sale of shares | | Strong | | |
| Dilution through executive compensation | | Moderate | | |
| Freezeouts | Moderate | Strong | None | None |
| Sales of control | | | | |
| Insider trading | | Moderate | | |
| **Mixed forms of tunneling** | | | | |
| Loans to directors and exec. officers | Strong | n.a. | n.a. | n.a. |
| Loans to other insiders or related firms | Weak | Weak | None | Moderate |

areas, all constraints are weak. Notably weak areas include asset tunneling; cash flow tunneling through transfer pricing, and loans to insiders other than directors and officers.

Overall, the US legal constraints on tunneling glass can be described as a glass at best half-full.[49] Atanasov et al. (2011b) illustrate via case studies that the gaps in US self-dealing rules can be exploited in the real world. For an aggressive insider, who will take whatever tunneling opportunities the legal system offers, the menu is rich, even if not unlimited. If the US remains a mostly low-tunneling place, the explanation may owe much to constraints other than formal rules.[50]

At the same time, informal constraints can weaken over time. Executive compensation offers an example. Thirty years ago, no one worried much about the compensation of large firm CEOs. To become seriously rich, one had to found a firm, not merely run it. Today, many non-founder CEOs do get seriously rich, and there is general, albeit not universal concern that executives are overpaid and pay is often loosely tied to performance or to a competitive market for executive talent. The difference lies not in law – flabby then and only slightly less flabby now – but in norms (Crystal 1991; Bebchuk & Fried 2004; Jensen et al. 2004).

Table 22.1 provides a research agenda in two ways. First, we predict that the principal gaps in tunneling protection will be exploited – that real-world examples will be found to correspond to those gaps. Atanasov et al. (2011b) offer specific examples. Second, although the cell entries are US-specific, Table 22.1 offers a template for assessing tunneling protections in other countries. No country, we predict, will provide strong tunneling protection across the board. Some will do better than the US in particular areas. Their rules might offer guidance on what one might call 'best practices' in anti-tunneling rules.

## 4.   IMPLICATIONS FOR THE DESIGN AND ENFORCEMENT OF LAWS AGAINST SELF-DEALING

Our principal goal in this chapter is to highlight areas of comparative strength and weakness in the regulatory control of self-dealing. Proposing detailed reforms to address specific weaknesses is well beyond our scope. Still, we can offer some general observations and recommendations:

*Reduce legal and accounting arbitrage opportunities*: tunneling, by its nature, is a transfer of wealth across boundaries. One motive for tunneling is arbitrage created by wedges in the law. One (now fortunately past) motive for use of executive stock options was that they allowed off-income-statement compensation, because the options were treated as not involving compensation expense if granted with an exercise price equal to current share price. Executive stock options remain favored by the rules governing cash flow disclosure – the company's tax deduction when an option is exercised boosts cash flow from operations, while

---

[49]     Our assessment of US rules is far more detailed than, but consistent in spirit with, the conclusion by Spamann (2010) that the US scores only 2/5 on a corrected 'LLSV' (La Porta et al. 1998) anti-director rights index.

[50]     Black (2001b) discusses the role of a variety of legal and market institutions in constraining self-dealing. For optimistic assessments of the overall level of tunneling by controllers at US firms, compared to other countries, see Nenova (2003); Dyck & Zingales (2004). For evidence suggesting significant private benefits of control, see Barclay & Holderness (1989).

the share repurchases needed to offset share dilution from option issuance are considered cash flow from financing.

Asset tunneling is encouraged by the different treatment of the transaction by seller and buyer. Atanasov et al. (2011b) illustrate how Coca-Cola could report large profits by selling bottling plants and franchise rights to Coke Enterprises for well above their value on Coca-Cola's books. Yet there was no offsetting expense for Coke Enterprises, which recorded goodwill and other intangible assets for the purchase (goodwill was written off at the time over 15 years; today it is not written off at all unless materially impaired).

Executives who defer their compensation or pension income often earn above-market interest rates. The company records the expense over time, and *not* as a compensation expense. The true compensation is hidden, so use of this disguise is encouraged.

Harmonizing tax rules will reduce incentives for arbitrage. For example, one motive for cash movement is tax arbitrage – transferring profits to an entity (or individual) paying a lower tax rate. Once transferred, the profits may be vulnerable to tunneling. In general, a flatter tax with broader applicability reduces this motive.

*Shareholder power to approve or challenge self-dealing transactions*: US corporate law is director-centric. What the outside directors approve, the shareholders can rarely contest. Thus, if a tunneler's dealings are approved by a passive board, shareholders have few remedies. Perhaps we should rethink the degree to which corporate law protects self-dealing transactions, especially large ones, even when approved by outside directors. Ex-post judicial remedies are only one response to self-dealing. Ex ante approval of significant transactions, by a majority of non-conflicted shareholders, has promise as well. The recent Dodd-Frank 'say on pay' reform moves in this direction for executive compensation, albeit not very far.

*Disclosure of self-dealing transactions*: the analysis suggests that self-dealing is often not effectively disclosed. There is clear need for more complete disclosure, for a broader range of related-party asset sales and purchases. Ideally, this disclosure should be close to real time, to allow shareholders to challenge the transaction before it is completed. Above a threshold size, disclosure might include the pro forma impact of the transaction on the company's financial statements, similar to pro forma financial statements for acquisitions. At present, disclosure often appears in opaque footnotes, in the next annual report or proxy statement. Enron was not alone in ensuring that these disclosures conveyed little or no information to shareholders about its related party transactions.

*Gatekeeper review for fairness*: disclosure helps, but without more may not ensure fairness. Moreover, even with better disclosure, fairness may be hard for shareholders to assess. One approach to improving the fairness of self-dealing transactions would be to require a company's auditors, or another 'gatekeeper', to assess the fairness of the terms for any transaction over a threshold size (Black & Kraakman 1996). The assessment would become public in the next annual report. But the insiders, knowing it was coming, would want to obtain the auditors' approval in advance, when the terms are still malleable and could be adjusted to make the auditors comfortable.

Today, fairness opinions are sometimes laughably far from the truth. A touch of direct liability to minority shareholders would reduce this problem, though how much liability would be optimal is a hard problem that we do not reach here. So would having the gatekeeper chosen, say, by major shareholders, instead of the board – a strategy that might also address the pro-management bias of compensation consultants (Bebchuk & Fried 2004; Crystal 1991).

## 5.   SUMMARY AND FUTURE RESEARCH

This chapter unbundles self-dealing by focusing first on what is being taken – cash flow, assets, or equity – and second on the different sources of regulation that constrain self-dealing. The result is a more granular understanding of how insiders can extract wealth from firms, how different laws and regulations affect self-dealing; and the self-dealing opportunities that US laws leave open for insiders who are willing to bear the reputational cost. We identify a number of gaps in legal protections against self-dealing, and offer preliminary suggestions for reforms to address these gaps.

## REFERENCES

Akerlof, George A., Paul M. Romer, Robert E. Hall & N. Gregory Mankiw (1993), 'Looting: The Economic Underworld of Bankruptcy for Profit', *Brookings Papers on Economic Activity*, 1993(2), 1–73.

Allen, William T., Jack B. Jacobs & Leo Strine (2000), 'Function Over Form: A Reassessment of Standards of Review in Delaware Corporation Law', *Business Lawyer*, 56, 1287–1322.

Allen, William T., Reinier Kraakman & Guhan Subramanian (2009), *Commentaries and Cases on the Law of Business Organization*, 3rd ed., Netherlands: Walters Kluwer.

Armour, John, Bernard Black, Brian Cheffins & Richard Nolan (2009), 'Private Enforcement of Corporate Law: A Comparative Empirical Analysis of the UK and the US', *Journal of Empirical Legal Studies*, 6, 687–722.

Atanasov, Vladimir (2005), 'How Much Value Can Blockholders Tunnel? Evidence from the Bulgarian Mass Privatization Auctions', *Journal of Financial Economics*, 76, 191–234.

Atanasov, Vladimir & Eric O'Brien (2010), 'Is a CEO Worth Ten Percent of Net Cash Flow? Analysis of CEO Compensation at Nabors Industries', Working paper. College of William and Mary.

Atanasov, Vladimir, Bernard Black & Conrad Ciccotello (2009), 'Unbundling and Measuring Tunneling', Working Paper, available at http://ssrn/com/abstract=1030529 (last accessed October 2011).

Atanasov, Vladimir, Bernard Black, Conrad Ciccotello & Stanley Gyoshev (2010a), 'How Does Law Affect Finance: An Examination of Equity Tunneling in Bulgaria', *Journal of Financial Economics*, 96, 155–73.

Atanasov, Vladimir, Audra Boone, & David Haushalter (2010b), 'Is There Shareholder Expropriation in the U.S.? An Analysis of Publicly-traded Subsidiaries', *Journal of Financial and Quantitative Analysis*, 45, 1–26.

Atanasov, Vladimir, Vladimir Ivanov & Kate Litvak (2011a), 'Does Reputation Limit Opportunistic Behavior in the VC Industry? Evidence from Litigation against VCs', *Journal of Finance*, forthcoming.

Atanasov, Vladimir, Bernard Black & Conrad Ciccotello (2011b), 'Law and Tunneling', *Journal of Corporation Law* 37, 1–49, also available at http://ssrn/com/abstract=1444414 (last accessed October 2011).

Baek, Jae-Seung, Jun-Koo Kang & Inmoo Lee (2006), 'Business Groups and Tunneling: Evidence from Private Securities Offerings by Korean Chaebols', *Journal of Finance*, 61, 2415–49.

Bank, Steven & Brian R. Cheffins (2010), 'The Corporate Pyramid Fable', *Business History Review*, 84, 435–58.

Barak, Ronen & Beni Lauterbach (2007), 'Estimating the Private Benefits of Control from Block Trades: Methodology and Evidence', Working Paper, available at http://ssrn.com/abstract=965668 (last accessed October 2011).

Barclay, Michael J. & Clifford G. Holderness (1989), 'Private Benefits from Control of Public Corporations', *Journal of Financial Economics*, 25, 371–95.

Bates, Thomas W., Michael L. Lemmon & James S. Linck (2006), 'Shareholder Wealth Effects and Bid Negotiation in Freeze-Out Deals: Are Minority Shareholders Left Out in the Cold?', *Journal of Financial Economics*, 81, 681–706.

Bebchuk, Lucian, Reinier Kraakman & George Triantis (2000), 'Stock Pyramids, Cross Ownership, and Dual Class Equity: The Mechanisms and Agency Costs of Separating Control from Cash Flow Rights', in Randall Morck (ed.) *Concentrated Corporate Ownership*, National Bureau of Economic Research.

Bebchuk, Lucian & Jesse Fried (2004), *Pay Without Performance: The Unfulfilled Promise of Executive Compensation*, Cambridge, M.A.: Harvard University Press.

Beck, Thorsten, Asli Demirguc-Kunt & Ross Levine (2003a), 'Law, Endowments and Finance', *Journal of Financial Economics*, 70, 137–81.

Beck, Thorsten, Asli Demirguc-Kunt & Ross Levine (2003b),'Law and Finance: Why Does Legal Origin Matter?', *Journal of Comparative Economics*, 31, 653–75.

Beny, Laura Nyantung (2008), 'Do Investors in Controlled Firms Value Insider Trading Laws? International Evidence', *Journal of Law, Economics and Policy*, 4, 267–310.

Berkman, Henk, Rebel Cole & Jiang Fu (2007), 'Expropriation through Loan Guarantees to Related Parties: Evidence from China', Working Paper, available at http://ssrn.com/abstract=981285 (last accessed October 2011).

Berkowitz, Dan, Katharina Pistor & Jean-François Richard (2003), 'Economic Development, Legality, and the Transplant Effect', *European Economic Review*, 47, 165–95.

Bertrand, Marianne, Paras Mehta & Sendhil Mullainathan (2002), 'Ferreting Out Tunneling: An Application to Indian Business Groups', *Quarterly Journal of Economics*, 119, 121–48.

Bhattacharya, Utpal & Hazem Daouk (2002), 'The World Price of Insider Trading', *Journal of Finance*, 57, 75–108.

Bhattacharya, Utpal & Hazem Daouk, (2009), 'When No Law is Better than a Good Law', *Review of Finance*, 13, 577–627.

Black, Bernard (2001a), 'The Legal and Institutional Preconditions for Strong Securities Markets', *UCLA Law Review*, 48, 781–855.

Black, Bernard (2001b), 'The Corporate Governance Behavior and Market Value of Russian Firms', *Emerging Markets Review*, 2, 89–108.

Black, Bernard (2006), Expert Report, *In re Enron Securities Litigation*, available on Westlaw at 2006 WL 2432018 and on SSRN, available at http://ssrn.com/abstract=1528457 (last accessed October 2011).

Black, Bernard & Reinier Kraakman (1996), 'A Self-Enforcing Model of Corporate Law', *Harvard Law Review*, 109, 1911–82.

Black, Bernard, Reinier Kraakman & Anna Tarassova (2000), 'Russian Privatization and Corporate Governance: What Went Wrong?', *Stanford Law Review*, 52, 1731–1808.

Burkart, Mike, Dennis Gromb & Fausto Panunzi (1998), 'Why Higher Takeover Premia Protect Minority Shareholders', *Journal of Political Economy*, 106, 172–204.

Cai, Jie & Ralph A. Walkling (2011), 'Shareholders' Say on Pay: Does It Create Value?', *Journal of Financial and Quantitative Analysis*, forthcoming, at http://ssrn.com/abstract=1030925 (last accessed October 2011).

Chazan, Guy (2009), 'Russian Tycoon's Fall Spurs Money Hunt', *Wall Street Journal*, September 8.

Cheung, Yan-Leung, P. Raghavendra Rao & Aris Stouraitis (2006), 'Tunneling, Propping and Expropriation: Evidence from Connected Party Transactions in Hong Kong', *Journal of Financial Economics*, 82, 343–86.

Ciccotello, Conrad, C. Terry Grant & Gerry H. Grant (2004), 'Cash Flow Impacts of Employee Stock Options', *Financial Analysts' Journal*, 60, 39–46.

Crystal, Graef (1991), *In Search of Excess: The Overcompensation of American Executives*, New York, N.Y.: W.W. Norton & Co.

DeAngelo, Harry, Linda DeAngelo & Edward Rice (1984), 'Going private: Minority freezeouts and stockholder wealth', *Journal of Law and Economics*, 27, 367–401.

Demirguc-Kunt, Asli & Vojislav Maksimovic (1998), 'Law, Finance, and Firm Growth', *Journal of Finance*, 53, 2107–37.

Deng, Jianping, Jie Gan & Jia He (2007), 'Privatization, Large Shareholders' Incentive to Expropriate, and Firm Performance', Working Paper, available at http://ssrn.com/abstract=970056 (last accessed October 2011).

Desai, Mihir, I.J. Alexander Dyck & Luigi Zingales (2007), 'Theft and Taxes', *Journal of Financial Economics*, 84, 591–623.

Djankov, Simeon, Rafael La Porta, Florencio Lopes-de-Silanes & Andrei Shleifer (2006), 'The Law and Economics of Self-Dealing', Working Paper, available at http://ssrn.com/abstract=864645 (last accessed October 2011).

Dyck, I.J. Alexander & Luigi Zingales (2004), 'Private Benefits of Control: An International Comparison', *Journal of Finance*, 59, 537–600.

Ertimur, Yonca, Fabrizio Ferri & Volkan Muslu (2011), 'Shareholder Activism and CEO Pay', *Review of Financial Studies*, forthcoming, at http://ssrn.com/abstract=1443455 (last accessed October 2011).

Feng, Yi & Yisong Tian (2009), 'Options expensing and managerial equity incentives', *Financial Markets, Institutions and Instruments*, 18, 195–241.

Ferri, Fabrizio & David Maber (2010), 'Say on Pay Votes and CEO Compensation: Evidence from the UK', Working Paper, available at http://ssrn.com/abstract=1420394 (last accessed October 2011).

Fried, Jesse & Mira Ganor (2006), 'Agency Costs of Venture Capitalist Control in Startups', *New York University Law Review*, 81, 967–1025.

Friedman, Eric, Simon Johnson & Todd Mitton (2003), 'Propping and Tunneling', *Journal of Comparative Economics*, 31, 732–50.

Gilson, Ronald J. & Bernard S. Black (1995), *The Law and Finance of Corporate Acquisitions*, 2nd ed., Westbury, N.Y.: Foundation Press.

Gilson, Ronald J. & Jeffrey N. Gordon (2003), 'Controlling Controlling Shareholders', *University of Pennsylvania Law Review*, 152, 785–850.

Goetzmann, William N., Matthew Spiegel & Andrey Ukhov (2003), 'Modeling and Measuring Russian Corporate Governance: The Case of Russian Preferred and Common Shares', available at http://ssrn.com/abstract=305494 (last accessed October 2011).

Gordon, Elizabeth A., Elaine Henry & Darius Palia (2004), 'Related Party Transactions and Corporate Governance', *Advances in Financial Economics*, 9, 1–27.

Gordon, Jeffrey (2009), '"Say on Pay": Cautionary Notes on the UK Experience and the Case for Shareholder Opt-In', Working Paper, available at http://ssrn.com/abstract=1262867 (last accessed October 2011).

Harvey, Campbell R., Karl V. Lins & Andrew H, Roper (2004), 'The Effect of Capital Structure When Agency Costs are Extreme', *Journal of Financial Economics*, 74, 3–30.

Heron, Randall A. & Erik Lie (2007), 'Does Backdating Explain the Stock Price Pattern Around Executive Stock Option Grants?', *Journal of Financial Economics*, 83, 271–95.

Jagolinzer, Alan D. (2009), 'SEC Rule 10b5-1 and Insiders' Strategic Trade', *Management Science*, 55, 224–39.

Jensen, Michael C., Kevin J. Murphy & Eric G. Wruck (2004), 'Remuneration: Where We've Been, How We Got to Here, What are the Problems, and How to Fix Them', Working Paper, available at http://ssrn.com/abstract=561305 (last accessed October 2011).

Jiang, Guohua, Charles M.C. Lee & Heng Yue (2010), 'Tunneling through Intercorporate Loans: The China Experience', *Journal of Financial Economics*, 98, 1–20.

John, Kose & Lubomir Litov (2009), 'Corporate Governance and Financial Policy', Working Paper, available at http://ssrn.com/abstract=637341 (last accessed October 2011).

Johnson, Simon, Rafael La Porta, Florencio Lopez-de-Silanes & Andrei Shleifer (2000), 'Tunneling', *American Economic Review*, 90, 22–7.

Kraakman, Reinier, John Armour, Paul Davies, Luca Enriques, Henry Hansmann, Gerard Hertig, Klaus Hopt, Hideki Kanda & Edward Rock (2009), *The Anatomy of Corporate Law: A Comparative and Functional Approach*, New York, N.Y.: Oxford University Press.

Lambert-Mogilansky, Ariane, Constantin Sonin & Ekaterina Zhuravskaya (2003), 'Capture of Bankruptcy: Theory and Russian Evidence', Working Paper, Center for Economic and Financial Research.

Landsman, Wayne R., Ken V. Peasnell, Peter F. Pope & Shu Yeh (2006), 'Which Approach to Accounting for Employee Stock Options Best Reflects Market Pricing?', *Review of Accounting Studies*, 11, 203–45.

La Porta, Rafael, Florencio Lopez-de-Silanes, Andrei Shleifer & Robert Vishny (1997), 'Legal Determinants of External Finance', *Journal of Finance*, 52, 1131–50.

La Porta, Rafael, Florencio Lopez-de-Silanes, Andrei Shleifer & Robert Vishny (1998), 'Law and Finance', *Journal of Political Economy*, 106, 1113–55.

La Porta, Rafael, Florencio Lopez-de-Silanes, Andrei Shleifer & Robert Vishny (2002), 'Investor Protection and Corporate Valuation', *Journal of Finance*, 57, 1147–70.

La Porta, Rafael, Florencio Lopez-de-Silanes & Andrei Shleifer (2006), 'What Works in Securities Laws?', *Journal of Finance*, 60, 1–32.

Levine, Ross (1998), 'The Legal Environment, Banks, and Long-Run Economic Growth', *Journal of Money, Credit & Banking*, 30, 596–613.

Levine, Ross (1999), 'Law, Finance, and Economic Growth', *Journal of Financial Intermediation*, 8, 8–35.

Marsh, Harold, Jr. (1966), 'Are Directors Trustees? Conflict of Interest and Corporate Morality', *Business Lawyer*, 22, 35–76.

Maug, Ernst (2006), 'Efficiency and Fairness in Minority Freezeouts: Takeovers, Overbidding, and the Freeze-in Problem', *International Review of Law and Economics*, 26, 355–79.

Ming, Jian Jane & T.J. Wong (2003), 'Earnings Management and Tunneling through Related Party Transactions: Evidence from Chinese Corporate Groups', Working Paper, Nanyang Technological University.

Morck, Randall (2004), 'How to Eliminate Pyramidal Business Groups – The Double Taxation of Inter-Corporate Dividends & Other Incisive Uses of Tax Policy', in James Poterba (ed.) *Tax Policy & the Economy*, National Bureau of Economic Research, 19.

Morck, Randall & Masao Nakamura (2007), 'Business Groups and the Big Push: Meiji Japan's Mass Privatization and Subsequent Growth', Working Paper, available at http://ssrn.com/abstract=989883 (last accessed October 2011).

Nenova, Tatiana (2003), 'The Value of Corporate Votes and Control Benefits: A Cross-Country Analysis', *Journal of Financial Economics*, 68, 325–51.

O'Neil, F. Hodge & Robert P. Thompson (2004), *Oppression of Minority Shareholders and LLC Members*, 2nd ed., St. Paul, M.N.: Thomson-West.

Rock, Edward L. (1997), 'Saints and Sinners: How Does Delaware Corporate Law Work?', *UCLA Law Review*, 44, 1009–1107.

Roe, Mark (2006), 'Legal Origins and Modern Stock Markets', *Harvard Law Review*, 120, 460–527.

Solomon, Deborah & Jared Sandberg (2002), 'Leading the News', *Wall Street Journal*, November 6.

Spamann, Holger (2010), 'The "Antidirector Rights Index" Revisited', *Review of Financial Studies*, 23, 467–86.

Subramanian, Guhan (2007), 'Post-Siliconix Freeze-Outs: Theory and Evidence', *Journal of Legal Studies*, 36, 1–26.

Teoh, Siew Hong, T.J. Wong & Gita Rao (1998a), 'Are accruals during initial public offerings opportunistic?', *Review of Accounting Studies*, 3, 175–208.

Teoh, Siew Hong, Iwo Welch, I. & T.J. Wong (1998b), 'Earnings management and the long-run underperformance of initial public offerings', *Journal of Finance*, 53, 1935–74.

# 23. Behavioral approaches to corporate law
### *Donald C. Langevoort*

## 1.  INTRODUCTION

In corporate legal scholarship, 'behavioral' analysis refers to using insights from psychology to address the relationships, rights and responsibilities among officers, directors, investors and other stakeholders. That does not make it a particularly well-defined subject. Psychology is a capacious field, running from the brain studies done by cognitive neuroscientists to the observations of interpersonal interactions in social cognition and social psychology laboratory experiments, the latter then bleeding into the separate field-study oriented research programs of sociology and cultural anthropology. In all these, there is so much – perhaps too much – for legal scholars to think about as potentially useful behavioral traits. Fortunately, researchers in business schools have for some time been using psychology as a tool for research specifically directed to organizational behavior and corporate governance, thereby giving legal scholars help in making connections of particular use to the analysis of corporate law-related issues (Camerer & Malmendier 2007).

My contribution reflects on the challenges of making these connections and some of the successes that have occurred so far. I make no effort to provide a thorough literature review – the number of published articles and works in progress that plausibly fall into the 'behavioral corporate law' category is sizable, and grows rapidly each year. The amount of contemporary scholarship in business, finance and economics that turns to psychology for insight relating to business institutions, from which legal research can then draw, is much larger.

What I want to outline here is an approach to using psychology for corporate legal analysis that addresses the obvious question: if persons (and presumably firms) are capable of acting rationally and have strong market-driven incentives to do so, why will that not drive out the irrational from having influence in a competitive marketplace? A plausible answer comes only if agents simply cannot act more rationally than their competitors or – more likely, in my view – there is something competitively adaptive about the particular heuristic or bias in question in business settings (which, of course, makes it unwise to label it 'irrational'). After exploring this question generally, I will turn to two subject areas to which behavioral corporate law scholarship has paid particular attention – the group behavior of corporate boards of directors, and the so-called 'inefficient markets' hypothesis that is the subject of modern behavioral finance. I conclude by briefly considering the relationship between psychology and culture, extending the approach put forth here to the place of corporate culture in legal analysis.

## 2.  THE BEHAVIORAL TURN

The 'behavioral' move in corporate and securities law scholarship is largely critical and reactive. Beginning largely with the seminal work of Henry Manne (1966) and continuing through a scholarly revolution in the 1970s that to this day still frames the scholarly enterprise of corporate legal research, the methodological assumptions of orthodox financial economics – individual rationality and market efficiency – came to dominate. This led to conclusions that, more often than not, criticized existing legal constraints as unnecessary or inefficient, and offered a deregulatory normative agenda in place of the legal status quo.

Critics of extensive reliance on these methodological assumptions, in corporate law and elsewhere, naturally turned to psychology to take aim at the rational actor paradigm. If people often predictably behave irrationally, then maybe these strongly deregulatory normative conclusions are unfounded. From the outset, however, this effort had trouble gaining traction because of a fairly obvious set of problems, with which the behavioral approach has struggled ever since. So-called 'irrationality' (or even bounded rationality) is hardly automatic or universal – the evidence we observe in the laboratory and the field varies considerably among the population, is highly situational and contingent, and institutionally constrained. That is to say, we observe a variable mix of rationality and suboptimal judgment and decision-making in our society and economy. And thus the orthodox economists can readily concede the irrationality of some people without in any way jeopardizing the basics conclusions of financial economics. Competitive markets reward rationality and penalize irrationality, they say, so that the cognitively weak should disappear from significance and institutions should develop to protect against bias. So long as arbitrage is possible in market settings, moreover, irrationality will not generate even short-term distortions, because any irrational price movements will immediately be exploited by the rational behavior of the so-called smart money, driving the price back to the rational expectations value. Richard Posner (1998), Roberta Romano (1986) and others have famously doubted the value of behavioral economics in business settings on grounds like these.

They are right to a point. For example, consider the challenge faced by an academic who wants to claim that because of some predictable behavioral or cognitive biases familiar in the psychology literature, corporate chief financial officers are likely to act in a certain legally problematic fashion. For this inference to be well-grounded, at least each of the following would have to be true:

(1)   the bias in question would have to be shown by researchers to be a commonly occurring phenomenon in the general population (not just an artifact of experimental design);
(2)   people who become CFOs would have to be at least as prone to the bias in question as the population that was studied in the experimental setting;
(3)   to the extent that the bias in question is situational or contingent, the setting in which the CFO makes the decisions would have to generate the right kinds of triggers;
(4)   the setting would not involve the kind of repeat play from which the CFO (maybe before she took on that role) would learn from experience so as to avoid these biases; and
(5)   the institutional environment in which these decisions are made would contain no 'debiasing' constraints, such as off-setting contractual incentives, peer review, external monitoring or structured group deliberation.

Usually, this will be hard to show. Among other things, CFOs – or CEOs, board members, portfolio managers, etc. – are not randomly drawn from the general population. Rather, they are survivors of high pressure employment and promotion tournaments that almost always took a significant degree of cognitive skill to win. Unless there is reason to believe that irrational bias could survive such a tournament, its presence among decision-makers at the top cannot be presumed. Moreover, the institutional incentive for firms to de-bias is well-recognized, as is the ability of institutional context to cue the pursuit of rational self-interest (Heath 1998; Arlen et al. 2002).

An inference of bias is questionable, then, but by no means impossible. There likely are cognitive biases that are adaptive enough in competitive settings to survive. For example, overconfidence and mildly inflated self-esteem (ego) are associated with greater risk tolerance, ambition, persistence and a host of other useful traits in a business environment (Goel & Thakor 2008; Malmendier & Tate 2008a, 2008b; Langevoort 1997). Here we see the interaction between luck and skill that is so important in psychology (fundamental attribution error, etc.) – many high-achieving individuals over-attribute success to skill, and put out of mind the situational randomness that sometimes generates good fortune. The over-confident may 'play' harder and more aggressively, producing more extreme positive and negative outcomes. Those lucky enough to get the positive outcome may play even harder and more aggressively the next round. If there are enough players in the tournament, there will be a lucky few who are rewarded repeatedly, more than their more realistic, conservative peers. So overconfidence could be highly adaptive, and if so we might expect CEOs to exhibit that particular bias (though whether that bias would persist after they have won the tournament and now are motivated to protect their status is itself open to question). We can imagine other adaptive traits as well. For example, the sunk cost bias – investing 'irrationally' after an earlier commitment to a choice – may relate closely enough to valued, observable consistency traits that it survives in repeat play. Or 'quick and dirty' heuristics that lead to good choices most of the time will produce quicker, more nimble behavior compared to the manager who (realistically) worries at length through every problem (Gigerenzer & Selten 2001).

To know whether cognitive and behavioral biases do affect judgment and decision-making in business settings, then, we cannot simply point to the existence of the bias in the general population and then assume that it automatically applies to any given business context – on the other hand, nor can we rule out its presence simply because of the marketplace. Fortunately, behavioral researchers in business schools have made substantial progress in addressing the problem through a number of strategies. One is to use experienced business people as subjects in laboratory experiments, to test for persistent 'expert' biases. Another is the increasing use of field studies looking at real decisions in economic settings (DellaVigna 2009). If we find on-the-ground evidence of suboptimal choice, researchers can then try to match the observations with theories of bias to find the best fit.

We can illustrate both the promise and challenges of using insights from psychology in corporate and securities law by looking at a recent legal controversy: the behavior of sell-side securities analysts, who advise brokerage firm customers and others about investment opportunities (Fisch & Sale 2003). Well before the scandals of the early 2000s, financial economists had found evidence that favorable recommendations significantly outnumbered unfavorable ones, especially with respect to issuers who were or might become investment banking clients of the analysts' employer. The standard economic account was one of deliberate skewing of recommendations because of the conflict of interest, which became the regulator's charge as well, and the basis for subsequent regulatory reform.

A competing explanation, however, is behavioral: that analysts with a good faith optimistic bias (i.e., true-believers, say, in the future of a particular technology in which the issuers they cover are heavily invested) are favored for a variety of reasons. For instance, issuers prefer them and thus provide them with superior access to information; they generate more retail commission business because of their infectious enthusiasm; they are willing to take greater risks in their recommendations and hence gain the halo of positive association for major strokes of luck, etc. The conflict of interest is not irrelevant, because it is part of the institutional environment that causes the optimists to be so favored. But the process by which the optimists thrive is natural selection, not (necessarily) savvy opportunism.

Economists might ask: so what? Outcomes are important, not motivations, and the outcomes arguably appear consistent with rational choice. But in the law, state of mind is usually crucial, with the standard varying depending on the legal rule invoked. Reliance on fraud-based prohibitions – as federal regulators did in the analyst cases – would be ineffective as applied to the true optimists. On the other hand, there would be the risk of unfair liability under a *scienter*-based regime if judges and juries disbelieve their good faith defenses based on a naively cynical assessment of their motivations. The difference would also be important in fashioning cures for the bias. For example, a certification that the analyst is being honest in her recommendation – as now required by SEC Regulation A-C – might work with respect to deliberate bias but be largely meaningless with respect to those simply prone to over-optimism.

One of the 'cures' for analyst bias – extended to many other settings as well as a result of recurrent financial scandals – is strengthened disclosure of conflicts of interest. Will this work? An interesting finding from psychological research is that persons who disclose conflicts may actually feel freer to act selfishly, because the disclosure gives them moral license by warning the counterparties of the risk (Cain et al. 2005). On the other hand, subsequent research has pointed out that in laboratory settings where there is repeat play and hence greater opportunities for those hurt by the selfishness to punish it later on, the opportunism diminishes (Church & Kuang 2009; Koch & Schmidt 2010). Given the stress placed in corporate and securities law on disclosure, understanding this dynamic more fully seems crucial to developing a coherent regulatory response to the problems of pervasive conflicts not only on the part of analysts but of many different kinds of economic actors.

All this, of course, simply emphasizes the need for corporate legal scholars to build their normative arguments on a solid base of empirical observation – preferably in the field – rather than simple borrowing from laboratory research in psychology generally. When some form of suboptimal decision-making is identified in practice, then the task turns to explaining why. As in the analyst context, it will often be the case that multiple behavioral and rational (e.g., agency cost) explanations are plausible, and again, it may be tempting to choose the more parsimonious rational explanation for purposes of legal analysis. But even putting aside the importance of inquiry into state of mind as a matter of law within that analysis, this can be dangerous. Imagine that we estimated that the likelihood of the behavioral effect being important is only 25%. If the regulatory intervention would fail because it ignores that effect even in a relatively small number of instances, the aggregate cost – the legal risk – might still be material. Simply assuming rationality because that is the best available description of behavior ignores the ecological diversity of outcomes in judgment and decision-making in social and economic settings, and hence the risk embedded in the broad societal 'portfolio' of choices.

## 3.   CORPORATE BOARDS: LOYALTY AND 'STRUCTURAL BIAS'

As modern corporate law developed, it has emphasized the adequacy of decision-making process over review of substantive outcomes. This is a natural response to the diversity of situations that challenge a corporate entity at any given time, and the need for flexibility, risk taking, etc., as well as the institutional incapacity of courts to second-guess business decisions particularly well. By and large, except in the case of the most severe conflicts, the key has been 'independence' (or 'disinterestedness') – so long as a sufficiently independent decision-maker within the approved corporate hierarchy has been given all the material facts and approved some action after due deliberation, the action is beyond serious judicial review. To this end, many contemporary corporate governance initiatives under both federal and state law seek to force greater independent director involvement at key decision points, and ex post judicial inquiry into independence can sometimes be quite robust.

Independence, however, is a fuzzy concept, and the temptation has long been to objectify the legal standard – independence is simply the absence of a certain level of self-interest in the outcome of the decision itself. To be sure, such an interest can take any number of forms but it remains focused largely on status or financial interest. This led to an outpouring of criticism from legal scholars using psychology research to call into question whether standards so based can reasonably assure the kind of objectivity that eliminates the need for judicial review of sensitive corporate decisions. The classic work by James Cox and Harvey Munsinger (1984) on judicial review of special litigation committee decisions recommending termination of a derivative lawsuit because of 'structural bias' was particularly influential, at least in academic circles (see also Hill & McDonnell 2007). Others are more willing to accept the desirability (or inevitability) of limited judicial review but then push for structural corporate governance reforms to create a better chance of independence ex ante. These, too, often invoke something from the psychology literature as justification.

An interesting example of the latter is the argument by Randall Morck (2008) in favor of separating the chair and CEO functions in corporate governance. His claim is that directors are psychologically susceptible to the kind of 'obedience' commands – submission to authority – demonstrated in the classic social psychology experiments by Stanley Milgram (1974). Hence the excessive deference to CEO influence, which could be counterbalanced by introducing a separate, equal authority figure in the person of the non-executive board chair.

This is a nice illustration of both the potential benefits and the challenges associated with psychology-based analysis of corporate legal issues. The Milgram results have been widely replicated, and are robust to a number of modifications to the original experimental design. But does the relationship between a CEO and other board members resemble closely enough the relationship between the 'teacher' and the experimental subjects? After all, especially in larger companies, independent board members are recruited based on their prior history of success in other endeavors, and are likely to be high-status, high self-esteem individuals. That they are prone simply to do what they are told by the CEO is doubtful.

Morck does offer some other psychological tendencies that might reinforce the deference to insider authority. For example, the inclination toward reciprocity might cause board members to defer – consciously or not – out of gratitude for the invitation to join the board and the perquisites of membership. Or in-group/out-group biases might cause board members to reject externally generated threats directed at others on the board 'team', especially if the board has developed a fairly close working relationship. These are somewhat more plausible as an explanation for excessive deference, but still seem incomplete: after all, we know that deference has its limits (boards do challenge and fire CEOs with increasing frequency) and these tendencies would not have much explanatory power as to the circumstances under which deference diminishes.

There is probably a deeper, more subtle cognitive dimension to excessive deference (see, e.g., Langevoort 2004). Businesses tend to be very complex, opaque and dynamic. The task of understanding any business deeply is perhaps beyond any person's capacity, even the company's senior executives. Outside directors come to the task with woefully little information of their own, and are highly dependent on a combination of reports generated (and controlled) by insiders and external cues such as press coverage and stock prices. This profound ambiguity suggests that key decisions – is the CEO doing a good job, how much should we pay her, etc. – will be made without a high degree of confidence, which leads naturally toward preserving the status quo. Absent real evidence of a problem, no director wants to throw a monkey wrench into the functioning corporate machinery where raising issues (for example, suggesting a leadership change or calling into question some corporate investment) might end up hurting rather than helping – nor does he or she want to display embarrassing ignorance by entering into a losing argument with someone far more familiar with the facts on the ground.

Other psychological tendencies can bolster this. When nothing is said or done to question some course of action, it becomes even harder to change later on. Commitment and sunk cost biases (cognitive dissonance, perhaps) make it hard to perceive or acknowledge that there is enough different to justify a reversal. And if individuals stay silent as a result, others on the board can easily interpret the silence as a signal that nothing is amiss, amplifying the status quo bias through a form of social proof. At the group level, this may take on the familiar form of 'groupthink' (Benabou 2009; O'Connor 2003). And to the extent that independent directors are drawn from the ranks of either current or former business executives, their natural frame is to see things in ways sympathetic to the challenges facing management (Hill & McDonnell 2007).

My point is simply that evidence of excessive deference is not necessarily the product of motivational influences like submission to authority or excessive loyalty. And this is important when we turn to proposed cures like separating the roles of CEO and board chair. Simply introducing a competing authority figure in the board setting does little to remedy information deficits or resolve ambiguity, unless that role is substantially empowered with full-time staff and other forms of support – which is bound to introduce a very different dynamic, and not necessarily in the direction of greater operational efficiency.

Morck acknowledges that the empirical evidence has not demonstrated any clear-cut benefits to separating the roles of CEO and board chair, which casts doubt on the simple Milgram hypothesis. His main interpretation, however, is that the authority of the CEO is too strong to be countered by simple separation, and that additional steps may be needed, like giving institutional shareholders greater nominating and election rights so as to create a more direct line of responsibility between independent board members and their constituents. While that may or may not be wise for a variety of other reasons, more powerful shareholder suffrage offers no solution to the informational problem, and might bring into the boardroom different heuristics, but not necessarily better ones. If – as many commentators have suggested – independent directors are particularly influenced by the stock price as the best test of managerial performance, then we might find greater pressure to do what the market values as opposed to what the company's own private stock of information would suggest. Or we might see more mimetic behavior as management fads and fashions spread through the empowered director community. Morck notes these risks, but suggests that this is the only way to stimulate open debate and questioning in the face of the CEO's overwhelming psychological authority.

While I am convinced that excessive deference at the board level is less about loyalty and subservience than many think, I think we may understate their significance as applied to executive behavior. To be sure, Milgram-like submission can readily be expected among subordinates in the corporate hierarchy. Key to the development of a strong, positive corporate culture is a willingness to sacrifice for the good of the team. Strong leaders build such teamwork by modeling the behavior themselves, and one can reasonably suspect that the best leaders take on the ethic of group care fairly naturally. To be sure, they may demand the outsized compensation package at a rate suitable for being the 'boss', but accepting that their loyalty must be commensurate.

In law, we are used to thinking about CEOs as self-aggrandizers, and hence the duty of loyalty is generally thought of in terms of conflicts between personal utility and shareholder wealth. It would not surprise me, however, if loyalty to other members of the team – fellow executives, valued assistants, and the like – was a strong driver of senior executive behavior. One of the important puzzles in corporate and securities law is why executives so often lie, putting at risk their reputations, wealth and sometimes, freedom. No doubt there are many possible explanations, but one could well be a willingness to 'take one for the team', trying to save the organization from competitive failure even if it takes violating the law to do so. Imagine, for example, Ken Lay of Enron, convicted of lying during the last stages of the company's deceptions when he returned to the role of CEO after some time away. By all accounts, the bulk of the fraud was engineered by others, mostly during Lay's absence. So assuming upon his return he discovered the fully contrived fraud, why not blow the whistle on it? My sense is that strong multi-directional loyalty is a big part of the explanation, because blowing the whistle would cause immediate and catastrophic harm to many people inside the corporate family, many of whom were not particularly guilty of any wrongdoing, and who had been very loyal to him. To avoid this harm to others, he might have been willing to try to continue the deception long enough to extract the company from it, at considerable personal risk.

A deeper understanding of loyalty inside the corporation is important for corporate law. If there are pathologies of loyalty, this would be important to the design of internal controls, which use motivational assessments as indicators for where resources are most needed. More generally from an academic perspective, it raises an interesting and underappreciated point about human behavior in economic settings: that some of what we regard as troubling conduct in terms of harm to certain stakeholders (e.g., harm to investors) is often other-regarding behavior vis-à-vis a different set of stakeholders. And that other-regarding behavior – organizational loyalty – is very functional and valuable most of the time, even for investors. Like intra-organizational trust (see Hill & O'Hara 2007), it is not something that investors should want to diminish appreciably, even if it has its risks.

## 4.   BEHAVIORAL FINANCE AND INVESTOR PSYCHOLOGY

The academic subspecialty of behavioral finance uses insights from cognitive and social psychology to analyze the behavior of investors, both in terms of individual investor decision-making and price formation in organized markets as a result of the interaction among many investors. The latter field responds to the prevalent assumption throughout most of the last four decades that organized markets are efficient, i.e., that stock prices are an unbiased estimate of value into which new information is promptly impounded. The empirical evidence about stock prices does not fit this paradigm particularly well, leading many financial economists to try to explain regularities in price movements, like momentum effects and investor over-reaction or under-reaction to particular kinds of news, by reference to psychological heuristics and biases (Baker et al. 2007). This effort relates back to Keynes' famous assumption that 'animal spirits' are deeply at work in the securities markets, which has become a well-worn cultural trope (Langevoort 2002). 'Noise trading' is the preferred description of non-rational activity that has the potential to affect market prices.[1]

Economists' work in behavioral finance divides into two main branches. One takes investor sentiment as an important driver of stock market prices, which rational managers exploit by timing important corporate transactions (issuances of new securities, repurchases, corporate takeovers) strategically. The other considers the possibility that managers are biased as well, so that investor and executive biases interact.

Given the role that market prices and efficiency-based theories have played in corporate law and economics over the last decades, this is an important body of research for corporate legal scholars. As Reinier Kraakman (1988) noted some time ago, optimal legal policy toward corporate takeovers rests heavily on one's assessment of whether a takeover bid necessarily rests on the bidder's (presumably rational) belief that it can add value to the target, thereby justifying the premium, or whether instead the bidder may simply be 'cherry-picking' a sentiment-driven drop in market value. Using market price as the best measure of managerial performance becomes increasingly risky as doubts about efficiency grow. The financial scandals – Enron and Worldcom in the early 2000s, in financial services more recently – have fueled fears that market prices can become a dangerous obsession, which the law should lean against (Stout 2003).

Behavioral finance needs to be used gingerly, because it remains a controversial subject and has not generated a tractable model of stock price behavior to substitute for the efficient market hypothesis. The general evolution of financial markets may well be toward efficiency, even if imperfections are readily observable right now, and the point is often made that behavioralists have not yet found investment strategies that produce supra-normal returns on a sustained basis. Normatively, it is not altogether clear that the presence of noise traders is problematic – they may simply be providing the liquidity that justifies investment by the smart money into the research that, in turn, moves stock prices toward more efficient levels. Moreover, the kinds of policy moves that seem logical as faith in markets prices diminishes – especially greater regulatory intervention – turn on the question of whether regulators are any less subject to cognitive bias or otherwise capable of improving on market-based results, even assuming the market is prone to mood swings.

Since the 1980s, corporate legal scholars have struggled with how to deal with empirical doubts about the strength of market efficiency. The obvious and important line of work is to identify those places in law or legal scholarship where efficiency has strongly been assumed,

---

[1]    For further discussion of behavioral finance in this volume, see Cunningham (Ch. 16) and Gilson and Kraakman (Ch. 24).

and show the risks associated with implementing legal norms that depend on the accuracy of that assumption and the consequences if that assumption is indeed misplaced. However, at least in law (as opposed to scholarship), strong claims of market efficiency are not necessarily essential to many of the rules that invoke the rhetoric of efficiency.

A good example of this – generating a great deal of unnecessary confusion in both law and scholarship – involves fraud-on-the-market litigation under the federal securities laws. Famously, in *Basic Inc. v. Levinson* (1988),[2] the Supreme Court embraced market efficiency in recognizing a presumption of reliance on market price integrity (and in dissent, Justice White criticized the embrace as too passionate given the lingering empirical doubts). Though seen today largely as a generous gift by the Court to private investor plaintiffs and their lawyers, that presumption was strongly urged at the time by notable conservatives, particularly Frank Easterbrook and Dan Fischel (1985). They strongly believed that markets were efficient, and that by making market price distortion the test for materiality, reliance and causation in these lawsuits – measured by econometric evidence – greater rigor and discipline would be imposed on this otherwise unruly litigation.

As a result, courts after *Basic* gradually came to assume that the presumption of reliance could only be justified if the market was in fact efficient (Langevoort 2009). So, as doubts about efficiency grew in the behavioral finance literature (Brav & Heaton 2003) and were voiced in the course of litigation by expert witnesses, courts began more aggressively to dismiss cases where efficiency was seriously put into question (i.e., for less widely traded securities). And they were forced to confront troubling questions about apparent inefficiencies even with respect to the biggest blue chip issuers. In the legal academic literature, more and more scholars invoked the behavioral finance research to suggest the need for a fundamental rethinking – if not outright abolition – of the fraud on the market presumption.

Given the language and reasoning in *Basic* and its progeny, this move seems to make sense. But if we think harder about the question, it is far from clear that it should. The presumption of reliance is essentially the creation of an entitlement to rely on the integrity of a stock's price even when any reasonable investor would have to admit that prices lack integrity with enough frequency that simply assuming integrity is foolish. Like the common law of fraud, it facilitates reliance and thus promotes capital formation by lowering the risk of investing. Nothing in that idea requires any assumption about market price, and it would be as well justified as applied to a relatively unknown mid-cap issuer as a blue chip stock.

The connection to market efficiency here is simply that the primary econometric tool used to test for and measure marketplace distortions – the event study, measuring the abnormal returns in the aftermath of corrective disclosure by the issuer – derives its power and elegance from assumptions about efficiency. But as Macey et al. (1991) showed in an important article shortly after *Basic*, the event study has sufficient power even when a market is well short of ideal. The level of confidence diminishes as volatility increases, but not so much as to render the event study unusable to make probabilistic assessments, and many kinds of fraud will generate dramatic enough price distortions that there simply is no close question at all. As they conclude, the fraud on the market suit need not strictly be limited at all to those markets that evidence very high levels of efficiency.

---

2   *Basic Inc. v. Levinson*, 485 U.S. 224 (1988).

So why has the law (and the academic literature) so confidently marched in the other direction? An important shift in thinking about the fraud on the market lawsuit has been toward doubting its efficacy, because of concerns about the incentives of plaintiffs' attorneys as well as the frustrations about the costs of litigation. Other countries – gaining competitively on the United States in capital markets activity – have nothing comparable as a compensatory vehicle, raising further questions about the balance of costs and benefits. In this setting, judicial and academic doubts about the efficacy of private securities litigation make it tempting to seize on questions about efficiency as a reason to resolve disputes against plaintiffs. Efficiency itself is neither necessary nor sufficient to this analysis, but offers rhetorical camouflage given its starring role in *Basic*.

My sense is that strong assumptions about marketplace efficiency in the law are often more about rent-seeking than empiricism. In the aftermath of the financial crisis that began in 2007, much has been said about the 'error' of thinking that markets were sufficiently self-disciplining and self-correcting that the regulation of financial institutions could take on a fairly light touch. But aside from some academic literature, it is far from clear how much policy was based on a bona fide belief in that. Mainstream work in financial economics, especially of the new institutional variety, has for some time emphasized informational imperfections, agency costs and moral hazards that interfere with optimal outcomes as measured in terms of either shareholder or societal interests. The behavioral literature added other reasons for skepticism. Bubbles, crashes and scandals repeatedly in the last two decades offered ample evidence of marketplace shortcomings. In the face of all this, such a bona fide belief would be naïve.

More likely, the rhetoric of the self-disciplining market was simply intended for external consumption as a means for achieving the preferred deregulatory outcome. One form of this is pure rent-seeking, but it need not be only that. Those with a bona fide skepticism of government intervention in markets have the incentive to overstate the market's capacity for self-cleansing – and to deny the human imperfections embedded in markets – to counter or diffuse political demands for heavier regulation. Perhaps they repeated it so much that they came to believe their own rhetoric, but my guess is that few proponents of deregulation seriously thought that markets work quite so perfectly.

The financial crisis should thus offer a boost to behavioral corporate and securities law. Understanding with greater precision why markets, firms and individuals made risky choices that they came to regret is the task at hand. As just suggested, many of the possible answers have nothing to do with psychology – these could have been rational choices (though perhaps self-serving ones for firm agents) under conditions of severe informational ambiguity. But behavioral explanations are likely candidates as well (Avgouleas 2009; Miller & Rosenfeld 2010; but see Posner 2009).

For example, investor sentiment might well have favored market leadership in the emerging 'shadow banking' sector and portfolio managers might have been reluctant to bet against that sentiment continuing, reducing the amount of arbitrage activity. Inside the firms, the kinds of biases discussed earlier (over-optimism, etc.) could have paid off handsomely in the short run, leading to the promotion of the more biased compared to the less, with an obvious effect on the internal culture. This is important, of course, because competition is so central to corporate economic activity, and by most accounts, increasing in most industries because of technology, globalization and the like. If competition induces – or favors – a particular mindset, producing judgment at odds with dispassionate rationality, then the law's efforts to respond with a fine-tuned set of rational incentives or disincentives will surely miss the mark. Nor will it be particularly easy to intervene by shifting greater responsibility to third-party actors (e.g., directors on an audit committee, accountants, lawyers), even though the benefits of involvement in risky decisions by the non-euphoric seem clear. There will be disagreement about the perception of risk that will turn conversations into power struggles, and unless the third-party actors have sufficient information at their disposal to hold their own in that struggle, the risk-seeking culture is likely to prevail in those struggles. The challenge for the law – and for the institutions of corporate governance – is to find steps toward detoxification without disabling the firm in the process.

## 5.   FROM PSYCHOLOGY TO CULTURE

Behavioral corporate law scholarship is generally viewed in distinction to the corporate law scholarship that uses the assumptions of conventional economic analysis. But a separate challenge comes from sociology, where there has been a long-standing skepticism about the methodological individualism in both psychology and economics. This is especially so when the subject of analysis is institutional. Thus, in management studies, there is a strong view of organizational behavior that rejects any substantial focus on individual actors, instead attending to the diffusion of norms and perceptions inside the firm as a matter of social construction (Weick 1995; Brown 1997). This critique is often anti-functionalist, rejecting the idea – dear to economists both orthodox and behavioral – that heuristics and norms develop and persist only to the extent that they serve a useful purpose.

As always, this controversy can be judged only by reference to empirical observation. My suspicion is that the economists have the better of the argument – it is hard to look at a successful business firm and believe that all is just myth, ceremony and mimetic diffusion of randomly generated beliefs – but that debate is beyond the scope of this chapter. What corporate legal scholars should find interesting and useful is that social constructs like culture can be examined through the lens of behavioral (as well as orthodox) economics in ways that respond to the sociologists' complaint about excessive individualism, while at the same time remaining faithful to a functionalist perspective. An important example of this, noted earlier, is the analysis by Akerlof and Kranton (2005) of organizational cultures that stress extreme loyalty, e.g., the US Marine Corps, showing that by conferring a strong sense of identity, such cultures are functional mechanisms for overcoming the temptation to defect in the face of danger, which is essential for group survival.

By and large, studies of organizational culture are about sense-making in the face of ambiguity, and the diffusion of beliefs among organizational stakeholders. Reality is not some exogenous state of affairs, just widespread social construal. If one then adds an insistence on some degree of functionalism for survival in a competitive market, it follows that cultural norms and beliefs will persist over time only to the extent that they are useful. Here we can build on the basic idea in the previous sections: there are certain kinds of beliefs that are adaptive in a competitive setting regardless of whether they are precisely accurate (e.g., over-optimism).

Consider corporate cultures generally. The basic challenge facing any organization is one of coordination: the interaction among multiple corporate agents will be unproductive to the extent that there are endless negotiations over what is happening, why and what is best now to do. Organizational hierarchies can try to impose order from above, but that is unlikely to be effective unless agents actually come to hold common beliefs. An organization that develops a common culture on matters relating to 'what', 'why' and 'should' will operate more efficiently in the short run and thus be more competitive than those that do not (Kreps 1990).

From this perspective, it is not hard to predict some of the substantive content of particularly productive corporate cultures (Langevoort 2006). Optimism and group self-efficacy are likely to be adaptive by enlarging the apparent pool of future rewards from cooperation. The simplification of perceptions of reality, rather than its complication, will also facilitate the coordination function – simple sense-making stories are more effective at allowing agents to get on with their business than complicated, ambiguous accounts. The problem, of course, is that as perceptions cohere in a way that promotes nimbleness and productivity, there may be a resistance to external signals that are inconsistent with prevailing beliefs. Risks, ethical challenges and the like are ruled out of order because they burden the negotiation of reality.

The relevance to legal analysis is thus clear. Legal scholars are used to discussing corporate cultures as either benign or corrupt, implicitly assuming that reality is well perceived so that the only remaining distinction reflects agency costs: the culture either promotes good ethics and law-abidingness or not. Taking culture seriously means accepting that reality is relative, and that unrealistic beliefs that are functional in the short run will not easily be challenged by outsiders.

There are a number of legal implications. One, relating back to the earlier discussion of state of mind, suggests that the notion of 'corporate scienter' is likely to be very difficult to assess – internally, firms may have ways of assessing information that is entirely genuine and in good faith, but unrealistic. Should a firm that trivializes risk in some corporate publicity or SEC filing bear liability under an intent-based legal regime upon a finding that the risk would have been palpable to an external observer? If the answer is no, the credibility of that disclosure drops considerably. But if the answer is yes, we are talking about liability for something other than corporate bad faith.

So, too, with corporate governance. One of the better arguments for enhanced shareholder suffrage rights is that firms can become captive to cultures that ignore change in the environment – indeed, an important line of thinking on organizational ecology is that most all firms eventually die because they lost the capacity to change as a result of the hardening of internal processes and beliefs. If one believes – admittedly it is far from clear – that institutional investors have a better capacity to perceive the need for a company to shift direction, then stronger outsider influence would be desirable. On the other hand, if corporate cultures are indeed so powerful, they will resist intervention from the top. The goal then is to find mechanisms of corporate governance that allow the reality that might be brought to bear by outside directors and others to seep into the culture slowly enough that it doesn't render it unable to do the essential work of simplification and coordination. This, for example, might be an argument for requiring – as some best practices are starting to encourage – more regular meetings and discussions directly between the independent directors and key managers (on matters of risk management, compliance, etc.), rather than allowing the CEO to define and control those interactions.

## 6.    CONCLUSION

Psychology offers useful insights to corporate law scholars in situations where the particular trait or tendency in question is empirically robust, situationally plausible, and either so hard-wired into the human brain that it will operate even in the face of substantial institutional constraints and disincentives or – better yet – actually be functional and adaptive in the marketplace. On both the individual and cultural level, it is not hard to identify traits and tendencies that might satisfy this test even though the behavior in question does not satisfy the formal demands of Bayesean rationality.

So stated, the apparent tension between psychology and economics diminishes considerably. New institutional economics has been more than willing to embrace psychology in the study of intra-firm behavior, for example. And behavioral finance has become important enough that the most respected journals in financial economics contain multiple contributions from this genre in nearly every issue. Again, the key is a plausible theory of frequency, adaptation and persistence.

Of these, frequency is probably the hardest, and something that can only be addressed empirically. Savvy behavior is commonplace, and evidence of the 'opportunism with guile' that describes the conventional economic approach is ample. For all the plausibility of the role of psychology in the recent financial crisis, for example, moral hazard and agency cost problems offer plausible explanations for what we observed, too. The task for corporate law scholarship in situations like these is to disentangle the rational from the biased to the greatest extent possible, and assess the efficacy of our toolkit of legal strategies in light of the resulting mix. Realistic approaches to corporate governance, regulation and liability depend on how well that assessment is done.

## REFERENCES

Akerlof, George & Rachel Kranton (2005), 'Identity and the Economics of Organizations', *Journal of Economic Perspectives*, 19, 9–32.
Arlen, Jennifer, Matthew Spitzer & Eric Talley (2002), 'Endowment Effects Within Corporate Agency Relationships', *Journal of Legal Studies*, 31, 1–37.
Avgouleas, Emilios (2009), 'The Global Financial Crisis, Behavioural Finance and Financial Regulation: In Search of a New Orthodoxy', *Journal of Corporate Legal Studies*, 9, 121–57.
Baker, Malcolm, Robert Ruback & Jeffrey Wurgler (2007), 'Behavioral Corporate Finance: A Survey', in B. Espen Eckbo (ed.) *The Handbook of Corporate Finance: Empirical Corporate Finance*, Amsterdam: Elsevier/North Holland, 145–89.
Benabou, Roland (2009), 'Groupthink: Collective Delusions in Organizations and Markets', National Bureau of Economic Research Working Paper w14764.
Brav, Alon & J.B. Heaton (2003), 'Market Indeterminacy', *Journal of Corporation Law*, 28, 517–39.
Brown, Andrew (1997), 'Narcissism, Identity and Legitimacy', *Academy of Management Review*, 22, 643–86.
Cain, Dylan, George Loewenstein & Daniel Moore (2005), 'The Dirt on Coming Clean: Perverse Effects of Disclosing Conflicts of Interest', *Journal of Legal Studies*, 34, 1–25.
Camerer, Colin & Ulrike Malmendier (2007), 'Behavioral Economics of Organizations', in P. Diamond and H. Vartanian (eds) *Behavioral Economics and its Applications*, Princeton: Princeton University Press, 235–90.
Church, Bryan & Xi Kuang (2009), 'Conflicts of Interest, Disclosure and (Costly) Sanctions: Experimental Evidence', *Journal of Legal Studies*, 38, 505–32.
Cox, James & Harvey Munsinger (1984), 'Bias in the Boardroom: Psychological Foundations and Legal Implications of Corporate Cohesion', *Law and Contemporary Problems*, 48, 83–135.
DellaVigna, Stefano (2009), 'Psychology and Economics: Evidence from the Field', *Journal of Economic Literature*, 47, 315–72.

Easterbrook, Frank & Daniel Fischel (1985), 'Optimal Damages in Securities Cases', *University of Chicago Law Review*, 52, 611–52.

Fisch, Jill & Hillary Sale (2003), 'The Securities Analyst as Agent: Rethinking the Regulation of Analysts', *Iowa Law Review*, 88, 1035–97.

Gigerenzer, Gerd & Richard Selten (eds) (2001), *Bounded Rationality: The Adaptive Toolbox*, Cambridge: MIT Press.

Goel, Anand & Anjan Thakor (2008), 'Overconfidence, CEO Selection and Corporate Governance', *Journal of Finance*, 63, 2737–84.

Heath, Chip (1998), 'Cognitive Repairs: How Organizational Practices can Compensate for Individual Shortcomings', *Research in Organizational Behavior*, 20, 1–37.

Hill, Claire & Brett McDonnell (2007), 'Disney, Good Faith and Structural Bias', *Journal of Corporation Law*, 32, 833–64.

Hill, Claire & Erin O'Hara (2007), 'A Cognitive Theory of Trust', *Washington University Law Quarterly*, 84, 1717–96.

Koch, Christopher & C. Schmidt (2010), 'Disclosing Conflicts of Interest – Do Experience and Reputation Matter?', *Accounting, Organizations and Society*, 35, 95–107.

Kraakman, Reinier (1988), 'Taking Discounts Seriously: The Implications of Discounted Share Prices as an Acquisition Motive', *Columbia Law Review*, 88, 891–941.

Kreps, David (1990), 'Corporate Culture and Economic Theory', in J. Alt & K. Shepsle, (eds), *Perspectives on Positive Political Economy*, Cambridge and New York: Cambridge University Press, 90–114.

Langevoort, Donald (1997), 'Organized Illusions: A Behavioral Theory of Why Corporations Mislead Stock Market Investors (and Cause Other Social Harms)', *University of Pennsylvania Law Review*, 146, 101–72.

Langevoort, Donald (2001), 'The Human Nature of Corporate Boards: Law, Norms and the Unintended Consequences of Independence and Accountability', *Georgetown Law Journal*, 89, 797–832.

Langevoort, Donald (2002), 'Taming the Animal Spirits of the Stock Markets: A Behavioral Approach to Securities Regulation', *Northwestern University Law Review*, 97, 135–88.

Langevoort, Donald (2004), 'Resetting the Corporate Thermostat: Lessons for Law from the Recent Financial Scandals About Self-Deception, Deceiving Others and the Design of Internal Controls', *Georgetown Law Journal*, 93, 285–317.

Langevoort, Donald (2006), 'Opening the Black Box of "Corporate Culture" in Law and Economics', *Journal of Institutional and Theoretical Economics*, 162, 80–96.

Langevoort, Donald (2009), '*Basic* at Twenty: Rethinking Fraud on the Market', *Wisconsin Law Review*, 2009, 151–98.

Macey, Jonathan, Geoffrey Miller, Mark Mitchell & Jeffry Netter (1991), 'Lessons from Financial Economics: Materiality, Reliance and Extending the Reach of Basic v. Levinson', *Virginia Law Review*, 77, 1017–49.

Malmendier, Ulrike & Geoffrey Tate (2008a), 'CEO Overconfidence and Corporate Investment', *Journal of Finance*, 60, 2661–2700.

Malmendier, Ulrike & Geoffrey Tate (2008b), 'Who Makes Acquisitions? CEO Overconfidence and the Market's Reaction', *Journal of Financial Economics*, 89(1), 20–43.

Manne, Henry G. (1966), *Insider Trading and the Stock Market*, New York: Free Press.

Milgram, Stanley (1974), *Obedience to Authority: An Experimental View*, London: Tavistock Press.

Miller, Geoffrey & Gerald Rosenfeld (2009), 'Intellectual Hazard: How Conceptual Biases in Complex Organizations Contributed to the Crisis of 2008', *Harvard Journal of Law and Public Policy*, 33, 807–31.

Morck, Randall (2008), 'Behavioral Finance in Corporate Governance: Economics and Ethics of the Devil's Advocate', *Journal of Management and Governance*, 12, 179–200.

O'Connor, Marleen (2003), 'The Enron Board: The Perils of Groupthink', *University of Cincinnati Law Review*, 71 1233–1319.

Posner, Richard (1998), 'Rational Choice, Behavioral Economics and the Law', *Stanford Law Review*, 50, 1551–75.

Posner, Richard (2009), 'Shorting Reason', *The New Republic*, April 15, 30–33.

Romano, Roberta (1986), 'A Comment on Information Overload, Cognitive Illusions and their Implications for Public Policy', *Southern California Law Review*, 59, 313–28.

Stout, Lynn (2003), 'The Mechanisms of Market Inefficiency: An Introduction to the New Finance', *Journal of Corporation Law*, 28, 635–69.

Weick, Karl (1995), *Sensemaking in Organizations*, Thousand Oaks: SAGE Publications.

# 24. Market efficiency after the fall: Where do we stand following the financial crisis?

*Ronald J. Gilson* *and Reinier Kraakman*

The financial crisis created a lot of losers. Investors, from individuals who thought that highly rated asset-backed securities were liquid, to German Landesbanks that purchased mortgage-backed securities that they did not and perhaps could not understand, lost very large amounts of money. Major financial institutions across the world were decimated, resulting in massive provision of government assistance and sometimes in full nationalization or failure. Further up the food chain, some large developed countries now face apparently unsustainable budget deficits, and some smaller European nations – examples to date include Greece, Iceland, Ireland and Portugal – have required large international aid packages to avoid defaults on sovereign debt. The resulting pressure to drastically reduce government spending threatens political stability across Europe and, should the United States seriously address budget deficits, perhaps there as well.

Against this backdrop, one might think it of small consequence that the financial crisis is also said to have dealt major setbacks to academic theories, most particularly the Efficient Capital Market Hypothesis (ECMH) (Fox 2010). After all, academic proponents of positions whose value the financial crisis is said to have degraded suffer no material losses other than to their egos. Indeed, academic theories by their nature operate to solicit their contradiction, a point famously stressed by Thomas Kuhn (1962) almost 50 years ago.

Nevertheless, two things make this iteration of theory and response to the ECMH different in the post-financial crisis context. The first is that the ECMH has moved beyond the academic community to spark debate as well as policy initiatives by the much larger political and professional communities. The ECMH, in one guise or another, has influenced regulatory policy for well over 30 years.[1] As a result, public understanding of the ECMH carries important economic consequences and is not simply a matter of academic debate.

The Kuhnian combination of assertion and critique gives rise to the second element that makes the interaction between the ECMH and the financial crisis of real, not just academic, significance. Once theory enters the realm of policy, it also enters the realm of politics, with that world's inexorable pattern of remaking theory into political argument. When the ECMH entered the political arena, it expanded from a narrow but important academic theory about the informational underpinnings of market prices into a broad 'faith-based' preference for relying on market outcomes over regulation.

---

The authors are grateful for the research assistance of Max Heurer and Rachel Gibbons.

[1] These range from Securities and Exchange Commission rules allowing corporations to incorporate by reference information contained in already filed documents into short form registration statements to the Supreme Court's decision in *Basic v. Levinson*, 485 U.S. 224 (1988), allowing reliance to be presumed in a securities fraud class action if the plaintiffs show that the relevant market was efficient.

In this important sense, the ECMH experienced a bubble itself. Its refraction from theory to policy through the prism of politics had inflated its claims far beyond what the original academic theory could support. After this ECMH bubble burst, however, we face the important task of guiding the concept back to its original scope without sacrificing its narrower but still important policy implications.

In the first section we address the principal cause of the ECMH expansion into a brief for broad deregulation: the confusion of informational and fundamental efficiency. As we argue, the difference between the two is easy to state but hard to define, especially as it is used casually by critics of the ECMH. At best, the question is whether there are verifiable circumstances in which regulatory implications follow from a potential difference between observable market prices and some concept of fundamental value. And here the question is always relative: the market can only be inefficient in comparison to some other, more plausible measure of fundamental value. We argue that once the ECMH is properly framed the comparison is context specific, depending on the information costs associated with valuing the asset in question, but with a strong – albeit rebuttable – presumption in favor of market price.

In the following section we trace the intellectual history of the ECMH, locating it among the cluster of models that together form the foundation of modern finance. The point of this capsulated account is to show that these models shared a common framework: they assumed perfect markets, in which nothing mattered because costless arbitrage eliminated mispricing and bad financial strategies. But this common framework raises an obvious question: what happens once frictions are added? The third section briefly reprises the authors' previous effort to assess the operation of these frictions in the context of the information efficiency of securities markets. Here the critical point is that market efficiency is a relative concept; a market is more or less informationally efficient depending on the cost characteristics of the information relevant to assessing market price. Conceptions of fundamental value that fail to consider the cost and the accessibility of information are simply implausible.

The fourth section then assesses the financial crisis in light of a properly conceived ECMH – that is, where a market's relative informational efficiency is a function of the level of frictions. We stress here that the information necessary to price many of the instruments associated with the financial crisis simply was unavailable; that is, it was extremely costly information indeed. In this setting, the ECMH predicts that markets will be relatively inefficient, as of course they were. We are then left with a less technical question. Knowing that the information necessary to properly price these instruments was not available, why were they bought and sold? One possibility is that even very large capital participants were, or acted as if they were, cognitively biased. In our view, however, frictions – institutional structures and poorly aligned incentives within and between the chain of institutions that comprised the sub-prime mortgage market, and the related information costs – provide a more compelling explanation and a better basis for future policy than does psychology when the task is assessing so sophisticated a market. The fifth section concludes.

## 1.  INFORMATIONAL VERSUS FUNDAMENTAL EFFICIENCY

Informational efficiency is straightforward to define: all publicly available information (past and current) is promptly incorporated into market price, reflecting the market's aggregate assessment of the value implications of that information.[2] Note that this proposition does not entail the stronger claim of fundamental efficiency – in our parlance, 'faith-based market efficiency' – that a market price that fully reflects all public information also accurately reflects an asset's 'fundamental value'; in colloquial terms, that the market price is right. To make this second claim requires another large step: one must be able to measure the fundamental value of the security in order to compare its value to market price. Only when the two are identical can we support the claim that market price is – or is not – fundamentally efficient.

Making this comparison presents difficult problems, both empirically and conceptually. The empirical problem is that we must be able to measure fundamental value if we are to determine whether it differs from market price. But as Richard Roll pointed out years ago with respect to empirically testing the Capital Asset Pricing Model (CAPM),[3] if we can't measure the price that CAPM dictates because the market portfolio is not observable, we cannot make the price-value comparison either with respect to magnitude or direction. A finding that market price differs from fundamental value (as measured by CAPM) is consistent either with an informationally inefficient market or an incorrect model of fundamental value (Roll 1977; Zingales 2010). Put simply, we have nothing against which to compare the market price.

But if we lack a Platonic measure of fundamental efficiency, what good is the concept of market efficiency? The price of residential housing during the bubble presents an example. Until mid-2007, a number of factors appear to have pushed prices up. A substantial increase in global liquidity reduced the price of credit, which in turn increased the demand – and hence the price – of homes. In addition, new mortgage products that required little or no down payment further expanded the availability of credit, and thus also increased demand with a similar effect on housing prices. In particular, mortgage products with low introductory interest rates encouraged home sales even when buyers would be very hard-pressed to service the mortgages after their initially low 'teaser' interest rates increased. These new products were rational insofar as lenders expected future housing prices to increase sufficiently to support future refinancing. Again, increasing the number of bidders, holding supply constant, inevitably increases price, at least in the short run. What was the fundamental value of housing? In light of what level of liquidity and over what range of mortgage products should it be measured?

Compare instead the observability of informational efficiency. The ECMH postulates that a stock price is efficient with respect to a particular information set – all publically available information – that can be observed. The assertion that fundamental value differs from an informationally efficient market price must mean one of two things. If the market is inaccurately assessing currently available information, then a profitable trading opportunity in fact exists[4] and the market is informationally inefficient. Alternatively, the difference between informational efficiency and fundamental efficiency can mean that someone has additional, non-public, information (including, for example, a better model of fundamental value) that

---

[2]   The definition in the text encompasses weak form and semi-strong form efficiency – that is, efficiency with respect to past and current information. Strong-form efficiency, in contrast, requires that the market price also reflects private information; that is, information that is not public at all

[3]   We discuss the Capital Asset Pricing Model below.

[4]   This is true absent a breakdown in the arbitrage mechanism that makes the correction unprofitable (see below).

demonstrates the inaccuracy of the current stock price – a circumstance that plainly does not call into question the market's informational efficiency, at least in the short run .

Although one could dismiss this distinction as hair splitting, it has important implications. Market prices can be said to be fundamentally inefficient only if we possess the yardstick for assessing fundamental efficiency; that is, only if there is a non-market institution whose estimate of current value we believe is systematically better – closer to fundamental efficiency – than the market price. For example, in *Smith v. Van Gorkom*,[5] the Delaware Supreme Court faulted the board of directors for relying on the market price of the company's stock in assessing an acquisition offer without securing a fairness opinion from an investment banker as to the 'fundamental' value of the company's stock. Is there reason to believe that investment bankers' calculations of fundamental value are systematically more accurate than market prices?[6] The Delaware Chancery Court, in contrast, expressed a much more skeptical view of investment bankers' valuations in *Paramount Communications, Inc. v. Time, Inc.*,[7] characterizing them as having 'a range that a Texan might feel at home'. If no existing institution can systematically predict the future cash flows of a security better than market price in light of the available information, the distinction between informational and fundamental efficiency begins to smack of the Nirvana fallacy.[8] We may have greater confidence in the acuity of central bankers than in that of investment bankers, but the problem remains: when can we confidently believe that central bankers' beliefs about fundamental value are better than those of the market?

Our point here is that less is gained analytically by distinguishing between informational and fundamental efficiency than is generally claimed. As we discuss in the next two sections, the extent to which market price asymptotically approaches fundamental value[9] results from trading mechanisms that push price in the direction of fundamental efficiency. Frictions that reduce the effectiveness of those mechanisms increase the divergence between informational and fundamental efficiency, but those frictions can be recognized and addressed without observing fundamental value directly.

---

[5]    488 A.2d 858 (Del. 1985).

[6]    A curiosity here is that Delaware Supreme Court presumably meant by fundamental value either some future market price or a future acquisition price. One presumes from the corpus of Delaware case law they meant a future acquisition price. Thus a claim about value may actually have been a claim about market structure: The *Van Gorkom* board failed to shop the company sufficiently. Given the qualifications that accompany a typical investment bankers' fairness opinion, it may be that even the investment bankers do not claim that they can specify a price more accurate than that of the markets. However, this does not mean that investment bankers' opinions have no information content (Cain & Denis 2010).

[7]    *Paramount Communications, Inc. v. Time Inc.*, Fed. Sec. L. Rep. (CCH) ¶94,514 (Del. Ch. 1989).

[8]    One can, of course, arbitrarily decide that one institution's estimate of fundamental value is best, as the Delaware Supreme Court has done by elevating board decisions backed by bankers' opinions over shareholder choice or market price in a wide range of fundamental transactions (Black & Kraakman 2002).

[9]    Grossman & Stiglitz (1980) demonstrate the intuitively obvious (at least after their article was published) result that prices cannot be perfectly efficient. They must reflect an equilibrium level of inefficiency – the point where additional expense in acting on new information or reassessing old information would exceed the gain from trading on it. The same phenomenon would operate with respect to fundamental efficiency.

No one – and certainly not the critics of market efficiency – claims to possess the model of fundamental value for a capital asset in the face of market frictions. Instead, the critics of the ECMH properly understood make a weaker but nonetheless important claim in the context of the financial crisis and earlier market bubbles. Implicitly, their real claim is that prices in a given market at a given time fail to respond to new and important information that should affect price under *any* rational model of fundamental value. It is this weaker and therefore less easily discounted concept that we will term 'fundamental value' in subsequent sections of this chapter. Market prices are not fundamentally efficient if they fail to meet the 'you-have-got-to-be-kidding' test in response to new and obviously relevant public information.

As we discuss below, security prices in the market for mortgage backed securities (MBS) failed to reflect increasingly shoddy underwriting practices in the mortgage market or the 'fact' that housing prices could not continue to rise indefinitely at their 2005–2007 rates and were likely to decline (or significantly slow their growth rate) (Lewis 2010) with devastating effects on the value of MBS securities. Assuming that these were facts known by large numbers of savvy investors, 'inefficient market prices' for MBS can only mean that the arbitrage mechanism broke down. In this account, traders knew that MBS prices were overpriced relative to fundamental value (even if this value was unobservable), and that these prices would therefore fall in the near term. However, without a low cost market vehicle to short MBS prices, traders were unable to impound this information into prices by their trading. How else should we understand John Paulson's need to cause Goldman Sachs to create a security that Paulson could short? And the internal incentives of the issuing financial institutions and the frictions associated with wholesale changes in those incentives and the business model that they implemented may keep the process going until arbitrage vehicles finally catch up.

If this was true, then the market price of MBS securities was informationally inefficient. But the appropriate inference to draw is not that animal spirits led market prices astray, but rather that an immature market lacked conduits for introducing new information into price, and therefore generated demonstrably inefficient prices.[10] The cure for this is not to abandon the ECMH, or any other hypothesis that assumes a frictionless market, but rather to improve the informational quality of prices by, for example, mandating disclosure of the assets underlying mortgage-based securities or derivatives, and encouraging short selling. As we argue, market frictions drive a wedge between market price and any measure of fundamental value. The ECMH then functions not as a claim that frictions do not exist or have no impact, but as a diagnostic tool for framing effective policy to improve informational efficiency.

## 2.   PUTTING MARKET EFFICIENCY IN AN INTELLECTUAL CONTEXT: THE RISE OF MODERN FINANCE

We argued above that a strong distinction between informational and fundamental efficiency is elusive because fundamental value is unobservable. Rather, a more fruitful focus is on fric-

---

[10]   Reflecting the informational foundation of the crisis, a member of the Federal Reserve's Board of Governors from 2006 to 2008, has stated that '[t]he financial system in mid-September 2008 was far more vulnerable than almost all policy makers and market participants realized at that time' (Mishkin 2012).

tions that increase the costs of information and block the conduits through which it enters market price – that is, what we have previously described as the mechanisms of market efficiency (Gilson & Kraakman 1984). While we cannot observe fundamental value except crudely and well after the fact, we can observe frictions in these conduits that presumptively drive a wedge between market price and fundamental value. This focus on the difference between analogues of market price and fundamental value in models that assume perfect markets – and the centrality of frictions to understanding why these two differ –is not peculiar to issues of market efficiency. Rather, it is shared by all of the foundational models of modern finance. Thus, to understand where market efficiency stands after the financial crisis, we first need a capsule account of the development of modern finance. As we will see, each of the foundational models of modern finance ultimately focuses our attention not on the tautological relation between fundamental value and market price in a perfect market, but rather on the frictions that explain the difference between the observed results in actual markets and the results that theory predicts we should observe in a world without financial and informational frictions.

A fair place to begin is 1960.[11] The *Journal of Finance* was launched only eight years before, and to that point had published no 'more than five articles that could be classified as theoretical rather than descriptive' (Bernstein 1992, 42). Thus, an opportunity existed to transform finance into a mathematically rigorous branch of microeconomics by developing theories that might be useful in explaining what had been observed. Science involves empirically testing hypotheses, but formulating the hypotheses to be tested requires a theory.

In setting the stage for our discussion of the financial crisis, we focus on three bodies of theory that arose between the late 1950s and the early 1970s. These theories sought to state rigorously how capital assets are priced, how a firm should choose which securities to issue (e.g., debt or equity) and in what quantities, and whether the market price of securities reflects all available information concerning their value. These three familiar theories – APM (Sharpe 1964), the Miller-Modigliani Irrelevance Propositions (Modigliani & Miller 1958; Miller & Modigliani 1961), and the ECMH (Fama 1970) – all obtain rigor by simplifying away from market imperfections. Put differently, they all assume markets with perfect information, no transaction costs, and rational investors who value capital assets based solely on their returns and their risk, which is measured as a linear function of variance in returns.

Start with CAPM. If investors value only risk and return –and diversification eliminates unsystematic risk – investors must logically price assets at the level dictated by expected systematic risk and return. CAPM merely takes the next step of postulating that what investors will pay for a given asset is the risk-free rate of return plus the value of the asset's systematic risk, as measured by 'beta' –a measure of how the asset's returns co-vary with those of the fully diversified market as a whole. Given the starting assumptions set forth above, CAPM is a tautology.[12]

---

[11] This section draws on Gilson & Kraakman (2004).
[12] Note that any number of other valuation models can be constructed by relaxing CAPM's assumptions about what investors value and how they value it. For example, while it is clear that investors value risk, whether variance is the right measure of risk for valuation purposes is an empirical matter. Empirical valuation models today use factors in addition to risk and return, giving rise to multiple 'betas'.

Similarly, the Miller-Modigliani (MM) Irrelevance Propositions are tautologies. As Miller (1988) was to put it 30 years later, the claim that debt-equity ratios do not affect firm value is no more (or less) than 'an implication of equilibrium in perfect capital markets'. Think of a simple balance sheet, with assets on one side and ownership interests – debt and equity – on the other. The balance sheet balances because the total value of the assets must correspond to the total ownership – debt and equity – interests. Why then should the divisions on the right side of the balance sheet – the manner in which ownership interests are divided – affect the left side of the balance sheet, that is, the value of the assets that derive from the firm's real activities?[13] If for some reason debt or equity is mispriced, costless arbitrage would restore the proper relation, so that increasing the amount of lower cost debt would result in an offsetting increase in the cost of equity or vice versa.

The ECMH also builds on perfect market assumptions. Commenting on Fama's (1970) seminal review article, William Sharpe (1970, 418) stated:

> simply put, the thesis is this: that in a well-functioning securities market, the prices … of securities will reflect predictions based on all relevant and available information. This seems to be trivially self-evident to most professional economists – so much so, that testing seems almost silly.

Ten years later, William Beaver (1981, 24) made much the same point: 'Why would one ever expect prices *not* to "fully reflect" publicly available information? Won't market efficiency hold trivially?' Absent frictions and with perfect information, the arbitrage machine logically ensures that price fully reflects available information.[14]

Market professionals initially responded angrily to the rapid academic acceptance of CAPM, the MM propositions, and the ECMH, notwithstanding the tautological character of these theories. If one imagined the theories' predictions survived the release of their perfect market assumptions, then each theory attacked the value of important capital market participants. CAPM called into question the value of highly paid portfolio managers – simply assessing the volatility of an asset relative to that of the market might not command the same rewards as firm specific assessments of risk and reward based on detailed fundamental analysis. The Irrelevancy Propositions were even more offensive. Crafting a corporation's debt-equity ratio was a central function of chief financial officers (and their highly compensated investment banker consultants); why pay large salaries or fees for an activity that does not increase the value of the firm? The ECMH completed the three-prong attack, calling into question not only the value of chartists (marginalized by weak form efficiency because the information content of historical prices already will be reflected in market price), but funda-

---

13    Miller (1988, 100) reports that even the tautological character of the propositions in a perfect capital market world was initially a difficult sell: 'We had first to convince people (including ourselves!) that there could be *any* conditions, even in a "frictionless" world, where a firm would be indifferent between issuing securities as different in legal status, investor risk and apparent cost as debt and equity'.

14    In addition to its prediction of the information content of stock prices, the ECMH also played a critical integrative role by linking asset pricing and capital structure choice through the medium of market prices. Both CAPM and the Modigliani-Miller propositions depend on an arbitrage mechanism for their proof: mispricing will be traded away. But for arbitrage to be triggered by mispricing, market prices must be reasonably informative. Thus, the positive power of the three theories rises and falls together.

mental analysis as well (marginalized by semi-strong form efficiency's claim that analysts cannot systematically profit by trading on newly released information).

While it is tempting to dismiss capital market professionals' hostile reaction as simply turf protection, that would miss the deeply felt belief that all three theories' perfect market elegance did not reflect the world in which the professionals worked. How predictive are the theories in the real world where information is costly and asymmetrically distributed, at least some investors are plainly irrational, and transactions costs are pervasive?

The transformation of finance into financial economics thus gave rise to a set of theories that explained the operation of asset pricing and capital structure in perfect capital markets and evoked a predictable reaction from those whose functions the theories implicitly questioned in actual markets. The next issue, clear in hindsight but less so at the time, was whether the real world capital market worked the way financial economics predicted. Put in terms of the controversy that came to a head with the financial crisis, the question is: were the frictions in the real world of a magnitude that they could drive a meaningful wedge between informational efficiency and fundamental efficiency, between market price and real value?[15] We have previously addressed this issue in an effort to link the level of market frictions to the level of informational efficiency by proposing a typology of 'mechanisms that operate to impound information into market price' (Gilson & Kraakman 1984, 557). We describe these mechanisms in the next section, and then turn in Section 4 to an examination of the information costs associated with pricing the assets that figured most prominently in the financial crisis.

## 3.   MARKET EFFICIENCY IS A RELATIVE CONCEPT: THE MECHANISMS OF MARKET EFFICIENCY

The lesson to be learned from the history of financial economics is that the foundational assumptions of its principal theories are not meant to describe real investors and real markets. Informational efficiency is not akin to gravity, a natural law of our universe. Rather, the prompt reflection of publicly available information in a security's price, and the extent to which that price approaches an unobservable fundamental value,[16] is the outcome of institutional and market interactions whose operation necessarily encounters numerous frictions. As we developed in 1984, once the perfect market assumptions are dropped, market efficiency necessarily becomes a relative concept, dependent on the level of frictions in a particular market: 'We need a concept of "relative efficiency" that distinguishes among and ranks the different market dynamics according to how closely they approximate the ideal of ensuring that prices *always* reflect all available information' (Gilson & Kraakman 1984, 557). Campbell, Lo, and MacKinley (1996, 25) echoed this conclusion 12 years later, in a standard econometrics of finance text: 'The notion of *relative* efficiency … may be a more useful concept than the all or nothing view taken by most of the traditional market efficiency literature.'

---

[15]   Here, again, 'real value' may be read in the strong sense of accepting CAPM or in the weaker sense of accepting any rational valuation model.

[16]   'Fundamental value' here is not discounted future market value, which only an omniscient market could provide, but the equilibrium price of numerous informed rational investors who share the same valuation model, whether it be CAPM or some more complex non-linear algorithms.

By the early 1980s, a large body of empirical work demonstrated that price responded extremely rapidly to most public and even 'semi-public' information – too rapidly to permit arbitrage profits. By and large, then, the public equities market appeared to be semi-strong form efficient, meaning that their relative efficiency for public information was high. But how was this possible, given that most traders, at least by number, were likely to be uninformed about the content of much of this information? What caused market prices to reflect new information ' "as if" they were set by the theorist's ideal of a market populated exclusively by fully-informed traders' (Gilson & Kraakman 2004, 720).

In prior work we addressed the determinants of relative market efficiency on two levels (Gilson & Kraakman 1984, 592–3). At the general level, we proposed that four increasingly costly mechanisms worked to incorporate information in market prices with correspondingly *decreasing* relative efficiency. First, and least remarkable, market prices immediately reflect information all traders really do know such as Federal Reserve announcements of interest rate changes; this information necessarily informs trading, as if the perfect market assumption were an accurate positive description of real markets in securities. Second, information that is public but less widely known is incorporated into share prices almost as rapidly as information that is universally known through the trading activity of savvy market professionals. This is the world of fundamental analysis, where relative efficiency is constrained by the need for analysts to earn a normal return, as described by Grossman and Stiglitz (1980). Third, inside information known to only a very few traders finds its way into prices more slowly, as uninformed traders learn about its content by observing tell-tale changes in the activity of presumptively informed traders or unusual price and volume movements. Finally, information as yet known to *no one* might be reflected, albeit slowly and imperfectly, in share prices that aggregated the forecasts of numerous market participants with heterogeneous information.[17] The arbitrage mechanism – aligning price with value – works on the level of all four mechanisms.

At the more specific level, we addressed how information comes to be distributed among traders in the market, and thus which of the four market mechanisms is likely to predominate in the incorporation of particular information into price. Simply put, relative market efficiency decreases as market frictions increase. The costs associated with frictions determine the range and distribution of information in the market; and the cost of information, in turn, depends on the market institutions that produce, verify, and analyze information – ranging from the *Wall Street Journal* to the exhaustive research of the best professional investors. While every step in the institutional pathways that channel information into price bears on the relative efficiency of market price, none is as important as the institutions that determine the transaction costs of acquiring and verifying information. As we argue below, the magnitude of these costs figured centrally in the pricing problems that underlay the claim that the Financial Crisis fatally undermined the ECMH. The ECMH, properly understood, focuses our attention on reducing these costs, to the end of reducing the gap between market price and a hypothetical fundamental value, whatever its unobservable structure may be.

---

[17]   We term this last mechanism 'uninformed trading'. It is the least efficient of the four market mechanisms, precisely because the true content of information is unknown and, as a result, price 'averages' the partial information and opinion of all investors democratically (Gilson & Kraakman 1984, 580–8). We term the other three mechanisms, respectively, 'universally informed trading', 'professionally informed trading', and 'derivatively informed trading'.

## 4. THE ECMH AND THE FINANCIAL CRISIS: INSTITUTIONAL FAILURE AND COSTLY INFORMATION

In an article published 20 years after our initial sketch of the mechanisms of market efficiency, we reconsidered the ECMH in light of the tech bubble of 1999–2000 and the rapidly developing field of behavioral finance (Gilson & Kraakman 2004). In this article, we argued that defective institutional channels of information were a proximate cause of distorted share prices – institutions ranging from auditors, investment banks and celebrity security analysts to legal and financial constraints on the ability of arbitrageurs to correct market prices. Put differently, agency costs were more pervasive, and reputational costs and civil damages proved to be less powerful deterrents, than we had supposed them to be twenty years earlier. Under these circumstances, arbitrage was less successful in buffering the distortion of market prices than we had previously assumed. This did not mean that our framework sketching the mechanisms of market efficiency was misguided, but only that the frictions and information costs were higher and, hence, the relative efficiency of equity prices lower, than we had implicitly supposed them to be in 1984. As we will see, the high information costs associated with the assets at the center of the financial crisis underscore our central theme in this chapter. A clear recognition of the mechanisms of market efficiency and the consequence of relative efficiency that entails the ECMH should be understood as one potential source of reform rather than as a 'refutation' of the ECMH. A regulatory strategy that reduces information and arbitrage costs increases future informational efficiency and thereby reduces the severity and frequency of divergences from fundamental value.

### Costly Information and the Pricing of Mortgage-backed Securities

Partly because of the enormous difference in scale between the tech bubble and the crisis of 2007–2009, many commentators today appear to believe that the crisis is an even more devastating blow to the ECMH than the tech bubble had been. In the crisis that was rooted in residential real estate, Keynes' 'animal spirits', working in tandem with unscrupulous bankers, are said to have not only discredited the ECMH once and for all, but also to have brought the world economy to the edge of an abyss comparable to the Great Depression. This bleak view rests on the assumption that savvy investors and banks knew – or should have known – and nevertheless persisted in investing with near certainty of the existence of a bubble in the residential real estate market.

After the fact, some say that the evidence of a bubble with potentially disastrous consequences for the US$ trillion market in mortgage-backed securities was written on the wall in day-glo colors. The S&P/Case-Shiller Index of prices had risen continuously between 1998 and 2007. Between 2001 and 2005, homeowners saw large average increases in house prices (Gorton 2008). An end to those increases would literally destroy the market. During the same five-year period, there was unprecedented experimentation in the design of unconventional mortgages and a similarly unprecedented reduction in the credit quality of borrowers. Between 2000 and 2007, the outstanding value of 'Agency' mortgages acquired by Fannie Mae and Freddie Mac – and implicitly guaranteed by the Federal Government – doubled, while the number of non-conforming 'private label' mortgages bundled by private financial institutions increased by 800% (Gorton 2008).

Of course such expansion could not go on forever. Not only were there more 'subprime' mortgages being written, but these mortgages themselves morphed from long-term to short-term financing instruments that combined a low, two- or three-year fixed interest rate ('teaser' rate) loans with a 27- or 28-year adjustable-rate mortgages (ARMs) whose rates hovered far above prominent market indexes. In addition, the new mortgage structure carried large prepayment penalties that barred subprime borrowers from refinancing with anyone other than their original lenders when their teaser periods ended and their interest rates jumped (Gorton 2008). Thus, original lenders acquired not just secured debt; they also (and perhaps only) acquired a long position in residential real estate that required periodic refinancing for stability – which was possible only if housing prices continued to rise. Viewed differently, teaser interest rates (and interest-only mortgages) increased demand for housing, particularly by subprime borrowers and speculators. Increased demand in turn inflated housing prices. And because the same phenomenon occurred nationally, residential lending risk was systematic and could not be reduced by regional diversification. This dynamic continued smoothly from 1998 through 2007 and then it failed precipitously as housing prices fell, much like the demand for shares in an over-levered company falls sharply when demand for its only product declines.

No doubt the crisis of 2007–2009 had many causes besides innovation in the MBS market and the collapse of demand in the housing market. Other plausible causes range from easy credit conditions driven by macro-economic factors (and/or the Fed's policy choices) to lax underwriting practices, self-interested credit ratings, inadequate reserve requirements for financial institutions, and sloppy regulation by federal agencies. We do not pretend to apportion responsibility for the crisis in this chapter. Rather our concern lies in dissecting the widespread view that the spike in mortgage defaults and corresponding decline in the market value of mortgage-based securities was clearly foreseeable beforehand, and therefore that even the 'science-based', as opposed to faith-based, formulation of the ECMH lacks value as a policy tool. If we are wrong and the critics are right, the strong implication is that no amount of additional market information would have dampened the demand for MBS, even though these were sold at manifestly unsupportable prices.

We begin by describing the production of MBS securities: that is, the institutional conveyer belt that converted residential mortgages (as well as commercial debt) into increasingly complex private-label investment products.[18] The private securitization process starts with a special purpose vehicle (SPV) – a holding entity or empty bucket – that buys mortgages originated either by the SPV's sponsor or acquired elsewhere with funds generated by selling claims against different slices or tranches of the cash flowing from these pooled mortgages. In a conventional multiple-tranche structure, the senior tranche carries the least risk, while subordinate tranches carry more, and the bottom tranche – the so-called 'toxic waste' – buffers against initial defaults or prepayment losses on the mortgage pool. But this is the plain vanilla model. More often the pooling entity's governing documents fix complex alter-

---

[18]   Securitized mortgage securities are generally divided into securities issued against Fannie Mae and Freddie Mac securities – i.e., securities funded by pools of government acquired mortgages – and private label securities that represent claims against pools of mortgages held by private trust-like entities termed 'Special Purpose Vehicles' (SPVs). While the Federal Government may be credited with creating the modern market in mortgage-backed securities, private financial institutions issued mortgage-based securitized products in this market as early as 1997 (Judge 2011, 17).

native channels for the 'waterfall' of cash to flow through the entity's tranche structure. One variation diverts returns from the mortgage pool to paying off the senior tranche in full before allowing cash to flow to other tranches in order of seniority (Frankel & Schwing 2005). Another variation allocates all returns to the senior tranche prior to some triggering event, such as a set term of years or specified performance threshold for the underlying pool of residential mortgages (Gorton 2010). Other structures included interest-only and principal-only tranches (Frankel & Schwing 2005), and still others had entirely bespoke tranche structures. Moreover, numerous devices other than tranche structure were used to enhance the security of the top tranche of claims against an SPV's mortgage pool, including the sponsoring organizations' retaining the riskiest tranche and most infamously the purchase by the SPV of credit default swaps (CDS) – a form of default insurance liberally issued by AIG, Lehman Brothers, and other storied players at the center of the crisis. Such additional credit enhancement generally aimed at earning a coveted AAA rating from a major credit-rating agency (Judge 2011).

One effect of structuring the cash flow rights of investors in an SPV mortgage pool was to distance investors from their underlying assets in a way that simpler structures, such as selling pro rata claims on returns from pooled mortgages, simply could not accomplish. Kathryn Judge (2011) has described this effect as the creation of a 'fragmentation node'.

In general, senior MBS claims backed by AAA ratings retained liquidity through the middle of 2007. They were sold in public offerings and frequently traded among dealers at real market prices. By contrast, claims against lower-ranked MBS tranches were difficult to sell and therefore lacked market prices. At least until 2004, sophisticated investors in high-risk securities imposed a natural limit on the growth of the residential mortgaged-back securities market by demanding high returns for purchasing claims on the subordinate tranches of MBS mortgage pools (Levitin & Wachter 2012). Rolling back through the supply pipeline, higher returns would have required higher interest rates on the underlying mortgages, which would have reduced the number of borrowers, and hence the supply of loans entering the pipeline.

This natural limit was breached, however, with the birth of a second-order securitization vehicle, the so-called collateralized debt obligation (CDO). By grouping claims against the middle tranches of numerous MBO mortgage pools, this vehicle expanded the market for high-risk mortgage-backed securities well beyond its 'natural' population of expert buyers in high-risk securities. Valuing these second derivative instruments was an order of magnitude more difficult than valuing their constituent MBO claims. To drill down to the quality of the collateral underlying such CDOs required first assessing the quality of the collateral comprising the hundreds of claims included in the CDOs' portfolios, and then further drilling to a second or third level, to assess the quality of the mortgages – and the structure of intra-MBO cash distribution rights – that were aggregated to form the asset pools of the CDOs. Valuation was possible as a practical matter only by making largely arbitrary assumptions. Nevertheless, numerous mortgages in privately-held MBO pools were resecuritized as CDOs by 2005 including, significantly, most MBO pools holding subprime mortgages. With the requisite 'credit enhancement', such as CDS backing, even the top tranches of CDOs that derived their cash flows from the middle tranches of MBOs that, in turn, depended on risky cash flows from pools of subprime mortgages, managed to obtain an AAA rating from at least one of the major rating agencies (Levitin & Wachter 2012). Oddly, new buyers seem to have underpriced the enormous leverage inherent in even the most senior tranche of these CDOs.

Only the market – or the lack thereof – seems to have registered the risk. Claims against the senior tranches of these CDOs were almost always sold to long-term institutional investors rather than traded. They were, in short, beyond the reach of even the most primitive of trading markets.

What lesson to draw for the ECMH after the disastrous performance of these securities during the crisis? For us, the lesson is that the crisis strongly supports the ECMH, at least if this hypothesis is construed as a scientific theory rather than as a broad assertion of 'faith-based' ideology. It is hard to imagine a market less informed than the 'market' in which claims on senior tranches of CDO asset pools were sold – but rarely traded. Moreover, in the rare event that these claims were priced in over-the-counter trades, the buyers and sellers who traded had little more than historical data on housing prices to rely upon – data that was obsolete once financial technology ensured a high correlation among regional housing prices. The rating agencies employed similar valuation models that suffered from the same defects and were additionally subject to issuer gaming (Lewis 2010). There were, finally, sequential informational asymmetries that replicated the second-order complexities of CDOs: the originators of mortgages knew their risks better than did their purchasers, who in turn understood their risks better than the credit rating agencies, and the investors – their ultimate purchasers of these securities – seem to have known very little beyond the reputations of rating agencies and of firms such as AIG and Lehman Brothers, that seemed to guarantee CDOs by writing credit default swaps.

Given the opacity and complexity of CDOs as well as the stable returns of MBOs in preceding years, the validation by rating agencies, and the informational asymmetries among the parties who manufactured these securities, nothing would be more surprising than to find that institutional buyers succeeded in pricing these securities accurately. This is especially so because CDOs were almost exclusively *sold* to institutional investors rather than traded in a market that might have tested their value periodically, if not continuously.

**Does the Opacity of the Assets Underlying CDOs Matter?**

Critics of the ECMH might acknowledge all of the arguments made in the preceding section and still insist that at least one fact – perhaps the most important fact – about the value of mortgage-backed securities was widely known and yet failed to enter market prices: namely, that housing prices could not continue to rise forever, and that prices in 2006 clearly reflected an enormous asset bubble. No matter what the underwriting quality or the proportion of subprime mortgages, the value of these securities would inevitably decline in the wake of a steep and sustained fall in housing prices (Lewis 2010). So here the question is whether a fact – vividly clear in hindsight – was widely known but simply ignored by the relevant market before the crisis?

The evidence suggests that the most astute investors did *not* forecast a steep fall in housing prices immediately prior to its actual occurrence. The significance of this evidence, however, might be read either as support for critics of the ECMH or, as we believe, as a reflection of the enormous information costs and the resulting relative inefficiency of prices in the market for mortgage backed securities. Allen Ferrell and Atanu Saha (2009) point out that it was not until 2006 that trading markets in housing futures and standardized CDS indexes developed. The Chicago Mercantile Exchange (CME) market in three-month housing futures, which first opened to trading in August of 2006, exhibited 'relative stability in market expectations until a decline in the fourth quarter of 2007 and then a precipitous drop at the very end of 2007 and beginning of 2008' (Ferrell & Saha 2009). Much the same result emerges from analysis of the several ABX indices, which first allowed trading on proxies for MBSs of various vintages and credit ratings. As Ferrell and Saha (2009) demonstrate, trading in AAA MBS securities failed to show any sign of sharp decline until October 2007.

If one were absolutely persuaded that the handwriting was on the wall months or even years before the onset of the crisis in late 2007, these results might seem to be the final proof of market inefficiency. To us, however, they indicate that the overwhelming consensus among professional traders using all available information was that a steep decline in housing prices was highly unlikely to occur within the foreseeable future circa early 2007. No doubt there were notable exceptions, as there are for every sharp turn of asset prices. Some traders have special insight (which might be described as non-public information) and other traders are gifted with great luck. Nevertheless, one must ask: how plausible can it be that prices fail to anticipate a radical reversal in future value that is obvious for all to see? When billions of dollars are at stake and assets are easily sold, what can it mean to say that professional investors ignore the obvious? The more plausible alternative is to hypothesize that the 'market' in which mortgage-backed securities were sold may have indeed been semi-strong form efficient in the sense that the impending decline in housing prices was not at all obvious after a long previous history of rising prices. Rather, information about an imminent crisis – as opposed to a distant decline – was neither obvious nor cheap. In this case the crisis is not a puzzle for a properly framed EMCH but instead it is powerful evidence of the central issue of information costs. It turns out that some information, even extremely important macro-level information, was very difficult to divine within an economically relevant time period. The market was relatively inefficient in information terms, which masked a large inefficiency in fundamental value.

## A Note on Behavioral Finance

As we noted earlier, critics of the ECMH have suggested that information related to the value of MBOs and CDOs was in fact obvious and yet failed to affect price for months or even years. The principal basis for this claim is a growing empirical literature that challenges financial economics, and in particular, challenges the underlying assumption of classical finance that investors buy and sell as if they are rational. In an earlier article we discussed the variety of behavioral hypotheses of cognitive bias that might plausibly interfere with rational pricing based on public information (Gilson & Kraakman 2004). This important literature identifying cognitive biases (which are sometimes termed 'animal spirits' in the financial discourse) grows out of work by cognitive psychologists Daniel Kahneman and Amos Tversky, which uses decision-making experiments to show how biases can lead individuals to systematically misassess an asset's value (Kahneman et al. 1982; Barberis & Thaler 2003; Hirshleifer 2001).

We do not wish to review our earlier discussion of cognitive biases here, much less the considerable progress that has been made in the field of cognitive finance since our past intervention. Instead we make a different point: Individuals whose decisions are subject to one or more cognitive biases are generally depicted as unsophisticated investors, or so-called 'noise traders', who make irrational investment decisions. Lee, Shleifer and Thaler's (1991) clever effort to explain the discount often associated with closed end mutual funds, one of the longstanding phenomena that conflicts with the implications of ECMH, aptly illustrates the potential for such misguided investors to influence price efficiency.[19] When an investor sells shares in a closed end mutual fund, she receives whatever a buyer is willing to pay, rather than a proportionate share of the fund's net asset value, as she would if she redeemed her interest in an open end mutual fund. Because the net assets of a closed end fund are observable, the ECMH predicts that the stock price of a closed end fund should reflect its net asset value. In fact, closed end funds systematically (but not uniformly) trade at a discount from their underlying asset value, which poses a serious problem for the claim that stock prices generally are the best estimate of a security's value. In the one case where we can actually observe underlying asset value, stock price diverges from it (Kraakman 1988).

For purposes of analyzing the mispricing of securitized assets during the financial crisis, however, evidence of noise trading – the single most important support for the proposition that cognitive biases distort prices in the securities markets – is singularly unhelpful. Ironically, the only actors in the crisis who come close to resembling conventional noise traders were the unfortunate homeowners who were forced to default on subprime mortgages and faced foreclosure as a result.[20] The principal players in the crisis were anything but 'noise traders' in the conventional sense; they were institutional investors and multinational banks. Nevertheless, it might be argued that these large and savvy investors might have been affected collectively by one or more of the proposed cognitive biases. Herding behavior by market insiders is the most plausible behavioral explanation, as might be suggested by the now iconic July 2007 comment by Chuck Prince, then Citigroup's CEO, that 'as long as the music is playing, you've got to get up and dance. We're still dancing.'[21] But the comment suggests even more strongly that herding behavior is by no means a necessary consequence of behavioral biases. It can also be an entirely rational decision by portfolio managers who seek to maximize their personal wealth or merely to survive. What is rational for the agent may be irrational for her principal – or if rational for her principal, irrational from the standpoint of the market as a whole (Hill 2011).

**The Limits of Arbitrage**

Even if high-end noise trading or rational herding inclined the institutional buyers and sellers to skew the valuation of mortgage-backed securities in the same way, one other element must be present to build a credible story based on either agency problems or behavioral finance. Arbitrageurs must be unable or unwilling to police the resulting price inaccuracies. Under perfect capital market assumptions, fully informed traders with unlimited access to capital immediately pounce on mispriced securities. If arbitrageurs were available to trade

---

[19]  For the heated debate over the econometrics in this article, see Chen et al. (1993a, 1993b); Chopra et al. (1993a), Zingales (2010) refers to the closed end mutual fund phenomenon in his recent account of the challenges to the ECMH.

[20]  Even in the case of borrowers who took on the unfavorably structured mortgages, there is a quite plausible case that these borrowers made fully rational decisions in buying homes they could not afford with money borrowed, at least for the teaser period, at greatly below market interest rates.

[21]  Available at http://dealbook.nytimes.com/2007/07/10/citi-chief-on-buyout-loans-were-still-dancing/ (last accessed March 2011). It should be obvious that the very popularity of the Prince quote demonstrates that this was not a noise trading phenomenon – Prince appears to have understood that the real problem was rational herding.

against the noise traders, then their action would suffice to return prices to their efficient level.

This limited arbitrage condition is critical to the behavioral finance perspective (Shleifer 2000), and the problem is more general than the simple case of closed end mutual funds. In the case of the crisis, the most plausible limits on arbitrage are the presence of fundamental risk; institutional limits, both regulatory and incentive based; and, as observed above, the potential that even large institutional traders may be subject to cognitive biases that reduce the ability of arbitrageurs to influence price.

The problem of *fundamental risk* simply reflects the fact that, unless hedged, the arbitrageur has a position in the stock of a particular company that is exposed to loss from a change in that company's fortunes. This can be avoided by holding an offsetting position in a substitute security. However, substitutes may not be available and in all events will be imperfect. Barberis and Thaler (2003) offer the illustration of an arbitrageur who believes that Ford is underpriced. To hedge the risk associated with purchasing Ford, the arbitrageur simultaneously shorts GM. But this strategy only provides a hedge against bad news in the automobile industry generally; it does not hedge against firm-specific bad news about Ford (and, to the extent that bad news for Ford is good news for GM, it may actually increase firm-specific risk). The arbitrageur must therefore expect a higher return to offset her basis risk, which in turn reduces arbitrage activity and lowers market efficiency. The result parallels Grossman and Stiglitz's (1980) point, to which we have already repeatedly referred, that moving prices in the informationally correct direction must be fueled by profits.

*Institutional limits* on arbitrage reflect barriers to arbitrageurs trading away information inefficiencies that result not from market risk, but from the structure of the institutions through which the arbitrageurs act. For our purposes, these limits fall into two categories: regulatory and market constraints on the mechanisms of arbitrage; and the structure of arbitrageurs' incentives. Each category restricts the extent to which arbitrage can correct mispricing. In the virtually unregulated market in mortgage-backed securities, market constraints created the most important limits on arbitrageurs. As Michael Lewis (2010) graphically explains, until 2006 there were no markets in which a deep-pocket arbitrageur could short MBOs and CDOs at low cost without having a very special relationship with a large investment banking firm. It was not until 2006 that two market makers emerged to provide non-insiders the ability to short classes of mortgage-backed securities if not particular issues: the Chicago Mercantile Exchange's market in housing futures and the ABX markets in MBOs by credit rating and issue date. At least one economist has argued that the emergence of the ABX markets in particular were responsible for bursting the real estate bubble and hence the bubble in the value of mortgage-backed securities (Genakopolos 2010). Even then, the account of John Paulson's need to enlist Goldman Sachs to raise and market an SPV just so Paulson had another vehicle to short the mortgage/housing market provides graphic evidence of the limited vehicles available to arbitrageurs to police prices.[22]

---

[22]   Goldman Sachs settled an SEC complaint with respect to the failure to disclose to potential buyers that Paulson had a role in selecting the securities to be included in the vehicle to make it most suitable for shorting for $500 million. Private litigation continues. On January 6, 2011, a German insurance company who invested in the SPV sued Goldman for failing to disclose Paulson's role in choosing securities. See http://www.marketwatch.com/story/goldman-sachs-is-sued-over-mortgage-debt-deals-2011-01-06 (last accessed March 2011).

Beyond the market constraints, we have thus far assumed a quite naïve relationship between information and the incentives of entrepreneurs. Recent work highlights a number of incentive problems associated with the arbitrageur's role. The first problem is that we have to this point treated arbitrageurs as a kind of market price police whose role is to enforce the efficiency of prices and whose efforts will be compromised to the extent that regulatory and transaction costs make short-selling costly. In fact, however, arbitrageurs have a much simpler goal: to make money. This, in turn, suggests that arbitrageurs act not only on a difference between a stock's market price and its fundamental value, but also on a difference between a stock's current market price and its future market price regardless of the relation between its future market price and its fundamental value.[23] Here the idea is simply that if overly optimistic noise traders (or badly informed or counseled institutional investors) are in the market, shorting the stock is not the only way to make money (and, indeed, may be a good way to lose money if the noise traders' persistence exceeds the arbitrageur's capital). Instead, one can profit by anticipating the direction of the noise traders' valuation error, and taking advantage of that error through long, not short, positions with the goal of selling the shares to noise traders at a higher future price. The result may be to drive up the price of already over-valued stocks, and to prolong the length and increase the extent of bubbles (De Long et al. 1990; Bulow & Klemperer 1994; Shleifer 2000).

The second problem is the agency costs of arbitrage, arising from, as Andrei Shleifer (2000) has nicely put it, the fact that 'brains and resources are separated by an "agency relationship"'. To see this, keep in mind that arbitrage positions are made based on ex ante expectations, but the gain realized depends on ex post outcomes. The two may differ, either because of the arbitrageurs' skill in identifying mispricing or because of fundamental or noise trader risk; that is, an investment may fail either because of bad judgment or because of bad luck.

For an arbitrageur trading for her own account, we can presume the explanation for a failed investment is observable. But now assume that the arbitrageur is instead an investment professional whose capital is raised from institutional investors and who receives a portion of the profits – the arbitrageur runs a hedge fund. Because the fund manager's ex ante assessment of the portfolio investment is not observable to the fund investor, the investor then may use the investment's ex post outcome as a proxy of the arbitrageur's skill, with the effect of exposing the arbitrageur's human capital to both fundamental and noise trader risk because the fund investor may mistakenly treat a loss that really results from bad luck as evidence of bad judgment. Arbitrageurs thought to have 'bad judgment' will have difficulty raising new funds or getting new jobs. This prospect, in turn, will cause the arbitrageur to reduce her risk by taking more conservative positions. Importantly, the personal risk to the arbitrageur increases as the importance of arbitrage as a means to correct market price increases. The greater the disagreement about a stock's price, the greater the bad luck risk that the arbitrage position turns out badly and, hence, the greater risk to the arbitrageur's human capital.[24]

---

23   Recall that fundamental value is not a single number but the arbitrageur's choice of value somewhere in the range of reasonable values.

24   This approach borrows from Andrei Shleifer & Robert Vishny (1997). In structure, this information asymmetry-based agency model should be familiar. In a somewhat different form, it has provided the economic basis for the business judgment rule that protects corporate directors from personal liability except in extreme circumstances: because courts and juries will find it difficult to distinguish between director decisions that result in bad outcomes because of bad judgment or because

This interaction between noise trader risk and the agency costs of arbitrage may promote bubbles. Once noise traders enter the market in large numbers, arbitrage risk increases, which in turn reduces the level of arbitrage. This reduction, one might imagine, is more or less linear. More important, the presence of a market driven by noise traders has the potential to create a kink in the arbitrage supply curve, when the potential profit from momentum trading exceeds the potential profit from short selling (Gilson & Kraakman 2004). From this perspective (and extrapolating from Lee, Shleifer and Charles' treatment of closed end mutual funds), a flood of liquidity turned institutional investors into noise traders, who relied on investment banks that profited from selling to these institutions investments that, because of their opacity, had to be sold not bought.

From the vantage point of the ECMH, it is not quite immaterial whether the high cost of information about the impending financial crisis together with the impact of institutional barriers to corrective arbitrage were sufficient to explain the crisis, or whether some cognitive bias is necessary to completely close the explanatory circle. The most important point is that the crisis challenges the ECMH much less than most boom and bust cycles because the quality of market-wide information was exceptionally poor and the institutional mechanisms for arbitrage and price correction were poorly developed. It may even be that the emergence of new market venues for arbitrage protected the economy from a later and even more serious market decline in mortgage-backed securities. In our view, the crisis provides evidence that, on balance, supports a properly framed ECMH rather than burying it.

## 5.   CONCLUSION

In this chapter, we have assessed the prominent post-financial crisis claim that the mispricing of subprime mortgages and related securities that gave rise to the financial crisis demonstrates, once and for all, the bankruptcy of the ECMH. We have argued that market efficiency has always been best understood as a relative matter. The perfect market roots of the ECMH serve to focus our attention on the institutional frictions that cause information to be incorporated into market price too slowly. The 'failure' of the ECMH was the failure of faith-based conviction that market price is fundamentally efficient, which provided the intellectual foundation for broad deregulation of the capital markets.

Properly framing market efficiency focuses our attention on the frictions that drive a wedge between relative efficiency and efficiency under perfect market conditions. So framed, relative efficiency is a diagnostic tool that identifies the frictions and information costs that reduce efficiency. Relative efficiency thus provides part of a regulatory strategy to address our last crisis. A market efficiency perspective on the financial crisis counsels in favor of, for example, required disclosure of the assets underlying asset-backed securities and derivatives so that the identity and condition of these assets can be tracked through layers of securitizations, as well as reduced barriers to short-selling. Reductions in information costs and frictions will not prevent future crises, but improving the performance of the mechanisms of market efficiency will make prices more efficient, frictions more transparent, and public sector agency costs more observable, which may allow us to catch the next problem earlier.

---

of bad luck, imposing liability on directors will result in conservatism to avoid the cost of the legal system making a mistake in assessing causation.

This would be no small accomplishment. Recall that as late as September 8, 2008, the Congressional Budget Office was still uncertain whether the 'period of slow growth … will ultimately be designated a recession', and was predicting 1.8% growth in 2009.[25] While perfect markets might be better, a strategy of improving the relative informational efficiency of markets would be a substantial improvement in a friction-filled world.

## REFERENCES

Barberis, Nicholas & Richard Thaler (2003), 'A Survey of Behavioral Finance', in George M. Constantinides, Milton Harris & Rene M. Stulz (eds) *Handbook of the Economics of Finance*, Amsterdam: Elsevier, 1053.
Beaver, William (1981), 'Market Efficiency', *Accounting Review*, 56, 23–37.
Bernstein, Peter L. (1992), *Capital Ideas: The Improbable Origins of Modern Wall Street*, New York: Free Press.
Black, Bernard & Reiner Kraakman (2002), 'Delaware's Takeover Law: The Uncertain Search for Hidden Value', *Northwestern University Law Review*, 96, 521–66.
Bulow, Jeremy & Paul D. Klemperer (1994), 'Rational Frenzies and Crashes', *Journal of Political Economy*, 112, 1–23.
Cain, Matthew D. & David J. Denis (2010), 'Do Fairness Opinion Valuations Contain Useful Information?', Purdue University, Purdue Economics Working Papers, No. 1244, available at http://ideas.repec.org/p/pur/prukra/1244.html (last accessed March 2011).
Campbell, John Y., Andrew W. Lo & A. Craig MacKinley (1996), *The Econometrics of Financial Markets*, Princeton, NJ: Princeton University Press.
Chen, Nai-Fu, Raymond Kan & Merton Miller (1993a), 'Are Discounts on Closed-end Funds a Sentiment Index?', *The Journal of Finance*, 48, 795–800.
Chen, Nai-Fu, Raymond Kan & Merton Miller (1993b), 'Yes, Discounts on Closed-end Funds are a Sentiment Index: A Rejoinder', *The Journal of Finance*, 48, 809–10.
Chopra, Navin, Charles M.C. Lee, Andrei Shleifer & Richard Thaler (1993), 'Summing Up', *The Journal of Finance*, 48, 801–8.
De Long, J. Bradford, Andrei Shleifer, Lawrence Summers & Robert Waldman (1990), 'Positive Feedback Investment Strategies and Destabilizing Rational Speculation', *The Journal of Finance*, 45, 379–95.
Fama, Eugene (1970), 'Efficient Capital Markets: A Review of Theory and Empirical Work', *The Journal of Finance*, 25, 383–417.
Ferrell, Allen & Atanu Saha (2009), 'Securities Litigation and the Housing Market Downturn', *Journal of Corporation Law*, 35, 97–122.
Fox, Justin (2010), *The Myth of the Rational Market: a history of risk, reward, and delusion on Wall Street*, New York: Harper Business.
Frankel, Tamar & Ann Taylor Schwing (2005), *Securitization: Structured Financing, Financial Asset Pools, and Asset-Backed Securities*, Anchorage, Alaska: Fathom Publishing Company.
Genakopolos, John (2010), 'Solving the Present Crisis and Managing the Leverage Cycle', Cowles Foundation for Research in Economics Discussion Paper Series, No. 1751, available at http://papers.ssrn.com/sol3/papers.cfm?abstract_id=1539488 (last accessed March 2011).
Gilson, Ronald J. & Reiner H. Kraakman (1984), 'The Mechanisms of Market Efficiency', *Virginia Law Review*, 70, 549–644.
Gilson, Ronald J. & Reiner H. Kraakman (2004), 'The Mechanisms of Market Efficiency Twenty Years Later', *Journal of Corporation Law*, 28, 715–42.
Gorton, Gary (2008), 'The Subprime Panic', Yale University ICF Working Paper Series, No. 08-25, available at http://papers.ssrn.com/sol3/papers.cfm?abstract_id=1276047 (last accessed March 2011).
Gorton, Gary B. (2010), *Slapped by the Invisible Hand: the Panic of 2007*, Oxford: Oxford University Press.
Grossman, Sanford & Joseph Stiglitz (1980), 'On the Impossibility of Informationally Efficient Markets', *The American Economic Review*, 70, 393–408.
Hill, Claire A. (2011), 'Why Didn't Subprime Investors Demand a (Much) Larger Lemons Premium?', *Law and Contemporary Problems*, 74, 47.

---

25   Congressional Budget Office, The Budget and Economic Outlook: An Update (2008), available at http://www.cbo.gov/doc.cfm?index=9706&type=0.[Q12]

Hirshleifer, David (2001), 'Investor Psychology and Asset Pricing', *The Journal of Finance*, 56, 1533–97.

Judge, Kathryn (2011), 'Fragmentation Nodes: A Study in Financial Innovation, Complexity, and Systematic Risk', *Stanford Law Review*, 64 (forthcoming).

Kahneman, Daniel, Paul Slovic & Amos Tversky (eds) (1982), *Judgment Under Uncertainty: Heuristics and Biases*, Cambridge: Cambridge University Press.

Kraakman, Reiner (1988), 'Taking Discounts Seriously: The Implications of "Discounted" Share Prices as an Acquisition Motive', *Columbia Law Review*, 88, 891–941.

Kuhn, Thomas (1962), *The Structure of Scientific Revolutions*, Chicago: University of Chicago Press.

Lee, Charles, Andrei Shleifer & Richard Thaler (1991), 'Investment Sentiment and the Closed-End Fund Puzzle', *The Journal of Finance*, 46, 75–109.

Levitin, Adam & Susan Wachter (2012), 'Explaining the Housing Bubble', *Georgetown Law Journal*, 100, forthcoming.

Lewis, Michael (2010), *The Big Short: Inside the Doomsday Machine*, New York: W.W. Norton.

Miller, Merton H. (1988), 'The Modigliani-Miller Propositions After Thirty Years', *The Journal of Economic Perspectives*, 2, 99–120.

Miller, Merton H. & Franco Modigliani (1961), 'Dividend Policy, Growth, and the Valuation of Shares', *The Journal of Business*, 34, 411–33.

Mishkin, Frederick S. (2012), 'Over the Cliff: from the Subprime to the Global Financial Crisis', *Journal of Economic Perspectives* (forthcoming).

Modigliani, Franco & Merton H. Miller (1958), 'The Cost of Capital, Corporation Finance, and the Theory of Investment', *The American Economic Review*, 48, 261–97.

Roll, Richard (1977), 'A Critique of the Asset Pricing Theory's Tests Part I: On Past and Potential Testability of the Theory', *Journal of Financial Economics*, 4, 129–76.

Sharpe, William (1964), 'Capital Asset Prices: A Theory of Market Equilibrium under Conditions of Risk', *The Journal of Finance*, 19, 425–42.

Sharpe, William (1970), 'Efficient Capital Markets: A Review of Theory and Empirical Work: Discussion', *The Journal of Finance*, 25, 418–20.

Shleifer, Andrei (2000), *Inefficient Markets: An Introduction to Behavioral Finance*, Oxford: Oxford University Press.

Shleifer, Andrei & Robert Vishny (1997), 'The Limits of Arbitrage', *The Journal of Finance*, 52, 35–55.

Zingales, Luigi (2010), 'Learning to Live with Not-so-Efficient Markets', *Daedalus*, 139, 31–40.

# Index

Printed and bound by CPI Group (UK) Ltd, Croydon, CR0 4YY

23/04/2025

14660990-0001